Financial Analysis and Ratios

ElioEndless

For more information, or to book an event, contact :

(elioendleeshouse@gmail.com)

Book design by kai

Cover design by Tyson

ISBN - Paperback: 123456789

ISBN – EbooK: 123456789

Hi, Dad!*waves* To my greatest father in the world and my mother.and my colleagues who assist me in creating this endeavor

Acknowledgment

I want to thank everyone who helped make this book. Their constant support, advice, and encouragement have been helpful.I am most grateful to those who gave me aspirational direction, constructive criticism, and kind advise. Their feedback shaped this book's content and direction. I appreciate their candid feedback on my project.I'm grateful for Mr. Jaffer and Mrs. Sameena's help at Endless publishers. They helped me overcome obstacles and improve my job. Their tremendous efforts are much appreciated.Mr. Ahmed, who works at Ahmed, was my project's external advisor. His advice and critique helped me refine my thoughts and improve my book. I appreciate his wisdom.Ms. Sultana and everyone else who helped get resources and make this initiative possible, thank you. Their assistance is much appreciated.The individual who motivated me to write a book deserves recognition. They have inspired me throughout this artistic process.I want to thank everyone who has helped me, no matter how tiny. You made this book possible.

Thank you all.

ElioEndless

Preface

Hey there, "wave"! How's it going? I'm your friendly neighborhood book editor, here to tell you about this amazing book that just landed on our shelves. It's a gem that our awesome publishing company has brought to life. Now, as part of my job, I get to dive into countless books, and I must say, this one is an absolute delight. No need for any unnecessary delay, let me give you a sneak peek into what makes it so worthwhile. Are you ready? Let's jump right in with the introduction!.Welcome to the captivating world of management and decision-making! In this book, we embark on a journey through the essential principles and strategies that drive successful firms. Whether you're a budding entrepreneur or a seasoned business professional, this comprehensive guide will equip you with the knowledge and tools to navigate the complexities of managing a firm effectively.

Part I sets the stage by delving into the fundamentals of the management process. In Chapter 1, we explore the crucial steps involved in shaping a firm's mission statement, defining its long-term strategic goals, and establishing short-term objectives. We also shed light on evaluating alternative strategies and implementing the preferred approach. Notably, we emphasize the relevance of these principles for managing the financial resources of small to medium-sized enterprises—a topic of utmost importance in today's dynamic business landscape.Recognizing that opportunities and threats often lie beyond a firm's immediate control, Chapter 2 uncovers different organizational structures and their impact on the firm's operations. Chapter 3 delves into the intricate world of tax regulations, highlighting the firm's ability to adapt and respond to the ever-evolving legal and tax environment.In a world filled with uncertainty, making informed financial decisions becomes an art. Chapter 4 focuses on the exploration of risk and its management within a firm. We delve into various risk responses, including formal insurance programs, as well as other alternatives. By equipping you with essential statistical tools and insights, this chapter empowers you to navigate the unpredictable landscape of risk and uncertainty with confidence.As you delve into the subsequent chapters, you will discover a wealth of knowledge and practical wisdom that will shape your understanding of management principles and inspire you to apply them in real-world scenarios. From strategic planning to risk management, each chapter holds valuable insights that will illuminate your path towards successWe invite you to embark on this enlightening journey, where theory meets practice, and innovation thrives. Prepare to unlock the secrets of effective management, cultivate your decision-making prowess, and embark on a transformative adventure that will elevate your professional endeavors.

Financial Analysis and Ratios

By C.miya

Contents

Part V. PART V: PRESENT VALUE MODEL APPLICATIONS

Preface

LINDON ROBISON

This book intends to help students and others learn how to successfully manage the finances of small to medium-size firms. The underlying assumption of this book is that successful financial managers need to master the construction and analysis of financial statements and present value models. Learning how to construct and analyze financial statements and present value models is the focus of this book that is divided into five parts.

Part I: Management

The chapters in Part I introduce management. Chapter 1 describes the firm management process—a process that includes identifying the firm's mission statement and strategic (long term) goals and tactical (short term) objectives; identifying the firm's strengths, weaknesses, opportunities, and threats; identifying and evaluating alternative strategies; and finally implementing and evaluating the preferred strategy. Chapter 1 notes that the management process has wide application including managing the financial resources of the small to medium-size firm.

The firm's opportunities and threats are most often nested in factors outside the firm's control. For example, different ways to organize the firm (Chapter 2) and the tax environment facing the firm (Chapter 3) are factors external to the firm. They are important to discuss, though, because the firm can adopt different responses to the legal and tax environment in which it operates.

We live in and make financial decisions in a world of risk and uncertainty. So how do we make choices when we can't be certain what the outcomes will be? Formal insurance programs are one way of addressing the risk firms face. However, there are other risk responses the firm can employ. Learning about risk and applying this knowledge to the purchase of insurance and adopting other risk management alternatives is the focus of Chapter 4. Some of the concepts covered in Chapter 4 are essential statistical tools needed to plan and make important decisions in a risky and uncertain world.

Part II: Strengths, Weaknesses, Opportunities, and Threats

Chapters in Part II focus on the internal financial strengths and weaknesses of the firm and its ability to respond to external opportunities and threats. Chapter 5 focuses on the construction, analysis, and interpretation of coordinated financial statements (CFS). CFS are the primary tools for answering the question: what is the financial condition of the firm and what are its financial strengths and weaknesses?

An important consideration, especially when the focus is on small to medium-sized firms, is how to construct financial statements when the firm has incomplete records. While the data used in the financial management process and the construction of financial statements are most often assumed to be obtainable and accurate, the reality may be quite different. Small to medium-sized firms often lack the financial records required to conduct the analyses described in Part II of this book. Acquiring and sometimes guesstimating the missing data is almost an art form—a process that forms the nexus between theory and practice.

An important lesson to be learned about financial statements—even when we can construct them accurately—is that financial statements alone do not completely reveal the financial strengths and weaknesses of the firm. A more complete view of the firm's strengths and weaknesses requires ratios be constructed using data included in the firm's CFS (Chapter 6). Ratios constructed using the firm's CFS can be compared with similar firms, and significant deviations from the norm can be noted and given further attention. Ratios describing the firm's financial well-being can be described by the acronym SPELL: (S)olvency, (P)rofitability, (E)fficiency, (L)iquidity, and (L) everage.

Chapter 7 notes that the firm's CFS is a system. An important characteristic of an open system is that its parts are connected internally with endogenous variables and externally—to factors outside of the firm—with exogenous variables. Therefore, a change in one or more of the firm's exogenous variables can change conditions inside the firm described by its endogenous variables.

Because CFS are a system, we can analyze the firm's opportunities and threats presented by forces outside the firm. For example, we can ask: what if there is a change in the firm's exogenous variables? Then, how will the financial condition of the firm change? Or we may ask: if the firm has a financial goal, then how much must an exogenous variable change for the firm to reach its goal? Finally, we may ask: if one part of the system changes, what will be the corresponding change? One way to think of the CFS system and what if and how much analysis is to compare it to a balloon: a squeeze somewhere in the balloon will produce a bulge somewhere else.

Throughout this book, we use data from a hypothetical (but not atypical) firm, HiQuality Nursery (HQN) to help make the analysis realistic. However, the financial analysis experience becomes authentic when those practicing financial management skills construct financial statements for actual firms, including ones in which the analyst has a personal interest.

Part III: Present Value Models

Chapters in Part III of this book introduce present value (PV) models. Chapter 8 provides the theoretical basis for PV models by demonstrating that PV models are multi-period extensions of a single period accrual income statement (AIS). To aid those preparing PV models, this chapter also introduces a generalized Excel template that can be used to solve practical PV problems. While PV models have the common feature of converting a challenger's future cash flow to its equivalent in the present, Chapter 9 introduces several different kinds of PV models distinguished by the questions they answer. Chapter 10 introduces one important distinction between PV models, whether the investment is an incremental change to an existing firm versus a stand-alone investment. Chapter 11, the last chapter in Part III of this book, describes forecasting methods useful for obtaining future cash flow estimates to populate PV models. Included in chapter 11 is a brief introduction to statistical regression methods, essential for forecasting.

Part IV: Homogeneous Measures

Chapters in part IV provide more detailed guidelines for constructing PV models. Chapter 12 compares a challenging investment to a defending one by converting a challenger's future cash flow to its equivalent in the present by exchanging cash flow between periods at the defender's internal rate of return. Chapters 13, 14, and 15 remind those solving PV problems that comparisons between challenger(s) and defenders(s) must use homogeneous measures. Chapter 13 describes how to compare investments with different sizes. Chapter 14 describes how to compare investments with different terms. Chapter 15 describes how to introduce taxes into PV models to produce consistent comparisons between challengers and defenders. Finally, chapter 16 introduces homogeneous currency and liquidity requirements when comparing challenging and defending investments.

Part V: Present Value Model Applications

Armed with a knowledge of PV model building principles and tools, the analyst is prepared to construct PV models for specific investments. Chapters in Part V note that specific investments, while similar, may have some distinct characteristics, depending on the type of investment activity under examination. Chapter 17 considers taking out and repaying loans, emphasizing that loan analysis is essentially a present value problem. Chapter 18 considers purchasing, using, or selling land. An important feature of land purchases and sales is transaction costs, which are included in the land models. Chapter 19 recognizes that the control and use of investments can be acquired through leases as well as through purchases. So, in this chapter, models are constructed that can be used to find the present values of leases. Chapter 20 reviews financial investments, a separate class of investments, especially relevant for personal financial management decisions. Chapter 21 prepares students to observe financial opportunities and threats using the term structure of interest rates, an important financial tool. Finally, Chapter 22 reminds readers that "money can't buy love" nor most other relational goods. Thus, Chapter 22 enlarges the management process to include relational goods as well as commodities.

PART I: MANAGEMENT

1. Financial Management and the Firm

LINDON ROBISON

Learning goals. After completing this chapter, you should be able to: (1) recognize the six steps included in the management process; (2) apply the management process to better manage the financial resources of the small to medium-size firm; and (3) apply the management process to other activities such as being a successful student.

Learning objectives. To achieve your learning goals, you should complete the following objectives:

- Understand the need for a concise firm mission statement.
- Learn how to distinguish between the firm's strategic (long-term) goals and its tactical (short-term) objectives.
- Learn how to choose goals and objectives that will successfully guide financial managers in the financial management process.
- Learn how to identify a firm's (internal) strengths and weaknesses.
- Learn how to identify a firm's (external) opportunities and threats.
- Learn how to develop a strategy to reach the firm's goals and objectives that take advantage of the firm's strengths and opportunities and minimize the limitations of its weaknesses and threats.
- Learn how to implement and evaluate outcomes of the firm's strategy for achieving its goals and objectives.
- Learn how to apply the management process to one's own efforts to succeed in this class.

Introduction to Management

Financial management is about, above all else, control. The word "manage" comes from an Italian word that means "to handle," like a horse rider. The management method can be used with a wide range of resources and organisations. In this book, the management process is used to manage a small business's finances instead of the finances of a big company.

The Management Process

There are six steps in the management process: 1) Make a mission statement for the company. 2) Choose the company's strategic (long-term) goals and tactical (short-term) goals. 3) Figure out the company's strengths, weaknesses, opportunities, and threats. 4) Make a plan for how the company will reach its strategic and tactical goals. 5) Put the plan into action. And 6) evaluate the company's performance.

Figure 1.1 shows a picture of these six steps, and then the text describes them in more depth. Figure 1.1 shows that as you move from one step of management to the next, you move towards the centre of the circle. And as you move closer to the middle of the circle, each action is limited by the choices made by management in the past.

Figure 1.1. The Managerial Process in Six Steps

So, what do we know now? We found out that there are six steps to the management process: 1) Make a purpose statement; 2) Choose strategic goals and tactical objectives; 3) Figure out the firm's strengths, weaknesses, opportunities, and threats; 4) Choose strategies; 5) Put strategies into action; and 6) Evaluate performance.

Develop the Firm's Mission Statement

A goal statement is the first step in the management process. In its goal statement, the company explains why it exists and what it stands for. The mission statement may also include criteria for how the business will choose which activities to take part in. Mission statements might also talk about the company's customers, the markets it will be in, and its social duties. Mission statements are usually short, to the point, easy to say and remember, clear, and broad enough to cover all of the things a company does. For example, a vegetable farm's purpose could be: "Our goal is to grow healthy, safe vegetables in a way that is good for the environment and our workers." When making the goal statement for a company, motives are very important. Motives come from physical and social/ emotional needs, and how the firm uses its resources to meet its needs will depend on how important these needs are. Because of this, the purpose statement should show how important the financial manager's goals are. Motives might include the need to increase one's own consumption, to act in accordance with one's internalised set of values, to earn the good will of others, to feel more like a part of one's community or other organisations, or to help a group that is struggling. The firm's attempts to manage its resources should be based on how important these competing goals are in   the   mission   statement.

One word that is sometimes used to describe management is "vision." Vision is the ability to picture in your mind something that hasn't been made yet. So, vision is a necessary part of any kind of physical creation, since we have to make an event, result, or thing in our minds before we can make it in the real world. An architect has to imagine what a building will look like and put that idea into plans that builders will use to make the building. Before an attacking play can be used in a game, a football coach thinks about it and draws it. Before putting time, energy, and other resources into a project, a financial manager needs to think about how it will benefit the business. The goal statement of a company shows what the manager wants the company to achieve. "Where there is no vision, the people perish"   (Proverbs   29:18)   is   a   Bible   verse   that   shows   how   important   vision   is.

So, what have we learned? We learned that the management process begins with a vision that describes what the firm wants to do and become. Without a vision, the firm is unlikely to succeed.

Choose the Firm's Strategic Goals and Tactical Objectives

Strategic goals set the long-term direction of the firm. Strategic goals are consistent with the firm's mission statement—what it values, why it exists, and what is its purpose. Strategic goals direct the firm's efforts toward achieving its mission over the long run. Strategic goals also call for tactical objectives, specific actions needed to achieve strategic goals. For example, a strategic goal may be to increase the firm's revenues by 10%. The objectives consistent with this goal may be to develop new products, to focus on a marketing strategy, or to increase the firm's sales force. The firm's objectives transform the firm's strategic goals into an action plan. Tactical objectives describe what short term actions are required if the firm is to reach its long-term goals.

The importance of goals and objectives

There are at least four reasons management requires the firm to choose goals and objectives:

1. Firm goals and objectives express what the firm believes is possible and desirable to achieve. By choosing the firm's goals and objectives, the manager is expressing confidence in what the firm can achieve. By declaring the firm's goals and objectives, the manager is also declaring its commitment of time, energy, and resources to achieve a desired end. Declaring the firm's confidence and commitments in the form of its goals and objectives is the first reason for setting strategic goals and tactical objectives.
2. As the firm works to achieve its goals and objectives, it faces a multitude of choices, including how best to allocate its limited resources. Goals and objectives guide the firm in its allocation decisions by asking: what choices and resource allocations will best enable the firm to reach its goals and objectives? Therefore, firm goals and objectives provide criteria for making choices, the second reason for setting goals and objectives.
3. Most firms include multiple actors with diverse assignments. Goals and objectives provide a means for rallying firm members to support a common cause. Goals and objectives provide a means for seeing one's individual efforts as part of and consistent with the firm's overall goals and objectives and to identify opportunities for synergism within the firm. Ideally, the firm's goals and objectives represent a consensus of firm members' beliefs in what is possible and desirable and how to best achieve them so that all parts of the firm work cooperatively and enthusiastically together. Providing a framework for firm members to work synergistically is the third reason for setting goals and objectives.
4. Finally, goals and objectives provide a measure against which the firm can evaluate its performance. It allows the firm to ask and answer questions such as: Where are we? How are we doing? Can we get where we want to be from here? Are we closer to reaching our goals than before? Measuring one's efforts against a standard is the fourth reason for setting goals and objectives.

The characteristics of good goals and objectives.

Some goals are better than others. The four reasons why we choose goals and objectives help us define the characteristics of good goals and objectives.

1. Good goals and objectives are realistic. They identify outcomes that are feasible for the firm to achieve given its environment and resources. It is not helpful to set unrealistic goals and objectives, even if they impress others. Unrealistic goals and objectives may create unrealistic expectations and lead to frustration later because they cannot be achieved. Good goals and objectives can be achieved with the wise use of resources available to the firm and the environment in which it exists.

2. Good goals and objectives answer the question: "What must the firm do to achieve its mission?" Goals and objectives that are consistent with the firm's mission statement provide the criteria for the management of the firm's energy and resources. If the firm goals and objectives fail to provide such criteria, then other goals and objectives should be selected.

3. Good goals and objectives reflect a consensus among those tasked with achieving them. People work hard for money. But they work harder when they feel they are part of a team—that their contributions are valued. Thus, good goals and objectives are the product of serious discussions intended to produce a consensus among those involved in reaching them. Therefore, at the end of the day, good goals and objectives provide a focus for synergistic efforts.

4. Finally, progress toward the achievement of good goals and objectives can be measured. Thomas S. Monson (1970) taught, "when progress is measured, progress improves. And when progress is measured and reported, the rate of improvement increases." Measuring the firm's progress helps guide the firm's future. If the measures signal that the firm is making adequate progress, then the firm is supported in its efforts to keep doing what it has been doing. If the measures signal that the firm is not making adequate progress, then the firm is supported in its efforts to change directions.

So, what have we learned? We learned that to realize the firm's vision we must choose goals that are realistic, describe what needs to be done, reflect a consensus, and can be measured. We need goals because they reflect what we believe is possible, they provide criteria for choosing between alternatives, they provide a rallying point for firm members to work together, and they provide measures against which performance can be evaluated.

Identify the Firm's Strengths, Weaknesses, Opportunities, and Threats.

Before developing strategies to accomplish the firm's goals and objectives, a manager needs to identify and evaluate the internal strengths and weaknesses of the firm. This evaluation should include an assessment of the firm's ability to survive financially in both the long run and the short run (solvency and liquidity); its profitability; its efficient management of its resources on which its profitability depends; and the risk inherent in its current financial state. External opportunities and threats that impact the firm's ability to accomplish its objectives also need to be considered. An external opportunity and threat analysis might include evaluating the behavior of close competitors or assessing the condition of the economy and business climate, or the impacts of the business cycle on clients' incomes and the resulting product demand.

> So, what have we learned? We learned that strengths, weaknesses, opportunities and threats analysis helps the firm understand the current constraints placed on it by both internal and external forces and enables the firm to take corrective action, when possible, to better position itself to accomplish its mission.

Develop and Evaluate the Firm's Strategy.

The firm's strategy is a plan that describes how it intends to achieve its strategic goals and its tactical objectives. Some have claimed that a goal or objective without a plan is only a wish. The firm's strategy is a plan of action that describes who will do what, when, and how. For each goal or objective, the firm must develop the corresponding strategy to accomplish it. The strategy development process includes collecting data and information about possible choices and likelihoods of possible events. Then, the information must be analyzed to determine the impact of a strategy on the firm's goals and objectives. Based on these analyses, management must select the proper strategy.

> So, what have we learned? We learned that unless we create a plan to achieve our goals and objectives consistent with our vision statement we have likely engaged only in wishful thinking. Planning who will do what, when, and how moves us in the direction of realizing our mission, goals, and objectives.

Implement the Firm's Strategy.

Once a strategy is selected, it must be administered throughout the firm. All relevant parts of the business (accounting, purchasing, manufacturing, processing, shipping, sales, administration) must support and take an active role implementing the strategy. There may be changes in the business that are necessary to implement the strategy such as changes in personnel, technology, or financial structure. Implementing the firm's strategy will require a carefully coordinated effort if the firm's strategy leads to the firm achieving its goals and objectives.

> So, what have we learned? We learned that there is often more said than done and more planned than executed. Implementing one's strategy is the sine qua non—unless the strategy is implemented, nothing else matters.

Evaluate the Firm's Performance.

Firm managers must continually evaluate the strategies they implemented to reach the firm's objectives and goals. They must determine if what the firm has achieved is consistent with its mission statement, goals, and objectives within an environment described by the firm's strengths, weakness, opportunities, and threats. Firm managers must also be prepared to alter strategies in response to changes in technologies, laws, market conditions, and personnel. These changes will make it necessary for the firm to continually reevaluate and adjust.

Evaluating the firm's performance must also include a review of its mission statement, goals, objectives, efforts to implement its strategies, and its strengths, weaknesses, opportunities and threats. Since the firm's mission statement and strategic goals are oriented toward the long term, they change infrequently. However, the firm's strategies may change as frequently as its internal strengths and weaknesses and external opportunities and threats change.

> So, what have we learned? We learned that life is like driving a car. Most of the time we look forward to where we are going. On occasion, however, it is important to look in our rear-view mirror to see where we have been and to learn from our journey.

The Firm Financial Management Process

The firm's financial management process involves the acquisition and use of funds to accomplish its financial goals and objectives consistent with its financial mission statement. The firm's financial management process essentially employs the same six management steps described earlier. The six steps of financial management include: 1) develop the financial mission of the firm; 2) choose the financial goals and objectives of the firm; 3) identify and evaluate the firm's financial strengths, weaknesses, opportunities and threats; 4) develop financial strategies including evaluating and ranking investment opportunities to achieve financial goals and objectives consistent with the firm's mission; 5) implement investment strategies by matching the liquidity of funding sources with cash flow generated from investments, by forecasting future funding needs, and by assessing the risk facing the firm; and, 6) evaluate the firm's financial performance relative to the goals and objectives of the firm. These six steps are described next in more detail.

(1) Develop the Firm's (Financial) Mission Statement.

While financial management usually plays a role in developing the firm's overall mission statement, there are other considerations shaping the firm's mission. As a result, the financial mission of the firm is usually nested within the more general mission of the firm. One financial mission of the firm may be to reach certain financial conditions that allow the firm's owners to pursue other goals and provide firm owners resources in the future. The firm's mission statement may lead naturally to important financial goals such as to maximize profit, reduce costs and increase efficiency, manage or increase the firm's market share, limit the firm's risk, or maximize the owner's equity in the firm. However, there may be a distinction between a firm's financial mission and the firm's overall mission. In other words, the firm's financial mission included in the strategic financial management process may be an objective in the firm's overall strategic management process.

(2) Choose the Firm's (Financial) Strategic Goals and Tactical Objectives.

The part of the firm's mission related to financial management must lead to the firm selecting financial goals consistent with the firm's mission statement and objectives likely to lead to the successful achievement of its strategic goals. The financial objectives may direct how the firm organizes itself, how it manages its tax obligations, and how it responds to risk—subjects discussed in Chapters 2, 3, and 4.

(3) Identify (Financial) Strengths, Weaknesses, Opportunities and Threats.

The use of coordinated financial statements (CFS) discussed in Chapter 5 can be used to evaluate the firm's internal strengths and weaknesses. We may need to look outside of the firm to identify external opportunities and threats facing the firm. Financial statements are used to formulate ratios that can be compared to other firms to determine how the firm's financial condition compares to normal—or average—firms, the subject of Chapter 6. Chapter 7 uses financial statements and ratios to demonstrate that the firm is a system with interconnected parts. As a result, each financial measure (e.g. solvency, profitability, efficiency, liquidity, and leverage) are connected to each other, and a change in one measure will change all the others.

(4) Develop and Evaluate the Firm's (Financial) Strategy.

Financial managers face an almost limitless set of investment opportunities with a wide variety of characteristics. Some investments will be liquid and easily converted to cash, such as inventories or time deposits. Other investments, such as real estate or production facilities, cannot be easily converted to cash and are considered illiquid. There are investments that provide fairly certain, low risk returns while others will provide uncertain, high risk returns. Some investments are depreciable while others increase in value over time. Firm budget resources for capital or long-term investments and evaluate them using present value (PV) tools. Many of the chapters that follow focus on PV models. Indeed, it may be correct to say that the focus of much of this book is on how to use PV models to evaluate a firm's financial strategy.

- PV models are similar in construction to accrual income statements (Chapter 8);
- PV models are distinguished by the questions they can answer (Chapter 9);
- PV models often evaluate incremental changes in a firm's portfolio of investments (Chapter 10)
- PV models project the future values of exogenous variables (Chapter 11)
- PV models need to be consistent, must be investments of homogeneous rates of return, size, term, tax treatment, and liquidity—requiring that we compare apples to apples and oranges to oranges (Chapters 12, 13, 14, 15, and 16);

Equipped with PV models and knowledge of how to conduct proper comparisons of investments using consistent measures, we are prepared to apply our tools to a wide range of investment problems that employ a variety of PV models. Included is a discussion of loan analysis in Chapter 17, land investments in Chapter 18, leasing options in Chapter 19, and investment in financial assets in Chapter 20. Then Chapter 21 introduces yield curves to help us identify outside-of-the-firm external threats and opportunities. Finally, the last chapter in this book, Chapter 22, ends with a cautionary note—there are relational goods that may be more important than money and should not be ignored.

(5) Implement the Firm's (Financial) Strategy.

Financial managers often play an important role in managing the implementation of an investment strategy. The implementation stage of financial management may include interacting with capital markets to raise funds required to support a strategy. Managers decide whether to acquire funds internally or borrow from other investors, commercial banks, the Farm Credit System, life insurance companies, or, depending on how the firm is organized, by issuing stocks or bonds.

In the process of obtaining and allocating funds, financial managers interact directly or indirectly with financial markets. This interaction could be simply obtaining a savings or checking account at your local bank. Or it could involve more sophisticated interactions such as raising funds by issuing ownership (equity) claims in your firm in the form of shares of stock.

Another part of implementing the financial strategy of the firm is to interact with various parts of the business and the household. For example, setting inventory policy is both a financial and business management decision and requires input from the production and sales departments of the firm as well as the firm's financial managers. In addition, financial managers must make trade-offs between risks and expected returns. One tool that can be used to evaluate future returns and risk is the term structure of interest rates, the subject of Chapter 21. There are other kinds of trade-offs as well. One important trade-ff is between commodities and relational goods. We will need both because they each satisfy different needs. This book is mostly about managing commodities, but Chapter 22 reminds us that "money can't buy love" or relational goods. Therefore, one more thing about management is to account for and manage relational goods.

(6) Evaluate the Firm's (Financial) Performance.

Finally, financial concepts and information are often used to evaluate a strategy's performance and to signal investment changes the firm needs to adopt in the future. In this effort, PV models will prove to be particularly helpful.

The relative importance of the six steps included in the management process will differ depending on what is being managed. In the case of financial management, the financial goals, the objectives, the strengths, weaknesses, opportunities, and threats analysis, and the strategies adopted and evaluated will differ from personnel management, for example. Like both financial management and other management efforts is their shared responsibility for the firm. What follows is strategic firm management applied to the financial resources available to the firm.

Our focus on firm financial management. While all six firm financial management processes are important and discussed in this book, we focus on two:

1. Assessing the firm's internal strengths and weakness through the use of coordinated financial statements, ratio analysis, and comparisons with 'average' firms; and

2. Developing strategies described by after-tax cash flow and evaluating them using PV models.

Of course the other parts of the management process are important, especially implementing strategic financial investment plans and evaluating the firm's performance. However, a thorough treatment of these topics which should be pursed in other venues.

---

1. Assessing the firm's internal strengths and weakness using coordinated financial statements, ratio analysis, and comparisons with 'average' firms; and
2. Developing strategies described by after-tax cash flow and evaluating them using PV models.

Of course, the other parts of the management process are important, especially implementing strategic financial investment plans and evaluating the firm's performance. However, a thorough treatment of these topics is better pursued in other venues.

Trade-offs between Financial Goals and Objectives

The firm's financial goals and objectives guide the financial manager. There are, of course, a wide range of possible tactical objectives that a firm may adopt to achieve its strategic goals and its mission. However, one maxim should guide the manager's choice of objectives: "There is no such thing as a free lunch!" Interpreted, this adage reminds us that nearly always, every objective comes at the cost of another objective

For example, consider the objective of maximizing the firm's profits. Increases in short-term profits may often reduce long-term profits. If the firm desires to reduce its risk, this may require that the firm reduce its profits by investing in less risky–but lower return–investments.

One often-stated firm financial management objective is to maximize the profits of the firm. However, the measure of profits can differ drastically across different accounting practices. For example, cash versus accrual accounting, different depreciation methods, and different inventory accounting methods all lead to different measures of profit. Maximizing profits using one accounting method may not maximize profits using another accounting practice. Furthermore, profits may be difficult to measure when the firm employs unpaid family labor. The real problem is that profits don't reflect the actual cash flow of the firm.

In addition, the traditional notion of profit ignores the timing of the cash flow received by a firm. Suppose you are given the choice of receiving $1,000 either today or one year from today. Which would you choose? Naturally, you would choose to get the money today because you could invest the money for some positive rate of return and earn more than $1,000 by the end of one year. For instance, suppose you could invest the money in the bank and earn a 5 percent return during the year. At the end of the year you would get back your $1,000 plus $1,000 x (.05) = $50 interest or a total of $1,050. Clearly, the $1,000 today is worth more than the $1,000 one year from today. The notion that dollars at different points in time are not worth the same amounts at a single point in time is known as the time value of money concept. Moreover, it underlies one of the most important financial trade-offs: present profits versus the present value of discounted future after-tax cash flow.

Another trade-off involving the maximize profit objective is that it ignores liquidity. Liquidity can be defined as a firm's ability to meet unexpected cash demands. These cash demands might be unexpected cash expenses for such things as repairs and overhead expenses, new investment opportunities, or unexpected reductions in revenue. The concept of liquidity is closely related to risk. Liquidity needs are usually met by holding salable assets and/or maintaining the capacity to borrow additional funds. Serious risks may reduce the value of some assets and make liquidation of the assets difficult. Likewise, serious risk may also make it difficult to borrow additional funds.

If you were a firm manager, would your objective be to maximize profits or would some other objective be preferable? In this class, we will argue that traditional profit maximization is not a very desirable objective for a financial manager. We will argue that in most cases, financial decisions should be made so they maximize the value of the firm, which turns out to be the same thing as maximizing the present value of all the future cash generated by the firm. Once again, it is important to note that "cash flow" is much different than "profit."

This concept of maximizing firm value is easy to defend in large firms where firm ownership is often separate from management. Owners of these firms generally want management to operate the firm in a way that maximizes the value of their investment; however, in smaller firms and households the value maximization principal is often constrained by other considerations such as concerns about quality of life. For example, you would likely be able to increase your personal wealth over time by driving a Chevrolet instead of a Cadillac (you could invest the cost savings), but you may gain enough satisfaction from driving a Cadillac (or a tractor with green paint) that you are willing to accept the lower wealth level. Nevertheless, for most of this course we will assume that financial decisions are made in a manner that is consistent with maximizing value. In cases where a firm does not maximize present value, it is still useful to estimate the present value maximizing decisions as a benchmark in order to understand the cost of alternative decision in terms of wealth loss.

Summary and Conclusions

Like it or not, we are all managers—if not managers of a firm then we are personal managers. We have important management responsibilities for our lives and resources. The management process is a universal process requiring that we first determine our mission and what goals and objectives are consistent with our mission? The goals and objectives we choose must declare what it is that we believe we can and should accomplish and the level of our commitment to reaching our goals and objectives. Finally, we cannot avoid setting goals and objectives because having no goal or objective is a goal or objective—to reach nowhere in particular.

Choosing our goals and objectives is crucial in the management process. We cannot achieve our mission without properly formulated goals and objectives. Goals and objectives lead us to conduct an honest evaluation of our internal strengths and weakness and external threats and opportunities, a process that identifies the resources and constraints likely to contribute to achieving our mission. After formulating our goals and objectives, and after conducting an honest evaluation of our strengths, weaknesses, opportunities and threats, we next decide on a strategy, a plan to follow that will enable us to accomplish our mission. Strategic management requires that we implement our plan, that we take specific actions to ensure we achieve our goal by implementing our strategies. And finally, we evaluate and, if necessary, modify our goals, objectives, and our understanding of our strengths, weaknesses, threats, and opportunities. Then, when we have completed the management process, we repeat it all over again, continually, and not necessarily following the steps in the management process in the same order. We end this chapter by emphasizing this truism: we are all managers, all the time.

References

Monson, T.M. (1970). "Thou Art a Teacher Come From God," Conference Report, Oct. 1970, 107.

Questions

1. What does the word management mean?
2. Discuss the six steps included in the management process. Should these steps be practiced sequentially? In any order? Or does it depend on the management problem? Defend your answer.
3. What features differentiate management and firm financial management?
4. Consider mission statements and strategic goals and tactical objectives. Is the following statement: "I want to obtain a college degree." a mission statement, a goal, or an objective? If it is a tactical objective, what strategic goals and mission statement are consistent with this tactical objective? If it is a strategic goal, what mission statement and tactical objectives are consistent with this strategic goal? Finally, if it is a mission statement, what strategic goals and tactical objectives are consistent with this mission statement?
5. Mission statements, strategic goals, and tactical objectives reflect motives. Several motives may explain one's desire to achieve a college degree. One motive for obtaining a college degree is to increase one's lifetime earnings. But there are other motives. To help you connect motives to your personal mission statement, goal, or objective to obtain a college degree, identify the relative importance of the five motives described below. To complete the questionnaire below, assume

you have 10 weights (e.g. pennies) to allocate among the five motives for attending the university. Distribute the 10 weights (pennies) according to the relative importance of each motive. Write your answer in the blank next to each question. There is no right or wrong allocation of weights among the motives except that the sum must add to 10. Each motive reflects the relative importance of one's need to increase one's own consumption, to earn internal/external validation, and to have a sense of belonging.

    a. I want a college degree so I can increase my lifetime earnings and get a better job.
    b. I want a college degree so important people in my life will be pleased with my achievements.
    c. I want a college degree to live up to the expectations I have for myself.
    d. I want a college degree so I will feel part of groups to which I want to belong.
    e. I want a college degree so that in the future, I will be better able to help others.

6. Develop a management plan for this class, this semester. This should include a brief discussion of each of the six steps in the strategic planning process including a mission statement, strategic goals and objectives, your strengths, weaknesses, opportunities, and threats, your strategies, your plan to implement your strategies, and, lastly, your evaluation process. Discuss what role financial management will play in your strategic planning process.

7. Imagine yourself as the financial manager of a small firm. Write a mission statement focused on profit maximization. What other considerations may be ignored if profit maximization were your primary mission? Suppose your mission statement was to "aid the disadvantaged"? Would profit or value maximization be part of your firm's goals and objectives? Please explain.

2. Exploring Diverse Business Structures: Alternative Forms of Business Organizations

LINDON ROBISON

Learning goals. After completing this chapter, you should be able to: (1) know the different forms of business organizations; (2) compare the advantages and disadvantages of alternative business organi-zations; and (3) identify how alternative business organizations can influence a firm's ability to achieve its financial goals and objectives.

Learning objectives. To achieve your learning goals, you should complete the following objectives:

- Learn about the advantages and disadvantages of a sole proprietorship.
- Study the characteristics of firms ideally organized as sole proprietorships.
- Learn about the advantages and disadvantages of partnerships.
- Study the characteristics of firms ideally organized as partnerships.
- Learn about the advantages and disadvantages of C corporations and S corporations.
- Study the characteristics of firms ideally organized as C corporations and S corporations.
- Learn about the advantages and disadvantages of a Limited Liability Company (LLC).
- Study the characteristics of firms ideally organized as LLCs.
- Learn about the advantages and disadvantages of a cooperative.
- Study the characteristics of firms ideally organized as cooperatives.
- Learn about the advantages and disadvantages of a trust.
- Study the characteristics of firms ideally organized as trusts.

Introduction

How a business is set up has an effect on how well it can meet its goals and objectives. This chapter is about the most common legal types of business organisations in the U.S. These are sole proprietorships, general and limited partnerships, limited liability companies (LLCs), S corporations, and C corporations. Partnerships, LLCs, and C corporations can be found in many different types and kinds of businesses. LLCs are becoming more and more important in the agricultural production sector, especially for family companies that have been in the same family for many generations. In family businesses, legal business arrangements that make it easy for assets to be passed down from one generation to the next have become very important.

The ability of a business to reach its goals and fulfil its mission depends on things like: 1) who makes the management decisions; 2) how flexible is it in its production, marketing, consumption, and financing activities; 3) its liability exposure; 4) its opportunities to get capital; 5) how long the business will last; 6) how it will end.

owners affects the firm; 7) methods available for transferring the current owners' interest to others; and 8) Internal Revenue Service definitions of business profits and their taxation. Thus, the way a firm is legally organized provides the framework for making financial management decisions.

Sole Proprietorship

The sole proprietorship is a common organization form especially used by small businesses. A sole proprietorship is a business that is owned and operated by a single individual. Most sole proprietorships are family-owned businesses. The advantages of a sole proprietorship business include:

1. It is easy and inexpensive to form and operate administratively (simplicity);
2. It offers the maximum managerial control; and
3. Business income is taxed as ordinary (personal) income to the owner.

The disadvantages of the sole proprietorship include:

1. It is difficult to raise large amounts of capital;
2. There is unlimited liability;
3. It is difficult to transfer ownership; and
4. The company's life is determined by the life of the owner.

Most sole proprietorships are set up loosely, and they don't need much paperwork to get started. It is the easiest to understand and use of the different business organisations. To start doing business, the person says that he or she is a business. In most situations, a licence is needed to run a business, but sometimes all it takes to start a business is "opening its door." The business's day-to-day operations are also run loosely, and the owner can run them however he or she wants, as long as they don't break any laws or tax rules. For example, you have to pay certain taxes by a certain date. Most rules that small businesses have to follow don't depend on how the business is set up legally. How many rules a business has to follow often depends on its size, number of workers, and location.

Since a sole proprietorship is owned by just one person, it gives that person the most power over how the business is run. In small businesses, the owner is often involved in all parts of the business, including buying, keeping track of inventory, production, sales, budgeting, dealing with employees and customers, and managing finances and the business as a whole. When a business is small, the fact that the owner has a lot of power can be a strength. However, as the business grows, the owner is often no longer able to handle all of the business's tasks. The owner must then hire knowledgeable people to run different parts of the business.

The resources of a sole proprietor business are the same as those of the owner. This can make it hard for a business to start up and slow its growth over time. In many cases, large amounts of money are needed to buy the land, buildings, tools, cars, and offices you need to start the business, as well as the salaries, wages, and supplies you'll need until the business gets going. Also, it often takes between two and three years for a business to start making money. The owner of the business has to get these funds from their own equity (money they own) or by borrowing money. When borrowing money, owner equity is used as collateral. How much you can borrow relies on how much equity you have and how much money you think your business will make. One of the biggest problems with being a sole proprietor is not having enough money to start and grow the business. The business owner has to pay taxes on the money he or she makes from the business.

The owner of a sole proprietorship is responsible for all of the business's bills, even if they are more than what they put into the business. For example, if a sole proprietorship can't pay its debts and obligations, creditors can take the owner's personal assets that aren't part of the business or other companies he or she owns. To pay the firm's debts, the owner may have to sell personal assets like a savings account, a holiday home, or other valuables.

One more thing that is bad about a sole proprietorship is that it only lasts as long as the owner does. The owner can sell the business's assets to a sole proprietorship or another company. But if the business isn't closed down before the owner dies, the assets that are still in the business will be divided according to the owner's will or another similar document. When the business owner dies, the business ends.

Partnerships

A business that is owned and run by two or more people is called a general partnership. The partners each put something into the business, help run it, and share any profits. Most partnerships start with a written agreement between the partners, but a partnership can be valid even without a written agreement. If the partnership owns real estate, the partnership agreement should be filed in the county where the land is. Some of the benefits of partnerships are:

1. They are easy and inexpensive to form and operate administratively;
2. They have the potential for large managerial control;
3. Business income is taxed as ordinary (personal) income to the owner; and
4. A partnership may be able to raise larger amounts of capital than a sole proprietorship.

The disadvantages of a general partnership include:

1. Raising capital can still be a constraint;
2. There is unlimited liability;
3. It is difficult to transfer ownership; and

4. The company has limited life.

The advantages and disadvantages of a general partnership are similar to the sole proprietorship. Partnerships are generally easy and inexpensive to set up and operate administratively. Partnership operating agreements are critical. Like sole proprietorships, profit allocated to the partners is based upon their share in the business.

Managerial control resides with the partners. This feature can be an advantage or disadvantage depending on how well the partners work together and the level of trust in each other. Control by any one partner is naturally diluted as the number of partners increases. Partnerships are separate legal entities that can contract in their own name and hold title to assets

The challenge to partnerships extends beyond possible conflicts with the partners. Divorce and other disputes may threaten the survival of the partnership when a claimant to a portion of the business's assets demands his/her equity.

Unlimited liability remains a strong disadvantage for a general partnership. All partners are liable for the debts of the firm. Due to this unlimited liability, the risks of the business may be spread according to the owners' equity rather than according to their interests in the business. This risk becomes an actual obligation whenever the partners are unable to satisfy their shares of the business's obligations.

Increasing the number of partners can increase the amount of capital that can be accessed by the firm. More partners tends to mean more financial resources and this can be an advantage of a partnership compared to a sole proprietorship. Still, it is generally difficult for partnerships to raise large amounts of capital—particularly when liability is not limited.

Ownership transfer and limited life continues to be a problem for partnerships; however, it may be possible to build provisions into the partnership that will allow it to continue operating if one partner leaves or dies. In some cases, parent-child partnerships can ease the difficulties of ownership transfer.

A *limited partnership* is another way businesses can organize. Limited partnerships have some partners (limited partners) who possess limited liability; limited partners do not participate in management of the firm. There must be at least one general partner (manager) who has unlimited liability. Because of the limited liability feature for limited partners, this type of business organization makes it easier to raise capital by adding limited partners. These limited partners are investors and make no management decisions in the firm.

One difficulty occurs if the limited partners wish to remove their equity from the firm. In this instance, they must find someone who is willing to buy their share of the partnership. In some cases, this may be difficult. Another difficulty is that the Internal Revenue Service (IRS) may tax the limited partnership as a corporation if it believes the characteristics of the business organization are more consistent with the corporate form of business organization.

In production agriculture, family limited partnerships serve a number of objectives. For example, parents contemplating retirement may wish to maintain their investment in a farm business but limit their liability and be free of management concerns. To reduce their liability exposure and be free of managerial responsibilities, parents can be limited partners in a business where younger family members are the general partner.

The joint venture is another variation of the partnership, usually more narrow in function and duration than a partnership. The law of partnership applies to joint ventures. The primary purpose of this form or organization is to share the risks and profits of a specific business undertaking.

Corporations

A *corporation* is a legal entity separate from the owners and managers of the firm. Three fundamental characteristics distinguish corporations from proprietorships and partnerships: (1) the way they are owned and managed, (2) their perpetual life, and (3) their legal status separate from their owners and managers.

A corporation can own property, sue and be sued, contract to buy and sell, and be fined—all in its own name. The owners usually cannot be made to pay any debts of the corporation. Their liability is limited to the amount of money they have paid or promised to pay into the corporation.

Ownership in the corporation is represented by small claims (shares) on the equity and firm's profit.

The two most common types of claims on the equity of the firm are common and preferred stock. The claims of preferred stockholders takes preference over equity claims of common stockholders in the event of the corporation's bankruptcy. Preferred stockholders must also receive dividends before other equity claims. The preferred stockholders' dividends are usually fixed amounts paid at regular intervals that rarely change. In most cases, preferred stock has an accumulated preferred feature. This means that if the firm fails to pay a dividend on preferred stock, at some point in time the corporation must make up the payment to its preferred stockholders holders before it can make payments to other equity claims.

Common stock equity claims are the last ones satisfied in the event of the corporation's bankruptcy. These are residual claims on the firm's earnings and assets after all other creditors and equity holders have been satisfied. Although it appears that common stock holders always get the "leftovers," the good news is that the leftovers can be substantial in some cases because of the nature of the fixed payments to creditors and other equity holders.

Large corporations are usually organized as Subchapter C corporations.

The advantages of a C corporation include:

1. There is limited liability;
2. The corporation has unlimited life;
3. Ownership is easily transferred; and
4. It may be possible to raise large amounts of capital.

The disadvantages of a C corporation include:

1. There is double taxation; and
2. It is expensive and complicated to begin operations and to administer.

Seeing Double

Earnings from the corporation are taxed using a corporate tax rate. When earnings are distributed to the shareholders in the form of dividends, the earnings are taxed again as ordinary income to the shareholder. For example, suppose a corporation, whose ownership is divided among its 3000 shareholders, earns $1,000,000 in taxable profits for the year and is in a flat 40-percent tax bracket. Profits per share equal $1,000,000/3000—or $333.33. The corporation pays 40% of $1,000,000—or $400,000—in taxes to the government. Taxes per share equal $400,000/3000—or $133.33.

Now suppose the corporation distributes its after-tax profits to its 3,000 shares in the form of dividends. Each shareholder would receive a dividend check of $600,000/3,000 = $200. The $200 dividend income received by each shareholder would then be taxed as ordinary personal income. If all the shareholders were in the 30-percent tax bracket, then each would pay 30% of $200 or $60 in taxes, leaving each shareholder with $140 in after-tax dividend income.

So what is the total tax rate paid on corporate earnings? Dividing the taxes paid by the corporation and the shareholder by the profit per share, the total tax rate is ($133.33+$60)/$333.33 = 58%, a higher rate than would be paid on personal income of the same amount.

One of the primary strengths of the corporate form of business organization is that the most the owners of the firm (shareholders) can lose is what they have invested in the firm. This limited liability feature means that as a shareholder, one's personal assets beyond the investment in the corporation can't be taken to satisfy the corporation's debts or obligations.

Ownership can easily be transferred by selling shares in the corporation. Likewise, the corporation has an unlimited life because when an owner dies, the ownership shares are passed to his/her heirs. The common separation of ownership and management in large corporations helps to ease the ownership transfer as the firm management process never ceases.

The easy transfer of ownership, separation of management and ownership, and limited liability features of a corporation combine to create a business structure that is designed to raise large sums of equity capital. Investors in large corporations don't have to become involved in management of the firm. Their risk is limited to the amount of funds invested in the firm, and their ownership interest can be transferred by selling their shares in the firm.

Corporations are more expensive and complicated to set up and administer than sole proprietorships or partnerships. Corporations require a charter, must be governed by a board of directors, pay legal fees, and meet certain accounting requirements. Despite the relatively high setup cost, the primary disadvantage of the corporate form of business is that income generated by the corporation is subject to double taxation.

However, there is a limit on corporate earnings that are double-taxed. The corporation may pay reasonable salaries, and these are deducted from the corporation's profits. Therefore, salaries paid to corporate workers and operators are not taxed at the corporate level. In some cases, the corporation's entire net profit may be offset by salaries to the owners so that no corporate income tax is due. On the other hand, if the corporation pays dividends to the shareholders, those payments are subject to corporate-level income tax. However, the individual does not have to pay self-employment tax on the dividends. And, qualifying dividends (and most United States Corporation dividends can fit into this definition) are taxed at capital gains rates and not the individual's top marginal tax rate. Finally, dividends paid to a shareholder that actively participates in the business are not subject to either the 0.9 percent Medicare surtax on earnings or the 3.8 percent tax on net investment income that are levied on higher-income taxpayers.

Another disadvantage of corporations has to do with the fact that the managers do not own the firm. Managers, who control the resources of the firm, may use them for their own benefit. For example, top management may build extravagantly large headquarters and buy fleets of jets and limousines for transportation. If less were spent on perquisites, then the income of the corporation would be higher. Higher income allows higher dividends to be paid to the owners (shareholder).

The (potential) self-serving behavior by management running contrary to the interests of stockholders is an example of a principal-agent problem. Methods of dealing with the principal-agent exist. One way is to hire auditors to monitor the use of firm resources. Further, a corporation has a board of directors responsible for hiring, evaluating, and removing top management. Boards are often ineffective because they meet infrequently and may not have access to the information necessary to fulfill their responsibilities. Additional problems exist if management personnel also sit on the board of directors.

Another way to deal with the principal-agent problem in corporations is to align the interests of management with those of shareholders. This is accomplished by basing the compensation of management on the value of the firm's stock. A chief executive officer could receive stock options as a part of his/her compensation package. If the stock price rises, the value of the options increase, which benefits the manager financially. The shareholders also benefit when the stock price increases. Such an arrangement may reduce the principal-agent problem. However, very high executive compensation can often trigger criticism from external groups such as consumer or labor activists.

Limitations of linking management's compensation to the value of its stock have been illustrated by Enron and Tyco corporations. These corporations inflated the value of their stocks and eventually bankrupted themselves and lost the investments of their employees. It seems there is still a lot to be learned about aligning the interests of corporate managers and shareholders.

Many small businesses, including farms, use the C corporation structure and operate much like partnership. This is frequently done for reasons of expensing and intergenerational transfer.

The corporation will need to be "capitalized" by some level of equity funds from the shareholders. It is common practice among lenders to require personal guarantees by the owners of small corporations before providing funds to the business. This essentially eliminates the limited liability features for those shareholders. As one might expect, due to these difficulties, many small corporations are not able to generate large amounts of capital by simply selling ownership shares. As a result, many small corporations do not really receive the full benefits of corporate organization but are still subject to the disadvantages, namely double taxation.

C corporations and S corporations. Any corporation is first formed under the laws of a particular state. From the standpoint of state business law, a corporation is a corporation. However, there are two types of for-profit corporations for federal tax law purposes:

- C corporations: What we normally consider "regular" corporations that are subject to the corporate income tax
- S corporations: Corporations that have filed a special election with the IRS. They are not subject to corporate income tax. Instead, they are treated similarly (but not identically) to partnerships for tax purposes.

There is an alternative form of corporate business organization that is often more desirable from a small business perspective. Subchapter S Corporations have limited liability protection, but the income for the business is only taxed once as ordinary income to the individual (Wolters Kluwer. n.d.).

Subchapter S Corporations are sometimes preferred by small businesses because they provide limited liability protection. Meanwhile the income for the business is only taxed once as ordinary income to the individual. There are requirements that must be satisfied for firms to be organized as Subchapter S corporations. These requirements include: (1) it cannot have more than 100 shareholders; (2) it may have only one class of stock; (3) it cannot have partnerships or other corporations as stockholders; and (4) it may not receive more than 20 percent of its gross receipts from interest, dividends, rents, royalties, annuities, and gains from sales or exchange of securities. In agriculture, these restrictions usually mean that only family or closely-held farm businesses can achieve Subchapter S status.

Federal income tax rules for Subchapter S corporations are similar to regulations governing partnerships and sole proprietors. However, corporations may provide certain employee benefits that are tax deductible. Accident and health insurance, group life insurance, and certain expenditures for recreation facilities all qualify. However, these benefits may be taxable to the employees and subsequently to the shareholders.

There is greater continuity for businesses organized under Subchapter S than for sole proprietorships or partnerships. Upon the death of shareholders, their shares of the corporations are transferred to the heirs and the Subchapter S election is maintained. Surveys suggest that the major reason farms incorporate is for estate planning. The corporate form allows for the transfer of shares of stock either by sale or gift. This is much easier than transferring assets by deed.

Limited Liability Company

The *Limited Liability Company (LLC)* is a relatively new form of business organization. An LLC is a separate entity, like a corporation, that can legally conduct business and own assets. The LLC must have an operating agreement which regulates its business activities and the relationship among its owners (referred to as members). There are no restrictions on the number of members or the members' identities. LLCs are subject to disclosure, record keeping, and reporting requirements that are similar to a corporation.

The attractive feature of the LLC is that all members obtain limited liability, but the entity is taxed as a general partnership. The LLC is similar in many respects to the Subchapter S corporation. The primary differences are: 1) the LLC has less restrictive membership requirements; and 2) the LLC is dissolved in the event of transfer of interest or death unless members vote to continue the LLC. Table 2.1 summarizes the primary characteristics of the business organizations discussed so far.

Table 2.1. Comparison of Business Organizations

Characteristic	Organization				
	Sole Proprietorship	Partnership	Limited Partnership	S Corporation	C Corporation
ownership	• single • individual	• two or more individuals	• two or more individuals • one or more general partners	• legal person • max 35 shareholders • individuals	• legal person
management decision	• proprietor	• partners	• general partner	• elected directors • management	• elected directors • management
life	• terminates at death	• terminates at death	• agreed term • terminates at death	• perpetual or fixed • transfer stock	• perpetual or fixed • transfer stock
transfer	• assets	• assets	• assets	• shares	• shares
income tax	• individual	• individual	• individual	• individual	• corporate • individual
liability	• unlimited	• unlimited	• general partners unlimited • limited partners limited	• limited	• limited
capital	• personal • loans	• personal • loans	• personal • loans	• shareholders • bonds • loans	• shareholders • bonds • loans

Cooperative

A *cooperative* is a business that is owned and operated by member patrons. Generally, cooperatives are thought to operate at cost, with all profits going to member patrons. The profits are usually redistributed over time in the form of patronage refunds. Cooperatives often appear to operate as profit making organizations much the same as other forms of business organization. Agricultural cooperatives do not face the same anti-trust restrictions as non-cooperative businesses, and they enjoy a different federal income tax status. In most instances, the concepts and analysis techniques covered in this course will be relevant to financial management in cooperatives.

Trusts

A *trust* transfers legal title of designated assets to a trustee, who is then responsible for managing the assets on the beneficiaries' behalf. The management objectives can be spelled out in the trust agreement. Beneficiaries retain the right to possess and control the assets of the trust and to receive the income generated by the properties owned by the trust. Beneficiaries hold the trust and personal property, rather than title to the assets. The legal status of certain types of land trusts are unclear in some states.

Farm Business Organization Types in US Agriculture

Gross cash farm income (GCFI) includes income from commodity cash receipts, farm-related income, and government payments. Family farms (where the majority of the business is owned by the operator and individuals related to the operator) of various types together accounted for nearly 98 percent of 2.05 million U.S. farms in 2018. Small family farms (less than $350,000 in GCFI) accounted for 90 percent of all U.S. farms. Large-scale family farms ($1 million or more in GCFI) accounted for about 3 percent of farms but 46 percent of the value of production.

The USDA defines a farm as a place that generates at least $1,000 value of agricultural products per year. In 2007, farms generating between $1,000 and $10,000 of agricultural products made up 60% of the 2.2 million U.S. farms. Farms producing $500,000 or more in 2007 dollars generated 96% of the value of U.S. agricultural production.[1]

1. https://www.ers.usda.gov/data-products/ag-and-food-statistics-charting-the-essentials/farming-and-farm-income

Table 2.2 shows the percentage of farms by organizational type and their share of aggregate agriculture product sales according to the 2007 Census of Agriculture. Sole proprietorships are the dominant form of business organization measured by farm count (86.5%) but have only 49.6% of the value of agricultural production. Partnerships and family corporations make up 20.8% of farms but have 43% of the value of agricultural production. Non-family corporations, part of the "other organization" category, accounted for 0.4% of farms and 6.5% of the value of agricultural production.

Table 2.2. Farm Business Organization Types (USDA Census of Agriculture, 2007. Farms in US 1,925,300)

Business Type	% of Farms	% of Cash Receipts
Sole Proprietorships	86.5%	49.6%
Partnerships	7.9%	20.9%
Family Corporations[2]	3.95	22.9%
Other[3]	1.2%	7.3%

More generally, about 80 percent of all businesses (agriculture and non-agriculture) are organized as sole proprietorships while only around 10 percent of businesses are organized as corporations. Conversely, about 80 percent of business sales come from corporations while sole proprietorships account for only about 10 percent of business sales.

> So, what have we learned? We learned that firms organize differently depending on the size, ability to manage, the need for internal versus external funding, and tax implications. Indeed, the need for different business organizations can be compared to the need for different kinds of transportation—it depends on where you are going.

2. More than 50% of the stock is owned by persons related by blood or marriage.
3. Nonfamily farms, estates or trusts, grazing associations, American Indian Reservations, etc.

Summary and Conclusions

Recognizing that we cannot offer financial management tools that meet the needs of all business organizations, we purposely focus in this text on small to medium-size businesses. As a result, we focus on firms that depend on internal capital and exercise the maximum control of the firm.

Questions

1. Describe the connection between how a business is organized and its ability to reach its goals and objectives.
2. Discuss the advantages and disadvantages of organizing a business as a sole proprietorship versus a C corporation.
3. Limited partnerships, limited liability companies, and Subchapter S corporations are alternative business organizations. Discuss the advantages and/or disadvantages these organizations offer relative to sole proprietorships, general partnerships, and C corporations.
4. Approximately 85% of all farm businesses in the US are organized as sole proprietorships. Explain why the organization form of farm businesses in the U.S. is dominated by sole proprietorships.
5. Can you explain in Table 2.2 why corporations tend to control more land than partnerships and sole proprietorships?
6. What are the advantages or disadvantages of a family corporation compared to a regular corporation?

3. Navigating Taxation: Understanding the Federal Tax System

LINDON ROBISON

Learning goals. At the end of this chapter, you should be able to: (1) describe the major components of the federal tax system; (2) know how the different forms of business organizations are taxed; (3) recognize the difference between a firm's gross income, adjusted gross income, and (4) understand how depreciation, capital gains, and depreciation recapture affect the amount of taxes a firm pays.

Learning objectives. To achieve your learning goals, you should complete the following objectives:

- Learn how to calculate the firm's tax liability by finding its taxable income
- Learn how to find the firm's average tax rate and marginal tax rates.
- Learn how to find a firm's tax liabilities by using tables of Federal Income Tax Rates.
- Learn how depreciation can reduce the firm's tax liabilities.
- Learn how to find the amount of taxes paid on interest and dividend income.
- Learn how to distinguish between capital gains and losses and depreciation recapture.
- Learn how taxes are calculated on depreciation recapture and capital gains and losses.
- Learn about the different ways depreciation can be calculated and the advantages and disadvantages of each depreciation method.

Introduction

One of the goals of financial management, according to Chapter 2, is to set up the business so that its worth is maximised. "The firm" could mean a big corporation, a small business, or even a single household. Later, we'll see that the firm's value is based on its cash flow after taxes, which can be very different from its accounting income-based profits. So, we need to know the difference between a company's cash flow and its financial income. We'll talk about this later. Luckily, for our purposes, we don't need to know a lot about how accounting is different for the different types of business organisations. So, we'll start by talking about some of the most important parts of the federal tax system that affect a company's cash flow after taxes. Because taxes have an effect on cash flow, it's important to know how the tax system works. This chapter will talk about some basic tax ideas that are important from a financial management point of view. Our attention is on the federal tax code because it is an important part of figuring out profit after taxes and cash flow after taxes. Still, there are a number of other taxes, such as state and local taxes, that can have a big effect on a company's profits.

and flow of money. When making financial choices, it is important to think about how all taxes will affect them. Congress writes the tax rules for the whole country. The Internal Revenue Service (IRS) is in charge of making sure that the code is followed and that federal income taxes are paid. The IRS makes rules that explain how the tax laws should be followed. The regulations are the tax laws that companies and people have to follow. One last word of caution: keep in mind that tax laws can and do change, and that these changes aren't always announced in a way that small businesses can understand. Still, not knowing what to do   is   not   an   excuse   for   filing   taxes   wrong.

Individual Taxes

Individual (ordinary) tax liabilities are determined by subtracting certain allowable deductions from one's total income to obtain taxable income. Taxable income is then used as the basis from which the tax liability is calculated. The general procedure is:

- *Gross income – Adjustments to income = Adjusted gross income.*
- *Adjusted gross income – Personal exemptions and deductions = Taxable income.*
- *(Taxable income) x (Average tax rate) = Tax liability.*

Gross income is all of the money, things, services, and property that you got during the tax year. Adjustments to income may include income that is not taxed, such as interest income from city bonds that are not taxed. Some past losses may also be included. No matter if you itemise or not, you can take personal exemptions and deductions out of your adjusted gross income. This includes business costs and some types of Individual Retirement Account (IRA) contributions. A personal exemption is the amount that can be taken off of your income based on how many people that income supports. You can get tax breaks for yourself, your spouse, and other people who depend on you if they meet certain requirements. From 2018 until 2025, the amount of the personal deduction is $0. You can also lower your taxable income by taking a standard deduction or listing all of your allowable costs.

The standard deduction is an amount that all taxpayers who don't itemise can take. It is the government's estimate of the typical tax-deductible costs you are likely to have. In 2018, the standard deduction is $12,000 for a single person, $18,000 for a person who is in charge of a family, and $24,000 for a married couple filing together. These are changed every year to keep up with inflation. If your tax-deductible costs are more than the standard deduction, you can list them separately and deduct the total amount of the itemised deductions. Expenses for things like hospital bills, certain types of taxes, mortgage interest, and donations to charity are some of the things that can be deducted. After taking personal exemptions and deductions out of Adjusted gross income, we get Taxable income, which is the amount of income that will be used to figure out your Tax bill.

In the United States, the Federal income tax is called a "progressive tax" because the percentage tax rate goes up as taxable income goes up. On the other hand, unfair taxes keep their tax rate the same.

stant or decrease as taxable income increases. State sales taxes, property taxes, social security taxes, and in some cases, state income taxes are regressive taxes because as a percentage of one's income paid as taxes they increase with a decline in one's income.

Two different tax rate measures include the Average tax rate and the Marginal tax rate defined below:

average tax rate = tax liability / taxable income

marginal tax rate = tax rate on the next dollar of taxable income.

The average tax rate represents the "average" tax rate that is paid on each dollar of taxable income. The marginal tax rate is the tax rate that is paid on the next dollar of taxable income. In a progressive tax system, the marginal tax rate will always be equal to or greater than the average tax rate.

The federal tax rate schedule for 2018 taxable income is shown in Table 3.1.

Table 3.1. Federal Income Tax Rates in 2018

Tax Bracket	Married Filing Jointly	Single
10% Bracket	$0 – $19,050	$0 – $9,525
12% Bracket	$19,050 – $77,400	$9,525 – $38,700
22% Bracket	$77,400 – $165,000	$38,700 – $82,500
24% Bracket	$165,000 – $315,000	$82,500 – $157,500
32% Bracket	$315,000 – $400,000	$157,500 – $200,000
35% Bracket	$400,000 – $600,000	$200,000 – $500,000
37% Bracket	Over $600,000	Over $500,000

Due to the progressive nature of the tax, the marginal tax rate increases as your income increases. The first $19,050 of taxable income for married couples filing a joint return are taxed at a rate of 10%, the next $58,350 ($77,400 – $19,050) of taxable income are taxed at a rate of 12%, and so on. Suppose a married couple had $120,000 of taxable income in 2018.

Their Federal tax liability would be calculated on each increment of income as follows: The average tax rate paid equals Total tax liability/taxable income = $18,279/$120,000 = 15.2% and the marginal tax rate paid on the last dollar earned would be 22%.

10% tax on first $19,050 ($19,050 – $0) = 10% x $19,050 = $1,905.00
12% tax on next $58,350 ($77,400 – $19,050) = 12% x $58,350 =$7,002.00
22% tax on next $42,600 ($120,000 – $77,400) = 25% x $44,700 = $9,372.00
Total Tax Liability on $120,000 = $18,279.00

It is important to distinguish between the marginal and average tax rate. The average tax rate is useful because it allows us, with a single number, to characterize the proportion of our total income that is taxed. In many cases, however, we are interested in the amount of tax that will be paid on any additional income that is earned, perhaps as a result of profitable investment. In these situations, the marginal tax rate is the appropriate rate to use. For example, suppose your average tax rate is 18.4 percent and you are in the 22 percent tax bracket, and you receive a $1,000 raise. The additional income you earn will be taxed at the marginal tax rate of 22 percent, regardless of the average tax rate, so that your increase in after-tax income is only $1,000(1 − .22) = $780. The marginal tax rate is also significant when considering the impact of tax deductions. Suppose you are in the 22 percent tax bracket and you contribute $2,000 to your favorite charity. This reduces your taxable income by $2,000, saving you $440 in taxes (22% times $2,000) so that your after-tax cost of your contribution is only $2,000(1 − .22) = $1,560.

Total Marginal Tax Rates

As we pointed out earlier, because of the progressive nature of the federal tax code, the effective marginal rate that individuals pay is nearly always greater than the federal marginal tax rate. However, there are more levels of government collecting tax revenues than just the federal government. In addition to the federal tax, most personal income is also subject to state taxes, Social Security taxes, Medicare taxes, and perhaps city taxes. State taxes vary but often run in the 4 − 6 percent range. Social Security (6.2 percent) and Medicare (1.45 percent) taxes are split between employer and employee, and the rate for most employees is 7.65 percent (self-employed pay both the employer and employee half, usually 15.3 percent). In 2018, the social security tax is imposed only on individual income up to $128,400. There is no maximum income limit on the Medicare tax. City taxes can run 3 − 4 percent. Therefore, the effective marginal tax rate for someone in the 24 percent federal tax bracket who pays social security tax will generally be over 37 percent. If the same person were self-employed they would be subject to an additional 7.65 percent, and a marginal tax rate that could exceed 50 percent of taxable income in some cases. It should be noted that one-half of "self-employment tax" is deductible from income subject to federal tax, so the effective marginal tax rate increases by only 7.65(1 − .24) = 5.81 percent for someone in the 24 percent tax bracket. As you can see, it is extremely important to understand what the effective marginal tax rate is when making financial management decisions.

Bracket Creep

Progressive tax systems are subject to an undesirable feature, often termed "bracket creep." *Bracket creep* is an inflation-induced increase in taxes that results in a loss in purchasing power in a progressive tax system. The idea is that inflation increases tend to cause roughly equal increases in both nominal income and the prices of goods and services. Inflation induced increases in income push taxpayers into higher marginal tax brackets, which reduces real after tax income. Consider an example of how inflation reduces real after-tax income and therefore purchasing power.

For the couple in our previous example with a taxable income of $120,000, their real after-tax income, their purchasing power in today's dollars, is equal to their *Gross income less* any *Tax liabilities* which in their case is: $120,000 – $18,279 = $101,721. Another way to calculate their purchasing power is to multiply (1 – average tax rate T) times their gross income: (1 – 15.2325%)$120,000 = $101,721.

Inflation is a general increase in price. Suppose that, as a result of inflation, that next year inflation will increase your salary 10%. However, suppose that inflation will also increase the cost of things you buy by 10%. As a result, to purchase the same amount of goods next year that were purchased this year will require a 10% increase in this year's expenditures. For the couple described in our earlier example, this will require expenditures of $101,721 times 110% = $111,893.10.

Now let's see what happens to our couple's after-tax income. A 10% increase in taxable income means they will have $120,000 times 110% = $132,000 in taxable income next year. Recalculating the couple's tax liabilities on their new income of $130,000:

The average tax rate paid equals Total tax liability/taxable income = $20,919/$132,000 = 15.85% while the marginal tax rate paid on the last dollar earned would be 22%. Subtracting couple's tax liabilities from their income leaves them $111,051, less than $111,893.10 which is the amount required to maintain the same purchasing power before inflation. In other words, as a result of the combination of inflation and bracket creep with increases on the average tax rate, the couple's purchasing power is reduced

The IRS recognizes the impacts of bracket creep, and periodically adjusts the tax schedules and/or deductions in an attempt to smooth or eliminate purchasing power losses due to bracket creep.

10% tax on first $19,050 ($19,050 – $0) = 10% x $19,050 = $1,905.00
12% tax on next $58,350 ($77,400 – $19,050) = 12% x $58,350 = $7,002.00
22% tax on next $54,600 ($132,000 – $77,400) = 25% x $54,700 = $12,012.00
Total Tax Liability on $132,000 = $20,919.00

Interest and Dividend Income

Interest and ordinary dividends earned by individuals are generally taxed as ordinary income. One exception is interest income earned on municipal bonds issued by state and local governments (bonds are promissory notes issued by a business or government when it borrows money). Municipal bonds are exempt from federal taxes, which makes them attractive to investors in high marginal tax brackets.

Suppose you are in a 25% marginal tax bracket and are considering investing $1,000 in either a corporate bond that yields 10% per year, (yield means the rate of return the investment provides) or a municipal bond yielding 8% each year. You can calculate your after-tax cash flow from each investment by subtracting the tax liability from the before-tax cash flow from each investment.

The corporate bond provides a $100 cash flow before taxes but only $75 is left after paying taxes. Meanwhile, the municipal bond is exempt from federal taxes and provides an $80 before and after-tax cash flow. This example illustrates the importance of considering after-tax cash flow as opposed to before-tax cash flow when considering investment opportunities.

Asset	Before-tax cash flow return	- Taxes	= After-tax cash flow
Corporate bond	$1,000(.10) = $100	$100(25%)	$75.00
Municipal bond	$1,000(.08) = $80	$0	$80.00

We can also measure an investment's return using percentages. Percentage measures standardize return measures so investments of different sizes can be compared. We calculate the percentage return during a period as the cash flow received during the period divided by the total amount invested. For example, the percentage rate of return on the corporate bond was $75/$1000=7.5%, while the percentage rate of return on the municipal bond was $80/$1000=8.0%.

When the returns on the bonds are expressed as rates of return, it is clear that the municipal bond is the preferred investment.

Suppose you wanted to find the before-tax rate of return on a corporate bond (rcb), a pre-tax equivalent rate of return that would provide the same after-tax rate of return as a tax free municipal bond (rmb). To find rcb , equate the after-tax rates of returns on the corporate and municipal bonds, rcb (1 − T) = rmb , and solve for the following:

$$r^{cb} = \frac{r^{mb}}{(1 - T)}$$
(3.1)

In our example municipal bond rate is 8% so that for an investor in the 25% marginal tax bracket, the pre-tax equivalent rate of return is:

$$r^{cb} = \frac{8\%}{(1 - 0.25)} = 10.67\%$$
(3.2)

In other words, a corporate bond yielding 10.67% would produce the same after-tax return as the municipal bond yielding 8% for an investor in the 25% tax bracket.

Interest Paid by Individuals

Interest paid by individuals is generally not tax deductible for personal expenditures, such as interest on a loan for a car used solely for personal travel. One primary, and important, exception to this is that interest on a home mortgage is usually deductible from taxable income if filing using itemized deductions. There is also a limited deduction available for student loan interest payments.

Capital Gains and Losses

From an accounting standpoint, we define *book value* (or basis) as acquisition cost less accumulated depreciation, which is determined by tax codes. (Book value may also be altered by improvements to depreciable assets.) For a variety of reasons, an asset's market value is usually different from its book value. When an asset is liquidated at a market value greater than its book value we say it has appreciated in value. If the appreciation is equal to or less than its original acquisition cost, we refer to the appreciation value as *depreciation recapture*. Appreciated value in excess of its acquisition value is referred to as *capital gains*.

Likewise, when an asset's liquidation value is less than its book value, we say that the asset has experienced *capital losses* and define: capital losses = book value − market value (if book value > market value). The tax rate for individuals on "long-term capital gains", which are gains on assets that have been held for over one year before being sold, depends on the ordinary income tax bracket. For taxpayers in the 10% or 15% bracket, the rate is 0%. For taxpayers in the 22%, 24%, 32%, or 35% bracket, it is 15%. For those in the 37% bracket, the rate is 20%. Other rates also exist under certain situations. The tax rate paid on depreciation recapture is the taxpayer's income tax rate since depreciation was used to shield income from income tax payments.

Suppose you are in the 24% tax bracket. You have just sold some land (a non-depreciable asset) for $50,000. The land was purchased 5 years ago for $30,000. Since you sold the land for more than its book value (the purchase price in this case) you will realize a capital gain of $50,000 − $30,000 = $20,000. Your tax liability on the sale will then be the capital gain times the capital gains tax rate or in this case $20,000(15%) = $3,000.

Capital losses must first be used to offset any capital gains realized that year; however, if you have any capital losses remaining after offsetting capital gains, you may offset ordinary income. If you still have capital losses remaining, you may carry the losses forward to offset future capital gains and income. This can be a powerful tool. Suppose the land in the above example brought a selling price of $20,000. Now you have realized a capital loss of $30,000 − $20,000 = $10,000. If you have not realized capital gains for the year, you can use the loss to offset your ordinary income, which in this example is being taxed at 24%. Your tax savings from the capital loss would be $10,000(24%) = $2,400. In other words, you can use the loss to reduce the level of taxable income by $10,000, which saves you $2,400 in taxes you would have been required to pay without the loss. If you had realized at least $10,000 in capital gains on assets held over 12 months during the year, your capital loss would have only saved you $10,000(.15%) = $1,500. It is clear that the current capital laws require some careful planning to capture the full benefits. (Note: some capital losses are limited to $3,000 per year to be taken against regular income. Anything left over can be carried forward to future years.)

Tax Credits

Tax deductions are subtracted from Adjusted Gross income and reduce the level of Taxable income. This results in a tax savings that is equal to the marginal tax rate for each dollar of allowable deduction. Tax credits, on the other hand, are direct deductions from one's Tax liability. Tax credits, therefore, result in a tax savings of one dollar for each dollar of tax credit. For example, consider the tax savings of a $1,000 deduction versus a $1,000 tax credit for an individual facing a 24% marginal percent tax rate:

tax deduction: tax savings = $1,000(24%) = $240; and
tax credit: tax savings = $1,000(100%) = $1,000.

Clearly, you would prefer one dollar of tax credits more than one dollar of tax-deductible expense. Tax credits come and go sporadically in the tax laws. They have been used in the past to stimulate investment in some types of assets. There are still some tax credits available today. For example, certain college tuition and child care expenses may be eligible for tax credits. Also, for each dependent child under age 17, up to $2,000 credit may be available.

Business Taxation

Remember that Subchapter S corporations, partnerships, and sole proprietorships are taxed according to the individual tax rate schedule the owner faces. Many Subchapter S corporations, partnerships, and sole proprietorships may get a 20% reduction of their Qualified Business Income, which might be their net business income. C corporations, on the other hand, are taxed according to corporate income tax rates. The corporate tax ate schedule for 2018 is now 21%.

Not all the income generated by a business's operations is subject to taxes. Most expenses incurred in order to generate the business income are deductible. In addition, there are a number of other adjustments to business income which deserve mention. Also be aware that many, but not all, states impose an additional tax on corporate income.

Depreciation

When a business purchases assets that can be used in the business for more than one year (often called capital expenditures), the business is generally not allowed to deduct the entire cost of the asset in the year in which it was purchased. *Depreciation* is an accounting expense that allocates the purchase cost of a depreciable asset over its projected economic life. This deduction acts as an expense for both accounting and tax purposes; so increases in depreciation expense result in decreased profit measures for a business. Nevertheless, depreciation expense is a *noncash expense*; that is, you aren't sending a check to anyone for the amount of the depreciation expense. This allows depreciation expense to act as a *tax shield*, which lowers taxable income, resulting in lower tax obligations and consequently higher after-tax cash flow. Accordingly, higher depreciation expenses result in lower profits but higher after-tax cash flow.

For tax purposes, there are rules that determine how you depreciate an asset. You can only depreciate an asset that has been *placed in service*, which means that it is available for use during the accounting period. There are also conventions that determine the point in time during the accounting period you must assume the asset was placed into service. Most depreciable assets are assumed to be placed into service at the mid-point of the year, regardless of the actual date they are placed in service. This is known as the *half-year convention*. There are also rules about the *recovery period* over which an asset can be depreciated. Table 3.2. shows the allowable recovery periods for different classes of farm property.

Table 3.2. Farm Property Recovery Periods[1]

Assets	Recovery Period in Years	
	Gen. Dep. System	Alter. Dep. System
Agricultural structures (single purpose)	10	15
Automobiles	5	5
Calculators and copiers	5	6
Cattle (dairy or breeding)	5	7
Communication equipment	7	10
Computers and peripheral equipment	5	5
Cotton ginning assets		
Drainage facilities	15	20
Farm buildings	20	25
Farm machinery and equipment	7	10
Fences (agricultural)	7	10
Goats and sheep (breeding)	5	5
Grain bin	7	10
Hogs (breeding)	3	3
Horses (age when placed in service)		
Breeding and working (12 yrs or less)	7	10
Breeding and working (more than 12 yrs)	3	10
Racing horses (more than 2 yrs)	3	12
Horticultural structures (single purpose)	10	15
Logging machinery and equipment	5	6
Nonresidential real property	39	40
Office furniture, fixtures and equipment (not calculators, copiers, or typewriters)	7	10

Paved lots	15	20
Residential rental property	27.5	40
Tractor units (over-the-road)	3	4
Trees or vines bearing fruit or nuts	10	20
Truck (heavy duty, unloaded weight 13,000 lbs. or more)	5	6
Truck (weight less than 13,000 lbs.)	5	5
Water wells	15	20

There are two depreciation methods that can be used for tax reporting purposes: *straight line* (SL) and *modified accelerated cost recovery system* (MACRS). Straight line allocates the depreciation expense uniformly each period. The amount of depreciation is found by multiplying the straight line recovery rate for each year times the asset's unadjusted basis (original cost). The SL recovery rate is simply the inverse of the number of years in the asset's recovery period adjusted by the required half-year placed in service convention. The straight recovery rates for 3-year, 5-year, and 7-year assets are shown in Table 3.3.

Table 3.3. Straight Line Recovery Rates for 3, 5, 7 Year Assets

Year	3-Year	5-Year	7-Year
1	16.67%	10%	7.14%
2	33.33%	20%	14.29%
3	33.33%	20%	14.29%
4	16.67%	20%	14.28%
5		20%	14.29%
6		10%	14.28%
7			14.29%
8			7.14%

As you might guess from its name, MACRS produces larger depreciation expenses in early years than the SL method of depreciation and lower depreciation expenses in the later years than the SL method of depreciation. The federal government specifies the allowable rates of MACRS depreciation. These rates are determined by using a combination of the declining balance (either 150% or 200%) and straight-line depreciation methods. Prior to 2018, farmers were not permitted to use 200% declining balance. The MACRS depreciation expense for each year is calculated by multiplying the unadjusted

1. Most assets use the General Depreciation System for recovery periods. See IRS guidelines for more information.

basis (acquisition cost) of the asset by the appropriate recovery rate for that year. The MACRS (200% method) recovery rates for the 3-year, 5-year, and 7-year asset classes are shown in Table 3.4.

Table 3.4. MACRS Recovery Rates for 3, 5, and 7-Year Assets

Year	3-Year	5-Year	7-Year
1	33.0%	20.00%	14.29%
2	44.45%	32.00%	24.49%
3	14.81%	19.20%	17.49%
4	7.41%	11.52%	12.49%
5		11.52%	8.93%
6		5.76%	8.93%
7			8.93%
8			4.46%

Suppose your business just purchased a $100,000 asset that has a 3-year useful life, and falls into 3-year class of assets. Using the SL method, the depreciation expense each year for the next 3 years would be:

Year	Recovery Rate	Unadjusted Basis	Depreciation Expense	Accumulated Depreciation
1	.1667	$100,000	$16,670	$16,670
2	.3333	$100,000	$33,330	$50,000
3	.3333	$100,000	$33,330	$88,330
4	.1667	$100,000	$16,670	$100,000

Note that the book value or basis of the asset (acquisition cost – accumulated depreciation) would be $0 after it has been fully depreciated at the end of 4 years. Because of the half-year convention, it takes 4 years to depreciate the asset, even though it falls into the 3-year classification.

Depreciation expense for the same asset using the MACRS method would be calculated as:

Year	Recovery Rate	Unadjusted Basis	Depreciation Expense	Accumulated Depreciation
1	.3333	$100,000	$33,333	$33,333
2	.4445	$100,000	$44,450	$77,780
3	.1481	$100,000	$14,810	$92,950
4	.741	$100,000	$7,410	$100,000

Note again that the depreciation expense using MACRS is higher in the early years and lower in later years than with the SL method and that the book value after 4 years is again zero. Businesses often use MACRS for tax purposes and SL for profit reporting. Can you think of any reasons why?

Some businesses that invest small amounts in capital assets are allowed to deduct up to $1,000,000 of the cost of acquired depreciable property as a current expenditure instead of a capital expenditure. This is known as *direct expensing*, and is available only to businesses that don't make large capital purchases each year. The allowable expensing amount is reduced by one dollar for each dollar of capital investment expenditure over $2,500,000 during the year. Other restrictions also apply.

Bonus or Additional Depreciation

Property purchased with a recovery period of 20 years or less may be eligible for 100% additional depreciation the year it is purchased. It is required unless the taxpayer elects out of it by class or recovery period (3, 5, 7, 10, 15, 20 year classes). It can be used on either new or used property but has limitations if purchased from a relative. Passenger automobiles may be limited to an extra $8,000 additional depreciation rather than 100%. The 100% depreciation decreases to 80% in 2024 and reduces by 20% each year after that until 2028 when it disappears.

Interest and Dividends Received

Interest and ordinary dividend income received by sole proprietorships and partnerships is taxed as ordinary income. Interest income received by corporations is taxed as corporate income. However, dividend income received by corporations is allowed eighty percent *tax exclusion* (only 20 percent is taxed) before being taxed as corporate income. The reason for the exclusion is that corporate income is already subject to double taxation, and taxing dividends as corporate income would result in triple (or more) taxation. Can you explain why?

Which is better for a corporation in a 21% marginal tax bracket: $1,000 of interest income or $1,000 of dividend income? Remember what we care about is after-tax cash flow (ATCF) so let's evaluate both investments:

Investment Income	− Taxes	= ATCF
Interest income $1,000	− $1,000(.21)	= $790
Dividend income $1,000	− $1,000(.20)(.21)	= $958

The ATCF from the dividends of $958 would be preferred to the $790 from the interest income. The dividends are effectively taxed at a lower rate than interest income. We can find the effective rate on each dollar of dividend income received by multiplying the two marginal tax rates by the proportion of income subject to tax: that is $1(.20)(T) = $1(.20)(.21) = 0.042 or 4.2%. Accordingly, the effective tax rate T for dividends in this case is 4.2% as opposed to 21% for interest income at this marginal tax rate. What incentives do federal tax laws give regarding the type of investments that corporate businesses make?

Interest and Dividends Paid

Interest expenses paid by businesses are tax deductible. Dividends or withdrawals paid by businesses are not tax deductible. Consider a firm in a 21 percent tax bracket that pays $1,000 in interest expense and $1,000 in dividends or withdrawals. What is the after-tax cost of each expense?

Expense Type	Expense	– Tax-savings	= After-tax expense
Interest expense	$1,000	– $100(.21)	= $790
Dividend expense	$1,000	– $0	= $1000

Dividends and withdrawals cost the firm $1 of after-tax income for each $1of dividend paid. Interest expense, on the other hand, costs the firm $1(1 – T) = $1(1 – .21) = $0.79 of after-tax income for each $1 of interest expense paid. Another way to think about it is to find out how much before-tax income it takes to pay $1 of both interest and dividend expenses. Using the formula discussed earlier:

Before-tax dividend expense = $1.00/(1 – .21) = $1.266
Before-tax interest expense = $0.79/(1 – .21) = $1.00

It takes $1.27 of before-tax income to pay $1 in dividend or withdrawal expense, while it takes only $1 in before-tax income to pay $1 in interest expense. The two ways for a firm to finance its assets are to use debt or equity financing. Which method of financing do the federal tax loans favor?

> So, what have we learned? It's not what you earn but what you get to keep that matters. And that's where tax management plays an important role. Taxes are an important difference between what you earn and what you get to keep. Thus, an important part of strategic financial management is managing one's tax obligations.

Summary and Conclusions

The main lesson for managing taxes is to look at investments and cash flow on an after-tax basis, and this requires that all tax obligations are accounted for in the tax management process. Management of the firm's taxes also requires managers to understand how different business organizations can create different tax obligations, the difference between average and marginal tax rates, the different tax obligations associated with interest versus dividend income, capital gains and capital losses, depreciation schedules, book value and market value of assets, tax deductions, and tax credits. Understanding these and other tax-related concepts will help financial managers manage the difference between what you earn and what you get to keep.

Questions

1. Tiptop Farms, a sole proprietorship, had a gross income of $600,000 in 2018. Tiptop Farms expenses were equal to $320,000. Tiptop had interest expenses of $80,000 and depreciation expenses of $75,000 during the year. Tiptop's owner withdrew $25,000 from the business during the year to help pay college expenses for the owners' children. The tax schedule for 2018 is:

Income	Tax Rate
$0 – 40,000	15%
$40,001 – 100,000	28%
$100,000 – 150,000	31%
$150,001 +	35%

   a. What was Tiptop's taxable income during 2018?
   b. What is Tiptop's tax liability for 2018?
   c. What is Tiptop's average and marginal tax rate for the year?
   d. If Tiptop is considering the purchase of a new investment, what tax rate should they use?

2. Consider a couple filing jointly, whose taxable income last year was $130,000. Assume that state taxes on their taxable earnings were 5%. The couple pays social security at the rate of 6.2%, and Medicare taxes at the rate of 1.45%. Half of the couple's social security and Medicare taxes are paid by their employer. Also recognize that social security was only charged on the first $128,400. Find the couples tax liability, its average tax rate, and its marginal tax rate. What is higher, the couple's average tax rate or their marginal tax rate? Explain your answer.

3. Suppose that last year, inflation was 8%, meaning that the price of every- thing you buy has increased by 8%. If your before-tax income increased by 8% would you be just as well off as before? If not, how much more than 8% would you need to increase to buy as much as you did before inflation?

4. A corporate bond is providing a yield of 12% per year, while at the same time, a municipal bond (which is tax exempt) is yielding 9% per year. Each bond only pays interest each year until the bond matures, at which time the principal investment will be returned. Each bond is equally risky, and your marginal tax bracket is 30%. You have $1,000 to invest.

   a. What is the after-tax cash flow from each bond? Which bond would you invest in?
   b. What is the percentage after-tax return on each bond?
   c. What before-tax equivalent on the corporate bond would make you choose it as an invest- ment?
   d. Suppose that you are also subject to a 5% state tax from which neither the corporate or municipal bond is tax exempt. What is the after-tax return on each bond?

5. Suppose you invest in a new tractor during the tax year that costs you $78,000, plus $2,000 for delivery and set up. Your marginal tax rate is 40%. Note: *new farm machinery has a class life of 5 years.*

    a. What is the depreciation expense each year using the straight line method of depreciation?

    b. What is the depreciation expense each year using the MACRS 200% declining balance method of depreciation?

    c. What is the tax shield each year from each method?

    d. Which method would you use for tax purposes? How about profit reporting? Explain.

6. Businesses often use MACRS for tax purposes and SL for profit reporting. Can you think of any reasons why?

4. Mitigating Uncertainty: Strategies for Managing Risk

LINDON ROBISON

Learning goals. After completing this chapter, you should be able to: (1) define and measure risk; (2) understand how a person's risk aversion affects his/her resource allocation; (3) distinguish between direct and indirect outcome variables; and (4) evaluate alternative risk response strategies available to firm and as managers including by assigning risk and outcome variable to a sking outcomes, diversifying investments, pauprobasibilityriskeredycfingatives(pdfi)tso the rchobasimg ariabteimal capital structure.

* Learn how measure the variability and central tendencies of random variables using the expected
Learning objectives. To achieve your learning goals, you should complete the following objectives: values and variances of their probability density functions.
* Learn how risk premiums can be used to measure the cost of risk.
* Learn how to describe the risky choice set facing firm managers using expected value-variance (EV) efficient sets.
* Learn about the normal probability density function and understand why it is so important when describing risky events.
* Learn how sharing risk with others can be a useful response to risk.
* Learn how purchasing insurance can be a useful response to risk.
* Learn how diversification can be a useful response to risk.
* Learn how purchasing risk-reducing inputs can be a useful response to risk.
* Learn how leverage affects the level of risk facing the firm.

Introduction

In this part, we look at how the company handles risk in order to reach its goals. Risk usually comes from things outside of the firm's control, but there are things the firm can do to reduce the harm it could do and put itself in a position to gain from the good it could do. Before we look at the different ways a company can deal with risk, we need to define it, figure out how to measure it, and then figure out how to include it when making business strategies.

The word "uncertain" is used to describe something like a hurricane or a football game whose result is not known for sure. There must be at least two possible results for something to be uncertain, and usually there are more. In the past, there was a difference between risky and uncertain events based on how much knowledge was available about the possible outcomes of an event and how likely those outcomes were. For example, when you flip a coin, there are two possible results.
:

"heads" (H) and "tails" (T) are the results. We can figure out that about 50 percent of the time, when a fair coin is tossed, it will land on either "heads" or "tails." Some people might call this event risky because we know a lot about the possible results and how likely they are to happen.

Now think about something else: the throw of a thumbtack1. How likely is it that the thumbtack will land on its side rather than its head? This event could be called unclear because we don't know much about it and can't figure out how likely it is to happen based on our past experiences or logic.

Many people no longer care about the difference between dangerous and uncertain events, and most researchers use the words uncertain and risky to describe the same things. One reason why many people don't know the difference between risky and uncertain events is that assigning probabilities to event outcomes is subjective. We never have enough information to be absolutely sure about either possible outcomes or their probabilities, and probabilities can be based on things other than logic and past observations, such as hunches, omens, the experiences of others in irrelevant situations, and the advice of people who aren't qualified.

Still, it might be helpful to tell the difference between dangerous and uncertain events. People seem to say that things are unclear when they don't know for sure what will happen. It also seems to be common to call uncertain events risky when they are uncertain and their occurrence changes the well-being of the person making the choice. So, only risky events matter, no matter how sure you are about the odds of different results (like the flip of a coin vs. the flip of a thumbtack).

The study of risky events is useful in financial management, especially when we need to estimate future cash flow to help us make decisions about capital planning.

Statistical Concepts Useful in Describing Risky Events and Risky Outcomes

Density function of probabilities. A probability density function (PDF) is a way to figure out how likely something is to happen. For example, the result of tossing a fair coin can be either "heads" (H) or "tails" (T). The file for this event may give H a 50% chance of happening and T a 50% chance of happening. A PDF can be either discrete or continuous. If the possible results of an event are limited, then a discrete pdf shows how likely they are to happen. If the possible results of an event are infinite, then a continuous pdf shows how   likely   they   are   to   happen.

Random factors. A random variable is a number that is given to the result of a risky event by a rule or function. The chance that a random variable will have a certain number is the same as the

1. The authors thank Jack Meyer for the thumbtack example of an uncertain event.

probabilities of its underlying event outcome. For example, suppose that an event were the toss of a coin. We might assign the outcome of heads the number one, and the outcome of tails the value of zero. Then the probability of a random variable taking on the value one is the same probability as H occurring when tossing a coin.

Expected values. An expected value is one measure used to describe the properties of a pdf. It is sometimes called the first moment of the pdf because it measures the center of a pdf's mass (like the fulcrum of a teeter totter).

The expected value of a pdf is determined by calculating a weighted average of the possible values of the random variable values times their likelihood of occurring. To illustrate, consider two possible investments A and B. The event is the operation of the economy with three possible outcomes: a recession with 20% likelihood, a stable economy with 60% likelihood, and a growth economy with 20% likelihood. The value of the random variables describing the three outcomes for investments A and B are described in Table 4.1 and represent alternative rates of return on the investments.

Table 4.1. pdfs and Random Variables Associated with Investments A and B

Economic outcomes	pdf associated with economic outcomes	Returns on investment A (a random variable)	Returns on investment B (a random variable)
Recession	20%	-20%	-40%
Stable	60%	20%	20%
Growth	20%	40%	60%
Expected values of investments A and B		16%	16%
Variances (standard deviations) of investments A and B		.039 (19.6%)	.103 (32.0%)

The expected value operator is expressed as E(). The expected value of investment A is the sum of A's random variables weighted by their respective probabilities and is written as:

$$(4.1) \quad E(\text{Investment A}) = (.2)(-.20) + (.6)(.20) + (.2)(.4) = 16\%$$

The expected value of investment B is written as:

$$(4.2) \quad E(\text{Investment B}) = (.2)(-.40) + (.6)(.20) + (.2)(.60) = 16\%$$

In general, the expected value of random variable y_j which occurs with discrete probability p_j with $j = 1, ..., n$ outcomes is expressed as:

$$(4.3) \quad E(y) = \sum_{j=1}^{n} p_j y_j$$

and where the sum of all probabilities of y_j occurring equal 1:

$$\sum_{j=1}^{n} p_j = 1$$
(4.4)

A special kind of expected value is the mean. A mean is calculated for n observations from an unknown pdf where every observation is equally likely. Suppose we observed five draws from an unknown distribution equal to 8, 4, 0, 2, and 6. Since we assume each observation was equally likely, $1/n$, or $1/5$, in this case the expected value is equal to the mean calculated as

$$\bar{x} = \frac{\sum x_i}{n}$$
(4.5a)

$$\bar{x} = \frac{8+4+0+2+6}{5} = \frac{20}{5} = 4.$$
(4.5b)

Variance and standard deviation. Even though the expected values of investments A and B described above are equal, most investors would not consider them equally attractive because of the wide differences in the variability of the values assumed by their random variables. One approach to measuring the variability of a random variable is to calculate its variance or the square root of its variance equal to its standard deviation. We can find the variance of a random variable y_j with n possible outcomes by summing y_j minus $E(y)$ quantity squared weighted by the probability of random variable occurring. We write the variance formula for random variable y_j as:

$$\text{Variance}(y) = \sigma_y^2 = \sum_{j=1}^{n} p_j [y_j - E(y)]^2$$
(4.6)

We illustrate the variance formula by calculating the variances and standard deviations for investments A and B. The variance for investment A is calculated as:

$$\sigma_A^2 = .2(-.2 - .16)^2 + .6(.2 - .16)^2 + .2(.4 - .16)^2 = .039$$
(4.7)

Meanwhile the standard deviation for investment A can be found by calculating the square root of the variance of investment A and is equal to:

$$\sigma_A = \sqrt{\sigma_A^2} = \sqrt{.039} = .196 \text{ or } 19.6\%$$
(4.8)

The variance for investment B is calculated as:

$$\sigma_B^2 = .2(-.4 - .16)^2 + .6(.2 - .16)^2 + .2(.6 - .16)^2 = .103$$
(4.9)

Meanwhile the standard deviation for investment B is found to equal:

$$\sigma_B = \sqrt{\sigma_B^2} = \sqrt{.103} = .320 \text{ or } 32\%$$

(4.10)

One reason for measuring the variability of the random variable by squaring its deviations from its expected value is because were we to find the average of the deviation of the random variable from their expected values, they would always sum to zero. They would sum to zero because probability weighted deviations above the expected value exactly equal probability weighted deviations below the expected value. Taking the square root of the variance of returns converts the deviation measure to units comparable with those of the original random variable. Thus, from the standard deviations calculated above, we can infer that, on average, the random variable representing investment A will deviate 19.6% from its expected value while the random variable representing investment B will deviate 32.0% from its expected value. Clearly, risky outcomes for investment B are more variable—and some would say more risky—than outcomes associated with investment A. We add to the descriptions in Table 4.1 of investments A and B their respective variances (standard deviations).

The variance of the sample is found as before by summing and squaring the deviations from the mean weighted by their probability of occurrence. However, for reasons not discussed here, the variance of the sample of observations is divided by $n-1$ instead of n where n is the number of observations. Thus the standard deviation from a sample distribution is denoted S_x for observations on the random variable x. Otherwise the variance of the random variable x drawn from the true population is divided by n. Therefore in our example, the sample standard deviation, the square root of the variance is:

$$S = \sqrt{\frac{(\sum x_i - \bar{x})^2}{n-1}}$$

(4.11a)

$$S = \sqrt{\frac{(8-4)^2 + (4-4)^2 + (0-4)^2 + (2-4)^2 + (6-4)^2}{4}}$$

$$= \sqrt{\frac{40}{4}} = \sqrt{10}$$

(4.11b)

Risk premiums and certainty equivalent incomes. While not properties of pdfs, important concepts connected to pdfs describing investments are risk premiums and certainty equivalent incomes. While these concepts are related to pdf properties, they also depend on risk preferences of individual decision makers for the variance and expected return inherent in the investment. Risk premiums, certainty equivalent incomes, and risk preferences can be easily explained.

Suppose an investor faced investment A described in Table 4.1 and had the opportunity to receive its expected value with certainty in exchange for paying a risk premium. What is the largest risk premium the investor would pay to receive the investment's expected value with certainty? The answer would depend on the investor's risk preferences. If the investor would pay a positive risk premium to receive investment A's expected value with certainty, then the investor is risk averse. If the investor would pay nothing to receive investment A's expected value with certainty, the investor is risk neutral. If the investor would pay to keep the variability (the investor enjoys gambling), we would say the investor is risk preferring.

Once we know the investor's risk premium for a particular investment's pdf, we can find their certainty equivalent income by subtracting it from the investment's expected value. We can describe the relationship between the ith investor's risk premium, certainty equivalent income, risk attitudes, and the expected value and variance of the random variable in the following expression:

$$(4.12) \quad y^i_{CE} = E(y) - \frac{\lambda^i}{2}\sigma^2_y$$

In equation (4.12), the ith investor's certainty equivalent income $y_{CE}{}^i$ for an investment whose possible values are represented by the random variable y is equal to the expected value of y less a risk premium. In equation (4.13), we can solve for the largest insurance premium the investor would be willing to pay to receive the investment's expected value with certainty.

$$(4.13) \quad \frac{\lambda^i}{2}\sigma^2_y = E(y) - y^i_{CE}$$

The ith's investor's risk premium is equal to the decision maker's risk preference measure λ^i divided by 2 times the variance of the random variable y. The investor's risk aversion coefficient $\lambda^i / 2$ is best understood as a slope coefficient that indicates the response on the investor's certainty equivalent income by an increase in a unit of variance of the random variable y.

Expected value–variance criterion. Suppose we had a set of pdfs each representing the likelihood of m alternative random variables. Furthermore, suppose each of the m investments were described using their expected values and variances. Then, assuming that all investors were risk averse and without knowing each investor's risk aversion coefficient, we know that for every two investments with equal expected values (variances) and unequal variances (expected values) the investor would prefer the investment with the smaller variance (largest expected value). On the other hand, we could not rank two investments in which one had a larger expected value and variance than the other. The set of investments and ranked preferred for risk averse decision makers is called the expected value-variance (EV) efficient set. The graph of a particular EV set follows.

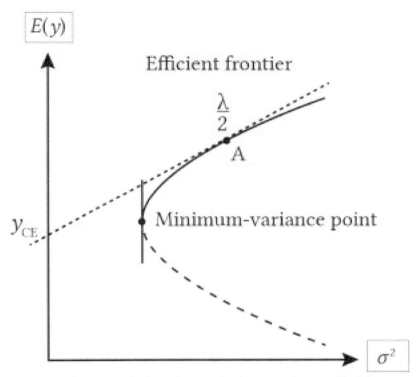

Figure 4.1 An Efficient Expected Value-Variance Frontier of Investments Represented by their Expected Values E(y) and Variances σ^2.

Suppose that we were to draw a line tangent to the relevant section of the EV at point A, representing an investment A. Then the slope of the line at point A would equal the decision maker's risk coefficient at the point. Furthermore, were we to extend the tangent line to intersect with the vertical axis, the point of intersection would equal the certainty equivalent of the investment.

The Normal Probability Density Function (pdf)

If you have a large enough sample of outcomes from a normal distribution, the distribution will look like a bell-shaped curve.

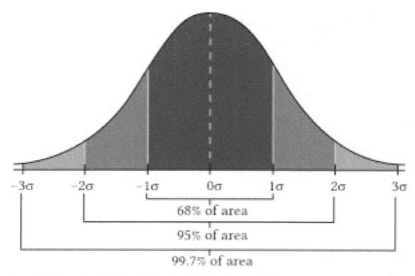

Figure 4.2. A normal probability distribution that describes probability in areas divided to standard deviations from the mean.

The normal distribution is symmetric about its expected value. The numbers in the graph correspond to standard deviations measured from the mean of the normal distribution. All of the characteristics of the normal distribution are completely described by the mean and variance (or equivalently, the standard deviation). The mean specifies the average value of the rate of return. The probability of getting a return above or below the mean by a certain amount is determined by the size of the standard deviation.

If the returns are normally distributed, there is a 68% chance that the return for any given period will be within one standard deviation of the expected value; a 95% probability that any particular observed return will be within 2 standard deviations of the expected value; and a 99.74% probability that any return will be within 3 standard deviations of the mean. Clearly, the larger the standard deviation, the more spread out the actual returns that occur will be. Suppose the common stock returns we looked at earlier were generated by a normal distribution. We estimated the expected value of the distribution to be $r = 18.92\%$ and the standard deviation to be $\sigma(r) = 16.18\%$. If we were interested in predicting what next year's return on common stocks will be, we could say that the expected value will be about 18.92%, but, in addition, there is a 68.26% probability that returns will be between 2.74% and 35.1%; a 95.44% probability that returns will be between –13.44% and 51.28%; and a 99.74% chance that the returns will be between –29.62% and 67.46%. The smaller the standard deviation, the less spread out the returns will be and the more accurate the mean will be as a predictor of future returns.

Sampling error. The normal distribution is an important distribution from both a theoretical and a practical standpoint. It is important to note that if you are looking at a small sample of data, its empirically based pdf is likely not to have the shape of a normal distribution even if it is actually generated from a normal distribution. In a small sample, the distribution will have gaps and holes in it and is unlikely have a shape that looks like the true distribution that generated the data. If you keep adding observations from the distribution, eventually the gaps will fill in, and it will start to look like the true distribution that generated the data. The point here is, even if the sample pdf generated by a normal distribution does look like a normal distribution, this may be because the sample size is too small. Therefore, because of its usefulness and tractability, we often assume that our sample pdfs are normally distributed.

Direct and Indirect Outcome Variables

Typically, we connect a risky event ϵ to a random variable $y(\epsilon)$. For example, ϵ may represent uncertain prices and $y(\epsilon)$ may represent income which depends on uncertain prices ϵ. We will refer to ϵ as the direct outcome variable and $y(\epsilon)$ as the indirect outcome variable over which the firm's utility is defined.

In most risk models, the relationship between ϵ and $y(\epsilon)$ is monotonic, if the direct outcome variable goes up (down) so does the indirect outcome variable. If prices increase, so does income; if the variance of ϵ increases, so does the variance of $y(\epsilon)$. However, one can easily construct examples in which the linkage is not so direct. For example, suppose the firm faces financial stress and that only very favorable outcomes will permit the firm to meet its cash flow obligations and survive. Under such circumstances, the firm may increase its expected income and its probability of surviving by choosing a strategy that increases its variance of direct outcomes. Consider such a problem by defining an indirect outcome variable $w = 0$ if the firm fails to survive and $w = 1$ if the firm survives. In this model the direct outcome variable is y. Then we connect the indirect outcome variable w to the direct outcome variable y by defining a survival income y_d and defining w in terms of y as follows:

$$w = \begin{cases} 0 \text{ for } y < y_d \\ 1 \text{ for } y \geq y_d \end{cases}$$

The ad hoc decision rule can be expresses as:

$$V(y) = \begin{cases} U(0) \text{ for } y < y_d \\ U(1) \text{ for } y \geq y_d \end{cases}$$

Since U(0) and U(1) are arbitrarily assigned values, let U(0) = 0 and U(1) = 1. Then, the ad hoc decision rule to be maximized is:

$$(4.14) \quad \text{Max } 1 - Pr(y < y_d)$$

which calls for minimizing $Pr(y < y_d)$. This rule is known as Roy's safety-first rule. When direct outcomes are defined in terms of winning or losing, Roy's safety-first rule is consistent with an expected utility model.

Of course, one can think of other direct and indirect outcome variable relationships. For example, y could represent uninsured income and w could represent insured income, or y could represent unhedged income and w could represent hedged income, or y could represent income produced without risk reducing inputs and w could represent income produced with risk reducing inputs.

So, what have we learned? We learned that risk responses are defined over direct outcome variables. Failure to distinguish between indirect and direct outcome variables may lead us to view responses to indirect outcome variables as risk preferring when they are indeed risk averting.

Firm Responses to Risk

Individuals and businesses all face risky events, including the possibility of losses that leave them less well off than before the outcome associated with the risky event occurred. These outcomes may include you or someone you care about becoming ill or unemployed. Business also face the possibility of losing customers, production failures, declining prices, and loss of financial support.

The next section describes alternative responses to risky events available to firms and individuals. If firms and individuals limit their risk responses described by alternatives on an EV frontier and select risky alternatives consistent with their underlying risk preferences, then they will maximize their certainty equivalent income. Higher risk-averse decision makers will select investments with lower expected values and variances. Less risk-averse decision makers will select investments with higher expected values and variances. If the firm's current risk position is an expected value-variance combination off the frontier, then the firm's risk responses may be designed to move the firm closer to a position on the EV frontier.

More to the point, a firm moving up or down its EV frontier involves paying another unit to absorb part or all of its risk (e.g. buying insurance) or changing the relative amount of safe and risky investments in its portfolio.

Someone once claimed that economists can predict the past correctly only 50% of the time. Imagine how successful economists are at predicting future outcomes for risky events? This should suggest that even though we present risk response solutions in closed forms, we should be cautious and explore alternative assumptions and predictions to explore the robustness of our estimates. With that caution in mind, we proceed to explore external risk responses (pay others to absorb our risk) and internal risk responses (change the firm's holdings of risky and safe investments).

Our discussion of risky and uncertain events and how to measure the probabilities of their outcomes has prepared us to evaluate alternative risk responses including: (1) sharing risk with others through various arrangements including forming partnerships and cooperatives, (2) buying insurance, (3) diversifying one's holdings of risky investments, (4) purchasing risk reducing inputs, and (5) choosing optimal capital structure. In addition, we will introduce the expected value-variance criterion for ranking alternative risky investments.

Sharing Risky Outcomes

One way to mitigate the impact of adverse outcomes associated with risky events is by forming risk sharing arrangements with others even when they are facing similar risks. The key to successful risk reduction combinations with others is to combine operations that are statistically independent of each other. Statistical independence has a precise meaning, but essentially it means that the expected value of the product of two random variables equals the product of their expected values. In a later section we will discuss combining firms' operations within other firms whose returns tend to move together.

To make the point that combining units experiencing independent risky outcomes can mitigate risk, consider the following. Let x be a random variable with expected value μ_x and variance σ_x^2 respectively. Let "a" and "b" equal numerical constants. Then, define a new random variable:

(4.15) $y = a + bx$

The variance of y, σ_y^2, is equal to:

(4.16) $\sigma_y^2 = b^2 \sigma_x^2$

The explanation for equation (4.16) is that the variance of the constant "a" or any constant is always zero while the variance of a constant times a random variable is the constant squared times the variance of the random variable.

In equation (4.15) we created a new random variable y by linearly transforming the random variable x. Now consider another way to create a new random variable—by taking the average of two (or more) random variables). For example, suppose two businesses were facing independently distributed risky earnings. One business owner faced the random variable x_1 and the second business owner faced the random variable x_2. Also suppose that the two business owners decided to combine their businesses and agreed that each would receive half of the average earnings. In this process we define a new random variable:

$$y = \frac{x_1 + x_2}{2}$$

(4.17)

First, recognize that each random variable is multiplied by the constant (1/2). Then each partner would earn on average the expected value

$$E\left(\frac{x_1 + x_2}{2}\right) = \left(\frac{\mu_{x_1} + \mu_{x_2}}{2}\right)$$

(4.18)

and the variance each owner would face would be the variance of the expected return multiplied by the constant (1/2) squared. The variance of the average earnings each firm would receive, σ_y^2, is equal to:

$$\sigma_y^2 = \left(\frac{1}{4}\right)\left(\sigma_{x_1}^2 + \sigma_{x_2}^2\right)$$

(4.19)

In the case that the distributions were identically distributed with expected value and variance of μ_x and σ_x^2, each partner would face the same expected value as before, μ_x. But, the variance of their individual earnings would be $(\sigma_x^2 + \sigma_x^2)/4 = \sigma_x^2/2$, half of what it was before without combining their businesses. Furthermore, the standard deviation of the earnings each partner would face would be:

$$\sqrt{\frac{\sigma_x^2}{2}} = \frac{\sigma_x}{\sqrt{2}}$$

(4.20)

And if n partners joined together, then they would each face the same expected value as before, but the variance each partner would receive is $\sigma_x/\sqrt{n}$. We now illustrate these important results.

Assume that business one's earnings are determined by outcomes associated with the toss of a fair coin. If the outcome of the coin toss is tails, the firm pays (loses) $5,000. If the toss is a heads, the firm wins $8,000. Thus, the firm wins either $8,000 or loses $5,000 and earns on average (.5) (−5,000) + (.5) (8,000) = $1500.

The standard deviation of this risky outcome is:

$$\sqrt{(.5)(-\$5,000 - \$1,500)^2 + (.5)(\$8,000 - \$1,500)^2} = \$6,500$$

(4.21)

Furthermore, assuming a normal distribution, 68% of the time, the average outcome will be between the mean and plus or minus one standard deviation: ($1,500 + $6,500) = $8,000 and ($1,500 − $6,500) = −$5,000.

Now suppose that two persons decide to combine their operations and share the average of the outcomes. Then the possible outcomes of two coin tosses are two heads (H, H) which earns on average

$16,000 / 2 = $8,000 and occurs with a probability of .25; two tails (T, T) which earns on average −$10,000 / 2 = −$5,000 and occurs with a probability of .25, and one head and one tail (H, T) or one tail and one head (T, H) which both earn on average $3,000 / 2 = $1,500 and each occurs with a probability of .25. The expected value for each of the two players can now can be expressed as:

(4.22)
$$(.25)(\$8,000) + (.25)(-\$5,000) + (.25)(\$1,500) + (.25)(\$1,500) = \$1,500$$

The two players now receive on average the same as before, $1,500, but consider the standard deviation of the average outcome:

(4.23)
$$\sqrt{(.25)(8,000 - 1,500)^2 + (.25)(-\$5,000 - 1,500)^2 + (.5)(\$1,500 - \$1,500)^2}$$
$$= \$4,596$$

Furthermore, assuming a normal distribution, 68% of the time, the average outcome will be between the mean and plus or minus one standard deviation: ($1,500 + $4596) = $6096 and ($1,500 − $4596) = −$3096. Note that even though the expected value did not change when outcomes were averaged over two persons, the standard deviation was reduced almost 30%. Also note that the results are in accord with equation (4.24):

(4.24) $$\frac{\sigma_x}{\sqrt{n}} = \frac{\$6,500}{\sqrt{2}} = \$4,596$$

Now imagine ten persons each facing independent and identical distributed earnings outcomes, then the standard deviation each would face would equal:

(4.25) $$\frac{\sigma_x}{\sqrt{n}} = \frac{\$6,500}{\sqrt{10}} = \$2,055$$

Furthermore, assuming a normal distribution, 68% of the time, the average outcome will range between ($1,500 − $2,055) = −$555.48 and ($1,500 + $2,055) = $3,555. Note that even though the expected value did not change when outcomes were averaged over ten persons, the standard deviation was reduced almost over 70%. Reducing the variability for each person by over 70% by combining ten independent risky events (facing each of 10 independent firms) illustrates the power of reducing risk by sharing independent risky events.

In the previous example we assumed that each partner contributed an equal share. Now assume two persons decided to form a partnership and share the risk and expected returns weighted by their shares contributed to the business. Assume partner 1 contributed w_1 = 30% of the assets and partner 2 contributed w_2 = 70% of the business. Each partner's business rate of return can be described by random variable y_1 and y_2 with expected values and variances for partner one of $\mu_1 = 10\%$ and $\sigma_1{}^2 = (5\%)^2$ for the first partner and $\mu_2 = 12\%$ and $\sigma_2{}^2 = (6\%)^2$ for the second partner. We want to find expected value of the partnership and each partner's share of the expected value. Then, we want to find the variance of the partnership and the variance of returns each partner would face.

First, to find the expected value of the partnership, we weight each partner's contribution by the percentage of their contributions. Call the expected return of the partnership $E(y_p)$:

$$(4.26) \quad E(y_p) = w_1\mu_1 + w_2\mu_2 = (.3)(10\%) + (.7)(12\%) = 11.4\%$$

Meanwhile, the variance of expected return from the partnership is the sum of the individual variances multiplied by the partners' shares squared:

$$(4.27) \quad \sigma_y^2 = w_1^2\sigma_{x_1}^2 + w_2^2\sigma_{x_2}^2 = (.3)^2(.05)^2 + (.7)^2(.06)^2 = .002 = (4.5\%)^2$$

Furthermore, the standard deviation of the portfolio is 4.5%. Thus, the partnership earns 11.4% on its investments and faces a standard deviation of returns equal to 4.5% which is less than their standard deviation of returns faced alone equal to 5.0% or 6.0%. Of course, they would have to agree on how to distribute profits, but we assume it would be based on the shares they contributed.

Reducing Risk by Purchasing Insurance

It may be difficult for an individual firm to agree with other independent firms on how to share profits and risk. However, an insurance company that absorbs individual firms' risk in exchange for an insurance premium can reduce the overall risk by combing the risk facing large numbers of individual firms. Furthermore, by carefully selecting businesses from different geographic areas and of different types, the risk absorbed by individual firms can be close to negligible.

For most individuals and businesses, insurance offers a way to reduce their risk when other measures are not available. Insurance is a practical arrangement by which a company or government agency provides compensation for a wide variety of losses and adverse outcomes. For example, we can purchase health insurance in case we become ill, fire insurance in case of a fire, term and whole life insurance for our heirs if we die, revenue insurance in case our expenses exceed income, trip insurance in case our flight gets canceled, and almost any other adverse outcome as long as we are willing to pay someone to assume the possibility of loss. This kind of insurance, discrete disaster event insurance, is described next.

Discrete disaster event insurance. Consider a firm with wealth comprised of a risky asset, whose value is W in the best state of nature and zero in the worst state of nature, and risk-free assets valued at W_0 regardless of the state of nature. An insurance company is willing to absorb the risk of possible losses of wealth in exchange for an insurance premium π_s. The firm must determine the maximum insurance premium π_b it can pay to avoid a disaster without reducing the level of its certainty equivalent wealth below the level attained with no insurance coverage. The firm can increase its certainty equivalent income by purchasing insurance if $\pi_s < \pi_b$.

Suppose the firm is considering a comprehensive fire insurance policy and W represents the value of the firm's flammable property being insured. To the find the maximum insurance premium π_b that the firm can pay without reducing its certainty equivalent income, we form the decision matrix displayed in Table 4.2.

The matrix has two possible states of nature, two choices, and four different possible outcomes. The states of nature are (1) a fire state s_1, and (2) a no-fire state s_2 . The choices are buy insurance (choice A_1) and remain uninsured (choice A_2). If choice A_1 is selected, the outcome in both states s_1 and s_2 is initial wealthy $W + W_0$ less an insurance premium π_s. This result is obtained because if a fire does occur, the insurance company reimburses the firm for its losses and receives a risk premium. If there is no fire, the insurance company pays for no losses while still earning the insurance premium. In both states the firm purchasing insurance pays a premium. If, on the other hand, the firm decides to remain uninsured (choice A_2) and no fire occurs, the firm will be left with both its safe wealth W_0 and its risky wealth W and will have saved the insurance premium because it didn't purchase insurance. However, if a fire does occur, the firm will lose its risky wealth W. These results are summarized below.

Table 4.2. Decision Matrix for Insurance Versus No Insurance with a Discrete Disaster Outcome.

States of nature	Probability of outcomes	Choices	
		A_1 (buy insurance) outcomes	A_2 (Don't buy insurance) outcomes
(s_1) fire	$0 < p < 1$	$W + W_0 - \pi_s$	W_0
(s_2) no fire	$1 - p$	$W + W_0 - \pi_s$	$W + W_0$

If the probability of fire is p and the probability of no fire is $1 - p$, the expected values of the two choices $E(A_1)$ and $E(A_2)$ are:

$$(4.28) \quad E(A_1) = W + W_0 - \pi_s$$

And

$$(4.29) \quad E(A_2) = pW_0 + (1 - p)(W + W_0) = W + W_0 - pW$$

The difference between $E(A_1)$ and $E(A_2)$ can be expressed as:

$$(4.30) \quad E(A_1) - E(A_2) = pW - \pi_s$$

If the decision maker was risk neutral and decided between options based on their expected value, the maximum the client would pay for the fire insurance would be $pW = \pi_b$, and as long as $\pi_b < \pi_s$ the client would be better off purchasing insurance than not purchasing insurance.

To illustrate, suppose that the flammable property was W = $100,000 and p = 1%. Then, the most a client could pay and break-even based on his or her expected values would be pW = (.01)($100,000) =

$1,000. If an insurance policy was available for less than $1,000, the client would be advised to purchase the insurance. Suppose the client is risk averse and lays awake at night worrying about the possibility of a fire, and perhaps the client is willing to pay an additional insurance premium based on some function of p and W equal to U(p,W) $150 to know that, no matter what, the outcome will be W + W$_0$ – π_b – U(p,W) = $100,00 + W$_0$ – $1,150.

Revenue insurance. One for the most important forms of insurance available to individual and firms is revenue insurance. The general principles of revenue insurance can be complicated. We describe a simplified version of revenue insurance with discrete outcomes.

Suppose an outcome from a crop operation is a risky event with three possible outcomes: normal income y, reduced income γy where γ is a percentage between one and zero, or a failed crop resulting in y = 0. Let the probability of y be p_1. Let the probability of γy be p_2. And let the probabilities of a failed crop and zero income be $(1 - p_1 - p_2)$.

The insurance provided does not fully compensate farmers for their losses for moral hazard reasons; they want the farmers to experience some losses for not producing a normal crop.

As a result, lost revenues are only compensated by δ percent. Furthermore, there is a complicated process to determine what is a normal yield that produces y. If a failed crop outcome occurs, the firm receives δy or δ percent of what it normally earns. If a partial crop outcome occurs, then the firm also earns δy because the insurance company pays δ of the firm's lost earnings equal to $\delta y(1 - \gamma)$.

To describe the revenue insurance program described above we construct Table 4.3.

Table 4.3. Decision Matrix for Revenue with Insurance Versus no Insurance with Discrete Outcomes.

States of nature	Probability of outcomes	Choices	
		A$_1$ (buy insurance) outcomes	A$_2$ (Don't buy insurance) outcomes
(s$_1$) full crop	p_1	$y - \pi_s$	y
(s$_2$) partial crop	p_2	$\delta y - \pi_s$	γy
(s$_3$) crop failure	$(1 - p_1 - p_2)$	$\delta y - \pi_s$	0

To solve for π_s we equate the expected value for the two choice options:

$$(4.31) \quad p_1(y - \pi_s) + (1 - p_1)(\delta y - \pi_s) = p_1 y + p_2(\gamma y)$$

And solving for the insurance premium π_s we find:

$$(4.32) \quad \pi_s = [\delta(1 - p_1) - p_2\gamma]y$$

To illustrate, suppose y = 100 and γy = 50 so that γ = 50%. Assume that the probability of a normal income is 60%, the probability of a partial crop and a reduced income is 30%, and the probability of a complete crop failure and no income is 10%. Finally, assume that your revenue insurance policy cov-ers δ = 80% of lost revenue. We restate these conditions in Table 4.4 and then solve for the break-even insurance premium π_s.

Table 4.4. Decision Matrix for Revenue Insurance Versus No Insurance with Discrete Outcomes.

States of nature	Probability of outcomes	Choices	
		A_1 (buy insurance) outcomes	A_2 (Don't buy insurance) outcomes
(s_1) full crop	$p_1 = 60\%$	$y - \pi_s = 100 - \pi_s$	$y = 100$
(s_2) partial crop	$p_2 = 30\%$	$\delta y - \pi_s = 80 - \pi_s$	$\gamma y = 50$
(s_3) crop failure	$(1 - p_1 - p_2) = 10\%$	$\delta y - \pi_s = 80 - \pi_s$	0

Finally, we solve for the break-even insurance premium πs:

$$(4.33) \quad \pi_s = [\delta(1 - p_1) - p_2\gamma)]y = [(.8)(.40) - (.30)(.5)]100 = 17$$

In other words, a manager could afford to pay up to 17% of its normal income as revenue insurance under the conditions described in Table 4.3.

Diversification of Firm Investments

Investors rarely hold investments in isolation. Indeed, holding a single investment by itself may be very risky. Most investors attempt to reduce risk by holding a portfolio of (two or more) investments. Adding a risky investment to a portfolio of investments may actually decrease the risk of the portfolio without adversely affecting the expected return on the portfolio. We illustrate the point that adding risky investments to one's portfolio may decrease risk with an example.

Umbrellas and sunglasses. Suppose that on any given day there are three possible weather outcomes: there may be rain, there may be a mix of clouds and sun, and there may be bright sunny skies. For simplicity, assume that the probability of each outcome is 1/3. A firm whose outcomes depend on the weather state can invest in umbrellas or sunglasses or a mix of the two. Both investments in umbrellas and sunglasses earn an expected rate of return equal to 10%. These results are summarized in Table 4.5 below:

Table 4.5. Expected Returns and Variances on Investments in Sunglasses and Umbrella

Weather states $i = 1,2,3$:	Probability of weather states	Random Returns on Sunglasses in the ith weather state: r_i^S	Random Returns on Umbrellas in the ith weather state: r_i^W	Return on portfolio
Rain	1/3	0%	20%	.5(0) +.5(20%) = 10%
Mix clouds and sunshine	1/3	10%	10%	.5(10) +.5(10%) = 10%
Sunny	1/3	20%	0%	.5(20) +.5(0%) = 10%
Expected return on investments:		$E(r_i^S)$ = (1/3)(0% + 10% + 20%) = 10%	$E(r_i^W)$ = (1/3)(20% + 10% + 0%) = 10%	.5E(r_i^S) + .5E(r_i^S) = (1/3)(10% + 10% + 10%) = 10%
Standard deviation of returns:		8.16%	8.16%	0%

Notice that when it rains, return on umbrellas is favorable (20%) but the return on sunglasses is low, 0%. The reverse is true when there are bright sunny skies; the return on umbrellas is low (0%) while the return on sunglasses is favorable, 20%. The standard deviation for both investments equals:

$$\text{(4.34a)} \quad \sqrt{.33(0 - .10)^2 + .33(.10 - .10)^2 + .33(.20 - .10)^2} = 8.16\%$$

Now assume that the firm diversified and created a portfolio in which 50% of its investments were in sunglasses and the other 50% were in umbrellas. The results are described in the last column of Table 4.5. Notice that the return in each state is 10% because when returns on low on sunglasses, return on umbrellas are favorable and vice versa. Note also that while each individual investment has a standard deviation of returns equal to 8.16%, the return on the portfolio is constant and the standard deviation of portfolio returns is zero.

$$\text{(4.34b)} \quad \sqrt{.33(.10 - .10)^2 + .33(.10 - .10)^2 + .33(.10 - .10)^2} = 0\%$$

This is an extreme example of how adding a risky investment may actually decrease the firm's risk. However, this favorable result occurred because the returns on umbrellas and sunglasses were perfectly and negatively correlated.

Covariance measures. To be perfectly and negatively correlated means that returns on one investment is above its mean by exactly same amount as the other investment is below its mean in the same state. One measure of correlation between two random variables is the covariance measure. Using the notation from the umbrellas and sunglasses example, we define the covariance as:

$$Cov(r_i^S, r_i^U) = E[(r_i^S - E(r_i^S))][(r_i^U - E(r_i^U))]$$

$$= \left(\frac{1}{3}\right)(0\% - 10\%)(20\% - 10\%)$$

$$+ \left(\frac{1}{3}\right)(10\% - 10\%)(10\% - 10\%)$$

$$+ \left(\frac{1}{3}\right)(20\% - 10\%)(10\% - 20\%)$$

$$= \left(\frac{2}{3}\right)(-10\%)(10\%) = -.00666$$

(4.35)

Notice that the covariance is similar to a variance measure except that instead of a deviation from the expected value being squared, the deviation for both variables in the same state are multiplied, so the covariance measures whether the two variables are moving in opposite directions from their means (negative covariance) or whether the two variables are moving in the same direction from their means (positive covariance). To emphasize the difference between variance and covariance measures, when calculating variance, we squared deviations from the mean, and as a result all variances are positive. In contrast, deviation in covariance measures are not squared which allows them to be positive or negative. Note that the first and third term in the covariance calculation in equation (4.35) were negative while the second term was zero. Thus, the covariance of investments in sunglasses and umbrellas is negative.

Obviously the sunglasses and umbrellas example is simplified to illustrate a point, that risk is completely eliminated because the returns from the two investments have perfect negative correlation. The level of correlation between returns is measured by the correlation coefficient ρ defined as:

$$\rho = \frac{Cov(r_i^S, r_i^U)}{\sigma_{r_i^S}\sigma_{r_i^U}}$$

(4.36)

Thus, in our example, the correlation coefficient is negative one:

$$\rho = \frac{Cov(r_i^S, r_i^U)}{\sigma_{r_i^S}\sigma_{r_i^U}} = \frac{-.00666}{(.0816)(.0816)} = -1.0$$

(4.37)

Obviously, other things being equal, we would prefer to add investments to our portfolio that are negatively correlated with our overall portfolio returns.

Let's return to our investigation of the partnership, only this time allow for a single firm to consider its rate of return on its portfolio of investments. Assume that it has two investments and the percent of the total portfolio invested in each investment is indicated by a weight w_1 and w_2 that sum to one. The expected value for the firm's portfolio can be expressed as before:

$$(4.38) \quad E(y_p) = w_1\mu_1 + w_2\mu_2$$

Now consider the variance of the investor's portfolio. If the investments are represented by independent random variables, the portfolio variance is as before—the weighted sum of the individual variances. When the investments are not independent, the portfolio variance also includes a covariance term. We can write the variance of the portfolio allowing for dependence between the two investments as:

$$(4.39) \quad \sigma_y^2 = w_1^2\sigma_{x_1}^2 + w_2^2\sigma_{x_2}^2 + 2w_1w_2Cov(r_i^1, r_i^2)$$

We now apply our portfolio approach to the umbrellas and sunglasses example. Recall that both investments earned an expected rate of return of 10% and their standard deviations were both equal to 8.16%. If the firm divided their portfolio between the two investments, then we would write the expected value and variance of the portfolio as:

$$(4.40) \quad E(y_p) = w_1\mu_1 + w_2\mu_2 = (.5)(10\%) + (.5)(10\%) = 10\%$$

And we write the portfolio variance as:

$$
\begin{aligned}
\sigma_y^2 &= w_1^2\sigma_{x_1}^2 + w_2^2\sigma_{x_2}^2 + 2w_1w_2Cov(r_i^1, r_i^2) \\
(4.41) \quad &= (.5)^2(.0816)^2 + (.5)^2(.0816)^2 + 2(.5)(.5)(-.00666) = 0
\end{aligned}
$$

In this special example, that the returns on sunglasses and umbrellas moved in perfectly opposite direction means that combining investments in both eliminated the variability of returns on the firm's portfolio.

Beta coefficients and risk diversification. An important risk concept applied to securities markets but which also has application to the firm is the beta coefficient (β). The beta coefficient is a measure associated with an individual investment which reflects the tendency of an investment's returns to move with the average return in the market. Applied to the individual firm, the beta coefficient measures the tendency of an individual investment's returns to move with the average return on the firm's portfolio of investments.

To explain beta coefficient, suppose we have past rate of return observations r_t^j on a potential new investment and on the firm's portfolio of returns r_t^p in time period t. Table 4.6 summarizes our observations:

Table 4.6. Observations of Returns on the Firm's Portfolio of Investments r_t^P and on a Potential New Investment (a Challenger).

Time t	Observed returns on the firm's portfolio over time r_t^P	Observed returns on a potential new investment for the firm's r_t^j
2012	10%	7%
2013	6%	8%
2014	7%	5%
2015	3%	2%
2016	5%	3%

Another way to represent the two rates of return measures and their relationship to each other is to represent them in a two dimensional scatter graph.

We may visually observe how the two sets of rates of return move together by drawing a line through the points on the graph in such a way as to minimize the squared distance from the point to the line. Our scatter graph is identified as Figure 4.3.

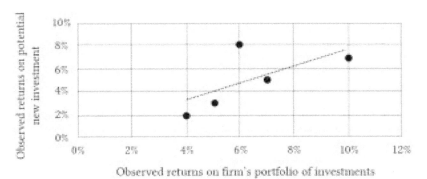

Figure 4.3. Scatter Graph of Returns on the Firm's Portfolio of Investments and Returns on the Potential New Investment

The relationship between the returns on the new investment and the firm's portfolio can be expressed as:

$$(4.42) \quad r_t^j = a + \beta r_t^p + \epsilon_t$$

Notice that the equation above describes the straight line drawn through the point plus the vertical distance from the line to each point. The slope of the line is the beta coefficient β and tells us how the returns on the portfolio and potential new investment have moved together in the past. We can find the equation for this line using a statistical method called "least squares" regression analysis. The method essentially finds a line so that the average squared deviations from the line, ε_t^2, are minimized. The formula for beta is equal to the covariance between the returns on the new investment r_t^j and the returns on the firm's portfolio r_t^p over some time period divided by the variance of portfolio returns:

$$\beta_j = \frac{Cov(r_t^j, r_t^p)}{\sigma_p^2}$$
(4.43)

Fortunately, the calculations for the beta coefficient as well as the coefficients in equation (4.16) can be found using Excel[2]. We find the beta coefficient and the coefficients for equation (4.16) using the data in Table 4.6.

The estimated equation for the line is:

$$\text{(4.44)} \quad E(r_t^j) = a + \beta r_t^p + E(\epsilon_t) = a + \beta r_t^p = .02 + .48 r_t^p$$

So, what have we learned? We learned that, in particular, a beta coefficient of .48 means that a 10% change in the return on the firm's portfolio will likely be accompanied by an increase of 4.8% in the expected returns on the potential new investment. Furthermore, a decrease of 10% in the returns on the firm's portfolio of investments will likely be accompanied by a 4.8% decrease in the expected returns on the potential new investment. It also means that the variability of the returns on the potential investment are less than the variability of returns on the firm's portfolio of returns. It also says that adding the potentially new investment will not diversify all of the firm's risk. There will still be 48% that is not diversified; it varies with the returns on the firm's overall rate of return. It reduces some of the risk faced by the firm, but not all of it—only about 52%.

Diversifiable and non-diversifiable risk. Assume a beta coefficient of minus one (–1). This would mean that for a 10% increase (decrease) in the firm's overall rate of return, that the expected rate of return on the potentially new investment decreases (increases) by 10%. Like investments in sunglasses and umbrellas, a sufficient investment in the new investment would eliminate the firm's risk. Thus, a beta of –1 means that all of its risk can be diversified. In contrast, assume a beta coefficient of one. This would

2. The linear regression equation that includes the Beta coefficient is found in Excel by first plotting a scatter diagram and then hovering over a data point in the graph. A complete discussion of linear regression models is outside the scope of this class. However, we will return to the subject of linear regression when we discuss forecasting.

mean that for a 10% increase (decrease) in the firm's overall rate of return, that the expected rate of return on the potentially new investment increases (decreases) by 10%. Unlike investing in sunglasses and umbrellas, adding the potentially new investment to the firm's portfolio of investment only accentuates its risk, and the new investment has no potential to diversify the firm's overall risk.

Purchase Risk Reducing Investments

It is useful to distinguish between two primary reasons for investing: first, to increase expected earnings for the firm and second, to reduce the variability of earnings. If one can increase expected returns without increasing variance of return, certainty equivalent income has increased. If one can reduce variance of returns without also reducing expected returns, certainty equivalent income has increased. See equation (4.12). Of course if from one's current expected value-variance position, one could increase one's expected value of returns without increasing the variance of returns—or if one could reduce one's variance without also reducing one's expected value—then the firm would be in an inefficient expected value-variance position off the EV frontier. However, we can identify investments whose primary purpose is to reduce variability even though they alter expected incomes. We call these risk reducing investments. We analyze risk reducing inputs using the certainty equivalent income model described in equation (4.12) that accounts for both variance and expected value in the ranking criterion.

We will illustrate risk reducing investments with a case study involving an irrigation investment. Consider a firm facing five moisture states with an equally likely chance of occurring: normal, low stress, moderate stress, high stress, and drought. The returns per acre with and without the irrigation system are reported in Table 4.7. The annualized cost of the irrigation system, which is expected to have a 20 year life and no liquidation value, is π per acre. We assume the defender's IRR associated with the certainty equivalent cash flow stream to be 8%.

Table 4.7. Returns per Acre under Alternative Moisture States with and without an Irrigation System.

Moisture states	Probability of moisture states	Return per acre without the irrigation investment $r_i^{w/0}$	Return per acre with the irrigation system r_i^w minus irrigation costs per acre π
Normal	20%	$128	$113– π
Low stress	20%	$105	$100 – π
Moderate stress	20%	$90	$80 – π
High stress	20%	$75	$75 – π
Drought	20%	$50	$70– π
Expected returns		$89.60	$87.60
Standard deviation of returns		$26.43	$16.28

Assume that π is $15 per acre. Then the expected value of the crop production per acre without irrigation is still $89.60 and greater than $87.60. If the decision maker were risk neutral, he or she would not invest in the irrigation system. Allow that the decision maker is risk averse and chooses between investments based on their certainty equivalent incomes rather than the difference in their expected values. If this were the case, then the certainty equivalent income without irrigation is:

$$\text{(4.45)} \quad y_{CE}^{w/0} = E(y) - \frac{\lambda}{2}\sigma_y^2 = \$89.60 - \frac{\lambda}{2}(26.43)^2$$

In contrast, the certainty equivalent income with the irrigation system is:

$$\text{(4.46)} \quad y_{CE}^{w} = E(y) - \frac{\lambda}{2}\sigma_y^2 = \$87.60 - \frac{\lambda}{2}(16.28)^2$$

We cannot decide between the two systems because one has a higher expected value and the other has a lower variance. It all depends on how risk averse the decision maker is. Recall that λ reflects the decision maker's preferred trade-off between expected return for variance. The break-even λ in this case is found by equating the two certainty equivalent incomes:

$$\text{(4.47)} \quad \$89.60 - \frac{\lambda}{2}(26.43)^2 = \$87.60 - \frac{\lambda}{2}(16.28)^2$$

and solving for λ:

$$\text{(4.48)} \quad \lambda = \frac{2(89.60 - 87.60)}{(26.43)^2 - (16.28)^2} = .009$$

Thus, all decision makers more risk averse than is reflected by the risk aversion coefficient of λ = .009 will be earning a lower expected value on average than would be earned without the irrigation system.

Choosing an Optimal Capital Structure

Leverage and risk. In an later chapter, we will use leverage as a measure of the firm's risk. We now make the connection between risk and leverage using a single period rate-of-return model that connects the rate of return on a firm's equity (ROE) to its rate of return on its assets (ROA). We call this relationship the rate of return identity (RORI). We define it here and explain it in more details in later chapters. We write the RORI equation as: :

$$\text{(4.49)} \quad ROE = (ROA - i)\frac{D}{E} + ROA$$

where i is the average interest rate the firm pays on its liabilities and D and E represent the firm's debt and equity respectively. In equation (4.49), note the leverage ratio D/E and that it multiplies the difference between the ROA and the average interest rate i. And now we return to a risk principle introduced earlier—that multiplying a random variable by a constant, in this case the leverage ratio, increases the variance of the random variable by the constant squared. Consider the application of this principle.

Suppose the random variable ROA is described by pdf $f(r^{ROA})$ with expected value r^{ROA} and variance σ^2. Now suppose that we were to multiply the random variable ROA by some scalar, say 2. Then the expected value of the random variable would be $2r^{ROA}$ and the variance would be $2^2\sigma^2$, or $4\sigma^2$.

In equation (4.49), the debt-to-equity ratio is the scaler that multiplies and exaggerates the difference between r^{ROA} and i. To illustrate, suppose that ROA can take on values of –8%, –3%, 3%, 5%, and 12% and i = 3%. Then in Table 4.8 we find ROE for leverage ratios of 0, 2, 5, and 10.

Table 4.8. ROEs whose Expected Values and Standard Deviations depend on Leverage Ratios.

Values of the random variable ROA (i = 3%)	ROE values for alternative Leverage Ratios (L = D/E) and values of the random variable ROA			
	L = 0	L = 2	L = 5	L = 10
–8%	–8%	-30%	-63%	-118%
–3%	–3%	-15%	-33%	-63%
3%	3%	3%	3%	3%
5%	5%	9%	15%	25%
12%	12%	30%	57%	102%
Standard deviations for ROEs associated with each leverage ratio L				
Expected values	1.8 %	-0.6%	-4.2%	-10.2%
Standard deviation σ	0.077	0.23	0.460	0.843

The first thing to note about the outcomes in Table 4.8 is that whenever the ROA exceeds the average interest rate i, that ROE > ROA. For example, for a leverage ratio of 2 and an ROA of 5%, ROE is 9%. The second point to observe is that even though the E(ROA) > 0, as the leverage ratio increased, the E(ROE) was mostly less than zero. In other words, the effect of leverage was more pronounced when the ROA < i than when ROA > i. Another thing to note is that if the ROA outcome is –8% and the firm has a leverage ratio of 10, it loses 118% of its equity. In other words, one unfavorable outcome with a high leverage ratio can destroy the firm. Finally, due to the cost of debt that must be paid regardless of ROA outcomes, ROA's less-than-average cost of debt with high leverage ratios have significant adverse effects on the firm's equity. Thus, we conclude that a high leverage ratio, even though it can exaggerate unusually high ROA outcomes, is still a risky state for the firm. For that reason, many firms view leverage reduction as an important strategy for reducing the riskiness of the outcomes they face.

Capital structure. A firm's capital structure is its combination of debt and equity used to finance its overall operations and growth. The small to medium-size firm may finance its overall operations and growth by using long-term debt, equity, and notes payable. We will discuss the small to medium-size firm's optimal capital structure using a simplified expected value-variance (EV) profit model.

In our simplified model, we let the firm's assets A be funded by a combination of debt D and equity E. We let $\tilde{r}^a$ be the stochastic rate of return on the firm's assets whose variance is $\sigma_a{}^2$ and whose expected rate of return is r^a. We let the average non-stochastic cost of debt per dollar be represented by the variable i^D. The firm decision maker's risk-return trade-off is measured by $\lambda/2$.

We represent the firm's stochastic profits π ˜to equal the stochastic rate of return on assets times assets less the firm's average cost of debt times the firm's debt. Then we substitute for assets A the sum of debt D plus equity E and collect like terms and express the stochastic results in equation (4.50).

$$(4.50) \quad \tilde{\pi} = \tilde{r}^a A - i^D D = \tilde{r}^a(D + E) - i^D D = (\tilde{r}^a - i^D)D + \tilde{r}^a E$$

We write the expected value of stochastic profits as:

$$(4.51) \quad E(\tilde{\pi}) = r^a A - i^D D = (r^a - i^D)D + r^a E$$

We write the variance of profits as:

$$(4.52) \quad \sigma^2(\tilde{\pi}) = (D + E)^2 \sigma_a^2$$

Finally, we substitute the expected value and variance of profits into equation (4.52) to find the firm's certainty equivalent of profits π_{CE} that we refer to as the EV model.

$$(4.53) \quad \pi_{CE} = E(\tilde{\pi}) - \left(\frac{\lambda}{2}\right)\sigma^2(\tilde{\pi}) = (r^a - i^D)D + r^a E - \left(\frac{\lambda}{2}\right)(D + E)^2 \sigma_a^2$$

Finding the firm's optimal capital structure.[3] Having our EV model defined over the expected value and variance of profits and accounting for the decision maker's risk attitudes, we use calculus to find the optimal debt level by differentiating the certainty equivalent function π_{CE} with respect to D.

$$(4.54) \quad \frac{d\pi_{CE}}{dD} = (r^a - i^D) - \lambda(D + E)\sigma_a^2 = 0$$

The second order conditions are satisfied allowing us to solve for the optimal debt D^* (assuming fixed equity). We find the optimal debt D^* to equal:

3. This section uses calculus to find the firm's optimal debt level and its optimal capital structure or leverage ratio (D/E). Those not interested in the derivation may skip to the next section without loss of continuity in the discussion.

$$D^* = \left(\frac{r^a - i^D}{\lambda\sigma_a^2}\right) - E$$

(4.55)

Equation (4.55) reveals an interesting detail. If the cost of debt equals the expected return on assets, the firm holds negative debt—preferring to lend out its equity at a safe rate i^D rather than earning a stochastic return on firm assets.

Dividing equation (4.55) by the firm's equity E, we can find its optimal leverage ratio l^* equal to:

$$l^* = \frac{D^*}{E} = \left(\frac{r^a - i^D}{\lambda\sigma_a^2 E}\right) - 1$$

(4.56)

We illustrate equation (4.56) using HQN's data described in Chapter 5. We substitute for r^a the ROA value equal to 6.5% (equation 6.13), the average cost of debt i^D equal to 6% (equation 6.20), equity E equal to $2,000 (Table 5.1), the risk aversion coefficient calculated in equation (4.48) equal to .009, and finally, we let the standard deviation—the amount that returns on assets vary on average—equal 1.25% or .0125 that we square to find the variance of profits $\sigma^2(\tilde{\pi})$ equal to .000156. Making the substitutions for the variables in equation (4.56) we find the firm's optimal leverage ratio equal to:

$$l^* = \frac{D^*}{E} = \left(\frac{r^a - i^D}{\lambda\sigma_a^2 E}\right) - 1 = \frac{(.065 - .06)}{(.009)(.000156)(\$2,000)} - 1 = 0.78$$

(4.57)

compared to the firm's actual leverage ratio of 4.0.

Changing variables affecting the optimal capital structure. We can imagine how the optimal leverage would change in response to changes in the value of the variables included in equation (4.57). In other words, we ask: how would the optimal leverage change if the value of one of the variables in equation (4.56) changed? We can infer the answer to this question by looking at changes in the optimal leverage ratio in response to a change in one of the variables holding the other variables constant.

Increasing the expected value of asset returns r^a makes it more profitable to use borrowed funds and increases the optimal leverage ratio. Increasing the average cost of debt i^D makes using debt less profitable and reduces the optimal leverage ratio. As a decision maker becomes more risk averse, represented by an increase in the risk aversion coefficient λ, the decision maker is less willing to risk losing equity with an unfavorable outcome and reduces leverage. As the firm's equity increases, it can achieve the same risk return combination with less debt and the optimal leverage ratio decreases. Finally, as the variance of return on firm assets σ_a^2 increases, the firm reduces its leverage ratio to return to its preferred trade-off between equity and debt.

We emphasize the importance of the decision maker's risk attitudes characterized by the risk aversion coefficient of .009. To illustrate, if we reduce the risk aversion coefficient to .003 and recalculate the optimal leverage ratio, we find it increased from 0.78 to:

$$\frac{(.065 - .06)}{(.003)(.000156)(\$2,000)} - 1 = 4.34.$$

(4.58)

This is close to HQN's actual leverage ratio. Alternatively, leaving HQN's risk aversion coefficient unchanged and increasing the expected value of the return on assets to 0.07. we find the new optimal leverage ratio to equal:

$$\frac{(.07 - .06)}{(.009)(.000156)(\$2,000)} - 1 = 2.56$$

(4.59)

We conclude with a note of caution. The calculation of risk aversion coefficients can be complicated and changed by the scale used to measure the random variable—dollars versus percentages. Our main message is that optimal leverage ratios are sensitive to not only rates of returns but also the decision maker's attitude toward risk.

So, what have we learned? We learned that firms generally dislike risk (however it is defined) and prefer expected earnings. Generally, we are willing to assume some risk if the increase in expected returns is sufficient. The firm selects its optimal combination of debt and equity to achieve its preferred expected profits and variance of profits. Increases in the value of variable that increase the firm's expected profits increase the firm's optimal leverage ratio. Increases in the value of variables that increase the firm's variance of profits reduce the firm's optimal leverage ratio.

Summary and Conclusions

Some sage is reported to have said that only death and taxes are certain. If that statement is anywhere close to being true, then risk and uncertainty fill the world we live in and try to manage. One important step toward managing the outcomes of risky events is to understand the tools that have been developed to report and measure it. In this effort, precision is not expected. It is best to explore the influence of risk in a variety of settings and assumptions.

The second thing to note about risk, emphasized in the irrigation example, is that individual risk preferences may have significant effects. As a result, two individuals facing the same investment opportunities may make different choices because of the different risk preferences. As a result, it is important for managers to explore their own risk preferences and apply them when making risky decisions.

References

Robison, Lindon J. and Peter J. Barry (1987). The Competitive Firm's Response to Risk. New York: Macmillan Publishing Co., 1987.

Questions

1. This question has several parts.
   1. What is the difference between a sample of observations and the population of possible values?
   2. Explain the difference between an expected value and variance (standard deviation) calculated from a sample and the expected value and variance (standard deviation) of a population.
   3. Find the expected value and variance (standard deviation) for the numbers 5, 8, –3, 9, and 0. Assume each number has an equally likely chance of being observed.
   4. Find the expected value and population variance (standard deviation) for the numbers 5, 8, –3, 9, and 0 if their probability of occurring were .1, .2, .4, .2, and .1 respectively.
   5. Compare the results obtained in parts 3 and 4.

2. Return to Table 4.1 in the text. Suppose that the investor decided to invest half of her assets in investment A and half in investment B. Describe the random variable for the combined investment. Then describe its pdf, expected value, and variance (standard deviation). Based on the respective expected values and variances for investment A, investment B, and the combined investment—which would you prefer, assuming you are risk averse?

3. Assume two people decide to form a partnership and share the risk and expected returns based on their shares contributed to the business. Assume partner 1 contributed 40% of the assets and partner 2 contributed 60% of the assets. Each partner's business can be described by random variables y1 and y2 with expected values and variances of $\mu_1 = 8\%$ and $\sigma_1^2 = 0.006$ for the first partner and $\mu_2 = 12\%$ and $\sigma_2^2 = .007$ for the second partner. Find the expected value standard deviation of the partnership.

4. Assume that Kelly wants to provide for her heirs in case she dies during the coming year. Therefore, she purchases a term life insurance policy that pays $1,000,000 in case she dies in return for an insurance premium of $800. Assuming Kelly is risk neutral, what must Kelly assume is the probability of her death in order for her to purchase the insurance policy?

5. Assume the conditions described in Table 4.3 except allow for the insurance coverage δ to increase from 80% to 85%. Find the increase in the break-even insurance premium.

6. Assume the conditions described in Table 4.4. Also assume that instead of purchasing revenue insurance the investor could purchase an irrigation system that would increase the probability of a normal revenue income year from 60% to 75%, reduce the probability of a reduced income year from 30% to 20%, and reduce the probability of zero income from 10% to 5%. What would be the most that the manager could pay to reduce its risk through the purchase of an irrigation system

and still be as well as he was before? (Hint: compare the value provided by the irrigation system less the cost of the irrigation system compared to the outcomes without an irrigation system.)

7. One of the differences between the purchase of an irrigation system and revenue insurance is that one has to purchase revenue insurance each year while the irrigation system continues to provide risk reduction services during its useful life. If the irrigation system described in the previous question were available for 10 years and the discount rate were 8%, what is the NPV of the irrigation system?

8. Use the data in Table 4.5 to find the beta coefficient for the investment in umbrellas and sunglasses.

9. A firm has two investments in its portfolio. The historical rates of return on the two investments are reported below. Find the expected rate of return for the firm's portfolio, the covariance between the two investments, and the variance of the portfolio returns. Rank investment 1, investment 2, and the combined investment using the EV criterion.

Table Q4.1. Observations of Returns on the Firm's Two Investments

Time t	Observed returns on investment one.	Observed returns on investment two.
2012	10%	7%
2013	6%	8%
2014	7%	5%
2015	3%	6%
2016	5%	4%

PART II: STRENGTHS, WEAKNESSES, OPPORTUNITIES, AND THREATS

5 Unveiling the Financial Picture: Decoding Financial Statements

LINDON ROBISON

Learning goals. After completing this chapter, you should be able to (1) construct consistent and accurate coordinated financial statements (CFS) (2) describe the differences and connections among balance sheets, accrual income statements (AIS), and statements of cash flows; and (3) distinguish between endogenous and exogenous variables and how they influence the construction of CFS.

• Learn how to construct the financial statements included in the CFS.

Learning objectives. To achieve your learning goals, you should complete the following objectives:

• Learn how the fundamental accounting equation organizes the firm's balance sheet.
• Learn how to organize a firm's cash flow data into a Sources and Uses of Funds (SAUF) statement.
• Learn how to distinguish between a firm's cash income statement and its accrual income statements (AIS).
• Learn how to compute a firm's cash income statement using cash flow and depreciation data.
• Learn how to distinguish between exogenous and endogenous variables.
• Learn how to compute a firm's statement of cash flow using data from its checkbook and other cash flow records.
• Learn the consistency requirements that connect data from the firm's balance sheets, AIS and statement of cash flow.
• Learn the distinction between consistency of financial statements and accuracy of financial statements.
• Learn how to organize firm financial data into a consistent and (as far as possible) accurate set of CFS.

Introduction

Balance sheets, the cash income statement, the annual income statement, the statement of cash flow, and the sources and uses of funds (SAUF) statement are all types of financial statements. The starting and ending balance sheets, an AIS, and a SCF are all parts of a coordinated financial statement (CFS). We are especially interested in the financial statements in CFS because they rely on each other and, when made the same way every time, can help us find mistakes in our data. The goal of financial statements is to give the company the information it needs to figure out what its strengths and weaknesses are, how well it's doing, how different futures might turn out, and how to choose the one that fits best with its mission, goals, and objectives.

The job of a financial manager is to do financial research. Financial managers need to know the basics of financial records, like how to make them and how to read them, in order to do their jobs well. The information below gives you a basic idea of what financial records are and how to make them. How to look at them will be the subject of later chapters. There are, of course, other reasons why it might be important to know how financial records work. We might want to know more about companies that do well, and one way to do this is to look at their financial records. We might want to invest in a company and want to find out how financially stable it is. We might have a job that needs us to know how to read financial statements. Or, we might just want to know enough to make decisions that affect the financial health of companies in which we have a stake. In an ideal world, companies would keep well-written financial statements that financial managers could use to do financial research. But the truth is that many companies, especially small ones, do not keep a set of financial records that is well-made. Also, a lot of companies don't keep track of all the information they need to in order to make true financial statements. On the other hand, almost all businesses keep records of their cash income and cash expenses, which are needed to figure out their income tax obligations. And the book worth of long-term assets, which is needed to make balance sheets, is written down in the same tax records. We can put together a set of financial statements, including an AIS, using data from the balance sheet and a cash income statement that we can get from tax records.

Financial Statements

The type of business can affect the financial records. For example, when making financial records for corporations, accountants must follow generally accepted accounting practises (GAAP), which say that shares of stock should be used to show ownership claims. GAAP doesn't have any rules about how financial records for sole proprietorships and partnerships have to be made. Also, some financial statements are based on accrual methods that record transactions as they happen, while others only record transactions when cash is traded. The value of an asset may be shown in a different way on different financial records. Some financial statements show how much an item is worth based on how much it could be sold for in the current accounting period. Market prices are the names for these numbers. Other financial statements show how much an object is worth based on how much it has lost value since it was bought. Most of the time, tax rules describe allowable depreciation in these statements. These amounts are called "book values."

So, what have we learned? We learned that financial managers need access to the follow-ing financial statements: book value balance sheets, accrual and cash income statements, sources and uses of funds (SAUF) statement, and statement of cash flow. Of these statements we make particular mention of the book value balance sheets, the accrual income statement (AIS) and the statement of cash flow. We refer to these as coordinated financial statements (CFS) because they are interdependent and their proper connections to each other—their consistency—can be easily checked. In addition, consistently constructed CFS can help us identify inaccuracies in our data. In what follows we describe firm financial statements.

The Balance Sheet

The balance sheet describes the firm's assets—what the firm owns or controls. It also lists the claims on the firm's assets from outside the firm called liabilities. The difference between assets and liabilities equals net worth and represents the firm's equity. The balance sheet is constructed at a point in time, e.g. the last day of the year, leading some to describe it as a snapshot of the firm's financial condition.

In the balance sheets presented in this class, the value of assets and liabilities is a combination of current and book values. Long-term assets are recorded at their book value—their purchase prices less accumulated depreciation determined by tax codes. Most liabilities and current assets are valued at their current values.

The underlying principal for constructing any balance sheet is the fundamental accounting equation: Assets = Liabilities + Equity. The fundamental accounting equation declares that each of the firm's assets must be financed either by liabilities (funds supplied by those outside the firm) or equity (funds supplied by the firm's owners). Moreover, the fundamental accounting equation separates the firm's assets from its liabilities and equity on the balance sheet. We can check the fundamental accounting equation by noting that the total value of assets equals the total value of liabilities and equity for each year the balance sheet is calculated.

Table 5.1 reports 2016, 2017 and 2018 year-end balance sheets for the hypothetical proprietary firm called HiQuality Nursery. Since we will repeatedly use data associated with this hypothetical firm and refer to the firm frequently, we will refer to it in the future using the acronym HQN. When reporting balance sheets for multiple years, the balance sheets in this text will appear in increasing time periods from least current to most current: 2016, 2017, and 2018 in the case of HQN.

Table 5.1. Year End Balance Sheet for HQN (all numbers in 000s)

Balance Sheet	Year		
	12/31/16	12/31/17	12/31,
Cash and Marketable Securities	$1,200	$930	$6
Accounts Receivable	$1,560	$1,640	$1,2
Inventory	$3,150	$3,750	$5,2
Notes Receivable	$0	$0	
CURRENT ASSETS	$5,910	$6,320	$7,0
Depreciable Long-term Assets	$3,270	$2,990	$2,
Non-depreciable Long-term Assets	$710	$690	$6
LONG-TERM ASSETS	$3,980	$3,680	$3,4
TOTAL ASSETS	$9,890	$10,000	$10,4
Notes Payable	$1,400	$1,500	$1,2
Current Portion LTD	$700	$500	$4
Accounts Payable	$2,400	$3,000	$4,0
Accrued Liabilities	$870	$958	$8
CURRENT LIABILITIES	$5,370	$5,958	$6,6
NONCURRENT LONG-TERM DEBT	$2,560	$2,042	$1,9
TOTAL LIABILITIES	$7,930	$8,000	$8,5
Contributed capital	$1900	$1900	$1,9
Retained earnings	$60	$100	($8
TOTAL EQUITY	$1,960	$2,000	$1,8
TOTAL LIABILITIES AND EQUITY	$9,890	$10,000	$10,4

Assets

Assets represent everything of value that the firm controls. Assets have value to the firm, mostly because they represent what can be used to generate earnings. The firm's assets are typically listed in order of liquidity, or nearness to cash. In most cases asset liquidity depends on the ease or cost of converting them to cash.

Current Assets. Current assets are cash and near-cash assets that are expected to be liquidated or converted to cash during the next year. Current assets are typically assets whose liquidation will not significantly disrupt the operation of the firm. We describe current assets next in their order of liquidity, or their nearness to cash.

- Cash balances are the firm's most liquid assets.
- Marketable securities are interest-bearing deposits with low risk of losing principal and can easily be converted to cash if needed.
- Accounts receivable include completed sales, for which payment has not been received.
- Notes receivable represent short-term loans the firm has made to others that are expected to be repaid during the coming year. Notes receivables are important for firms for whom lending money and earning interest on their loans is a significant source of income.
- Finally, inventories may be of two kinds. One kind of inventory represents the value of inputs on hand that can be used in future production or manufacturing of goods. A second kind of inventory are products available for sale. Inventories are often the least liquid of the firm's current assets, and their value is often not known until they are sold.

Long-term assets. Long-term assets yield services over several time periods. Liquidation of long-term assets would typically disrupt the operations of the firm and would occur only if the firm were facing a solvency crisis or replacing long-term assets with more productive ones.

Some balance sheets distinguish long-term assets by the length of time they will be held by the firm before being liquidated, referring to them as intermediate versus long-term assets. We prefer to distinguish between long-term assets by whether or not they depreciate. Depreciable long-term assets include machinery, equipment, breeding stock, contracts, long-term notes receivable, building and improvements. Non depreciable long-term assets are mostly land.

Book value versus market value of long-term assets. The book value of long-term assets is equal to their purchase price less accumulated depreciation: book value = acquisition cost − accumulated depreciation.

Accumulated depreciation is intended to reflect the loss in value of long-term assets due to use or the passage of time. As a practical matter, the depreciation rate is usually determined by tax codes.

While long-term assets are valued at their book value in the balance sheet, firms are also interested in the market value of their long-term assets. An asset's market value is the price at which it could be sold in the current market. An asset's book value is almost always different than its market value, the price at which the asset could be sold in the current period. Two reasons why an asset's book value and market value differ are because an asset's book value ignores appreciation and its depreciation is set by predetermined rates (rather than market forces), most often reflected in tax codes.

Tax consequences created by depreciable assets are complicated. Consider an example. Suppose a firm purchased a depreciable asset for $1,000 and then depreciated its value by $100 for four years and then sells the asset for $1,300. The difference between the realized market value of $1,300 and its book value of $600 consists of recaptured depreciation of $400 and capital gains of $300. The $300 of capital gains are taxed at the capital gains tax rate. Because the depreciation shielded the firm's income from income tax, the tax savings from $400 of depreciation is recaptured at the firm's income tax rate.

To better understand why book value is not equal to market value, think about what determines market value. As will be demonstrated later, the market value of an asset generally depends on the discounted value of future cash flow the asset is expected to generate. The cash flow characteristics that are important in establishing the market value of an asset include:

- the size and/or number of expected future cash flow;
- the timing of expected future cash flow; and
- the risk and variability of future cash flow.

In general, the larger the size and/or number of expected future cash flow, the larger will be the market value of the asset. Likewise, the sooner the asset is expected to generate cash flow, the higher will be the asset's market value, because a dollar today is generally preferred to a dollar later. Finally, as the risk or variability of an asset's future cash flow increase, the lower will be the asset's market value. To account for the influence of the size, timing, and risk of an asset's cash flow on an asset's value, later chapters will introduce the concepts of the time value of money. The concept of certainty equivalent measures was introduced in the chapter Managing Risk.

> So, what have we learned? We learned that with so many variables affecting the market value of an asset, we cannot expect that any predetermined depreciation schedule will accurately predict a depreciable asset's market value. Therefore, depreciable assets are valued at their book value in our balance sheets.

Liabilities

Liabilities are obligations to repay debt and accrued interest charges. They are listed according to the date they become due. Current liabilities are debt and interest payments due during the current period and pose the greatest liquidity demands on the firm's resources. Long-term liabilities are debts that will come due after the current year. Equity, which represents residual ownership of the firm's assets, has no fixed due date and is consequently listed after current and fixed liabilities.

Current liabilities. Current liabilities include the following:

- Notes payable are short-term debt (written promises) the firm is obligated to pay during the current year.
- The current portion of long-term debt (LTD) is the portion of LTD that is due during the upcoming year.
- Accounts payable equal the value of purchases made for inputs but not paid.
- Accrued liabilities are expenses that have been incurred through the operation of the firm and the passage of time, but have not been paid. Examples of accrued expenses include taxes payable, interest payable, and salary and wages payable.

Non-current long-term debt is the final category of liabilities, a long-term liability. Non-current long-term debt is that portion of the firm's debt due after the current period. These are usually long-term notes payable, mortgages, or bond obligations.

Equity

Equity, or net worth, is the difference between assets and liabilities, the difference between what one owns and what one owes. The firm's equity is an estimate of what owners of the firm would have left if they sold all their assets at their book value and paid all their liabilities valued at their market value. Therefore, equity is an important indicator of a firm's financial health.

The actual difference between what one owns and what one owes, if required to sell all of one's assets and repay one's liabilities, depends not only on the difference between the market value and book value of assets but also on the liquidity of the firm. Therefore, some caution is called for when interpreting the equity appearing on the firm's balance sheet as an indicator of its financial well-being.

Equity consists of accumulated retained earnings reported in the AIS and contributed capital by the firm's owners. One practical note is that when reconciling assets and liabilities, contributed capital is sometimes treated as a residual variable.

Checkbooks and Sources and Uses of Funds (SAUF) Statement

Most small firms record cash flow data in checkbooks, credit card statements, or other financial worksheets. These data are important for the construction of financial statements. They also supply the information needed to construct the firm's income tax returns. Consider HQN's cash flow data recorded in its checkbook reported in Table 5.2. To simplify the reporting of cash flow data, individual entries of the same kind have been combined into general categories.

Checkbooks

Beginning cash balance. Beginning cash balance is the cash the firm had on hand at the end of the previous period. It also appears on the first line of the firm's checkbook.

Cash receipts. Cash receipts may include cash received from the sale of tangible products like grain and livestock. Cash receipts may also include cash received from services the firm sells to other firms such as tiling, harvesting, and veterinary services. Cash receipts may include government payments from sponsored activities and insurance payments. Finally, cash receipts include reductions in accounts receivables and inventories that represent previous sales and production converted to cash in the present period.

Cash cost of goods sold (COGS). Cash COGS reflect the direct cost of materials and labor used to produce the goods that were sold to generate the firm's revenue. Cash COGS vary with the production levels and are usually the largest expense in most businesses. Finally, cash COGS include reductions in accounts payable that represent expenses incurred in the previous periods paid for in the present period.

Cash overhead expenses (OE). Cash OE represent the cost of operating and administrating the business beyond those included in COGS. These expenses typically include such things as administrative expenses, general office expenses, rents, salaries, and utilities. OE are difficult to assign to a particular production activity because they contribute to more than one project. Moreover, they tend not to vary with changes in production levels although they may vary over time. Cash OE may also include payments on accrued liabilities. Finally, cash OE include reductions in accrued liabilities incurred in previous periods paid for in the present period.

Taxes. Taxes include all compulsory contributions to and determined by governmental units. Taxes may be imposed on property, profits, and some goods used in production and sales.

Interest. Interest is the cost paid to use money provided by others during the current period. We sometimes distinguish between interest paid on long-term and short-term debt obligations.

Cash purchases or sales of long-term assets. Depreciable and non-depreciable long-term assets provide services for more than one period providing the firm a measure of control over its capital service flow not afforded by rental agreements.

Loan payments and account and note payments. Loan payments and account and note payments reflect payments on the amount of financial resources owed others. Sometimes referred to as principal payments, in the case of loans, note payment reflect reductions in the financial obligations of the firm as opposed to interest payments charged for the use of the financial resources of others.

Owner draw. Owner draw represents funds withdrawn from proprietary firms by its owners. These payments may be in exchange for services rendered by the firm's owner. In other cases, owner draws are funds withdrawn from the firm to meet financial needs of the firm's owner.

Table 5.2. HQN's 2018 Checkbook

Date	Item	Withdrawal	Deposit	Balance
12/31/17	Beginning cash balance			$930
	Cash receipts		$38,990	$39,920
	Cash cost of goods sold (COGS)	$27,000		$12,920
	Cash overhead expenses (OE)	$11,078		$1,842
	Interest paid	$480		$1,362
	Taxes paid	$68		$1,294
	Purchase of long-term assets	$100		$1,194
	Sale of long-term assets		$30	$1,224
	Current portion of long-term debt paid	$157		$1,067
	Long-term borrowings		$50	$1,117
	Notes payable	$230		$887
	Owners' draw	$287		$600
12/31/18	Ending cash balance			$600

The Sources and Uses of Funds (SAUF) statement.

The data recorded in the firm's checkbook and other cash flow records can be organized as an SAUF statement that identifies sources of cash for the firm (cash inflows) and uses of funds (cash outflows). The SAUF statement is consistent with the cash flow data reported in HQN's checkbook in Table 5.2. HQN's SAUF statement is reported in Table 5.3.

At the beginning of the period, firm managers make cash flow projections recorded in the SAUF statement. These projections allow the firm to plan in advance for cash flow shortages or for investment and savings opportunities. Obviously, a negative ending cash balance is not possible; therefore, the firm adjusts its cash expenses or cash receipts so that the firm remains solvent. In the last column of HQN's SAUF, ending period cash balances were projected to equal $51.

Table 5.3. HQN's 2018 SAUF Statement

Date	Sources of Cash	Actual	Projected
12/31/17	Beginning cash balance	$930	$930
	Cash receipts	$38,990	$39,000
	Sale of long-term assets	$30	$50
	Long-term borrowing	$50	$25
12/31/18	Total sources of funds	$40,000	$40,005
	Uses of Cash		
	Cash COGS	$27,000	$25,000
	Cash OE	$11,078	$12,000
	Interest paid	$480	$480
	Taxes paid	$68	$70
	Cash purchases of long-term assets	$100	$150
	Pay current portion of long-term debt payment	$157	$1,067
	Notes payable	$230	$887
	Owners' draw	$287	$300
12/31/18	Total uses of funds	$39,400	$39,954
12/31/18	Ending cash balance (Total sources – total uses of funds)	$600	$51

Notice that the entries in the Checkbook reported in Table 5.2 match those in the SAUF statement reported in Table 5.3, except that they are organized as sources of funds coming into the firm and uses of funds representing funds flowing out of the firm. Consistency between the firm's SAUF statement and its checkbook requires cash at the ending periods in the balance sheet and the SAUF are equal.

So, what have we learned? We learned that records of cash flow whether recorded in checkbooks or similar records is one of the most important data sources for constructing CFS for the firm. This data can be used to construct SAUF statements and statements of cash flow.

Statement of Cash Flow (SCF)

The firm's balance sheet describes its financial position at a point in time while the firm's statement of cash flow (SCF) describes the firm's cash flow over a period of time between the firm's beginning and ending balance sheets. The main purpose of the SCF is to find the change in the firm's cash position during the accounting year.

Three major cash flow activities. The firm's SCF is similar to its SAUF statement except that it separates cash flow into the three categories: (1) cash flow from operations, (2) cash flow from investments, and (3) and cash flow from its financing activities.

The cash flow from operations reflect the cash flow generated by the firm in producing and delivering its goods and services. Cash flow from operations reflect the firm's management of its production and marketing activities.

The cash flow from investment activities result from the firm's sale and purchase of long-term assets. Sales of long-term assets whose market value exceeds its book value create realized capital gains and depreciation recapture. Cash flow from investment activities reflect the firm's investment management strategies.

The cash flow from financing activities result from borrowing new debt, repaying old debt, raising new equity capital, and returning capital to owners. Cash flow from financing reflect the firm's management of its debt and equity.

Cash flow for the firm during the accounting period are summarized by its change in cash position. By adding cash on hand at the end of the previous period to the change in cash position reported in the statement of cash flow, we obtain cash on hand at the end of the period. As a result, the change in cash position links the beginning and ending cash on hand reported in the balance sheet.

The SAUF statement derived from the checkbook contains all the data required to construct a statement of cash flow (SCF) for the firm. While cash flow can occur in any order in real life, we have arranged them in the SAUF statement by categories: cash flow associated with operations, cash flow associated with investment, and cash flow associated with financing.

Net cash flow from operations. The first entry in HQN's checkbook is cash receipts of $38,990. This represents a source of cash, and is therefore entered in the "credit" or "deposit" column of the checkbook. The next items that appear in the checkbook are cash COGS of $27,000, cash OE of $11,078, interest paid of $480, and taxes paid equal to $68. We find net operating cash flow by subtracting from cash receipts, cash expenditures or COGS, cash OE, interest and taxes.

+	Cash receipts	$38,990
−	Cash COGS	$27,000
−	Cash OE	$11,078
−	Interest paid	$480
−	Taxes paid	$68
=	*Net Cash Flow from Operations*	$364

Net cash flow from investments. Net cash flow from investment activity is calculated from checkbook entries equal to $70 which corresponds to net cash flow from investment. It is calculated as the difference between purchases of long-term assets ($100) less sales of long investments assets equal to $30. These calculations for HQN in 2018 are recorded below.

+	Realized capital gains + depreciation recapture	$0
+	Sales of non-depreciable assets	$0
−	Purchases of non-depreciable assets	$0
+	Sales of long-term assets	$100
−	Purchases of long-term assets	$30
=	Net Cash Flow from Investments	($70)

It is important to recognize that some purchases may be paid for with borrowed funds. In this case the borrowed funds would be entered in the SAUF as a source of funds while the purchase reflects own plus borrowed funds expended to acquire the long-term asset.

Net cash flow from financing. Cash flow from financing activities recorded in the checkbook reflect the difference between borrowing and repayment of long-term debt and payments of notes payable. Interest paid on long-term debt and notes payable is included in net cash flow from operations. Finally, dividends paid and owner draw are subtracted and the difference between new equity contributed and purchased is reflected in the net cash flow from financing. HQN's 2018 net cash flow from financing are recorded below.

−	Long-term debt payments	$157
+	Long-term borrowings	$50
−	Payments on notes payable	$230
−	Owner draw	$287
=	Net Cash Flow from Financing	($624)

An alternative to calculating net cash flow from financing is to use the difference between the ending and beginning balance sheet to the find the change in long-term debt and current long-term debt plus the change in notes payable. Finally, we subtract payment of dividends and owner draw. Net cash flow calculated using the balance sheet rather than the checkbook is reported next.

+	Change in non-current LTD	($57)
+	Change in current portion of LTD	($50)
+	Change in notes payable (borrowing less payments)	($230)
−	Payment of dividends and owner draw	$287
=	Net Cash Flow from Financing	($624)

We demonstrate that cash flow associated with borrowing LTD, repaying current and noncurrent portions of LTD, and converting noncurrent LTD to current LTD are properly accounted for by adding changes in current and noncurrent LTD. To this end, consider the following. We assume transactions occur at the end of each period. Current and noncurrent LTD at the end of the previous period are designated LTD_0^C and LTD_0^N respectively. Current and noncurrent LTD at the end of the current period are designated LTD_1^C and LTD_1^N respectively. Assume that at the end of the current period: (1) the firm reduces its outstanding LTD by paying amounts LTD^{PayN} and LTD^{PayC} on noncurrent and current LTD balances respectively ; (2) it increases its LTD by borrowing amount LTD^{Borrow}; and (3) some noncurrent LTD^N becomes current LTD^C—an amount equal to $LTD^{Converted}$. We can now write the identity:

$$(5.1) \quad LTD_1^C = LTD_0^C + LTD^{Converted} - LTD^{PayC}.$$

In words, current LTD at the end of the period equals current LTD at the beginning of the period plus noncurrent LTD converted to current LTD less current LTD payments made at the end of the period. Then we find the difference between current LTD at the end of the previous and current periods as:

$$(5.2) \quad \Delta LTD^C = LTD_1^C - LTD_0^C = LTD^{Converted} - LTD^{PayC}.$$

Similarly, we write the identity

$$(5.3) \quad LTD_1^N = LTD_0^N + LTD^{Borrow} - LTD^{Converted} - LTD^{PayN}.$$

In words, noncurrent LTD at the end of period one is equal to noncurrent LTD at the beginning of the period plus additional LTD borrowings, less noncurrent LTD converted to current LTD minus noncurrent LTD payments. Then we find the difference between noncurrent LTD at the end of the previous and current periods as:

$$(5.4)$$
$$\Delta LTD^N = LTD_1^N - LTD_0^N = LTD^{Borrow} - LTD^{Converted} - LTD^{PayN}$$

Finally we add $\Delta LTD^C + \Delta LTD^N$ to find:

$$(5.5) \quad \Delta LTD^C + \Delta LTD^N = LTD^{Borrow} - LTD^{PayC} - LTD^{PayN}$$

Since $LTD^{Converted}$ cancels when the two equation are added together, we prove that including the difference in current and noncurrent LTD in the financing cash flow section of the statement of cash flow properly accounts for borrowing and payment of LTD and transferring funds from noncurrent to current LTD.

We are now prepared to calculate the change in the net cash position of the firm by combining HQN's cash flow from operations, investing, and financing.

Table 5.4a. HQN's 2018 Statement of Cash Flow

+	Cash receipts	$38,990
–	Cash COGS	$27,000
–	Cash OE	$11,078
–	Interest paid	$480
–	Taxes paid	$68
=	**Net Cash Flow from Operations**	**$364**
+	Realized capital gains / depreciation recapture	$0
–	Purchases of long-term assets	$100
+	Sales of long-term assets	$30
=	**Net Cash Flow from Investments**	**($70)**
+	Long-term borrowing	$50
–	Long-term debt payments	$157
–	Note payments	$230
–	Dividends and owner's draw	$287
=	**Net Cash Flow from Financing**	**($624)**
	Change in Cash Position of the Firm	**($330)**

An alternative statement of cash flow calculates Net Cash Flows from financing, logically equivalent to Table 5.4a, using changes in Current and Non-current LTD and Changes in notes payable, including as before dividends and owner's draw. The alternative to Table 5.4a, especially useful when data on borrowings and payment data is not available, is reported below:

Table 5.4b. HQN's 2018 Statement of Cash Flow

+	Cash receipts	$38,990
−	Cash COGS	$27,000
−	Cash OE	$11,078
−	Interest paid	$480
−	Taxes paid	$68
=	**Net Cash Flow from Operations**	**$364**
+	Realized capital gains / depreciation recapture	$0
−	Change in non-depreciable long-term assets	$0
−	Change in depreciable long-term assets + depreciation	$70
=	**Net Cash Flow from Investments**	**($70)**
+	Change in noncurrent LTD	($57)
+	Change in current portion of LTD	($50)
+	Change in notes payable	($230)
−	Payment of dividends and owner's draw	$287
=	**Net Cash Flow from Financing**	**($624)**
	Change in Cash Position of the Firm	**($330)**

Since the ending cash position of the firm in the previous period was $930, a change in the cash position associated with the firm's cash flow implies that the ending cash position of the firm is: $930 − $330 = $600. This amount, $600, corresponds to the cash balance appearing at the end of the current period's balance sheet. Indeed, a check on the consistency of the calculation that uses a checkbook to construct a statement of cash flow is that the change in cash position reconciles the cash balances appearing in the end of period balance sheets. Furthermore, the beginning and ending cash balances in the checkbook must equal the ending cash balances in the end of period balance sheets. In this case, the beginning and ending cash balances in the checkbook are $930 and $600, respectively, which matches the ending cash balances in the previous and current end of period balance sheets.

So, what have we learned? We learned that it is essential to understand that the individual financial statements included in CFS are interdependent and all are important for describing the financial condition of the firm. Their interdependence can be verified with the following consistency checks. The fundamental accounting identity requires that total assets equal liabilities plus net worth. The change in cash position calculated in the SCF equals the difference in cash and marketable securities in the beginning and ending period balance sheets. And finally, the change in retained earnings calculated in the AIS must equal the change in retained earnings in the ending and beginning period balance sheets.

Cash Income Statements

Unlike the balance sheet—which is a picture of the firm's assets, liabilities, and net worth at a point in time—the firm's income statement is a record of the firm's income and expenses incurred between two points in time. Profits (losses) reported in the firm's income statement are reflected in the firm's balance sheet as an increase (decrease) in the firm's equity. Therefore, the firm's income statement provides the details that explain changes in the firm's equity. To complicate matters, there are two distinct income statements, cash and accrual. We first discuss the firm's cash income statement.

Cash income statements record the firm's income and expenses when they generate a cash flow. One of the most important uses of a cash income statement is to determine the firm's tax obligations. The cash income statement is also an important tool for determining the liquidity of the firm—to determine if its cash receipts are sufficient to meet its cash expenses.

HQN's 2018 *Cash income statement*. Using data from the firm's checkbook or its SAUF statement plus the ending balance sheets, we are prepared to complete a cash income statement. Sometimes the cash income statement is referred to as a modified cash income statement because it includes depreciation which is not a cash flow event but which is an expense allowed when computing taxable income. The 2018 HQN cash income statement constructed using data from HQN's checkbook plus book value asset data from ending balance sheets used to calculate depreciation is reported below:

Table 5.5. HQN's 2018 Cash Income Statement (all number in $000s)

	Cash receipts	$38,990
+	Realized Cap. Gains and Depreciation Recapture	0
−	Cash COGS	$27,000
−	Cash Overhead Expenses	$11,078
−	Depreciation	$350
=	**Cash Earnings Before Interest and Taxes (CEBIT)**	**$562**
−	Interest paid	$480
=	**Cash Earnings Before Taxes (CEBT)**	**$82**
−	Taxes paid	$68
=	**Cash Net Earnings After Taxes (CNIAT)**	**$14**
−	Dividends and Owner Draws	$287
=	**Cash Additions to Retained Earnings**	**($273)**

Notice that all of the entries in the cash income statement are entries in the firm's checkbook and SAUF statement except for realized capital gains and depreciation recapture and depreciation. Depreciation is listed as an expense even though it may not reflect a cash flow event because it represents a loss in value to the firm of assets previously purchased. To find the depreciation for HQN we begin with a fundamental relationship that applies to all depreciable long-term assets (DLTA):

Beginning DLTA + purchases of DLTA − sales of DLTA (book value) − depreciation = Ending (book value) DLTA

Notice that the sale of DLTA is listed at their book value. This is necessary to maintain the value of DLTA at their book value in the balance sheets. Solving for depreciation in the identity above and substituting data from the checkbook and balance sheets we find:

Depreciation = Beginning DLTA + purchases of DLTA − sales of DLTA (book value) − Ending DLTA

Depreciation = $2990 + $100 − $30 − $2710 = $350.

Finally, depreciation recapture is treated a separate category of cash receipts to the firm because it represents a value that was previously deducted as an expense included in depreciation and is now received as an unexpected income (or loss). Depreciation recapture plus capital gains is equal to the market value of DLTA sold less the book value of DLTA sold provided the sale price is not greater than the original purchase price.

Realized capital gains (losses) + depreciation recapture = Sale of DLTA (market value) − sale of DLTA (book value)

= $30 − $0 = $30.

In this example, we assume that DLTA were sold at their book value so realized capital gains plus depreciation recapture are zero.

Accrual Income Statement (AIS)

HQN's 2018 accrual income statement (AIS) is reported in Table 5.6. Because the accrued income statement is the more common of the two income statements, we sometimes drop the word accrual and refer to it as the firm's income statement. We create HQN's income statement by adding to cash transactions non cash exchanges affecting the financial condition of the firm.

Table 5.6. HQN's 2018 Accrual Income Statement
(all numbers in $000s)

+	Cash receipts	$38,990
+	Δ Accounts Receivable	($440)
+	Δ Inventories	$1450
+	Realized Capital Gains / Depreciation Recapture	$0
=	**Total Revenue**	**$40,000**
+	Cash COGS	$27,000
+	Δ Accounts Payable	$1,000
+	Cash OE	$11,078
+	Δ Accrued Liabilities	($78)
+	Depreciation	$350
=	**Total Expenses**	**$39,350**
	Earnings Before Interest and Taxes (EBIT)	**$650**
−	Interest	$480
=	**Earnings Before Taxes (EBT)**	**$170**
−	Taxes	$68
=	**Net Income After Taxes (NIAT)**	**$102**
−	Dividends and owner draws	$287
=	**Additions To Retained Earnings**	**($185)**

An important check on the consistency of HQN's balance sheets and its AIS is that additions to retained earning of ($185) should equal the difference between beginning and ending retained earning in the balance sheet.

We now explain in more detail the calculation of the individual entries in the AIS. In addition, by rearranging the numbers used to find AIS entries, we can find cash income statement entries.

Finding accrued income. Our first checkbook entry records cash receipts of $38,990. So, what is the difference between cash receipts and accrued income? Accrued income includes cash receipts from the sale of products, insurance, and government payments plus credit sales—creating accounts receivable. In addition, accrued income includes inventory increases—production essentially sold into inventory. Both increases in accounts receivable and inventory increase accrued income. While cash receipts are recorded in the checkbook, changes in accounts receivable (Δ Accounts Receivable) and changes in inventories (Δ Inventories) are found as the differences between accounts receivable and inventory entries in the two ending period balance sheets. Since we can find changes in accounts receivable and changes in inventories, we can now calculate accrued income equals the following:

Accrued Income = Cash Receipts + Δ Accounts Receivables + Δ Inventories

$40,000 = $38990 + ($440) + $1450

Notice that cash receipts understate actual income in this example.

Total revenue. Adding cash receipts, realized capital gains / depreciation recapture, changes in inventory, and changes in accounts receivable provides a measure of the firm's total accrued income.

Finding accrued COGS. The checkbook records cash COGS of $27,000. But accrued COGS must add to cash COGS the COGS that the firm purchased on credit which increased the firm's accounts payable. The amount of goods the firm purchased on credit can be calculated as the difference between accounts payable at the beginning and at the end of the year recorded in the firm's balance sheets. For HQN, changes in accounts payable (Δ Accounts Payable) equal $1,000, allowing us to find accrued COGS as:

Accrued COGS = Cash COGS + Δ Accounts Payable

$28,000 = $27,000 + $1000

Note that cash COGS understate actual COGS.

Finding accrued OE. The checkbook records cash OE of $11,078. But accrued OE must add to cash OE the overhead expenses that were purchased on credit increasing the firm's accrued liabilities. In general, changes in accrued liabilities (Δ Accrued Liabilities) equal the difference between accrued and cash overhead expenses, and can be found as the difference between accrued liabilities recorded in the ending period balance sheets. The difference between ending period accrued liabilities equals ($78), meaning that the firm actually paid off some accrued liabilities incurred in earlier periods in addition to paying for overhead expenses incurred during the current period. We express accrued overhead expenses as:

Accrued OE = Cash OE + Δ Accrued Liabilities

$11,000 = $11,078 + ($78)

Note that cash OE overstate actual overhead expenses.

Calculating depreciation in the accrual income statement. We previously calculated depreciation in the cash income statement and found it to equal to $350. The calculation of depreciation is the same in both the accrual and cash income statement.

Earnings Before Interest and Taxes (EBIT). After subtracting from the firm's total revenue, its cash COGS, change in accounts payable, cash OE, changes in accrued liabilities and depreciation, we obtain a measure of the firm's profits (total revenue minus total expenses). But the profit measure obtained is before subtracting interest costs and taxes. Therefore, we call this profit measure Earnings Before Interest and Taxes are paid (EBIT).

Earnings Before Taxes (EBT). Subtracting interest expenses from EBIT gives the firm's earnings before taxes (EBT), which are the firm's profits after paying all expenses except taxes.

Net Income After Taxes (NIAT). Subtracting the firm's tax liabilities from EBT gives the firm's net income after taxes (NIAT), generally referred to as the firm's profits. NIAT is also what is available to be reinvested in the firm or withdrawn by the owners.

Interest costs, taxes, and withdrawals. The checkbook records interest costs of $480, taxes equal to $68, and withdrawals of $287. These are paid in cash and can be entered directly in the AIS.

Dividends and owner draw. Dividends and owner draw represent payments make to owners of the firms from the firm's profits. In the case of dividends, these reflect payments made to compensate owners of the firm for their investments in the firm. In the case of owner draw, these may include payments to owners for services rendered or to meet the financial needs of the firm's owners.

Finding Cash Receipts, Cash COGS, and Cash OE from the accrual statement. Usually, firms have access to cash receipts, cash COGS, and cash OE from which it can find accrued income, accrued COGS, and accrued OE. This was our approach in the previous section. However, we could reverse the calculations beginning with accrued income, accrued COGS, and accrued OE and then solve for cash receipts, cash COGS, and cash OE. These calculations are described next and are essential in order to complete the firm's statement of Cash Flow when we begin with accrual data rather than cash flow data.

Suppose that we knew that accrued income were equal to $40,000. We could find cash receipts by subtracting from accrued income, change in accounts receivable and change in inventory:

$38,990 = $40,000 − ($440) − $1450

Finding cash COGS. Suppose that we knew that accrued COGS were equal to $28,000. We could find cash COGS by subtracting accrued COGS change in Accounts Payable:

$27,000 = $28,000 − $1,000

Finding accrued OE. Suppose that we knew that accrued OE were equal to $11,078. We could find cash OE by subtracting from accrued OE, change in accrued liabilities.

$11,078 = $11,000 − ($78)

More Complicated Financial Statements

Compared to HQN's balance sheets, income statements, and SCF described in this chapter, balance sheets, income statements, and SCF for an actual firm are often much more complicated. In what follows, we highlight the main differences between HQN's financial statements and financial statements of actual firms.

Level of detail. One of the main differences between HQN's financial statements and financial statements of actual firms is the level of detail. For example, the income statement may separate total sales into sales of livestock and livestock products, crops sales, and sales of services. Expenses may be separated into seed, fertilizer, other crop supplies, machinery hire, feed purchased, feeder livestock purchased, veterinary services, livestock supplies, fuel and oil, utilities, machinery repairs, insurance, rents, hired labor to name a few. Additional inventory details may include livestock and crops held for sale and feed, value of growing crops, farm supplies, and prepaid expenses.

Data deficiencies. Another difference between HQN's financial statements and financial statements of actual firms is the quality of the data. HQN's data are assumed to be accurate and consistent. Data supplied by actual firms is sometimes neither accurate nor consistent. Other data deficiencies of actual firms may include the following. 1) The data are rarely complete, especially for large complex firms with several activities. 2) Data from the firm's activities may be reported by different persons using different metrics. 3) Some of the same data are provided from different sources and are not equal. 4) Personal data may be confounded with firm data.

Exogenous and endogenous variables. There are two types of variables in CFS: exogenous versus endogenous. The value of exogenous variables are determined outside of the CFS . It can be observed and supplied by sources other than the firm. Endogenous variables are calculated using exogenous variables so that any change in exogenous variables produces changes in endogenous variables. For example, the cash flow variable is an exogenous variable because it can be observed and recorded. Other data, such as firm's equity or additions to retained earnings are computed using exogenous and sometimes other endogenous variables. The problem occurs where the value in the CFS can be observed and calculated. For example, end of period cash is calculated from beginning period cash plus change in cash position. But end of period cash may be observed by referring to the firm's checkbook. If the exogenous variable is accurate, then the observed and calculated numbers will be equal and consistent. But in some cases they are not equal and the firm will be required to take steps designed to reconcile the differences.

Consistency versus accuracy. Two words describe financial statements: "consistency" and "accuracy". Consistency means that we compute values for variables in the CFS in the same way every time so that changes in primary data produce predictable changes in calculated data. Accuracy means that our measurement conforms to the correct value of what is being measured. The financial statements are consistent if the following are true: "additions to retained earnings" reported in the accrued income statement reconciles retained earnings in the ending period balance sheets. The reconciling equation is: beginning retained earnings plus additions to retained earnings equals retained earnings in the ending period balance sheet. A second consistency requirement is that the change in cash position reported in the statement of cash flow reconciles cash balances in the ending period balance sheets. The reconciling equation is: beginning cash plus change in cash position equal ending cash. Finally, the third consistency condition is that the fundamental accounting identity is true; namely, that assets equal liabilities plus equity.

The financial statements may be consistent, but not all the data may be accurately recorded. On the other hand, if the financial statements are not consistent, we can be sure they are not accurate. We summarize our description of financial statements by declaring that consistency is a necessary condition for an accurate set of financial statements but consistency is not sufficient for an accurate set of financial statements.

Hard and soft data. Faced with the data challenges described above, financial managers are charged with the task of preparing the most accurate and consistent set of CFS possible. Guidelines for this task include determining which data is "soft" and which data is "hard." Soft data is estimated or may lack a supporting data trail. Still, it represents the best guesstimates available. Hard data has a reference or an anchor. For example, the sale of a product is usually recorded although there may be some benefits or costs associated with the sale that are not recorded. Interest costs and taxes are recorded and can be considered hard data. Inventories are more difficult to determine if they are hard or soft because they change over a reporting cycle and their estimated value at the beginning and ending balance sheets may not be available. So, an important task of the financial manager is to assess the reliability of the different data.

Over-identified Variables

An over-identified variable is one whose endogenously calculated value can be observed and recorded as an exogenous variable. For example, consider ending cash balances recorded in the ending period balance sheet. Calculated as an endogenous variable, ending cash balances equal beginning cash balances recorded in the beginning period balance sheet plus changes in cash position calculated in the statement of cash flow. In addition, the financial manager may observe the ending cash balance recorded in the firm's checkbook. In some cases, however, the financial managers can observe data reflecting the value of endogenous variables. For example, financial managers may observe ending cash balances and have calculated them as an endogenous value using consistency conditions of coordinated financial statements. In this case, values for the variable ending cash balances are over identified. When entries in the CFS can be both observed as an exogenous variable and calculated as an endogenous variable, the CFS variables are over identified.

Ideally, the observed exogenous variable value equals the endogenous variable value. In such fortunate cases, the datum is most likely accurate and consistent with other variable values. When the values for the over-identified variables are not equal, the financial manager can be assured that either the endogenous or the exogenous variable values or both are inaccurate. If the observed value is from hard data, then the financial manager must revisit the values of other exogenous data that were used to calculate the endogenous variable value. Therefore, over-identified variables provide a useful means for evaluating the accuracy of one's financial statements and exogenous data values used to find the values of endogenous variables.

Constructing Consistent Coordinated Financial Statements (CFS): A Case Study

We now construct a consistent set of financial statements for an actual firm using the data they supplied. In the process, we will experience some of the data deficiencies described earlier and the challenge of having our CFS be both accurate and consistent. We will call our case study firm, Friendly Fruit Farm (FFF) because producing and selling fruit is the firm's main commercial activity.

To assure that our financial statements are consistent, we will use the template prepared for analyzing HQN and described in more detail in the appendix to the chapter System Analysis. The categories in the HQN template are aggregated compared to actual firms. To fit the data supplied by FFF to the HQN template will require side-bar calculations that organize the data to correspond with the general categories described in Tables 5.1, 5.4, 5.5, and 5.6. The general rule for deciding when side-bar calculations are required is the following: if for any given entry of the CFS there are two or more instances of that item supplied by FFF, a side bar calculation is required. Therefore, the number of side-bar calculations will depend on the firm being examined and the data which the firm supplies.

FFF balance sheets. FFF supplied the following balance sheet data.

Table 5.7. FFF supplied Ending Period Balance Sheets

	12/31/17	12/31/18
Cash and checking balance	($7,596)	($24,333)
Prepaid expenses & supplies	$7,467	$15,369
Growing crops	$0	$0
Accounts receivable	$33,400	$45,668
Hedging accounts	$0	$0
Crops held for sale or feed	$178,098	$204,530
Crops under government loan	$0	$0
Market livestock held for sale	$7,933	$6,500
Other current assets	$278	$278
Total current farm assets	**$219,581**	**$248,011**
Breeding livestock	$10,583	$18,019
Machinery and equipment	$85,001	$87,387
Titled vehicles	$2,889	$2,667
Other intermediate asses	$9,689	$8,893
Total intermediate farm assets	**$108,162**	**$116,966**
Farm Land	$166,200	$179,348
Buildings and improvements	$76,852	$81,021
Other long-term assets	$6,229	$6,229
Total long-term assets	**$249,281**	**$266,599**
Total Farm Assets	**$577,023**	**$631,576**
Accrued interest	$1,078	$1,487
Accounts payable	$2,080	$1,637
Current notes	$67,935	$74,644
Government crop loans	$0	$0
Principal due on term debt	$28,511	$30,072
Total current farm liabilities	**$99,604**	**$107,840**
Total intermediate farm liabilities	**$43,793**	**$31,782**
Total long-term farm liabilities	**$118,617**	**$124,420**
Total Farm Liabilities	**$262,015**	**$264,042**

Having collected financial data for FFF's balance sheets we proceed to organize it into categories described by the balance sheets prepared for HQN. The main reason for doing so is to insure consistency. The second reason for doing so is to organize it into categories amenable to ratio analysis important for financial analysis and management. The balance sheet categories used by HQN which we want to duplicate for FFF are described in Table 5.1 .

Cash and marketable securities. We begin by noting that ending period cash balances cannot be negative. Otherwise they are liabilities. But in the balance sheets provided by FFF, they report negative cash balances in both end of period balance sheets. We set them to zero and include them as liabilities included in accounts payable. Our first line in FFF's ending period balance sheets is:

	12/31/17	12/31/18
Cash and marketable securities	$0	$0

Accounts receivable. FFF lists accounts receivables. They also lists prepaid expenses and hedging accounts that have properties similar to accounts receivable. All three measures represent short-term sacrifices by the firm for benefits they have not yet received. Usually, accounts receivables reflect firm sales for which it has not yet been compensated in cash. In the case of prepaid expenses, it represents payments for goods they have not yet received. In the case of a hedging account, they represent funds paid for options not yet exercised. Adding to accounts receivable, prepaid expenses and hedging funds produces a more inclusive measure of accounts receivable equal to:

	12/31/17	12/31/18
Accounts receivable	$33,400	$45,668
Prepaid expenses and supplies	$7,467	$15,369
Hedging accounts	$0	$0
Accounts receivable	$40,867	$61,037

Inventories. FFF lists several inventories in its ending period balance sheets. We list and sum these below.

	12/31/17	12/31/18
Growing crops	$0	$0
Crops for sale or feed	$178,098	$204,530
Crops under government loan	$0	$0
Market livestock for sale	$7,933	$6,500
Other current assets	$278	$278
Inventories	$186,309	$211,308

We now find the sum of FFF's current assets by adding cash and marketable securities, accounts receivable, and inventories and report the results below.

	12/31/17	12/31/18
Cash and marketable securities	$0	$0
Total accounts receivable	$40,867	$61,037
Total inventories	$186,298	$211,308
Current assets	$227,165	$272,345

We now find FFF's depreciable long-term assets. Note that FFF listed intermediate and long-term assets. In the HQN template, we distinguish long-term as either depreciable or non-depreciable. We consider property, plant, and equipment as depreciable long-term assets and land and buildings as non-depreciable long-term assets. Note that in the FFF supplied balance sheets, they list non-farm assets, which we ignore since our analysis is focused on the farm firm. We now list FFF's depreciable and non-depreciable long-term assets and find their sum.

	12/31/17	12/31/18
Breeding livestock	$10,583	$18,019
Machinery and equip.	$85,001	$87,387
Titled vehicles	$2,889	$2,667
Other intermediate assets	$9,689	$8,893
Depreciable long-term assets	**$108,162**	**$116,966**
Land	$166,200	$179,348
Buildings and improvements	$76,852	$81,021
Other long-term assets	$6,229	$6,229
Non-depreciable long-term assets	**$249,281**	**$266,598**
Total long-term assets	**$357,443**	**$383,564**

We find FFF's total assets as the sum of current and long-term assets and report the result below.

	12/31/17	12/31/18
Total current assets	$227,165	$272,345
Total long-term assets	$357,443	$383,564
Total assets	**$584,608**	**$655,909**

Notice that the total firm assets calculated above do not match the total firm assets calculated by FFF. This is because the negative cash balances have been shifted to the liabilities section of the balance sheet.

Next we prepare FFF's liabilities data to match HQN's reduced categories template. We begin by listing notes payable. We include in this category current notes payable and government loans.

	12/31/17	12/31/18
Current notes	$67,935	$74,644
Government crop loans	$0	$0
Notes payable	$67,935	$74,644

Next we include accrued interest and current portion of the long-term debt and current payments on loans in the category current portion of long-term debt.

	12/31/17	12/31/18
Accrued interest	$1,078	$1,487
Principal due on long-term debt	$28,511	$30,072
Current portion of long-term debt	$29,589	$31,559

Next we list FFF's accounts payable including negative balances in cash reported in the asset portion of the balance sheet.

	12/31/17	12/31/18
Accounts payable	$2,080	$1,637
Negative cash balances	$7,596	$24,333
Accounts payable	$9,676	$25,970

Combining our current liabilities entries and summing we find the sum of FFF's current liabilities:

	12/31/17	12/31/18
Notes payable	$67,935	$74,644
Current portion of LTD	$29,589	$31,559
Accounts payable	$9,676	$25,970
Accrued liabilities	$43,793	$31,782
Total current liabilities	**$150,993**	**$163,955**

Now we consider our long-term liabilities described as long-term debt. The first long-term liabilities is noncurrent long-term debt which is listed below.

	12/31/17	12/31/18
Noncurrent long-term debt	$118,617	$124,420

We add current liabilities to noncurrent long-term debt to find FFF's total liabilities.

	12/31/17	12/31/18
Current liabilities	$150,993	$163,955
Noncurrent long-term debt	$118,617	$124,420
Total Liabilities	$269,610	$288,375

Finally, we compute FFF's equity as the difference between its total assets and it total liabilities and find it equal to:

		12/31/17	12/31/18
+	TOTAL ASSETS	$584,608	$655,909
−	TOTAL LIABILITIES	$269,610	$288,375
=	EQUITY	$314,998	$367,534

Table 5.8. FFF's 2018 Ending Period Balance Sheets

	12/31/17	12/31/18
Cash and marketable securities	$0	$0
Accounts receivable	$40,867	$61,037
Inventories	$186,298	$211,308
Total current assets	$227,165	$272,345
Depreciable long-term assets	$108,162	$116,966
Non-depreciable long-term assets	$249,281	$266,598
Total long-term assets	$357,443	$383,564
TOTAL ASSETS	**$584,608**	**$655,909**
Notes payable	$67,935	$74,644
Current portion of LTD	$29,589	$31,559
Accounts payable	$9,676	$25,970
Accrued liabilities	$43,793	$31,782
Total current liabilities	$150,993	$163,955
Noncurrent long-term debt	$118,617	$124,420
TOTAL LIABILITIES	**$269,610**	**$288,375**
EQUITY	**$314,998**	**$367,534**
TOTAL LIABILITIES AND EQUITY	**$584,608**	**$655,909**

Populating FFF's Cash Income Statements to Conform to HQN's Income Templates

To enable FFF to populate its income statements, it supplied the following data.

+	Apples	$274,069
+	Cherries	$52,123
+	Peaches	$23,046
+	Grapes	$1,467
+	Pears	$638
+	Plums	$508
+	Raspberries	$2,580
+	Blueberries	$900
=	**Total cash fruit sales**	**$355,331**
+	Asparagus	$7,872
+	Cordwood	$31
+	Pumpkins	$360
+	Rhubarb	$179
+	Squash	$246
+	Sweet corn	$1,666
+	Tomatoes	$429
+	Other crops	$7,560
=	**Total cash crops and vegetable sales**	**$18,343**

Finally we sum the cash receipts categories:

+	Total cash fruit sales	$355,331
+	Total cash crops and vegetable sales	$18,343
+	Total cash receipts of finish beef calves	$1,898
+	Government payments	$5,376
+	Dividend and Insurance Payments	$1,651
+	Other farm income	$7,144
=	Cash farm income	$389,743
+	Seed	$2,039
+	Fertilizer	$4,652
+	Chemicals	$55,640
+	Crop insurance	$4,523
+	Packaging and supplies	$7,266
+	Marketing	$137
+	Crop miscellaneous	$31,940
+	Feed	$128
+	Livestock supplies	$794
=	**Total Cash COGS**	**$107,119**
+	Supplies	$638
+	Fuel	$13,458
+	Repairs	$19,882
+	Custom hire	$3,317
+	Hired labor	$99,671
+	Land rent	$29,777
+	Machinery lease	$2,827
+	Insurance	$8,593
+	Utilities	$7,177
+	Hauling	$86
+	Dues	$4,288
+	Miscellaneous	$7,092
=	**Total Cash OE**	**$196,806**

FFF also reported that in 2018 it paid $12,712 in interest charges, $4,628 in taxes, and that the owners withdrew $44,402. FFF also reported the purchase and sale of assets as $57,048 and $1,185 respectively. We assume that the sale of assets was at their book value.

We now populate FFF's AIS, using cash receipts and expense data supplied by FFF and changes in FFF's completed balance sheet entries.

Table 5.9. FFF's 2018 Accrual Income Statement
(all numbers in $000s)

+	Cash receipts	$389,743
+	Change in Accounts Receivable	$20,170
+	Change in Inventories	$25,010
+	Realized Capital Gains / Depreciation Recapture	$0
=	**Total Revenue**	**$434,923**
+	Cash Cost of Goods Sold (COGS)	$107,119
+	Change in Accounts Payable	$16,294
+	Cash Overhead Expenses (OE)	$196,806
+	Change in Accrued Liabilities	($12,011)
+	Depreciation	$47,059
=	**Total Expenses**	**$355,267**
	Earnings Before Interest and Taxes (EBIT)	**$79,656**
−	Interest	$12,712
	Earnings Before Taxes (EBT)	**$66,944**
−	Taxes	$4,628
	Net Income After Taxes (NIAT)	**$62,316**
−	Dividends and owner draws	$44,402
	Additions To Retained Earnings	**$17,914**

Detailed explanations of the AIS entries follow.

- FFF reported total cash receipts equal to $389,743.
- Change in accounts receivables was calculated by finding the difference between accounts receivable in FFF's ending period balance sheets equal to ($61,037 − $40,867) = $ 20,170.
- Change in inventory was calculated by finding the difference between inventories in FFF's ending period balance sheets equal to ($211,308 − $186,298) = $25,010.
- FFF reported Cash COGS equal to $107,119.
- Change in Accounts Payable was calculated by finding the difference between accounts payable reported in FFF's ending period balance sheets equal to $25,970 − $9,676 = $16,294.
- FFF reported Cash OE equal $196,806.
- Change in accrued liabilities was calculated by finding the difference between accrued liabilities in FFF's ending period balance sheets equal to ($31,782 − $43,793) = ($12,011).

The next expense category required by FFF's AIS is depreciation. The data for calculating the change in long-term assets was available in FFF's balance sheets. FFF also reported its sale and purchases of long-term assets as $57,048 and $1,185 respectively. The formula for depreciation is:

Purchases of depreciable LTAs − sales of depreciable LTAs (book value) − Δ depreciable LTAs (book) = depreciation.

Making the necessary substitutions, we find FFF's 2018 depreciation:

$57,048 − $1,185 − ($116,966 − $108,162) = $47,059.

- Summing cash and noncash receipts we find total revenue.
- Summing cash and noncash expenses we find total expenses.
- Subtracting total expenses from total revenue, we find earnings before interest and taxes (EBIT) equal to $79,656.
- FFF reported interest costs equal to $12,712 which were subtracted from EBIT to obtain Earning Before Taxes (EBT) equal to $66,944.
- FFF reported taxes equal to $4,628 which were subtracted from EBT to obtain Net Income after paying interest and taxes (NIAT) of $62,316.
- FFF reported paying dividends and owner withdrawals of $44,402 which were subtracted from NIAT to find changes in retained earnings of $17,914.

Cash income statement. Using the cash receipts and expense data supplied by FFF, we can easily find its cash income statement

Table 5.10. FFF's 2018 Cash Income Statement

	Cash receipts	389,743
+	Realized Capital Gains	$0
−	Cash COGS	$107,119
−	Cash overhead expenses	$196,806
−	Depreciation	$47,059
=	**Cash Earnings Before Interest and Taxes (CEBIT)**	**$38,759**
−	Interest paid	$12,712
=	**Cash Earnings before Taxes (CEBT)**	**$26,047**
−	Taxes paid	$4,628
=	**Cash Net Earnings After Taxes (CNIAT)**	**$21,419**
−	Dividends and owner draws	$44,402
=	**Cash Additions to Retained Earnings**	**($22,983)**

Statement of Cash Flow. We now have all of the data required to find FFF's statement of cash flow. We begin by finding FFF's net cash flow from operations.

+	Cash receipts	$389,743
−	Cash COGS	$107,119
−	Cash OE	$196,806
−	Interest paid	$12,712
−	Taxes paid	$4,628
=	**Net Cash Flow from Operations:**	**$68,478**

Net cash flow from investment activity is calculated from data used to find depreciation and equals

+	Sale of long-term assets	$1,185
–	Purchases of long-term assets	$57,048
=	**Net Cash Flow from Investments**	**($55,863)**

Net cash flow from financing activities reflects the difference between borrowing of long-term debt and notes payable and principal and interest payments on long-term debt and notes payable. Finally, dividends paid are subtracted and the difference between new equity contributed and purchased is computed.

	Change in non-current LTD (borrowing less payments)	$5,803
+	Change in current portion of LTD	$1,970
+	Change in notes payable (borrowing less payments)	$6,709
–	Payment of dividends and owner withdrawal	$44,402
=	**Net Cash Flow from Financing**	**($29,920)**

Table 5.11. Statement of Cash Flow

+	Cash receipts	$389,743
–	Cash COGS	$107,119
–	Cash OE	$196,806
–	Interest paid	$12,712
–	Taxes paid	$4,628
=	**Net Cash Flow from Operations**	**$68,478**
+	Realized capital gains + depreciation recapture	$0
–	Purchases of depreciable long-term assets	$57,048
+	Sales of depreciable long-term assets	$1,185
=	**Net Cash Flow from Investments**	**($55,863)**
+	Change in non-current long term debt	$5,803
+	Change in current portion long term debt	$1,970
+	Change in notes payable	$6,709
–	Dividends and owner's draw	$44,402
=	**Net Cash Flow from Financing**	**($29,920)**
	Change in cash position of the firm	**($17,305)**

What to do? Consider the following example. You are visiting in a new town and are trying to find your way to an important site. Suppose that you stop a person you assume is familiar with the location and ask for directions which the person provides. You thank the person for directions and begin your journey to your destination. But just to make sure you are on the right path, you consult your map and find that the directions you just received are in conflict with your map. You are faced with a choice. Which set of directions do you choose? They both can't be correct.

We face a similar problem when our completed financial statements aren't consistent. Somewhere in our entries there is an error(s). Therefore to populate our template we have to decide what numbers to believe.

In our case the conflict arises when reported primary data and calculated data required to reconcile the various financial statements are inconsistent. The first requirement is to establish consistency beginning with the calculated entries. Consistency is a necessary condition for accuracy and makes it a logical place to begin. Then we determine if the primary data that conflicts with the calculated number is hard or soft. If it is reasonably hard data, and is higher that the calculated data we explore the data for under estimates of cash inflows and over estimates of cash outflows. We follow the reverse process if the primary data is less than the calculated data. If we can find soft data that can be changed to make the calculated data consistent with the primary data—we make the changes.

So, what have we learned? We learned from the FFF example that actual firms have more complicated data sets that we illustrated using the HQN example. Yet, the variable categories we used when computing the HQN study apply generally even though some side-bar calculations may be required to reduce actual firm data to the variable categories used to describe HQN.

Summary and Conclusions

In this chapter we have learned how to construct CFS. Coordinated financial statements are tools that we will use in the next chapter to analyze the firm's strengths and weaknesses. Constructing financial statements for actual firms with less than perfect and complete data is somewhat of an art.

Questions

1. Define the differences between consistent financial statements and accurate financial statements.
2. Discuss the statement: "consistent financial statements are necessary but not sufficient for accurate financial statements."
3. What are some conditions required for financial statements to be consistent?
4. In a typical data set provided by a farm firm, what data is most reliable (hard) and which data is

least likely to reliable (soft)?

5. Below is a completed 2018 checkbook and 2017 and 2018 ending period balance sheets for the "Grow Green" vegetable farm. Use the numbers in their checkbook and their two balance sheets to create a 2018 cash and AIS and statement of cash flow.

Grow Green 2018 Checkbook				
Date	Item	Check amount	Deposit amount	Checkbook balance
12/31/17	Beginning cash balance			$930
	Cash receipts		$40,940	$41,870
	Seed, feed, fertilizer	$20,000		$21,870
	Labor cost of producing products	$8,350		$13,520
	Insurance	$2,000		$11,520
	Utilities	$9,632		$1,888
	Purchase of LTAs	$100		$1,788
	Sale of LTAs (at book value)		$30	$1,818
	Interest paid	$504		$1,314
	Taxes paid	$71		$1,243
	Payment on current-term debt	$50		$1,193
	Long-term debt payments	$57		$1,139
	Payment on notes	$230		$906
	Owner draw	$390		$516
12/31/18	Ending cash balance			$516

Grow Green Balance Sheet		
	12/31/17	12/31/18
Cash and Marketable Securities	$930.00	$516.00
Accounts Receivable	$1,640.00	$1,200.00
Inventory	$3,750.00	$5,200.00
Total Current Assets	**$6,320.00**	**$6,916.00**
Depreciable long-term assets	$2,990.00	$2,800.00
Non-depreciable long-term assets	$690.00	$600.00
Total Long-term Assets	**$3,680.00**	**$3,400.00**
Total Assets	**$10,000.00**	**$10,316.00**
Notes Payable	$1,500.00	$1,270.00
Current Portion of LTD	$500.00	$450.00
Accounts Payable	$3,000.00	$4,000.00
Accrued Liabilities	$958.00	$880.00
Total Current Liabilities	**$5,958.00**	**$6,600.00**
Noncurrent Long-term Debt	**$2,042.00**	**$1,985.00**
Total Liabilities	**$8,000.00**	**$8,585.00**
Other Capital	$1,900.00	$1,689.00
Retained Earnings	$100.00	$42.00
Equity	**$2,000.00**	**$1,731.00**
Total Liabilities and Equity	**$10,000.00**	**$10,316.00**

6. Compare the differences and the advantages and disadvantages of cash and AIS.
7. In problem 5, you should have found ending cash to equal $630 which is the same as the observed ending cash. Instead assume that the ending cash balance recorded in the balance sheets provided was equal to $650. Describe the possible adjustments you might make to observed variables to make consistent observed ending cash and the calculated ending cash. Provide a revised set of CFS that are consistent with ending cash calculated and observed.
8. Most firm managers who are also the firm's financial manager keep less than the complete data set required to construct a complete set of financial statements. And even the data they collect are not in the format we expect, requiring us to reformat the data we do have. With less than complete data sets, we are forced to do the best we can with what we have. What follows is a typical data set which ABM 435 teams have used in the past to construct a set of consistent and accurate set of financial statements. Using the data provided, construct a consistent and, to the extent possible, accurate set of financial statements.

Farm A	12/31/18
Acres owned	488
Acres rented	449
Machinery investment / crop acre @ cost	$95
Machinery investment / crop acre @ market	$520
Average price received	
Corn	$6
Soybeans	$13
Wheat	$7
Hay	$97
Average yield	
Corn	$175
Soys	$54
Wheat	$76
Gross Cash farm income including government payments & patronage dividends	$863,561
Cash Farm Expense including land rent but excluding interest	$637,231
Interest	$23,232

Other balance sheet related data include the following:

	12/31/17	12/31/18
Cash and checking	$63,211	$66,696
Crops and Feed	$470,632	$430,532
Market livestock	46,696	$55,463
Accounts receivable	$34,062	$44,550
Prepaid expenses and supplies	$104558	$101,381
Hedging activities	$1916	$2374
Other current assets	$18,901	$15,822
Other capital assets	$29,140	$36,539
Breeding livestock	$29,140	$40,053
Accounts payable	$26,149	$29,789
Accrued interest	$7,222	$7470
Current notes	$111,819	$127,402
Government crop loans	$1,400	$1,733
Loan principal due	$59,849	$68,559
Intermediate liabilities	$130,409	$124,872
Long-term liabilities	$344,658	$347,834
Machinery and Equipment (book)	$132,656	$179,366
Titled vehicles (book)	$3,096	$3,563
Buildings/improvements (book)	$105,559	$110,232
Land (book)	$508,571	$574,410

Purchases of Breeding Livestock	$901
Sale of Breeding Livestock	$291
Purchases other capital assets	$11,924
Sale of other capital assets	$8,443
Land sales (50% of sale were realized cap. Gains	$21,970
Purchase of titled vehicles	$1,948
Sale of titled vehicles	$636
Investments in buildings/improvements	$21,970

6. Unlocking Insights: Analyzing Financial Ratios

LINDON ROBISON

Learning goals. After completing this chapter, you should be able to: (1) calculate financial ratios using information included in a firm's coordinated financial statements (CFS); and (2) answer the question: "what are the firm's financial strengths and weaknesses?"

Learning objectives. To realize your learning goals, you should complete the following objectives:

- Learn how financial ratios allow us to compare the financial condition of different firms.
- Learn how to construct (S)olvency, (P)rofitability, (E) fficiency, (L)iquidity, and (L)everage ratios—what we refer to collectively as SPELL ratios.
- Learn how SPELL ratios help us describe the financial strengths and weaknesses of a firm.
- Learn how the times interest earned (TIE) ratio and the debt-to-service (DS) ratio can provide information about the firm's solvency.
- Learn how the profit margin (m) ratio, the return on assets (ROA) ratio, and the return on equity (ROE) ratio can provide information about the firm's profitability.
- Learn how to find the after-tax ROE where T is the average tax rate paid by the firm on its earnings before taxes (EBT).
- Learn how to relate ROE and ROA to each other.
- Learn how the inventory turnover (ITO) ratio, the inventory turnover time (ITOT) ratio, the asset turnover (ATO) ratio, the asset turnover time (ATOT) ratio, the receivable turnover (RTO) ratio, the receivable turnover time (RTOT) ratio, the payable turnover (PTO) ratio, and the payable turnover time (PTOT) ratio can provide important efficiency information about the firm.
- Learn how the current ratio (CT) and the quick ratio (QK) can provide information about the firm's liquidity.
- Learn how leverage ratios including the debt-to-equity (DE) ratio and the equity multiplier (EM) ratio can be used to monitor and measure the firm's risk.
- Understand how comparing the firm's SPELL ratios to industry standard ratios can help answer the question: what are the financial strengths and weaknesses of the firm?
- Learn how to construct after-tax ROE and after-tax ROA measures.
- Learn how unpaid family labor affects ROE and ROA measures.
- Learn why the firm may consider profit and solvency ratios key to a firm's survival and success.
- Learn how the DuPont ratio demonstrates the interdependencies of some SPELL ratios.

Introduction

Ratios, percents, and rates. Coordinated financial statements (CFS) include both outside and inside factors. Exogenous variables have numbers that can be seen or that are set by things that happen outside the firm. Endogenous variables get their values from what is going on inside the company and from the values of foreign   variables.

When the CFS factors are turned into ratios, they are more useful, especially for figuring out what the firm's strengths and weaknesses are. We could look at the variables in the CFS and compare them to other firms to figure out what the firm's strengths and flaws are, but our conclusions would be limited because no two firms are the same. Ratios, on the other hand, let you compare the success of different companies using a standard,   easy-to-understand   measure.

When you split one number by the other, you get a ratio, which is made up of two numbers. Let's say that the terms X and Y stand for two numbers that make up a ratio (X/Y). The number tells us how many Xs there are for every Y. This standard number, which is the number of units of X for each unit of Y, lets us compare companies with ratios that are built the same way. We can tell the difference between numbers and rates.

When ratios are measured in the same units (dollars, inches, pounds, etc.), the units in the ratio cancel out, leaving a decimal number that, when multiplied by 100, becomes a percentage. Since all of the numbers in the CFS are measured in dollars, all of the rates of numbers in the CFS are percentages. So, financial numbers   tell   us   how   much   Y   of   X   there   is.

Now, think about a ratio that is made up of two numbers that are split by each other but are measured in different ways. In this case, the units don't cancel each other out, so the answer is a rate. For example, y/x tells us the price per ounce if y is measured in dollars and x is measured in ounces. To show how important numbers are, think about buying a box of breakfast cereal. Let's say you go to the grocery store to buy Super Sweet Sugar Snacks, your favourite morning cereal. You find a 10-ounce box of Super Sweet Sugar Snacks for $3.20 and a 15-ounce box of the same cereal for $4.50. What is the best box of cereal to buy? The answer can't be found in the price of each box of cereal, because the more expensive box also has more cereal in it. But if we split the price of each box by the amount of cereal in each box, we can compare "apples to apples," or in this case, we can compare the price per ounce of cereal in each box, which is a similar rate. Using the ratio of dollars to ounces in the box, we can see that cereal in the small box costs $0.32 per ounce ($3.20 for 10 oz.) but costs $0.30 per ounce ($4.50 for 15 oz.) in the large box. The big box   of   cereal   is   the   better   buy   because   each   ounce   of   cereal   costs   less.

The cereal case shows a very important point: a ratio is not very helpful if you don't have another ratio to compare it to. When you know how much cereal costs per ounce in the small box, you can better understand how much cereal costs per ounce in the big box. In the same way, having business standards ratios against which we can compare our ratios is important for a financial manager's efforts to discover the firm's strengths and weaknesses.

> So, what have we learned? We learned that when answering the question what the firm's financial strengths and weaknesses are, it is important that we look at the firm from several different points of view represented by the SPELL ratios.

We discuss next the different views required to adequately describe the firm's financial condition. Each of the different views are represented by a set of ratios. As is customary, it is understood that financial ratios are really percentages or decimal representations of two numbers measured in the same units.

Financial Ratios

Five groups can be made from the different kinds of financial ratios that can be made from the factors in a coordinated financial statement. You can remember the groups with the acronym SPELL. (S)olvency ratios, (P)rofitability ratios, (E)fficiency ratios, (L)iquidity ratios, and (L)everage ratios are the five types of financial ratios. Each of these five types of ratios shows something different about the firm's financial strengths and flaws.

Ratios and time measurement points. When using CFS data to make financial ratios, it's important to pay close attention to the "point in time" or "period of time" that the ratio shows. Numbers on balance sheets show how a company's finances were doing at a certain point in time. Numbers from income statements and cash flow statements show how money has been used over time. When you use two numbers from the balance sheet to make a ratio, the numbers should be from the same time. Measures of ratios of points and lengths of time. There are two ways to make a ratio. One uses a number from the income statement or statement of cash flow to show how things have changed over time. The other uses a number from the balance sheet to show how things are financially at a certain point in time. One way is to use a number from the end-of-period balance sheet from the previous period that matches the time when the actions shown on the income statement start. The second method takes the average of the measures on the balance sheet at the beginning and end of the time period that includes the events on the income statement. We'll talk more about when each of the two ways is better in the future.

Cash-to-accruals rates. In this chapter, we make a number of ratios that use an income or a COGS variable. The question is whether these should be cash income and cash cost of goods sold (COGS) or accrued income and accrued COGS. We use accrual variables, which look at when a financial deal happened instead of when it was turned into cash.

Useful comparisons. The usefulness of ratios depends on having something useful to compare them to. Suppose we wish we compare ratios of different firms. Obviously, we would expect ratios constructed for different firms to have been calculated at comparable points and periods of time. We would also expect that firms being compared are of the same size and engaged in similar activities. Fortunately, we can often find such measures described as industry average ratios.

Sometimes the relevant comparison for the firm is with itself at different points in time. Having the same ratio over a number of time periods for the same firm allows the firm manager to identify trends. One question trend analysis may answer is: in what areas is the firm is improving (not improving) compared to past performances. Of course, trend analysis can be performed using absolute numbers as well as ratios.

What follows. In what follows, we will introduce several ratios from each of the "SPELL" categories. Then we will discuss how each of them, alone and together with other SPELL ratios, can help answer the question: what are the firm's financial strengths and weaknesses. Since data from HQN's financial statements will be used to form the SPELL ratios, HQN's balance sheets, AIS, and statement of cash flow for 2018 are repeated in Table 6.1.

So, what have we learned? We learned that the ratio of variables X and Y (X/Y) tells us how many units of X are associated with each unit of Y. As a result we can compare the ratio X/Y in firms A and B because the two ratios provide the same information about the same variable in the two firms—the number of units of X that exist for each unit of Y.

Table 6.1. Coordinated financial statement for HiQuality Nursery (HQN) for the year 2018
Open HQN Coordinated Financial Statement in MS Excel

BALANCE SHEET				ACCRUAL INCOME STATEMENT			STATEMENT OF CASH FLOW	
	12/31/17	12/31/18			2018			2018
Cash and Marketable Securities	$930	$600	+	Cash Receipts	$38,990	+	Cash Receipts	$38,990
Accounts Receivable	$1,640	$1,200	+	Δ Accounts Receivable	($440)	–	Cash COGS	$27,000
Inventory	$3,750	$5,200	+	Δ Inventories	$1450	–	Cash OE	$11,078
Notes Receivable	$0	$0	+	Realized Capital Gains / Depreciation Recapture	$0	–	Interest paid	$480
CURRENT ASSETS	$6,320	$7,000	=	Total Revenue	$40,000	–	Taxes paid	$68
Depreciable Long-term Assets	$2,990	$2,710	+	Cash Cost of Goods Sold (COGS)	$27,000	=	Net Cash Flow from Operations	$364
Non-depreciable Long-term Assets	$690	$690	+	Δ Accounts Payable	$1,000	+	Realized capital gains + depreciation recapture	$0
LONG-TERM ASSETS	$3,680	$3,400	+	Cash Overhead Expenses (OE)	$11,078	+	Sales non-depreciable assets	$0
TOTAL ASSETS	$10,000	$10,400	+	Δ Accrued Liabilities	($78)	–	Purchases of non-depreciable assets	$0
Notes Payable	$1,500	$1,270	+	Depreciation	$350	+	Sales of depreciable assets	$30
Current Portion LTD	$500	$450	=	Total Expenses	$39,350	–	Purchases of depreciable assets	$100
Accounts Payable	$3,000	$4,000		Earnings Before Interest and Taxes (EBIT)	$650	=	Net Cash Flow from Investments	($70)
Accrued Liabilities	$958	$880	–	Interest	$480	+	Change in noncurrent LTD	($57)
CURRENT LIABILITIES	$5,958	$6,600		Earnings Before Taxes (EBT)	$170	+	Change in current portion of LTD	($50)

NONCURRENT LONG-TERM DEBT	$2,042	$1,985	−	Taxes	$68	+	Change in notes payable	($230)
TOTAL LIABILITIES	$8,000	$8,585		Net Income After Taxes (NIAT)	$102	−	Payment of dividends and owner's draw	$287
Contributed Capital	$1,900	$1,900	−	Dividends and owner draws	$287	=	Net Cash Flow from Financing	($624)
Retained Earnings	$100	($85)		Additions To Retained Earnings	($185)		Change in cash position of the firm	($330)
TOTAL EQUITY	$2,000	$1,815						
TOTAL LIABILITIES AND EQUITY	$10,000	$10,400						

Solvency Ratios

Solvency ratios, sometimes called repayment capacity ratios, can be used to answer questions about the firm's ability to meet its long-term debt obligations. Here we will examine two solvency ratios: (1) times interest earned (TIE) and (2) debt-to-service ratio (DS).

Times interest earned (TIE) ratio

The TIE ratio measures the firm's solvency or repayment capacity. The TIE ratio combines two period of time measures obtained from the firm's income statement and is defined as:

$$TIE = \frac{EBIT}{INT}$$
(6.1)

In the above formula, INT represents the firm's interest obligations accrued during the period. EBIT measures the firm's earnings during the period before paying interest and taxes. The TIE ratio answers the question: how many times can the firm pay its interest costs using the firm's operating profits (for every dollar of interest costs how many dollars of EBIT exist? Generally, a healthy firm's TIE ratio exceeds one (TIE > 1), otherwise the firm won't be able to pay its interest costs using its current income. HQN's TIE ratio for 2018 is:

$$TIE = \frac{\$650}{\$480} = 1.35$$
(6.2)

HQN's 2018 TIE ratio indicates for every dollar of interest the firm owes, it has $1.35 dollars of EBIT to make its interest payments.

Debt-to-service (DS) ratio

Like the TIE ratio, the DS ratio answers questions about the firm's ability to pay its current long-term debt obligations. In contrast to the TIE ratio, DS ratio recognizes the need to pay the current portion of its long-term debt in addition to interest. Finally, the DS ratio (in contrast to the TIE ratio) adds depreciation to EBIT because depreciation is a non-cash expense. Subtracting depreciation from revenue to obtain EBIT understates the liquid funds available to the firm to pay its current long-term debt obligations.

To illustrate the logic behind this formula, assume that cash receipts equals $100, depreciation equals $30, other expenses equal $10, and EBIT is equal to $60. But more than $60 is available to pay interest and principal because depreciation of $30 is a non-cash expense. Thus we add depreciation to EBIT to improve our measure of income available for interest and debt repayment: $60 + $30 = $90, which is the numerator in the DS ratio equation.

This book recommends that the current portion of the long-term debt at the beginning of the current period be used to calculate the denominator in the firm's DS ratio. After making these adjustments, we obtain the firm's DS ratio equal to:

$$DS = \frac{EBIT + Depreciation}{INT + Current\,portion\,long - term\,debt}$$
(6.3)

If the DS < 1, a firm will not be able to make principal and interest payments using EBIT plus depreciation. In this case, the firm will be required to obtain funding from other sources such as restructuring debt, selling assets, delaying investments in assets, and/or increasing EBIT to meet current debt and interest obligations. If the firm were unable to meet its interest and principal payment over the long term, the firm's survival would be threatened.

We can solve for HQN's 2018 DS ratio. According to HQN's income statement EBIT was $650 and depreciation was $350. Interest paid equaled $480 and the current portion of the long-term debt listed on the firm's 2017 end of period balance sheet was $500. Making the substitutions into equation (6.3) we find HQN's DS ratio equal to:

$$DS = \frac{\$650 + \$350}{\$480 + \$500} = 1.02$$
(6.4)

According to HQN's DS ratio, its EBIT plus depreciation are sufficient to meet 102 percent of its interest and current principal payments, a more accurate reflections of its solvency than its TIE ratio of 1.35.

Profitability Ratios

Profitability ratios measure the firm's ability to generate profits from its assets or equity. The firm's accrual income statement (AIS) provides three earnings or profit measures useful in finding rates of return: earnings before interest and taxes (EBIT), earnings before taxes (EBT), and net income after interest and taxes (NIAT).

We examine three profitability ratios: (1) profit margin (m), (2) return on assets (ROA), and (3) return on equity (ROE). In some cases, the profitability measures are reported on an after-tax basis requiring that we know the average tax rate for the firm which we calculate next.

Finding the average tax rate. In some cases, particularly with profitability measures, we need to know the average tax rate paid by the firm. We find the average tax rate by solving for T in the following formula that equates net income after taxes (NIAT) to EBT adjusted for the after-tax rate T:

$$(6.5) \quad NIAT = EBT(1 - T)$$

And solving for T in equation (6.5):

$$(6.6) \quad T = 1 - \frac{NIAT}{EBT}$$

Solving T for HQN in 2018 using EBT and NIAT values from Table 6.1 we find:

$$(6.7) \quad T = 1 - \frac{102}{170} = .4$$

Profit margin (m) ratio

The ratio m measures the proportion of each dollar of cash receipts that is retained as profit after interest is paid but before taxes are paid.

The ratio m, is defined as:

$$(6.8) \quad m = \frac{EBT}{Total\ Revenue}$$

In 2018, HQN had a before-tax profit margin equal to:

$$\underset{(6.9)}{m} = \frac{\$170}{\$40,000} = .00425 = .425\%$$

In other words, for every $1 of revenue earned by the firm, HQN earned $0.00425 in before-tax profits. Meanwhile, the after-tax profit margin m is defined as:

$$\underset{(6.10)}{m(1-T)} = \frac{EBT(1-T)}{Total\ Revenue} = \frac{NIAT}{Total\ Revenue}$$

In 2018, HQN had an after-tax profit margin equal to:

$$\underset{(6.11)}{m(1-.4)} = \frac{\$102}{\$40,000} = .00255 = .255\%$$

In other words, for every $1 of cash receipts, HQN earned $0.00255 in after-tax profits.

Return on assets (ROA) ratio

The ROA measures the amount of profits generated by each dollar of assets and is equal to:

$$\underset{(6.12)}{ROA} = \frac{EBIT}{A}$$

HQN's 2018 before-tax ROA using beginning period assets is equal to:

$$\underset{(6.13)}{ROA} = \frac{\$650}{\$10,000} = 6.5\%$$

Interpreted, each dollar of HQN's assets generates $.065 cents in before-tax profits.

Return on equity (ROE) ratio

The ROE ratio measures the amount of profit generated by each dollar of equity after interest payments to debt capital are subtracted but before taxes are paid. Profits after interest is subtracted equals EBT (earnings before taxes). The ROE ratio can be expressed as:

$$ROE = \frac{EBT}{E}$$

(6.14)

HQN's 2018 before-tax ROE using beginning period equity is equal to:

$$ROE = \frac{\$170}{\$2,000} = 8.5\%$$

(6.15)

After-tax return on equity, ROE(1 – T), can be expressed as EBT adjusted for taxes, or NIAT. Therefore, ROE(1 – T) can be expressed as NIAT divided by equity:

$$ROE(1 - T) = \frac{NIAT}{E}$$

(6.16)

HQN's 2018 after-tax ROE is equal to:

$$ROE(1 - T) = \frac{\$102}{\$2,000} = 5.1\%$$

(6.17)

Interpreted, each dollar of equity generated about $0.085 in before-tax profits and $0.051 in after-tax profits during 2018.

The relationship between ROE and ROA. Before leaving profitability ratios, there is one important question: which is greater for a given firm: ROE or ROA? To answer this question, we simply define (ROE)/(E) as equal to the return assets (ROA)(A) less the cost of debt (i)(D):

(6.18) $$(ROE)(E) = (ROA)(A) - (i)(D)$$

After substituting for A, (D + E) and collecting like terms and dividing by equity E, we obtain the result in equation (6.19):

$$ROE = (ROA - i)\left(\frac{D}{E}\right) + ROA$$

(6.19)

Equation (6.19) reveals ROE > ROA if ROA > i; ROE = ROA if ROA = i; and ROE < ROA if ROA < i.

If ROE is not greater than ROA, then the firm is losing money on every dollar of debt. For HQN, ROE is 8.5% and greater than its ROA of 6.5%. Meanwhile HQN's average interest rate on its debt (total interest costs divided by debt at the beginning of the period equal to i) during 2018 was equal to:

$$i = \frac{int}{debt} = \frac{\$480}{\$8,000} = 6\%$$

(6.20)

Efficiency Ratios

Efficiency ratios compare outputs and inputs. Efficiency ratios of outputs divided by inputs describe how many units of output each unit of input has produced. More efficient ratios indicate a unit of input is producing greater units of outputs than smaller efficiency ratios.

Consider two types of efficiency ratios: turnover (TO) ratios and turnover time (TOT) ratios. The turnover ratios measure output produced per unit of input during the accounting period, in our case 365 days. For example, suppose our TO ratio is 5. A TO ratio of 5 tells that during 365 days, every unit input produced 5 units of output.

We may want to find the number of days required for a unit of input to produce a unit of output. We can answer the question by dividing 365 days by the number of turnovers that occurred during the year. This tells us the number of days required for a unit of input to produce a unit of output, what we call a turn over time, or TOT, ratio. Continuing with our example, if an input was turned into an output 5 times during the year, then dividing 365 days by 5 tells us that every turnover required (365 days)/5 = 73 days.

We now consider four TO efficiency measures: (1) the inventory turnover (ITO) ratio, (2) the asset turnover (ATO) ratio, (3) the receivable turnover (RTO) ratio, and (4) the payable turnover (PTO) ratio. We also find for each TO ratio their corresponding TOT ratio.

Inventory turnover (ITO) ratio

The ITO ratio measures the output (total revenue) produced by the firm's inputs (inventory). Total revenue is a period of time measure. Inventory is a point-in-time measure. We use the beginning of the period inventory measure because it reflects the inventory on hand when revenue generating activities began. ITO is defined below.

$$ITO = \frac{Total\ Revenue}{Inventory}$$
(6.21)

The 2018 ITO ratio for HQN is:

$$ITO = \frac{\$40,000}{\$3,750} = 10.67$$
(6.22)

The ITO ratio indicates that for every \$1 of inventory, the firm generates an estimated 10.67 dollars of revenue during the year. A small ITO ratio suggests that the firm is holding excess inventory levels given its level of total revenue. Likewise, a large ITO ratio may signal potential "stock outs" which could result in lost revenue if the firm is unable to meet the demand for its products and services.

We can find the number of days required to sell a unit of the firm's beginning inventory, its inventory turnover time (ITOT) ratio, by dividing one year (365 days) by the firm's ITO:

$$
\text{(6.23)} \quad ITOT = \frac{365}{ITO}
$$

The ITOT ratio for HQN in 2018 is equal to:

$$
\text{(6.24)} \quad ITOT = \frac{365}{10.67} = 34.21
$$

In other words, a unit of inventory entering HQN's inventory is sold in roughly 35 days.

Asset turnover (ATO) ratio

The ATO ratio measures the amount of total revenue (output) for every dollar's worth of assets (inputs) during the year. The ATO ratio measures the firm's efficiency in using its assets to generate revenue. Like the ITO ratio, the ATO ratio reflects the firm's pricing strategy. Companies with low profit margins tend to have high ATO ratios. Companies with high profit margins tend to have low ATO ratios.

Let A represent the value of the firm's assets. The ATO ratio is calculated by dividing the firm's total revenue by its total assets:

$$
\text{(6.25)} \quad ATO = \frac{Total\ Revenue}{A}
$$

Using beginning of the period assets, HQN's 2018 ATO ratio is equal to:

$$
\text{(6.26)} \quad ATO = \frac{\$40,000}{\$10,000} = 4.0
$$

We can find the firm's asset turnover time (ATOT) ratio, the number of days required for a dollar of assets to generate a dollar of sales, by dividing 365 by the firm's ATO ratio. Using the ATO previously calculated for HQN in 2018 we find:

$$
\text{(6.27)} \quad ATOT = \frac{365}{ATO} = \frac{365}{4.0} = 91.3
$$

In other words, a dollar of HQN's assets generates a dollar of cash receipts in roughly 91 days.

Receivable turnover (RTO) ratio

The RTO ratio measures the firm's efficiency in using its accounts receivables to generate cash receipts. The RTO ratio is calculated by dividing the firm's total revenue by its accounts receivables. Using account receivables measured at the beginning of the year, the firm's RTO ratio measures how many dollars of revenue are generated by one dollar of accounts receivables held at the beginning of the period. The RTO reflects the firm's credit strategy. Companies with high RTO ratios (strict customer credit policies) tend to have lower levels of total revenue than those with low RTO ratios (easy credit policies). We express the RTO ratio as:

$$RTO = \frac{Total\ Revenue}{Account\ Receivables}$$
(6.28)

Using data from HQN for 2018, cash receipts from the income statement, and accounts receivables from the ending 2017 balance sheet, we find HQN's RTO to equal:

$$RTO = \frac{\$40,000}{\$1,640} = 24.39$$
(6.29)

In the case of HQN during 2018, every dollar of account receivables generated $24.39 in revenue or an output to input ratio of 24.39.

We can estimate the firm's receivable turnover time (RTOT) ratio or what is sometimes called the firm's average collection period for accounts receivable ratio, the number of days required for a dollar of credit sales to be collected, by dividing 365 by the firm's RTO ratio.

$$RTOT = \frac{365}{RTO}$$
(6.30)

In the case of HQN during 2018, we find its RTOT ratio equal to:

$$RTOT = \frac{365}{24.39} = 14.96$$
(6.31)

Interpreted, it takes an average of nearly 15 days from the time of a credit sale until the payment is actually received. The RTOT ratio, like the RTO ratio, reflects the firm's credit policy. If the RTOT is too low, the firm may have too tight of a credit policy and might be losing revenue as a result of not offering customers the opportunity to purchase on credit. On the other hand, remember that accounts receivable must be financed by either debt or equity funds. If the RTOT is too high, the firm is extending a lot of credit to other firms, and the financing cost may become excessive. Another concern is that the longer a firm extends credit, the greater is the risk that the firm's accounts receivable will ever be repaid.

In some cases, it is useful to construct a schedule that decomposes accounts receivable into the length of time each amount has been outstanding. For example, the schedule might break the accounts receivable into: 1) the amount that is less than 30 days outstanding, 2) the amount that is 30–60 days outstanding, and 3) the amount that is more than 60 days outstanding. This breakdown provides additional information on the risk of the firm's accounts receivable and the likelihood of repayment.

Payable turnover (PTO) ratio

The PTO ratio measures the firm's efficiency in using its accounts payable to acquire its accrued COGS. The PTO is calculated by dividing accrued COGS (equal to cash COGS plus change in account payable) by accounts payable measured at the beginning of the year. The firm's PTO ratio measures how many dollars of accrued COGS are generated by one dollar of accounts payable held at the beginning of the period. The PTO reflects the firm's credit strategy. Does it prefer equity or debt financing. Firms with low PTO ratios tend to favor the use of debt to finance the firm which tends to generate higher variability in its ROE. The PTO ratio is expressed as:

$$PTO = \frac{Accrued\,COGS}{AP}$$
(6.32)

Using data from HQN for 2018, we find its PTO to equal:

$$PTO = \frac{\$28,000}{\$3,000} = 9.33$$
(6.33)

In the case of HQN, every dollar of accounts payable produced 9.33 dollars in accrued COGS.

We can estimate the firm's payable turnover time (PTOT) ratio by dividing 365 days by the firm's PTO ratio.

The PTOT ratio measures the number of days before a firm repays its credit purchases. The PTOT formula, like the other average period ratios, is found by dividing 365 by the PTO ratio. The PTOT ratios can be expressed as:

$$PTOT = \frac{365}{PTO}$$
(6.34)

HQN's 2018 PTOT ratio is calculated as:

$$\underset{(6.35)}{PTOT} = \frac{365}{9.33} = 39.12$$

Interpreted, HQN's PTOT ratio of nearly 39 days implies that it takes the firm an average of 39 days from the time a credit purchase is transacted until the firm actually pays for its purchase. The PTOT ratio, like the PTO ratio, reflects the firm's credit policy. If the PTOT is too low, the firm may not be using its available credit efficiently and relying too heavily on equity financing. On the other hand, PTOT ratios that are too large may reflect a liquidity problem for the firm or poor management that depends too much on high cost short term credit.

Note of caution. Economists and others frequently warn against confusing causation and correlation between variables. Descriptive data reflected in the ratios derived in this section on efficiency ratios do not generally reflect a causal relationships between variables nor should they be used to make predictions. For example, in the previous section, we are not suggesting that PTOT can be predicted by the PTO or vice versa. The only thing that can be inferred is that PTOT times PTO will always equal 365 days.

Liquidity Ratios

A firm's liquidity is its ability to pay short-term obligations with its current assets. Also implied by liquidity is the firm's ability to quickly convert assets into cash without a loss in their value which would be the case if the exchange of an asset for cash required a large discount. However, before we review important liquidity ratios, we review an important liquidity measure that is not a ratio: a firm's net working capital.

Net working capital (NWC). Even though NWC is not a ratio, it provides some useful liquidity information that should not be ignored. If NWC is positive, then CA which are expected to be converted to cash during the upcoming year will be sufficient to pay for CL, those liabilities expected to come due during the upcoming year. HQN's net working capital, described in Table 6.2, is positive for years 2016, 2017, and 2018, suggesting the firm was capable of meeting its short-term debt obligations by using only the assets expected to be liquidated during the upcoming year.

Table 6.2. Net Working Capital for HQN

Year	Current Assets	–	Current Liabilities	=	Net Working Capital
2016	$5,910,000	–	$5,370,000	=	$540,000
2017	$6,320,000	–	$5,958,000	=	$362,000
2018	$7,000,000	–	$6,600,000	=	$400,000

Another aspect of HQN's NWC is its trend. Is NWC increasing or decreasing over time? We measure the trend in NWC by calculating the change in NWC between calendar years. HQN's NWC decreased by $178,000 during 2017 ($362,000 – $540,000). It increased by $38,000 during 2018 ($400,000 – $362,000).

The decrease in NWC during 2017 and the slight increase in 2018 calls for an explanation. Was the drop in NWC justified? Did it represent a conscious liquidity decision by the firm? Was it due to external forces? It is the duty of financial managers to find answers to these questions.

Current (CT) ratio

Liquidity ratios measure a firm's ability to meet its short-term or current financial obligations with short-term or current assets. The CT ratio is the most common liquidity measure. It combines two point-in-time measures from the balance sheet, current assets (CA), and current liabilities (CL). The point-in-time measures of the two numbers must be the same. We write the CT ratio as:

$$CT = \frac{CA}{CL}$$
(6.36)

In principle we would like to see the CT ratio exceed one (CT > 1), because it suggests that for every dollar of CL there is more than one dollar of CA sufficient to cover the liquidation of CL if necessary. If the CT ratio is less than one (CT < 1), then liquidating current assets will not generate enough funds to pay for the firm's maturing current liabilities obligations which may create a significant problem. If the firm's current liabilities exceed its current assets, the firm may have to liquidate long-term assets to meet it current obligations. But liquidating long-term (usually illiquid) assets is often costly to do because they cannot be easily converted to cash and end up being sold for a price less than their value to the firm.

The current ratio is constructed from the firm's balance sheet (see Table 6.1). The CT ratio for HQN at the beginning of 2018 (the end of 2017) was:

$$CT = \frac{\$6,320}{\$5,958} = 1.06$$
(6.37)

HQN's beginning 2018 CT ratio value of 1.06, suggests that its current liquid resources were just sufficient to meet its current obligations.

As with all the ratios we will consider, there is generally no "correct" CT ratio value. Clearly a firm's CT ratio can be too low, in which case the firm might have difficulty paying its maturing short-term liabilities. Nevertheless, a CT < 1 does not mean that a firm will not be able to meet its maturing obligations. The firm may have access to other resources that can be used to help meet maturing obligations, such as earnings from operations, long-term assets that could be liquidated, debt which could be restructured, and/or investments in depreciating assets which can be delayed.

On the other hand, a firm's CT ratio can be too high. CA usually earn a low rate of return and holding large levels of current assets may not be profitable to the firm. It may be more efficient to convert some of the CA to long-term assets that generate larger expected returns. To illustrate, think of the extreme case of a firm that liquidates all of its long-term assets and holds them as cash. The firm might have a large CT ratio and be very liquid, but liquid assets are unlikely to generate a high rate of return or profits.

Quick (QK) ratio

The QK ratio is sometimes called the acid-test ratio. The QK ratio is very similar to the CT ratio, except that inventories (INV), another point-in-time measure obtained from the firm's balance sheet, are subtracted from CA. The QK ratio is defined as:

$$QK = \frac{CA - INV}{CL}$$

(6.38)

In forming the QK ratio, inventories are subtracted because inventories are most often the least liquid of the current assets, and their liquidation value is often the most uncertain. Thus the QK ratio provides a more demanding liquidity measure than the firm's CT ratio.

Using balance sheet data from Table 6.1, we find the beginning 2018 QK ratio for HQN equal to:

$$QK = \frac{(\$6,320 - \$3,750)}{\$5,958} = 0.43$$

(6.39)

In other words, liquidating all current assets except inventory will generate enough cash to pay for only 43 percent of HQN's current liabilities. Once again, there is no right or wrong QK ratio. This partly depends on the form of one's inventories. Product inventories are liquid. Inventories of inputs are less liquid. Clearly, HQN's liquidity is much lower if its inventory is not available to meet currently maturing obligations. Nevertheless, similar to the CT ratio, a QK ratio of less than one does not necessarily mean the firm will be unable to meet the maturing obligations.

Leverage Ratios

A lever is bar used for prying or dislodging something. We can move more weight with a lever than by applying force directly. The concept of leverage has application in finance. In finance, we define leverage ratios as those ratios used to describe how a company obtains debt and assets using its equity, as a lever. There are several different leverage ratios, but the main components of leverage ratios include debt, equity, and assets. A common expression that associates leverage with equity and debt is: How much debt can we raise (leverage) with our equity?

In general, higher leverage ratios imply greater amounts of debt financing relative to equity financing and greater levels of risk. Greater levels of firm risk also imply less ability to survive financial reversals. On the other hand, higher leverage is usually associated with higher expected returns. Here, we consider two key leverage ratios: (1) debt-to-equity ratio (DE) and (2) equity multiplier ratio (EM).

Debt-to-equity (DE) ratio

This image demonstrates leveraging equity to acquire loan funds. DE ratios are the most common leverage ratios used by financial managers. They combine two point-in-time measures from the same balance sheet. The DE ratio measures the extent to which the firm uses its equity as a lever to obtain loan funds. As the firm increases its DE ratio, it also increases its control over more assets.

The DE ratio is equal to the firm's total debt (D) divided by its equity (E). If dollar returns on assets exceed the dollar costs of the firm's liabilities, having higher DE ratios (greater leverage) increases profits for the firm. We write the firm's DE ratio as:

$$DE = \frac{D}{E}$$
(6.40)

In general, having a lower DE ratio is preferred by creditors, because more equity funds are available to meet the firm's financial obligations. (Why?) HQN's DE ratio at the beginning of 2018 was:

$$DE = \frac{\$8,000}{\$2,000} = 4.0$$
(6.41)

Interpreted, HQN's DE ratio of 4 implies that each dollar of its equity has leveraged $4.00 of debt. As with liquidity ratios, there is no magic value for DE ratios. If too much debt is used per dollar of equity, the risk of being unable to meet the fixed debt obligations can become excessive. On the other hand, if too little debt is used, the firm may sacrifice returns that can be realized through leverage.

Equity multiplier (EM) ratio

This image demonstrates leveraging equity to acquire assets. The EM ratio is equal to the firm's total assets A divided by its equity E. The EM ratio tells us the number of assets leveraged by each dollar of equity. The EM ratio like the DE ratio combines two point-in-time measures from the balance sheet. The EM ratio is a financial leverage ratio that evaluates a company's use of equity to gain control of assets. The EM ratio is particularly useful when decomposing the rate of return on equity using the DuPont equation that we will discuss later in this chapter. The formula for EM can be written as:

$$EM = \frac{A}{E}$$
(6.42)

HQN's assets and equity are used to calculate its EM at the beginning of 2018, and can be expressed as:

$$EM = \frac{\$10,000}{\$2,000} = 5.00$$
(6.43)

Leverage ratios are often combined with income statement measures to reveal important information about the riskiness of the firm beyond those provided by leverage ratios. We need to include income and cash flow data to answer the question: what is the optimal leverage ratio? We considered these issues when we earlier examined repayment capacity ratios.

Other Sets of Financial Ratios

Other sets of financial ratios besides SPELL ratios have been proposed and used elsewhere. For example, one popular set of ratios is referred to as the Sweet 16 ratios. These are compared to the SPELL ratios in Table 6.3.

Table 6.3. Comparing Sweet 16 Ratios with SPELL ratios

SPELL Ratios	Sweet 16 List	Comments
(S)olvency	Solvency	Same ratios.
(P)rofitability	Profitability	Same ratios.
(E)fficiency	Efficiency	Same ratios.
(L)iquidity	Liquidity	Same ratios.
(L)everage	Repayment Capacity	Different interpretation. Equates repayment capacity with leverage.

The DuPont Equation

The DuPont equation equals ROE multiplied by two identities assets (A) over A and total revenue over total revenue.

$$\text{(6.44)} \quad ROE = \frac{EBT}{E}\frac{A}{A}\frac{total\,revenue}{total\,revenue} = \frac{EBT}{total\,revenue}\frac{total\,xrevenue}{A}\frac{A}{E}$$

The second half of equation (6.44), after substituting and rearranging ratios, shows that ROE depends on the asset turnover ratio (ATO), sales margin (m) and the equity multiplier (EM) ratio:

$$\text{(6.45)} \quad ROE = \frac{EBT}{total\,revenue}\frac{total\,revenue}{A}\frac{A}{E} = m(ATO)(EM)$$

The DuPont equation is important because it provides a detailed picture of the firm's ability to generate profits efficiently from its equity across several of the SPELL ratios. The first ratio measures operating efficiency using the firm's profit margin ratio m. The second ratio measures asset use efficiency using the firm's asset turnover ratio ATO. And the third ratio measures financial leverage or risk using the firm's equity multiplier ratio EM.

ROE depends on =	(Efficiency in generating profits from sales)	(Efficiency in generating sales from assets)	(Amount of assets leveraged by each dollar of equity)

The DuPont is only one of a large number of DuPont-like equations. Multiplying by ROE assets/assets and one of the following: accounts receivables/accounts receivables, inventories/inventories, and accounts payables/accounts payables produces many versions of the DuPont equation. We list a few possibilities below:

$$ROE = (m)(ATO)(EM) = (m)(RTO)(EM)$$
$$\text{(6.46)} \quad = (m)(ITO)(EM) = (m)(PTO)(EM)$$

The interdependencies described in the DuPont equation help us to perform strengths and weaknesses analysis. HQN's DuPont equation for 2018 is found using previously calculated values for m, ATO, and EM:

$$\text{(6.47)} \quad ROE = (m)(ATO)(EM) = (.00425)(4.0)(5.0) = 8.5\%$$

Since our ROE calculation of 8.5% equals the DuPont calculation of ROE, we are confident that our calculations, which mix point and period of time measures, are consistently calculated and reflect the interdependencies of the system. Comparing the components of the DuPont equation with industry standards we find:

ROE depends on =	(m: lowest quartile of the industry)	(ATO: highest quartile of the industry)	(EM: significantly higher than the highest quartile of the industry)

Based on the above analysis, the ROE is at or near the industry average despite a weak profit margin because its ATO and EM are both high. HQN is efficient in its generation of cash receipts from assets and it is also highly leveraged so that as long as its average cost of debt is less than its ROA, its ROE increases.

To explore the profit margin further, note that the low profit margin is determined by EBT that in turn depends on the level of cash receipts and the cost to generate that level of cash receipts. Our earlier analysis suggested that operating costs and interest costs were relatively high, and these may be having a major impact on the profit margin.

Looking at the ATO ratio, we see that fixed assets impact the ratio, and we were concerned that the firm may not be reinvesting enough in replacing assets. Failing to replace assets as they are used up would artificially inflate the ATO and the firm's ROE. Also, the inventory levels may be too high. Lowering the inventory levels would increase the ATO and improve ROE. Finally, the high level of leverage helped ROE but is putting the firm in a risky position. The large withdrawal of equity in 2018 has further increased this risk.

Comparing Firm Financial Ratios with Industry Standards

Financial ratios calculated for an individual firm can be made more useful by having a set of standards against which they can be compared. One might think of the limited usefulness of one's blood pressure readings without some reference level of what is considered a normal of healthy blood pressure. Consider how one can learn more about a firm by comparing it to similar firms in the industry or by comparing it to the distribution of ratios of similar firms.

Major sources of industry and comparative ratios include: Dun and Brad- street, a publication of Dun and Bradstreet, Inc.; Robert Morris Associates, an association of loan officers; financial and investor services such as the Standard and Poor's survey; government agencies such as the Federal Trade Commission (FTC), Securities and Exchange Commission (SEC), and Department of Commerce; trade associations; business periodicals; corporate reports; and other miscellaneous sources such as books and accounting firms. Table 6.4 shows selected HQN's ratios for 2018, as well as ratios for other firms in the industry. The industry ratios are broken into quartiles. For example, 1/4 of the firms in the industry have current ratios above 2.0.

Table 6.4. HQN ratios for 2018 & Industry Average Ratios in Quartiles
Open HQN Coordinated Financial Statement in MS Excel

Ratios	HQN for 2018	Lower Quartile	Median	Upper Quartile
SOLVENCY RATIOS				
TIE (times interest earned)	1.35	1.6	2.5	5.8
DS (debt-to-service)	1.02	0.9	1.4	3.3
PROFITABILITY RATIOS				
m (margin)	0.43%	0.44%	1.03%	1.79%
ROA (return on assets)	6.50%	0.66%	3.30%	7.00%
ROE (return on equity)	8.50%	2.10%	10.70%	17.20%
EFFICIENCY RATIOS				
ITO (inventory turnover)	10.67	4.8	7.7	14.9
ITOT (inventory turnover time)	34.21	76.04	47.40	24.50
ATO (asset turnover)	4	1.5	3.2	3.9
ATOT (asset turnover time)	91.25	243.33	111.06	93.59
RTO (receivables turnover)	24.40	15.21	11.41	8.90
RTOT (receivables turnover time)	14.96	24	32	41
PTO (payable turnover)	9.33	9.36	12.59	15.21
PTOT (payable turnover time)	39.12	39	29	24
LIQUIDITY RATIOS				
CT (current)	1.06	0.9	1.3	2
QK (quick)	0.43	0.5	0.7	1.1
LEVERAGE RATIOS				
DE (debt-to-equity)	4	2.8	1.9	0.9
EM (equity multiplier)	5	3.8	2.2	3.24

Using Financial Ratios to Determine the Firm's Financial Strengths and Weaknesses

Comparing SPELL ratios with industry standards. In what follows we compare the ratios computed for HQN with the ratios calculated for similar firms. Comparing HQN's SPELL ratios with industry standards is the essence of strengths and weaknesses analysis and answers the question: what is the financial condition of the firm?

In Table 6.4, the industry is described by the ratio for the firm, the median firm, and the average of firms in the upper and lower quartile of firms. Consider how comparing HQN to the other firms in its industry might allow us to reach some conclusions about HQN's strengths and weaknesses and to determine its financial condition.

Solvency ratios. HQN's solvency ratio compared to its industry indicates that it may have a difficult time paying its fixed debt obligations out of earnings. The TIE ratio in 2018 is 1.35 which is less than the industry's lowest quartile. HQN's DS ratio in 2018 is 0.94, which implies that only about 94 percent of the firm's interest and principal can be paid out of current earnings which is only slightly higher than the industry's lowest quartile. In effect, compared to industry standards, HQN's significant weakness is its solvency. HQN will need to refinance, raise additional capital, or liquidate some assets in order to make the interest and principal payments and remain in business.

Profitability ratios. Compared to industry averages, HQN is profitable. Its ROE is reasonably close to the industry average and its ROA is close to the upper quartile industry average. Paradoxically, HQN's m margin is close to the industry's lowest quartile average.

Efficiency ratios. Compared to the industry averages, HQN is very efficient. Both HQN's ITO and ATO ratios are near the top in its industry. Its ITO ratio in 2018 was 10.67, indicating that HQN has sold its inventory over 10 times during the year. This ITO ratio is above the median value for firms in this industry of 7.7, and strong. The ATO ratio has a 2018 value of 4.0, indicating the firm had sales of 4 times the value of its assets, compared to an industry median of 3.2 which is in the upper quartile of firms in its industry. The firm appears to be using assets efficiently which undoubtedly contributes to HNQ's profitability even though its margin in low.

The RTOT ratio has a 2018 value of 14.96. This value is well below industry averages, and raises a question about the firm's credit policies. The industry average RTOT was 32 and suggests that HQN might consider a more generous credit policy. On the other hand, HQN's PTOT ratio is 39 and is in the lowest quartile for the industry. This suggests that HQN is depending on dealer supplied credit more than other firms in its industry because of its low solvency. Still, HQN's strength may be its efficiency.

Liquidity ratios. The current ratio is 1.06, which suggests the firm is liquid, but barely. Its ratio is near the lower quartile of firms in the industry. The quick ratio is 0.43, suggesting the firm cannot meet its short-term obligations without relying on inventory. HQN's quick ratio is in the lower quartile of firms in the industry, indicating that the firm is less liquid than most of its competitors and is an HQN weakness.

Leverage ratios. The leverage ratios indicate that the HQN's use of debt is high. Comparison with industry ratios shows that HQN is highly leveraged relative to other firms in the industry. As long as ROA exceeds the average interest costs of debt, high leverage increases the firm's profitability—but increases its risk associated with adverse earnings.

Limitations of Ratios

While ratio analysis can be a powerful and useful tool, it does suffer from a number of weaknesses. We discussed earlier how the use of different ac- counting practices for such items as depreciation can change a firm's financial statements and, therefore, alter its financial ratios. Thus, it is important to be aware of and understand accounting practices over time and/or across firms.

Difficult problems arise when making comparisons across firms in an industry. The comparison must be made over the same time periods. In addition, firms within an "industry" often differ substantially in their structure and type of business, making industry comparisons less meaningful. Another difficulty is that a departure from the "norm" may not indicate a problem. As mentioned before, a firm might have apparent weaknesses in one area that are offset by strengths in other areas.

Furthermore, things like different production practices in a firm may require a different financial structure than other firms in the industry. Additionally, shooting for financial ratios that look like the industry average may not be desirable. Would you want your business to be average?

Inflation can have a significant impact on a firm's balance sheet and its corresponding financial ratios. As a results, it is important to keep in mind the difference between a capital item's book value and it market value. Firms that keep a set of market value financial statements in addition to their book value financial statements should conduct financial analysis with both their book value and market value financial statements.

We should recognize that a single ratio does not provide adequate information to evaluate the strength or weakness of a firm. A weak ratio in one area might be offset by a strong ratio in another area. Like- wise, a perfectly healthy firm, from a financial standpoint, may have some special characteristics which result in a ratio which would be out of line for other firms in the industry who do not have these char- acteristics.

Finally, it must be understood that financial analysis does not in itself provide a management decision. The analysis provides information which will be a valuable input into making management decisions, but there is no "cook book" formula into which you plug the financial analysis number and produce the correct management decisions.

Financial ratios can be an effective strengths and weaknesses analysis tool. However, not all ratios are equally important. Their principal use is to assess the firm's ability to survive. To survive in the long term, the firm must be profitable and solvent. Profitability is defined as the difference between a firm's revenues and its expenses. Solvency is the firm's ability to meet its cash obligations when they become due. Solvency depends on the firm's holdings of liquid assets—assets that can easily and with little expense be converted into cash in the current period.

If a firm is not both profitable and solvent, it cannot survive in the long term. In the short term, a firm can be solvent but not profitable. For a limited time, an unprofitable firm can convert assets to cash and remain solvent by borrowing, refinancing existing debt, selling inventory, liquidating capital assets, increasing accounts payable, or depleting its capital base. These acts may improve the firm's solvency in the short run, but are likely to erode the firm's future profitability.

In contrast, a firm may be profitable and not solvent, in which case it cannot survive even in the short term. Once a firm fails to meet its cash flow obligations, even if it is profitable, in most cases it loses control over its assets. Therefore, short-term survival may require some firms to sacrifice profitability for solvency. Thus, financial managers must monitor both the firm's solvency and profitability. An appropriately constructed set of financial ratios will allow financial managers to monitor both the firm's profitability and solvency.

Financial ratios may also provide information about the liquidity of the firm, which is related to the firm's solvency because the firm's liquidity position tells us something about the firm's ability to meet unforeseen outcomes and survive. Also related to the firm's solvency and liquidity is the probability of achieving different rates of return. Measures of the probability of alternative rates of return are sometimes examined under the general heading of risk, a subject examined in Chapter 4.

Strengths and Weaknesses Summary

How do we summarize our strengths and weaknesses analysis? One way is to assign a grade to each of the SPELL categories ranging from 5 (superior) to 1 (on life support). Clearly, the grades assigned are somewhat subjective, but perhaps useful, in summarizing a great deal of financial information. Then what? Do we assign equal weight to each of the SPELL categories depending on their relative importance? The answer to this question depends on the vision, goals, and objectives of the firm manager. To complete this discussion of how to assign weights to the SPELL categories, we treat them equally important in this example—although a strong case exists for assigning a greater weight to profitability measures. In Table 6.5 we summarize our strengths and weaknesses ratings.

Table 6.5. Summary of HQN's 2018 Financial Strengths & Weaknesses

SPELL Category	weights	Grades: 5 (very strong) to 1 (very weak)
Solvency	.2	2.0
Profitability	.2	3.0
Efficiency	.2	4.0
Liquidity	.2	3.0
Leverage	.2	2.0
Weighted Summary		2.8

So, what have we learned? We learned that a firm's SPELL ratios can be compared to financial ratios of similar firms to determine the firm's financial strengths and weaknesses. In the case of HQN, we assign to it a strengths and weaknesses score of 2.8 which is less than the median or average financial conditions of similar firms in its industry. Significant in arriving at an overall financial strengths and weaknesses score of 2.8 was HQN's high leverage that places it in a risky position and its weak solvency condition.

Summary and Conclusions

When using financial ratios from one's own firm and comparing them with industry standard ratios, it is often useful to take notes or summarize the major points as you work through the ratio analysis. In our analysis of HQN, the firm is highly leveraged and is in a risky position. We might ask why is the firm relying so heavily on debt and why is its equity being withdrawn at such a high rate? The overhead expenses seem to be too high. Why? How can the situation be improved? Why are the firm's assets being depleted? What is the cause of the increasingly high level of inventory being held?

After gathering information on these questions and others, the firm's financial manager may produce a detailed strengths and weaknesses report. In the report, key financial management issues can be explored, and forecasts of future financial needs and situations can be made. Continued monitoring of the firm's financial statements and ratios will allow the firm's management to gain solid understanding of the relationship between the firm's operations and its financial performance and to recommend changes when required.

So, what have we learned? We learned that by using the information contained in its CFS, firms can construct financial ratios that provide five different views of the firm's financial condition: its solvency, its profitability, its efficiency, its liquidity, and its leverage. A logical next step is to a assign a weight to each of the firm's financial conditions reflected by its ratios after comparing them to industry standards. The overall weighted average reflects the firm's financial strengths and weaknesses and answers the question: what is the financial condition of the firm.

Questions

When calculating 2018 ratios, please refer to Tables 5.1, 5.4A or 5.4B, and 5.6 in Chapter 5. When asked for industry standard comparisons, use industry measures provided in Table 6.4.

1. In this chapter we identified two kinds of ratios: percentages and rates. Please distinguish between rates and percentages.
2. Explain why financial statement data is made more useful by forming SPELL ratios?
3. Describe the kinds of questions related to the firm's financial strengths and weaknesses each of the SPELL ratios can help answer.
4. Calculate the 2018 SPELL ratios for Friendly Fruit Farm (FFF) described in Chapter 5.
5. Do FFF's DS and TIE ratios, both solvency ratios, tell consistent stories? Defend your answer.
6. Explain why a firm might be reluctant to meet its short-term liquidity needs by liquidating long-term assets.
7. Describe the connections between the m ratio and FFF's ROE.
8. What is the essential difference between ROA and ROE profit measures? What do they each measure?
9. What conditions guarantee that ROE > ROA or that ROA > ROE?
10. Explain the connections between efficiency and ROE or ROA measures.
11. Create an efficiency ratio for your class preparation efforts? (Hint: what are the inputs and what are the outputs?) What could you do to improve the efficiency of your class preparation efforts?
12. What might be implied by very high or very low ITO ratios?
13. Calculate ITO ratios using 2018 total revenue measures for FFF. Then compare your results with ITO ratios using accrued COGS. Explain the differences.
14. The optimum RTOT ratio seeks to balance the need to generate cash receipts by offering easy credit versus the need to meet liquidity need by limiting its accounts receivable. Looking at the financial statements for HQN, what is an ideal RTOT ratio (state a number)? Defend your ideal number RTOT number, and if it is different than HQN's actual number, what actions could you take to align HQN's actual RTOT to its ideal RTOT?
15. Explain why it is difficult to compare net working capital numbers between firms.
16. The DuPont equation allows us to decompose the ROE measure. Replace total revenue with COGS in equation (6.45) and recalculate the components of the revised DuPont equation. Interpret the results. Does the resulting equation still equal HQN's ROE?
17. Using FFF's QK ratios at the end of years 2017 and 2018, what strengths and weaknesses score would you assign to its liquidity?
18. Suppose FFF's long-term debt was 10% above the book value of their long-term assets and only 50% of the current value of their long-term assets. Calculate DE ratios using current and book values of their long-term assets. If FFF were applying for a loan, which DE ratios would they most likely present?
19. If ROA exceeds the average costs of the firm's liabilities, having higher DE ratios (greater leverage) increases profits for the firm. Why might lenders want lower DE ratios while borrowers may want higher DE ratios?

20. Compare firms with low ITO ratios such as jewelry stores with firms with high ITO ratios like grocery stores or gas stations. How might their profit margin requirements for success differ? Explain.

21. Using FFF's SPELL ratios and the industry standards used to evaluate HQN's strengths and weaknesses, write a brief report of FFF's financial strengths and weaknesses. Organize your report into the five SPELL categories: solvency, profitability, efficiency, liquidity, and leverage. Complete a table similar to Table 6.5 that was prepared for HQN. What is the summary measure of FFF's financial strengths and weaknesses?

7. Optimizing Efficiency: Systems Analysis for Business Success

LINDON ROBISON

Learning goals. After completing this chapter, you should be able to (1) define a system; (2) recognize system properties included in coordinated financial statements (CFS); (3) connect changes in exogenous variables and parameters determined outside the CFS system to changes in endogenous variables calculated inside the CFS system; (4) conduct scenario analysis by answering "what-if" and "how-much" kinds of questions; (5) endogenize exogenous variables to improve the credibility of opportunity and threat analysis; (6) simplify financial ratio analysis by exogenizing endogenous variables; and (7) satisfy system-off companion ratios using common size balance sheets and income statements. Describe how (S)olvency, (P)rofitability, (E)fficiency, (L)iquidity, and (L)everage (SPELL) ratios answer the question: "what-is" the financial condition of the firm.

Learning objectives. To achieve your learning goals, you should complete the following objectives:

- Learn how to answer the question: what-if the value of an exogenous variable or parameter changes, then how will the values of endogenous variables change.
- Learn how to answer the question: how-much the value of an exogenous variable or parameter needs to change for the value of an endogenous variable to equal a specified value.
- Learn how to evaluate scenarios and evaluate the firm's strengths and weaknesses using what-if and how-much analysis.
- Learn how to endogenize exogenous variables within a CFS system to increase the credibility of opportunity and threat analysis.
- Learn how to create subsystems of the CFS system that describes a firm's rate of return on equity (ROE) and solvency by exogenizing certain endogenous variables.
- Learn how to find common size balance sheet ratios equal to balance sheet entries divided by total assets.
- Learn how to find common size income statement ratios equal to income statement entries divided by total revenue.
- Learn how to use common size balance sheets, income statements composed of common size ratios to examine financial trade-offs when conducting what-if and how much analysis.
- Learn how to use pro-forma common size statement to forecast future CFS values.

Introduction

In what follows we define and distinguish between different kinds of systems. Then we make the point that CFS are a system. Indeed, we have already used CFS system properties to answer the question:

what-is the financial condition of the firm. We answered that question by using CFS data to find the firm's SPELL ratios. However, the value of information gained from SPELL ratios has its limits. Answering what-is kinds of questions is a static (timeless) analysis because it focuses on the current financial condition of the firm. We also need information that is forward looking such as knowing how the financial condition of the firm may change in response to changes in its external environment described by exogenous variables and parameters.

The CFS system allows us to examine alternative scenarios by allowing us to answer what-if questions: what if a change in the firm's exogenous variables occurs, how will its endogenous variables and SPELL ratios change. The CFS system also allows us to examine how-much questions: how-much an exogenous variable must change to produce a specified value for an endogenous variable. The CFS system allows us to change the relationship between exogenous and endogenous variables by endogenizing certain exogenous variables. The CFS system allows us to focus our analysis on key SPELL ratios by exogenizing certain endogenous variables. Finally, the CFS system allows us to create common size balance sheets and income statements that focus on common size ratios. These common size ratios are helpful because they provide comparisons of balance sheet and income statement entries relative to total assets and total revenue. As a result, the ratios can help describe the financial trade-offs facing the firm. To begin our applications of the CFS system, we must first describe the properties of a system.

Understanding Systems

What is a system. A system is an interacting and interdependent group of items forming a unified whole serving a common purpose. Every system has boundaries that separate activities that occur within the system from those that occur outside of the system. There are several kinds of systems. An abstract system uses variables to represent tangible or intangible things and may or may not have a real-world counterpart. On the other hand, physical systems are generally concrete operational systems made up of people, materials, machines, energy, and other physical things. Physical systems are the systems that abstract systems may attempt to represent.

Finally, systems may be closed or open. Open systems allow for exogenous forces outside of the system to influence activities within the system. Closed systems are immune to exogenous forces. Finally, systems may be stochastic or nonstochastic. For stochastic systems, endogenous outcomes within the system and their exogenous causes are described with probabilities. Meanwhile, nonstochastic systems connect endogenous and exogenous variables and parameters with certain (nonprobabilistic) relationships.

System Metaphors

A metaphor compares two ideas or objects that are dissimilar to each other in some ways and like each other in other ways. We introduce three metaphors to describe how changes in an exogenous variable or parameter—a shock—can change endogenous variables.

Balloons. One might compare the CFS to a balloon. If you squeeze one part of the balloon (an exogenous force), there will be an (endogenous) bulge somewhere else in the balloon. This action-reaction nature of a system (and balloons) leads to us examine shocks in pairs and answer the question: "what-if" a change in an exogenous variable occurs, "then" what happens to the endogenous variables of the system?

Predicting the weather. Predicting the financial future of the firm has characteristics in common with predicting the weather. Meteorologists look at where the weather fronts have been, the direction they have been traveling, and then predict where they will likely be in the future. To hedge their bets, they often predict future weather patterns with probabilities. Predicting the future financial condition of the firm also looks at the condition of the firm now, how it has changed over time, and then predicts with probabilities where it will be in the future.

The detective. Trying to describe how changes in an exogenous variable will affect endogenous variables is like a detective trying to put all the clues together to solve a case that explains who committed a crime. The detective observes a crime—an unusual condition different than what existed before the crime occurred. The financial manager observes changes in the firm's endogenous variables and attempts to link them to changes in one of the exogenous variables and parameters. Most importantly, a detective (and a financial manager) compares the firm's financial condition with industry standards or with other firms and asks: what is unusual, what is out of place?

Understanding the CFS System

CFS are a system. The CFS are an abstract system whose variables and statements describe the financial condition of a firm using mathematical equations and numbers. The CFS are designed to represent the financial condition of the firm at the beginning and ending of a period with balance sheets and financial activities between the beginning and ending balance sheets using an AIS and a statement of cash flow (SCF). The CFS are an open system. They allow for an external environment represented by exogenous variables and parameters to influence activities within the firm represented by endogenous variables. Finally, for our purposes, we assume that the relationships between CFS and variable values included in the CFS system are deterministic.

CFS and Strengths, Weaknesses, Opportunities, and Threats (SWOT) analysis. Because CFS are a system, we can use them as our primary strengths, weaknesses, opportunities, and threats analysis tool. We summarize several reasons why the CFS system is important for financial managers conducting SWOT analysis:

- because it allows us to answer the question: what-is the financial condition of the firm reflected by its SPELL and common size ratios. Answering the what-is question is the primary means for conducting strengths and weakness analysis;
- because the relationships between CFS variables and financial statements are consistent (they don't change and cannot produce a contradiction), we can check the accuracy of our data by looking for unusual numbers in the statements. If we observe unrealistic results, they can only be attributed to data inaccuracies;
- because it allows us to conduct opportunities and threats analyses by asking what-if questions. What-if analysis considers a possible change (opportunity or threat) in the external environment of the firm and noting changes in the financial condition of the firm;
- because it allows us to ask how-much questions and determine how-much of an external change is needed to change a particular endogenous variable by a specific amount. Answering how-much questions allows us to find the required response to opportunities and threats to achieve a firm's goal;
- because it allows us to define subsystems to focus on parts of the system such as profitability and solvency;
- and, because it allows us to examine important financial trade-offs using common size balance sheets and income statements.

Endogenous and exogenous variables and parameters. To understand the CFS system, we must be able to distinguish between endogenous and exogenous variables and parameters. One way to distinguish between CFS endogenous and exogenous variables is to ask: was this variable calculated somewhere in the system? Or, was its value determined outside of the system? If the variable was calculated within the system, it is an endogenous variables. If the variable or parameter was determined outside of the system, it is an exogenous variable.

To illustrate, cash and marketable securities in the beginning period balance sheet is an exogenous variable. Its value was determined by activities in previous time periods. In contrast, ending period cash and marketable securities depend on their beginning period values and changes in the firm's cash position calculated in the SCF. Therefore, the firm's ending period cash and marketable securities is an endogenous variable.

Endogenous and exogenous variables and parameters also create interdependencies between CFS. In general, financial activities described by CFS link beginning and ending period balance sheet with an income statement and SCF. We illustrate these connections with two of several possible examples.

1) The difference in cash balances reported in the beginning and ending period balance sheets equals the change in cash position calculated in the SCF.

2) The difference in retained earnings reported in the beginning and ending period balance sheets equals the addition to retained earnings calculated in the firm's AIS.

HQN exogenous variables and parameters. We illustrate CFS exogenous variables and parameters using HQN's exogenous variables and parameters in Table 7.1. A special kind of exogenous variables are side-bar sums of exogenous variables. Because they are summed outside of CFS, side-bar calculations are also exogenous variables. One reason we sum exogenous variables in side-bar calculations is to create categories that can be used to compare a firm's financial performance with similar firms, with the industry average in which it operates, and with its own performance over time. These comparisons could not occur unless financial data were organized into comparable categories. Another special kind of exogenous variables are parameters used to endogenize an exogenous variable such as the average tax rate.

Table 7.1. Exogenous variables and parameters used to compute HQN's Coordinated Financial Statements (CFS)
Open HQN Coordinated Financial Statement in MS Excel

	A	B	C	E	F	H	I
1	**Balance Sheet**			**Statement of Cash Flow Exogenous**		**Sidebar Calculations**	
2	Date	12/31/17	12/31/18	Cash Receipts	$38,990.00	*Cash Receivables*	
3	Cash & Market Securities	$930		Cash COGS	$27,000	Sales	$18,000
4	Accounts Receivable	$1,640	$1,200	Cash OEs	$11,078	Landscaping	$15,000
5	Inventory	$3,750	$5,200	Interest Paid	$480	Consultation	$5,990
6	Notes Receivable	$0	$0	Taxes Paid	$38	Total	$38,990
7	Total Current Assets						
8	Depreciable Assets	$2,990		Realized Capital Gains	$0	*Cash COGS*	
9	Non-depreciable Assets	$690		Sale of Non-depreciable LTA	$0	Fertilizer	$5,000
10	Total Long-Term Assets			Purchase of Non-depreciable LTA	$0	Maintenance	$7,000
11	**TOTAL ASSETS**			Sale of Depreciable LTA	$30	Labor	$8,000
12				Purchase of Depreciable LTA	$100.	Transportation	$5,000
13	Notes Payable	$1,500	$1,270	Dividend/Owner Draw	$287	Repairs	$2,000
14	Current Portion LTD	$500	$450			Total	$27,000
15	Accounts Payable	$3,000	$4,000	Average Tax Rate on ROA T*	0.10		
16	Accrued Liabilities	$958	$880	Average Tax Rate on ROE T	0.40	*Cash OES*	
17	Total Current Liabilities			Average Interest Rate of Liabilities	0.06	Utilities	$6,000
18	Non-Current LTD	$2,042	$1,985			Office Rent	$4,000
19	**TOTAL LIABILITIES**			Depreciation	$350	Cleaning	$1,078
20	Contributed Capital	$1,900	$1,900			Total	$11,078
21	Retained Earnings	$100					

	A	B	C	E	F	H	I
1	Balance Sheet			Statement of Cash Flow Exogenous		Sidebar Calculations	
22	TOTAL EQUITY	$					
23	TOTAL LIABILITIES & EQUITY	$					

Over-identified variables and systems. Suppose that we use the system properties of the CFS to find ending period cash and marketable securities. Then suppose we observe ending cash and marketable securities reported in our check book or other financial reports. What happens if ending cash and marketable securities determined within the CFS differs from ending cash and marketable securities reported by our bank statement and other financial records are not the same?

The problem is that the ending cash and marketable securities value is over identified. It can be calculated as an endogenous variable within the CFS or observed externally as an exogenous variable. When the two values differ, we say the system is inaccurate because the two values for the over-identified variables don't agree. In such circumstances, the financial manager must employ his/her best effort to find the error in the data. Resolving data errors revealed by over-identified variables may be the most challenging task facing financial managers whose data is often incomplete and sometimes inaccurate. In some cases, the data errors revealed by over-identified variables provides financial managers opportunities to encourage the principals of the firm to reexamine their financial records and look for errors or missing data.

What-Is Analysis and SPELL Ratios

SPELL ratios and what-is analysis. Chapter 6 described the firm's financial system using SPELL ratios. Alone, SPELL ratios help describe the financial condition of the firm and reveal its strengths and weaknesses. However, SPELL ratios are more useful when their interdependence are recognized. In other words, a change in the firm's solvency is likely to change the firm's liquidity. A change in the firm's efficiency is likely to change the firm's profitability. And the list of possible interdependencies continues. Since the variables in the financial system are interdependent, the SPELL ratios composed of system variables are also interdependent.

Profitability and solvency ratios. How do we proceed to examine the interdependencies of the firm? One approach is to focus on the firm's bottom line—its profitability and solvency ratios. A firm can exist for many reasons. It may satisfy the firm owners' desires to engage in a production activity. (For example, I just want to farm!) It may be organized to provide family members and others employment. It may exist to provide some public service. There are undoubtedly other reasons why firms exist. However, the firm financial manager is usually charged with only one mission—to ensure the firm's survival and its profitability. This requires a proper balance between the firm's return and its solvency.

In our view, solvency ratios described by the times interest earned (TIE) and debt-to-service (DSR) ratios and profitability ratios described by margin (m), return on equity (ROE), and return on asset (ROA) ratios are the most important SPELL ratios. However, efficiency, leverage, and liquidity ratios also matter to the firm because they influence its profitability measured by its ROE and ROA ratios and its solvency measured by its TIE and DSR ratios.

So, what have we learned? We have learned that since the CFS are a system, we can ask and answer questions related to changes in the values of exogenous variables and parameters and observe how these changes produce changes in the values of endogenous variables within the system. Furthermore, because the CFS are a system, they provides consistent relationships between CFS variables so that unusual values of endogenous variables may call attention to the accuracy of exogenous variables and parameters that determines its value. It may be helpful when considering the properties of a system to compare them to others systems described by a balloon or other activities that predict the weather based on known information or activities of a detective that looks for unusual values (clues) the solve the questions.

What-if Analysis and SPELL Ratios

We emphasized earlier the interdependencies between endogenous and exogenous variables and parameters in the CFS system. Therefore, any change in an exogenous variable or parameter in one part of the CFS system will produce changes in endogenous variables in other parts of the system. Tracing the impact of a change in an exogenous variable on endogenous variables in the system is referred to here as what-if analysis.

What-if analysis may help the firm anticipate and plan for opportunities and threats. What-if analysis may also permit firm managers to virtually experiment with changes in exogenous variables before implementing an actual financial plan.

The first step in what-if analysis is to introduce the change in an exogenous variable. The second step is to recalculate the endogenous variables in the financial statements. The third step is to recalculate the SPELL ratios and compare them to the previous ratio values and to industry averages. Finally, the fourth step is to interpret the results described by changes in the firm's SPELL ratios. Fortunately, steps one, two, and three can be automated using Excel CFS spreadsheets described in an Appendix to this chapter.

Describing the results of what-if analysis. To help analyze the results of what-if analysis, we use an Excel spreadsheet that describes exogenous variables and the CFS. We illustrate how to use an Excel spreadsheet to describe what-if analysis using HQN's CFS. We represented HQN's CFS for years 2017 and 2018 in Table 6.1. We repeat it here as Table 7.2 for convenience. It represents the financial conditions of HQN before any changes in exogenous variables and parameters are considered.

Table 7.2a. HQN's Coordinated Financial Statements (CFS).

	A	B	C	D	E	F	G	H	I
1	BALANCE SHEET				ACCRUAL INCOME STATEMENT			STATEMENT OF CASH FLOW	
2	DATE	12/31/2017	12/31/2018		DATE	2018		DATE	2018
3	Cash and Marketable Securities	$930	$600	+	Cash Receipts	$38,990	+	Cash Receipts	$38,990
4	Accounts Receivable	$1,640	$1,200	+	Change in Accounts Receivable	($440)	-	Cash Cost of Goods Sold	$27,000
5	Inventory	$3,750	$5,200	+	Change in Inventories	$1,450	-	Cash Overhead Expenses	$11,078
6	Notes Receivable	$0	$0	+	Realized capital gains (losses)	$0	-	Interest Paid	$480
7	Total Current Assets	$6,320	$7,000	=	Total Revenue	$40,000	-	Taxes	$68
8	Depreciable Assets	$2,990	$2,710				=	Net Cash Flow from Operations	$364
9	Non-depreciable Assets	$690	$690	+	Cash Cost of Goods Sold	$27,000			
10	Total Long-Term Assets	$3,680	$3,400	+	Change in Accounts. Payable	$1,000	+	Realized Capital Gains and Depreciation Recapture	$0
11	TOTAL ASSETS	$10,000	$10,400	+	Cash Overhead Expenses	$11,078	+	Sales of Non-depreciable Assets	$0
12				+	Change in Accrued Liabilities	($78)	-	Purchases of Non-depreciable Assets	$0
13	Notes Payable	$1,500	$1,270	+	Depreciation	$350	+	Sales of Depreciable Assets	$30
14	Current Portion Long-Term Debt	$500	$450	=	Total Expenses	$39,350	-	Assets	$100
15	Accounts Payable	$3,000	$4,000				=	Net Cash Flow from Investment	($70)
16	Accrued Liabilities	$958	$880		Earnings Before Interest and Taxes (EBIT)	$650			
17	Total Current Liabilities	$5,958	$6,600	-	Less Interest Costs	$480	+	Change in Non-current Long-term Debt	($57)
18	Non-Current Long Term Debt	$2,042	$1,985	=	Earnings Before Taxes (EBT)	$170	+	Change in Current Portion of Long-term Debt	($50)
19	TOTAL LIABILITIES	$8,000	$8,585	-	Less Taxes	$68	+	Change in Notes Payable	($230)

20	Contributed Capital	$1,900	$1,900	=	Net Income After Taxes (NIAT)	$102	–	Less Dividends and Owner Draw	$287
21	Retained Earnings	$100	($85)	–	Less Dividends and Owner Draw	$287	=	**Net Cash Flow from Financing**	($624)
22	Total Equity	$2,000	$1,815		Addition to Retained Earnings	($185)			
23	**TOTAL LIABILITIES & EQUITY**	$10,000	$10,400				=	**Change in Cash Position**	($330)

Table 7.2b. HQN's Base SPELL ratios.

	A	B	C
1		**12/31/2018**	**Industry**
2	**SOLVENCY RATIOS**		
3	Times Interest Earned (TIE)	1.35	2.5
4	Debt Service Ratio (DSR)	1.02	1.40
5	**PROFITABILITY RATIOS**		
6	Profit margin (m)	0.43%	1.03%
7	Return on assets (ROA)	6.50%	3.30%
8	After-tax ROA [ROA(1-T*)]	5.82%	
9	Return on equity (ROE)	8.50%	10.70%
10	After-tax ROE [ROE(1-T)]	5.10%	
11	**EFFICIENCY RATIOS**		
12	Inventory Turnover (ITO)	10.67	7.7
13	ITOT (365/ITO)	34.22	47.4
14	Asset Turnover (ATO)	4.00	3.2
15	ATOT (365/ATO)	91.25	114.1
16	Receivable Turnover (RTO)	24.39	11.41
17	RTOT (365/RTO)	14.97	32
18	Payable Turnover (PTO)	9.33	12.59
19	PTOT (365/PTO)	39.11	29.00
20	**LIQUIDITY RATIOS**		
21	Current ratio (CR)	1.06	1.30
22	Quick ratio (QR)	0.43	0.70
23	**LEVERAGE RATIOS**		
24	Debt/Asset (D/A)	0.80	0.91
25	Debt/Equity (D/E)	4.00	2.00
26	Equity multiplier (A/E)	5.00	2.20

Now consider what-if cash sales increased by $1,000. The first thing to observe is that increasing cash sales by $1,000 increased cash receipts by the same amount, from $38,990 to $39,990. We report the what-if analysis results in Table 7.3.

Table 7.3a. HQN's Coordinated Financial Statements (CFS) after increasing sales by $1,000.

	A	B	C	D	E	F	G	H	I
1	BALANCE SHEET				ACCRUAL INCOME STATEMENT			STATEMENT OF CASH FLOW	
2	DATE	12/31/2017	12/31/2018		DATE	2018		DATE	2018
3	Cash and Marketable Securities	$930	$1,600	+	Cash Receipts	$39,990	+	Cash Receipts	$39,990
4	Accounts Receivable	$1,640	$1,200	+	Change in Accounts Receivable	($440)	–	Cash Cost of Goods Sold	$27,000
5	Inventory	$3,750	$5,200	+	Change in Inventories	$1,450	–	Cash Overhead Expenses	$11,078
6	Notes Receivable	$0	$0	+	Realized capital gains (losses)	$0	–	Interest Paid	$480
7	Total Current Assets	$6,320	$8,000	=	Total Revenue	$41,000	–	Taxes	$68
8	Depreciable Assets	$2,990	$2,710				=	Net Cash Flow from Operations	$1,364
9	Non-depreciable Assets	$690	$690	+	Cash Cost of Goods Sold	$27,000			
10	Total Long-Term Assets	$3,680	$3,400	+	Change in Accounts. Payable	$1,000	+	Realized Capital Gains and Depreciation Recaputre	$0
11	TOTAL ASSETS	$10,000	$11,400	+	Cash Overhead Expenses	$11,078	+	Sales of Non-depreciable Assets	$0
12				+	Change in Accrued Liabilities	($78)	–	Purchases of Non-depreciable Assets	$0
13	Notes Payable	$1,500	$1,270	+	Depreciation	$350	+	Sales of Depreciable Assets	$30
14	Current Portion Long-Term Debt	$500	$450	=	Total Expenses	$39,350	–	Assets	$100
15	Accounts Payable	$3,000	$4,000				=	Net Cash Flow from Investment	($70)
16	Accrued Liabilities	$958	$880		Earnings Before Interest and Taxes (EBIT)	$1,650			
17	Total Current Liabilities	$5,958	$6,600	–	Less Interest Costs	$480	+	Change in Non-current Lont-term Debt	($57)

18	Non-Current Long Term Debt	$2,042	$1,985	=	Earnings Before Taxes (EBT)	$1,170	+	Change in Current Portion of Long-term Debt	($50)
19	**TOTAL LIABILITIES**	$8,000	$8,585	–	Less Taxes	$68	+	Chage in Notes Payable	($230)
20	Contributed Capital	$1,900	$1,900	=	Net Income After Taxes (NIAT)	$1,102	–	Less Dividends and Owner Draw	$287
21	Retained Earnings	$100	$915	–	Less Dividends and Owner Draw	$287	=	**Net Cash Flow from Financing**	($624)
22	Total Equity	$2,000	$2,815		Addition to Retained Earnings	$815			
23	**TOTAL LIABILITIES & EQUITY**	$10,000	$11,400				=	**Change in Cash Position**	$670

Table 7.3b. HQN's Base SPELL ratios after increasing sales by $1,000.

	A	B	C
		12/31/2018	**Industry**
1			
2	**SOLVENCY RATIOS**		
3	Times Interest Earned (TIE)	3.44	2.5
4	Debt Service Ratio (DSR)	2.04	1.40
5	**PROFITABILITY RATIOS**		
6	Profit margin (m)	2.85%	1.03%
7	Return on assets (ROA)	16.50%	3.30%
8	After-tax ROA [ROA(1-T*)]	15.82%	
9	Return on equity (ROE)	58.50%	10.70%
10	After-tax ROE [ROE(1-T)]	55.10%	
11	**EFFICIENCY RATIOS**		
12	Inventory Turnover (ITO)	10.93	7.7
13	ITOT (365/ITO)	33.38	47.4
14	Asset Turnover (ATO)	4.10	3.2
15	ATOT (365/ATO)	89.02	114.1
16	Receivable Turnover (RTO)	25.00	11.41
17	RTOT (365/RTO)	14.60	32
18	Payable Turnover (PTO)	9.33	12.59
19	PTOT (365/PTO)	39.11	29.00
20	**LIQUIDITY RATIOS**		
21	Current ratio (CR)	1.06	1.30
22	Quick ratio (QR)	0.43	0.70
23	**LEVERAGE RATIOS**		
24	Debt/Asset (D/A)	0.80	0.91
25	Debt/Equity (D/E)	4.00	2.00
26	Equity multiplier (A/E)	5.00	2.20

After an increase in sales and cash receipts of $1,000, earnings before interest and taxes (EBIT) and earnings before taxes (EBT) all increased by $1,000. Change in cash and marketable securities also increased by $1,000 as did additions to retained earnings. Importantly, ROE increased from 8.5% to 58.5% while ROA increased from 6.5% to 16.5%.

Representing outcomes of what-if analysis using SPELL ratios. While we can report the results of what-if analysis as numbers in CFS, these are difficult to compare with other firms. Instead, we present the results using SPELL ratios. We want to compare SPELL ratios before and after the change described in the what-if analysis has occurred. The table that compares SPELL ratios before and after the change described in the what-if analysis has occurred is called an Activity table. An Activity table is described here and in the appendix to this chapter. An Activity table has four columns. The first column describes the SPELL ratios being compared. The second column describes the industry average SPELL ratios against which the firm can compare its own SPELL ratios. The third column describes the ratio's value recalculated as a result of the what-if analysis. And finally, the fourth column presents the firm's base—its SPELL ratios before the what-if changes were considered. We present an Activity table for HQN in Figure 7.4 that describes an in sales of $1,000. Note the changes in SPELL ratios ROE, ROA, TIE, and DSR. We present Activity Table 7.4 below. All the key ratios improve with an increase in sales.

Table 7.4. HQN's Activity Table: SPELL ratios before and after a $1,000 increase in Cash Receipts

	A	B	C	D
1	Ratios	Industry Average	Activity Ratios	HQN Base
2	**Solvency**			
3	TIE	2.50	3.44	1.35
4	DSR	1.40	2.04	1.02
5	**Profitability**			
6	Profit margin (m)	0.290	0.028	0.004
7	ROA	0.33	0.165	0.065
8	ROE	0.107	0.585	0.085
9	**Efficiency**			
10	ITO	7.7	10.93	10.67
11	ITOT	47.4	33.38	34.22
12	ATO	3.2	4.10	4.00
13	ATOT	114.1	89.02	91.25
14	RTO	11.41	25.00	24.39
15	RTOT	32	14.60	14.97
16	PTO	12.59	9.33	9.33
17	PTOT	29	39.11	39.12
18	**Liquidity**			
19	Current Ratio	1.30	1.06	1.06
20	Quick Ratio	0.70	0.43	0.43
21	**Leverage**			
22	Debt/Assets	0.91	0.80	0.80
23	Debt/Equity	2.00	4.00	4.00
24	Asset/Equity	2.20	5.00	5.00

Endogenizing Exogenous Variables and Parameters

CFS systems are not unique because every financial system may define its endogenous and exogenous variables differently. As a result, each system may define its interdependencies differently, which in turn defines how consistency is achieved in the system. One way we can change the nature of a system is by endogenizing an exogenous variable.

Endogenizing an exogenous variable. System definitions of endogenous and exogenous variables and parameters are arbitrarily defined depending on data availability and analytic needs of the firm's financial manager. We illustrate next, using HQN data, how exogenous variables may be endogenized. In Figure 7.4, we described the what-if analysis of increasing sales by $1,000 which in turn increased cash receipts from $38,990 to $39,990. In this case, sales is considered an exogenous variable as is COGS. However, we should be concerned with the credibility of the results since we are confident that increasing sales will require an increase in COGS and possibly OEs, AR, interest, and taxes—to name a few exogenous variables affected by an increase in sales. The question is how-much do these other exogenous variables and parameters change and do they change in a systematic way with increases in sales?

To account for changes in exogenous variables and parameters expected with an increase in sales, we begin by considering how to internalize our exogenous variables and parameters when conducting what-if analysis. This is a critical task facing financial managers.

First consider the connection between current receipts and COGS. In 2018 cash COGS was 69% of original cash receipts ($27,000/$38,990). We might consider endogenizing cash COGS by replacing it with 69% of projected cash receipts. Then if cash receipts increase, so will COGS. We express the endogenized value of COGS below:

$$(7.1) \quad COGS = (.69)(CR) = (.69)(\$39,900) - \$27,351$$

Taxes for the previous year were reported to be $68, but this amount assumes original EBT of $170 and an average tax rate of 40%. We endogenize taxes in HQN's income statement by replacing taxes in the exogenous variable page with the average tax rate parameter of 40% times projected EBT:

$$(7.2) \quad \text{Taxes} = (.4)(EBT) = (.4)(\$1,170) - \$468$$

After endogenizing taxes and COGS, we resolve the HQN-CFS template and find new ratios for the "what-if" analysis and report the results in the Activity Table below.

Table 7.5. HQN's Activity Table: What-if Analysis after Endogenizing COGS and the average tax rate

	A	B	C	D
1	Ratios	Industry Average	Activity Ratios	HQN Base
2	**Solvency**			
3	TIE	2.50	2.20	1.35
4	DSR	1.40	1.44	1.02
5	**Profitability**			
6	Profit margin (m)	0.290	0.014	0.004
7	ROA	0.033	0.105	0.065
8	ROE	0.107	0.288	0.085
9	**Efficiency**			
10	ITO	7.7	10.93	10.67
11	ITOT	47.4	33.38	34.22
12	ATO	3.2	4.10	4.00
13	ATOT	114.1	89.02	91.25
14	RTO	11.41	25.00	24.39
15	RTOT	32	14.60	14.97
16	PTO	12.59	9.53	9.33
17	PTOT	29	38.30	39.12
18	**Liquidity**			
19	Current Ratio	1.30	1.06	1.06
20	Quick Ratio	0.70	0.43	0.43
21	**Leverage**			
22	Debt/Assets	0.91	0.80	0.80
23	Debt/Equity	2.00	4.00	4.00
24	Asset/Equity	2.20	5.00	5.00

The main result of endogenizing taxes and COGS was to reduce ROE from 16.5% to 10.57% and ROA from 58.5% to 28.85%.

So, what have we learned? We have learned what it means to endogenize exogenous variables and parameters. On occasion, we may have overidentified variables that provided a check on the accuracy of exogenous variables and parameters. However, overidentified variables means that we can arbitrarily decide if variables is to be treated as endogenous or exogenous within the CFS system. One thing we also learned is that there may exist inter-dependencies in exogenous variables and parameters not captured in CFS systems that must be addressed when performing what-is analysis if our results are to be credible.

What-If Analysis and Scenarios

What-if analysis often begins when the financial manager considers possible scenarios facing its firm. As the financial manager attempts to describe scenarios and consider possible responses, the manager may do so using what-if analysis after changing one or more exogenous variables. Following these changes in exogenous variables we may follow these changes throughout the CFS using what-if analysis. Consider several scenarios that a typical firm might face. Also consider several questions firm managers might want to answer about the scenario using what-if analysis.

Scenario 1. The firm has not been replacing its long-term assets. As a result, its cost of goods sold (COGS) has been increasing due to increased repairs and maintenance costs. What conditions may have prompted the firm to not replace its long-term assets. What are the consequences of this scenario on the financial condition of the firm reflected in its SPELL ratios?

Scenario 2. A financial manager is risk-averse and decides to increase the firm's current assets to reduce the risk of insolvency. What actions can the firm manager take to increase its level of current assets. What are the consequences of this scenario on the financial condition of the firm reflected in its SPELL ratios?

Scenario 3. Suppose the firm decides to increase the time it takes to repay its notes payable. What are the advantages/disadvantages of adopting such a strategy? What conditions facing the firm might prompt it to increase the time it takes to repay its notes payable? What are the consequences of this scenario on the financial condition of the firm reflected in its SPELL ratios?

Scenario 4. To boost its revenue, the firm offers easy credit terms to its customers. What are the implications for the firm? How would you expect the firm's credit policies to be reflected in the firm's financial statements? What are the consequences of this scenario on the financial condition of the firm reflected in its SPELL ratios?

Scenario 5. Market conditions have reduced the demand for the firm's products. As a result, cash receipts are falling. Unfortunately, most of the firm's overhead expenses (OE) are fixed and don't adjust to changing output levels. What are the consequences of this scenario on the financial condition of the firm reflected in its SPELL ratios?

Scenario 6. The firm's owners face serious medical costs and to pay for these, they must extract funds from the business. They want to know how to extract the required funds in such a way that least jeopardizes the firm's rate of return and solvency. What are the consequences of this scenario on the financial condition of the firm reflected in its SPELL ratios?

Scenario 7. The firm makes a major investment in long-term assets to improve its efficiency. One impact of the change is to reduce its taxes because of increased depreciation. The firm owners are interested in knowing what other changes in the firm's financial condition if it makes major investments in long-term assets. What are the consequences of this scenario on the financial condition of the firm reflected in its SPELL ratios?

Scenario 8. Hard economic times have reduced the firm's customers' ability to pay for their purchases in the usual amount of time. The firm wants to know how to respond to its decreased liquidity. What are the consequences of this scenario on the financial condition of the firm reflected in its SPELL ratios?

Scenario 9. Cash receipts have been inadequate for the firm to meet its notes payable and current long-term liabilities. As a result, it is forced to sell off some of its long-term assets at values less than reported on its balance sheet. The firm wants to know what other strategies it can adopt to meet its solvency demands. What are the consequences of this scenario on the financial condition of the firm reflected in its SPELL ratios?

Scenario 10. Reduced sales without changes in production levels have led to increased inventories. To meet its financial demands, the firm has restructured its debt, decreasing the current portion of the long-term debt. The firm wants to know how these changes will be reflected in its SPELL ratios.

Scenario 4 analysis. Performing what-if analysis for each scenario requires that we assume specific numbers for our exogenous variables. This approach is an alternative to endogenizing one or more of its exogenous variables. In our illustration assume that as a result of offering easy credit terms, cash receipts (CR) increased by 5% from $38,990 to $40,940. Then, because production has increased, assume that cash COGS increase by 8% from $27,000 to $29,160. There may be other changes in exogenous variables and parameters, but these are enough to illustrate how to conduct scenario analysis. After making the changes, we resolve the CFS template and report the consequences in Activity Table 7.6.

Table 7.6. HQN's Activity Table: What If Analysis of Scenario 4.

	A	B	C	D
		Industry Average	Activity Ratios	HQN Base
1	Ratios	Industry Average	Activity Ratios	HQN Base
2	**Solvency**			
3	TIE	2.50	0.92	1.35
4	DSR	1.40	0.81	1.02
5	**Profitability**			
6	Profit margin (m)	0.290	-0.001	0.004
7	ROA	0.033	0.044	0.065
8	ROE	0.107	-0.020	0.085
9	**Efficiency**			
10	ITO	7.7	11.19	10.67
11	ITOT	47.4	32.63	34.22
12	ATO	3.2	4.20	4.00
13	ATOT	114.1	87.01	91.25
14	RTO	11.41	25.58	24.39
15	RTOT	32	14.27	14.97
16	PTO	12.59	10.05	9.33
17	PTOT	29	36.31	39.12
18	**Liquidity**			
19	Current Ratio	1.30	1.06	1.06
20	Quick Ratio	0.70	0.43	0.43
21	**Leverage**			
22	Debt/Assets	0.91	0.80	0.80
23	Debt/Equity	2.00	4.00	4.00
24	Asset/Equity	2.20	5.00	5.00

Note that increasing HQN's cash receipts by 5% and it COGS by 8% reduced its ROA from 6.5% to 4.4% and turned its ROE from 8.5% to a negative two percent.

How Much Analysis and Goal Seek

CFS system's properties allow us to ask and answer important what-if kinds of questions by changing an exogenous variable or parameter and observing its effect on the endogenous variables of the system. Goal Seek is an important Excel function that allows us to ask and answer how-much kinds of questions that take the form: how much of a change is required in an exogenous variable x for variable y to reach a specified value, a goal, equal to a? To illustrate using HQN data, suppose we asked: how much must HQN's CR increase for ROE to equal 9%?

To answer this question using an Excel spreadsheet that describes HQN's CFS, we press the [Data] tab and the [What-if Analysis] button. Finally, we press "Goal Seek" in the drop-down menu. Goal Seek asks us to supply three pieces of information: the cell where the goal value is located, the numeric value for the variable identified in the goal cell, and the cell location of the variable we wish to change to achieve our goal. The number we wish to change must be an exogenous variable. We want to change the endogenous variable ROE located in cell H50 to a value of 9% by changing cash sales of landscaping services an exogenous variable located in cell J4 located on the exogenous variables and parameters page. We record this information in the Goal Seek menu below.

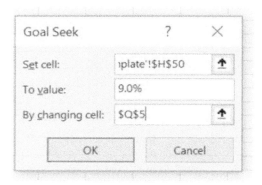

Figure 7.1. Goal Seek Pop-up Menu

Then we click [OK] and that find cash receipts from landscaping services must increase to $30,010 for HQN to earn an ROE of 9%. Furthermore, increasing cash receipts from landscaping services to $30,010 increases total cash receipts to $39,000. Changes in the endogenous variables included in system are described next in Activity Table 7.7.

Table 7.7. HQN's Activity Table: Using Goal seek to find the increase in cash receipts required for ROE to equal 9.0%.

	A	B	C	D
		Industry Average	Activity Ratios	HQN Base
1	Ratios	Industry Average	Activity Ratios	HQN Base
2	**Solvency**			
3	TIE	2.50	1.38	1.35
4	DSR	1.40	1.03	1.02
5	**Profitability**			
6	Profit margin (m)	0.290	0.0045	0.0043
7	ROA	0.033	0.066	0.065
8	ROE	0.107	0.090	0.085
9	**Efficiency**			
10	ITO	7.7	10.67	10.67
11	ITOT	47.4	34.21	34.22
12	ATO	3.2	4.00	4.00
13	ATOT	114.1	91.23	91.25
14	RTO	11.41	24.40	24.39
15	RTOT	32	14.96	14.97
16	PTO	12.59	9.33	9.33
17	PTOT	29	39.11	39.12
18	**Liquidity**			
19	Current Ratio	1.30	1.06	1.06
20	Quick Ratio	0.70	0.43	0.43
21	**Leverage**			
22	Debt/Assets	0.91	0.80	0.80
23	Debt/Equity	2.00	4.00	4.00
24	Asset/Equity	2.20	5.00	5.00

Note that increasing CR from landscaping services to $39,000 increased of ROE to 9.00%. Of course, there were other consequences. ROA increased to 6.6%. The TIE solvency ratio increased slightly from 1.35 to 1.38. These and other changes we observe by comparing the activity and goal seek columns with the HQN base column.

Creating Subsystems by Exogenizing Endogenous Variables

Sometimes, it is helpful to answer what-if and how-much questions in simpler terms. We can simplify our analysis by creating subsystems of CFS. Indeed, all systems are reduced versions of some larger system. One method for creating subsystems from larger systems is to exogenize some endogenous variables.

We can construct many subsystems. However, we focus on the two that matter most to the firm: those that describe the firm's ROE and those that describe its solvency. To illustrate, suppose we wanted to build a subsystem around the firm's ROE. We might begin by assuming that the firm sells each item of what it produces at an exogenously determined price p, whose marginal cost is c, whose fixed overhead expense is b, and whose interest costs are iD where i is the average cost of its debt and D is the sum of the firm's liabilities determined in the previous period. Finally, letting the number of physical units sold equal S, we define our ROE subsystem by assuming all other variables except ROE to be exogenous. To create an ROE subsystem, we first define EBT as:

(7.3) $$EBT = (p - c)S - b - iD.$$

Now we can write the ROE subsystem as:

(7.4)
$$ROE = \frac{EBT}{Equity} = \frac{(p-c)S - b - iD}{Equity}$$
$$= \frac{EBT}{Total\ Revenue} \frac{Total\ Revenue}{Assets} \frac{Assets}{Equity} = m\ ATO\ EM$$

Having defined an ROE subsystem, we are prepared to ask what-if questions such as: what would happen to the firm's ROE if we could increase the ATO by increasing cash receipts? Since our subsystem has defined all its interdependencies, we can find the answer to this what-if question by observing the change in the firm's ROE in response to changes in the system's exogenous variables and parameters. We illustrate this approach using HQN's data. Initially, HQN's ROE equals:

(7.5)

$$ROE = \frac{EBT}{Equity} = \frac{(p-c)S - b - iD}{Equity} = \frac{\$40,000 - \$39,350 - \$480}{\$2,000} = 8.5\%$$

Suppose the value of the exogenous variable cash receipts increased to $40,100? The results on the firm's ROE can be found to equal:

(7.6)

$$ROE = \frac{EBT}{Equity} = \frac{(p-c)S - b - iD}{Equity} = \frac{\$40,100 - \$39,350 - \$480}{\$2,000} = 13.5\%$$

Another subsystem might involve solvency and the TIE ratio. To analyze this subsystem, we begin with the EBT defined earlier and remove interest costs to obtain earnings before interest and taxes (EBIT) equal to:

(7.7) $$EBIT = (p-c)S - b$$

Next we write a DuPont type equation focused on TIE equal to:

(7.8)

$$TIE = \frac{EBIT}{Interest} = \frac{EBIT}{Assets} \frac{Assets}{Interest} = ROA\frac{(D+E)}{iD} = \frac{ROA}{i}\left(1 + \frac{1}{D/E}\right)$$

where D/E is the debt-equity leverage ratio. Having now defined a solvency subsystem reflected by the firm's TIE ratio, we can ask the following what-if question. What-if the firm increased its debt D? Then, what would be the effect on the firm's solvency? To answer this what-if question, we substitute the simplified EBIT formula into equation (7.8) to obtain:

$$TIE = \frac{(p-c)S - b}{i}\left(1 + \frac{1}{D/E}\right)$$
(7.9)

To illustrate, we substitute HQN's data into equation (7.8) to find its initial TIE value. Making the substitution we find:

$$TIE = \frac{ROA}{i}\left(1 + \frac{E}{D}\right) = \frac{6.5\%}{6\%}\left(1 + \frac{\$2,000}{\$8,000}\right) = 1.35$$
(7.10)

Now suppose we ask: what-if the firm's equity falls by \$1,000? In response to this change in an exogenous variable, HQN's TIE ratio would decline to:

$$TIE = \frac{ROA}{i}\left(1 + \frac{E}{D}\right) = \frac{6.5\%}{6\%}\left(1 + \frac{\$1,000}{\$8,000}\right) = 1.22$$
(7.11)

And what-if the firm's interest rate increased by one percent to 7.0%? Then its TIE ratio becomes:

$$TIE = \frac{ROA}{i}\left(1 + \frac{E}{D}\right) = \frac{6.5\%}{7\%}\left(1 + \frac{\$1,000}{\$8,000}\right) = 1.16$$

(7.12)

It is important to recognize that the answers to our what-if questions provided by our subsystems are only approximations of what would happen if we considered the entire system. Nevertheless, the subsystem approach provides some useful intuitive explanations that may be disguised in a full system analysis.

So, what have we learned? We learned that open systems like CFS require endogenous variables whose values are determined within the system and exogenous variables and parameters whose values are determined outside the system. However, systems are arbitrary constructs and we can create open subsystems including one that describes the firm's ROE and TIE ratios by arbitrarily exogenizing what were previously endogenously determined variables.

Common Size Balance Sheets and Income Statements

When comparing a firm's financial condition with other firms, with itself over time, or with the average firm in the industry in which it operates, it is often useful to make comparisons using standardized measures such as SPELL ratios. But what if the comparisons we wish to make involves entries in the firm's financial statements, including balance sheets and income statements? To address the need for standardized measures of balance sheet and income statement entries, we express all items in the balance sheet as a percentage of total assets and all items in the income statement as a percentage of total revenue. We refer to the results as common size balance sheets and common size income statement ratios. Common size balance sheets and income statements are composed of common size ratios that sum to 100%.

Common size balance sheet insights. Consider what we can learn from common size balance sheets and their common size ratios. Suppose that a firm's cash and marketable securities was $100,000 at the end of 2017 and $110,000 at the end of 2018. In addition, suppose the firm's total assets were $2,000,000 at the end of 2017 and $3,000,000 at the end of 2018. The firm's cash and marketable securities increased by $10,000 over the year which might suggest the firm is now more liquid. However, the firm's cash and marketable securities must now support a larger amount of total assets. The common size cash and marketable securities ratio was 5% at the end of 2017 and only 3.67% at the end of 2018. Thus, the amount of cash and marketable securities available per dollar of assets decreased during the year. Stated differently, cash and marketable securities relative to total assets declined between 2017 and

2018 while increasing in absolute amounts. We report HQN common size balance sheets and ratios in Table 7.8.

Table 7.8. Common Size Balance Sheets for HQN

	Year			
ASSETS	2016	2017	2018	Ind. Ave.
Cash and Marketable Securities	12.13%	9.30%	5.77%	6.3%
Accounts Receivable	15.77%	16.40%	11.54%	26.4%
Inventory	31.85%	37.50%	50.00%	25.6%
CURRENT ASSETS	59.76%	63.20%	67.31%	58.3%
Depreciable long-term assets	33.06%	29.90%	26.92%	35.7%
Non-depreciable long-term assets	7.18%	6.90%	5.77%	6.0%
LONG-TERM ASSETS	40.24%	36.80%	32.69%	41.7%
TOTAL ASSETS	**100.00%**	**100.00%**	**100.00%**	**100.00%**
LIABILITIES				
Notes Payable	14.15%	15.00%	12.21%	13.9%
Current Portion LTD	7.08%	5.00%	4.33%	3.6%
Accounts Payable	24.27%	30.00%	38.46%	18.7%
Accrued Liabilities	8.80%	9.58%	8.46%	6.8%
CURRENT LIABILITIES	54.30%	59.58%	63.46%	43.0%
NON-CURRENT LONG-TERM DEBT	25.88%	20.42%	19.09%	13.4%
TOTAL LIABILITIES	80.18%	80.00%	82.55%	56.4%
Equity	19.82%	20.00%	17.45%	43.6%
TOTAL EQUITY	19.82%	20.00%	17.45%	43.6%
TOTAL DEBT AND EQUITY	**100.00%**	**100.00%**	**100.00%**	**100.00%**

Common size balance sheets and what-is analysis. HQN's common size balance sheet ratios can be examined by comparing them with other firms in the industry described in the last column of Table 7.8. Doing so provides information critical for what-is analysis. HQN's common size current asset ratio is above the industry average and rising primarily as a result of relatively high and increasing common size inventories ratio. Accounts receivable ratios are low compared to the industry's average as are long-term asset ratios. Current liabilities ratios are well above the industry average and rising mostly as a result of increasingly accounts payable ratios. Although falling, long-term debt ratios are still above the industry average; owner equity ratios are well below the average firm in the industry. Finding where one's firm differs from the industry or from other firms using common size balance sheets is one way for understanding what-is the financial condition of the firm.

Common size income statements and what-is analysis. HQN's common size income statement ratios can be examined by comparing them with other firms in the industry described in the last column of Table 7.9. HQN's COGS common size ratio in 2018 was close to the industry average. However, its overhead expenses ratio (OE) were much higher than the industry average in both 2017 and 2018. As a result, its EBIT ratios were much lower than the industry average. Furthermore, its interest costs ratios were almost double the industry average. HQN's high OE and high interest costs ratios relative to the industry average were somewhat mitigated by HQN's lower than industry ratios for depreciation and taxes. Still, HQN's net income after taxes (NIAT) ratio in 2018 was low compared to the industry average: 0.25% for HQN versus 2.28% for the industry.

Finding where one's firm differs from the industry or from other firms using common size income statements common size income statement ratios is one important way to determine what-is the financial condition of the firm.

Table 7.9. HQN's Common Size Income Statement

	Year		
	2017	**2018**	**Ind. Ave.**
Total Revenue	100.00%	100.00%	100.00%
Cost of Goods Sold (COGS)	67.37%	70.00%	71.40%
Overhead Expenses	29.82%	27.50%	22.50%
Depreciation	1.24%	0.88%	1.75%
EARNING BEFORE INTEREST AND TAXES (EBIT)	1.57%	1.62%	4.35%
Interest	1.22%	1.20%	0.55%
EARNINGS BEFORE TAXES (EBT)	0.35%	0.42%	3.80%
Taxes	0.17%	0.17%	1.52%
NET INCOME AFTER TAXES (NIAT)	0.18%	0.25%	2.28%

What-if Analysis and Trade-offs

Common size statement ratios sum to 100%. This fact implies that we cannot increase one variable in the statements without decreasing the relative importance of other variables. This required trade-off in response to changes in exogenous variable provides us an important tool for conduction what-if analysis using common size statements. There are various ways we can describe these trade-offs.

The squeeze versus the bulge. One way to examine trade-offs in common size ratios is to assume the financial system has some characteristics similar to a balloon. If we squeeze a balloon, a corresponding bulge will occur—because balloons require equal pressure on its surface. This balloon-like characteristic is evident in common size financial statements because common size ratios must sum to 100%.

For example, suppose the firm wishes to increase its liquidity by increasing its accounts receivable ratio. However, increasing the accounts receivable and depreciable assets ratios will require that the long-term assets ratio decreases—and profitability and perhaps efficiency may suffer.

CFS and trade-offs. Trade-offs are obvious within common size statements. Some usual trade-offs are summarized in the table that follows. Consider the left-hand column as the "squeeze" and the right-hand column as the "bulge." However, the "squeeze" and "bulge" comparisons described below are only qualitative possibilities. To find out the quantitative connections, we must look at the change in common size ratios after a change in an exogenous variable or parameter has occurred.

Table 7.10. The Squeeze vs. The Bulge

The Squeeze	The Bulge
leverage ratio (D/E): High	rate of return on equity (ROE): High
cash receipts/inventory ratio (ITO): High	cash receipts/accounts receivable (RTO): Low
cash receipts/inventory ratio (ITO): Low	profit margin (m): Low
current assets/current liabilities ratio (CR): High	rate of return on equity (ROE): Low
cash receipts/assets ratio (ATO): High	operating and repair: High
COGS/notes payable (PTO): High	interest costs: High

Companion ratios. We now conduct what-if analysis using common size ratios by looking for interesting things in pairs. To begin, look at HQN's common size inventories ratio: 50% in 2018 versus an industry average of 25.6%. We have found a squeeze. The bulge? Look at its accounts receivable ratio: 11.54% versus an industry standard of 26.4%. Does this suggest that the firm has adopted a stringent credit policy that has discouraged some customers by forcing them to pay in cash, reducing sales and increasing unsold inventories? Perhaps. It's an area the firm should explore. If HQN's stringent credit policy were indeed affecting cash receipts, then its inventory turnover ratio (ITO) would be affected. Compare, but this ratio isn't too far from the industry average: 10.67% versus the industry average of 7.7%. However, the ITO upper quartile for the industry is 14.9%, suggesting a large variability for the industry. So, the firm's credit policy is still a concern.

Consider companion SPELL ratios. HQN's debt to equity ratio is 4.0 in 2018 versus the industry average of 1.9. Unfortunately for HQN, a high leverage ratio hasn't increased profits or rates of return as much as might be expected because of its low efficiency. Continuing, if HQN has unusually high levels of debt relative to its equity, we should expect its interest payments to be above the industry average. They are 1.2% of cash receipts in 2018 versus an industry average of .55%. Already we are alarmed; high leverage is usually accompanied by high risk. One reason that high leverage implies high risk is that the firm's equity relative to its liability is small and not able to survive a market reversal. Is HQN's equity low relative to the industry? Very much so: 17.45% in 2018 versus the industry average of 43.6%.

Common Size Statements and Forecasting

Using historical data, we attempt to look ahead to financial conditions the firm is likely to experience in the future. This effort is different than what-if analysis because we are predicting what-is likely to be the financial conditions of the firm in the future. Common size statements can sometimes be helpful when forecasting the future. We introduce the topic of forecasting here and in more detail in Chapter 11. In what follows we describe two forecasting method using common size statements. The first one is trend analysis. The second method is pro-forma analysis.

Trend analysis. Consider the common size balance sheets reported earlier in Table 7.8. Trend analysis begins by looking for significant changes or trends in the asset or liability ratios. Current asset ratios have increased over the three-year period mostly due to increases in inventory levels. Cash and marketable securities common ratios declined during the three years for the same reason—current assets being tied up in inventory. Long-term assets have fallen primarily as a result of declining values of the firm's property, plant, and equipment. The worrisome result of this trend is that it may project increased maintenance costs associated with aging machinery.

On the debt side of the balance sheet, current liabilities ratios have increased during the three-year period mostly as a result of increases in accounts payable ratios. Long-term debt ratios have declined, and owner equity ratios have remained relatively constant. The question associated with these trends is, can increasing dependence on notes payable be sustained? Are there less expensive sources of financing available?

Examining HQN's common size income statement, reported in Table 7.9, we see that both EBIT and NIAT ratios increased in 2018. Comparing HQN's income statement ratios with other firms in the industry, we note that HQN's EBIT and NIAT ratios were low compared to industry averages, primarily as a result of relatively high overhead expenses and interest expenses ratios. High OE, COGS, and interest costs ratios have reduced HQN's taxes ratio. Trends in both common size balance sheets and income statements can be used to predict their future value, assuming the trends continue; or, they may be used to identify barriers to the trends continuing.

Pro forma financial statements. Pro forma income statements and balance sheets are forecasts of what these statements will look like in the future and provide essential planning information. There are several ways to construct pro forma statements. The usual technique is to select a key variable and predict its future value. Then assume constant SPELL ratios which include the key variable and solve for other values using other ratios. We demonstrate this approach in what follows.

Assume that HQN wants to achieve a projected level of cash receipts. Also assume that SPELL ratios will remain constant even in the face of projected total revenue increases. Specifically, assume that next year's projected total revenue for HQN will equal $42,000, an increase of 5%. What does this imply for HQN's level of inventory? From HQN's SPELL ratios, we see that the inventory turnover ratio was 10.67%. Assuming this year's ratios will not change next year, we can use the projected level of cash receipts to forecast the pro forma levels of inventories (INV). The first step in these types of problems is to write out the definition of each ratio and their assumed values:

$$ITO = \frac{\text{Total Revenue}}{INV} = \frac{\$40,000}{\$3,750} = 10.67\%$$
(7.13)

From the inventory turnover (ITO) equation we find:

$$INV = \frac{\text{Total Revenue}}{ITO}$$
(7.14)

Next, we use the projected cash receipts level of $42,000 and divide by ITO to find projected HQN's inventory in 2019:

$$INV = \frac{\text{Total Revenue}}{ITO} = \frac{\$42,000}{10.4\%} = \$4,038.46$$
(7.15)

We observe an interesting result. Inventories increased by 5% to $4,038.46, the same percentage increases as was projected in total revenue. This result, of equal percentage increases, occurs whenever the ratio is held fixed. When one number of the ratio is increased by some percent, the other number in the ratio must increase by the same percent. To illustrate, consider the m ratio:

$$m = \frac{EBIT}{\text{Total Revenue}} = \frac{\$170}{\$40,000} = 0.00425$$
(7.16)

If the m ratio is constant and cash receipts increases to $42,000, then EBIT will increase by 5% to $178.50. Again, the technique is to assume that the historical financial relationships will hold in the future and then project the future value of one variable, usually cash receipts. This allows us to calculate the projected values of the remaining financial variables based on the historical financial relationships. Of course, we could create pro forma income statements and balance sheets by increasing all the variables by some common percent, or just the exogenous variables by the common percent. However, increasing all the exogenous variables by a common percent is confusing, and it is highly unrealistic. That explains why what-if analysis is often applied to the firm's CFS.

Summary and Conclusions

We began this chapter by describing the CFS as a system in which changes in one part of the system affect other parts of the system. We answered the question, what-is the financial condition of the firm by computing SPELL ratios using CFS data and comparing these with industry averages of similar firms. Because SPELL ratios are computed using CFS data, they reflect the interdependencies inherent in the CFS.

While SPELL ratios can describe what-is the firm's strengths and weaknesses, they can also answer what-if and how-much kinds of questions by changing CFS exogenous variables that reflect scenarios the financial managers may face—and recomputing the SPELL ratios. Comparing SPELL ratios before and after the changes in exogenous variables and parameters allows us to examine the firm's strengths and weaknesses. We also answered how-much questions with the help of Excel's goal seek. How-much questions help us find the requirements for reaching specific financial goals.

What-is analysis assumes relationships among exogenous variables are fixed. However, when we change an exogenous variable required by what-if and how-much analysis, we may need to consider interdependencies between exogenous variables. We demonstrated this interdependencies when we considered an increase in cash sales that would require an increase in COGS and taxes. As a result, to improve the credibility of our scenario analysis using what-if and how-much, we may need to endogenize certain exogenous variables.

We faced the fact that the world is a complicated system and we can sometimes gain insights about it by creating subsystems that assume or define some endogenous variables as exogenous variables and parameters. In effect, we create subsystems from systems by reducing the number of endogenous variables and increasing the number of exogenous variables and parameters—allowing us to describe a subsystem within a system with a reduced number of endogenous variables.

We found our subsystems to be useful because they allow us to understand the connections between some of the most important parts of the financial system such as a firm's rates of return and solvency. While there are many subsystems we could create and examine, we emphasized the firm's TIE ratio and its ROE ratios that reflect a firm's solvency and rate of return on equity. We expressed our subsystems using DuPont type equations.

Another important set of ratios we considered was common size ratios. We found common size ratios by dividing CFS balance sheet entries by total assets and CFS income statement entries by total revenue. As a result, common size balance sheet ratios and common size income statement ratios sum to 100%. They reflect what-is the financial condition of the firm by comparing the relative important of each balance sheet and income statement entry to total assets or total revenue.

That common size ratios in balance and income statements sum to 100% facilitates a special kind of what-if analysis: the analysis of trade-offs in the relative importance of common size ratios. We perform trade-off analysis by changing an exogenous variable and recalculating common size ratios and noting the changes in relative importance of each ratio relative to total assets or total revenue.

Finally, we facilitated what-is, what-if, and how much analysis using CFS and common size statements entered into Excel spreadsheets described in the appendix to this chapter.

Questions

1. Describe a system that is different than the CFS system described in this chapter.
2. Refer to Table 7.1 that lists exogenous variables and parameters. Since determining which variables are endogenous and exogenous is somewhat arbitrary, especially when some variables are overidentified, describe factors that influence which variables are exogenous in any particular CFS.
3. SPELL and common size ratios can be used to describe what-is the financial condition of the firm. What-if and how-much analysis examine possible scenarios, counter-factual conditions that differ from the actual condition of the firm. Explain the benefits and limitations of what-is versus what-if analysis.
4. Explain why it may be necessary to endogenize some exogenous variables and parameters when conducting what-if and how-much analysis to improve credibility. Explain why it may be necessary to exogenize some endogenous variables when the goal is to provide a simpler view of the firm. Give examples from the text of endogenizing some exogenous variables and exogenizing some endogenous variables.
5. Choose three of the ten scenarios described in the text. Then perform what-if analysis using the Excel CFS template described in the appendix to this chapter. Describe what changes in exogenous variables or what exogenous variables should be endogenized to improve the credibility of the analysis. Recognize that some scenario analyses may require more than one exogenous variable be changed. Finally, write a brief opportunities and threats report about how the conditions described in the scenario would change the firm's opportunities and threats.
6. Compare HQN's 2017 and 2018 common size balance sheet in Table 7.8 with the industry average. Based on these comparisons, describe what is the financial condition of the firm. How does what-is analysis using common size balance sheets and income ratios differ from conducting what-is using SPELL ratios.
7. Refer to Table 7.8 that describe HQN's common size balance sheets at the end of years 2016, 2017, and 2018. Notice that cash and marketable securities were well above the industry average in 2016 and then declined in both 2017 and 2018 to percentages below the industry average.
8. Common size statement are interdependent. And increase in one common size ratio requires corresponding decreases in other ratios. By referring to other ratios in the common size balance sheet, explain what changes in the firm likely account for HQN's decline in liquidity reflected by a decrease in the relative importance of cash and marketable securities.
9. Refer to Table 7.8 and observe that HQN's current liabilities increased from 59.58% in 2017 to 63.46% in 2018. In all years, current liabilities were well above the industry average of 43%. If high levels of current liabilities in HQN's balance sheets (the squeeze), what is other ratios are below the industry average that would be the companion ratio (the bulge). Is this change a strength or weakness for HQN?
10. Focusing on HQN's common size income statement in Table 7.9, observe that overhead expenses were increasing between 2017 and 2018 while depreciation was low. Are the two connected? Can you connect this change to changes in the firm's long-term assets in the common size balance sheets?

11. The common size income statement's base is cash receipts. Recalculate the common size income statements for 2017 and 2018 using COGS as the new base. What is the effect of changing the base in the calculation of the common size income statement?

12. In Table 7.9, NIAT is especially low compared to the industry average. Can you explain why?

13. Compute a pro forma income statement for HQN for 2019. Assume cash receipts equals $42,000 and the relationships described by the common size income statement for 2018 are maintained.

Appendix to System Analysis

Coordinated financial statements (CFS) and ratios. This appendix operationalizes the calculation of CFS using HQN data reported in Chapter 5, calculates SPELL ratios derived in Chapter 6, and common size ratios derived in this chapter. CFS include interdependent beginning and ending period balance sheets linked with income and cash flow statements. CFS for HQN described in Chapter 5 and HQN SPELL ratios described in Chapter 6 are reported below. Open the HQN Coordinated Financial Statement template in MS Excel.

Table 7.A1. HQN Coordinated Financial Statement Template

Exogenous and endogenous data. Data included in CFS and used to find SPELL ratios can be separated into endogenous and exogenous variables and parameters. Exogenous variables and parameters and their values are determined outside of CFS. These are used to find the values of endogenous variables whose values are calculated within CFS. It is somewhat arbitrary which variables are endogenous and endogenous. The distinction depends on what data are available outside of CFS and which data must be calculated. A third data category included in CFS are repeated values of endogenous and exogenous variables and parameters that are reported in more than one location. For example, cash receipts are calculated using exogenous data that are summed and then reported in the statement of cash flow and the income statement. Table 7.A2 below describes exogenous data included in CFS.

Table 7.A2. Exogenous Variables

Exogenous data reported in Table 7.A2 can be separated into three categories. The first category includes exogenous data included in beginning and ending balance sheets. The second category includes exogenous data included in the statement of cash flow, and the third category includes exogenous data used for side-bar calculations required to combine multiple entries of similar data into a single category that can be used to facilitate comparisons between firms, a firm and the industry in which it operates, and the same firm over time. Side-bar calculated sums are treated as exogenous data in CFS. There is no exogenous data included in income statements in Table 7.A2 since it is created using data transferred from the balance sheets or statement of cash flow or calculated. Exogenous data reported in Table 7.A2 are collected from outside of CFS from such sources as tax records, records of financial transactions including purchases and sales of depreciable and non-depreciable assets, and operating data include product sales receipts and records operating expenses.

Whenever there is a question about a datum source in the CFS, one need only hover the cursor over the cell in question. If the source refers one back to the exogenous data sheet, the variables is an exogenous variable including side bar calculations. If the cell begins with an "=" sign indicating a calculation, the datum is an endogenous variable. If the cell indicates another cell location within the CFS, the data is being transferred from another location and may be either an exogenous or endogenous variable.

SPELL *ratios.* SPELL ratios included in the CFS were described in Chapter 6. Figure 7.A1 reports two categories of SPELL ratios. The first category describes exogenously determined values that report industry standard ratios. The second SPELL ratios category describes endogenously determined values that reflect the financial condition of the firm being examine. Comparing the two categories of SPELL ratios helps financial managers determine the financial condition of the firm. The formula for each financial ratio reported in the CFS for the firm being examined can be discovered by hovering over the cell containing the ratio of interest. For example, hovering over the ROE cell, we find the ratio is calculated as: J21/C28. Then referring to the CFS, we find J21 equals Earnings Before Taxes of $170 divided by C28 equal to total equity at the beginning of the period of $2,000. ROE then is found as the ratio $170/$2000=8.5%.

What-if analysis. One of the many advantages of using an Excel spreadsheet to describe CFS and SPELL ratios is the ability to considers the consequences of changes in exogenous variables and parameters on the value of endogenous variables. We describe the consequences of change(s) in the value of exogenous variable(s) on endogenously determined SPELL ratios and report the results in Table 7.A3.

Table 7.A3. HQN's Activity Table: What-if Analysis Before Changes

	A	B	C	D
		Industry Average	Activity Ratios	HQN Base
1	Ratios	Industry Average	Activity Ratios	HQN Base
2	**Solvency**			
3	TIE	2.50	1.35	1.35
4	DSR	1.40	1.02	1.02
5	**Profitability**			
6	Profit margin (m)	0.290	0.004	0.004
7	ROA	0.033	0.065	0.065
8	ROE	0.107	0.085	0.085
9	**Efficiency**			
10	ITO	7.70	10.67	10.67
11	ITOT	47.40	34.22	34.22
12	ATO	3.20	4.00	4.00
13	ATOT	114.10	91.25	91.25
14	RTO	11.41	24.39	24.39
15	RTOT	32.00	14.97	14.97
16	PTO	12.59	9.33	9.33
17	PTOT	29.00	39.12	39.12
18	**Liquidity**			
19	Current Ratio	1.30	1.06	1.06
20	Quick Ratio	0.70	0.43	0.43
21	**Leverage**			
22	Debt/Assets	0.91	0.80	0.80
23	Debt/Equity	2.00	4.00	4.00
24	Asset/Equity	2.20	5.00	5.00

The first column in Table 7.A3 describes the financial ratio being reported. The second column describes the average ratio value for the industry to which the firm belongs. Ratios in this column provides the firm a standard against which it can compare itself. The third column describes the value of the firm's SPELL ratios after the change in the exogenous variable has occurred. We refer to this column as the activity column. Finally, the fourth column describes the value of the ratios before the change in the exogenous variable has occurred. We label this column base values. Of course, what-if analysis can accommodate more than one exogenous variable change. For example, the scenarios described in Chapter 7 may require several changes in exogenous variables and parameters to be adequately described.

For Table 7.A3, the activity column and the base column are equal since no change in an exogenous variable or parameter has been introduced. Now introduce a change. Suppose that cash sales increased from $18,000 to $18,100. We describe the consequences of this change in an exogenous variable will influence HQN's SPELL ratios in Table 7.A4. While several SPELL ratios change, the most important change increased ROA from 6.5% to 7.5% and increased the ROE ratio from 8.5% to 13.5%. Since the activity column is updated after each "what-if" analysis, it may be convenient to copy each "what-if" table and record it in a separate Excel page.

Table 7.A4. HQN's Activity Table: What If Analysis: Increasing Cash Sales to $18,100.

	A	B	C	D
		Industry Average	Activity Ratios	HQN Base
1	Ratios			
2	**Solvency**			
3	TIE	2.500	1.563	1.354
4	DSR	1.400	1.122	1.020
5	**Profitability**			
6	Profit margin (m)	0.290	0.007	0.004
7	ROA	0.033	0.075	0.065
8	ROE	0.107	0.135	0.085
9	**Efficiency**			
10	ITO	7.700	10.693	10.667
11	ITOT	47.400	34.133	34.219
12	ATO	3.200	4.010	4.000
13	ATOT	114.100	91.022	91.250
14	RTO	11.410	24.451	24.390
15	RTOT	32.000	14.928	14.965
16	PTO	12.590	9.333	9.330
17	PTOT	29.000	39.107	39.120
18	**Liquidity**			
19	Current Ratio	1.300	1.061	1.061
20	Quick Ratio	0.700	0.431	0.431
21	**Leverage**			
22	Debt/Assets	0.910	0.800	0.800
23	Debt/Equity	2.000	4.000	4.000
24	Asset/Equity	2.200	5.000	5.000

Goal seek and "how-much" analysis. Finally, we introduce "Goal Seek", an Excel function that allows us to ask the question: how-much of a change in exogenous variable X is required for an endogenous variable Y to equal a specified value? We refer to this analysis as how-much analysis. The details of how to use Goal Seek and how-much analysis were described in Chapter 7. The main point here is that Goal Seek and how much analysis, like what-if analysis, analyzes the consequences of a change in an exogenous variable on an endogenous variable. The difference is that the size of the change in the exogenous variables is determined by a separate analysis that uses goal seek. The values of SPELL ratios after introducing a change in an exogenous variable whose amount was determined by goal seek is reported in the what-if table, Table 7.A3. For example, suppose we are interested in discovering how-much of a change in labor costs is required to increase ROE to 9.0%. Using goal-seek, we find that decreasing labor costs to $7990 will increase ROE to 9%. Other changes associated with decreasing labor costs to $7,990 are reported in Table 7.A5.

Table 7.A5. HQN's Activity Table: Goal Seek Reducing Labor Costs to $7,990 Increases ROE to 9%

	A	B	C	D
1	Ratios	Industry Average	Activity Ratios	HQN Base
2	**Solvency**			
3	TIE	2.500	1.375	1.354
4	DSR	1.400	1.031	1.020
5	**Profitability**			
6	Profit margin (m)	0.290	0.005	0.004
7	ROA	0.033	0.066	0.065
8	ROE	0.107	0.090	0.085
9	**Efficiency**			
10	ITO	7.700	10.667	10.667
11	ITOT	47.400	34.219	34.219
12	ATO	3.200	4.000	4.000
13	ATOT	114.100	91.250	91.250
14	RTO	11.410	24.390	24.390
15	RTOT	32.000	14.965	14.965
16	PTO	12.590	9.330	9.330
17	PTOT	29.000	39.121	39.120
18	**Liquidity**			
19	Current Ratio	1.300	1.061	1.061
20	Quick Ratio	0.700	0.431	0.431
21	**Leverage**			
22	Debt/Assets	0.910	0.800	0.800
23	Debt/Equity	2.000	4.000	4.000
24	Asset/Equity	2.200	5.000	5.000

Common size statements and "what-is" analysis. Common size statements introduced in this chapter are an important financial analysis tool that can be used for what-is, what-if, and how-much analysis. Entries in common size statements are ratios like the SPELL ratios but differ because they sum to 100% and therefore emphasis trade-offs between elements of common size balance sheets and income statements. The only point that distinguishes SPELL ratios from common size ratios is that the latter set of ratios care created using the same base for balance sheet and income statement ratios, total assets versus total revenue. Common size ratios using CFS base numbers provide the basis for what-is analysis. Conducting what-if and how-much analysis using CFS after changes in exogenous variables provide the basis for common size statement what-if and how-much analysis. We include an Excel template that describes common size balance sheets in Figure 7.A6. The activity column headed 12/31/2018 reflects a what-if analysis that examines an increase in sales of $1,000.

Table 7.A6. HQN Common size balance sheets for December 31, 2017 and 2018.

	Activity		Activity		
ASSETS	12/31/2017	base 2017	12/31/2018	base 2018	Ind. Ave.
Cash and Marketable Securities	9.30%	9.30%	7.93%	5.77%	6.30%
Accounts Receivable	16.40%	16.40%	11.27%	11.54%	26.40%
Inventory	37.50%	37.50%	48.85%	50.00%	25.60%
CURRENT ASSETS	63.20%	63.20%	68.06%	67.31%	58.30%
Depreciable long-term assets	29.90%	29.90%	25.46%	26.06%	35.70%
Non-depreciable long-term assets	6.90%	6.90%	6.48%	6.63%	6.00%
LONG-TERM ASSETS	36.80%	36.80%	31.94%	32.69%	41.70%
TOTAL ASSETS	**100.00%**	**100.00%**	**100.00%**	**100.00%**	**100.00%**
LIABILITIES					
Notes Payable	15.00%	15.00%	11.93%	12.21%	13.90%
Current Portion LTD	5.00%	5.00%	4.23%	4.33%	3.60%
Accounts Payable	30.00%	30.00%	37.58%	38.46%	8.70%
Accrued Liabilities	9.58%	9.58%	8.27%	8.46%	6.80%
CURRENT LIABILITIES	59.58%	59.58%	62.01%	63.46%	43.00%
NON-CURRENT LONG-TERM DEBT	20.42%	20.42%	18.65%	19.09%	13.40%
TOTAL LIABILITIES	80.00%	80.00%	80.65%	82.55%	56.40%
TOTAL EQUITY	20.00%	20.00%	19.35%	17.45%	43.60%
TOTAL DEBT AND EQUITY	**100.00%**	**100.00%**	**100.00%**	**100.00%**	**100.00%**

Finally, we include a common size income statement in Table 7.A7. Note that we have few industry averages to compare the AIS entries, partly because there is less standardization for income statements than for balance sheets.

Table 7.A7. HQN's Common size income statement for 2018 reflecting an increase in sales of $1,000.

Date		AIS Activity	Activity 2018	Base 2018	Industry Average
+	Cash Receipts	$39,990	97.54%	97.48%	
+	Change in Accounts Receivable	($440)	-1.07%	-1.10%	
+	Change in Inventories	$1,450	3.54%	3.63%	
+	Realized Capital Gains (Losses	$0	0.00%	0.00%	
=	**Total Revenue**	$41,000	100.00%	100.00%	100.00%
+	Cash Cost of Goods Sold	$27,593	67.30%	67.50%	71.40%
+	Change in Accounts Payable	$1,000	2.44%	2.50%	
+	Cash Overhead Expenses	$11,078	27.02%	27.70%	22.50%
+	Change in Accrued Liabilities	($78)	-0.19%	-0.20%	
+	Depreciation	$350	0.85%	0.88%	1.75%
=	**Total Expenses**	$39,943	97.42%	98.38%	
	Earnings Before Interest and Taxes (EBIT)	$1,057	2.58%	1.63%	4.35%
−	Less Interest Costs	$480	1.17%	1.20%	0.55%
=	**Earnings Before Taxes (EBT)**	$577	1.41%	0.43%	3.80%
−	Less Taxes	$231	0.54%	0.17%	1.52%
=	**Net Income After Taxes (NIAT)**	$346	0.84%	0.26%	3.80%
−	Less Dividends and Owner Draw	$287	0.70%	0.72%	
=	**Addition to Retained Earnings**	$59	0.14%	-0.46%	

PART III: PRESENT VALUE MODELS

8. Valuing Future Cash Flows: Present Value Models & Accrual Income Statements

LINDON ROBISON

Learning goals. After completing this chapter, you should be able to: (1) construct present value (PV) models that are multi-period extensions of accrual income statements (AIS); (2) demonstrate how to properly represent the financial characteristics of an investment using PV models; (3) distinguish between PV models by associating them with AIS earnings and rates of return; and (4) clarify the con-ditions required for earnings and rates of return on assets and equity to provide consistent rankings. These contributions are intended to help financial managers make better investment decisions.

Learning objectives. To reach your learning goals, you should complete the following objectives:

- Describe the similarities and differences between AIS and PV models.
- Demonstrate that before and after-tax rates of return on assets (ROA) and equity (ROE) derived from AIS are equivalent to before and after-tax internal rate of return on assets (IRR^A) and equity (IRR^E) derived from multi-period IRR models.
- Demonstrate that net present value (NPV) models can be viewed as multi-period present value extensions of EBIT, EBT, and NIAT earning measures.
- Solve NPV and IRR models using a generalized Excel template.
- Identify the conditions required for consistent earnings and rates of return on assets and equity rankings.

Introduction

1

The development of PV models has a long history. Some of that history is reviewed by Robison and Barry (2020). Relevant to this chapter is work by Osborn (2010), Graham and Harvey (2001), Scott and Petty (1984), and a host of other authors have focused on the possible inconsistency between NPV and IRR rankings and how to resolve the possible conflict. One resolution to the ranking conflict focused on reinvesting cash flow, producing a new class of PV models that Lin (1976) and others have referred to as modified PV models. Related to modified PV models, Beaves (1988) and Shull (1994) describe implicit

1. The material in this chapter was adapted from Robison, L.J. and P.J. Barry (2020). "Accrual Income Statements and Present Value Models." Agricultural Finance Review.

and clear rates of reinvestment. Magni (2013) suggested a weighted average IRR as a way to fix the problems with PV and IRR. Robison, Barry, and Myers (2015) stated conditions for homogeneous size that would guarantee that IRR and NPV rankings would be the same. Recent research has found connections between PV models and other fields. Magni (2020) connected accounting, finance, and engineering to PV models. Robison and Barry (2020) linked AIS accounting measures to PV models by pointing out that changes in running accounts and the liquidation of capital accounts need to be taken into account in PV models. This chapter emphasises that if we pay attention to the connections between the AIS model and the PV model, we can make more accurate and clear PV models and better understand how rankings can be in conflict based on whether we are looking at assets or equity.

AIS and PV Models

Income Statements for Earnings. AIS figures out how much money is made from assets and shares before and after taxes are paid. AIS earning measures can also predict return on assets (ROA), return on equity (ROE), and after-tax return on equity (ROE(1–T)), where T is the average tax rate, when used with balance sheet data. AIS measures income and costs when events happen, not just when cash payments are processed or received (see Harsh, Connor, and Schwab (1981) and Lazarus (1987) for more information). To achieve this end, AIS include changes in working and capital accounts that do not produce cash flow. PV types defined. This study says that PV models are just AIS models with more than one time period. This description is correct because AIS earnings and rates of return can be measured with PV models. ROA, ROE, and ROE(1-T) from the AIS are the same as IRRA, IRRE, and IRRE(1-T) from the PV model. Also, NPV for asset earnings (NPVA), equity earnings (NPVE), and after-tax equity earnings (NPVE(1-T)) are the same as AIS EBIT, EBT, and NIAT. AIS and PV models are not the same. Even though AIS and PV models are similar in some ways, there are some important differences. Think about two. First, AIS are made to measure how well a company is doing financially. Because of this, they tend to be about the past. PV models look at whether or not it makes financial sense to make an investment whose reward depends on cash flows in the future. Because of this, PV models often centre on the past.

Second, AIS can be built to measure rates of return and earnings on assets and equity both before and after taxes are paid in one time. PV models can be used to figure out the rates of return and earnings on assets and equity before and after taxes are taken out for businesses that make money over a long period of time. So, at the end of the first quarter, AIS reports its earnings. At the end of the analysis, PV models show the present value of the cash flow made over several time periods and the liquidated value of the operating and capital accounts. Both AIS and PV models have details. Both the AIS and PV models match and agree with each other. So that everything is the same, we need to add the same details and differences to PV models as we do to AIS models. This means that we must first decide if we are exploring or not.

gain or loss on assets or stock. Second, both AIS and PV models need to take into account changes in accounts received, inventories, accounts payable, accrued liabilities, and capital accounts. Lastly, you need both earnings data and the amounts of assets and equity to figure out rates of return on assets and equity. AIS need information from balance sheets about the assets and stock at the start. To figure out how investments are supported, PV models also need information about assets and ownership.

> So, what have we learned? PV models are multi-period generalizations of AIS whose future cash flows are evaluated as though they were received in the present period. As a result, we need to be prepared to construct PV models with the same detail included in an AIS. If we fail to include these details, we may misrepresent the present value of the investment's earnings and rates of return.

AIS Earnings and Rates of Return on Assets and Equity

Earnings on assets. AIS earnings on beginning assets equals:

- the difference between cash receipts and the sum of cash cost of goods sold (COGS) and cash overhead expenses (OE), and
- changes in the value of the firm's operating and capital accounts.

A *numerical example.* We illustrate how to find AIS earnings and rates of return on assets using data that describes the fictional firm Hi-Quality Nursery (HQN) described in Chapter 5. We report the AIS for HQN in Table 8.1.

Table 8.1. HQN's 2018 Accrual Income Statement

	2018
+ Cash Receipts	$38,990
+ Change in Accounts Receivable	($440)
+ Change in Inventories	$1,450
+ Realized capital gains (losses)	$0
Total Revenue	$40,000
+ Cash Cost of Goods Sold	$27,000
+ Change in Accounts Payable	$1,000
+ Cash Overhead Expenses	$11,078
+ Change in Accrued Liabilities	($78)
+ Depreciation	$350
Total Expenses	$39,350
Earnings Before Interest and Taxes (EBIT)	$650
– Less Interest Costs	$480
Earnings Before Taxes (EBT)	$170
– Less Taxes	$68
Net Income After Taxes (NIAT)	$102
– Less Dividends and Owner Draw	$287
Addition to Retained Earnings	($185)

The AIS reported in Table 8.1 organizes cash flow and changes in operating and capital accounts into total revenue and total expenses and reports the difference as EBIT. The HQN EBIT calculation is summarized in equation (8.1). Total revenue equals cash receipts (CR), plus the change in accounts receivable (ΔAR), plus the change in inventory (ΔInv), plus realized capital gains (losses) (RCG). Total expenses equal the sum of cash COGS, plus the change in accounts payable (ΔAP), plus the change in cash overhead expenses (ΔOE), plus the change in accrued liabilities (ΔAL), plus the change in the book value of capital assets or depreciation (Dep). EBIT represents HQN's earnings from its beginning assets that include assets supported by its liabilities or debt.

$$EBIT = \text{total revenue} - \text{total expense}$$
$$= (CR + \Delta AR + \Delta Inv + RCG)$$
$$- (COGS + \Delta AP + OE + \Delta AL + Dep)$$
(8.1)
$$= \$40,000 - \$39,350 = \$650$$

Rates of return on assets. We find HQN's ROA by dividing HQN's EBIT of $650 by its beginning assets (A_0) of $10,000 reported in Table 8.2. HQN's ROA equals:

$$ROA = \frac{EBIT}{A_0} = \frac{\$650}{\$10,000} = 6.5\%$$

(8.2)

Table 8.2. HQN's Beginning and Ending Balance Sheets

DATE	12/31/2017	12/31/2018
Cash and Marketable Securities	$930	$600
Accounts Receivable	$1,640	$1,200
Inventory	$3,750	$5,200
Notes Receivable	$0	$0
Total Current Assets	$6,320	$7,000
Depreciable Assets	$2,990	$2,710
Non-depreciable Assets	$690	$690
Total Long-Term Assets	$3,680	$3,400
TOTAL ASSETS	$10,000	$10,400
Notes Payable	$1,500	$1,270
Current Portion Long-Term Debt	$500	$450
Accounts Payable	$3,000	$4,000
Accrued Liabilities	$958	$880
Total Current Liabilities	$5,958	$6,600
Non-Current Long-Term Debt	$2,042	$1,985
Total Liabilities	$8,000	$8,585
Contributed Capital	$1,900	$1,900
Retained Earnings	$100	($85)
Total Equity	$2,000	$1,815
TOTAL LIABILITIES AND EQUITY	$10,000	$10,400

Earnings and rate of return on equity. We find HQN's earnings on its beginning equity by subtracting from EBIT interest costs (Int) that represent payments for the use of debt and other liabilities and refer to the result as EBT, earnings after interest and before taxes are paid. We find ROE for HQN by dividing EBT by the firm's beginning equity (E_0) of $2,000 reported in Table 8.2. HQN's ROE equals:

$$ROE = \frac{EBIT - Int}{E_0} = \frac{EBT}{E_0} = \frac{\$170}{\$2,000} = 8.5\%$$

(8.3)

Earnings and changes in beginning assets and equity. EBIT and EBT earnings on the firm's beginning assets and equity respectively. These earnings estimates may not equal the actual changes in assets and equity between periods reported in HQN's balance sheets. To explain, the change in equity between periods reported in Table 8.2 equals ($185), ($1815 – $2,000). However, this value is not equal to EBT of $170 estimated from HQN's AIS in Table 8.1. The difference between the change in equity and EBT can be attributed to sum of taxes paid equal to $68 and owner draw equal to $287. If we subtract taxes and owner draw from EBT, we find the change in equity between periods of ($185) equal to the actual change in equity reported in Table 8.2.

(8.4)
$$\Delta \text{Equity} = EBT - \text{taxes} - \text{owner draw} = \$170 - \$68 - \$287 = (\$185)$$

Table 8.3 reports a change in HQN's assets of $400, ($10,400 – $10,000). Meanwhile, HQN's AIS reports EBIT equal to $650. We can explain part of the difference between EBIT and the actual change in assets by accounting for interest and taxes paid and owner draw. These describe how operating activities can explain the difference between beginning and ending assets. Then if we add the effect of increased liabilities of $585, ($8585 – $8000), and the corresponding increase in assets, we explain the discrepancy. We summarize these results in the Table 8.3.

Table 8.3. HQN's EBIT and Change in Assets

	EBIT	$650
–	Interest paid	$480
–	Taxes paid	$68
–	Owner draw	$287
=	Change in retained earnings	($185)
+	Changes in total liabilities	$585
=	Change in total assets	$400

The main point is that while rates of return on assets and equity reflect some changes in beginning assets and equity—they do not necessarily equal the differences between beginning and ending assets and equity reported in balance sheets. Therefore, we cannot measure rates of return on assets and equity as percentage changes in ending and beginning assets and equity reported in balance sheets.

So, what have we learned? We have learned that EBIT and EBT estimate earnings on beginning assets and equity respectively. EBIT and EBT should be used rather than changes in assets and equity to estimate asset and equity earnings because some changes in assets and equity may be unrelated to investment earnings. We estimate of ROA and ROE by dividing EBIT by A_0 and EBT by E_0 respectively.

AIS and IRR Models

IRR model definition. To build an IRR model, we reorganize an AIS into cash flow and changes in operating and capital accounts. This reorganization allows us to extend an AIS into an n period IRR model by separating n periods of cash flow from the liquidation of operating and capital accounts in the nth period.

Table 8.4 divides cash flow into cash receipts (CR) and cash expenses (CE). CR include cash sales from operations, reductions in accounts receivable ($\Delta AR < 0$), reductions in inventories held for sale ($\Delta Inv < 0$) and realized capital gains (RCG). CE include cash COGS, cash OEs, reductions in accounts payable ($\Delta AP < 0$), and reductions in accrued liabilities ($\Delta AL < 0$).

Table 8.4. HQN 2018 Cash Flow (Cash Receipts minus Cash Expenses)

+	Cash Receipts from Operations	$38,990
+	Realized Capital Gains (RCG)	$0
=	Cash Receipts (CR)	$38,990
+	Cash Cost of Goods Sold (COGS)	$27,000
+	Cash Operating Expenses (OE)	$11,078
=	Cash Expenses (CE)	$11,078
	CR – CE	$912

Table 8.5 records changes in operating accounts and depreciation. Changes in operating accounts include ΔAR, ΔInv, ΔAP, and ΔOE. Note that we include negative changes in operating accounts that produce CR and CE cash flow. We include changes in operating accounts regardless of their sign in Table 8.5 to assure that we are measuring returns and expenses when they occur.

Table 8.5. HQN 2018 Changes in Operating and Capital Accounts

+	Change in accounts receivable (ΔAR)	($440)
+	Change in inventories (ΔInv)	$1450
–	Change in accounts payable (ΔAP)	$1,000
–	Change in accrued liabilities (ΔAL)	($78)
=	Changes in operating accounts	$88
–	Depreciation (Dep)	$350
=	Changes in capital accounts	$350
=	Changes in operating and capital accounts	($262)

To summarize the calculations included in Tables 8.4 and 8.5 we express HQN's EBIT as the sum of cash flow and changes in operating and capital accounts:

$$EBIT = (CR - CE) + (\Delta AR + \Delta INV - \Delta AP - \Delta AL - Dep)$$

(8.5) $$= \$912 + (\$262) = \$650$$

Notice that the sum of cash flow (CR – CE) recorded in Table 8.4 of \$912 plus changes in operating and capital accounts ($\Delta AR + \Delta INV - \Delta AP - \Delta AL - Dep$) recorded in Table 8.5 of (\$262) equal EBIT of \$650 reported in Table 8.1. Were the capital assets sold and their liquidation value not equal to their book value, the difference in capital accounts would be recorded as realized capital gains or losses (RCG) and included in our cash flow measure.

Finally, the EBIT estimate of change in assets minus interest costs equals EBT, the estimate of HQN's change in equity:

(8.6) $$EBT = EBIT - Int = \$650 - \$480 = \$170$$

So, what have we learned? Total revenue in AIS include the difference between CR and CE and changes in operating and capital accounts plus RCG. CR includes cash sales plus reductions in AR ($\Delta AR<0$) and Inv ($\Delta Inv<0$) accounts. Cash expenses include cash COGS and OEs and reductions in AP ($\Delta AP<0$) and AL ($\Delta AL<0$) accounts. Changes in operating account include changes between the ending and beginning AR, Inv, AP, and AL accounts over the life of the analysis. When we do not intend to liquidate capital assets at the end of the analysis, we value them at their book value rather than their market value.

AIS and IRR^A Models

Single period IRR^A models. We found ROA and ROE from an AIS by dividing EBIT and EBT by beginning assets A_0 and equity E_0 respectively. We follow a similar procedure when we build PV models. We must account for the beginning value of assets and equity as well as relevant changes in their ending values, including only those changes that affect EBIT or EBT. We are not interested in explaining total changes in equity and assets over the periods of analysis, but only those changes that we can attribute to operating, investing, and financing activities. To that end, we rearrange equation (8.2) and write:

(8.7) $$A_0 ROA = EBIT$$

Now suppose that we add A_0 to both sides of equation (8.7) and after factoring, divide both sides of equation (8.7) by (1 + ROA) to obtain:

(8.8)

$$A_0 = \frac{A_0 + EBIT}{(1 + ROA)}$$
$$= \frac{A_0 + (CR_1 - CE_1) + (\Delta AR_1 + \Delta Inv_1 - \Delta AP_1 - \Delta AL_1 - Dep_1)}{(1 + ROA)}$$

We simplify equation (8.8) by substituting for A_0, the value of capital accounts V_0 plus the value of current asset accounts AR_0 and Inv_0 plus beginning cash balance Csh_0.

(8.9)

$$A_0 = \frac{V_0 + AR_0 + Inv_0 + Csh_0 + (CR_1 - CE_1) + (\Delta AR_1 + \Delta Inv_1 - \Delta AP_1 - \Delta AL_1 - Dep_1)}{(1 + ROA)}$$

We simplify equation (8.8) still more by recognizing that the value of capital assets V_0 less depreciation, Dep_1, equals the book value of capital assets V_1^{book} at the end of the period. However, if the capital assets are actually liquidated, then the liquidation value of capital assets can be written as $V_1^{liquidation}$ = V_0^{book} - Dep_1 + RCG. Furthermore, $AR_0 + \Delta AR_1 = AR_1$, and $Inv_0 + \Delta Inv_1 = Inv_1$. Now we can rewrite equation (8.9) as:

(8.10)

$$A_0 = \frac{(V_1^{liquidation} + AR_1 + Inv_1 + Csh_0 + (CR_1 - CE_1) - (\Delta AP_1 + \Delta AL_1)}{(1 + ROA)}$$

To write the multi-period equivalent of equation (8.10), we allow time subscripts to range from $t = 1$, ..., n periods. To convert cash flow and liquidated values of noncash operating and capital accounts to their present value, we discount them by $(1 + ROA)$. However, the discount rate in the multi-period equation is not the ROA derived from the one-period AIS but IRR^A, a multi-period average internal rate of return on assets, that we substitute for ROA. We summarize our results in equation (8.11):

$$A_0 = V_0 + AR_0 + Inv_0 + Csh_0$$
$$= \frac{CR_1 - CE_1}{(1 + IRR^A)} + \cdots + \frac{CR_n - CE_n}{(1 + IRR^A)^n}$$
$$+ \frac{V_n^{liquidation} + AR_n + Inv_n + Csh_0 - (AP_n - AP_0) - (AL_n - AL_0)}{(1 + IRR^A)^n}$$

To demonstrate equation (8.11) with data from HQN, we set n=1, replace IRR^A with ROA and write:

(8.12)

$$A_0 = \frac{CR_1 - CE_1}{(1 + ROA)}$$
$$+ \frac{V_1^{liquidation} + (AR_1 + Inv_1 + Csh_0) - (AP_1 - AP_0) - (AL_1 - AL_0)}{(1 + ROA)}$$
$$= \frac{\$38,990 - \$38,078}{(1.065)}$$
$$+ \frac{(\$3,400 - \$70) + (\$1,200 + \$5,200 + \$930) - \$1000 - \$78)}{(1.065)}$$
$$= \frac{\$10,650}{1.065} = \$10,000$$

To explain equation (8.12), we compare the result with HQN's AIS. We observe CR_1 less CE_1 produces $38,990 – $38,078 = $912 (see Table 8.1). Ending period long-term assets (LTA) equal $3,400 (see Table 8.2) from which we subtract purchases minus sales of LTA equal to $100 – $30 = $70. Ending account balances AR1 + Inv1 equal $1,200 + $5,200, and the beginning cash balance is $930. Next, we subtract changes in accounts payable of $1,000 and changes in accrued liabilities of ($78).

AIS and IRR^E Models

We computed ROE by subtracting from EBIT interest paid for the use of debt and divided the result by beginning equity, E_0. To find the multi-period IRR for equity, IRR^E, we subtract in each period t interest cost iD_{t-1} where D_{t-1} equals the firm's debt at the end of the previous period and i equals the average cost of debt. To find the amount of equity invested, we subtract from initial assets initial debt D_0. Outstanding debt during the period of analysis collects interest. No changes in debt occur in the last period and debt at the end of the t–1st period, D_{n-1}, is retired in the last period. Revising equation (8.10) to account for interest costs and debt and replacing ROE with IRR^E, we can find the multi-period equivalent of ROE, IRR^E. We write:

(8.13)

$$
\begin{aligned}
E + 0 &= V_0 + AR_0 + Inv_0 + Csh_0 - D_0 \\
&= \frac{(CR_1 - CE_1 - iD_0)}{(1 + IRR^E)} + \cdots + \frac{(CR_n - CE_n - iD_{n-1})}{(1 + IRR^E)^n} \\
&\quad + \frac{V_n^{liquidation} + AR_n + Inv_n + Csh_0 - (AP_n - AP_0) - (AL_n - AL_0) - D_0}{(1 + IRR^E)^n}
\end{aligned}
$$

To illustrate equation (8.13) with data from HQN, we set $n = 1$, replace IRR^E with ROE and write:

$$E_0 = \frac{CR_1 - CE_1 - iD_0}{(1 + ROE)}$$

$$+ \frac{V_1^{liquidation} + AR_1 + Inv_1 + Csh_0 - (AP_1 - AP_0) - (AL_1 - AL_0) - D_0}{(1 + ROE)}$$

$$= \frac{\$38,990 - \$38,078 - \$480}{(1.085)}$$

$$+ \frac{(\$3,400 - \$70) + \$1,200 + \$5,200 + \$930}{(1.085)}$$

$$- \frac{\$1,000 + (\$78) + \$8,000}{(1.085)}$$

$$= \frac{\$2,170}{1.085} = \$2,000$$

So, what have we learned? We have learned that the multi-period IRR^A and IRR^E models described in equations (8.11) and (8.13) follow AIS construction principles. Investing and borrowing recorded in AIS occur at the beginning of the period. Liquidation of investments and repayments occur at the end of the period. When we extend single period AIS to multi-period PV models, we must allow for multi-period repayments and borrowings and investing and disinvesting. We can easily extend equations (8.11) and (8.13) to account for these possibilities. However, wanting to maintain the focus of this paper on AIS and PV model connections, we omit these complications for now.

AIS Earnings and NPV Models

In the previous sections we derived multi-period IRR^A and IRR^E that correspond to ROA and ROE derived from a one period AIS and beginning assets and equity. Now we introduce multi-period NPV models that correspond to one period AIS earnings, EBIT, EBT, and NIAT. We begin by emphasizing the main difference between IRR and NPV models. IRR models find the rate of return earned by the investment or equity supporting the investment. NPV models measure the earnings realized by transferring funds from a defending investment, the investment in place, to a challenging investment, the investment being considered to replace the defending investment. Thus, NPV models convert multi-period future cash flow and changes in operating and capital accounts from a challenging investment for present dollars at the rate of one plus the defender's IRR, $(1 + IRR)$.

EBIT and NPV^A *earnings on assets.* We write NPV for asset earnings by rearranging equation (8.10) and by reinterpreting IRR^A as the internal rate of return on a defending investment.

(8.15)

$$
\begin{aligned}
NPV^A = -A_0 &+ \frac{CR_1 - CE_1}{(1 + IRR^A)} + \cdots + \frac{CR_n - CE_n}{(1 + IRR^A)^n} \\
&+ \frac{V_n^{liquidation} + AR_n + Inv_n + Csh_0 - (AP_n - AP_0) - (AL_n - AL_0)}{(1 + IRR^A)^n}
\end{aligned}
$$

To demonstrate equation (8.15) with HQN data, we set $n = 1$, replace IRR^A with ROA, and write:

(8.16)

$$NPV^A = -A_0 + \frac{CR_1 - CE_1}{(1 + ROA)}$$

$$+ \frac{V_1^{liquidation} + AR_1 + Inv_1 + Csh_0 - (AP_1 - AP_0) - (AL_1 - AL_0)}{(1 + ROA)}$$

$$= -\$10,000 + \frac{\$38,990 - \$38,078}{(1.065)}$$

$$+ \frac{(\$3,400 - \$70) + \$1,200 + \$5,200 + \$930}{(1.065)}$$

$$- \frac{\$1,000 + (\$78)}{(1.065)} = -\$10,000 + \frac{\$10,650}{1.065} = \$0$$

Notice that the NPV^A after exchanging funds from a defender with an identical challenger is zero. But if we found NPV at the end of one period, $(IRR^A)(A_0)$, the product would equal EBIT: $(.065)(\$10,000) =$ $\$650$ (see equation 8.5). These results emphasize that one important difference between AIS and NPV earnings is that AIS value earnings at the end of the period while PV models value earnings in the present. NPVs value earnings in the present because the present is where we live and make decisions. It should be obviously that if the defender's IRR were not equal to the challenger's IRR, then NPV^A would not equal zero. For example, suppose that in equation (8.15), the defender's IRR were 6%. Then NPV^A would equal $47.17.

EBT and NPVE earnings on equity. We write the NPV for equity earnings by rearranging equation (8.14) and by recognizing that IRR^E is the internal rate of return on equity for a defending investment.

(8.17)

$$
\begin{aligned}
NPV^E &= -(A_0 - D_0) \\
&= -(V_0 + AR_0 + Inv_0 + Csh_0) + D_0 \\
&\quad + \frac{(CR_1 - CE_1 - iD_0)}{(1 + IRR^E)} + \cdots + \frac{(CR_n - CE_n - iD_{n-1})}{(1 + IRR^E)^n} \\
&\quad + \frac{V_n^{liquidation} + AR_n + Inv_n + Csh_0 - (AP_n - AP_0) - (AL_n - AL_0) - D_0}{(1 + IRR^E)^n}
\end{aligned}
$$

To illustrate equation (8.17) with data from HQN, we set n=1, replace IRR^E with ROE, and write:

(8.18)

$$NPV^E = -E_0 + \frac{CR_1 - CE_1 - iD_0}{(1 + ROE)}$$

$$+ \frac{V_1^{liquidation} + AR_1 + Inv_1 + Csh_0 - (AP_1 - AP_0) - (AL_1 - AL_0) - D_0}{(1 + ROE)}$$

$$= -\$2,000 + \frac{\$38,990 - \$38,078 - \$480}{(1.085)}$$

$$+ \frac{(\$3,400 - \$70) + \$6,400 + \$930}{(1.085)}$$

$$- \frac{\$1,000 + (\$78) + \$8,000)}{(1.085)}$$

$$= -\$2,000 + \frac{\$2,170}{1.085} = \$0$$

Like the results obtained for NPV^A, NPV^E from exchanging funds from a defender with an identical challenger is zero. But if we found NPV^E at the end of one period, $(IRR^E) \times (E_0)$, the product would equal EBT: $(.085) \times (\$2,0000) = \$170$ (see equation 8.6). It should be obvious that if the defender's IRR were not equal to the challenger's IRR, that NPV^E would not equal zero. For example, suppose that in equation (8.18), the defender's IRR were 8%. Then NPV^E would equal $9.26.

So, what have we learned? We have learned that EBIT corresponds to NPV^A. EBT corresponds to NPV^E. We have also learned that IRR and NPV models are distinguished by their reinvestment rate assumptions. IRR models assume that cash flow is reinvested in the challenger and earn the challenger's IRR. NPV models assume that cash flow is reinvested in the defender and earn the defender's IRR. Because cash flow in IRR models is discounted and reinvested at the same rate, NPVs or IRR earnings either from assets or equity are always zero.

After-tax ROE and ROA

PV models often focus on after-tax cash flow because it represents what firms/investors keep after paying all their expenses including taxes. In what follows we present tax obligations in a simplified form to illustrate their impact on earnings and rates of return. Our goal is to find the average tax rate T that adjusts ROE to ROE(1–T) and T* that adjusts ROA to ROA(1–T*). We do not try to duplicate the complicated processes followed by taxing authorities to find T and T*. Instead we suggest that the firm pays an average tax rate T or T* on EBT and EBIT respectively.

AIS report taxes paid by the firm and subtracts them from EBT to obtain NIAT. We calculate interest costs by multiplying the average interest rate i times beginning period debt D_{t-1} (iD_{t-1}) and subtract them from earnings to reduce tax obligations. As a result, NIAT represents changes in equity after both interest and taxes have been paid. In 2018, HQN paid $68 in taxes. To find the average tax rate HQN paid on its changes in equity we set taxes equal to the average tax rate T times EBT:

$$\text{(8.19)} \quad \text{Taxes} = (T)(EBT) = \$68$$

Solving for the average tax rate T that HQN paid on its earnings we find:

$$\text{(8.20)} \quad T = \frac{\text{Taxes}}{EBT} = \frac{\$68}{\$170} = 40\%$$

Finally, we adjust ROE for taxes and find HQN's after-tax ROE to be:

$$\text{(8.21)} \quad ROE(1-T) = \frac{NIAT}{E_0} = \frac{\$102}{\$2,000} = 5.1\%$$

AIS and After-tax ROAs. An AIS computes taxes paid by the firm on its return to equity but not on its return to assets. They record only one value for taxes paid and these estimates account for tax saving resulting from interest payments. As a result, we cannot use the average tax rate T calculated for taxes paid on equity earnings to adjust ROA for taxes. To find the average tax rate T* that adjusts ROA to ROA(1 − T*), we calculate taxes "as if" there were no interest costs to reduce the average tax rate to T*. We find ROA(1 − T*) in equation (8.16) as:

$$(8.22) \quad ROA(1 - T*) = \frac{(EBIT - \text{Taxes})}{A_0} = \frac{(\$650 - \$68)}{\$10,000} = 5.8\%$$

Solving for T* we find:

$$(8.23) \quad T* = 1 - \frac{(EBIT - \text{Taxes})}{EBIT} = 1 - \frac{(\$650 - \$68)}{\$650} = 10.5\%$$

Equation (8.23) emphasizes an important point: adjusting ROE and ROA for taxes nearly always requires different average tax rates. The only time that T = T* is when interest costs are zero. In that case, we can easily demonstrate that T* = T since EBIT = EBT:

$$(8.24) \quad T = T* = \frac{\text{Taxes}}{EBIT} = \frac{\text{Taxes}}{EBT} = 10.5\%$$

After-tax Multiperiod IRR$^{E(1-T)}$ Model

We are now prepared to introduce taxes into the IRR^E model described in equation (8.13). We begin by solving for NIAT in equation (8.21) and replacing ROE(1-T) with IRR^E(1 − T):

$$(8.25) \quad NIAT = E_0 ROE(1 - T) = E_0 IRR^E(1 - T)$$

Next, we write NIAT as EBIT adjusted for both interest costs and taxes:

$$(8.26) \quad NIAT = (EBIT - Int)(1 - T)$$

Then, we substitute for EBIT the right-hand side of equation (8.5) and for NIAT, the right-hand side of equation (8.25) and add time subscripts. The result is equation (8.27).

$$(8.27) \quad \begin{aligned} E_0 ROE(1 - T) \\ = [(CR_1 - CE_1 - Int_1) \\ + (\Delta AR_1 + \Delta Inv_1 - \Delta AP_1 - \Delta AL_1 - Dep_1)](1 - T) \end{aligned}$$

Finally, we add E_0 to both sides of equation (8.27) and after factoring $[1 + ROE(1 - T)]$ and dividing both sides of equation (8.27) by the factor, we obtain:

(8.28)

$$E_0 = \frac{E_0 + [(CR_1 - CE_1 - Int_1) + (\Delta AR_1 + \Delta Inv_1 - \Delta AP_1 - \Delta AL_1 - Dep_1)](1 - T)}{[1 + ROE(1 - T)]}$$

Replacing E_0 with $Csh_0 + AR_0 + Inv_0 + V_0 - D_0$ in the numerator of (8.28), we can write:

$$E_0 = \frac{Csh_0 + AR_0 + Inv_0 + V_0 - D_0 + [(CR_1 - CE_1 - Int_1)}{[1 + ROE(1 - T)]}$$
$$+ \frac{(\Delta AR_1 + \Delta Inv_1 - \Delta AP_1 - \Delta AL_1 - Dep_1)](1 - T)}{[1 + ROE(1 - T)]}$$

(8.29)

Finally, we simplify equation (8.29) by recognizing that

(8.30) $\quad V_0 - Dep_1(1 - T) = V_1^{book} + TDep_1,$

(8.31) $\quad Int_1 = iD_0,$ and

$$AR_0 + Inv_0 + (\Delta AR_1 + \Delta Inv_1)(1 - T)$$
(8.32) $\quad = T(AR_0 + Inv_0) + (1 - T)(AR_1 + Inv_1).$

These simplifications allow us to rewrite equation (8.29) as:

(8.33)

$$E_0 = \frac{Csh_0 - D_0 + T(AR_0 + Inv_0) + (1-T)(AR_1 + Inv_1) + V_1^{book} + TDep_1}{[1 + ROE(1-T)]}$$
$$+ \frac{[(CR_1 - CE_1 - iD_0) - (\Delta AP_1 + \Delta AL_1)](1-T)}{[1 + ROE(1-T)]}$$

To verify our results, we substitute HQN numerical values into equation (8.33) and find:

$$E_0 = \frac{\$930 - \$8,000 + [.4(\$1,640 + \$3,750)]}{(1.051)}$$
$$+ \frac{[.6(\$1,200 + \$5,200)] + (\$3,400 - \$70) + [.6(\$350)]}{(1.051)}$$
$$+ \frac{[(\$38,990 - \$38,078 - \$480) - (\$1,000 - \$78)].6}{(1.051)} = \$2,000$$

(8.34)

To write the multi-period equivalent of equation (8.34) we discount n periods of operating income and in the nth period we liquidate operating and capital accounts and replace ROE(1 – T) with IRR^E(1 – T).

$$E_0 = \frac{(CR_1 - CE_1 - iD_0)(1 - T) + TDep_1}{[1 + IRR^E(1 - T)]}$$

$$+ \cdots + \frac{(CR_n - CE_n - iD_{n-1})(1 - T) + TDep_n}{[1 + IRR^E(1 - T)]^n}$$

$$+ \frac{Csh_0 - D_0 + T(AR_0 + Inv_0) + (1 - T)(AR_n + Inv_n)}{[1 + IRR^E(1 - T)]^n}$$

$$(8.35) \qquad + \frac{V_n^{book} - (AP_n - AP_0 + AL_n - AL_0)(1 - T)}{[1 + IRR^E(1 - T)]^n}$$

Capital gains (losses) and taxes. At the end of the analysis, PV models value their capital assets at their book value, or if they liquidate them, they value them at their liquidation value $V_n^{liquidation}$. For tax purposes, if the difference between the liquidation and book value of capital assets is positive, $(V_n^{liquidation} - V_n^{book}) > 0$, the firm or the investment has realized capital gains whose after-tax value is $(1 - T)(V_n^{liquidation} - V_n^{book}) > 0$. On the other hand, if the difference is negative $(V_n^{liquidation} - V_n^{book}) < 0$, then the firm has realized a capital loss and earned tax credits whose after-tax value loss is $(1 - T)(V_n^{liquidation} - V_n^{book}) < 0$. To simplify the tax discussion, we ignore the tax rate differences between income, capital gains, and depreciation recapture and apply only one tax rate T, the average of all tax rates. Finally, to adjust capital accounts for taxes, we replace V_n^{book} in equation (8.28) with what follows:

$$(8.36) \qquad (1 - T)(V_n^{liquidation} - V_n^{book}) + V_n^{book} = (1 - T)V_n^{liquidation} + TV_n^{book}$$

Now we can write the after-tax IRRE model for changes in equity consistent with AIS construction principles.

(8.37)

$$E_0 = \frac{(CE_1 - CE_1 - iD_0)(1 - T) + TDep_1}{[1 + IRR^E(1 - T)]}$$
$$+ \cdots + \frac{(CR_n - CE_n - iD_{n-1})(1 - T) + TDep_n}{[1 + IRR^E(1 - T)]^n}$$
$$+ \frac{Csh_0 - D_0 + T(AR_0 + Inv_0) + (1 - T)(AR_n + Inv_n)}{[1 + IRR^E(1 - T)]^n}$$
$$+ \frac{(1 - T)V_n^{liquidation} + TV_n^{book} - (AP_n - AP_0 + AL_n - AL_0)(1 - T)}{[1 + IRR^E(1 - T)]^n}$$

So, what have we learned? We have learned that taxes are intended to be charged on earnings including the cost (interest) of using borrowed funds that support the investment. While most expenses are incurred in exchanges for nondurable goods that are used up in the period's production, capital investments are only used up over several periods. To account for the periodic costs of using capital assets, we include depreciation as a cost when finding earnings and rates of return. We also use depreciation to generate tax savings.

After-tax Multi-period $IRR^A(1-T^*)$ Model

There is no explicit measure for T* that can be used to find ROA(1 − T*). This peculiar result occurs because taxes must account for interest costs that we do not consider when finding EBIT. Yet, many applied IRR models solve for after-tax return on assets that assume we can measure ROA(1 − T*). Still, we can find such a measure from an AIS allowing us to write:

(8.38)

$$
\begin{aligned}
A_0 &= \frac{(CR_1 - CE_1)(1 - T*) + T * Dep_1}{[1 + IRR^A(1 - T*)]} \\
&+ \cdots + \frac{(CR_n - CE_n)(1 - T*) + T * Dep_n}{[1 + IRR^A(1 - T*)]^n} \\
&+ \frac{Csh_0 + T * Accts_0 + (1 - T*)Accts_n}{[1 + IRR^A(1 - T*)]^n} \\
&+ \frac{(1 - T*)V_n^{liquidation} + T * V_n^{book} - (AP_n - AP_0 + AL_n - AL_0)(1 - T*)}{[1 + IRR^A(1 - T*)]^n}
\end{aligned}
$$

The main difference between equations (8.37) and (8.38) is that T is replaced with T*, interest charges are not subtracted from periodic cash flow, and initial liabilities are no longer subtracted. All these changes are required so that earnings can be attributed to beginning assets rather than beginning equity.

Although there is no explicit AIS measure corresponding to equation (8.38), we do know the value of beginning assets A_0 and IRR^A (1 − T*) so we can write the one period HQN numerical equivalent of (8.38) assuming capital assets are valued at their book value:

$$A_0 = \frac{Csh_0 + T * Accts_0 + (1 - T*)Accts_1 + V_1^{book} + T * Dep_1}{[1 + ROA(1 - T*)]}$$
$$+ \frac{[(CR_1 - CE_1) - (\Delta AP_1 + \Delta AL_1)](1 - T*)}{[1 + ROA(1 - T*)]}$$
$$= \frac{\$930 + \$565.95 + \$5,728 + \$3,330 + \$36.75}{(1.058)}$$
$$+ \frac{[(\$38,990 - \$38,078) - (\$1,000 - \$78)].895}{(1.058)}$$

(8.39)
$$= \$10,000$$

So, what have we learned? We have learned that AIS do not find after-tax earnings on assets because tax laws account for interest payments which are not considered on returns to assets. Still, it is popular to find after-tax rates of return and earnings on assets which requires a special calculation to find the equivalent average after-tax rate.

Rates of Return on Assets and Equity

Miller and Bradford (2000) reviewed and compared rates of return on assets and equity. We agree with their conclusion that the two measures should be viewed as complementary. To describe the relationship between ROE and ROA, we begin with equations (8.2) and (8.3) that employ AIS definitions of ROA and ROE. From these two equations we deduce the rates of return identity:

(8.40)

$$ROE = \frac{EBIT - Int}{E_0} = \frac{(ROA)(A_0) - (i)(D_0)}{E_0} = \frac{(ROA - i)D_0}{E_0} + ROA$$

Note that in equation (8.40) if i = ROA or if D_0 = 0 then ROE = ROA. Note also that ROE and ROA are positively related. Furthermore, if we solve for ROA as a function of ROE, we find the familiar weighted cost of capital (WCC) equation that we illustrate using HQN data:

$$ROA = ROE\left(\frac{E_0}{A_0}\right) + i\left(\frac{D_0}{A_0}\right)$$

$$= 8.5\%\left(\frac{\$2,000}{\$10,000}\right) + 6\%\left(\frac{\$8,000}{\$10,000}\right) = 6.5\%$$

(8.41)

Of course, we are less confident about the relationships in equations (8.40) and (8.41) when measured in multi-period settings where ROA is replaced with IRR^A and ROE is replaced with IRR^E and interest rates and asset and debt levels may vary over time.

We emphasize that both ROA and ROE provide interesting and important information. Financial managers should be interested in what firms and investments can earn independent of how they are financed. Then, if the difference between return on assets and the cost of debt matters, as it should, ROE provides important information for choosing between alternative financing options.

So, what have we learned? We have learned that by adjusting liabilities, interest costs, and tax rates, we can derive PV earning measures corresponding to NIAT, EBIT, and EBT measures calculated in AIS. This provides us an interesting interpretation of PV models. Discounting after-tax multi-period earnings on equity provides a measure corresponding the present value of future NIAT calculations. Discounting before-tax multi-period earnings on assets provides a measure corresponding the present value of future EBIT calculations. Finally, discounting before-tax multi-period earnings on equity provides a measure corresponding the present value of future EBT calculations

Conflicting Asset and Equity Earnings and Rates of Return Rankings

Suppose we are comparing two mutually exclusive challengers, 1 and 2, funded by the same defender and earning rates of return on invested assets of $ROA^1 > ROA^2$. Do these results imply that $ROE^1 > ROE^2$? That NPV earnings from assets invested in challengers 1 and 2 satisfy $NPV^{A1} > NPV^{A2}$? Or, that NPV earnings from equity invested in challengers 1 and 2 satisfy $NPV^{E1} > NPV^{E2}$?

The answer is that earnings and rates of return on assets and equity are consistent only under limited conditions. These include, A_0 and E_0 must satisfy homogeneity of size conditions and the average interest cost i must be the same for both investments. We demonstrate that if the homogeneity and average interest rate conditions are satisfied, then $ROA^1 > ROA^2$ implies $ROE^1 > ROE^2$, $NPV^{A2} > NPV^{A1}$, and $NPV^{E1} > NPV^{E2}$. To begin, recall equation (8.41) that allows us to write:

(8.42)

$$ROA^1 - ROA^2 = ROE^1 \left(\frac{E_0}{A_0} \right) + i \left(\frac{D_0}{A_0} \right) - ROE^2 \left(\frac{E_0}{A_0} \right) + i \left(\frac{D_0}{A_0} \right)$$
$$= (ROE^1 - ROE^2) \left(\frac{E_0}{A_0} \right)$$

Therefore, if $ROA^1 > ROA^2$, then $ROE^1 > ROE^2$. Next, if $ROA^1 > ROA^2$, then from equation (8.2), it follows that $EBIT^1 > EBIT^2$ and $NPV^{A1} > NPV^{A2}$ since:

$$NPV^{A1} - NPV^{A2} = \frac{EBIT^1 - EBIT^2}{(1 + ROA)} > 0$$
(8.43)

Finally, if $EBIT^1 > EBIT^2$ and interest costs are the same for both investments, then $EBT^1 > EBT^2$ and $NPV^{E1} > NPV^{E2}$ since:

$$NPV^{E1} - NPV^{E2} = \frac{EBIT^1 - EBIT^2}{(1 + ROE)}$$
(8.44)

Conflicting rankings may occur when interest rates or debt levels financing the two challengers differ. To illustrate, suppose we decided to rank challengers 1 and 2 that satisfied homogeneity of size conditions for assets and equity and whose ROA1 and ROA2 were equal. Now assume that interest costs for the two investments differed. Then we would rank the two investments based on their asset earnings and rates of return as equal. But for rankings based on equity earnings and rates of return, the investment with the lower interest cost would be preferred. The consequence is that asset-based rankings would be equal and equity-based rankings would be unequal and asset and equity-based rankings would be inconsistent.

To make clear that asset and equity earnings and rates of return may produce conflicting rankings, consider HQN's one-period ROA of 6.5% ($650/$10,000) and its one-period ROE of 8.5% ($170/$2,000) respectively. Let HQN's beginning assets and EBIT describe both investments 1 and 2. Now suppose that interest costs for investments 1 and 2 differed. For example, let the average interest rate charged on investment 1 be 6% and 0% for investment 2. As a result, the IRR^E and NPV^E rankings would no longer be consistent with IRRA and NPV^A rankings for investments 1 and 2. We summarize these results in Table 8.6.

Table 8.6. HQN's Inconsistent rankings based on asset and equity earnings and rates of return.

	Investment 1	Investment 2
Asset earnings and rates of return (rankings)		
NPV^A (rankings)	EBIT=$650 (1)	>EBIT=$650 (1)
IRR^A (rankings)	$650/$10,000=6.5% (1)	>$650/$10,000=6.5% (1)
Equity earnings and rates of return (rankings)		
NPV^E (rankings)	EBT=$170 (2)	EBT=$650 (1)
IRR^E (rankings)	$170/$2,000=8.5% (2)	$650/$2,000=32.5% (1)

One can imagine other less extreme cases in which asset and equity rankings could be inconsistent simply because interest cost influence earnings and rates of return on equity but not for assets.

So, what have we learned? We have learned that earnings and rates of return measures for assets and equity need not provide consistent rankings. As a result, financial managers must carefully whether investment decisions should depend on asset or equity earnings. At the heart of this decision is the importance of debt and interest charges in making investment decisions.

Summary and Conclusions

We now make explicit the main point of this paper. PV models should be constructed as multi-period extensions of AIS. Otherwise, they may misrepresent the financial characteristics of investments and may lead to less than optimal investment decisions. Furthermore, different AIS earnings and rates of return help us distinguish between different NPV models and IRR. These distinctions are important since asset and earning measures on assets and equity may lead to different recommendations.

We emphasize that AIS help us recognize the conditions required for asset and equity earnings and rates of return rankings to be consistent. These insights that we learn from AIS and multi-period extensions of AIS, we believe will help financial managers better understand, build, and interpret PV models. However, these results, also task financial managers with the responsibility to carefully decide whether to base their recommendation on asset or equity earnings and rates of return.

Using the PV models developed in this paper, we can imagine financial managers building Excel templates or similar computerized support systems to solve applied investment problems that include more details than we were able to include in our demonstrations. These details may include more complete description of taxes and allow more investments and disinvestments to occur during the analysis. We wish you all success in this effort—to develop and apply PV models that represent multi-period extensions of AIS.

Questions

1. How does this chapter define present value models?
2. Describe two similarities and distinctions between AIS and PV models.
3. Discuss the following statement. AIS find earnings at the end of the period. PV models value earnings in present dollar equivalents.
4. AIS EBIT and EBT measure earnings on beginning assets and equity respectively. Do these measures equal the actual change in beginning assets and equity? If not, explain why not?
5. Please consider the following statement. AIS value cash flows and liquidation of operating and capital accounts at the end of one period. IRR models find the present value of cash flow earnings over several periods and the liquidation of operating and capital account that occurs in the last period. Explain why this difference between AIS and PV models is required. (Hint: why do we limit AIS earning measures to one period while PV models find the present value of investment earnings over several periods.
6. What is the main difference between IRR^A models and IRR^E models?
7. One important difference between IRR models and NPV models is their reinvestment rate assumptions. Please describe the reinvestment rate assumptions for IRR and NPV models. What is the NPV value for IRR models?
8. The cost of operating inputs is included in PV models in the period in which they are paid for with cash. Explain how depreciation estimates the cost of using up capital inputs.
9. Explain the difference between the average tax rate used to find the after-tax rate of return on equity versus the average tax rate used to find the after-tax rate of return on assets. Also explain why AIS compute earnings on assets (EBIT), equity (EBT), and after-tax earnings on equity (NIAT)–but do not calculate after-tax earnings on assets?
10. Using the rate of return identify find ROE if ROA=7%, beginning assets are $10,000, the average interest rate is 6%, and liabilities are 75% of assets.
11. List sufficient conditions that guarantee that earnings and rates of return on asset will generate the same rankings as earnings and rates of return on equity.

12. If earnings and rates of return on assets and equity provided conflicting rankings, which earnings and rates of return measures would you rely on to choose your investment, on assets or on equity? Defend your preference for either asset or equity rankings.
13. Use the template described in the appendix to this chapter to find NPV on assets for the following investment.

Appendix to Present Value Models & Accrual Income Statements

Open Green & White Services Excel PV Template

A *generalized NPV equation*. This appendix operationalizes the concepts presented in this chapter by presenting a generalized present value (PV) template. The PV template corresponds to an accrual income statement (AIS) that measures after-tax returns on equity described in equation (8.37). To solve equation (8.37) for NPVE(1–T) using a generalized PV template, we replace beginning equity E_0 with beginning assets A_0 minus beginning liabilities D0 and discount future cash flow using the defender's after-tax internal rate of return on equity IRRE(1–T) and by subtracting equity $(A_0 - D_0)$ from both sides of the equation. We rewrite the results as:

(8.A1)

$$NPV^{E(1-T)} = -(A_0 - D_0) + \frac{(CR_1 - CE_1 - iD_0)(1-T) + TDep_1}{[1 + IRR^E(1-T)]}$$
$$+ \cdots + \frac{(CR_n - CE_n - iD_{n-1})(1-T) + TDep_n}{[1 + IRR^E(1-T)]^n}$$
$$+ \frac{Csh_0 - D_0 + TAccts_0 + (1-T)Accts_n}{[1 + IRR^E(1-T)]^n}$$
$$+ \frac{(1-T)V_n^{liquidation} + TV_n^{book} - [AP_n - AP_0 + AL_n - AL_0](1-T)}{[1 + IRR^E(1-T)]^n}$$

A generalized PV template for finding rolling earnings and rates of return on equity. We now introduce the generalized NPV template corresponding to equation (8.A1). To demonstrate the template, we use data from the Green and White Services investment problem to be introduced in Chapter 10 and re-present the defender by solving HQN's ROE, ROA, T, and T*.

Table 8.A1. A generalized PV model template wit

	A	B	C	D	E	F	G	H	I	J	
1	Year	Assets	Debt Capital	Capital Accounts Liquidation Value	Capital Accounts book value	Depreciation (Dep=ΔE)	Asset Operating accounts (AR+INV)	Sales	Cash Receipts (CR=H+ΔG)	Liability Operating Accounts (AP+AL)	Ex (CC OE
2	0	$40000	$32000	$40000	$40000						
3	1	$0	$27200	$30000	$30000	$10000	$1000	$20000	$19000	$0	
4	2	$0	$22200	$15000	$15000	$15000	$1200	$30200	$30000	$0	$
5	3	$0	$17200	$5000	$5000	$10000	$800	$35600	$36000	$0	$
6	4	$0	$12200	$0	$0	$5000	$400	$39600	$40000	$0	$

Defender data obtained from HQN is represented in Table 8.A2 below.

Table 8.A2. Defender's IRR^E, average tax rate T paid on its equity earnings, and average interest "i" rate paid on its liabilities.

	A	B
1	IRR^E	0.085
2	T	0.4
3	$IRR^E(1-T)$	0.051
4	average interest rate i	0.06

Finally, we present in Table 8.A3 GWS equity generated after-tax cash flow during its four years of operation and corresponding after-tax internal rates of return.

Table 8.A3. GWS equity generated after-tax cash flow during its four years of operations and corresponding after-tax internal rates of return.

	A	B	C	D	E
1	Economic Life	1 year	2 years	3 years	4 years
2		-$8,000.00	-$8,000.00	-$8,000.00	-$8,000.00
3		$7,448.00	$4,048.00	$4,048.00	$4,048.00
4		-6.90%	$3,440.80	$9,920.80	$9,920.80
5			3.03%	-$1,819.20	$9,900.80
6				31.67%	-$2,379.20
7					64.79%

The results of Table 8.A3 should remind us of the nature of the IRR calculation. After having calculated an investment's IRR in year t, any positive cash flow in later periods, will increase the investment's IRR. In the case of GWS, cash flow differ in the last year but still add to the calculated IRR value.

Detailed description of Table 8.A1. The column headings in Table 8.A1 describe exogenous and endogenous variables used to find rolling (every year) NPV and annuity equivalent (AE) estimates and correspond to variables in equation (8.A1). Highlighted data are exogenous often obtained from coordinated financial statements or projected. Data not highlighted are endogenous or calculated. Projecting values in Table 8.A1 is a subject to which we will return in Chapter 11. Now we will describe in more detail the values in Table 8.A1 and their correspondence to variables in equation (8.A1). Columns are indicated by highlighted letters in column titles.

- Column A indicates the period t at the end of which financial activity occurs and values are recorded.
- Column B line 4 lists total investment amount A_0 including beginning cash C_0, beginning accounts receivable and inventories $(AR_0 + Inv_0)$, plus capital investments V_0.
- Column C line 4 lists beginning current liabilities and noncurrent long-term liabilities D_0 supporting the firm's assets on which interest is paid. Subsequent values in Column C list the amount of outstanding liabilities in each period.
- Column D lists the liquidation value of capital investments. Since Table 8.A1 calculates rolling after-tax estimates of NPV, AE, and IRR, we are required to estimate the liquidated value of the investment in each period.
- Column E lists the book value of capital investments determined by the initial purchase price and depreciation percentages reported by taxing authorities.
- Column F calculates depreciation equal to the change in the investment's book value.

- Column G lists the value of accounts receivable AR_t and inventory Inv_t at the end of period t.
- Column H lists total sales during period t.
- Column I calculates cash receipts CR_t in period t by adjusting total sales for changes in inventories and accounts receivable.
- Column J lists the value of accounts payable AP_t and accrued liabilities AL_t at the end of period t.
- Column K lists expenses in period t equal to the cost of goods $COGS_t$ plus overhead expenses OE_t.
- Column L calculates cash expenses CE_t in period t adjusted for changes in accounts payable and accrued liabilities.
- Column M calculates interest costs iD_{t-1} by multiplying periodic liabilities at the end of the previous period D_{t-1} by the average interest rate i.
- Column N calculates tax savings from depreciation equal to the average tax rate time depreciation in the previous period
- Column O calculates after-tax cash flow from operations in period t, equal to $(CR_t - CE_t - iD_{t-1})(1-T) + TDep_{t-1} + \Delta D_t)$. Note that the change in outstanding debt is included because of its impact on cash flow.
- Column P calculates cash flow from after-tax liquidation of changes in asset operating accounts $(AR_n + Inv_n - AR_0 - Inv_0)(1 - T)$.
- Column Q calculates cash flow from after-tax liquidation of changes in liability operating account $(AP_n - AP_0 + AL_n - AL_0)(1 - T)$.
- Column R calculates the cash flow from after-tax liquidation of capital and asset and liability operating accounts.
- Column S sums cash flow from after-tax liquidations plus operating cash flow in the last period, required for finding rolling NPV, AE, and IRR values.
- Column T calculates rolling after-tax NPVs as though the investment ended in each year using Excel NPV equation by finding the NPV from operations and liquidations.
- Column U calculates rolling after-tax AEs associated with the after-tax NPVs for each period using Excel PMT function by finding the payment whose present value equals after-tax NPV for the corresponding period.
- Column V calculates rolling after-tax IRRs for each year using Excel IRR function. To find the annual IRRs we calculate the after-tax cash flow for each possible age of the investment reported in Table 8.A2.

Adjusting the PV template to calculate after-tax earnings and rates of return on assets. AIS statements compute earnings before interest and taxes (EBIT), earnings before taxes (EBT), and net income after taxes (NIAT). Table 8.A1 finds the PV model equivalent of NIAT. However, there is no AIS equivalent earnings measure that corresponds to after-tax NPV measures reported in Table 8.A4. This is because taxes paid are reduced by interest costs. However, in this chapter, Chapter 8, we found a method for finding the equivalent average tax rate paid on earnings from assets that enabled us to find rolling after-tax NPVs, AEs, and IRRs for assets.

To adjust equation 8.A1 to find the after-tax earnings and rates of return for assets, we set D_0 equal to zero, we replace the defender's after-tax IRR for equity $IRR^E(1-T)$ with the defender's after-tax return on assets IRR^A(1–T*), and we replace the average tax rate T on equity with the average tax rate T* on assets. The revised after-tax NPV calculation for assets is reported as equation 8.A2:

(8.A2)

$$
\begin{aligned}
NPV^{A(1-T*)} = -A_0 &+ \frac{(CR_1 - CE_1)(1 - T*) + T * Dep_1}{[1 + IRR^A(1 - T*)]} \\
&+ \cdots + \frac{(CR_n - CE_n)(1 - T*) + T * Dep_n)}{[1 + IRR^A(1 - T*)]^n} \\
&+ \frac{Csh_0 + T * Accts_0 + (1 - T*)Accts_n}{[1 + IRR^A(1 - T*)]^n} \\
&+ \frac{(1 - T*)V_n^{liquidation} + T * V_n^{book} - [AP_n - AP_0 + AL_n - AL_0](1 - T*)}{[1 + IRR^A(1 - T*)]^n}
\end{aligned}
$$

The PV template equivalent to equation 8.A2 is reported in Table 8.A4.

Table 8.A4. A generalized PV model template wit

	A	B	C	D	E	F	G	H	I	J	
1	Year	Assets	Debt Capital	Capital Accounts Liquidation Value	Capital Accounts book value	Depreciation (Dep=ΔE)	Asset Operating accounts (AR+INV)	Sales	Cash Receipts (CR=H+ΔG)	Liability Operating Accounts (AP+AL)	Exp (CO OE)
2	0	$40000	$0	$40000	$40000						
3	1	$0	$0	$30000	$30000	$10000	$1000	$20000	$19000	$0	$
4	2	$0	$0	$15000	$15000	$15000	$1200	$30200	$30000	$0	$
5	3	$0	$0	$5000	$5000	$10000	$800	$35600	$36000	$0	$
6	4	$0	$0	$0	$0	$5000	$400	$39600	$40000	$0	$

Defender data obtained from HQN is represented in Table 8.A5 below.

Table 8.A5. Defender's IRR[A], average tax rate T* paid on its assets earnings and average interest i (although irrelevant for the calculations in Table 8.A4).

	A	B
1	IRR[A]	0.065
2	T*	0.105
3	IRRA(1-T*)	0.0582
4	average interest rate i	0.06

Finally, we present GWS asset generated after-tax cash flow during its four years of operation and corresponding after-tax internal rates of return.

Table 8.A6. GWS asset generated after-tax cash flow during its four years of operations and corresponding after-tax internal rates of return.

	A	B	C	D	E
1	Economic Life	1 year	2 years	3 years	4 years
2		-$40,000.00	-$40,000.00	-$40,000.00	-$40,000.00
3		$40,600.00	$10,000.00	$10,000.00	$10,000.00
4		1.50%	$31,620.00	$15,900.00	$15,900.00
5			3.03%	$21,180.00	$15,700.00
6				7.63%	$15,440.00
7					14.85%

So, what have we learned? This appendix demonstrated how the PV equations consistent with AIS earnings and rates of return can be operationalized using Excel formulas. The corresponding PV templates demonstrated here could be found at links to this chapter. In general, the templates employ the same level of aggregation as employed when calculating AIS statements. This level of aggregation can be adapted depending on the user's needs. However, it should be kept in mind that financial ratios used to compare firms within the industry also employ the level of aggregation employed here.

9. Evaluating Investment Opportunities: Applying Present Value Models   LINDON ROBISON

Learning goals. At the end of this chapter, you should be able to: (1) organize present value (PV) models by the questions they answer; (2) organize PV models by their unknown endogenous variables; and (3) solve practical PV problems using appropriate PV models.

Learning objectives. To reach your learning goals, you should complete the following objectives:

- Distinguish between different kinds of PV models including:
  - net present value (NPV),
  - internal rate of return (IRR),
  - maximum (minimum) bid (sell),
  - annuity equivalent (AE),
  - loan formula,
  - optimal term,
  - replacement,
  - incremental,
  - capitalized value,
  - break-even,
  - payback.
- Describe the unknown endogenous variable that defines PV models.
- Describe the kinds of questions different PV models can answer.
- Use Excel financial formulas to solve the different kinds of PV models described in this chapter.

Introduction

Earlier, we said that a PV model is a multi-period extension of an accrual income statement (AIS) that rates future cash flows as if they were received in the present. Just like different AISs find different ways to measure earnings and rates of return, different PV models find different ways to measure earnings, rates of return, and more. Also, different kinds of PV models are made to answer different kinds of questions.

Kinds of PV Models

Comparative advantage. Think about yourself driving a fancy car or a tractor across the country. Imagine yourself pulling a plough with a luxury car or truck instead. Even though both a high-end car

Even though both a car and a truck can move things and pull things, they are not equally good at each job. Economists use the term "comparative advantage" to talk about activities that a company can do, but not all of them are as good as others. Luxury cars are great for cross-country trips, but not for pulling a snow plough. A tractor is made to pull a plough, but it isn't good for going far distances. In the same way, there are different types of PV models. Each model is better than the others at answering different kinds of questions. In the next section, we'll look at some of the most important PV models and how they can be used to answer questions.

What sets one PV model apart from another. PV models have one equation and are made to find one unknown variable. Different types of PV models can be told apart by the one unknown variable they're trying to find. The PV model and unknown variable we want to find depend on the questions we want to answer. Here, we'll talk about the NPV, IRR, maximum (minimum) bid (sell), annuity equivalent (AE), break-even, optimum life and replacement, and payback models. We also say what question each is meant to solve. We stress that each type of PV model solves for one unknown variable that tells us what type of PV model it is.

Net Present Value Models

NPV models find the difference between the earnings of the challenger and the earnings of the defence. These differences in pay can be good or bad. Positive (negative) NPV returns show that the challenging (defending) investment makes more money in present value dollars than the challenging (defending) investment. When comparing more than one attacker to the same defender, the NPVs of the challengers must be calculated and compared.
The main difference between NPV models and AIS profit calculations is that AIS calculations can include non-cash returns and costs, such as rises in inventory and depreciation. The discount rate and the exponents of the discount rate are not the only numbers that go into NPV models. Cash flow is another important number. The only exception is the investment's value at the end of its economic life, which is viewed as if it had been turned into cash.
An example of an NPV calculation. Let's say that an investment in a challenger costs V0 dollars up front and brings in R1 dollars plus the investment's liquidation value S1 in the next period. For now, imagine that the exchange rate between current defender dollars and future challenger dollars is r percent. This is the opportunity cost of giving up the defender to invest in the challenger. The NPV tells us if the benefits of the challenger are greater than the potential costs of not investing in the defender.

$$NPV = -V_0 + \frac{R_1 + S_1}{(1+r)}$$
(9.1)

Suppose a challenging investment costs $100 and returns R_1 = $100 and S_1 = $20 in period one while the defending investment earns r equal to 10%. Then the NPV of this investment would be:

$$NPV = -100 + \frac{\$100 + \$20}{1.1} = \$9.09$$
(9.2)

For this investment, NPV is positive, and present profits from the challenger outweigh the present loss in profits from sacrificing the defender. Another way to describe this result is that the challenger earned a higher rate of return than the defender. How much more? The exchange rate for the challenger is ($100 + $20)/$100 = 1.20 compared to $110/$100 = 1.10 for the defender.

But what does it mean to say that the challenger earned a higher rate of return than the defender? An investment is a commitment one makes to a project. If the project pays more than the rate of return on the defender, then the investment's NPV is positive. In our example the project pays at the rate of 20%. In NPV models, think of the discount rate as the rate earned by the defending investment. And if NPV is positive, the challenger will earn a rate of return higher than could be earned by continuing to invest in the defender.

Of course, investments can be much more complicated than described above. For example, an investment may generate (positive and negative) cash flows for n periods (R_1, R_2, $\cdots$, R_n) rather than just one period. Furthermore, most capital assets generate a positive or negative liquidation value (S_n) at the end of its economic life which should be accounted for explicitly.

An Excel template solution. Suppose a firm can invest V_0 = $1,000 present dollars in exchange for three future period dollars R_1 = $200, R_2 = $250, R_3 = $350, and salvage value V_3 = $950. Also assume that the defender exchanges dollars between time period at the rate of (1.08). Excel finds the NPV of the investment just described using its NPV equation described below in Table 9.1 equal to $431.50. To make the Excel solution transparent, the function f_x= NPV(B1,B3:B4,(B5+B6))−B2 describes the cell location of the variables included in the solution. Meanwhile, an explanatory equation containing variable names is listed to the right of the NPV equation, =PV(r,V_0,R_1,R_2,R_3+V_3) . We follow this pattern in describing future Excel solutions.

B7		fx	=NPV(B1,B3:B4,(B5+B6))-B2
	A	B	C
1	rate	0.08	
2	V_0	$1000	
3	R_1	$200	
4	R_2	$250	
5	R_3	$350	
6	V_3	$950	
7	NPV	$431.50	=NPV(r,V_0,R_1,R_2,R_3+V_3)-V_0

Internal Rate of Return (IRR) Models

Assume that an investment's acquisition, salvage, and cash flow are known and that we want to determine the rate of increase in the investment's beginning equity or assets from operations and investment activities. Compared to equation (9.2), NPV is zero and r is replaced with IRR. We write:

$$V_0 = \frac{R_1 + S_1}{(1 + IRR)}$$
(9.3)

Next we solve for the IRR in equation (9.3) and find:

$$IRR = \frac{R_1 + S_1}{V_0} - 1$$
(9.4)

The unknown variable in equation (9.3) describes the rate of return on the challenger. NPV is known to be zero since there is no comparison between the challenger and a defender. We are not comparing two investments as was the case of NPV models. We are only interested in finding the rate of return for a single investment. Of course, an investment's IRR can be compared to the IRRs of other investments or can be used to discount another challenging investment's cash flow, in which case it is referred to as the opportunity cost of capital or the discount rate. In such a model, the IRR will be equal to the defender's rate of return on equity (IRR^E) or its rate of return on its assets (ROA^A) depending on the focus of the PV model. Consider the PV equation below.

An Excel template solution. Suppose a firm can invest V0 = $1,000 present dollars in exchange for future dollars R1 = $200, R2 = $250, R3 = $350, and salvage value V3 = $950. The firm's financial manager wants to know what is the investment's internal rate of return? Excel find the IRR of the investment just described using its IRR equation described below in Table 9.2 equal to 24.28%. Note that the template requires that cash flow in each period are summed.

Open Table 9.2 in Microsoft Excel.

Table 9.2. An Excel Template Used to Find an IRR.

	B5	fx	=IRR(B1:B4)
	A	**B**	**C**
1	-V$_0$	-$1,000	
2	R$_1$	$200	
3	R$_2$	$250	
4	R$_3$ + V$_3$	$1,300	
5	IRR	24.28%	=IRR(V$_0$,R$_1$,R$_2$,R$_3$+V$_3$)

More complicated IRR models. Suppose that we wanted to find the IRR for an n period PV model such as the one written below:

$$V_0 = \frac{R_1}{(1 + IRR)} + \cdots + \frac{R_n}{(1 + IRR)^n}$$
(9.5)

Equation (9.5) is an nth degree polynomial with multiple possible solutions. But we need only one. To reduce equation (9.5) to a single IRR solution, it has become standard to specify a reinvestment rate r and compound cash flow to the last period allowing us to write:

$$V_0 = \frac{(1 + r)^{n-1} R_1 + \cdots + (1 + r) R_{n-1} + R_n}{(1 + IRR)^n}$$
(9.6)

From equation (9.6) we find the solution for IRR equal to:

$$IRR = \left[\frac{(1 + r)^{n-1} R_1 + \cdots + (1 + r) R_{n-1} + R_n}{V_0} \right]^{(1/n)}$$
(9.7)

Break-Even Models

Fundamental to PV models is the concept of break-even. Break-even refers to an equality between rates of return and earnings between a defending investment and a challenging investment. If the break-even solution compares the present earnings on the defender and challenger and if the NPV was positive (negative), the NPV could be reduced (increased) by changing the price of the challenger. Alternatively, we could find the break-even rates of return on the defender and challenger by altering the defender's IRR or changing any of the challenger's cash flow including salvage values, tax rates, and any periodic cash flow. We will discuss several break-even models in what follows, beginning with maximum (minimum) bid (sell).

Maximum Bid (Minimum Sell) Models

Different kinds of investment questions create the need for different kinds of PV models. The maximum bid (minimum sell) model assumes the defender's IRR r and the challenger's cash flow are known. The models then solve for the purchase (sell) price of an investment that equates NPV to zero. In a maximum bid (minimum sell) price model, the solution is the maximum price the buyer (seller) can offer and still earn the defender's IRR. To repeat, from the buyer's perspective, the solution is the most that can be offered and still earn the IRR rate r on the challenger. Or, from the seller's perspective, the minimum sell price is the lowest price a seller can accept in exchange for the cash flow stream generated by the investment and still earn the IRR rate r earned on the challenger.

To illustrate, begin by assuming that r, the IRR of the defender, is known as well as the cash flow that can be earned by the challenger. Now find the challenger's maximum bid price, V_0^B (minimum sell price V_0^S) by setting NPV equal to zero and finding the maximum bid V0B (minimum sell V0S) price. We write the maximum bid (minimum sell) price as:

$$V_0^B(V_0^S) = \frac{R_1 + S_1}{(1 + r)}$$
(9.8)

An Excel template solution for a Maximum (Minimum) bid (sell) model. Suppose a firm can invest V_0 = $1,000 present dollars in exchange for future dollars R_1 = $200, R_2 = $250, R_3 = $350, and salvage value V_3 = $950. Also assume that the defender exchanges present dollars for future challenger dollars at the rate of (1.08). Excel finds the NPV of the investment just described using its NPV equation described below in Table 9.3 equal to $431.50. To find the maximum bid (minimum sell) price, we sum the V_0 and NPV. The solution is described in Table 9.3.

Table 9.3. An Excel Template Used to Find an NPV and a Maximum Bid (Minimum Sell) Price

Open Table 9.3 in Microsoft Excel.

	B8	fx	=B7+B2
	A	B	C
1	r	0.08	
2	V_0	$1,000	
3	R_1	$200	
4	R_2	$250	
5	R_3	$350	
6	V_3	$950	
7	NPV	$431.50	
8	max bid	$1,431.50	=V_0 + NPV

Break-even Cash Flow Models

Assume that the investor knows the investment's cost V_0, its liquidation value S_1, and the IRR of the defender r but doesn't know the challenger's cash flow R_1 that would be required for the investment to earn an IRR equal to the defender's. The firm can find the cash flow amount required to break-even earnings by setting NPV to zero and solving for R_1 in equation (9.1) as follows:

(9.9) $$R_1 = (1 + r)V_0 - S_1$$

If r were 10%, and if the liquidation value were zero, and the initial investment were $100, then the break-even cash flow would be $100(1.1) = $110, the amount the investment would be required to earn to break-even. Break-even here has a specific meaning which is for the challenger to earn the defender's IRR.

An Excel template solution for a Break-Even cash flow model. Suppose a firm can invest V_0 = $1,000 present dollars in exchange for future dollars R_1 = $200, R_2 = $250, R_3 = $350, and salvage value V_3 = $950. Also assume that the defender exchanges dollars between time period at the rate of (1.08). The financial manager wants to know the salvage value that would allow the challenger to break even—to earn the defender's IRR of 8 percent. To find the break-even salvage value solution, we introduce Excel's goal seek solution described in the Excel appendix to this book.

We begin with the solution in Table 9.3. Then Goal Seek asks, if we require the value in cell B7, the investment's NPV, to be set equal to zero, how much would we need to change the investment's salvage value in cell B6 (the salvage value V_3)?

B7		fx	=NPV(B1,B3:B4,(B5+B6))–B2
	A	B	C
1	r	0.08	
2	V_0	$1,000	
3	R_1	$200	
4	R_2	$250	
5	R_3	$350	
6	V_3	$950	
7	NPV	$431.50	=NPV(r,V_0,R_1,R_2,R_3+V_3)–V_0
8	max bid	$1,431.50	=V_0 + NPV

Goal Seek   ?   ✕

Set cell: B7   ⬆

To value: 0

By changing cell: $B$6| ⬆

        OK   Cancel

We report the goal seek solution in Table 9.5. We find that the salvage value could fall from $950 to $406.43 and still break-even, i.e., the challenger could earn the defender's IRR of 8 percent and an NPV equal to zero.

	A	B
1	r	0.08
2	V_0	$1,000
3	R_1	$200
4	R_2	$250
5	R_3	$350
6	V_3	$406.43
7	NPV	$0.00

Annuity Equivalent (AE) Models

An annuity is a financial product sold by financial institutions. The essence of an annuity is this: an individual or firm pays into a fund that is invested and grows until some point when the investment is paid back to the investor as a constant stream of payments for a specified period. In this book we define a related concept, an annuity equivalent. An annuity equivalent is a constant stream of payments whose present value is equivalent to some other stream of payments that may not be constant. The annuity equivalent model finds an annuity associated with an investment. An annuity is like a time adjusted average. Suppose we wished to find the annuity equivalent associated with the generalized NPV model below:

$$
\begin{aligned}
NPV &= -V_0 + \frac{R_1}{(1+r)} + \frac{R_2}{(1+r)^2} + \cdots + \frac{R_n + S_n}{(1+r)^n} \\
&= \frac{R}{(1+r)} + \frac{R}{(1+r)^2} + \cdots + \frac{R}{(1+r)^n}
\end{aligned}
$$

(9.10)

The value for R in equation (9.10) is the annuity equivalent (AE) cash flow. The discounted PV of the constant cash flow R yields an amount equal to NPV.

An Excel template solution for an AE model. Suppose a firm can invest V_0 = $1,000 present dollars in exchange for future dollars R_1 = $200, R_2 = $250, R_3 = $350, and salvage value V_3 = $950. Also assume that the defender exchanges dollars between time period at the rate of 8 percent. Under this scenario, the firm estimates its NPV to equal $431.50. The financial manager wants to know what is the AE for an NPV of $431.50 over 4 years? The AE solution for this investment over 4 periods is $130.28, negative since it represents funds being withdrawn from the investment. We find AE using Excel's PMT function.

Table 9.6. Finding an Annuity Equivalent for an NPV over 4 years.
Open Table 9.6 in Microsoft Excel.

B9		fx	=PMT(B1,B8,B7)
	A	B	C
1	r	0.08	
2	V₀	$1,000	
3	R₁	$200	
4	R₂	$250	
5	R₃	$350	
6	V₃	$950	
7	NPV	$431.50	
8	n	4	
9	AE	($130.28)	=PMT(r,n,NPV)

The PMT solution informs us that an NPV of $431.50 could pay $130.28 for four years in the future before exhausting its value.

Capitalization Formulas

Long-lived assets, often non-depreciable, require a special PV model. Long-lived assets will be discussed in more detail in Chapter 14 on investment terms. But for now, consider the following. Suppose that we can considered the future cash flow of a long-lived asset to be represented by the annuity equivalent model described in equation (9.10). Now let n, the term of the investment, get very large. Then the present value of the present value of the AE can be written as:

$$\lim_{n\to\infty} NPV_n = -V_0 + \frac{R_1}{(1+r)} + \frac{R_2}{(1+r)^2} + \cdots + \frac{R_n + S_n}{(1+r)^n}$$

$$= \frac{R}{(1+r)} + \frac{R}{(1+r)^2} + \cdots + \frac{R}{(1+r)^n} = \frac{R}{r}$$

(9.11)

The capitalization formula, like all PV models that depends on future forecasts, is an approximation. In this case the approximation improves with increases in n. To illustrate suppose that we found the PV for $n = 30$, $r = 8\%$, and AE = $130.28. The Excel solution is PV(.08,20,130.28) = $1,466.66. The capitalization approximation is $130.28/.08 = $1628.50. If n increases to 40, PV equals $1,553.54.

Optimal Life Models

Optimal life models ask what is the optimal life of this investment? We may want to ask if the NPV of the investment in equation (9.9) would be increased if the economic life of the investment were increased to the $(n + 1)$ period or reduced to the $(n - 1)$ period. The optimal life model in continuous time can be written as:

$$NPV = -V_0 + \int_0^n R(t)e^{-rt}dt + S_n e^{-rn}$$

(9.12)

Where $R(t)$ equals the cash flow in the tth period and S_n is the salvage value in the nth period. The optimal solution has a specific meaning in the context of the optimal life model. It is that value of n that maximizes the NPV. Formally, the solution employs the calculus to optimize the NPV. In the discrete time model which is most often employed in practice, the optimal value is found through trial and error or through repeated calculations of alternative values for n.

A related optimal life model asks: what is the optimal value of n that maximizes NPV if there are replacements for the investment? In this case, NPV is the sum of NPVs from individual investments. Such a replacement model will be described in more detail in Chapter 14.

The Payback Model

While PV models are generally carefully deduced and the data required to solve them is explicit, sometimes decision makers just want a "ball-park" estimate of the desirability of a financial strategy. In such cases, decision makers are willing to sacrifice rigor and precision for approximations. When this is the case, the payback model is often employed. To obtain an approximation, it assumes the discount rate in PV models is zero. In other words, the payback model assumes that present and future dollars are valued the same—a very unrealistic assumption. Then the payback model calculates the number of periods required to earn the investment's present value. The number of periods required to earn the investment's value is the payback period, the criterion used to rank investments. All cash flow after the payback period is assumed to have no influence on the criterion. To illustrate, n is the payback period in the payback model that follows.

(9.13) $V_0 = R_1 + R_2 + \cdots + R_n$

And if periodic cash flows are constant we can express the payback period as:

$$\text{Payback period} = \frac{(\text{initial investment})}{(\text{periodic cash flows})}$$

(9.14)

To illustrate, consider an initial outflow of $5,000 with $1,000 cash inflows per month. In this case, the payback period would be 5 months. If the cash inflows were paid annually, then the result would be 5 years. More generally, cash flows will not equal one another. If $10,000 is the initial outflow investment, and the cash inflows are $1,000 in year one, $6,000 in year two, $3,000 in year three, and $5,000 in year four, then the payback period would be three years, as the first three years are equal to the initial outflow.

Despite its popularity, the payback model is not recommended for several reasons. Mainly, ignoring the time value of money basically treats an inter temporal investment as though it were a static profit problem. Furthermore, it treats cash flow earned after the payback period as not important. In sum, in many respects, the pay-back method inadequately accounts for important details of the investment problem.

Present Value Models and Rates of Return

So far, the opportunity cost of capital has been introduced without specifying whose capital is being invested. Is it equity capital, debt capital, or a combination of debt and equity capital? Or does it matter? The short answer is that it does matter as we demonstrated in Chapter 8. If the focus is on the return on equity, then the discount rate represents the return on equity ROE in a one-period model and IRR^E in a multi-period model. When focused on the rate of return on equity, interest costs on debt are subtracted from the cash flow included in the model. If the focus is on the return on assets ROA in a one-period model and IRR^A in a multi-period problem, then the cost of the investment is subtracted at the beginning of the model and earnings reflect a return to the assets, and interest costs are irrelevant since the asset is treated as though it were purchased at the beginning of the investment.

The difference between the two approaches matter because most firms rely on a combination of debt and equity to fund assets. Reduced to its essence, the issue is whether the opportunity cost of capital reflects the rate of return on the firm's assets or equity. Both approaches apply under different circumstances. For example, interest costs may be subsidized so that ROE estimates may be distorted compared to what they would be if the firm paid the market rate of interest. In this case, a return to asset approach may be appropriate. In other circumstances, the firm may indeed want to know their earnings and rate of return independent of contributions from debt capital. In this case, a return on equity approach may be appropriate. We now describe the two approaches in more detail using a one-period model to make the results transparent.

Internal rate of return on assets (ROA). In the return to asset model, we charge the entire investment at the beginning of the period and include its liquidation value as a return at the end of the period. This approach ignores the fact that investments may be financed and paid for over the life of the investment and charging for the investment at the beginning of the project doesn't accurately reflect its cash flow. However, in the ROA approach, we ignore financing because our interest is in the productive capacity of the long-term asset, independent of the terms under which it can be financed. The advantage of the

ROA approach is that the analysis considers the rate of return on the entire investment made at the beginning of the period. The NPV for the ROA approach for a single period can be expressed as:

$$NPV = -V_0 + \frac{R_1 + S_1}{1 + ROA}$$

(9.15)

Note that in equation (9.15), if NPV = 0, as it would in an IRR model, then $(1 + ROA)V_0$ is equal to $R_1 + S_1$. If we replace V_0 with $E_0 + D$, we can write $R_1 + S_1 = (1 + ROA)(E_0 + D)$. This fact will be helpful as we connect ROA and ROE measures.

We illustrate how to find ROA in a simple one-period example. Suppose the firm's defender is a $1,000, non-depreciable investment that will earn $100 for one period and then will be liquidated at its acquisition price. We find the ROA associated with $1,000 of assets invested in the defender by setting its NPV equal to zero in equation (9.15) and solve for ROA.

$$\begin{aligned} ROA &= \frac{R_1 + S_1}{V_0} \\ &= \frac{\$1,100 - \$1,000}{\$1,000} = 10\% \end{aligned}$$

(9.16)

Internal rate of return on equity (ROE). In the ROE approach, the analysis depends on how the asset is financed. In this approach, the cost of interest and debt payments are subtracted explicitly. Moreover, the initial investment is equal to the amount of equity invested since the debt is paid directly to whoever supplies the investment. However, the debt D plus average interest costs charged at interest rate i (iD) are subtracted at the end of the period. The NPV for the one-period ROE model is expressed as

$$NPV = -E_0 + \frac{R_1 + S_1 - (1 + i)D_0}{1 + ROE}$$

(9.17)

Now reconsider the same example, except that the $500, or half of the defender, is financed at 9%. The other half of the investment, $500, is financed by the firm's equity. We continue to assume that, after one period, the investment is liquidated for its acquisition value, the loan of $500 is repaid, and the firm recovers its investment of $500. The firm also earns in one period, $100, the same as before. But now it pays a rental fee for the use of the loan's funds of 9% times $500, or $45. By setting the NPV model of the defender in equation (9.17) equal to zero, we can find its ROE associated with the firm's equity (IRR^E) in the project equal to.

$$ROE = \frac{(R_1 + S_1) - (1 + i)D_0 - E_0}{V_0}$$

$$= \frac{\$1,100 - \$45 - \$500}{\$500} = 11\%$$

(9.18)

We find the defender's ROE to equal 11%. In this case, the firm gained access to the use of an asset because of financing. The gains from a lender providing the firm access to $500 of debt capital to acquire a $1,000 investment using only $500 of its own money increased its earnings on its equity from 10% to 11%. Meanwhile the investment as a whole continued to earn only 10%. The value of the financing increased the rate of return on equity by 1%.

For a variety of reasons, financial managers may prefer to represent the defender's rate of return using ROA. However, this same manager must be careful to make sure that the cash flow associated with the challengers are consistent and measure cash flow earned by assets. On the other hand, if the defender's rate of return is represented by its ROE, then debt and interest costs should be accounted for explicitly.

In practice, most PV modelers appear to prefer the ROA approach, even though both approaches are valid and provide unique information. Nevertheless, the dominance of the ROA approach has resulted in the identification of ROAs as simply the IRR of the investment, a practice we will also adopt in the remainder of this book.

> So, what have we learned? We have learned that single equation PV models can solve for at most one unknown variable that defines what kind of PV model is represented. You will be asked to summarize the different kinds of PV models, the unknown variable that defines the PV model, and the kinds of questions each model is designed to answer in the chapter questions section.

Summary and Conclusions

This chapter reviewed several different kinds of PV models. They differ because they are designed to answer different kinds of questions. Some PV models, NPV and IRR, help us rank alternative investments. Others like AE models can be used to find the optimal time for replacing an investment—or what our periodic loan payments will be. And still other PV models like the maximum bid (minimum sell) models help us know the maximum (minimum) we can offer to purchase (sell) an investment and still earn the defender's IRR. Finally, still other PV models such as capitalization formulas and payback models offer at most a rule of thumb for evaluating and making investment decisions.

Questions

1. PV models can be identified by the questions they are designed to answer. Please complete the table below by identifying the unknown variable and the question the solution to the unknown variables is designed to answer:

Question you want to answer	Unknown Variable	Appropriate PV Model to Answer your Question
What is the rate of return I can expect from my equity invested in a lawn care business?		
What will be my loan payment for a $10,000 loan to be repaid in 10 annual installments at an interest rate of 6%?		
How much will the value of my assets change if I disinvest $50,000 from a defender and reinvest the funds in a challenger, assuming my defender is earning an IRR of 9%?		
What is the most I can pay for a challenging investment and break-even or earn my defender's IRR?		
I own an aging orchard. I need to know the optimal time to replace my orchard with new tree varieties.		
I am considering the purchase of beef feeder operation. I want to know the value of the operation realizing that I will earn returns on many beef-feeder cohorts.		
If the discount rate is zero, how many periods will be required to recover my original investment.		

2. Compare the implied reinvestment rates for NPV and IRR models.
3. IRR models measure an investment's internal rate of return. NPV models measure the difference in present earnings between the defender and the challenger. Both NPV and IRR models can be used to rank investments. Would you expect them to ranking investments consistently? Defend your answer.
4. To find the present value of a stream of future income for a long-lived asset, I capitalize the constant or first period's cash flow. What are the key assumptions employed that permit us to use the capitalization formula?
5. Suppose you found the maximum bid price for a purchase you are considering. How would you

use this information in your negotiations with the seller?

6. Suppose that you found that an investment's AE reached its maximum at year 10 while its NPV reached its maximum at 15 years. How would you use these results to determine the optimal life of the investment?

7. When finding the ROE, we explicitly accounted for the debt used to finance the investment. However, when finding the ROA measure, we did not account for the debt used to finance the investment. Explain the difference between the two approaches. Which one would you recommend?

8. Provide numerical PV models in which you find an investment's IRR and NPVs using IRR^A and IRR^E.

9. Most of the time, we don't identify discount rates in PV models as being either a ROE or a ROA. Instead we seem to prefer to identify the defender's ROA with the letter "r". Why do we tend to prefer ROA to ROE measures? Can you describe a case when it would be important to evaluate the projects using the defender's ROE instead of its ROA?

10. Assume you were considering one investment that could be financed from two different financial institutions. Thus, the only difference between the projects were their cash flow associated with their use of debt capital. How would you proceed to rank the two investments?

10. Growth and Decision-Making: Assessing Incremental Investments

LINDON ROBISON

Learning goals. After completing this chapter, you should be able to: (1) distinguish between incremental and stand-alone investments; (2) understand how time and use costs determine the optimal service extraction rates; and (3) find internal rates of return on incremental investments.

Learning objectives. To achieve your learning goals, you should complete the following objectives:

- Learn how to find contributions from incremental investments by finding changes in the firm's cash receipts (CR), cash cost of goods sold (COGS), cash overhead expenses (OE), and change in operating and capital asset accounts.
- Learn how to use Excel templates to find net present value (NPV), annuity equivalent (AE), and internal rate of return (IRR) measures earned by incremental investments.

Introduction

NPV models figure out the difference between how much the challenger makes and how much the defender makes. Different pay can be a good or a bad thing. Positive (negative) NPV results show that the investment being defended makes more money in terms of present value dollars than the investment being challenged. When comparing more than one attacker to the same defender, the NPVs of the attackers must be calculated and compared.

The main difference between NPV models and AIS profit calculations is that AIS calculations can include non-cash returns and costs, such as increases in inventory and depreciation. NPV models use more numbers than just the discount rate and the exponents of the discount rate. Another important number is cash flow. The only exception is the value of the investment at the end of its economic life, which is treated as if it had been turned into cash.

An example of how to figure out NPV. Let's say an investment in a challenger costs V0 dollars up front and brings in R1 dollars plus the investment's disposal value S1 in the next period. For now, let's say that the exchange rate between present defender dollars and future challenger dollars is r percent. This is the cost of giving up the defence in order to put your money into the challenger. The NPV tells us if the benefits of the challenger are bigger than the costs of not investing in the defence.

start assets and equity, and then give the results as measures of return on assets (ROA) and return on equity (ROE). AIS doesn't try to figure out how much a single capital asset or subset of the firm's assets adds to earnings predictions. But when we build PV models for firm investments, we try to separate the return from the investment(s) added to the output unit or the firm. How else could we decide whether to invest in the competitor or not?

But when we try to measure the return on an additional investment, we run into trouble. The problem is that a firm's best response to a new investment is often to change the amount of non-durable assets and services it gets from other durables it operates. This makes it hard to tell how much of a change in output is due to the new investment and how much is due to changes in how the firm uses its other inputs. In this chapter, we will spend a lot of time figuring out how to measure the contributions of incremental spending.

What comes next. In what follows, we explain how to use incremental budgeting analysis to look at small purchases. We explain the incremental investment analysis with the help of simpler math and graphical analysis. Then, we show how incremental budgeting analysis works with an example from Green & White Services and the generalised PV template from this book's Appendix to Chapter 8.

Counting the contributions of small investments

This is an example of a small purchase. As an example of an incremental investment, let's say that Hi Quality Nursery (HQN) is thinking about buying a sprinkler system to cut down on the number of casual workers it needs. HQN asks: Will spending money on the new water system help my company's finances?

How are gradual investments different from investments that stand on their own? Or, in our case, how do we figure out how much the investment in sprinklers and the drop in hired help cost? To find the answer, we have to figure out how the investment in sprinklers and the loss of investment in hired labour will affect HQN's income and costs.

We know that HQN will need less wage workers to water its plants during the growing season now that it has a new sprinkler system. Also, it's possible that HQN's operating procedures will stay the same for a long time after this change. Some new costs may be needed to run and manage the new sprinkler system, but these are likely to be much less than the amount saved on hired help because of the investment in sprinklers. It's not clear how revenue would change if a new method for watering was used. If running costs go down, it's possible that some plants and shrubs that didn't make money before may now do so because it costs less to make them.

Because the consequences of the sprinkler/hired labor changes will likely have long-term consequences, this problem can't be analyzed using a single period financial tool such as CFS. Instead the problem requires that we employ multi-period PV model templates. The answers that can be supplied by PV models include: how will an incremental investment change the capital structure of the firm? How will incremental investment change the equity of the firm? How will the incremental investment change the internal rate of return on the firm's assets and equity?

Contributions from existing investments. Suppose that we have a profit function π that depends on the revenue and costs associated with an independent profit generating plant described as f(x) where the variable x represents the existing asset and liability configuration of the firm:

(10.1) $\quad \pi = f(x)$

Analyzing the firm as a function of its current asset and liability configuration described as x in equation (10.1) is what we do when we construct coordinated financial statements (CFS). Rates of return on assets and equity as well as our other ratio calculations all reflect the current financial condition of the firm. To find rates of return on assets or equity, we divide equation one by its assets or by its equity.

Now suppose that we want to analyze how profits will respond to a change in x. Using the delta notation, Δ to reflect change, we write the effect of a change in x on profits as:

(10.2) $\quad \Delta\pi = f(x + \Delta x) - f(x)$

What we have described is a stand-alone investment that allows us to examine the effects on profits in response to a change in x without being required to consider other changes in the firm. To complicate the analysis, suppose that the firm's asset and liability configuration are describe by two interdependent variables x and y so that when we change x, to maximize profits we must also change y. Indeed, it is hard to imagine any change in x that doesn't require adjustments in other inputs to achieve the most beneficial outcomes. (If we purchase a sprinkler to reduce labor costs, we would surely expect labor costs to be reduced). To account for the simultaneity of x and y, we write the profit function as:

(10.3) $\quad \pi = g(x, y)$

Since x and y are interdependent, any change in x must also consider a change y to optimize its firm profits, so that to analyze a change in profits attributable to a change in x and y, we must calculate:

(10.4) $\quad \Delta\pi = h(x + \Delta x, y + \Delta y) - h(x, y)$

Equation (10.4) essentially describes incremental analysis. In accounts for changes in revenue and expenses associated with the incremental investments plus changes in the costs and revenue associated with other variables essential to the firm's operations.

A *graphical approach.* We now present the earlier results using graphical analysis familiar to students of microeconomics. Assume that a firm produces output using a combination of capital services and other inputs x and y. We graph the combinations of capital services and other inputs that produce the same output and call the result an isoquant (i.e. same quantity). In Figure 10.1 we represent two levels of output by isoquants Q1, and Q2 drawn convex to the origin to reflect diminishing marginal productivity.

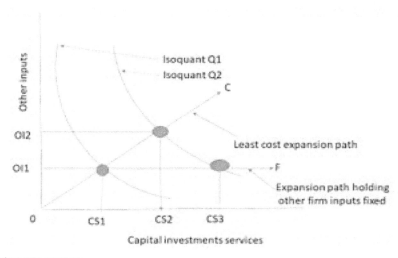

Figure 10.1. Isoquants

Now suppose that the firm considers an incremental investment, a capital investment that will allow the firm to increase its supply of capital services from CS1 to CS3 and increase output from Q1 to Q2. In this case, we hold constant the level of other inputs constant at OI1. However, economic production theory teaches that increasing production from Q1 to Q2 holding other inputs constant would be inefficient. Instead, the theory teaches that the firm should increase capital services and other inputs along some least cost line AC determined by the relative costs of increasing both the capital services from the new investment and from the other inputs.

Increasing production along the least cost line AC, the firm would increase capital service from CS1 to CS2 an amount less that was required to reach Q2 when we held other inputs constant. In other words, increasing the use of other inputs allows the firm to use less capital services from the new investment compared to the capital services required if other inputs were held constant (CS2 – CS1) < (CS3 – CS1) while still producing the same level of output. Furthermore, expanding other inputs and services from the new durable along the least cost expansion path assures us that the cost of increasing other inputs from OI1 to OI2 is more than offset by reducing the cost of capital services from (CS3 – CS1) to (CS2 – CS1).

Which expansion path? We have demonstrated that whether to measure the cost of increasing production along the least cost line AC or the expansion path AF that holds other inputs constant at OI1 depends on the nature of the costs of increasing the use of other inputs depends mostly on the passage of time or use. If increases in other inputs makes the investment more productive, this productivity increase is credited to the investment. Finally, if we measure changes along the least cost path, we must recognize that we are answering a different kind of question than "what are the unique returns to a challenging investment?" When performing PV analysis on a stand-alone investment, we ask: does the investment earn a positive net present value (NPV)—greater than the PV sacrificed by liquidating the defender. In contrast, the incremental investment analysis asks: is this change in the capital structure of the firm and use of other inputs more efficient and profitable than before the change?

It is not a settled matter whether to measure the cost of increasing production along the least cost line AC or the expansion path AF that maintains other inputs constant at OI1. We come down on the side of measuring increases in production attributable to increases in durable services and other inputs because that is what the firm does. If the increased durable services make other inputs more productive, then why not include their contributions along with those of the increased durable services?

However, if we measure changes along the least cost path, we must recognize that we are answering a different kind of question than "what are the unique returns to a challenging investment?" When performing PV analysis on a stand-alone investment, we ask, does the investment earn a positive present value return—greater than the present value sacrificed by liquidating the defender. In contrast, the incremental approach asks: is this change in the capital structure of the firm and use of other inputs more efficient and profitable than before the change?

To emphasize the challenges of measuring the contributions of incremental investments, consider a scissors type of investment. With only one scissor blade, not much cutting occurs. Add a blade to an existing blade, and the scissor output returns to normal. The increase in the scissor production was because we changed the use of both blades. And the decision to add a second blade is made based on the change in output using one scissor blade to two and the change in output must be attributed to them both. If we analyzed the contribution of the second blade keeping the first blade idle, output would have remained at zero. Is it fair to attribute to the second blade the contributions of the first blade? Yes, if one treats the investment in the first blade as a sunk cost and not relevant for answering the question. On the other hand, the service extraction rate from the first blade increases when one adds a second blade. Part of the increased output must be attributed to increased services provided by the first blade. The scissor example is an extreme case. However, it illustrates the difficulty of applying the incremental approach if all other inputs are held constant.

Optimal Service Extractions Rates from Stand-alone and Incremental Investments

When analyzing incremental investment problems, we often assume that the investment being analyzed provides services at its optimal rate. Finding the optimal service extraction rate for capital investments is complicated and we often employ complex computer programs to find these optimal rates. Yet it is important to understand what determines optimal service extraction rates even though the focus of our analysis is on the investment's earnings and rates of return.

To be clear, when we discuss the cost of extracting services from our capital investment, we include the change in its salvage value, the cost of using other nondurable inputs, and the change in the value of other capital investments whose services support our investment. As it turns out, the costs of using a capital investment within a period conform to the categories already identified in our PV templates. The cost of using nondurable inputs are measures as cash costs of goods sold (COGS). The cost of extracting capital investment services that depend mostly on the passage of time, we measure as cash overhead expenses (OE). The cost equal to the change in the liquidation value of the capital investment we measure as depreciation (Dep) and most of the time we assume that this rate of depreciation is determined by the passage of time.

Service extraction rates when the cost of using the investment depends mostly on the passage of time. Consider, for example, an investment whose use cost depends mostly on the passage of time such as a storage facility. The roof, for example, has a finite time during which it can provide services. It simply wears out over time. Much the same is true for other parts of the building including its painted surfaces, floors, and other building features. While there may be some important costs associated with heating, ventilation, and air conditioning services, these costs depend mostly on the passage of time and weather conditions than on the number of items stored or the activity that occurs in the building. Finally, investments in buildings are usually fixed because their liquidation value is often low. To use a building requires that the new owner relocate to the building site. Thus, location fixity reduces the liquidity of the investment and contributes to its fixity in the firm's investment portfolio.

So, what is the optimal use of an investment whose costs depend mostly on the passage of time? Since its marginal use cost is usually low, their optimal use is their maximum capacity if the investment is making some positive contributions to the firm. For investments whose use costs depend mostly on the passage of time, we are not likely to change their use when adding an incremental investment to the firm unless we operate them at less than full capacity before the incremental investment.

Service extraction rates when the cost of using an investment depends mostly on its use. Consider another kind of investment whose use costs depends mostly on services provided by other capital investments, including maintenance costs, and nondurable inputs. Electric motors or gasoline powered equipment have their cost of service extraction dependent mostly on the cost of using nondurable inputs and services from other durables.

So, what determines the optimal service extraction rates from investments whose cost depends mostly on use and other inputs? The optimal service extraction rate depends mostly on the marginal use costs. Furthermore, we expect that service extraction rates change when incremental investments are added to the firm that alter these marginal use costs. In sum, investments whose costs depends mostly on their use will find that their optimal use is not fixed nor at their maximum capacity.

Opportunity costs. All investments that provide services for one period or more incur opportunity costs equal to the defender's IRR times the value of the investment at the beginning of the period. We incur the cost when we sacrifice a defending investment to employ a challenging one. We account for these costs when discounting future costs and returns to their present value.

So, what have we learned? We learned that the optimal service extraction rate from durables depends on the nature of costs (and returns). If costs vary with use, marginal cost and marginal returns play an important role in determining the optimal use of the durable in the short run. If costs are mostly time dependent, in the short run the durable's optimal service extraction rate is its maximum if each service unit provides value. However, in the long term, both time and use cost matter and determine whether the firm invests or disinvests in the durable.

Incremental Investments and Homogeneity of Size

We established earlier that comparing two challenging investments with different initial and periodic sizes could produce conflicting net present value (NPV) and internal rate of return (IRR) rankings. Incremental analysis violates the homogeneity of size condition and can produce conflicting NPV and IRR rankings. Consider the following.

Suppose a small firm has a profit function $\pi(x,y)$ where x and y represent the firm's existing assets (inputs). Next suppose that the firm is considering an incremental investment such that the new profit function will be $\pi(x + \Delta x, y + \Delta y)$. To decide whether to commit to the incremental investment or not, the firm has the following options: compare (1) incremental investment contributions $[\pi(x + \Delta x, y + \Delta y) - \pi(x,y)]$ versus (2) comparing whole firm profits before the incremental investment $\pi(x,y)$ and after the incremental investment: $\pi(x + \Delta x, y + \Delta y)$. An example follows.

Consider a firm with initial investments of $1,000 expected to produce cash flow for the next periods of $750 and $500. The firm is considering an incremental investment of $100 expected to produce an incremental change in cash flow for the next two periods of $64 and $51 respectively. The total cash flow after the incremental investment for the next two periods are $750 + $64 = $814 and $500 + $51 = $551.

Assuming the defender's IRR is 8%, we compare IRR and NPV for the incremental investment with IRR and NPV for the firm's profits before and after the incremental investment. At first, one might conclude that the two approaches should produce identical rankings. They don't. Because they violate homogeneity of size condition, comparing the cash flow differences versus the cash flow of the entire firm before and after the investment, they need not produce consistent rankings and Table 10.1 demonstrates.

Table 10.1. Comparing NPV versus IRR Rankings for an incremental Investment

	Incremental Investment cash flow	Investment cash flow before the incremental investment	Investment cash flow after the incremental investment
Amount	$100	$1,000	$1,000
R1	$64	$750	$814
R2	$51	$500	$551
NPV @ r = 8% (rankings)	$2.98 (invest)	$123.11 (2)	$126.10 (1)
NPV @ r = 12% (rankings)	-$2.20 (don't invest)	$68.24 (1)	$66.04 (2)
IRR (rankings)	10.26% (invest if r=8%; don't invest if r=12%)	17.54% (1)	16.86% (2)

The lesson from Table 10.1 is this. Incremental investment analysis recommends investing if the defender's IRR is 8% because it is greater than its IRR of 10.26% and produces a positive NPV of $2.98. Incremental investment analysis recommends not investing if the defender's IRR is 12% because it is less than its IRR of 10.26% and produces a negative NPV of -$2,20. In contrast, comparing whole firm NPVs and IRRs before and after the investment, NPV criterion recommends investing for a defender's IRR of 8% but not if the defender's IRR is 12%. Based on the IRR criterion, whole firm comparisons recommends against investing. In summary, NPV criterion produce consistent recommendation using incremental budgeting and whole firm comparisons. Incremental and whole firm IRR provide consistent recommendations if the defender's IRR is 8% but provide conflicting recommendation is the defender's IRR is 12%. Whole firm comparisons before and after the incremental investment based on their IRRs unambiguously recommend not investing: the IRR for not investing is 17.54% and greater than the IRR for investing of 16.88%.

We can produce consistent IRR and NPV results if we adjust for size—requiring us that we compare investments of the same size. This we achieve homogeneity of size by investing the differences in size between the incremental investment and the whole firm investments at the defender's IRR of 8% or 12%. When we do this, we create a disadvantage for incremental investments because it ignores returns from the firm greater than the defender's returns and instead assumes all the difference between the incremental investment and the whole firm earns the discount rate. To demonstrate, in Table 10.2 we compare the incremental method and whole firm approach adjusted for size differences at the discount rates of 8% and 12%.

Table 10.2. Comparing NPV versus IRR Ranking for an incremental Investment after adjusting for size differences assuming the defender's IRR is 8%

	Incremental Investment cash flow	Investment cash flow before the incremental investment	Investment cash flow after the incremental investment
Amount	$100	$1,000	$1,000
R1	$0	$750	$814
R2	$1,287	$500	$551
NPV @ r = 8% (rankings)	$2.98 (invest)	$123 (2)	$126 (1)
IRR (rankings)	8.15% (invest)	13.88% (2)	14.02% (1)

For a discount rate of 8% and equal size investments, incremental and whole firm comparisons produce consistent results.

Table 10.3. Comparing NPV versus IRR Ranking for an incremental Investment after adjusting for size differences assuming the defender's IRR is 12%

	Incremental Investment cash flow	Investment cash flow before the incremental investment	Investment cash flow after the incremental investment
Amount	$100	$1,000	$1,000
R1	$0	$750	$814
R2	$1,377.08	$1,465.44	$1,462.68
NPV @ r = 8% (rankings)	-$2.20 (don't invest)	$68.24 (1)	$66.04 (2)
IRR (rankings)	11.89% (don't invest)	15.42% (1)	15.31% (2)

For a discount rate of 12% and equal size investments, incremental and whole firm comparisons produce consistent results.

So, what have we learned? We learned that without adjusting for size differences, IRR and NPV may produce inconsistent ranking results when comparing before and after an incremental investment analysis. Adjusting for size differences produce consistent rankings. However, it is important to note that whether to make the incremental investment or not depends on the discount rate. The discount rate of 8% leads to an invest decision. A discount rate of 12% leads to a don't invest decision.

Ranking two investments using differences. Incremental budgeting analysis leads to a more general question. In some cases, applied researchers compare two challenging investments by finding the NPV or IRR of their difference. The problem as we just demonstrated is this. If we violate homogeneity of size requirement, NPV and IRR rankings may be inconsistent when comparing the cash flow differences of two investments versus investment rankings of whole firms. In other words, IRR and NPV ranking of investments of A and B may be inconsistent with investment A–B without making appropriate size adjustment.

So why do some investors perform incremental investments? The answer is the same one we used to justify the payback method for ranking investments. It is perceived to be less data demanding than solving for an entire firm's cash flow before and after an incremental investment because independent effects need not be considered.

So, what have we learned? We learned that incremental analysis and whole firm comparisons may produce conflicting rankings. If performing incremental budgeting and comparing investment differences, we generally advise financial managers to use NPV because one will obtain the same rankings as one would obtain using NPV whole firm comparisons. A justification for this approach is that an incremental investment is not generally a scalable investment, otherwise it wouldn't be incremental.

Green and White Services: A Stand-Alone Investment

Lon is considering investing in a lawn care and snow removal business that will require he purchase lawnmowers, snow blowers, and other equipment. Lon intends to name his business Green and White Services (GWS). Assume that Lon has hired you to advise him on whether he should invest in the business. To solve Lon's investment problem, you intend to solve equation (A8.1) repeated here as equation (10.5) below:

(10.5)

$$NPV = -(A_0 - D_0) + \frac{(CR_1 - CE_1 - iD_0)(1-T) + TDep_1}{[1 + IRR^E(1-T)]}$$
$$+ \cdots + \frac{(CR_n - CE_n - iD_{n-1})(1-T) + TDep_n}{[1 + IRR^E(1-T)]^n}$$
$$+ \frac{Csh_0 - D_0 + TAccts_0 + (1-T)Accts_n}{[1 + IRR^E(1-T)]^n}$$
$$+ \frac{(1-T)V_n^{liquidation} + TV_n^{book} - [AP_n - AP_0 + AL_n - AL_0](1-T)}{[1 + IRR^E(1-T)]^n}$$

Equation (10.5) is a generalized NPV equation that is used as the basis for the PV template that is used in this section. By setting debt to zero, using the tax rate for assets and the defender's IRR for return on assets—we can find NPV and IRR for assets. By account for debt, using the tax rate for equity and the defender's IRR for return on its equity—we can find NPV and IRR for equity. We can solve for IRRs by setting NPVs equal to zero. We illustrate how to operationalize equation (10.5) using the PV template described at the end of Chapter 8 by solving Lon's investment in GWS.

To complete the PV template corresponding to equation (10.5) Lon provides the information.

Acquisition and depreciation. Lon estimates the initial investment for GWS will cost $40,000. We enter that number in cell B4. Since the focus is on return to assets, we ignore debt levels, leaving column C equal to zero. The equipment falls into the MACRS 3-year depreciation class (25%, 37.5%, 25%, and 12.50%). We calculate depreciation by multiplying MACR 3-year class rates (25%, 37.5%, 25% and 12.5%) times the value of the capital accounts equal to $40,000. Depreciation is ($40,000 x 25%) = $10,000 in year one; $40,000 x 37.5% = $15,000 in year two, $40,000 x 25% = $10,000 in year three, and $40,000 x 12.5% = $5,000 in year four. Depreciation in each year is recorded in column F. Investment book value equals the initial purchase price less accumulated depreciation is recorded in column E. To simplify, we set liquidated value of the investment equals to its book value and reported the results in column D.

Operating income and expenses. Lon recognizes that not all his customers will pay for his services when he provides them. As a result, he expects his accounts receivable (AR) to equal $1,000 at the end of his first year of operation, to grow to $1200 at the end of year two, to decline to $800 at the end of year three, and to decline to $400 at the end of year four. The outstanding $400 balance at the end of year four, he expects to liquidate when he sells his business. Inventories (INV) are expected to equal zero. The sum of asset operating account balances (AR + INV) are reported in column G.

Lon intends to charge $40 per service for both lawn care and snow removal. He estimates that his expenses (labor, fuel, main-tenance) will average $18 per service. Lon projects the number of services for the next four years to be 500 in year one, 750 in year two, 900 in year three, and 1,000 in year four. To find sales we multiply the number of services per year by the price paid per service. We find that sales equal $40 x 500 = $20,000 in year one; $40 x 750 = $30,000 plus $200 of miscellaneous income in year two ($30,200); $40 x 900 = $36,000 plus $600 in miscellaneous income in year three ($36,600); and $40 x 1000 = $40,000 less $400 of promotional discounts in year four ($39,600). We report sales in column H.

We adjust sales to find cash receipts by accounting for changes in (AR+ INV) and report the results as cash receipts (CR) in column I. In year one AR increased by $1,000. As a result, CR equal sales of $20,000 less $1,000 increase in AR or $19,000. In year two AR increased by $200 so that CR equal sales of $30,000 less $200 increase in AR or $29,800. In year three, AR declined by $400 so the CR was greater than sales of $36,000 by $400: $36,000 + $400 equals $36,400. Finally, at the end of year four, the last year Lon intends to operate his business, he expects that AR will decline to $400 increasing CR by $400 to $4,400. Finally, the remaining $400 balance of CR Lon liquidates when he sells the business.

We assume that the sum of outstanding liability operating accounts, account payable (AL) and accrued liabilities (AL) equal zero and report the results in column J. We find COGS by multiplying the number of services provided times the cost to deliver a service unit. We find they equal $18 x 500 = $9,000 in year one; $18 x 750 = $13,500 in year two; $18 x 900 = $16,200 in year three, and $40 x 1000 = $18,000 in year four. We report expenses in column K. And because there are no changes in operating account, cash expenses equal expenses are reported in column L. Interest costs reported in column M equal debt at the beginning of the period times the average interest rate. Since our focus in on earnings and rates of return on equity, we set debt to zero and as a result, interest costs are zero.

Depreciation tax savings. Tax savings from depreciation recorded in column N equal depreciation recorded in column F times the average tax rate. Column O records annual cash flow equal to cash receipts (column I), less cash expenses (column L), minus interest costs (column M) whose sum is multiplied by one minus the average tax rate, plus depreciation tax savings (column N), plus change in outstanding debt (ΔColumn C).

Liquidation values. We find the after-tax liquidated value of asset operating accounts (Column P), after-tax liquidated value of liability operating accounts (Column Q), and the after-tax difference between the market and book value of capital assets (Column R). Finally, we sum cash flows from liquidations and cash flow in the last period (Column S).

Other exogenous variables. We report the defender's IRR on assets, average tax rate, and average interest rate in Table 10.4 below:

Table 10.4. Green and White Services (GWS) Asset Variables: Defender's IRR[A], Average Tax Rate, After-Tax Discount Rate, and Average Interest Rate on Debt.

	A	B
1	r	0.05
2	T	0.2
3	r(1-T)	0.04
4	Average interest rate	0.06

To simplify, we assume that Lon's marginal tax rate and capital gains tax rate both equal 20%. Lon also assumes that the before-tax IRR of the defending investment equals 5%. As a result, the after-tax IRR of the defending investment is 4%. The average interest rate (not relevant in this case because of the focus on assets) is 6%.

Rolling NPV, AE, and IRR calculations. Rolling NPVs, IRRs, and AEs equal their values calculated as if the term ended in each year. Lon assumes he will operate GCS for four years. He might have asked: what is the optimal life of GCS? To answer the optimal life question, we need to find annual or rolling NPV and AE values. In this case, Lon is correct, four years is preferred to one, two, or three years of operation. Rolling NPV reported in column N increased from a negative NPV of ($769) if he operated the business for one year to an NPV of $16,412 if he operated his business for four years as planned. Meanwhile rolling AEs increase from a negative ($800) to a positive $4,521 while rolling IRRs increase from 2% to 18.67%.

Table 10.5. PV template used to find drolling estimates for NPVAs, IRRAs, and AEA

s e a r n e d o n G W S ' s a s s e t s . .

Open PV Template in Microsoft Excel.

A

B

C

D

E

F

G

H

I

J

K

L

M

N

O

P

Q

E

S

T

U

V

1

Year Assets Debt capital Capital accounts liquidation value Capital accounts book value Depreciation (Dep= ΔE) Asset Operating accounts (AR + INV) Sales Cash Receipts (CR = H+ Δ G) Liability Operating Accounts (AP+AL) Expenses (COGS + OEs) Cash Expenses (CE=K+Δ J) Interest costs (Int=i*C (t-1)) Depreciation tax savings (TxF) After-Tax Cash flow= (I-L-M)(1-tax rate) +N+ΔC After-tax Liquidation asset operating accounts=[G(t)-G(0)](1-tax rate) Afer-tax Liquidation liability operating accounts: [J(n)-J(0)](1-tax rate) Sum liquidating Capital, operating, and debt accounts = (D-E)(1-tax rate)+P-Q+E-C Sum liquidations + last period cash flow = 0+R Rolling afer-tax NPV Rolling after-tax AE Rolling after-tax IRR

2

0

$40,000

$0

$40,000

$40,000

3

1

$0

$0

$30,000

$30,000

$10,000

$1,000

$20,000

$19,000

$0

$9,000

$9,000

$0

$2,000

$10,000

$800

$0

$30,800

$40,800

-$769

-$800

2.00%

$0

$0

$15,000

$15,000

$15,000

$1,200

$30,200

$30,000

$0

$13,500

$13,500

$0

$3,000

$16,200

$960

$0

$15,960

$32,160

-$651

-$345

3.03%

5

3

$0

$0

$5,000

$5,000

$10,000

$800

$35,600

$36,000

$0

$16,500

$16,500

$0

$2,000

$17,600

$640

$0

$5,640

$23,240

$5,253

$1,893

9.93%

6

4

$0

$0

$0

$0

$5,000

$400

$39,600

$40,000

$0

$18,000

$18,000

$0

$1,000

$18,600

$320

$0

$320

$18,920

$16,412

$4,521

Cash flow used to Find Lon's Rolling NPV and IRRs. It may be helpful to make explicit the cash flow used to find the rolling NPVs, IRRs and AEs. Recall that in the last year, cash flow sums operating cash flow for that year and the liquidation of operating and capital accounts. The cash flow per year are summarized in Table 10.6.

Table 10.6. Cash flow used to find Lon's Rolling NPV^A, ^{IRRA}, and AE^A on his assets. IRR^A are calculated at the end of each year.

	A	B	C	D	E
1	Economic Life	1 year	2 years	3 years	4 years
2		-$40,000.00	-$40,000.00	-$40,000.00	-$40,000.00
3		$40,800.00	$10,000.00	$10,000.00	$10,000.00
4		2.00%	$32,160.00	$16,200.00	$16,200.00
5	...		3.03%	$23,240.00	$17,600.00
6	...			9.93%	$18,920.00
7	...				18.67%

Earnings and rate of return on Equity. Once we have solved for Lon's earnings on his assets, (NPV^A) and rate of return on assets (IRR^A) we can easily find Lon's earnings and rate of return on his equity, NPV^E and IRR^E respectively. To do so we enter his defender's IRR^E equal to 9%, his average tax rate equal to 40%. As a result, his after-tax IRR^E on his defender is 5.4%. We assume that Lon borrows $30,000 to finance his new business and retires the loan in equal installments of $10,000 over the next three years.

Table 10.7. Green and White Services (GWS) Equity Variables: Defender's IRR^E, Average Tax Rate, After-Tax Discount Rate, and Average Interest Rate on Debt.

	A	B
1	r	0.09
2	T	0.4
3	r(1-T)	0.054
4	Average interest rate	0.06

The annual cash flow used to find Lon's rolling NPV^{E}s, IRR^{E}s, and AE^{E}s on his equity is reported in Table 10.8.

Table 10.8. Cash flow used to find Lon's Rolling NPV^E, IRR^E, and AE^E on his equity. IRR^E are calculated at the end of each year.

		A	B	C	D	E
1	Economic Life	1 year	2 years	3 years	4 years
2		-$40,000.00	-$40,000.00	-$40,000.00	-$40,000.00
3		$40,800.00	$10,000.00	$10,000.00	$10,000.00
4	IRR% (last entry)	1.50%	$31,620.00	$15,900.00	$15,900.00
5	...		3.03%	$21,180.00	$15,700.00
6	...			7.63%	$15,440.00
7	...				14.85%

After making the necessary changes, we resolve the PV model template and obtain the results in Table 10.9.

Table 10.9. PV template used to find ▶

	A	B	C	D	E	F	G	H	I	J	K	
1	Year	Assets	Debt capital	Capital accounts liquidation value	Capital accounts book value	Depreciation (Dep= ΔE)	Asset Operating accounts (AR + INV)	Sales	Cash Receipts (CR = H+ Δ G)	Liability Operating Accounts (AP+AL)	Expenses (COGS + OEs)	
2	0	$40,000	$30,000	$40,000	$40,000							
3	1	$0	$20,000	$30,000	$30,000	$10,000	$1,000	$20,000	$19,000	$0	$9,000	
4	2	$0	$10,000	$15,000	$15,000	$15,000	$1,200	$30,200	$30,000	$0	$13,500	
5	3	$0	$0	$5,000	$5,000	$10,000	$800	$35,600	$36,000	$0	$16,500	
6	4	$0	$0	$0	$0	$5,000	$400	$39,600	$40,000	$0	$18,000	

An Incremental Investment Problem: Adding Landscaping Services to GWS

Partial budget analysis. We emphasize that we recommend incremental investment analysis compare before and after whole firm investments after making appropriate size adjustments. On the other hand, we recognize that sometimes an approximation result is adequate and that examining the changes in before and after whole firm's NPV and IRR results may be enough, especially if the incremental investment is small and likely to have limited influence in the firm.

Examples of when partial budgeting has been employed include incremental investments that: expand an existing enterprise, purchase new equipment, change the commodity being produced when equipment requirements are similar, participating in a government program, and changing a production practice.

The most significant limitations are partial budgeting analysis as it is typically employed is that it ignores the time value of money and is limited to comparing two investments. Furthermore, it is often limited to analyzing benefits and costs in a single period, making it ineffective for long term investments[1]. Were we to make an inter-temporal adaptation of partial budgeting analysis, we would find in each period the change in cash receipts less the change in cash expenses. Alternatively, Benefits = increased return from the new activity plus reduced costs of the replaced activity less Costs=reduced returns from old activity + increased costs associated with new activity Or, as suggested in partial budgeting analysis, the increase in cash costs from the new investment

GWS's *incremental investment*. Before finalizing his investment, Lon wonders about an adjustment to his financial plan. If he adds a trailer and a small tractor to his investment, he can perform not only yard care services but some basic landscaping services as well. The additional investment would equal $30,000 that is also depreciable over the next four years. Comparing the four-year cash flow associated with GWS, Lon wonders what percent change would be required to break-even? In other words, Lon wants to find α in the following equation:

$$\text{(10.6)} \quad \$30,000 = \frac{\sigma x\$10,000}{1.04} + \frac{\sigma x\$16,200}{1.04^2} + \frac{\sigma x\$17,600}{1.04^3} + \frac{\sigma x\$18,920}{1.04^4}$$

1. A reference to partial budgeting analysis is: https://sustainable-farming.rutgers.edu/wp-content/uploads/2014/09/Partial-Budgeting-Manual.pdf

Table 10.10. Cash Flow Required to Break-Even with a $30,000 Incremental Investment

	A	B	C
1	Year	Cash Flow	Cash Flow(a)
2	0	($30,000)	($30,000)
3	1	$10,000	$5,318
4	2	$16,200	$8,615
5	3	$17,600	$9,360
6	4	$18,920	$10,062
7	r(1-T*)	0.04	0.04
8	NPV^A	$26,412.43	$0.00
9	AE^A	-$7,276.36	$0.00
10	IRR^A	33.38%	4%
11	a		0.531798

The goal-seek results confirm that for a $30,000 incremental investment would need to earn roughly 53% of the original cash flow to break-even, that is, earn the defender's IRR^A of 4%.

Brown and Round Doughnuts

An important kind of incremental investment is one that to adapt means replacing or modifying an existing investment. In this section we consider a doughnut machine replacement. Although less preferred, we can make incremental investment analyzes without using the PV model template. In this section we demonstrate how to perform incremental investment analysis without using the PV model template.

Brown and Round Doughnuts. We next consider two alternative machines for making doughnuts. One machine is the one already in operation. In this case the challengers are an older version of the original machine and a new machine. Should you continue with the used machine, buy a new machine, or get out of the doughnut business?

Continuing to make doughnuts with the old machine.

In this example the challenger is an older version of the original investment. To be specific, suppose you bought a doughnut machine 3 years ago for $90,000. You are depreciating the machine over 5 years using the MACRS method, and the expected market value 5 years from today is $10,000. The machine generates $30,000 in cash revenues and produces $15,000 in cash expenses each year. If you sold the machine today, you could get $30,000 from a local competitor.

Your after-tax IRR^A, $r(1 - T)$, is 10%, your marginal tax rate is 40%, and the capital gains tax is 20%. Assume book value depreciation can be used to offset ordinary income.

Let's begin with the old machine. Keeping the old machine is equivalent to reinvesting its $30,000 current value ($V_0$) in the business and forfeiting the tax refund from capital losses. To determine the tax refund forfeited, recall that the used machine was purchased 3 years earlier for $90,000, and has been depreciated using 5-year MACR, so the machine's book value is $90,000(100\% - 15\% - 25.5\% - 17.85\%)$ = $37,485.

Since book value exceeds liquidation value, a tax credit is owed to the seller equal to $T(V_0 - V_0^{book})$ = .4(30,000 - 37,485) = $2,994. Now we can write the acquisition ATCF as $ATCF_0$ = - $30,000 - $2,994 = - $32,994. Finally, 5 year MACR depreciation rates on the old machine equal: 16.66%, 16.66%, and 8.33%. We write the ATCF for the tth period as:

$$ATCF_t = (CR_t - CE_t - Dep_t)(1 - T) + Dep_t - n$$

(10.7)
$$= (CR_t - CE_T)(1 - T) + TDep_t - \Delta V_n$$

However, because ATCF per period differs, we describe it using Table 10.11. below.

Table 10.11. Finding ATCF for Continuing to Operate with the Old Doughnut Machine

Year	CR_t	CE_t	Dep_t (MACR)	$(CR_t - CE_t)(1-T) + TDep_t$	ΔV_n	$ATCF_1$
1	30,000	15,000	14,994 (16.66%)	(15,000 x .6) + (14,994 x .4) = 14,998	0	$14,998
2	30,000	15,000	14,994 (16.66%)	(15,000 x .6) + (14,994 x .4) = 14,998	0	$14,998
3	30,000	15,000	7,470 (8.33%)	(15,000 x .6) + (7470 x .4) = 11,988	0	$11,988
4	30,000	15,000	0	(15,000 x .6) = 9,000	0	$9,000
5	30,000	15,000	0	(15,000 x .6) = 9,000	0	$9,000

Finally, we write the salvage value for the old machine. Recalling that the salvage value of the old machine, V_5, is $10,000, that the old machine is completely depreciated, and the capital gains tax rate T_g is 0.2, we can write the salvage value as:

$$ATCF_5 = V_5(\text{old}) - T[V_5(\text{old}) - V_5(\text{book of old})]$$

(10.8)
$$= \$10,000 - .2(\$10,000 - 0) = \$8,000$$

Finally, we are prepared to combine the ATCF from the acquisition, operation, and liquidation of the old doughnut machine. We express these in Table 10.12.

Table 10.12. Old Doughnut Machine Operating ATCF

Year	CR_t	CE_t	Dep_t (MACR)	$(CR_t-CE_t)(1-T) + TDep_t$	ΔV_n	$ATCF_1$
0						

Year	CR_t	CE_t	Dep_t (MACR)	$(CR_t-CE_t)(1-T) + TDep_t$	ΔV_n	$ATCF_1$
0	$-V_0 - T(V_0 - V_0^{book})$ = -$30,000 - (.4)($30,000 - $37,485) = - $30,000 - $2,994 = - $32,994					-$32,994 (Acquisition)
1	30,000	15,000	14,994 (16.66%)	(15,000 x .6) + (14,994 x .4) = 14,998	0	$14,998
2	30,000	15,000	14,994 (16.66%)	(15,000 x .6) + (14,994 x .4) = 14,998	0	$14,998
3	30,000	15,000	7,470 (8.33%)	(15,000 x .6) + (7470 x .4) = 11,988	0	$11,988
4	30,000	15,000	0	(15,000 x .6) = 9,000	0	$9,000
5	30,000	15,000	0	(15,000 x .6) = 9,000	0	$9,000
6	$V_5 - T(V_5 - V_5^{book})$ = $10,000 - (.2)($10,000 - 0) = $10,000 - $2,000 = $8,000					$8,000 (Liquidation)

The only other calculation left is to compute the NPV of the old doughnut machine which we complete using our Excel spreadsheet.

Table 10.13. Old Doughnut Machine
Open Table 10.13. in Microsoft Excel

	A	B	C
1	variables	data	formulas
2	rate	0.1	
3	Acquisition cost	-$32,994	
4	ATCF1	$14,998	
5	ATCF2	$14,998	
6	ATCF3	$11,988	
7	ATCF4	$9,000	
8	ATCF5	$9,000	
9	Salvage value	$8,000	
10	NPV	$18,745	=-V_0+NPV(rate,ATCF1:ATCF5)+V_n/(1+rate)^nper
11	IRR	30%	=IRR(Acquisition cost, ATCF1:ATCF5,salvage value)
12	AE	($4,944.92)	=PMT(rate,nper,NPV)
13	nper	5	

A new doughnut machine.

Assume that, after completing the PV analysis of the old doughnut machine, a salesman for a "new and improved" doughnut machine stops by and wants to sell you a new machine. The new machine will increase your revenues to $45,000 each year, and decrease your expenses to only $10,000 each year. The new machine costs $90,000 and will require $10,000 for delivery and installation costs. Thus, the acquisition ATCF0 = $100,000. The machine will fall into the MACRS five-year depreciation class (15%, 25.5%, 17.85%, 16.66%, 16.66%, and 8.33%). The machine is expected to have a $40,000 salvage value after 5 years.

Next, we need to determine the operating ATCF for the new machine. Tax rates, the defender's after-tax IRR, and MACR depreciation rates are the same as before—equal to those used to evaluate the continued use of the old doughnut machine. Because of the level of sales, accounts receivable and accounts payable increase by $5,000 and $2,000 in the first year respectively. They are reduced by the same amount in the fifth year. The formula for operating ATCF is the same as before except that sales and expenses are no longer just cash items and must be adjusted by the term $\Delta V_n = \Delta CA - \Delta CL = \$5,000 - \$2,000 = \$3,000$

$$ATCF_t = (\text{Sales}_t - \text{Expenses}_t - Dep_t)(1 - T) + Dep_t - \Delta V_n$$

(10.9)
$$= (\text{Sales}_t - \text{Expenses}_t)(1 - T) + TDep_t - \Delta V_n$$

The new machine will be depreciated using the 5-year MACRS method. The depreciation for each machine, and the change in depreciation each year for the next 5 years is:

Table 10.14a. New Doughnut Machine
Depreciation

Year	$100,000 x MACR rate	=	Depreciation
1	$100,000 x 15%	=	$15,000
2	$100,000 x 25.5%	=	$25,500
3	$100,000 x 17.85%	=	$17,850
4	$100,000 x 16.66%	=	$16,660
5	$100,000 x 16.66%	=	$16,660

Remember that depreciation expense is a noncash expense, which by itself doesn't generate a cash flow. However, you can use the depreciation expense to reduce taxable income. As a result, the firm realizes an additional tax savings from depreciation. The amount of the tax savings are described below.

Table 10.14b. New Doughnut Machine Tax Savings

Year	Tax Savings	=	(Depreciation)(T = .4)
1	$15,000 x (.4)	=	$6,000
2	$25,500 x (.4)	=	$10,200
3	$17,850 x (.4)	=	$7,140
4	$16,660 x (.4)	=	$6,664
5	$16,660 x (.4)	=	$6,664

Finally, we find the salvage value as follows. We first recognize that the sale of the doughnut machine in 5 years will increase cash flow by $40,000. Next, we find the asset's book value in year five as the difference between its acquisition value less its accumulated depreciation: $100,000 – ($15,000 + $25,500 + $17,850 + $16,600 + $16,660) = $8,330. Since the asset's book value is less than its salvage value, there are capital gains taxes to be paid. Therefore, the salvage value ATCF can be written as the salvage value less the capital gains tax:

$$ATCF = V_5 - T[V_5 - V_5(\text{book})]$$

(10.10)
$$= \$40,000 - .2(\$40,000 - \$8,330) = \$33,666$$

Finally, we combine acquisition, operation, and liquidation ATCF associated with the new doughnut machine in Table 10.15.

Table 10.15. New Doughnut Machine Operating ATCF

Year	Sales	Expense	Dep$_t$ (MACR)	(Sales – Expenses) x (1 – T) + T Dep.	ΔV_n	ATCF$_1$
0 ATCF$_0$	(Acquisition) = –V$_0$ =					–$100,000
1 ATCF$_1$	45,000	10,000	15,000 (15%)	(35,000 x .6) + (15,000 x .4) = 27,000	3,000	$24,000
2 ATCF$_2$	45,000	10,000	25,500 (25.5%)	(35,000 x .6) + (25,500 x .4) = 31,200	0	$31,200
3 ATCF$_3$	45,000	10,000	17,850 (17.85%)	(35,000 x .6) + (17,850 x .4) = 28,140	0	$28,140
4 ATCF$_4$	45,000	10,000	16,660 (16.66%)	(35,000 x .6) + (16,660 x .4) = 27,664	0	$27,664
5 ATCF$_5$	45,000	10,000	16,660 (16.66%)	(35,000 x .6) + (16,660 x .4) = 27,664	–3,000	$30,664
5 ATCF$_5$	(liquidation) = V$_5$ – T[V$_5$ – V$_5$(book)] = $40,000 – .2($40,000 – $8,330) =					$33,666

We find the NPV for the new doughnut machine in Table 10.16:

Table 10.16. New Doughnut Machine NPV

Year	$\dfrac{1}{(1+r(1-T))^2} = \dfrac{1}{1.10^t}$	ATCF	$\dfrac{ATCF}{(1+r(1-T))^t}$
0	1	-$100,000	-$100,000
1	.91	$24,000	$21,840
2	0.83	$31,200	$25,896
3	0.75	$28,140	$21,105
4	0.68	$27,664	$18,812
5	0.62	$30,664 + $33,666 = $64,330	$39,885

$$NPV = \sum_{t=0}^{5} \frac{ATCF_t}{1+r(1-T)^2} = \quad \text{\$27,538 (27,584 using CF worksheet)}$$

Finally, we find the NPV for the new doughnut machine using our Excel Spreadsheet.

Table 10.17. New Doughnut Machine
Open Table 10.17. in Microsoft Excel

	A	B	C
	variables	data	formulas
1			
2	rate	0.1	
3	Acquisition cost	-$100,000	
4	ATCF1	$24,000	
5	ATCF2	$31,200	
6	ATCF3	$28,140	
7	ATCF4	$27,664	
8	ATCF5	$30,664	
9	Salvage value	$33,666	
10	NPV	$27,584	=-V0+NPV(rate,ATCF1:ATCF5)+Vn/(1+rate)^nper
11	IRR	18%	=IRR(Acquisition cost, ATCF1:ATCF5,salvage value)
12	AE	($7,276.60)	=PMT(rate,nper,NPV)
13	nper	5	

So, what have we learned? NPV will be positive for both options, continuing to use the old machine or investing in the new one. However, the firm's NPV will increase the most if it adopts the new machine—an increase of $8,839 ($27,584 - $18,745) over continuing to use the old machine. However, the IRR of the old machine is greater, and we have a conflict between IRR and NPV rankings. The ranking is resolved by deciding on the reinvestment rate for the differences in funding required by the two investments. If the difference in funding levels is invested at the discount rate, the NPV rankings are appropriate. If the investments can be scaled, then the IRR rankings are appropriate. It is assumed here that the reinvestment rate is the after-tax IRR of the defender, 10%, so that any differences in size would not change their respective NPVs, and NPV rankings are appropriate.

Summary and Conclusions

This chapter has reviewed two stand-alone and incremental investments. Of the two types of investments, incremental one may be the most common and therefore merit a separate chapter calling attention to there special nature.

Of importance, incremental investments require that its optimal use requires that the use of existing services and nondurable inputs be changed to accommodate the incremental investment. As a result, it has become a somewhat common approach to analyze incremental investments by measuring changes in all the variables used in the PV template and calculating NPVs, IRRs, and AEs based on the changes in cash flow.

We wondered how the rankings before and after the incremental investment would compare to the NPV, IRR, and AE of the difference? We note that the rankings might be inconsistent because the homogeneity of size condition was violated. NPV rankings generally were consistent.

So, we ask: why perform incremental investment at all? What not just compare the firm's financial rates of return and earnings before and after the investment? While we recommend this approach, we also recommend that PV problems are solved by practical people solving practical and immediate problems and may lack the resources required to solve a complete firm investment analysis. In these cases, reverting to incremental investments with perhaps less data requirements is the preferred approach.

Questions

1. Please describe the difference in investment focus between an AIS and a PV model?
2. What is the main difference between a stand-alone versus an incremental investment? Explain why some sources describe incremental investment analysis as incremental budgeting analysis.

3. This chapter presented two main PV model templates. One focused on analyzing investments. The second one focused on analyzing equity committed to the investment. Describe the differences between the two templates. Then explain how these differences permit us to calculate returns associated with investments versus returns on equity committed to investments. 4. Describe the nature of a fixed investment.

4. A capital investment provides services over several periods. A nondurable provides services once. Explain how this difference in capital goods and nondurable inputs are recognized in PV models.

5. A capital investment provides services for more than one period without losing its identity. The cost of providing these services is the change in the liquidation of the capital asset and the use of nondurable goods. The change in the liquidation value of a capital asset may mostly depend on the passage of time and the intensity of its use. Please explain how these two costs that result from the passage of time an use influence the optimal service extraction rate from the capital asset.

6. Operating accounts include AR, INV, AP, and AL. Describe how decreases (increases) in capital accounts influence operating and liquidation ATCF.

7. What is the difference between exogenous and endogenous variables used to solve for NPV, AE, and IRR in PV models?

8. Solving PV models requires that we forecast the values of exogenous and endogenous variables for the economic life of the investment. Describe how these forecasts might vary in their sophistication.

11. "Anticipating the Future: Forecasting and Present Value Models

LINDON ROBISON

Learning goals. At the end of this chapter, you should be able to: (1) distinguish between deterministic and statistical forecasts; (2) recognize the difference between endogenous and exogenous variable forecasts; (3) recognize the difference between dependent and independent variables in statistical forecasts; (4) recognize the value of quantitative forecasts; (5) understand how to apply econometric methods to forecast; and (6) be able to complete present value (PV) models by forecasting endogenous and exogenous variables.

Learning objectives. To achieve your learning goals, you should complete the following objectives:

- Understand the difference between deterministic and statistical forecasts.
- Recognize the difference between exogenous and endogenous variables and forecasts.
- Distinguish between independent and dependent variables in regression equations.
- Learn the difference between quantitative forecasts and qualitative predictions.
- Understand why present value (PV) models require cash receipts and cash expense forecasts.
- Learn how to find forecast confidence intervals.
- Utilize information about time and use costs to forecast cash costs of goods sold (COGS) and overhead expenses (OEs).
- Understand how to use correlations among variables to make forecasts.
- Practice forecasting techniques for simple investment problems.

Introduction

1

Forecasts and predictions. This chapter is about forecasting. Forecasts use observations and perceptions about the past to predict the future. The origin of the word forecast comes from the word "fore" which means before plus the word "casten" which means to scheme, plan, or prepare. Thus, when we forecast, we predict something before it happens so that we can plan or prepare for it.

1. Much of the material in this chapter was developed in an article under review by the Agricultural Finance Review titled: "Coordinated Financial Statements: What-is, What-if, and How-much Questions" by Lindon J. Robison and Peter J. Barry submitted January 2021.

Forecasts and guesses go together. A comment about what someone thinks will happen in the future is also a prediction. We sometimes tell the difference between predictions and forecasts by how we got to our idea of what will happen in the future. A prediction is less scientific and more emotional than a forecast. It is based on an educated guess. From this point of view, predictions use a wider range of information to describe the future, such as past observations, expert views, conditional relationships, signs, impressions, and other hints about the future.

Forecasts for every day. Everyone makes predictions. We have to have them. In fact, almost every choice we make is based on what we think will happen. We count on our almost "every moment" forecasts so much that we may not pay much attention to them. For example, we might not think much about our prediction that water will pour out of the tap when we turn it on. Still, our forecast comes before turning on the tap, and it's what makes us do it.

How important predictions are in general. Some forecasts are more important than others because they lead to big investments of money or time that are hard or expensive to take back. Buying a house, a new car, or picking a partner may be examples of important predictions. When making important predictions, we might need to make more than one prediction. When we buy a car, we might want to guess how often it will need repairs, how well it will use gas, how comfortable it will be to drive, and whether or not it will please our partner. We might talk to friends who have bought cars like ours to get a better idea of what to expect. We might look at professional car-buying guides that compare the performance and price of cars that interest us. We might even rent the car of interest to get a feel for it firsthand. But at the end of the day, we predict how buying a car will go and make a choice based on what we think will happen.

Good predictions. The accuracy of our predictions depends on the quality of the information and research we use to make them, as well as how far in the future the predictions are made. Think about what comes next. We may be almost sure that turning on the tap makes water flow because we have been doing this for a long time. In this case, our prediction is very likely to come true. On the other hand, we may have heard that a restaurant serves a tasty Rueben sandwich, and based on the "expert" opinions of our friends, we may think that if we eat the Rueben at the restaurant, we will be happy with the experience. In this case, our prediction is about half right. (Who's to say our friends don't like sandwiches as much as we do?) Some ads include predictions, like that if you buy a certain product, you'll become popular and rich, and your skin's spots will go away. If these predictions aren't backed up by double-blind studies, they should be questioned because the people making them have no reason to give correct results.

Forecasting is done in two steps. Forecasting is done in two steps. In the first step, we gather and look at data to see how different variables change over time. Let's say we look at an exogenous variable at time t, x_t, and find that it is strongly linked to the same variable from earlier times. Then we could write: $x_t = f(x_{t-1}, x_{t-2,}) + t$, where t is an error term that shows what the external variable doesn't explain in the current time period and the ones before and after it.

In the first step, let's say we guess a value for x_t, which we'll call x_t since it's just a guess and we don't know what the real value is. Then, we solve 274 | Ch. 11 to guess two times in the future. Models for Forecasting and Present Value

Find: $x_{t+1} = f(x_t, x_{t-1},)$ by using the coefficient we found in step 1. If $x_{t+1} - x_t = c$, then our prediction for k periods from now is: $x_{t+k} = x_t + kc$. What comes next. In what comes next, we'll talk about how different forecast equations are based on the almost certain knowledge that we use to make our predictions. All forecast models give estimates of what will happen in the future, but some of them are based on facts and some on statistics. In statistically estimated forecast equations, it will be important to tell the difference between factors that are dependent and those that are independent. We will use the words from Chapters 5 and 7 to tell the difference between exogenous and endogenous variables when we talk about the types of variables we will be forecasting. At the end of the day, the goal of this chapter is to find the forecasted endogenous and exogenous factors that are needed to finish PV models. You can use the questions at the end of the chapter to practise and learn more about forecasts. Equations for the Future

Exogenous and endogenous factors. Variables that come from outside a system are called exogenous. Endogenous variables are ones that are set up by the system itself. When we made coordinated financial statements (CFS) and PV templates, we made a distinction between endogenous variables, whose values were set by the CFS and PV template, and exogenous variables, whose values were set by something outside the CFS and PV template. Both the CFS system and the PV templates use deterministic equations to show how endogenous and exogenous variables are linked to each other. Dependent and independent factors. People often talk about dependent and independent factors when doing experiments. Statistical models let the experimenter change the independent variables to see how they affect the dependent variables that are tied to the independent variables. But sometimes the link between dependent and independent variables can't be found through experiments. Instead, it has to be inferred and seen. This is the sense that we use depen-dent and independent factors in forecast equation. Variables that work on their own, and what do we know for sure? We require independent variables to forecast dependent variables. Our independent variables are those that are used as exogenous variables in the CFS and PV models that are used to find endogenous variables. So, what do we know for sure about the different factors? There are only two things we know for sure that can be used as independent variables in our prediction equation: the amount of time until a future date and the values of variables that have already happened, including lagged values of the dependent variable. If we added a contemporaneous variable to our independent factors in our forecast equation, we would have to predict it along with the dependent variable. This can happen when big forecasting models use multiple equations to predict a lot of dependent factors. In our conversation, we only use one equation to make a prediction. Lastly, our confidence in the connection between our dependent variables and time and lagged values grows with the quality and amount of information used to figure out the correlations.

Still, human behavior can often be predictable—we often act the same way in similar circumstances, and we develop habits that seem ingrained. We often use these tendencies to aid us in our forecasts. One important category of events that we use to guide our forecasts are commitments and covenants to perform in a predictable way in the future. For example, most have borrowed and agreed to repay on loans following specified terms. These performance commitments can be treated as nearly time dependent exogenous variables.

Forecasting endogenous variables. While forecasts mostly focus on exogenous variables when used within CFS and PV templates, we may find it useful to forecast endogenous variables. Forecasting endogenous variables is usually not necessary because they are determined by relationships established within the CFS and PV template. However, we recognize that our exogenous variables are estimated with error so that endogenous variable forecasts derived from the exogenous variable forecasts also contain errors. As a result, we may find it useful to over-identify some endogenous variables and a check on accuracy of our exogenous variables.

So, what have we learned? We learned that system variables may be either exogenous variables determined outside of the system or endogenous variables determined within the system by exogenous variables. Exogenous variables used to determine endogenous variables are dependent variables forecast by statistical or other models using independent variables that have been observed or that are highly correlated with the passage of time. In sum, we are mostly interested in forecasting exogenous variables (for our purposes) to use in CFS or PV templates. While we could technically, forecast endogenous variables, and sometimes we do, they are not our primary concern because they are determined within the CFS or PV templates.

In what follows, we will organize our forecast equation around what we know for sure. As a result, some forecast equations depend only on the passage of time. Others depend on the lagged values of a dependent variables. And still others depend on the lagged values of independent variables. Finally, we may create hybrid forecast equations that combine time and lagged values of dependent and independent variables. Forecasts that combine contemporaneous independent variables require accompanying equations that forecast their values—forecast equations in which they are the dependent variables.

Forecast Equations and What we Know

Trend lines. Consider forecasting exogenous variables that are highly correlated with or are dependent on the passage of time. Time may enter the forecast equation in several different forms, but to forecast future periods only requires time as the independent variable. An example may be an equation that forecasts the condition of a building's roof k periods in the future. The condition of the roof and its remaining life might both be expressed as a function of the roof's age. Consider such an expression:

A roof's remaining useful life equals its useful life when constructed – it age.

Forecast equations that depend mostly on the passage of time are often referred to as trend lines. In this case, the endogenous variable y depends only on a constant and the independent variable t. This forecast equation can be expressed as:

(11.1) $y_t = \theta_0 + \theta_1 t + \epsilon_t$

The trend line forecast k periods in the can simply be written as:

(11.2) $\hat{y}_{t+k} = \theta_0 + \theta_1(t + k)$

In equation (11.2), the hat over the endogenous variable signifies that we have an estimate, not an actual value.

Lagged dependent variable. Suppose that Lon wants to forecast the demand for his services next season. His forecast might begin with the demand for his services he experienced during the previous period. One reason to emphasize the demand for Lon's services in the previous period is because so many conditions that existed last year will exist this year. To reflect the connection between this year's forecast and what happened last year, we specify:

Services in period t = services provided in period $(t - 1)$ + an error term

To complicate our forecasts, we recognize that the change in demand for Lon's services in period t will depend on the number of new lawn care providers (Lon's competition) plus change in the number of potential customers measured by the number of new households in Lon's service area with a yard. Call these changes in the demand less changes increases in services provided by others equal to change in services Δs_t and write the result as:

Services in period t =services provided in period $t - 1 + \Delta s_t$ + error.

Distributed lags of independent variables. Closely related to forecasts that depend on the passage of time and lagged values of depend variables are lagged values of independent variable on which the dependent variable depends. This forecast equation is relevant when the dependent variable depends on the outcome of other independent variables. Some variables such as costs of goods sold (COGS), depend on production activities in the previous period. So, if we intend to forecast COGS, we may want to relate them to some function of production activities in the previous period.

COGS this period = some function of production activity levels in the previous period.

A popular forecast equation that combines both the lagged dependent variable and independent variables is the infinite geometric distributed lag (IGL) forecast equation. We derive it next.

Suppose we want to forecast a dependent variable at the end of period t, y_t, whose value we assume depends on the infinite lagged values of an independent variable z, $z_{t-1}, z_{t-2}, z_{t-3}, \cdots$ weighted by the geometric factor $|\rho| < 1$. In this case we can write our forecast equation as:

$$(11.3) \quad y_t = \alpha + \beta(z_t + \rho z_{t-1} + \rho^2 z_{t-2} + \cdots) + \epsilon_t$$

where α, β, and ρ are estimated coefficients. Without simplifying (11.3), it would be nearly impossible to estimate. However, using the geometric series sum technique, we can simplify (11.3) to an equation that we can estimate. To simplify, we lag (11.3) to obtain

$$(11.4) \quad y_{t-1} = \alpha + \beta(z_{t-1} + \rho z_{t-2} + \rho^2 z_{t-3} + \cdots) + \epsilon_{t-1}$$

Then if we multiply (11.4) with ρ and subtract the result from (11.3), we obtain the geometric sum of the lagged values of z and an equation that we can estimate:

$$(11.5) \quad y_t - \rho y_{t-1} = \alpha - \rho\alpha + \beta z_t + \epsilon_t - \rho\epsilon_{t-1}$$

Solving for the current value of the endogenous variable and letting the error term equal $v_t = \epsilon_t - \rho\epsilon_{t-1}$ we can write:

$$(11.6a) \quad y_t = \alpha(1 - \rho) + \rho y_{t-1} + \beta z_t + v_t$$

And

$$(11.6b) \quad y_t = \gamma_0 + \rho y_{t-1} + \beta z_t + v_t$$

and where $\alpha = \gamma_0 / (1-\rho)$. In addition, the proper estimation of equation (11.6b) and other linear regression models requires that the error term, in this case v_t, is distributed normally with a zero mean and a variance of σ^2, a condition we express as $N(0,\sigma^2)$.

The geometric lag. The geometric lag structure that produced equation (11.6b) is specific. More general lag structures can be estimated. Indeed, another geometric lag structure is $(z_{t-1} + \rho z_{t-2} + \rho^2 z_{t-3} + \cdots)$ that produces the model in equation (11.7) that doesn't require a forecasted value of z to estimate y and can be expressed as:

$$(11.7) \quad y_t = {}_0 + \gamma_1 y_{t-1} + \gamma^2 z_{t-1} + v_t$$

Forecasting exogenous variables using time and lagged values as independent variables. We have already described forecasting as a two-step procedure. The first step requires that we find the relationship between dependent variables and lagged dependent variables, time and/or lagged value of other relevant variables calculated using past observations. The second step requires that we project the forecast dependent or exogenous variable into the future. If the independent variable is time, then to find a forecast requires only that we update our time variables. On the other hand, if our independent variable includes lagged values, then we must forecast using a stepwise procedure. In the first step we find our next period forecast. In the second step our forecast becomes the independent variable in our two-period future forecast—and so on to obtain future in the future forecasts. To illustrate, suppose that in the first-step we estimated that:

(11.8) $\hat{x}_t = a + bx_{t-1}$

Then in the second step, our first period forecast becomes the independent variable is our two- period forecast allowing us to write:

(11.9) $\hat{x}_{t+1} = \alpha + \beta\hat{x}_t$

Repeating the substitution process, we obtain a k period in future forecast equal to:

(11.10) $\hat{x}_{t+k} = \alpha + \beta\hat{x}_{t+k-1}$

It should be noted that in equation (11.8), the forecast was only one period away from something we knew for sure, the lagged value of dependent variable. In equation (11.9) we were two periods away and in equation (11.10) we were k periods away from something we knew for sure. Therefore, we might conclude that the further away from lagged values we know for sure, the less confidence we should have in the accuracy of our forecast.

Deterministic versus linear regression forecasting equations. There are two ways to process data that describes the relationships between dependent and independent variables. The first method assumes that our relationship that describes the connection between dependent and independent variables is measured without error and the forecast is deterministic. The second method assumes that the relationship between dependent and independent variables approximates the true relationship which we don't know. So, in this second case, the best we can do is to estimate statistically the relationship between the dependent and independent variable(s) and recognize that the actual forecast is a sophisticated guess. We will refer to these methods here that explicitly recognize we are not completely accurate in our estimation of the dependent and independent variable relationship as a statistical regression model.

Several factors determine whether we should forecast using a deterministic or a regression model. These factors may include our confidence in our data, the importance of our forecasts, and difficulty and cost of gathering and processing the data. In what follows, we describe and give examples of both deterministic and linear regression models.

Deterministic Forecasts

A naïve forecast. Assume that the relationship between a dependent variable y is a linear function of itself lagged equal to:

(11.11) $y_t = a + by_{t-1}$

If we are unable or unwilling to estimate coefficient a and b in equation (11.11), we may assume their values to equal: $a = 0$ and $b = 1$. This assumption implies that $y_t = y_{t-1}$. We call this a naïve forecast.

Even though the deterministic naïve forecast is our simplest forecast, it has its place. Suppose our question is: what would be the consequences on the investment's value if everything continued as it is right now? The answer to that question may indeed be a naïve (constant value) forecast. We demonstrate a naïve forecast using Lon's services provided during the previous four years. These are represented in Table 11.1. Our forecast description includes the actual value x_t, the forecast $x_{\hat{t}}$, and the error of the forecast ϵ_t.

Table 11.1. Deterministic naïve forecasts of Lon's service calls

Time period	Actual value x_t	Forecast vales $x_{\hat{t}}$	Forecast error: $\epsilon_t = x_t - x_{\hat{t}}$
0	525	n.a.	
1	755	525	230
2	890	755	135
3	990	890	100
Forecast	n.a.	990	n.a.

One test of the accuracy of one's forecast is the pattern of the forecast error. We expect it to be randomly distributed about zero—in this case the sum of errors should be close to zero. In this case the sum of errors equal 365. In this case, our forecast model fails the test, and so we try a different forecast model.

Moving average forecasts. A step up in forecast sophistication that does not rely on statistical methods is the moving average. Suppose that we are interested in predicting the amount of services Lon could provide if the business continued another year. If we truly believed there was no trend in the data and the variation was due to random events, we might reduce the random effects on the forecast by averaging the previous four period $(990 + 890 + 725 + 525)/4 = 782.5$ or possible the last three $(990 + 890 + 755)/3 = 878.3$ or perhaps the most recent two observations $(990 + 890)/2 = 940$. However, because there is a positive trend, a weighted average forecast is even less accurate than the naïve forecast of 990 over the sample period, and we have no way of knowing its accuracy of the forecast beyond the sample period.

Geometric forecasts. PV models by their nature are geometrically designed created by compounding discount rates of the form ab, ab^1, $ab^2, \cdots$, ab^n where a and b are constants and superscripts represent the geometric factor. As a result, we may assume that our forecasts should also follow some form of a geometric series.

To make geometric forecasts, we begin by observing previous values of exogenous variable values reported in current and past Coordinated Financial Statements (CFS). To illustrate, suppose that over the past 10 years, corn yields $g_1, g_2, \cdots, g_{10}$ have increased by 13%. Then letting $\bar{g}$ equal the average percentage increase in corn yields we find the average yield in equation (11.12) equal to:

$$(11.12) \quad (1 + g_1)(1 + g_2) \cdots (1 + g_n) = (1 + \bar{g})^n$$

Where g_t is the actual growth rate in the exogenous variable for periods $t = 1, \cdots, n$ and the average geometric growth rate is $\bar{g}$. To illustrate suppose we had growth rates of corn yields for 10 year that we represent as:

$$(11.13) \quad (1 + g_1)(1 + g_2) \cdots (1 + g_1 0) = (1.13) = (1 + \bar{g})^n$$

Then solving deterministically for the average geometric mean over the past ten years of yields, we find:

$$(11.14) \quad (1 + \bar{g}) = (1.13)^{0.1} = 1.0123$$

Or an average, for the past 10 years, yields in period t that we represent with the variable y_t increased by 1.23%. Assuming the past trends in yield continue and if the yield last year were 140 bushels per acre, in 5 years we would expect yields to have increased to:

$$(11.15) \quad y_5 = 140(1.0123)^5 = 148.82$$

In other words, corn yields in period 5, assuming the average yield trend for the past ten years continues will equal 148.82 bushels per acre. In the case of Lon's services, over four years services have increased by $990/525 = 200\%$ or $1.89^{0.3} = 1.26$ of that services have increased on average by 26 percent per year so that next year's forecast for Lon's business is $(990)(1.26) = 1,221$.

Linear Regression Forecasts

What is a linear regression forecast? The second forecasting method is the statistical procedure referred to as multiple linear regression or in the case of a single explanatory variable, linear regression. Regression analysis finds a coefficient for a line (plane) through points representing values of a dependent variable such that the squared differences between the line and the values of the regression line are minimized. Hence, the regression method is sometimes referred to as least squares regression analysis.

Regression models can also be used to measure the percentage of the total variation around the mean of the data explained by regression equation using what is referred to as an R^2 that is between zero and 100 percent. Obviously, as we add more independent variables to our regression equation, we can increase the value of R^2. However, as we add independent variables to our regression equation, the significant of each individual independent variable will likely decrease, a significance measured by t-tests. Eventually, we can add enough independent variables that our relationships is deterministic. When conducting regression analysis, we assume that independent variables are measured without error and not influenced by each other. Dependent variables are related to the independent variables and we expect them to be forecast with some error.

Finally, the ability to estimate regression equations are often complicated by missing variables, non-normal distributions of υt, autocorrelations between the error terms and correlations between the error terms and the exogenous variables and other properties keep econometricians occupied. These complications and others encountered when estimating regression equations, we ignore in this chapter in order to emphasize the fundamental concepts of forecasting.

A *Lagged Regression Model and Forecast*. Suppose we return to equation (11.11) and instead of assuming coefficient values of $a = 0$ and $b = 1$ we estimate coefficients a and b in regression equation (11.16).

$$(11.16) \quad y_t = a + by_{t-1} + \epsilon_t \text{ where } \epsilon_t \; N(0, \sigma^2)$$

Fortunately, Excel has a statistical function that can estimate a and b so that the sum of ${\epsilon_t}^2$ is is minimized and the sum of ϵ_t's is zero. To access regression analysis for estimating regression coefficient a and b in Excel we select Data and regression from the drop-down menu. If the Analysis tab does not appear, it may be necessary to access it from your options. Instructions to enable this option are in the appendix at the end of this chapter.

Figure 11.1. Data Ribbon for Excel Spreadsheet

After selecting the Data tab, select regression from the drop-down menu.

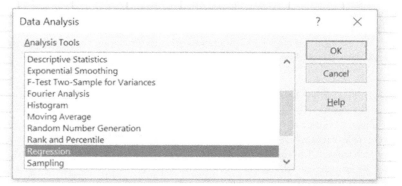

Figure 11.2. Data Analysis Pop-up Menu

After selecting regression from the drop-down menu, we are asked for regression analysis data. The lagged independent values for x_{t-1} (A2:A4) are entered in the Input X Range. The current or dependent values x_t (B2:B4) are then entered as the Input Y Range:

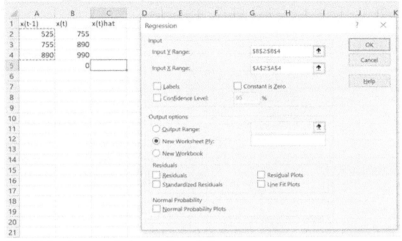

Figure 11.3. Data input page for the regression analysis.

We include a request that the regression equation find the constant value a. Clicking OK returns the regression estimates for our forecast equation equal to:

Open Table 11.2 in Microsoft Excel.

Table 11.2. The results from a linear regression analysis for Lon's sales.

	A	B	C	D	E	F	G
1	Summary Output						
2							
3	Regression Statistics						
4	Multiple R	0.997992					
5	R Square	0.995989					
6	Adjusted R	0.991978					
7	Standard	10.56297					
8	Observation	3					
9							
10	ANOVA						
11		df	SS	MS	F	Significance F	
12	Regression	1	27705.09	27705.09	248.3061	0.040346	
13	Residual	1	111.5763	111.5763			
14	Total	2	27816.67				
15							
16		Coefficients	Standard Error	t Stat	P-value	Lower 95%	Upper 95%
17	Intercept	417.0247	29.90354	13.94567	0.045572	37.06427	796.9852
18	X Variable (t)	0.637754	0.040472	15.75773	0.040346	0.123503	1.152005

Interpreting all the output described above is beyond the scope of this discussion and the proper topic for a beginning econometrics class. However, note that R^2 accounts for most of the variation in the data and the t-tests for the coefficients a and b are greater than 1.9 which is often reported as the minimum required for the independent variables to be retained.

Having found the forecast equation, we use the results to obtain our forecasts. To do so, we focus on the estimates of coefficient a reported in cell B17 equal to 417.02 and coefficient b reported in cell B18 equal to .638.

(11.18) $\quad \hat{x}_t = a + bx_{t-1} = 417.2 + .638x_{t-1}$

Next we create our table of lagged values, estimated values, errors, and a forecast value.

Table 11.3. Naïve forecasts of Lon's service calls

Time period	Actual value x_t	Estimated and Forecast vales $x_{\hat{t}}$	Forecast error: $\epsilon_t = x_t - x_{\hat{t}}$
0	525	n.a.	
1	755	752	3
2	890	899	-9
3	990	985	5
Forecast	n.a.	1049	n.a.

Notice that we obtain our forecast for x_{t-1} by substituting our last observed value of 990 into our forecast equation:

$$(11.19) \quad \hat{x}_t = a + bx_{t-1} = 417.2 + .638(990) = 1049.$$

Notice that accounting for a trend line significantly improved our estimated values over the sample range compared to previous forecast equations. Furthermore, the error term appears more nearly random and sums to a number close to zero: 3 – 9 + 5 = 1. However, before we become too impressed with our estimates compared to our actual values, we must acknowledge that we have only three estimated values to estimate the two unknown parameters "a" and "b". In other words, we almost have a perfectly identified systems so there is really no estimating challenge at all leaving us with a lack of confidence that our three-year trend will really continue.

Nonlinear trend lines. It is common for most new business to make impressive gains early on and then see gains level off. Indeed, it appears that for many processes, growth appears to follow a concave down pattern as might be described in the graph below.

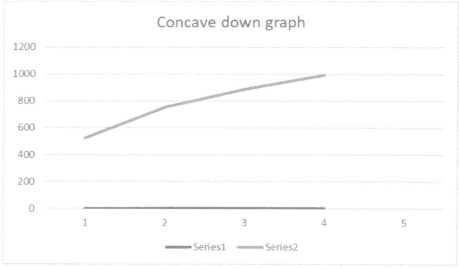

Figure 11.4. Quadratic Trend Line.

Such a function can be represented with a more complicated mathematical representation like the one below:

(11.20) $y_t = \beta_0 + \beta_1 t + \beta_2 t^2$

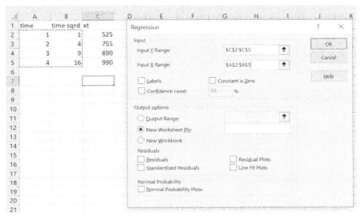

Figure 11.5. Data input page for a quadratic trend line.

Notice for the exogenous variable time and time squared, we entered the data matrix. Next we click OK to obtain the result:

Table 11.4. Regression results for forecasting Lon's services using a quadratic time function.
Open Table 11.4 in Microsoft Excel.

	A	B	C	D	E	F	G
1	Summary Output						
2							
3	Regression Statistics						
4	Multiple R	0.999259					
5	R Square	0.998518					
6	Adjusted R	0.995554					
7	Standard	13.41641					
8	Observation	4					
9							
10	ANOVA						
11		df	SS	MS	F	Significance F	
12	Regression	2	121270	60635	336.8611	0.038498	
13	Residual	1	180	180			
14	Total	3	121450				
15							
16		Coefficients	Standard Error	t Stat	P-value	Lower 95%	Upper 95%
17	Intercept	245	37.3497	6.559625	0.09631	-229.573	719.5729
18	X Variable (t)	315.5	34.07345	9.259409	0.068488	-117.444	748.4442
19	X Variable (t^2)	-32.5	6.708204	-4.84481	0.129583	-117.736	5273581

We are particularly interested in the coefficient for our estimated equation (11.21). We write the results as:

(11.21) $\hat{x}_t = a + bt + ct^2 = 245 + 315.5t = 32.5t^2.$

We create our table of lagged values, estimated values, errors, and a forecast value.

Table 11.5. Forecasts of Lon's service calls based on a quadratic function of time.

Time period	Actual value x_t	Estimated and Forecast vales $\hat{x_t}$	Forecast error: $\epsilon_t = x_t - \hat{x_t}$
1	525	528	-3
2	755	746	9
3	890	899	-9
4	990	987	3
Forecast	n.a.	1010	n.a.

Note that the forecast based on a quadratic function of time is 1010 compared to 1049 based on a linear function of time. Since both equations report significant R^2 and t-values—we must choose between them based on economic logic—which model best fits the reality on the ground?

Confidence intervals. Assume the new potential owner is unsure about the reliability of the forecasts and asks what are the high and low forecast values? Using the forecast.confidence function, we can find statistical bounds around the projected trend line using the standard deviation of values around the trend link. Then we add and subtract the standard deviation multiplied by a constant such that given data and assuming the trend continues, we can be 95% sure that the "true" projection is included in the bounded confidence interval. Below we include the forecast values for Lon's services during the next four year. Then we graph the original values, their forecasted values and the confidence intervals.

C6		f_x	=FORECAST.ETS(A6,$B$2:$B$5,$A$2:$A$5,1,1)	

	A	B	C	D	E
1	yr	value	Forecast(value)	Lower Confidence Bound(value)	Upper Confidence Bound(value)
2	1	575			
3	2	755			
4	3	890			
5	4	990	990	990.00	990.00
6	5		1136.801056	1082.95	1190.65
7	6		1273.468975	1217.94	1328.99
8	7		1410.136894	1352.98	1467.30
9	8		1546.804813	1488.04	1605.57
10					

Table 11.6. Forecast values for the demand for Lon's Green & White Services for the next four years, and 95% confidence intervals around the forecasts.

Forecasts and Shocks

Exogenous variable forecasts and shocks. Now suppose that in time $t + k$ we forecast the value of our dependent variable but something we call a shock, s_{t+k}, occurs that hasn't occurred in the past. Because the shock hasn't occurred in the past, we don't account for it in our forecast. Or suppose something that has occurred in the past that helped us forecast y_{t+k} doesn't occur? This is another kind of a shock.

To illustrate the first kind of shock, consider Christmas tree sales. Based on our past experiences, we forecast a significant rise in Christmas tree sales in December. But suppose this year, the world experiences a pandemic and tree-harvesters are quarantined and unable to supply the usual number of Christmas trees. Then we may find that our Christmas tree sales forecast to be widely inaccurate.

Shocks may have two kinds of consequences. And the kinds of forecasting consequences shocks may produce depend on what we are forecasting. If we are forecasting a quantitative value—e.g. Christmas tree sales, our forecast may be inaccurate such as we observe a reduction is sales of 50% below our forecast. Or, if we are forecasting an event with only two possible outcomes, e.g. win or lose, then our forecast is either right or wrong, correct or incorrect, true or false. Such would be the case if we forecast the winner of the Super Bowl and the wrong team wins. In this case, are forecast was not merely inaccurate, it was wrong.

Getting real. Before proceeding, we need to get real. Relationships between endogenous and exogenous variables are hardly ever stable or easily identified. Remember shocks? To illustrate, assume that we intended to forecast future corn prices. We begin by identifying the connection between past corn prices and other past exogenous variables. But then, we might find the relationship that we thought we had estimated was not stable and susceptible to forces not included in our model including shocks. Corn prices fell by two and one-half times in the 1970s leading to a fall in related prices and the financial crisis of the 1980s. Land values fell as much as 50 percent during the same time period. Later, in the 2006–2013 period corn prices nearly doubled over the previous twenty-year period only to fall again in 2013 with input prices substantially higher than in the previous period. In real terms, current profitability was lower than it was in the post 1980's period. Historically, it has taken grain and oilseed markets six to twelve years to find their "new normal" following large, sustained shocks. History again provides a guide to the future, but the internal confidence around these future projections should be wide.

Recognizing the difficulty of what we're about, in what follows we employ equation (11.1) beginning with its most simple form and then consider increasing complicated forecast equations. Our goal is to find first the relationship between endogenous and exogenous variables to forecast their future values.

So, what have we learned? We have learned that forecasts depend on their values being highly correlated with the passage of time where we determined the correlation between t and independent variables by past observations. However, things in the future may not be just like they were in the past. Things that happened in the past that we assumed will happen in the future, don't. Or things that didn't happen in the past, do happen in the future. Both unplanned events we call shocks. So, in time period $t+k$, instead of observing y_{t+k}, we observe $y_{t+k} + s_{t+k}$. What is the influence of a shock on our forecast depends on if we are forecasting discrete outcomes (win versus lose) or continuous values (the level of Christmas tree sales).

Forecasting Exogenous Variables and the Accuracy of Endogenous Variables

Earlier we distinguished between dependent and independent variables in forecast equations and exogenous and endogenous variables in CFS and PV templates. When the exogenous variables are known in CFS and PV templates, endogenous variables are found using deterministic equations. We now ask, what about exogenous and endogenous variables in CFS and PV models when exogenous variables are forecast with error. Now we are less confident that the deterministic relationships from which we find endogenous variables as some deterministic function of exogenous variables can still be relied on?

We propose that we establish some over-identified checks on the values of our endogenous variables as means of validating our exogenous variable forecasts. In practice this proposal means that we use economic reasoning and other established relationships between endogenous and exogenous variables to obtain independent estimates of our exogenous variables besides the deterministic one obtains from CFS and PV templates. In other words, once we have obtained forecasts for our exogenous variable(s) x_t, we are prepared to use these forecasts to find the future values of our endogenous variables $\hat{y}_t$.

These conditional forecasts of our endogenous variables take the form: if $x(t)$ then $y(t)$. To illustrate, we may forecast umbrella sales to increase if it rains—if it rains then umbrella sales will increase. We may not be able to predict the weather, but we can predict how consumer purchases will likely respond to the occurrence of rain. In the statement, if $x(t)$ then $\hat{y}(t)$, $x(t)$ is the exogenous variable forecast and $\hat{y}(t)$ is the endogenous variable forecast.

Another illustration of a conditional forecast, the forecast of an endogenous variable, may be the firm's profit forecasts. An agricultural firm's profit forecast may depend on several factors including weather, crop yields, trade policies, inventory levels, input costs, revenue and expense margins, and national economic variables such as stock market indices, consumer price indices, consumers' disposable incomes, the interest rate, and the level of consumer confidence to name a few.

Once we have obtained our exogenous variable forecasts from deterministic or regression equations, we now intend to use these to forecast future values of endogenous variables. The connection between exogenous and exogenous variables may be deterministic as was their calculations in CFS and PV templates. In other cases, they simply may be related to each other statistically even though economic logic may lead to the equation that forecasts endogenous variables from the base of exogenous variables.

Sometime correlations with exogenous variables can be useful even if the exogenous variable is not one with which we are directly interested. This is because several exogenous variables may be influenced in similar ways by time. Prices are a case in point. Some prices seem to move together through time and this correlation may be particularly helpful in our endogenous variable forecasts. In these cases, the relationship between exogenous and endogenous variables are not deterministic and must be estimated.

Price forecasts. In our original study of Lon's service, we predicted prices to be constant over the four years of Lon's operations. This forecast is naïve. Instead, suppose that we believed that Lon's prices for services would follow national price trends. One national price trend is the consumer price index (CPI). The CPI measures changes in the price level of a weighted average market basket of representative consumer goods and services purchased by households. There are, of course, several different CPI indexes. To calculate the CPI, we designate a base year for prices and assign it an index of 100. Then the updated value of the index is found by dividing the index of prices is the updated period by the index of prices in the base year:

$$(11.22) \quad \frac{CPI_t}{CPI_{base}} = \frac{\text{Average Prices}_t}{\text{Average Prices}_{base}} \approx \frac{\text{Lon's prices}_t}{\text{Average Lon's Prices}_{base}}$$

Suppose that we wish to know the average percentage increase from the base year to year t. If the current CPI were 123% and the base year were 10 years earlier, we could find the average geometric increase in prices to be those we found earlier:

$$(11.23) \quad (1 + \bar{g}) = (1.23)^{(1/10)} = 1.02$$

In other words, prices (including the price of lawn care services) have increased by 2% per year. If we applied this estimated average of prices to yard care services, we can forecast Lon's future price for yard care services:

Table 11.7. Forecast values for the price of Lon's Green & White Services Assuming a 2.1% increase

Year	Forecast Service Prices	Service times forecast price = sales	COGS = .45 x sales
Base	$40		
1	$40.84	$40.84 x 525 = $21,441	$965
2	$41.69	$41.69 x 755 = $31,476	$14,164
3	$42.67	$42.67 x 890 = $37,976	$17,089
4	$43.46	$43.46 x 990 = $43,025	$19,361

Percentage forecasts and margins. One of the main ways we can forecasts endogenous variables outside of the CFS and PV template is to observe the relationships between them and exogenous variables in the past—and the more observations, the better. One observation that is important using past data is the margin between revenue and costs. We can be confident that this difference is bounded, otherwise, competitors would flock to join our industry and begin replicating our operations. If the difference is negative for some time, we will become insolvent and forced to leave the industry. Sometimes, if we can discover the connection between margins and time—we may forecast margin as a function of time. For example, suppose we are interested in the price of hard red winter wheat but can only observe past prices of corn and soybeans. Using linear regression, a statistical technique that allows us to relate an endogenous variable to one or more exogenous variable—we can use the future estimates of corn and soybean prices to predict hard red winter prices.

Sales data. In column three of Table 11.1 and beginning in year one, we estimate cash sales or cash cost reductions. We can employ several assumptions about future cash flow associated with sales or reduced costs. The first one is that there is no change from data entered in year one. This assumption is consistent with capitalization formula that assume zero change in future cash flow. It may also be relevant if the model assumes that data are in real numbers so that numbers do not change with inflation. Furthermore, we may assume the future is represented by the present and these relationships between variables in the present should be preserved.

Economic logic and margins. Economic logic and margins may guide our endogenous variable forecasts. Recall that common size income statements provide us percentage relationships between endogenous and exogenous variables. Consider the common size income statement for HQN. Such a statement could, of course, be acquired for other industries more nearly like the industry in which we are focused.

Table 11.8. (Table 7.9) HQN's Accrued Common-Size Income Statements

Year	2017	2018	Industry Average
Total Revenue	100.00%	100.00%	100.00%
Cost of Goods Sold (COGS)	67.37%	70.00%	71.40%
Operating Expenses	29.82%	27.50%	22.50%
Depreciation	1.24%	0.88%	1.75%
EARNING BEFORE INTEREST AND TAXES (EBIT)	1.58%	1.62%	4.35%
Interest	1.22%	1.20%	0.55%
EARNINGS BEFORE TAXES (EBT)	0.36%	0.42%	3.80%
Taxes	0.17%	0.17%	1.52%
NET INCOME AFTER TAXES (NIAT)	0.19%	0.25%	2.28%

Economic logic suggests that some relationships between exogenous and endogenous variables may continue in the future. For example, taxes are likely to be function of the difference between revenue and sales. Another class of relationships likely to persist over time are margins, 100% minus the percent of costs as a function of revenue. Economic logic tells us that margins can't be zero or negative or the firm wouldn't survive. Nor can they be excessively high without inviting competitors and innovators to join the industry. Of course, changing competitive advantages and innovations may temporarily affect margins, in the short run and will likely encourage changes in the industry as firms expand to take advantage of the innovations. And as we increase in sophistication, we might. worry about local, national, and international politics that may influence tariffs and the challenges of competing in a global economy—ultimately affecting our margins.

COGS and Revenue. The foundation for our forecasts is the economic relationship between the variables in our industry. Once we have price and/or yield forecasts, we can add other forecasts by treating them as dependent variables. Two variables of economic necessity must be highly correlated are costs and revenue. For example, we may expect to find that COGS has a predictable relationship to sales since the more we produce and sale the more expenses we are likely to occur. Therefore, once we have sales forecasts, we can forecast COGS using established relationships observed from past data.

One other relationship is the difference between revenue and costs. We can be confident that this difference is bounded. Otherwise, if the difference were strongly positive, competitors would flock to our industry and begin replicating our operations. If the difference is negative for a significant period of time, we will become insolvent and leave the industry. Taxes will be some function of the difference between revenue and sales. Changes in comparatives advantages and preferences may also be included in the description of how the variables are related. Future preferences will influence demand for what we produce.

Changes in comparative advantage—who can produce least expensively and where—will also influence revenue and expenses. Favorable increases in comparative advantage will reduce our costs and put us in a position to expand our operation. And as we increase in sophistication, we might worry about local, national, and international politics that may influence tariffs and the challenges of competing in a global economy.

Consider COGS in Table 11.1. In this example, we estimated COGS to be on average 45% of sales. Sales have been forecast to increase by 3 percent from base sales we observed in the CFS that described the firm. As a result, COGS will also increase by 3% maintaining a constant relationship of 45% between sales and COGS.

Still another method for estimating future cash revenue and expense cash flow is to employ someone else's guesses about the future. This is difficult because our investment and earning potential is often unique to our own firm. Still there are guesses about the future that are related to our own investment's future. And there are sophisticated forecasting firms and experts who make predictions about the future relevant to our own investment. For example, a dairy firm might be interested in forecasted milk prices or the expected cost of feed. Firms related to home sales would find future interest rate forecasts to be relevant since the demand for homes can be expected to be related to the cost of home financing. Indeed, most investments can be tied to some future forecast that is relevant.

COGS and OE. Associated with the business include what economists refer to as fixed and variable costs. We treat COGS as variable costs that follow the investment's cash revenue. In addition, we impose on the relationship between CR and COGS the restriction that long-term, Sales>COGS. OE are costs difficult to assign to any one production activity and vary over time. In our simplified analysis, we did not assume any OE. This is an unreasonable assumption since such fixed costs such as insurance, rental of office and storage space, and licenses all produce fixed costs. In the previous four years, fixed costs were $350, $390, $450, $515. In addition, in the most recent two years, Lon was required to rent addition space that cost $100 in each period. We use the OE observations and estimate the following equation using our observed data.

(11.24) $OE = \alpha_0 + \alpha_1 \text{time} + \alpha_2 \text{ additional storage}$

The way our forecasts work in practice is that we find some historical basis for the equation and from those relationships estimate our coefficients.

Now we illustrate the various forecasting methods using the data in our example template. To begin, suppose that we are confident in the cash flow data appearing in year two since year one may be a transition year. Dividing cash COGS by cash sales we find:

(11.25) $0 < \gamma < \dfrac{COGS}{\text{Cash Sales}} = \dfrac{\$106,913}{\$137,068} = 78\%$

As a result, in the future, we will assume that COGS equal 78% of whatever we estimate sales to equal. Whatever we estimate sales to equal, we will assume that COGS equal

Other forecasts. Sometimes, failing to find forecasts of direct interest to the calculation of our investment's NPV, AE, and IRR—we can often find forecasts highly correlated with our forecasts of interest. For example, suppose we are interested in the price of hard red winter wheat but can only observe past prices of corn and soybeans. Finding past relationships between the price of hard red winter wheat and corn and soybean prices, we can use forecasts of corn and soybean prices to forecast future prices of hard red winter wheat.

Real versus nominal data values. In our PV templates, we project CR, cash COGS and cash OE. We can employ several assumptions about future cash flow associated with these values. The first one is that there is no change from data entered in year one. This assumption is consistent with capitalization formula that assume zero change in future cash flow. It may also be relevant if the model assumes that data are in real numbers so that numbers do not change with inflation. Furthermore, we may assume that the future is represented by the present and these relationships between variables in the present should be preserved.

Testing for robustness. That we populate our PV templates with estimates suggests that our templates will not be completely accurate. They will be consistent because the templates relate variables to each other consistently, but they are not likely to be completely accurate. We simply are not likely to estimate all of the future values of our variables correctly. As a result, we should calculate NPV, AE, and IRR under a variety of assumptions about future values so that we have some impression about the robustness of our estimates.

> So, what have we learned? We have learned that forecasting recognizes two different kinds of statements. The first of these is of the form: if t then y_t. From this relationship between t and y_t, we make forecasts that include linear trend lines and other more complicated functions of time. Other kinds of forecast depend on lagged values of the dependent and independent variables.

We have been careful to distinguish between dependent and independent variables in forecast equations and exogenous and endogenous variables in CFS and PV templates. In the latter case, the relationship between exogenous and endogenous variables are deterministic that depend on accounting identities. The problem occurs that when we forecast exogenous variables, these are estimated with error that implies that our endogenous variables in CFS and PV templates are also estimated with error. Then it may be useful to find overidentified estimates of our endogenous variables to validate our exogenous variable forecasts—using the structure of our CFS and PV templates to check for accuracy. These require that we forecast our endogenous variables as well as our exogenous variables using economic and other logic to guide our estimation of endogenous variables. This type of estimation, like other forecasts will be of the form if x_t then y_t.

Qualitative Forecasts

Not everything we know can be reduced to a number. If all the lessons learned from the past could be translated into a quantitative forecast function, we could leave much of forecasting to computers (they already carry a significant forecasting role). But such is not the case. We all know much more that can be represented by a numerical forecast. When historical data is not available, we generally employ qualitative forecasting techniques that most often depend on the judgment of experts—that may be aided by quantitative forecasts.

Experts and all the rest of us observe, absorb, and process informative through our multiple sources and senses. So how do we do it? We may not be able to describe the process because our intuitive sense are complicated and profound. Book like "Thinking Fast and Slow" try to describe some aspects of our capacity to analyze and predict using information much more sophisticated that has been described in this chapter. This is not to disrespect the amazing information captured by digital coding, especially in the sciences, but when it comes to the "animal spirits" that operate in interpersonal interaction, it pays to leave room for qualitative judgments and forecasts.

So, we employ and appreciate professional forecasters to share their qualitative forecasts, sometimes augmented by quantitative forecasts. In may be the case that we will increasing translate qualitative forecasts into quantitative ones—and multitude are the examples of qualitative forecasts being improved using quantitative information.

Professional forecasts are usually experts in their specialty such a yields and prices of agricultural and forestry products as well as margins between revenue and cost. An example of expert forecast services are those offered by the Food and Agricultural Policy Research Institute (FAPRI) at the University of Missouri. FAPRI makes annual 10-year baseline projections for grain, oilseed, livestock markets, and a variety of other indicators. Even here, it is important to moderate forecasts using microeconomic principles and experience in making projections including a range of scenarios. Understanding intermediate and longer-term industry supply curves including regional and international dimensions is very important for most projects. Extension specialists, such as Dr. Jim Hilker, who have distinguished themselves with accurate forecasts can also be an invaluable resource.

One advantage of professional forecasts is that they account for so many influences that uncomplicated forecasters may ignore. The other advantage is that when we present our forecasts and responses to our forecasts are important—it is always helpful to have a reliable source for support.

PV Models and Forecasts

Forecasts and present value models. While this chapter is about forecasting, we are most interested in forecasting PV model exogenous variables. Solving PV models requires that we forecast the future value of cash flow generated by an investment. PV models include exogenous and endogenous variables.

PV models discount future cash flows to find their equivalent worth in the present—since it is in the present where we live and make decisions. To repeat for emphasis, we cannot solve PV models without forecasting future exogenous variable cash flow on which the present value of an investment depends. When we invest in the present, all we know for sure is the cost of the investment, the time distance to different futures, lagged values of endogenous and exogenous variables, and future commitments like loan terms. Every other piece of data requires us to solve the PV problem and exogenous variable forecasts.

To illustrate, the template below is identified as: PV Template: Green & White Services. It will be helpful in our forecasting discussions in this chapter to continue using Lon's yard care investment example. We will embellish it somewhat to focus on certain aspects of forecasting while maintaining the main characteristics of the problem.

Table 11.9. PV Template: Green & White Services Open PV Template in Microsoft Excel.

Data for Green & White Services. Looking to the future, Lon is considering the purchase of a lawn care/snow removal business. He will purchase the good will (customer base) of the previous owner of the business and equipment for $40,000. His expected service calls, service prices and variable cost per service are reported below:

Table 11.10. Endogenous and exogenous variable forecasts for Green & White Services.

	A	B	C	D	E	F	G	H	I	J	K	L	
1	Year	Number of Services	Price/ Service	Cost/ Service	Sales	AR+INV	CR	Expenses	AP+AL	CE	Depreciation Rates	V0	D
2	1	525	40	18	21000	1000	20000	9450	100	9350	0.25	40000	
3	2	755	40	18	30200	1200	30000	13590	200	13490	0.375	40000	
4	3	890	40	18	35600	800	36000	16220	100	16120	0.25	40000	
5	4	990	40	18	39600	400	40000	17820	100	17820	0.125	40000	

Forecast number of services are described Table 11.10 column B. Prices and cost per service forecasts are described in columns C and D and when multiplied by projected services produce sales revenue in column E and expenses in column H. Note that these are accumulated sales and costs, not cash. The sum of accounts receivable (AR) and inventory (INV) at the end of the period are reported in column F while the sum of accounts payable (AP) and accrued liabilities (AL) are reported in column I. Cash receipts (CR) and cash expenses (CE) are found by adjusting sales and expenses for changes in asset and liability accounts and the results are recorded in columns G and J respectively. Allowable depreciation rates are recorded in column K and when multiplied by the capital asset purchase of $40,000 produce depreciation amounts recorded in M. Finally, debt outstanding is recorded in Column N.

Besides the annual data forecasts, we also record certain rate forecasts for Green & White Services. Some of these as well as some of the annual forecasts may be either exogenous or endogenous variables depending on how the endogenous defining equations are define. We include the current exogenous rates as:

Table 11.11. IRRs, average tax rate, average interest rate, and growth rates is applicable for Green & White Services.

	A	B
1	ROA	0.08
2	T	0.2
3	ROE(1-T)	0.064
4	Average Interest Rate	0.06
5	Debt Growth Rate	0
6	Liquid Growth Rate	0
7	Book Value Growth Rate	0
8	Account Balance Growth Rate	0
9	CR Growth Rate	0
10	COGS Growth Rate	0
11	OE Growth Rate	0
12	Beginning Cash	0
13	Liability op. Account Rate	0

We now ask, where can we find future values for template variables that will permit us to solve multi-period PV problems? The answer is that we forecast or estimate (guess) the value of exogenous variables in the template and based on these exogenous variable forecasts, we solve for the endogenous forecast variables.

Populating the PV template with exogenous and exogenous variables. Like Coordinated Financial Statements (CFS), we populate PV templates with exogenous and endogenous variables. The columns of data in Table 11.9 are organized into exogenous and endogenous variables. The exogenous variables are highlighted. Endogenous variables are not. The main distinction between exogenous and endogenous variables within the template is the following. The values of exogenous variables are determined outside of the template. The values of endogenous variables are determined within the main template. Excel makes it easy to distinguish between exogenous and endogenous variables. We can identify endogenous variables within the template because they require an operations such as +,-,*,^, or /. They may also require an operation embedded in an Excel function such as PV, PMT, NPER, RATE, IRR, or NPV.

Otherwise, they are exogenous. If the cell requires an operation, it will be signaled by an "=" sign that references other cells included in an operation. Exogenous variables may reference cells outside of the PV model with an equal sign when they contain values on which an operation will be performed. Alternatively, exogenous data cells in the template may include a number. The exception to this means for identifying endogenous variables is when they are calculated in separate pages and then copied into the main template.

We now describe in more detail the variables and data needed to populate our PV templates that enable us to find rolling NPV, AE, and IRR estimates for investments and invested equity. We begin with the only information we know for sure, future dates: 2019, 2020, 2021, etc. Therefore, we begin populating our PV templates with the one thing we know about the future: future dates recorded in column 1.

The investment acquisition amount. We record the investment acquisition amount in cell B4. Its value is determined outside of the template making it an exogenous variable. We treat the investment's acquisition value as though it were a cash expenditure unless funded by debt, an amount recorded in cell C4. When we employ debt to acquire the investment, the focus is on the equity invested—equal to the investment amount less the debt used to acquire the investment.

If we purchased the investment(s) on credit, we enter the loan principal and interest payments in the years they are paid. We don't enter the loan amount because money came from a lender and was received by the seller of the investment—Lon is only an intermediary in the exchange

The investment amount is also a well-documented number. Durable sellers post their offer prices. Markets establish and record the prices at which durables are exchanged. References for used durable prices like Kelly's Blue Book for cars are generally available. Salvage values that occur sometime in the future are much harder to estimate. The IRS provides some economic life estimates and depreciation data equal to percent changes in the value of the original durable. Theses may help us establish book values and may provide some guide for determining the durables' liquidation value.

Complicating our investment data are projects that incur investments costs over several time-periods. Indeed, one might consider repair and maintenance expenditures designed to improve the life and durable performance to represent additional investments. In other cases, the investment includes several durable that we replace at different intervals. For example, feeder calf operations routinely replace one cohort of calves with another but the feeding equipment and physical facilities we replace less often than the feed calves.

Liquidation values. To find rolling NPV, AE, and IRR estimates, we require not only an investment acquisition amount, but investment liquidation and market values over time. An investment's acquisition value, V_0, is the amount of money exchanged to acquire the investment. An investment's book value in period t, V_t^{book}, equals it acquisition value minus its accumulated depreciation. An investment's liquidation value in period t, $V_t^{liquidation}$, is the amount of money a buyer is willing to exchange for the investment when it is sold. If an investment's liquidation value is greater than its acquisition value, we refer to the difference as capital gains. If an investment's liquidation value is less that its acquisition value but greater than its book value, we refer to the difference as depreciation recovery. Finally, if the liquidation value is less than its book value, we refer to the difference as capital losses. We describe capital gains, depreciation recovery, and capital losses in the following equations:

for $V_t^{liquidation} > V_0 > V_t^{book}$, capital gains = $V_t^{liquidation} - V_0 > 0$,

for $V_0 > V_t^{liquidation} > V_t^{book}$, depreciation recapture = $V_t^{liquidation} - V_t^{book} > 0$, and

for $V_0 > V_t^{book} > V_t^{liquidation}$, capital losses = $V_t^{book} - V_t^{liquidation} > 0$.

We determine accounting book values by applying tax regulations that specify depreciation amounts depending on the type and age of the investment. Since depreciation forecasts depend on the age and amount of the investment, we generally consider them endogenous variables. Furthermore, we recognize that liquidation values of investments are also generally determined by projecting market values and cost data and may be endogenously or exogenously variables. When we do not expect to liquidate the investments, but want to estimate their NPV, AE and IRR, we may equate market liquidation value with book values. That we populate our PV templates with forecasts, sophisticated guesses, suggests that our template is not completely accurate. As a result, we should calculate NPVs, AEs, and IRRs under a variety of guesses so that we have some impression about the robustness of our estimates.

Summary and Conclusions

We conclude this chapter with the observations that we are all forecasters—all the time. We are all today making decisions and plans that will influence our conditions in the future–and these require forecasts. As we review the nature of forecasts, we should be humbled by the process and two factors. The first one is that forecasts have been often wrong. As evidence, review the forecasts that predicted the great recession of 2008. And the second factor that should humble us is that the only thing we know for certain about the future is the time it will take us to get there.

We emphasize here that there exist many potential forecast equations. These should be evaluated based on their accuracy, their implementation difficulty, availability of data, and the importance of the forecast. Still, we need to accept that what should determine our confidence in the accuracy and correctness of our forecasts is finding exogenous variables highly correlated with the passage of time. Fortunately, there are several exogenous variables that are satisfy this requirement. Most natural phenomenon have some predictable life cycle patterns of growth, production, and decay. We all make commitments that commit us to some action in the future that we often complete. As a result, our own actions in the future can often be predicted. Still shocks often leave disturbs our confident in our forecasts.

Still, we must make decisions in the present that commit us to outcomes in the future—and there is no alternative. We will all continue to forecast and hope to become better in the effort. Hopefully, this chapter has provided some ideas on how we can all make better forecasts.

Questions

1. Describe the differences between forecasts and predictions.
2. How would you characterize the main business of forecasters?
3. List five forecasts and five predictions that you have made during the last week. Describe your confidence in the accuracy of your forecasts and predictions and what determined your confidence.
4. Forecasts can be accurate or inaccurate or wrong and right. Explain.
5. Evaluate the following forecast. A turkey woke up on Thanksgiving Day and forecast that it would be like every other day?
6. List two kinds of shocks. Provide an example from the nation news of the shocks.
7. Given the likelihood that not all of our forecasts will be accurate or correct, how can we plan these eventualities?
8. What is the difference between dependent and independent variables in forecast equations?
9. Explain the difference between exogenous and endogenous variables in the context of CFS and PV templates.
10. We may forecast exogenous and endogenous variables. Explain the difference in these forecasts and how they may be used.
11. Forecasting can be described as a two-step process.
12. The commodity price index is today 123 percent of its base 10 years ago.

    1. Using a deterministic method, forecast the price index next year. If corn prices today are $3.18 forecast next year's corn prices using the following methods:
    2. Using a naïve forecast.
    3. Using a geometric average forecast based on the commodity price index.
    4. Assume that corn prices during the past four years were: $2.56, $3.90, $2.89. $3.25, and $2.89. Use a linear regression model to forecast corn prices next year and the year after next.
    5. Using a regression equation with independent variables t and t^2 to forecast corn prices next year and the year after that.
    6. Compare and comment of the R^2 for the linear and quadratic function and the t statistics for coefficients of the independent variables in the equations.
13. Consider the PV template described in Table 11.1. Then resolve the template assuming that expenses (COGS +OEs) were an endogenous variable. Find the value of expenses using the exogenous variable sales data. Determine the relationship between COGS that vary with sales and OEs that mostly vary with the passage of time.

14. Assume the following endogenous and exogenous variables have been observed in the past. Forecast Y(7) using the data below. Determine the accuracy of your forecast and the confidence interval around your forecast.

Time Period	Y(t)	Y(t-1)	X(t-1)
1	45	35	44
2	52	45	39
3	67	52	33
4	68	67	34
5	80	68	26
6	78	80	21
7			

Appendix

If the Data menu ribbon does not show the Data Analysis button at the far right, you can enable it in the Excel Options.

Figure 11.A1. Excel Data Menu Ribbon without the Data Analysis option.

Select File and then Options.

Figure 11.A2. Excel File Menu Options Selection

In the Excel Options popup window, first select the Add-ins menu, and then select the Go... button to Manage Excel Add-ins.

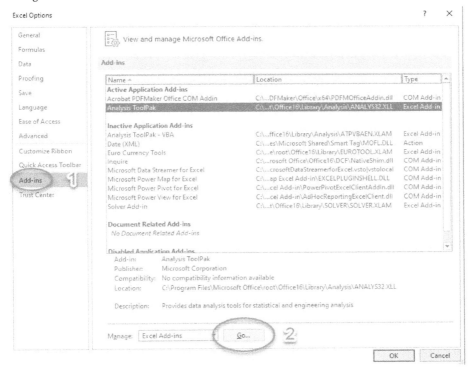

Figure 11.A3. *Excel Options to Manage Add-ins.*

Finally, in the Add-ins popup window, check the Analysis ToolPak option and select OK.

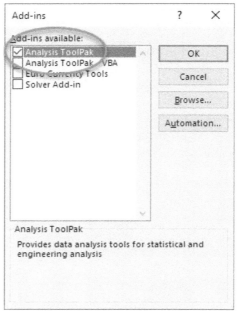

Figure 11.A4. Enable Analysis Toolpak.

When you return to the Excel spreadsheet Data menu ribbon, the Data Analysis button is now available.

Figure 11.A5. Data Ribbon with Data Analysis option enabled.

PART IV: HOMOGENEOUS MEASURES

12. "Prioritizing Investments: Ranking and Comparable Measures"

LINDON ROBISON

Learning goals. At the end of this chapter, you should be able to: (1) explain why unambiguous rankings require one-dimensional measures; (2) understand why consistent rankings require homogeneous measures; and (3) describe present value (PV) model dimensions that require homogeneous measures.

Learning objectives. To achieve your learning goals, you should complete the following objectives:

- Understand the need for one-dimensional ranking criterion.
- Evaluate and distinguish between one-dimensional net present value (NPV) and internal rate of return (IRR) ranking measures.
- Learn about PV model homogeneous measures that are required for consistent NPV and IRR rankings that include:
  - homogeneous funding sources;
  - homogeneous initial and periodic sizes;
  - homogeneous terms;
  - homogeneous tax rates; and
  - homogeneous liquidity and currency.

Introduction

Financial managers must decide whether to continue their commitment to an existing investment called a defender or disinvest in the defender and commit resources to a new investment called a challenger. More complicated investment problems may require that we choose between a defender and several challengers—mutually exclusive challengers, challengers that can be acquired in combination with other challengers, and time sequenced challengers. To describe the nature of defenders and challengers and the need for homogeneous measures, we introduce a simple one-period present value (PV) model.

Suppose we have already committed V_0^d to a defending investment in exchange for its future cash flow equal to R_1^d. Now suppose that the rate $(1 + r^d)$ at which the defender exchanges present and future dollars is:

$$(1 + r^d) = \frac{R_1^d}{V_0^d}$$

(12.1)

Now consider an alternative challenging investment. The rate at which the challenger's investment funds V_0^c are exchanged for future cash flow R_1^c is:

$$(1 + r^c) = \frac{R_1^c}{V_0^c}$$

(12.2)

In equations (12.1) and (12.2), r^c and r^d equal the defender's and challenger's internal rates of return. We cannot really say much about the relative internal rates of returns of the defender and challenger unless we require that the two investment amounts V_0^d and V_0^c are equal. If the investment amounts are equal and if ($R_1^c > R_1^d$), then we can make a definitive statement about their relative IRRs, ($r^c > r^d$).

Now suppose that we equate $r^c = r^d + \alpha$ and rewrite equation (12.2) as:

(12.3) $$(1 + r^d + \alpha)V_0 = R_1^c$$

Finally, we divide both sides of equation (12.3) by $(1 + r^d)$ and write:

(12.4) $$\frac{\alpha V_0}{1 + r^d} = -V_0 + \frac{R_1^c}{1 + r^d} = NPV$$

where the present value of earnings, $\alpha V_0 / (1 + r^d)$, will be referred to net present value, NPV.

So, what have we learned? By means of this example, we introduce some of the main themes of this chapter. Comparisons between defenders and challengers require homogeneous measures. Assuming homogeneous measures, challengers and defenders can be ranked for investment preference by their individual IRRs. Or, we can combine a defender and a challenging investment into one ranking equation we refer to as the NPV equation. NPV and IRR equations are the fundamental PV equations from which most others can be derived and extended for several periods. To ensure that they provide consistent rankings, we measure the characteristics of defenders and challengers in homogeneous units.

Opportunity Costs

An opportunity cost is a benefit, profit, or value of something that must be given up in order to acquire or achieve something else. An economic couplet declares that there is no free lunch. If you want lunch, you must pay for it—sacrifice something to obtain it. The opportunity cost, the cost of lunch, of investing in a challenger is the IRR of the defender. NPVs measure the difference in the present value of future earnings if the investor sacrificed the defender to invest in the challenger.

Prices are not opportunity costs. The price of a good is the amount of money, or money equivalent, paid to obtain it. The amount of money or money equivalent paid to obtain the good represents the direct cost of what is given up to acquiring something desired or to avoid something disliked. However, there may be other costs incurred to acquire a good—or to avoid a bad—besides the price paid. For example, one might consider the cost of attending a movie to be the price of the ticket. However, transportation costs to and from the theater could add to the actual value of what must be exchanged to attend the movie. And there may be other costs of attending the movie such as lost earnings as a result of missing work. Or, suppose the movie was playing while the moviegoer ate his or her prepaid dinner meal. Now the cost of the movie includes not only the price of the ticket plus transportation costs and lost wages but also the value of the skipped meal. The cost of the ticket, transportation costs, lost wages, and the skipped meal together represent the opportunity cost of attending the movie, which is different from the price of the movie ticket.

Opportunity costs and perfect capital markets. The capital (or financial) market is where people trade today's present dollars for future dollars and vice versa. In a perfect capital market, dollars trade between adjacent time-periods at the (same) market rate of interest. For a perfect capital market to exist, the following conditions are required: no barriers to entry; no participant can influence the price; transactions are costless to complete; relevant information about the market is widely and freely available; products and services are homogeneous; no distorting taxes exist; and investment possibilities are continuously divisible. Finally, the firm's opportunity cost of capital is the same regardless of the size or purpose of the amount being borrowed or lent. Finally, in perfect capital markets, investment NPVs are zero.

Though markets for some financial investments are considered highly efficient, they are not perfect. Rates of return on savings rarely equal the rate paid to borrow funds. Moreover, rates of return on investments typically depend on the size and economic lifetime of the investments. Hence, in the real world, investors face imperfect capital markets. We allow for imperfections in capital markets in our PV models by allowing the rate of return on an investment being considered for adoption, a challenger, to differ from the rate of return on an investment that must be sacrificed to adopt the challenger, a defender, to vary. In imperfect markets, the opportunity cost of the defender and the market rates of interest on loans are rarely equal.

So, what have we learned? We have learned that adopting a challenging investment requires that we sacrifice a defending one and what the defending investment earns. That's right, there is no free lunch. As a result, we recognize that opportunity costs are much more (and sometimes less) than just prices.

One-dimensional Ranking Measures

An analogy. To uniquely rank defending and challenging investments requires a one-dimensional ranking measure. To make this point, that unique investment rankings requires a one-dimensional measure, assume that we determined the winner and loser of a sporting event by several different measures.

To illustrate, suppose that the winner of the Super Bowl football game depended on the following measures: points earned, yards gained, yards earned on the ground divided by the yards earning passing, yards penalized, injuries sustained, and the number of persons viewing the contest. Most football sports fans would agree that the success measures just described matter—but they would also agree that we would be unable to determine who wins and who loses with such multi-dimensional measures unless in some rare event one team dominated in all dimensions. So, we must decide which measure matters most and in the case of football—the measure that matters most is points earned. Hopefully, all other measures are subsumed in the one defining measure.

We rank most investments using one of two one-dimensional measures, NPVs and IRRs. What does it mean that NPVs and IRRs provide one-dimensional measures? It means that they can be represented by a location along a straight line. Consider other details about NPVs and IRRs as ranking measures. NPVs measure the difference between a challenger and a defender described in present value dollars. Positive (negative) NPVs imply that the investors will increase (decrease) their earning by exchanging the defender for the challenger. Percentage rates of return measure the internal rate of return (IRR) of a single investment. Any comparison between defenders and challengers using IRRs will require an IRR be calculated for each investment.

NPV rankings. To rank investments uniquely using NPV measures requires that we reduce their current and future earning to a single number in the same period. Alternatively, we could compare two investments' future cash flow in each period of their economic lives. Then, we would likely be unable to rank them because one investment may earn more in one period and less in another that a challenging investment. To avoid the indecisiveness of multi-dimension metrics, we convert future cash flow to their present value creating a one-dimensional number that allows us to uniquely rank defender and challenging investments. To reduce future cash flow to equivalent in the present we assume that a challenger's earnings are reinvested in the defender and earn the defender's rate of return.

IRR rankings. Alternatively, investments can be ranked by their IRRs, a percent. But to find a percentage to represent the PV model, we treat each periodic cash flow as equally important by converting them to their present value equivalent. We use the word internal to describe the second ranking method because the earnings from the investment are reinvested in the challenger rather than being reinvested in the defending investment. IRRs have two possible interpretations. One, it is the (internal) rate of return earned by the challenger. Or, it is the defender's IRR that produces an NPV of zero. Of course, if the defender's IRR produces an NPV of zero, it means that the defender and challenger's IRR are equal. If the NPV is positive (negative), then the IRR of the challenger is greater than (less than) that of the defender although there may be some strange exceptions.

The idea that future cash flow can be ranked by their NPVs or IRRs may be one of the most important and pervasive concepts in financial management. It is the basis for ranking nearly every investment with future cash flow including physical investments, bonds, stocks, insurance, pension funds, housing, land, cars—and almost anything that has more than one period of economic life generating cash flow.

The problem of IRR and NPV rankings. There is a problem with having IRR and NPV ranking measures. We don't have just one—one-dimensional ranking number (points earned in a football game). We have two and possibly more. And when we have more than one, one-dimensional ranking measure, we have the possibility for inconsistent rankings. And we do.

IRR and NPV ranking criteria routinely produce inconsistent rankings and provide unlimited opportunities for academics to argue about their relative virtues. And here is the main point of this chapter, if we compare challengers and defenders using homogeneous measures, we can guarantee that IRR and NPV rankings will provide consistent rankings.

So, what have we learned? Unambiguous investment rankings require that we agree on one, one-dimensional ranking measure. And failing that, having more than one one-dimensional ranking measure, we must describe challengers and defenders using homogeneous measures to guarantee that we will have consistent IRR and NPV measures.

Homogeneous Measures

What adds complexity to choosing between a defender and a challenger and among challengers is that they often have different characteristics that make comparisons between and among them difficult. Moreover, these differences between challenging and defending investments, unless addressed, may result in inconsistent rankings. As a result, we may be unsure which is the preferred investment decision. This chapter intends to describe how we can avoid inconsistent investment rankings by requiring homogeneous (same) values for some investment characteristics. We do allow for some investment characteristics to be unequal–the ones that lead us to prefer one investment over another.

What is homogeneity? Homogeneity is the quality or state of being equal or of the same kind. Homogeneity synonyms include uniformity, equality, consistency, and harmony. Employed in our investment ranking discussion, homogeneity means that measures not relevant to the rankings of investments should be equal and not allowed to influence ranking outcomes. Homogeneous measures can be of two kind. We are measuring the same thing, inches, pounds, days of the year, time in the mountain time zone, etc. The second meaning of a homogeneous measure is that the value of the same characteristic being compared is the same across investments.

On the other hand, not all measures used to describe need or should be homogeneous, at least in the second meaning of the word. If all the measures were used to describe defending and challenging investments were homogeneous, they would be the same value and we would not be able to distinguish between investments. To emphasize the need for homogeneous measures, we introduce a horse racing analogy.

An analogy. To make the point that a lack of homogeneous (same) measures may create ranking conflicts, even when the comparisons involve one-dimensional measures, we compare ranking investments to a horse race. We organize horse races so that other factors besides the horses' speed do not influence the horse race outcome. For example, we expect that only horses enter the race. We require that the horses all begin the race at the same time and place. We expect that all horses will run the same distance and at the same time—that implies that not only has the starting point and time has been determined but the finish line as well. We require the jockey's weight not be a factor. Finally, we expect that everyone agrees that the criterion for ranking horses is the time interval between when each horse starts and finishes the race.

Ranking investments is, of course, not a horse race. Yet, the process of ranking investments according to their rates of return or earnings and horses according to their speed have many elements in common. First, we assume that we are comparing investments of the same size (only horses run the race). We also assume that we are comparing investments over the same time-period or term, (the length of the race is the same for all horses). Finally, we assume that the criterion used to rank investments (NPVs or IRRs) would provide the same rankings for each investment just as we would agree that timekeepers would agree on which horse crossed the finish line first. For the horse race to be fair, i.e. that the outcome is not influenced by irrelevant factors unrelated to the horses' speed, we control for as many differences as possible and meaningful. Only when controlling for irrelevant factors can we make the horse's speed the most important factor, the one nonhomogeneous factor that determines the winner.

To continue our analogy, suppose we wanted to compare the average speed on horses in different races. That may be difficult because so many conditions may not be controlled or made the same between races. Different locations, different conditions and length of the track, different weather conditions and time of day and time of year—all these and others may all influence the speed of the horses in that race. And if those difference between races were not enough to complicate the comparisons, consider the differences between horses: their age, weight, gender, genealogy, races run previously during a set period, their diets, and overall health, how it was trained—to name a few. All these differences may lead us to ask—what can we infer from race outcomes? What we want to know is what variables should not be measured in homogeneous measures? It may be that what we don't want to make homogeneous is something intangible—the horse's desire and will to win. Like we meant to say, it can be complicated.

Homogeneous Cash Flow Measures

We have emphasized that for NPV and IRR to provide consistent rankings, defender and challenger investments must be measured in homogeneous units. Perhaps the two most important homogeneous characteristics is that the economic activity of the defender and challenger must be both represented by cash flow. And secondly, the cash flow used to represent the economic activity of the defender and challenger must be measured in common present value units.

The cash flow principle. One investment dimension that both the defender and challenger must adopt to represent their economic activity, is the cash flow it generates and when. We refer to this requirement as the cash flow principle. When building a PV model, we represent economic activities of the firm by their cash flow. In our horse race analogy, the cash flow principle is equivalent to letting only horses run the race. Some activities of the firm produce what we characterize as noncash outcomes such as appreciation (depreciation) of assets, increases in inventories of unsold goods, and increases in accounts receivable and payable. But these events are not included in PV models because they do not produce cash flow.

One justification for the cash flow principle is that, at some point, we expect all economic activities to generate cash flow. At some point, we expect inventories to be liquidated and generate cash. At some point, we expect accounts receivable and accounts payable to be settled for cash. At some point we expect long-term assets that have appreciated (depreciated) to be sold and the difference between their acquisition and sale price to capture the noncash flow of depreciation (appreciation). Thus, in effect, we do count all economic activities of the firm by recognizing only cash flow; however, we count them only when they create cash flow.

The cash flow principle requires that careful distinction be made between a cash transaction and a noncash transaction. Sometimes the distinction is not always clear. For example, an asset's book value depreciation does not itself generate a cash flow. Depreciation expenses of an investment do, however, generate a tax shield that creates a cash flow in the form of reduced tax payment. Thus, we include the cash flow associated with tax savings resulting from depreciation of an asset but not the depreciation.

Present value equivalent cash flow. We already determined the need for homogenous measures to unambiguously rank investments using either NPVs or IRRs. Furthermore, we earlier accepted that a dollar in the present in not the same as a future dollar. But how do we reconcile that our NPV and IRR models consist of time-dated cash flow that are inherently differ from each other? The answer is that we exchange them with their present value equivalent by discounting them either with at the defender's or the challenger's IRR.

Consider a percent that describes the exchange between future dollars (A) and present dollars (B). We exchange future and present dollars every time we lend or borrow money, make or liquidate an investment, or invest in or withdraw money from a retirement account.

To illustrate, suppose I borrow present dollars V_0 now from a lender and in one year from now, I repay the lender future dollars R_1 where the subscript indicates the end of the time-period in which the cash flow occurs. Since the ratio contains numbers of the same units, the rate of exchange between me and a lender is (R_1/V_0) equal to the decimal $(1 + r)$ or as sometime reported, as r percent. We summarize the ratio of future to present dollars expressed as a decimal equal to:

$$\underset{(12.5)}{\frac{R_1}{V_0}} = (1 + r)$$

To illustrate, suppose V_0 equals $100 and R_1 equals $110. In this example the ratio of future to present dollars is: $110/$100 = 1.10 or 110% and we could say that one present dollar can be exchanged for 1.10 future dollars.

Now suppose I want to receive R_1 dollars one period in the future in exchange for V_0 now. The percentage describing the exchange is (V_0/R_1) equal to $1/(1 + r)$ or if multiplied by 100%, I could say that I can exchange future dollars for present dollars at $(1/1 + r)$ percent.

$$\underset{(12.6)}{\frac{V_0}{R_1}} = \frac{1}{(1 + r)}$$

To illustrate, suppose V_0 equals $100 and R_1 equals $110. In this example the percentage of present to future dollars is $100/$110 = 0.91 and we could say that one future dollar can be exchanged for present dollars at .91 percent. Sometimes we say that one dollar in the future can be discounted to 0.91 present dollars, expressing our ratio as a decimal.

The variable r appears frequently in PV models that describe money exchanged across time. It is important to recognize that r is a decimal. However, when it is used in a ratio or equation with dollars—it is often referred to as a rate. For example, consider equation (12.7).

$$\underset{(12.7)}{V_0(1 + r)} = R_1$$

In equation (12.7) r is a decimal or percent that multiplies present dollars to find future dollars and we refer to it as the rate of return earned on initial investment V_0.

Exchanging present dollars for a future dollar over more than one period. If we know the exchange rate r and are willing to assume it is constant over time, it is a small step to convert present dollars to their equivalent in the future or to convert future dollars to their equivalent in the present. We simply multiply or divide by the appropriate rate. To convert present dollars to their one period in the future value we multiply by $(1 + r)$. To convert future dollars to their present worth, we divide or discount by $1/(1 + r)$.

To illustrate the importance of calculating the present value of future cash flow, suppose that a "down-on-her-luck friend" approaches you. She explains that her wealthy aunt has promised her $100 in one year, but she needs the money now. She asks you what you would offer in present dollars in return for her future $100 dollars. You quickly calculate (assuming an exchange rate of 110% or 1.10), and report that the present value of $100 future dollars (received in one period from now) is $90.91. Or, we might say that the discounted present value of $100 future dollars is $90.91.

Just as we found the present value of one period in future dollars, we can also find the present value of future cash flows received in two or more periods in the future. Returning to our earlier example, suppose this same down-on-her luck friend offers you R_1 dollars in one period and R_2 dollars two periods in the future and asks how many present dollars would you offer for the exchange if the exchange rate is $(1 + r)$.

We can find the present value of R_2 in two steps. First, convert R_2 to its equivalent value in period one dollars by discounting at the rate of $1/(1 + r)$ or $[R_2/(1 + r)]$. Then we discount $[R_2/(1 + r)]$ by dividing again by $(1 + r)$ to convert period one dollars to present period dollars. Important to note is that the exchange rate is assumed to be $(1 + r)$ between any two periods, including between periods one and two. We summarize our two period future cash flow discounted to their present value as:

$$V_0 = \frac{\left[R_1 + \dfrac{R_2}{(1+r)}\right]}{(1+r)} = \frac{R_1}{(1+r)} + \frac{R_2}{(1+r)^2}$$

(12.8)

We would follow a similar procedure to find the present value of dollars received in three periods from the present. Suppose you were offered $100 for the next three periods. What is the present value of these future cash flows if the exchange rate were 110 percent between any two periods? The answer is:

$$V_0 = \frac{\$100}{1.1} + \frac{\$100}{1.1^2} + \frac{\$100}{1.1^3}$$
$$= 90.91 + \$82.64 + \$75.13 = \$248.68$$

(12.9)

> So, what have we learned? We learned that we can find the present value of future dollars by discounting them using one plus the appropriate discount rate r. Furthermore, we can find the value of present dollars in the future by compounding or multiplying then using one plus the appropriate reinvestment rate r. All this assumes, of course, that the exchange rate of dollars between time periods is a constant $(1 + r)$. By means of the exchange rate, we convert cash flow either in NPV or IRR models to their equivalent (homogeneous value) in the present.

Homogeneous measures and winning horses. In sum, when comparing horse races and investments, we try and make homogeneous any many irrelevant factors as possible. If we do not, the results will be influenced, biased, by factors we don't want to determine the outcome. And there is more. Not only do irrelevant non-homogeneous investment dimensions bias rankings, that may also produce inconsistent IRR and NPV rankings. In other words, if we allow to many factors to vary, we may get a decisive race outcome but not be able to determine if it was meaningful. In the remainder of this chapter and in the following chapters, we focus on several investment dimensions that must be measured the same, homogeneously, so that our investment rankings will be unbiased and that NPV and IRR rankings will be consistent.

So, what have we learned? When ranking investments, we must decide which factors influencing the investment's performance should be made equal and which factors should be allowed to vary between defenders and challengers. Choosing which factors, we should hold constant or not, is somewhat of an art. There is no book of investment principles that we know of that can guide our choices. The best we can offer is a reasoned approach to help us determine what factors should be allowed vary and to determine investment rankings and which ones should not be allowed to vary. The criteria we adopt for requiring homogeneous measures is this: we require homogeneous measures for those factors that allow IRR and NPV rankings to be inconsistent. We describe next those factors that if allowed to vary may produce inconsistent rankings.

Other Homogeneous Measures

In what follows, we briefly introduced those investment dimensions that should be made homogeneous to produce consistent NPV and IRR rankings. Later, each dimension will be emphasized in a separate chapter. We have already noted that PV models should measure economic activity using only cash flow and convert them to their present value equivalent. We also described in Chapter 8 the need to measure earnings and rates of return from either assets or equity. We should also compare investments of the same initial and periodic sizes, terms, tax codes, and liquidity and currency.

PV models are designed to measure time-dated cash flow in homogeneous units by converting them to their equivalent present value. This is key and fortunately is inherent in PV models. But there are other investment dimensions besides their time dated cash flow that may not only be measured in different units but may be measured in the same weight but given different values. As a result, investments not measured in homogeneous unit may produce inconsistent IRR and NPV rankings. We describe these next and they are so important that in what follows we devote a separate chapter to each measure.

Homogeneous funding sources. An important characteristic of an investment that should be homogeneous across investments being compared is the investment's funding source. This topic is covered in Chapter 8, but homogeneous funding sources is not the only focus of chapter 8. Homogeneity of investment funding requires that both defenders and challengers must attribute their earning and rates of return to either its equity or assets. To be specific, if two investments are being ranked using their IRRs, then cash flow for the investments must be either attributed to cash flow from equity or assets. If two or more investments are being ranked using NPVs, then cash flow for challengers and the defender's discount rate must be attributed to either equity or assets. To avoid confusion, we will describe the rate of return on equity as ROE or IRR^E. And we will describe the return to the firm's assets or investment as ROA or IRR^A. If we wish to compare earnings on the investment or assets, we will compare NPV^A. If we wish to compare earnings on equity, we will compare NPV^E for the different investments.

So how do we build PV models that measure earnings and rates of return on assets or equity? When finding the ROA for the defender, we ignore cash flow that includes borrowing or lending activities. The advantage of this approach is that it measures the rate of return on assets independent of the returns from the loan used to finance the investment. We write the defender's cash flow and its corresponding IRR that measures ROA as:

$$(12.10) \quad V_0 = \frac{R_1}{(1 + ROA)}$$

where V_0 is the initial investment, R_1 is net cash flow earned in the first period, and S_1 is the liquidation value of the investment after one period. Then we write the ROA as:

$$(12.11) \quad ROA = \frac{R_1 - V_0}{V_0}$$

Interpreted, equation (12.11) equates ROA to cash returns R_1 including cash value of capital gains (losses) equal to the difference between the liquidation value and the beginning value of the asset all divided by the beginning value of the assets. It measures the rate of return on the firm's assets including returns generated by human capital, manufactured capital, social capital, natural capital, and financial capital.

In this approach, we do not account for the source of funding for the investment—equity or assets. Unless otherwise specified, it includes both debt and equity funding. In this calculation, we do not charge for interest costs charged on debt capital because the entire investment is charged at the beginning of the investment cycle and to charge for interest costs would double count the cost of using debt capital.

To measure the rate of return on the firm's equity, we only charge for equity initially invested and charge principal and interest payment in the time period they are repaid and the loan balance and the end of the analysis. In this formulation we net out the cost of using debt capital and attribute the remaining earnings to invested equity.

To calculate returns to earning by subtracting out the use of debt, assume that an asset is acquired using debt D_0 plus equity E_0 whose sum is equal to V_0. At the beginning of the project, the firm supplies equity capital to purchase the investment creating a negative cash flow of E_0 dollars in the beginning period.

Then it receives D_0 from the lender and pays D_0 to the seller to complete the purchase of the investment. Since the investor receives D_0 from the lender and pays debt capital D_0 to the seller of the asset at the beginning of the period, they cancel out making net cash flow from debt capital at the beginning of the investment zero. At the end of the period, the investment repays debt capital D_0 plus interest iD_0 to the lender. In a one period model, the investor pays back to the lender, debt capital D_0. Thus, we can express these cash flow as:

$$(12.12) \quad E_0 = \frac{R_1 - (1+i)D_0}{(1 + ROE)}$$

And we can write the ROE as follows:

$$(12.13) \quad ROE = \frac{R_1 - (1+i)D_0 - E_0}{E_0}$$

We are interested in the relationship between ROA and ROE. To determine that relationship, we first solve for R_1 in equation (12.11) and find that it equals:

$$(12.14) \quad R_1 = (1 + ROA)V_0$$

Then we make the substitution for R_1 in equation (12.13) using equation (12.14) and replacing V_0 with (D_0 + E_0) we again the rates of return identity (RORI) result:

$$(12.15) \quad ROE = \frac{(ROA - i)D_0 + ROA}{E_0}$$

What equation (12.15) reveals is that ROE > ROA as long as the firm earns a positive return on its debt capital (ROA > i).

Homogeneous initial and periodic investment sizes. Homogeneous size measures (Chapter 13) require that initial and periodic investment sizes for challengers and defenders must be equal. This seems like an obvious requirement. Nevertheless, it is routinely ignored and often produces conflicting NPV and IRR rankings. To apply the homogeneity of size requirements, initial investment differences must be resolved. We resolve initial size difference by accounting for their earnings especially that remain invested in a defender. Periodic cash flow in PV models represent investment withdrawal that alter the size of the investment. To maintain periodic size homogeneity, cash flow is compounded until a common ending period.

Our goal is to obtain unbiased investment and cash flow measures. This requires not only homogeneous measures but that all cash costs and cash returns associated with an investment should be included when determining an investment's present value. Consider how the total costs and returns principle is applied in several practical situations. Whenever low-interest loans or preferential tax treatments are tied to the ownership of a durable, these concessions will influence the present value of the investment. To ignore these benefits (costs) would lead to an under or over evaluation of the worth of the investment.

Sometimes an investment such as land has more than one source of returns. Mineral deposits, potential recreational use, and urbanization pressures may create expected returns over and above those associated with agricultural use. Pollution standards may impose costs in addition to those normally experienced. All these expected cash costs and returns that influence the value of the durable should be included in the PV model. And cash flow associated with decreased accounts and inventories should also be included.

Requiring initial and periodic size equality is analogous requiring horses in the same race to be of the same size.

Homogeneous terms. Just as we would expect horses in the same race to run the distance, we would expect that investments being compared would be measured over the same term. Chapter 14 describes how we implement the homogeneity of term requirement. Similar to the method used when satisfying the homogeneity of size condition, when comparing investments of two different terms, we must account for the investments' earning between the term of their investments.

Complicating the application of the homogeneity of term requirement are sequenced investments, one s that cannot occur without a similar disinvestment. For example, we cannot invest in a new orchard or cohort of animals without deciding the term of the existing investments.

Homogeneous tax rates. Taxes represent withdrawal from the firm's earning by government. Homogeneous tax-rate measures (Chapter 15) require that we account for differences in effective tax rates for defenders and challengers that depend on cash flow patterns and capital gains (loses). The main point here, is that tax considerations should be equally considered when evaluating the challenger as well as the defender. On the other hand, some taxes may not be identically applied to both defenders and challengers and require a careful consideration of the effects of taxes.

Homogeneous liquidity and currency measures. Homogeneous liquidity measures (Chapter 16) recognize that firms and investments can be differentiated by their liquidity. This is a difficult concept to apply when ranking investments. And perhaps the best we can offer is to provide liquidity measures that differ by investment types.

A different homogeneity measure applies why engaged in global trade across countries and currencies. Now the rate of currency exchange becomes and important consideration and even more so when it varies over time.

> So, what have we learned? To compare the value of a potentially new investment, a challenging investment, with an investment to be sacrificed, a defending investment, we need to apply homogeneous measures to both. Included in the list of homogeneous measures

required for meaningful and consistent rankings include: using only cash to represent economic activity, using homogeneous funding sources, using homogeneous initial (and periodic) investment sizes; using homogeneity investment terms; homogeneous currency and liquidity measures; homogeneous risk measures; homogeneous tax rate measures; and homogeneous measures of funding sources (assets versus equity).

Summary and Conclusions

The discount rate in a PV model represents the defender's IRR. It is the rate of return sacrificed by disinvesting in the defender to acquire the challenger. The defender's rate of return measures either its ROA or ROE. Choosing the appropriate discount rate for NPV models describing a challenger is perhaps the most difficult task of investment analysis. The choice essentially involves the identification of challengers and opportunity costs associated with defenders.

When ranking investments, we have available one of two possible one-dimensional ranking criterion, NPVs or IRRs. Ideally, these should provide consistent rankings regardless of whatever method we use. Unfortunately, this is not always the case and to be true in general requires that we adopt homogeneous measures for describing challenging and defending investments. These homogeneous measures are so important that they occupy much our effort in chapters 13, 14, 15 and 16 that follow. Our goal is that by using homogeneous measures to construct PV models we can obtain consistent, stable, and accurate investment ranking. Knowing that one's investment rankings are stable, accurate, and consistent is essential for the success of a financial manager whose goal is to maximize the present value of the firm's investments.

Questions

1. The fundamental concept of PV analysis is that a dollar today is not valued the same as a dollar received in the future. List several reasons that might explain why a dollar today may not be valued the same as a dollar in the future.
2. The idea that the value of a good today is not the same as the value of the good in the future is a universal concept. Suppose you were offered a 2020 Ford F-150 pickup truck for delivery today or the same truck in the same condition delivered in 2023. If the price today for the truck were $40,000, what would you offer today for the truck to be delivered in 2023? If the prices you would offer are different, please explain why?
3. Explain the importance of valuing future cash flow in one single period, e.g., the present period.

4. Explain the difference between ratios, percentages, and rates.
5. To test your understanding of exchange rate between present and future dollars, please answer the following. Suppose that you could exchange one apple for 1.1 oranges. What is the exchange rate between apples and oranges, between oranges and apples? Compare the exchange rates between apples and oranges and oranges to apple to the exchange between present and future dollars is $r=.1$ or 10%.
6. Two important economic concepts associated with PV models and investments in general are price and opportunity costs. Opportunity costs are the sacrifices required to obtain a good. The market price of the good may be part of the opportunity cost, but likely not the entire opportunity cost. Consider the opportunity cost of attending the university. These may include income sacrificed. Then compare the opportunity cost of attending the university with the tuition costs, a direct cost. Describe the differences between opportunity costs versus direct costs in other personal activities.
7. Suppose that you invest $100 today. Then assume that one year later your investment returns $110 in cash. Assume that your opportunity cost of capital is 12%.
   1. What is the NPV of the investment?
   2. What is the IRR of the investment?
   3. What is the ratio that converts dollars received one period in the future to their present value?
   4. What is the ratio that converts present dollars to their value one period in the future?
8. A financial manager believes that a defending investment can earn $500 for the next six years. He also believes that his defending investment can be sold today for $2,500. What is the opportunity cost of sacrificing the defender to invest in a challenger? In other words, find the IRR of the defending investment.
9. Briefly distinguish between a defending and a challenging investment. Suppose you are considering replacing an outdated piece of equipment with two different pieces of equipment of difference sizes, efficiency, and useful life. In addition, one company offers financing while the other one assumes buyers will provide their own financing. Describe the challenging you might face comparing and deciding between the two investments.
10. In practice, financial managers face more complicated investment problems than deciding between a single defender and a single challenger. Describe how you might solve an investment problem with more than one challenger? One challenger but more than one defender? When choosing between multiple defenders, what would be the appropriate criterion for the preferred defender? How would you analyze a problem consisting of multiple challengers and defenders? What principle from micro economic theory might guide you in preparing your answer?
11. Describe the fundamental different between rates of return and earnings on assets versus equity. Can you think of different considers when earnings and rates of return on assets would be the preferred measures versus conditions when earnings and rates of return on equity would be the preferred measure?
12. Explain how violating homogeneity of size may lead to inconsistent NPV and IRR rankings. (Hint: how do rankings based on a percent (IRRs) versus rankings based on dollar amounts (NPV) permit inconsistent rankings when initial investment sizes are different.)

13. Compare investments of different terms to two horses running a race of different lengths.
14. Since only death and taxes remain a constant, explain why it is important to measure a defender's and challenger's cash flow in both before and after-taxes. Suppose that the before and after-tax rankings were inconsistent, what would you conclude. Would you base your investment decision on before or after-tax results?
15. Suppose that you make a significant investment in U.S. currency in a foreign country factory that produces products that are sold and denominated in the currency of the host country? Homogeneous measures require that the investment be evaluated in the same currency. How would you convert a foreign currency to U.S. dollars?

13. "Equalizing Scale: Assessing Investments of Homogeneous Sizes"

LINDON ROBISON

Learning goals. At the end of this chapter, you should be able to: (1) understand how internal rate of return (IRR) and net present value (NPV) models can produce inconsistent rankings; (2) produce con-sistent IRR and NPV rankings by adjusting for investment size differences and by adopting common reinvestment rate assumptions; (3) understand why some NPV and IRR rankings are unstable; (4) rec-ognize how different initial size adjustment methods (addition, scaling, or some combination) include IRR and NPV ranking may be inconsistent and that NPV rankings and (5) recognize how investment type dif-ferences can be used to identify the proper size adjustment method.

Learning objectives. To achieve your learning goals, you should complete the following objectives:

- Recognize that IRR and NPV rankings may be inconsistent and that NPV rankings may be unstable.
- Understand the difference between periodic investment sizes and initial investment sizes.
- Describe how different reinvestment rate assumptions can produce inconsistent IRR and NPV rankings.
- Show how resolving periodic and initial size differences and a common reinvestment rate pro-duce consistent challenging investment rankings.
- Illustrate the different methods available for resolving periodic size investment differences.
- Demonstrate how scaling and addition can be used to resolve initial size differences in invest-ments.
- Demonstrate that while different methods for resolving periodic and initial size differences can each produce consistent rankings, the consistent rankings may not be the same.
- Understand the conditions under which IRR and NPV provide the same rankings as the size adjusted IRR and NPV models.
- Recognize the four basic investment models
- Recommend the appropriate investment model based on challenger characteristics.

Introduction

1

1. Some of the material in this chapter was adapted from Robison, Myers, and Barry (2015).

In the single equation NPV model, we assumed that cash flow was exchanged between time periods at the defender's IRR. In the single equation IRR model, we assumed that cash flow was exchanged between time periods at the challenger's IRR. In the NPV model, the challenger (defender) was preferred to the defender (challenger) if the NPV were positive (negative). Furthermore, the NPV ranking of the defender and challenger was the same ranking obtained by comparing their respective IRRs. As a result, both IRR and NPV criteria produce the same ranking.

This chapter recognizes that when we rank multiple challengers funded by one defender, their IRR and NPV rankings may be different. Furthermore, we observe that changes in the defender's IRR may produce unstable NPV rankings. We demonstrate these results in Table 13.1 that ranks three challengers.

Table 13.1. Inconsistent IRR and NPV rankings and unstable NPV rankings among three mutually exclusive investments of different initial and periodic cash flows.

initial investments V_0^i where $i = 1,2,3$	period one cash flows R_t^i where $t = 1$ generated by initial investments V_0^i where $i = 1,2,3$	period two cash flows R_t^i where $t = 2$ generated by initial investments V_0^i where $i = 1,2,3$	NPV^i earned by initial investments V_0^i where $i = 1,2,3$ assuming $r = 5\%$ (ranking)	NPV^i earned by initial investments V_0^i where $i = 1,2,3$ assuming $r = 10\%$ (ranking)	IRR^i earned by initial investments V_0^i where $i = 1,2,3$ (ranking)
$1,000	$800	$400	$124.72 (3)	$57.85 (2)	14.8% (1)
$2,000	$1,560	$800	$211.34 (2)	$79.34 (1)	13.3% (2)
$3,000	$2,250	$1,200	$231.29 (1)	$37.10 (3)	11.0% (3)

We describe the challenging investments' NPV rankings in columns 4 and 5 for investments of $1,000, $2,000, and $3,000. The investments' IRR rankings appear in column 6. We indicate investment rankings by parenthesized numbers in columns 4, 5, and 6.

If the defender's IRR is 5% for challenging investments 1, 2, and 3, their NPV rankings are 3, 2, and 1 respectively. If the defender's IRR is 10% for challenging investments 1, 2, and 3, their NPV rankings are 2, 1, and 3 respectively. Meanwhile, for challenging investments 1, 2, and 3 their IRR rankings are different still: 1, 2, and 3 respectively. These results demonstrate that IRR and NPV rankings may provide inconsistent rankings and NPV rankings may vary with the defender's IRR.

The inconsistent IRR and NPV rankings require decision makers to choose between conflicting recommendations. They must decide: which ranking method should they believe. Among practitioners, the NPV approach is considered more reliable for wealth maximization. However, the ease in which decision makers can interpret IRRs has made it the more popular of the two ranking methods. Both ranking methods, however, have their drawbacks. Investments may have multiple IRRs and NPV rankings may be unstable—varying with changes in the defender's IRR what is often referred to as the discount rate.

The problem produced by inconsistent IRR and NPV rankings is obvious—it leaves decision makers without a clear recommendation. On the other hand, NPV rankings that vary with the discount rate (see columns four and five) can be just as problematic. The reason is that if we are not sure of the discount rate, then we cannot be sure of the NPV rankings either.

The purpose of this chapter is to demonstrate that by resolving periodic and initial investment size differences between challenging investments and by adopting a common reinvestment rate, we can guarantee consistent IRR and NPV rankings. We will also explain why some NPV rankings vary with changes in the defender's IRR. Finally, we show that depending on how we adjust for size differences and the reinvestment rate we adopt, we an produce four different present value (PV) models. We also discuss the conditions under which each investment model is appropriate for ranking challenging investments—rankings that will be consistent but possibly different across models.

Periodic and Initial Investment Sizes

Sometimes when IRR and NPV methods produce inconsistent rankings, it is because the challenging investments being ranked lack investment size homogeneity. Challenging investments may lack investment size homogeneity in two ways. First, their initial investment sizes may be different. In Table 13.1 note that challenging investments 1, 2, and 3 invested initial amounts of $1,000, $2,000, and $3,000 respectively.

The second way challenging investment sizes may differ is their periodic cash flows. These differences change periodic investment amounts between challenging investments. Notice that in Table 13.1 cash flows in period one are different: $800, $1,560, and $2,250 for investments 1, 2, and 3 respectively. Differences in initial and periodic investment sizes contribute directly to inconsistent and unstable rankings.

Notation. This chapter employs more than the usual amount of mathematical notation. It is required to tell the story about consistent and stable IRR and NPV rankings. The good news is that there are no complicated mathematical operations besides adding, subtracting, canceling like terms, and factoring. The notation that will be used throughout this chapter includes variables with subscripts and superscripts. The superscript on a variable associates it with an investment, $i = 1, 2, ..., m$. The subscript on a variable associates it with a time period $t = 1, ..., n$. If a superscripted variable is raised to a power, the variable is placed in parentheses and the power to which the variable is raised is placed outside of the parentheses. To illustrate, the variable $(R_5^2)^3$ describes the value for the variable R associated with investment $i = 2$ in the $t = 5$ time period raised to the third power. Finally, when we write an expression like $S(r, R_n^i)$ we are saying that function S depends on values assumed by variables r and R_n^i without specifying the exact nature of the function or the values of the variables represented by r and R_n^i. When we want to represent a vector of values for investment i we bold **R** and write $\mathbf{R} = R_1^i, R_2^i, ..., R_n^i$.

How differences in periodic cash flow can create periodic investment size differences. Applying the notation described earlier, we now demonstrate how differences in cash flow create differences in investments sizes over time. Assume that initial investments of V_0^i for investments $i = 1$ and $i = 2$ equal V_0. Also assume that cash flows in period one earned by investments one and two are equal to R_1^1 and

R_1^2 respectively. These positive (negative) cash flows represent investments (disinvestments) in the underlying investment. If the initial investments earned a rate of return equal to the defender's IRR equal to r, then beginning in period two, investment one equals $V_0 (1 + r) - R_1^1$ and investment two equals $V_0 (1 + r) - R_1^2$ which are not equal if $R_1^1 \neq R_1^2$. As a result, unequal periodic cash flows create unequal periodic investments, even if their initial investments are equal, a cause of inconsistent rankings.

To illustrate numerically, suppose that $V_0 = \$100$ and $R_1^1 = \$15$ and $R_1^2 = \$20$. If r is 10% then after one period the amount invested in investment one is $\$100(1.1) - \$15 = \$95$ and the amount invested after one period in investment two is $\$100(1.1) - \$20 = \$90$. After one period the investment amounts are unequal and violate the homogeneity of measures requirement.

The implication of these results is that even though two investments begin with equal initial investments, IRR and NPV rankings may still be inconsistent and unstable if periodic cash flows are unequal.

> So what have we learned? We've learned that the two homogeneous investments size conditions required for consistent NPV and IRR rankings are 1) equal initial challenging investments sizes, and 2) equal periodic cash flows except in the last period. We require equal periodic cash flows except in the last period to ensure that the challenging investments will satisfy equal periodic investment sizes. Besides these two size conditions, one of two reinvestment rate assumptions must be adopted for both NPV and IRR rankings. These two reinvestment rate assumption are that cash flow are either reinvested at the defender's IRR or at the challengers' respective IRRs.

Consistent IRR and NPV Rankings When the Reinvestment Rate is the Defender's IRR

To be clear, reinvestment rates indicate where periodic cash flows will be reinvested. If the reinvestment rate is the defender's IRR, then we assume that earnings from the challenging investments will be reinvested in the defender. If the reinvestment rates are the challenging investments' respective IRRs, then we assume that earnings from the investments will be reinvested in the challenging investments. If there is some other reinvestment rate, it must correspond to a separate investment and be evaluated as another challenger. Hence, the only reinvestment rates we consider are the defender's IRR and the challenging investments' IRRs.

NPV models implicitly assume that the reinvestment rate is the defender's IRR and earnings from the investment will be reinvested in the defender. IRR models assume that the reinvestment rate is the investment's own IRR and that the funds will be reinvested in itself. However, to remove ranking inconsistencies, we impose the same reinvestment rate across IRR and NPV models and produce what others have referred to as modified IRR (MIRR) and modified NPV (MNPV) models.

Next we demonstrate that if the two sufficient size conditions are satisfied and challenger earnings are reinvested in the defender, we are guaranteed consistent NPV and IRR rankings. NPV rankings will be consistent and under some conditions stable.

NPV rankings. Consider ranking two mutually exclusive n period investments in a similar risk class by their respective NPVs. The NPV model for investment one is described as:

$$NPV^1 = -V_0^1 + \frac{R_1^1}{(1+r)} + \cdots + \frac{R_n^1}{(1+r)^n}$$

(13.1a)

The NPV model for investment two is described as:

$$NPV^2 = -V_0^2 + \frac{R_1^2}{(1+r)} + \cdots + \frac{R_n^2}{(1+r)^n}$$

(13.1b)

In the equations above, r is the defender's IRR, V_0^1 and V_0^2 are initial investments one and two respectively, and R_t^1 and R_t^2 are periodic cash flows in periods $t = 1, \cdots, n$ generated by mutually exclusive investments one and two. We assume that the terms of the two investments are equal.

To resolve size differences caused by differences in periodic cash flows, we set them equal to zero in every period except the last one by reinvesting them at rate r until the last period. Generally, the discount rate and the reinvestment rate in NPV models are equal. To distinguish the original NPV model with the NPV model with funds reinvested until the last period, many finance scholars refer to the later model as the modified NPV model or the MNPV model. We write the MNPV model as:

$$MNPV^1 = -V_0^1 + \frac{(1+r)^{n-1}R_1^1 + (1+r)^{n-2}R_2^1 + \cdots + R_n^1}{(1+r)^n}$$

$$= -V_0^1 + \frac{S(r, \mathbf{R}^1)}{(1+r)^n}$$

(13.2a)

where $S(r, \mathbf{R}^1) = (1+r)^{n-1}R_1^1 + (1+r)^{n-1}R_2^1 + \cdots + R_n^1$. Similarly the MNPV model for investment two can be rewritten as:

$$MNPV^2 = -V_0^2 + \frac{(1+r)^{n-1}R_1^2 + (1+r)^{n-2}R_2^2 + \cdots + R_n^2}{(1+r)^n}$$

$$= -V_0^2 + \frac{S(r, R^2)}{(1+r)^n}$$

(13.2b)

where $S(r, \mathbf{R}^2) = (1+r)^{n-1}R_1{}^2 + (1+r)^{n-2}R_2{}^2 + \cdots + R_n{}^2$. Finally, we impose the additional condition that $S(r, \mathbf{R}^1)$, $S(r, \mathbf{R}^2) > 0$, otherwise the investment decision is no longer interesting.

The difference between $MNPV^1$ and $MNPV^2$ which ranks the two investments can be expressed as:

$$MNPV^2 - MNPV^1 = [V_0^1 - V_0^2] + \frac{[S(r, \mathbf{R}^2) - S(r, \mathbf{R}^1)]}{(1+r)^n}$$

(13.3)

If the initial investment sizes are the same as required by the homogeneity of measures principle, then the difference in the first bracketed expression in equation (13.3) is zero and the rankings will depend only on the difference between the sums of reinvested cash flows:

$$MNPV^2 - MNPV^1 = \frac{[S(r, \mathbf{R}^2) - S(r, \mathbf{R}^1)]}{(1+r)^n}$$

(13.4)

Equation (13.4) provides an interesting result. We obtained these results by reinvesting and discounting cash flow at the same rate so NPVs of the two investments are unaffected allowing us to write:

$$\frac{[S(r, \mathbf{R}^2) - S(r, \mathbf{R}^1)]}{(1+r)^n} = NPV^2 - NPV^1.$$

(13.5)

We now illustrate the results of equation (13.5). Let the initial investment equal \$100 and cash flows in periods one and two equal \$50 and \$70 respectively. Finally let the discount rate and the implied reinvestment rate equal 10%. Then we write:

$$NPV = -\$100 + \frac{\$50}{(1 + 10\%)} + \frac{\$70}{(1 + 10\%)^2} = \$3.31$$

(13.6a)

Then we write the equivalent MNPV model as:

$$MNPV = -\$100 + \frac{(\$50)(1 + 10\%) + \$70}{(1 + 10\%)^2} = \$3.31$$

(13.6b)

The results illustrate NPV and MNPV models are equal and provide the same rankings when the reinvestment rate is the same as the discount rate.

Finally, it should be noted that the difference between the NPVs in equation (13.5) may be unstable and change as the defender's IRR changes as we demonstrated in Table 13.1.

IRR rankings. Consider ranking two mutually exclusive n period investments in a similar risk class by their respective IRRs. If the IRR rankings are to be consistent with the NPV rankings, they must satisfy the sufficient conditions described earlier, including assuming the same reinvestment rate r. The IRR model for investment one is described as:

$$(13.7a) \quad V_0^1 = \frac{R_1^1}{(1 + IRR^1)} + \cdots + \frac{R_n^1}{(1 + IRR^1)^n}$$

The IRR model for investment two is described as:

$$(13.7b) \quad V_0^2 = \frac{R_1^2}{(1 + IRR^2)} + \cdots + \frac{R_n^2}{(1 + IRR^2)^n}$$

In the equations above, V_0^1 and V_0^2 are initial investments one and two respectively, and R_t^1 and R_t^2 are periodic cash flows in periods $t = 1, \cdots, n$ generated by mutually exclusive investments one and two.

To resolve differences in periodic cash flows, we set them equal to zero in every period except the last period by reinvesting them at rate r until the last period. Generally, the discount rate and the reinvestment rate in IRR models are equal. Here, the reinvestment rate is r rather than their respective IRRs. To distinguish the original IRR model from the IRR model with funds reinvested until the last period, many finance scholars refer to the later model as the modified IRR model, the MIRR model. We write the MIRR model as:

$$(13.8) \quad V_0^1 = \frac{S(r, \mathbf{R}^1)}{(1 + MIRR^1)^n}$$

Solving for MIRR[1] in equation (13.8) we obtain:

$$(13.9) \quad MIRR^1 = \left[\frac{S(r, R^1)}{V_0^1} \right]^{1/n} - 1$$

which has one positive root.

Investment two is described as:

$$V_0^2 = \frac{S(r, \mathbf{R}^2)}{(1 + MIRR^2)^n}$$

(13.10)

Solving for $MIRR^2$ in equation (13.9) we obtain:

$$MIRR^2 = \left[\frac{S(r, R^2)}{V_0^2}\right]^{1/n} - 1$$

(13.11)

which has one positive root.

Finally, we write the difference between $MIRR^1$ and $MIRR^2$ assuming initial investments V_0^2 and V_0^1 are equal to V_0 as:

$$MIRR^1 - MIRR^2 = \left[\frac{S(r, R^1)}{V_0^1}\right]^{1/n} - \left[\frac{S(r, R^2)}{V_0^2}\right]^{1/n}$$

$$= \left\{[S(r, R^2)]^{1/n} - [S(r, R^1)]^{1/n}\right\} \left(\frac{1}{V_0}\right)^{1/n}$$

(13.12)

If the initial sizes and terms of investments one and two are equal, then their MIRR ranking will depend on the same criterion that ranked the investments' MNPVs—the difference in the sum of their reinvested cash flows $S(r, \mathbf{R}^1)$ and $S(r, \mathbf{R}^2)$ and the MIRR rankings and MNPV rankings will be consistent. However, we cannot be certain that the MIRR rankings will equal the IRR rankings because we changed the reinvestment rate assumption in the IRR models.

Consistent IRR and NPV Rankings Assuming Reinvestment Rates are the Challenging Investments' IRRs

In this section, we demonstrate that we can also guarantee consistent NPV and IRR rankings by imposing the second reinvestment rate assumption—that periodic cash flows are reinvested in the challenging investments' IRRs.

Suppose the reinvestment rates were the IRRs of the challengers being evaluated. This reinvestment rate is appropriate under the condition that the cash flows are reinvested in the challengers as opposed to being reinvested in the defending investment. To demonstrate the consequences of assuming that the reinvestment rates equal the challengers' IRRs, consider the following.

Assume that the initial sizes of the challenging investments are equal and that their cash flows are reinvested in themselves earning their respective IRRs and the discount rate applied to the NPVs is the defender's IRR. Then we could write the difference between MNPVs as:

$$MNPV^2 - MNPV^1 =$$

$$\frac{[S(MIRR^2, \mathbf{R}^2) - S(MIRR^1, \mathbf{R}^1)]}{(1+r)^n}$$

(13.13a)

Meanwhile, we can write the difference between MIRRs as:

$$MIRR^2 - MIRR^1 =$$

$$\left\{ [S(MIRR^2, \mathbf{R}^2)]^{1/n} - [S(MIRR^2, \mathbf{R}^1)]^{1/n} \right\} \left(\frac{1}{V_0} \right)^{1/n}$$

(13.13b)

Notice that the MNPV and MIRR rankings depend on the same sums making their rankings consistent. However, in contrast to the NPV model, the MNPV rankings are stable and likely different that the original NPV rankings. But there is one thing more. Look at the original IRR equations. They are equivalent to the MIRR equations. Reinvesting and discounting by the challengers' IRRs are offsetting operations and don't change the original IRRs. Therefore, if the initial sizes are equal, and the assumption is that cash flows are reinvested in the challenging investments, then IRR and MIRR rankings are equivalent! This is such an important point, we illustrate it with an example.

Assume net cash flows of $50 and $70 in periods one and two respectively, an initial investment of $100, and a reinvestment rate of the investment's IRR or MIRR. Then we can write the IRR as:

$$\$100 = \frac{\$50}{(1+IRR)} + \frac{\$70}{(1+IRR)^2} \text{ and } IRR = 12\%$$

(13.14a)

Now we can write the MIRR model as:

$$\$100 = \frac{(\$50)(1+MIRR) + \$70}{(1+MIRR)^2} \text{ and } MIRR = 12\%$$

(13.14b)

Because the IRR and MIRR values are the same, they will return identical rankings. To emphasize the main point, if the periodic cash flows are reinvested in the challengers, then ranking investments using the investments' IRR is the same as ranking them with their MIRRs.

So what have we learned? We learned that when we satisfy the two sufficient size conditions required for consistent rankings, equal initial and period investment sizes (except in the last period), and satisfy the second reinvestment rate assumption that we reinvest in the challenging investments—then MNPV and MIRR rankings of the challengers will be consistent. And there is one thing more, the MIRR rankings will be the same as the original IRR rankings.

We have also learned that inconsistent challenging investments IRR and NPV rankings are often the results of the two ranking methods adopting different reinvestment rate assumptions. NPV models assume the reinvestment rate is the defender's IRR. IRR models assume the reinvestment rate is the challenger's IRR for the same investment. Consistency requires that the reinvestment rate for each investment be the same regardless of whether the ranking tool is IRR or NPV. Once we have satisfied initial and periodic investment size differences and adopted a consistent reinvestment rate assumption, investments can be ranked consistently using IRR or NPV methods.

Reinvestment rates and inconsistent rankings. To make clear that consistent IRR and NPV rankings require that the same reinvestment rate for each investment regardless of the ranking methods, IRR or NPV, we describe three investments with the same initial sizes and assume the defender's IRR is 5%. We allow NPV models to reinvest at the defender's IRR rate of 5%. We allow the challenger's cash flow to be reinvested at their respective IRRs. The inconsistent rankings produced by allowing investments' reinvestment rate to be different when using IRRs versus NPVs, we describe in Table 13.2. The results demonstrate that even if we adjust for initial and periodic size differences but fail to require consistent reinvestment rates, IRR and NPV rankings could still be inconsistent.

Table 13.2. Rankings Allowing NPV models (IRR models) to reinvest periodic cash flows at the defender's IRR (challengers' IRRs). Investment rankings indicated in parentheses below NPVs and IRRs values.

Period	Variables	Challenger 1 cash flow	Challenger 2 cash flow	Challenger 3 cash flow
0	V_0	– $3,000	– $3,000	– $3,000
1	R_1	– $100	$2,010	$2,250
2	R_2	$3,800	$1,560	$1,200
	NPVs assuming r=5%	$351.47 (1)	$329.25 (2)	$231.29 (3)
	IRRs	10.89% (3)	13.01% (1)	11.03% (2)

Now assume that investment three was the defender and we used its IRR equal to 11.03% to reinvest period one cash flow to period two. Then because we employed the same reinvestment rate for each model regardless of whether we used IRR or NPV ranking models, consistency is restored. We describe these results in Table 13.3.

Table 13.3. Allowing NPV and IRR models to reinvest periodic cash flows at same reinvestment rate equal to challenger 3's IRR. Investment rankings indicated in parentheses below NPVs and IRRs values.

Period	Variables	Challenger 1 cash flow	Challenger 2 cash flow	Challenger 3 cash flow
0	V_0	– $3,000	– $3,000	– $3,000
1	R_1	$0	$0	$2,250
2	R_2	$3,800 – $100 x 1.1103 = $3688.97	$1,560 + $2010 x 1.1103 = $3791.70	$1,200
	NPVs assuming r=11.03%	– $7.57 (3)	$83.82 (1)	$0 (2)
	IRRs assuming r=11.03%	10.89% (3)	12.57% (1)	11.03% (2)

So what have we learned? We learned that when we rank challengers using their NPVs and IRRs even when we adjust for initial and periodic size differences—we can produce conflicting rankings because IRR and NPV models assume different reinvestment rates. For IRRs and NPVs to produce consistent rankings, each investment must assume the same reinvestment rates. Different investments may assume different reinvestment rates; however, if IRR and NPV ranking are to be consistent, they must be the same reinvestment rate for the same investment regardless of whether the ranking models are IRRs or NPVs.

Resolving Initial Size Differences by Scaling

Scaling and a reinvestment rate equal to the defender's IRR

Consider the possibility of eliminating initial investment size differences between mutually exclusive investments by scaling the challengers to a common initial size. To scale challengers requires that they are available in continuous sizes. To scale an investment requires that it leaves the relative size of the investment and its cash flows constant over the continuous sizes. For example, scaling an investment by two assumes that there exists an investment twice the size that produces twice the cash flow of the original investment in each period. To illustrate, assume net cash flows of $50 and $70 in periods one and two respectively, an initial investment of $100, and assume the reinvestment rate equals the defender's IRR of r = 10%. Then we can write the MIRR model as:

$$MIRR = \left[\frac{(\$50)(1 + 10\%) + \$70}{\$100}\right]^{1/2} - 1 = 12\%$$

(13.15a)

Suppose now that we scale the MIRR model by 2. Then we can rewrite the model as:

$$\text{scaled } MIRR = \left\{\frac{2[(\$50)(1 + 10\%) + \$70]}{(2)\$100}\right\}^{1/2} - 1 = 12\%$$

(13.15b)

Notice that the scaling factor "2" cancels so we are left with the original MIRR equation in (13.15a). And even if the reinvestment rate is the IRR, the scaling factor still cancels. Thus, the MIRR and the scaled MIRR are equal. (Can you demonstrate that the scaling factor cancels regardless of the reinvestment rate?)

Scaling and a reinvestment rate equal to the challengers' IRR

What if the reinvestment rate is the challenger's own IRRs, which assumes that the funds are reinvested in the challengers, then MIRRs, scaled MIRRs and the IRR equations are the same.

To make the point absolutely clear, that scaling will not change MIRRs or IRRs when the reinvestment rate is the investment's IRR, we illustrate these results by comparing the original IRR calculations from Table 13.1 with MIRRs, and scaled MIRRs calculated in Table 13.4.

Table 13.4. Consistent MIRR, scaled MIRR, and IRR rankings obtained by scaling initial investment sizes and periodic cash flows assuming the reinvestment rates are equal to the investments' IRR^i where $i = 1,2,3$.

initial investment V_0^i and scaling factor γ_i where $i = 1,2,3$	period one cash flows γ_i R_t^i where $t = 1$	period two cash flows R_2^i + (1 + $IRR^i)R_1^i$ where $i = 1,2,3$	period two cash flows $\gamma_i R_2^i$ + $\gamma_i(1 + IRR^i)R_1^i$ where $i = 1,2,3$	$MIRR^i$ where $i = 1,2,3$ assuming $r = IRR^i$ (ranking)	Scaled $MIRR^i$ where $i = 1,2,3$ assuming $r = IRR^i$ (ranking)	IRR^i where $i = 1,2,3$ assuming $r = IRR^i$ (ranking)
$V_0^1 = \$1,000$ $\gamma_1 V_0^1 = \$3,000$ $(\gamma_1 = 3)$	0	$\$400 +$ $(1.148)\$800 =$ $\$1,318.40$	$(3)\$400 +$ $(3)(1.148)\$800$ $= \$3,955.20$	14.8% (1)	14.8% (1)	14.8% (1)
$V_0^2 = \$2,000$ $\gamma_2 V_0^2 = \$3,000$ $(\gamma_2 = 3/2)$	0	$\$800 +$ $(1.133)\$1,560 =$ $\$2,567.48$	$(3/2)\$800 +$ $(3/$ $2)(1.133)\$1,560$ $= \$3,851.22$	13.3% (2)	13.3% (2)	13.3% (2)
$V_0^3 = \$3,000$	0	$\$1,200 +$ $(1.110)\$2,250 =$ $\$3,652.50$	$\$1,200 +$ $(1.110)\$2,250$ $= \$3,652.50$	11.0% (3)	11.0% (3)	11.0% (3)

We next demonstrate how scaling achieves ranking consistency between MNPVs and MIRRs and scaled MNPVs when the reinvestment rate is the defender's IRR. The MIRR, scaled MIRR and MNPV rankings in Table 13.5 are consistent because the MNPV rankings have been scaled to conform to the MIRR, and scaled MIRR.

Table 13.5. Consistent size adjusted MIRR and MNPV rankings obtained by scaling initial investment sizes and periodic cash flows assuming the reinvestment rate equal to the defender's IRR of r = 5%.

initial investment V_0^i and scaling factor γ_i where $i = 1,2,3$	period one cash flows γ_i R_t^i where $t = 1$	period two cash flows γ_i R_2^i + $\gamma_i(1 + r)R_1^i$ where $i = 1,2,3$	Scaled MNPV^i where $i = 1,2,3$ assuming $r = 5\%$ (ranking)	MIRRs and Scaled MIRR^i where $i = 1,2,3$ assuming $r = 5\%$ (ranking)
$\gamma_1 V_0^1 = \$3,000$ ($\gamma_1 = 3$)	0	(3)$400 + (3)(1.05)$800 = \$3,720	$374.15 (1)	11.4% (1)
$\gamma_2 V_0^2 = \$3,000$ ($\gamma_2 = 3/2$)	0	(3/2)$800 + (3/2)(1.05)$1,560 = \$3,657	$317.01 (2)	10.4% (2)
$V_0^3 = \$3,000$	0	$1,200 + (1.05)$2,250 = \$3,562.50	$231.29 (3)	9.0% (3)

While MIRRs are not affected by scaling, even when the reinvestment rate is the defender's IRR, scaling does have an effect on MNPVs. We observe the effect of scaling on MNPVs by rewriting equation (13.4) as:

$$NPV^2 - NPV^1 = [\gamma V_0^1 - V_0^2] + \frac{[S(r, \mathbf{R}^2) - \gamma S(r, \mathbf{R}^1)]}{(1 + r)^n}$$

$$= \frac{[S(r, \mathbf{R}^2) - \gamma S(r, \mathbf{R}^1)]}{(1 + r)^n}$$

(13.16)

Note that the scaling factor does not cancel out in equation (13.19) and may affect the values and rankings of scaled and unscaled MNPVs. To summarize, scaled and unscaled MIRRs are equal in rank and amount. However, scaled and unscaled MNPVs are not necessarily equal in rank or amount.

To illustrate, consider the earlier example reconstructed as an MNPV model. Assume an MNPV model with an initial investment of $100, and cash flows in periods one and two of $50 and $70 respectively and a reinvestment rate $r = 10\%$ and a discount rate of $r = 8\%$

$$MNPV = -\$100 + \frac{(\$50)(1 + 10\%) + \$70}{(1 + 8\%)^2} = \$7.17$$

(13.17a)

Suppose now that we scale the MNPV model by 2. Then, we can rewrite the model as:

$$\text{scaled } MNPV = -(2)\$100 + \frac{(2)[(\$50)(1+10\%)+\$70]}{(1+8\%)^2} = \$14.34$$

(13.17b)

Notice that the scaling factor "2" no longer cancels so we are left with a different MNPV equations before and after scaling. And even if the reinvestment rate is the same as the discount rate, the scaling factor still does not cancel. (How can you demonstrate that the scaling factor does changes the MNPV regardless of the reinvestment rate?) Notice something else that is very important: the scaled MNPV is equal to the unscaled MNPV times the scaling factor which in this case is two: $14.34 = (2) $7.17

> So what does this mean? If the reinvestment rate is the investment's IRR which assumes that cash flows are reinvested in the challenger, then we should rank investments using IRRs. Even if the investments are of unequal size which can be resolved by scaling, IRR rankings will still be consistent with scaled MNPV rankings which can be obtained by multiplying the unscaled MNPVs by their respective scaling factors.

Resolving Initial Size Differences by Addition

Suppose that the defender is scalable but that the challenging investments are unique and cannot be scaled. Since initial investment size equality is one of the conditions required for consistent MIRR and MNPV rankings, we must adopt an alternative to the scaling method to achieve initial size equality. One approach is to add sufficient amounts of the scalable defender to the smaller challenging investment so that its size equals the size of the larger challenger. For example assume that $(V_2 - V_1) = \delta$ is added to V_1 where it earns the defender's IRR equal to r until the nth period. This allows us to rewrite equation (13.4) as:

$$MNPV^2 - MNPV^1 = [V_0^1 + \delta - V_0^2]$$
$$+ \frac{[S(r, \mathbf{R}2) - S(r, \mathbf{R}1) - \delta(1+r)^n]}{(1+r)^n}$$

(13.18a)

Because compounding and discounting δ are offsetting effects, we can rewrite equation (13.18a) as (13.18b):

$$MNPV^2 - MNPV^1 = [V_0^1 - V_0^2]$$
$$+ \frac{S(r, \mathbf{R}^2) - S(r, \mathbf{R}^1)}{(1+r)^n}$$

(13.18b)

But this ranking would have been obtained by comparing the MNPVs before adjusting for size differences by addition. Therefore, equation (13.18b) can be rewritten as:

$$MNPV^2 - MNPV^1 = NPV^2 - NPV^1$$
$$= [V_0^1 - V_0^2] + \frac{S(r, \mathbf{R}^2) - S(r, \mathbf{R}^1)}{(1+r)^n}$$

(13.18c)

These results demonstrate that when the reinvestment rate is the defender's IRR then NPV, MNPV, and added MNPV rankings will all be equal in amount and rank.

We can write the added MIRRs as:

$$\text{added } MIRR^2 - \text{added } MIRR^1$$
$$= \left[\frac{S(r, \mathbf{R}^2)}{V_0^2}\right]^{1/n} - \left[\frac{S(r, \mathbf{R}^1) + \delta(1+r)^n}{(V_0^1 + \delta)}\right]^{1/n}$$

(13.19)

Furthermore, these added MNPV and added MIRR rankings will be consistent because the ranking criterion are the same (see Table 13.6). Note, however, that the consistent rankings obtained through addition are not the same as those obtained when initial size differences were resolved through scaling. Clearly, the final rankings depend on what methods we use to adjust for initial size differences and what reinvestment rate we assume.

Table 13.6. Added MIRRs and added MNPVs assuming the reinvestment rate is the defender's IRR of r = 5%.

initial investment V_0^i and addition amount δ_i where $i = 1,2,3$	period one cash flows R_{ti} where $t = 1$	period two cash flows R_2^i + $\delta_i(1+r)^2$ + $R_1^i(1+r)$ where $i = 1,2,3$	MNPV^i where $i=1,2,3$ assuming $r=5\%$ (ranking)	MIRR^i where $i=1,2,3$ assuming $r=5\%$ (ranking)
$(\delta_1 + V_0^1) = \$3,000$ $(\delta_1 = \$2,000)$	0	\$400 + \$2,000(1.05)2 + \$800(1.05) = \$3,445	\$124.72 (3)	7.2% (3)
$(\delta_2 + V_0^2) = \$3,000$ $(\delta_2 = \$1,000)$	0	\$800 + \$1,000(1.05)2 + \$1,560(1.05) = \$3,540.50	\$211.34 (2)	8.6% (2)
$V_0^3 = \$3,000$	0	\$1,200 + \$2,250(1.05) = \$3,562.50	\$231.29 (1)	9.0% (1)

Four Consistent Investment Ranking Models

We have demonstrated that differences in initial and periodic sizes can cause inconsistent ranking. We resolved differences in periodic sizes by reinvesting cash flow until the last period. However, we noted that the reinvestment rate for each investment could be the challenger's IRR or the defender's IRR.

Then we noted that consistency requires that their initial sizes are equal as well as their periodic sizes. Several methods can be employed to resolve initial size differences. We emphasized two: scaling and addition. Each of these methods will generate consistent initial size adjusted MIRR and MNPV rankings as long as cash flows are reinvested until the last period.

The methods employed to adjust for periodic and initial size differences produce four distinct ranking models that depend on which size adjustment method and reinvestment rate we adopt. We describe the four investment ranking models in Table 13.7 below.

Table: 13.7. Alternative methods for adjusting challenging investments to resolve periodic and initial size differences assuming equal term and risk.

	Assume the reinvestment rate is the defender's IRR equal to r	Assume the reinvestment rate is the challengers' IRR
Resolve initial size differences by scaling the smaller challenger with a factor equal to $\gamma > 1$	model 1	model 2
Resolve initial size differences by adding amount δ to the smaller challenger	model 3	model 4

We now list below the PV models consistent with models 1 through 4. We first write the unadjusted IRR and NPV models as:

$$(13.20) \quad V_0 = \frac{R_1}{(1 + IRR)} + \frac{R_2}{(1 + IRR)^2} + \cdots + \frac{R_n}{(1 + IRR)^n}$$

And

$$(13.21) \quad NPV = -V_0 + \frac{R_1}{(1 + r)} + \frac{R_2}{(1 + r)^2} + \cdots + \frac{R_n}{(1 + r)^n}$$

Model 1. We write the adjusted IRR* and NPV* model 1 as:

(adjusted IRR model 1)

$$(IRR\ 1) \quad \gamma V_0 = \frac{(1 + r)^{n-1}\gamma R_1 + (1 + r)^{n-2}\gamma R_2 + \cdots + \gamma R_n}{(1 + IRR^*)^n}$$

(adjusted NPV model 1)

$$NPV^* = -\gamma V_0 + \frac{(1+r)^{n-1}\gamma R_1 + (1+r)^{n-2}\gamma R_2 + \cdots + \gamma R_n}{(1+r)^n}$$

(NPV 1)
$$= \gamma NPV$$

Model 2. We write the adjusted IRR and NPV as:

(adjusted IRR model 2)

$$\gamma V_0 = \frac{(1+IRR)^{n-1}\gamma R_1 + (1+IRR)^{n-2}\gamma R_2 + \cdots + \gamma R_n}{(1+IRR)^n}$$

(IRR 2)

(adjusted NPV model 2)

$$NPV^* = -\gamma V_0$$
$$+ \frac{(1+IRR)^{n-1}\gamma R_1 + (1+IRR)^{n-2}\gamma R_2 + \cdots + \gamma R_n}{(1+r)^n}$$

(NPV 2)

Model 3. We write the adjusted IRR* and NPV* model 3 as:

(adjusted IRR model 3)

$$V_0 + \delta = \frac{(1+r)^{n-1}R_1 + (1+r)^{n-2}R_2 + \cdots + R_n + \delta(1+r)^n}{(1+IRR^*)^n}$$

(IRR 3)

(adjusted NPV model 3)

$$NPV^* = -(V_0 + \delta)$$
$$+ \frac{(1+r)^{n-1}R_1 + (1+r)^{n-2}R_2 + \cdots + R_n + \delta(1+r)^n}{(1+r)^n}$$

(NPV 3)
$$= NPV$$

Model 4. We write the adjusted IRR* and NPV* model 4 as:

(adjusted IRR model 4)

$$(\text{IRR 4}) \quad V_0 + \delta = \frac{(1+IRR)^{n-1}R_1 + (1+IRR)^{n-2}R_2 + \cdots + R_n + \delta(1+IRR)^n}{(1+IRR)^n}$$

(adjusted NPV model 4)

(NPV 4)

$$NPV^* = -(V_0 + \delta)$$
$$+ \frac{(1+IRR)^{n-1}R_1 + (1+IRR)^{n-2}R_2 + \cdots + R_n + \delta(1+IRR)^n}{(1+r)^n}$$
$$= MNPV$$

Comments on the Four Investment Models and Ranking Consistency

A comment about ranking consistency. Before commenting on models 1 through 4, we note the following. In some cases periodic and initial size-adjusted IRRs and NPVs produce the same rankings as the original IRRs and NPVs. In these cases, it simplifies our efforts to be able to use the original NPV or IRR rankings knowing they will provide the consistent rankings produced by the size adjusted IRR and NPV models.

Comments on model 1. Notice that we can factor out the scaling factor in NPV model 1 producing the original NPV multiplied by the scaling factor—γ NPV. Moreover, ranking investments by γ NPV provides the same ranking as size adjusted IRRs and NPVs. So, if ranking needs to occur under conditions consistent with model 1, our recommendation is to rank challengers using γ NPV.

Comments on model 2. Notice that the scaling factor in IRR model 1 cancels so that we are left with our original IRR model except that periodic cash flow are reinvested until the last period. But, compounding and discounting by the same term are offsetting actions. As a result, the IRR rankings provides the same ranking as the adjusted IRR model. So, if ranking needs to occur under conditions consistent with model 2, our recommendation is rank challengers using their original IRRs.

Comments on model 3. Notice that compounding and discounting by the factor $(1 + r)$ in model 3 are offsetting actions so that the adjustment produces the original NPV model except for the added factor δ that is added at the beginning and subtracted at the end of the period—eliminating it's influence in the model. As a result, the original IRR rankings are the same as the size adjusted IRR and NPV models. So, if ranking needs to occur under conditions consistent with model three, our recommendation is rank challengers using their original IRRs.

Comments on model 4. Notice that compounding and discounting using the challenger's IRR are offsetting actions so that the adjustment produces the original IRR model except for the added factor δ. However, δ is added at the beginning and subtracted at the end of the period eliminating it from the model. As a result, the IRR rankings are the same rankings provided by the size adjusted IRR and NPV models. So, if ranking needs to occur under conditions consistent with model four, our recommendation is rank challengers using their original IRRs.

Other size adjustment models. For completeness, it is important to note that there are a number of other size adjustment methods we could employ. For example, we could combine challengers 1 and 2 in Table 13.1 to achieve initial size consistency with challenger 3. Or we could use some combination of scaling and addition to adjust for initial size differences. And the alternative reinvestment rates we could employ to resolve periodic size differences is large indeed. The only consideration when employing these nonstandard size adjustments is that the recommendations included in comments for models one through four no longer apply, requiring decision makers to find size adjusted NPVs or IRRs.

When to Rank Challengers Using Four Models

Adjusting initial investment sizes: scaling versus addition. The appropriate initial size adjustment method depends on the characteristics of the challengers in which investments are made. To compare challengers of different initial sizes, scaling to achieve initial size differences is appropriate when the challengers are available in continuous sizes or approximately so. We describe such investments as producing constant returns to scale. For constant returns to scale, the relationship between the investment and the cash flow it produces is constant. To illustrate, hours of services may often be purchased in divisible units, each unit producing the same output as earlier ones. In sum, models 1 and 2 apply when the investments are models available in continuous sizes.

On the other hand, some investments are available only in a few sizes. Machinery is available in a limited number of sizes. Sometimes, land may be purchased in fixed quantities depending on physical configurations. The same is true for buildings. So how do we compare investments available in a few sizes?

Suppose we are comparing two investments of different sizes. Assume we find the difference in their initial cost and ask: if the smaller challenger is adopted, where is the difference in their initial cost employed and what does it earn? The answer is it remains invested in the defender and these must be included with the earnings of the smaller challenger. In this way we achieve initial size consistency while allowing the underlying investments to be different in their initial sizes.

Adjusting periodic size differences: reinvestment rate assumptions. We resolved periodic size differences by setting cash flow in all of the periods to zero except cash flow in the last period. We set all of the cash flow in all but the last period equal to zero by reinvesting them. The implicit reinvestment rate for NPV and IRR models is the defender's or the challengers' IRRs.

Ranking Investments when the Challengers are not Mutually Exclusive

So far we have treated our challengers as mutually exclusive investments—only one can be chosen. For firms with a fixed investment budget, treating investments as mutually exclusive may be justified. Suppose that we face a set of challenging investments that are not mutually exclusive and their adoption depends on their passing some IRR hurdle. How should the investment problem be analyzed? In other words, suppose that we have a portfolio of different investment challengers and of different sizes. How big or how many challengers should be adopted ?

Economic theory can help us answer this question. Usually we array our challengers according to their IRRs and invest in the most profitable ones first. Of course, the size of the defender must match the size of the challenger, but the criterion for arranging defenders to match the size of our challenger is somewhat different. We give up, sacrifice, the defender with the smallest IRR first. To assume that defenders are infinitely scalable is to believe that the firm is in a perfect market, an assumption we earlier rejected.

Of course, investments may not come in infinitely small amounts; one large investment may be more profitable than a small investment because it is larger. If challengers come in lumpy amounts, that is the size of the challenger we investigate.

So, we are back to the place we started. Begin with the highest rate of return challenger, and sacrifice the lowest rate of return defender. Then analyze the next highest rate of return challenger and sacrifice the next lowest rate of return defender, all the time maintaining size equality. Keep analyzing challengers and defenders sequentially, maintaining size homogeneity, until you fail to adopt the next highest rate of return challenger compared to the next lowest rate of return defender.

This rule is comparable to the marginal cost equals marginal return rule employed in comparative economic static analysis.

The logic behind this arrangement is that we begin by considering the most favorable challenger, and compare it with the least favorable defender. Then we continue to the next most favorable challenger and second least favorable defender. Once we have found a challenger unable to earn a higher IRR than the IRR of the defender being sacrificed, we end our investment analysis.

Common Practice, Common Problems, and Reinvestment Rates

Common practice is to rank challengers using IRR or NPV methods. We have emphasized that this common practice can frequently produce a common problem of inconsistent rankings. Then we made the point that when challengers were adjusted for initial and periodic size differences and employed a common reinvestment rate—either the defender or the challengers' IRRs—then the ranking were consistent. The question is, can consistent IRR and NPV rankings be achieved under fewer restrictions? For example, could we relax the common reinvestment rate assumption and still find consistent rankings—all the time? The answer is no!

Since we require only one counter-example to disprove the general claim, we provided one in Table 13.2. Consider three challengers of equal initial size and different periodic cash flow. Since reinvesting the cash flow to achieve periodic size equality at the defender's IRR doesn't change NPV rankings and reinvesting at the challenger's IRR doesn't change IRR rankings, we can rank the three challengers using NPV and IRR under initial and periodic size equality. We reported the results of such a comparison earlier in Table 13.2.

Note the conflicting NPV and IRR rankings. NPV ranks the three challengers 1, 2, and 3. IRR ranks the three challengers 3, 1, and 2. These results provide the one counter example needed to disprove the claim that different reinvestment rates are not required for consistent rankings. Furthermore, since we are describing the reinvestment rate for the same investment and are only changing the ranking method, consistency would require the same reinvestment rate assumption regardless of the ranking method employed.

Summary and Conclusions

This chapter has demonstrated that equal initial investments and periodic cash flows reinvested until the last period plus a common reinvestment rate across IRR and NPV models are sufficient conditions for consistent MIRR and MNPV investment rankings. We can make unequal initial investments equal by scaling or adding investments to the small challengers—and by some other methods, if required. Whether or not initial size differences are resolved by scaling or by addition depends on whether the challenger is available in continuous sizes in which case scaling is appropriate. Otherwise, if it is unique and cannot be scaled, size differences are resolved by additions. All other methods for resolving initial size differences ultimately create additional challengers.

Resolving periodic size differences required that we reinvest cash flow until the final period. We considered the defender's IRR and the challengers' IRRs as possible reinvestment rates. Of course, there are a number of other possible reinvestment rate choices. The important point is that if the discount rate and the reinvestment rate are different, then the NPV rankings will be stable and will not vary with the discount rate.

So what have we learned? As long as the homogeneity of size principle is observed, whatever common reinvestment rate is assumed or whatever initial size adjustment method is employed will generate consistent rankings. These possibilities we described as four basic models. In addition, while all size adjusted PV models will produce consistent rankings, the ranking may vary with the methods adopted. The main implication of these results is to shift the debate from which ranking method to use, IRR versus NPV, to what is the appropriate size adjustment model to adopt?

Questions

1. Discuss why some investment analysts prefer NPV methods to rank investments while others prefer IRR methods. Which do you prefer? Defend your answer.
2. Provide three reasons why NPV and IRR rankings may be inconsistent.
3. Refer to the investment problems described in Table Q13.1 below. Notice that initial investment sizes are unequal as are the periodic cash flows in period one which produce the inconsistent NPV and IRR ranking reported in the last two columns and rows of Table Q13.1. We will refer to the results in Table Q13.1 in several questions that follow.

Table Q13.1. NPVs and IRRs for two mutually exclusive investments assuming a discount rate equal to the defender's IRR of r = 5%.

initial investments V_0^i where $i = 1,2$	period one cash flows R_t^i where $t = 1$ generated by initial investments V_0^i where $i = 1,2$	period two cash flows R_t^i where $t = 2$ generated by initial investments V_0^i where $i = 1,2$	NPV^i earned by initial investments V_0^i where $i = 1,2$ assuming $r = 5\%$ (ranking)	IRR^i earned by initial investments V_0^i where $i = 1,2$ (ranking)
$V_0^1 = \$3,000$	$2,000	$1,500	$265.31 (1)	11.51% (2)
$V_0^2 = \$1,000$	$800	$400	$124.72 (2)	14.83% (1)

    a. Complete Table Q13.2 by finding MNPVs and MIRRs for the two investments assuming a discount rate and reinvestment rate equal to the defender's IRR, of $r=5\%$. Include the investment rankings in the parentheses.

Table Q13.2. MNPVs and MIRRs for two mutually exclusive investments assuming a discount and reinvestment rate of $r = 5\%$.

initial investments V_0^i where $i = 1,2$	period one cash flows R_t^i where $t = 1$ generated by initial investments V_0^i where $i = 1,2$	period two cash flows R_t^i where $t = 2$ generated by initial investments V_0^i where $i = 1,2$	$MNPV^i$ earned by initial investments V_0^i where $i = 1,2$ assuming $r = 5\%$ (ranking)	$MIRR^i$ earned by initial investments V_0^i where $i = 1,2$ assuming $r = 5\%$ (ranking)
$V_0^1 = \$3,000$		$\$1,500 + \$2,000(1.05)$ $= \$3,600$	\$ ( )	% ( )
$V_0^2 = \$1,000$		$\$400 + \$800(1.05) =$ $\$1,240$	\$ ( )	% ( )

b. Complete Table Q13.3 by finding MNPVs and MIRRs for the two investments assuming a discount rate and reinvestment rate equal to the defender's IRR, of $r = 5\%$ and a reinvestment rates equal to the investments' IRRs. Include the investment rankings in the parentheses.

Table Q13.3. MNPVs and MIRRs for two mutually exclusive investments assuming a discount and reinvestment rate of $r = 5\%$. and reinvestment rates equal to the investments' IRRs

initial investments V_0^i where $i = 1,2$	period one cash flows R_t^i where $t = 1$ generated by initial investments V_0^i where $i = 1,2$	period two cash flows R_t^i where $t = 2$ generated by initial investments V_0^i where $i = 1,2$	$MNPV^i$ earned by initial investments V_0^i where $i = 1,2$ assuming the discount and reinvestment rate equal $r = 5\%$ (ranking)	$MIRR^i$ earned by initial investments V_0^i where $i = 1,2$ assuming the reinvestment rate equals $r = 5\%$ (ranking)
$V_0^1 = 3,000$		$\$1,500 +$ $\$2,000(1.1151) =$ $\$3,730.20$	\$ ( )	% ( )
$V_0^2 = \$1,000$		$\$400 + \$800(1.1483)$ $= \$1,318.64$	\$ ( )	% ( )

c. Complete Table Q13.4 by finding scaled MNPVs and scaled MIRRs for the two investments assuming a discount rate and reinvestment rate equal to the defender's IRR, of $r=5\%$. What is the scaling factor you are using? Include the investment rankings in the parentheses.

Table Q13.4. Scaled MNPVs and MIRRs for two mutually exclusive investments assuming a discount and reinvestment rate of $r = 5\%$.

initial investment $\gamma_i V_0^i$ where $i = 1,2$	period one cash flows $\gamma_i R_t^i$ where $t = 1$ generated by initial investments $\gamma_i V_0^i$ where $i = 1,2$	period two cash flows $\gamma_i R_t^i$ where $t = 2$ generated by initial investments $\gamma_i V_0^i$ where $i = 1,2$	Scaled $MNPV^i$ earned by scaled initial investments $\gamma_i V_0^i$ where $i = 1,2$ assuming the discount and reinvestment rate equal $r = 5\%$ (ranking)	Scaled MIRRs earned by scaled initial investments $\gamma_i V_0^i$ where $i = 1,2$ assuming the discount and reinvestment rate equal $r = 5\%$ (ranking)
$V_0^1 = 3,000$		$\$1,500 +$ $[\$2,000(1.05)]$ $= \$3,600$	\$ ( )	% ( )
$\gamma_2 V_0^2 =$ $\$3,000$ $\gamma_2 = 3$		$[(3)\$400] +$ $[(3)\$800(1.05)]$ $= \$3,720$	\$ ( )	% ( )

d. Complete Table Q13.5 by finding scaled MNPVs and scaled MIRRs for the two investments assuming a discount rate equal to the defender's IRR, of $r = 5\%$ and reinvestment rates equal to the investments' IRRs. Include the investment rankings in the parentheses.

Table Q13.5. Scaled MNPVs and MIRRs for two mutually exclusive investments assuming a discount rate of $r = 5\%$ and reinvestment rates equal to the investments' IRRs

initial investment $\gamma_i V_0^i$ where i = 1,2	period one cash flows $\gamma_i R_t^i$ where $t = 1$ generated by initial investments $\gamma_i V_0^i$ where $i = 1,2$	period two cash flows $\gamma_i R_t^i$ where $t = 2$ generated by initial investments $\gamma_i V_0^i$ where $i = 1,2$	Scaled MNPV^i earned by scaled initial investments $\gamma_i V_0^i$ where $i = 1,2$ assuming the discount rate $r = 5\%$ and reinvestment rates equal to the investments' IRRs (rankings)	Scaled MIRRs earned by scaled initial investments $\gamma_i V_0^i$ where $i = 1,2$ assuming the reinvestment rate equals $r = 5\%$ (ranking)
$V_0^1 =$ $3,000	$1,500 + [$2,000(1.1151)] = $3,730.20		$ ( )	% ( )
$\gamma_2 V_0^2 =$ $3,000 where $\gamma_2 =$ 3	[(3)$400] + [(3)$800(1.1483)] = $3,955.92		$ ( )	% ( )

e. Complete Table Q13.6 by finding added MNPVs and MIRRs for the two investments assuming a discount and reinvestment rate equal to the defender's IRR, of $r = 5\%$. What is the additional investment amount γ_i added to the smaller investment? Include the investment rankings in the parentheses.

Table Q13.6. Added MNPVs and MIRRs for two mutually exclusive investments assuming a discount rate of $r = 5\%$ and reinvestment rates equal to the defender's IRR of $r = 5\%$.

Initial plus added investments $(V_0^i + \delta_i)$ where i = 1,2	period one cash flows R_t^i where $t = 1$ generated by initial plus added investments $(V_0^i + \delta_i)$ where $i=1,2$	period two cash flows $R_t^i + \delta_i(1 + r)^2$ where $t=2$ generated by initial plus added investment $(V_0^i + \delta_i)$ where $i = 1,2$	Added MNPV^i earned by initial plus added investments $(V_0^i + \delta_i)$ where $i = 1,2$ assuming the discount rate and reinvestment rate $r = 5\%$ (rankings)	Added MIRR^i where $i = 1,2$ earned by initial plus added investments $(V_0^i + \delta_i)$ where $i = 1,2$ assuming the reinvestment rate $r = 5\%$ (rankings)
$V_0^1 =$ $3,000		$1,500 + $2,000(1.05) = $3,600	$ ( )	% ( )
$(V_0^2 + \delta_2) =$ $3,000 where $\delta_2 =$ $2,000		$400 + $800(1.05) + $2,000(1.05)^2 = $3,445	$ ( )	% ( )

f. Complete Table Q13.7 by finding added MNPVs and MIRRs for the two investments assuming a discount rate equal to the defender's IRR, of $r = 5\%$ and reinvestment rates equal to the investments' IRRs. Include the investment rankings in the parentheses.

Table Q13.7. Added MNPVs and MIRRs for two mutually exclusive investments assuming a discount rate of $r = 5\%$ and reinvestment rates equal to the investments' IRRs

Initial plus added investments $(V_0^i + \delta_i)$ where $i = 1,2$	period one cash flows R_t^i where $t = 1$ generated by initial plus added investments $(V_0^i + \delta_i)$ where $i=1,2$	period two cash flows R_t^i where $t=2$ generated by initial plus added investment $(V_0^i + \delta_i)$ where $i = 1,2$	Added MNPV^i earned by initial plus added investments $(V_0^i + \delta_i)$ where $i = 1,2$ assuming the discount rate $r = 5\%$ and reinvestment rates equal to the investments' IRRs (rankings)	Added MIRR^i earned by initial plus added investments $(V_0^i + \delta_i)$ where $i = 1,2$ assuming the reinvestment rate $r = 5\%$ (rankings)
$V_0^1 =$ $3,000		$1,500 + [$2,000(1.1151)] = $3,730.20	$ ( )	% ( )
$(V_0^2 + \delta_2) =$ $3,000 where $\delta_2 =$ $2,000		$400 + [$800(1.1483)] + $2,000(1.1483)2 = $3,955.83	$ ( )	% ( )

4. To answer the questions that follow, first complete Table Q13.8 using data from the completed Tables in question 3. Cells indicated with an "n.a." do not require an answer.

Table Q13.8. Summary of rankings described in Tables Q13.1 through Q13.7

Table provide the data	Type of ranking	Assuming reinvestment rate is defender's IRR		Assuming reinvestment rate is investments IRR	
		Investment 1	**Investment 2**	**Investment 1**	**Investment 2**
Q13.1	NPV			n.a.	n.a.
	IRR	n.a.	n.a.		
Q13.2	MNPV			n.a.	n.a.
	MIRR			n.a.	n.a.
Q13.3	MNPV	n.a.	n.a.		
	MIRR	n.a.	n.a.		
Q13.4	Scaled MNPV			n.a.	n.a.
	Scaled MIRR			n.a.	n.a.
Q13.5	Scaled MNPV	n.a.	n.a.		
	Scaled MIRR	n.a.	n.a.		
Q13.6	Added MNPV			n.a.	n.a.
	Added MIRR			n.a.	n.a.
Q13.7	Added MNPV	n.a.	n.a.		
	Added MIRR	n.a.	n.a.		

a. Referring to your completed Table Q13.8, which ranking methods produce consistent results? Please explain your answer.

b. Referring to your completed Table Q13.8, which consistent ranking method(s) are consistent with NPV rankings? Please explain your answer.

c. Referring to your completed Table Q13.8, which consistent ranking method(s) are consistent with scaled NPVs? Please explain your answers.

d. Referring to your completed Table Q13.8, which consistent ranking method(s) are consistent with IRRs? Please explain your answers.

5. Explain why investments of unequal term can be examined using the ranking methods described in this chapter.

14. "Aligning Timelines: Evaluating Investments with Homogeneous Terms"

LINDON ROBISON

Learning goals. Assuming reinvestment rate is investments IRR After completing this chapter, you should be able to: (1) consistently rank one-time investments using internal rate of return (IRR) or net present value (NPV) methods; (2) find time adjusted cash flow averages called annuity equivalents (AE); (3) use AE to find methods for ranking repeatable investments with (4) use capitalising IRR rates to find NPV present value of long-lived investments and repeatable investments.

- Learn how to represent the time adjusted average of an investment's cash flow using AE.

Learning objectives. To achieve your learning goals, you should complete the following objectives:

- Learn how IRR and NPV methods may provide conflicting optimal replacement ages for repeatable investments.
- Learn how to use an investment's cash flow patterns and its AE to determine the optimal life of a repeatable investment.
- Learn how to find the present value of future earnings from repeatable investments using the capitalization formula.

Introduction

The word term refers to the length of time an object is expected to last. An investment refers to a commitment of resources from which investors expect to earn a return. The term of an investment refers to the length of time investor commit resources to a project. In this chapter we explore the connections between investments and their terms. We begin by considering different kinds of investments.

One-time investments. In the previous chapter, we developed methods for ranking one-time mutually exclusive investments with unequal initial and periodic sizes. In that effort, we employed a simplifying assumption: that the terms of the competing challengers and the defender were equal. This assumption allowed us to rank investments consistently using IRR and NPV methods. This assumption is frequently violated. Not all challengers and defenders have equal terms. Therefore, we develop methods for ranking one-time mutually exclusive challengers of unequal terms which is the first goal of this chapter. An important characteristic of one-time investments is that owning a one-time investment does not require replacement in order to invest in a similar investment.

Repeatable investments. Some investments provide essential services. As a result, when they wear out, they need to be replaced (think of a light bulb). What replaces the existing investment may be an identical, improved, or remodeled version of the original investment. We call these investments that require replacement, repeatable investments because they are owned in sequence rather than simultaneously. Examples of repeatable investments include orchards, breeding livestock, roofs on houses, and equipment. Since repeatable investments are owned in sequence, we must determine what is the optimal time to replace a repeatable investment.

Finding the optimal life of a repeatable investment requires that we review the concept of a time-adjusted average cash flow, an AE. AE, of course, change as new periods of cash flow are included in its calculation. Using AE for different time periods and patterns of cash flow, we can determine the optimal life of the investment.

Long-lived investments. While the term of an investment refers to the length of time investors are committed to the project, the economic life of an investment refers to the length of time an investment has the potential to generate economic services. As a result, the economic life of an investment can exceed the term of an investment and in fact does when it is sold to a subsequent owner. Sometimes we account for the difference between the economic life and term of an investment by including salvage value when finding the NPV or IRR of an investment for a particular owner. In this chapter we explicitly account for salvage value by finding the present value of an investment's cash flow over its economic life. This approach requires that we discuss the concept of capitalization and capitalized values.

In what follows we first discuss how to value long-lived assets and capitalization of an investment's earning. We begin with discussing how to value long-lived assets because in that discussion we review capitalization and AEs, concepts important for finding optimal terms and ranking repeatable investments later on.

Present Values and Capitalization Rates

The economic life and term of an investment. The term of an investment is the number of periods the financial manager expects to manage an investment. The economic life of an investment is the number of periods the investment is expected to generate cash flow. The PV of an investment for an individual depends on its cash flow during the term of the investment plus its liquidation value. The liquidation value of the investment depends on its economic life. Therefore, to estimate the present value for an investment, we must find the discounted present value of all future cash flows. In practice, we often estimate the present value of an investment using the capitalization formula.

The capitalization formula and capitalization rate. Consider a challenging investment that earns R constant cash flow dollars for n period and is liquidated at the end of the nth period for V_n. We assume that the defender funding the investment has an IRR of r. We write the maximum bid (minimum sell) price PV model that equates V_0 to its discounted future earnings over a term of n periods discounted by its defender's IRR as:

$$V_0 = \frac{R}{(1+r)} + \cdots + \frac{R+V_n}{(1+r)^n}$$
(14.1)

Now assume that the second owner of the investment has the same earnings expectations as the first owner of the durable so that we can write:

$$V_n = \frac{R}{(1+r)} + \cdots + \frac{R+V_{2n}}{(1+r)^{2n}}$$
(14.2)

Finally, substituting for V_n in equation (14.1) the right hand side of equation (14.2) we obtain:

$$V_0 = \frac{R}{(1+r)} + \cdots + \frac{R+V_{2n}}{(1+r)^{2n}}$$
(14.3)

And if the investment's salvage value were continually exchanged with its expected cash flows we could write:

$$V_0 = \frac{R}{(1+r)} + \frac{R}{(1+r)^2} + \cdots$$
(14.4)

Clearly, the farther away from the present is the constant cash flow R, the less it contributes to the present value of the investment. To demonstrate the diminishing contributions of future cash flow, note how the value of discount rate that multiplies R decreases with n. To illustrate we let $r = 10\%$, R=100, and alternative values of n.

$$\frac{\$100}{(1.1)^{20}} = \$14.86$$

$$\frac{\$100}{1.1)^{40}} = \$2.21$$

$$\frac{\$100}{(1.1)^{60}} = \$0.33$$

$$\frac{\$100}{(1.1)^{80}} = \$0.05$$

And

$$\frac{\$100}{(1.1)^{100}} = \$0.01$$

So what is the sum of an infinite stream of constant payments R discounted by r percent? To find that sum, multiply both sides of equation (14.1) by $(1 + r)$ and subtract from the result the original equation:

$$V_0(1+r) - V_0 = R - \frac{R}{(1+r)} + \frac{R}{(1+r)} - \frac{R}{(1+r)^2} + \frac{R}{(1+r)^2}$$

$$- \cdots - \frac{R}{(1+r)^{mn}} + \frac{V_{mn}(1+r) + V_{mn}}{(1+r)^{mn}}$$

(14.5)

After subtracting and simplifying and letting m get very large, we find the sum of the infinite series to equal:

$$V_0 = \lim_{m \to \infty} \frac{R}{r}\left[1 - \frac{1}{(1+r)^{mn}}\right] + \frac{V_{mn}}{(1+r)^{mn}} = \frac{R}{r}$$

(14.6)

The far right-hand side of equation (14.6) we refer to as the capitalization formula where the investment's constant earnings R is divided by the defender's IRR equal to r, the capitalization rate. The capitalization formula allows us to relate the present value of all future cash flow to the value of the investment.

$$V_0 = \frac{R}{r}$$

(14.7)

To illustrate the capitalization formula, suppose that you purchase an annuity for $100 that pays you and your heirs $5 a year forever. The capitalization formula for this investment is equal to:

$$V_0 = \frac{R}{r} = \frac{\$5}{r}$$

(14.8)

If we knew the investment's initial value and its infinite stream of earnings, we could always estimate the capitalization rate as:

$$r = \frac{R}{V_0} = \frac{\$5}{\$100} = 5\%$$

(14.9)

Comments about the capitalization formula and capitalization rate. In textbooks and references to the capitalization rate, it is often expressed as:

$$r = \frac{\text{annual cash income}}{\text{purchase price}}$$

(14.10)

Then when practitioners implement the capitalization formula, equation (14.9), they estimate R as the first period's net cash flow and an industry capitalization rate for r. For example, if the industry standard were 5%, we would write the capitalization formula that estimates the maximum bid price for the investment as:

$$\text{(14.11)} \quad V_0 = \frac{R}{r} = \frac{\$5}{.05} = \$100$$

PV models and capitalization formulas. The capitalization formula is a PV model. The unknown variable in the capitalization formula identifies the kind of PV model represented. If the unknown variable is the discount rate or the capitalization rate r, the capitalization formula is an IRR model. Most often, capitalization formulas solve for V_0 making them maximum bid (minimum sell) type models.

> So what have we learned? We learned that we can best understand the capitalization formula and the capitalization rate in the context of a PV model. Despite its various descriptions in applied publications, the capitalization formula is the constant income or AI of the investment earned over its economic life divided by defender's IRR.

Present Value (PV) Models and Averages

In the previous section, we described how the capitalization formula depended on a constant R. However, this is an unrealistic assumption since an investment's cash flow is hardly ever (never) equal to a constant. So instead, we assume that R is a time adjusted cash flow measure, an AE that we describe next.

Arithmetic means, expected values, geometric means and AEs. There are several measures of central tendency in a numeric series that include arithmetic means, expected values, and geometric means. An example of an arithmetic mean or average follows. Consider three numbers 3, 5, and 7. The average of these numbers can be calculated by dividing their sum by 3 since there are three numbers: $(3 + 5 + 7) /$ 3 = 5. This is the average of this series. Now suppose we wanted to find the mean of the three numbers weighted by their probability of occurring. If the probability of 3 occurring were 25%, if the probability of 5 occurring were 25%, and the probability of 7 occurring were 50%, then the expected value of the series would be: [(.25)3] + [(.25)5] + [(.5)7] = 5.50. This is the weighted average or expected value of the series.

Next consider an example of a geometric mean. Consider three rates of return: 105%, 110% and 115%. The geometric mean is that number which, when multiplied together three times, equals the product of 105%, 110%, and 115%: $[(1.05)(1.10)(1.15)] = (1.0991)^3$. Alternatively, the geometric mean is

$[(1.05)(1.10)(1.15)]^{1/n} = 1.33^{1/n} = 1.0992$ where $n = 3$ because there are three numbers in the series. Note that the geometric mean is not equal to the arithmetic mean: $[(1.10 + 1.11 + 1.12)] / 3 = 1.11$. It is also not necessarily equal to the expected value.

To illustrate AE, the constant R in equation (14.9) is an AE whose present value sum equals the present value of the sum of discounted cash flow R_1, R_2, $\cdots$, R_n.

(14.12)

$$\frac{R_1}{(1+r)} + \frac{R_2}{(1+r)^2} + \cdots + \frac{R_n}{(1+r)^n} = \frac{R}{(1+r)} + \frac{R}{(1+r)^2} + \cdots + \frac{R}{(1+r)^n}$$

For example, consider the AE in the following problem:

$$\frac{15}{(1.1)} + \frac{20}{(1.1)^2} = \frac{17.38}{(1.1)} + \frac{17.38}{(1.1)^2}$$
(14.13)

On the left hand side of equation (14.12) is a stream of unequal periodic cash flow. On the right hand side of equation (14.12) is a stream of equal periodic cash flow each of which is an AE. The important fact, however, is that the discounted AE on the right-hand side of equation (14.12) equals the discounted periodic cash flow on the left-hand side of equation (14.12). The AE for the series on the right-hand side of equation (14.12) is 17.38. We demonstrate how to find an AE using Excel as follows.

Calculating AE from an irregular stream of cash flow is a two-step procedure. The first step is to find the net present value (NPV) of the irregular cash flow stream. We illustrate this step using Excel's NPV function. In our example, the NPV of $15 received at the end of period one and $20 received at the end of period two is $30.17.

Table 14.1a. How to Find an AE for an Irregular Stream of Cash Flow
Open Table 14.1a. in Microsoft Excel

B5		f_x	=NPV(B1,B2:B3)
	A	B	C
1	rate	0.1	
2	R1	15	
3	R2	20	
4	nper	2	
5	NPV	$30.17	=NPV(rate,R1:R2)

The next step is to find the AE, a constant payment, for the NPV equal to $30.17. Using Excel's PMT function we find the AE for an NPV of $30.17 equal to $17.38. We display the Excel solution below.

Table 14.1b. How to Find an AE for an Irregular Stream of Cash Flow

Open Table 14.1b. in Microsoft Excel

	B6		f_x	=PMT(B1,B4,B5,,0)
	A	B		C
1	rate	0.1		
2	R1	15		
3	R2	20		
4	nper	2		
5	NPV	$30.17	=NPV(rate,R1:R2)	
6	AE	($17.38)	=PMT(rate,nper,NPV,,0)	

So, what have we learned about AE? An AE is a constant cash flow stream whose discounted value is to equal the present value of another stream of unequal cash flow. Each value in the stream of equal cash flow is an AE. If one calculated the arithmetic mean of the AE in the steam of cash flow, the arithmetic average would also equal the value of any other AE in the series. If the discount rate were an interest rate and V0 were an amount borrowed, then AE would be the constant loan payment whose present value would equal the original loan amount.

Some observations on NPV and AE rankings. Consider an NPV model and its value expressed as the present value of a series of AE in equation (14.14). Since the present value of the AE is equal to the NPV of the investment, then the two sums must provide equal NPV rank. Important to note, however, is that it is the present value of the series of AE payments that is equal to the NPV, while a number of unequal payments could equal the same NPV. Therefore, there is a direct relationship (i.e. they both go up or down together) between NPVs and AEs. Furthermore,

$$
\begin{aligned}
NPV &= -V_0 + \frac{R_1}{(1+r)} + \frac{R_2}{(1+r)^2} + \cdots + \frac{R_n}{(1+r)^n} \\
&= \frac{R}{(1+r)} + \frac{R}{(1+r)^2} + \cdots + \frac{R}{(1+r)^n}
\end{aligned}
$$

(14.14)

any change in NPV must be matched by a corresponding change in the AE and in the same direction. For any two investments of equal size and term, and where investment one has a larger NPV than investment two, then investment two must increase its AE in order for it to equal the higher NPV amount. We illustrate this point in more detail.

Consider again the expression:

$$NPV = \frac{R}{(1+r)} + \frac{R}{(1+r)^2} + \cdots + \frac{R}{(1+r)^n}$$

(14.15)

Then, suppose the term of the model in equation (14.15) is increased by one period. Then the equality in equation (14.15) no longer holds:

$$NPV < \frac{R}{(1+r)} + \frac{R}{(1+r)^2} + \cdots + \frac{R}{(1+r)^n} + \frac{R}{(1+r)^{n+1}}$$

(14.16)

To preserve the equality in equation (14.15), the AE equal to R must be decreased by some amount δ to reestablish the equality allowing us to rewrite the earlier equality:

$$\begin{aligned} NPV &= \frac{R}{(1+r)} + \frac{R}{(1+r)^2} + \cdots + \frac{R}{(1+r)^n} \\ &= \frac{R-\delta}{(1+r)} + \frac{R-\delta}{(1+r)^2} + \cdots + \frac{R-\delta}{(1+r)^{n+1}} \end{aligned}$$

(14.17)

So, what have we learned? We learned that NPVs and the present value of their AE provide equal rankings. Furthermore, any sum or vector of cash flow can be converted to its present value equivalent annuity. To maintain the equality between a present value and a stream of annuities requires the following. If the present value sum is increased, then either the term or the amount of the annuity must increase.

More Complicated Capitalization Formulas

In the discussion to this point, we implemented the capitalization formula by assuming that the future cash flow were constants, AEs. This of course, is rarely the case. We now ask: how can we find the capitalization formula if future cash flow are expected to increase (decrease) at $g\%$ over time as you might expect on rental property? To answer this question we return to our PV model.

Suppose that we wanted to find the capitalization formula for an investment whose cash flow are expected to increase (decrease) at an average rate of g percent ($g < 0$ percent). Then the capitalization formula that accounts for R is increasing (decreasing) at rate g ($g < 0$) as:

$$(14.18) \quad V_0 = \frac{R(1+g)}{(1+r)} + \frac{R(1+g)^2}{(1+r)^2} + \cdots = \frac{R(1+g)}{(r-g)}$$

Now the capitalization rate, the defender's IRR is equal to: $(r - g)/(1 + g)$. We write the capitalization rates depending on alternative values of g and $r = 10$ in Table 14.2

Table 14.2a. Alternative percentage capitalization rates $(r - g)/(1 + g)$ depending on alternative values of $g > 0$ and r

	$g = 0\%$	$g = 1\%$	$g = 2\%$	$g = 3\%$	$g = 4\%$	$g = 5\%$
$r = 10\%$	0.1	0.089	0.078	0.068	.058	0.048
$r = 9\%$	0.09	0.079	0.069	0.058	0.048	0.038
$r = 8\%$	0.08	0.069	0.059	0.049	0.038	0.029
$r = 7\%$	0.07	0.059	0.049	0.039	0.029	0.019
$r = 6\%$	0.06	0.050	0.039	0.029	0.019	0.01

Table 14.2b. Alternative percentage capitalization rates $(r - g)/(1 + g)$ depending on alternative values of $g < 0$ and r

	$g = 0\%$	$g = -1\%$	$g = -2\%$	$g = -3\%$	$g = -4\%$	$g = -5\%$
$r = 10\%$	0.10	0.111	0.122	0.134	0.146	0.158
$r = 9\%$	0.09	0.101	0.112	0.124	0.135	0.147
$r = 8\%$	0.08	0.091	0.102	0.113	0.125	0.137
$r = 7\%$	0.07	0.081	0.092	0.103	0.115	0.126
$r = 6\%$	0.06	0.071	0.082	0.093	0.104	0.116

So, what have we learned? We have learned that expected increases in cash flow decrease capitalization rates and increase the value of capitalized income. For example if R = $100, r = 10% and g = 0% so that the capitalization rate is 10%, then V_0 = $1000. If R = $100, r = 10%, and g = 5% then the capitalization rate is 4.8%, and V_0 = $2,083.33. We have also learned that expected decreases in cash flow increase capitalization rates and decrease the value of capitalized income. For example, if R = $100, r = 10%, and g = –5% then capitalization rate is 15.8%, then V_0 = $632.91.

Ranking One-time Investments with Unequal Terms using NPV Models

Notation. Before proceeding to the first focus of this chapter, ranking one-time investments, we confirm the notation used earlier and which will be used again in this chapter. The mathematical notation will describe two challenging investments and a defender. We assume that the initial investment sizes are equal to V_0. The defender's IRR for the two investments is r. The term of investments one and two are n_1 and n_2 respectively. Periodic cash flows for investments $i = 1, 2$ in period $t = 1, ..., n_i$ can be expressed as R_t^i. And the vector of cash flows is represented as: $\mathbf{R}^i = R_1^i, R_2^i, \cdots, R_{n_i}^i$ for $i = 1, 2$.

Finally, we define the sum S of compounded periodic cash flows at rate r as: $S(r, \mathbf{R}^i, n_{in}) = (1 + r)^{(n_i - 1)} R_1^i + (1 + r)^{(n_i - 2)} R_2^i + \cdots + R_{n_i}^i$. We also define the sum of periodic cash flows compounded at the investment's IRR as: $S(IRR^i, \mathbf{R}^i, n_i) = (1 + IRR^i)^{(n_i - 1)} R_1^i + (1 + IRR^i)^{(n_i - 2)} R_2^i + \cdots + R_{n_i}^i$. Note that the value of the function S depends on three variables defined in the equation: the reinvestment rate r or IRR^i, the vector of periodic cash flows $\mathbf{R}^i$, and the term of the investment n_i.

Sufficient conditions for consistently ranking mutually exclusive one-time investments using IRRs and NPVs. We discovered in Chapter 13 that there are two sufficient conditions for consistently ranking investments using NPVs and IRRs—assuming their terms were equal. These two sufficient conditions are equal initial investment sizes and equal periodic cash flows except in their common last period.

In this chapter we will assume that initial sizes of investments are equal. However, we will allow for differences in periodic cash flows because investment terms differ. As a result, we can no longer be sure that the NPVs and IRRs rank investments the same. To solve the problem of unequal periodic cash flows, we need to rationalize investment term differences. Our focus in the first part of this chapter is on how to create equal terms and periodic cash flows except for the last period for mutually exclusive challengers.

Compounding and discounting by the same rate are offsetting operations. Essential to rationalizing term differences is the obvious fact that NPVs for investment one and two compounded and discounted at rate r have the same value as their original NPV function. We demonstrate this point using the following equations. For investment one, the result is:

$$NPV^1 = -V_0 + \frac{R_1^1}{(1+r)} + \cdots + \frac{R_{n_1}^1}{(1+r)^{n_1}}$$

$$= -V_0 + \frac{(1+r)^{(n_1-1)}R_1^1 + (1+r)^{(n_1-2)}R_2^1 + \cdots + R_{n_1}^1}{(1+r)^{n_1}}$$

$$= -V_0 + \frac{S(r, \mathbf{R}^1, n_1)}{(1+r)^{n_1}}$$

(14.19a)

Similarly, for investment two:

$$NPV^2 = -V_0 + \frac{R_1^2}{(1+r)} + \cdots + \frac{R_{n_2}^2}{(1+r)^{n_2}}$$

$$= -V_0 + \frac{(1+r)^{(n_2-1)}R_1^1 + (1+r)^{(n_2-2)}R_2^2 + \cdots + R_{n_2}^2}{(1+r)^{n_2}}$$

$$= -V_0 + \frac{S(r, \mathbf{R}^2, n_2)}{(1+r)^{n_2}}$$

(14.19b)

What equations 14.19a and 14.19b illustrate is the obvious: multiplying by one, the compound rate divided by the identical discount rate, cannot change the value of what is being multiplied.

In Chapter 13, we created equal periodic cash flows by reinvesting the periodic cash flows until the last period, creating MNPV and MIRR models. Then we learned that if the reinvestment rate was equal to the discount rate that NPV and MNPV and IRR and MIRR models produced identical results because reinvesting and discounting by the same rate are offsetting operations. What we learn in this chapter confirms this principle, that reinvesting and discounting by the same rate are offsetting operations. Furthermore, this principle can be used to resolve differences in investment terms.

Resolving term differences. We can convert challengers to the same term by reinvesting and discounting their cash flow to a common term. The compound factor that converts the periodic cash flows and the discount rate from period n_2 to n_1 is $(1 + r)^{(n_1-n_2)}$. This is applied to the extreme right-hand side of equation (14.19b) resulting in the expression:

$$NPV^2 = -V_0 + \frac{(1+r)^{(n_1-n_2)}S(r,\mathbf{R}^2,n_2)}{(1+r)^{(n_1-n_2)}(1+r)^{n_2}}$$

$$= -V_0 + \frac{(1+r)^{(n_1-n_2)}S(r,\mathbf{R}^2,n_2)}{(1+r)^{n_1}} = -V_0 + \frac{S(r,\mathbf{R}^2,n_1)}{(1+r)^{n_1}}$$

(14.20)

Equation (14.20) confirms once again that compounding and discounting by the same rate are offsetting operations even when used to extend the term of investments. Nevertheless, by compounding and discounting by the same rate (multiplying by one), we convert the term of investment two to the term of investment one without changing the value of the function. It is still equal to the original NPV equation.

The rankings of investments one and two—assuming their reinvestment rates and discount rate are the defender's IRR, r—can be expressed as:

$$NPV^1 - NPV^2 = \frac{S(r,\mathbf{R}^1,n_1)}{(1+r)^{n_1}} - \frac{S(r,\mathbf{R}^2,n_1)}{(1+r)^{n_1}}$$

(14.21)

Clearly, the only difference between the two NPVs are their vector of cash flow since they have equal initial investments, discount (reinvestment) rates, and terms.

So, what have we learned? We learned that it is okay to compute and rank mutually exclusive investments using their original NPV equations even though their terms are not the same as long as the reinvestment rate is the defender's IRR. In other words, the compounding and discounting are offsetting operations so that NPV models that convert future streams of cash flow to the present are unaffected.

IRR and NPV Models for Analyzing Repeatable Investments

In our earlier discussions, we showed that IRR and NPV rankings were consistent as long as certain size conditions were satisfied and the investments were equal terms. We can no longer claim IRR and NPV provide consistent ranking when their terms are different.

The two preceding sections resolve term differences by assuming the reinvestment rates were either the defender's or the challengers' IRRs. The problem is that we can no longer be certain that the NPV and IRR methods rank the challengers consistently since we violated the common reinvestment rate assumption—the reinvestment rates were the challengers' own IRRs. If we allow each investment to reinvest in itself, we lose our consistency guarantee.

Another problem using IRR methods besides losing consistency with NPV rankings is that methods for finding the optimal term involve finding the term with the greatest IRR instead of finding the term with the largest AE. This complicates an already complicated subject.

For these and several other reasons, in the remainder of this chapter we will analyze repeatable investments using NPV model assumptions, the most notable of which is that the reinvestment rate is the defender's IRR common to both challengers. To be clear, we could assume a common defender's IRR or each challenger's IRR but having more than one challengers' IRR may produce inconsistent rankings and asymmetry in exchanges. Were we to assume a still different reinvestment rate besides these, the defender's or the challengers' IRR would imply there exists another challenger besides those being considered and, if so, should be considered as a separate challenger.

So in what follows, we assume that earnings from the challengers are reinvested in the defender and asymmetry between exchanges of dollars between time periods. In the next section we begin building the AE tool using NPV assumptions required to analyze repeatable investments.

Ranking One-Time Investments

Term difference and inconsistent rankings. Consider Table 14.3. Note that the two challengers are not periodic size consistent because they withdraw funds at different rates. Challenger one withdraws all of its earnings after one period. Meanwhile, challenger two withdraws some of its earnings in period one and the remainder in period two. As a result, the two investments have unequal terms.

In Table 14.3 panel a, we rank the two challengers using their NPV, IRR, and AE assuming that the discount rate and the reinvestment rate is 10%. In Table 14.3 panel b, we make the two challengers periodic size-consistent by reinvesting period one earnings for one period at the defender's IRR. This operation also resolves term differences between the two investments.

Table 14.3. The Influence of periodic Size and Term Differences Created by Differential Withdrawals.

Panel a. NPV, IRR and AE rankings assuming different periodic cash flows and terms for challengers one and two and a discount rate equal to the defender's IRR of 10%.

Challengers	Initial Outlay	Cash Flows in period one	Cash Flows in period two	NPV (rankings)	IRR (rankings)	AE (rankings)
C1	$1,000	$1,180	$0	$72.73 (2)	18% (1)	$72.73 (1)
C2	$1,000	$160	$1,160	$104.13 (1)	16% (2)	$60.00 (2)

Panel b. NPV, IRR, and AE rankings assuming equal periodic cash flows and terms for challengers one and two where equal periodic cash flows and terms are achieved by reinvesting period one cash flows at the defender's IRR rate of 10% to a common ending period. NPV and IRR rankings after adjusting for term differences assuming a reinvestment rate of r.

Challengers	Initial Outlay	Cash Flows in Period one	Cash Flows in Period two	NPVs and MNPVs (rankings)	IRR (rankings)	AE (rankings)
C1	$1,000	$0	$1,180 (1.10) = $1,298	$72.73 (2)	6.7% (2)	$49.91 (2)
C2	$1,000	$0	$160 (1.10) + $1,160 = $1,336	$104.13 (1)	15.6% (1)	$60.00 (1)

Panel c. NPV, IRR, and AE rankings assuming equal periodic cash flows and terms for challengers one and two where equal periodic cash flows and terms are achieved by reinvesting cash flows at the investments' IRRs. The discount rate is assumed to equal the defender's IRR of 10%

Challengers	Initial Outlay	Cash Flows in Period one	Cash flows in Period two	NPV (MNPV) (rankings)	IRR (rankings)	AE (rankings)
C1	$1,000	$0	$1,180 (1.18) = $1,392.40	$150.74 (1)	18% (1)	$86.66 (1)
C2	$1,000	$0	$160 (1.16) + $1,160 = $1,345.60	$112.07 (2)	16% (2)	$64.57 (2)

Term and periodic cash flow differences in Table 14.3 panel a produced inconsistent rankings using NPV versus IRR and AE methods. However, in Table 14.3 panel b, when term and periodic cash flow differences were eliminated except for the common last period through reinvesting at the defender's IRR of 10%, NPV, IRR, and AE rankings were consistent. In Table 14.3 panel c, when term and periodic cash flow differences were eliminated through reinvesting at the challengers' respective IRRs of 18% and 16%, NPV, IRR, and AE rankings were again consistent but changed from the rankings produced when the reinvestment rate was the defender's IRR.

There are two things to be emphasized about Table 14.3. First, NPVs in panel a and panel b are the same even after adjusting for differences in periodic cash flows and terms. This is because the reinvestment rate was the defender's IRR, and reinvesting and discounting cash flows are offsetting operations. Second, when we adjusted for periodic size inconsistencies using the investments' IRRs as the reinvestment rate, NPVs changed but the investments' IRRs were equal to their MIRRs in panels a and c. This is again the result of reinvesting and discounting by the same rate—the investments' IRRs.

> So what have we learned? We learned that if investments have term differences and the reinvestment rate is the defender's IRR then NPV rankings are appropriate. If investments have term differences and the reinvestment rates are the investments' IRRs then IRR rankings are appropriate.

Alternative reinvestment rate assumptions. In Table 14.3, we made the first challenger into a two-period model by reinvesting its earnings at the defender's IRR. Suppose the one-period challenger was available for investment in each period. In other words, suppose that challenger one could be repeated. Since challenger one is an investment of size $1,000, then only $1,000 of period one earnings could be reinvested in the one-period challenger. The difference between the challenger's first-period earnings and $1,000 we assume will be invested at the defender's IRR. The new investment problem is summarized in Table 14.4.

Table 14.4. Resolving Term Differences Between Two Challengers by Reinvesting $1,000 of Period One Earnings at its One-period IRR of 18% and Reinvesting other Funds at the Defender's IRR of 10%.

Challengers	Initial Outlay	Cash Flow in period one	Cash Flow in period two	NPV assuming defender's IRR is 10% (rankings)	IRR(rankings)	AE (rankings)
C1	$1,000	$0	$1,000 (1.18) + $180 (1.1) = $1,378	$138.84 (1)	17.4% (1)	$80.00 (1)
C2	$1,000	$0	$1,160 + $160 (1.1) = $1,336	$104.13 (2)	15.6% (2)	$60.00 (2)

The interesting result of Table 14.4 provides an example of a blended reinvestment rate not equal to either the defenders IRR of 10% or the investment's own IRR but a weighted average of them both equal to 17.4% for investment one and 15.6% for investment two. However, viewing investment opportunities as combinations of investments in the defender and the challenger must be considered to be a new challenger with a unique reinvestment rate.

Using Annuity Equivalents (AE) to Rank Repeatable Investments

The difficulty of finding finite number of replacements to resolve term differences. In our previous example, we resolved term differences between a one-period investment and a two-period investment by repeating the first investment. Now suppose we have a more complicated term inconsistency problem. For example, assume challenger one's term is 7 periods while challenger two's term is 8 periods. Now repeating an investment one or several times won't resolve term differences. Indeed, to resolve term differences in this problem would require that challenger one be repeated 8 times and challenger two be repeated 7 times. Now we have a 58-period model—which requires a lot of work.

Using Annuity Equivalents (AE) to rank repeatable investments. We can resolve term differences by calculating and comparing the AE of the investments, even though they have different terms. The reason we can use the AE to rank investments of different terms is because the annuity equivalent doesn't change when you increase the term by repeating investments. Thus, the AE from one investment repeated 2, 3, 4, 7, 8, m, or an infinite number of times is the same. This is an important fact because the AE calculated over the lives of multiple (infinite) replacements can be compared to the AE of another repeatable investment and the two investments can be ranked by their difference.

We now support the claim that we can rank repeatable investments by their AE. We write the one-period model as:

$$NPV = -V_0 + \frac{R_1}{(1+r)} + \frac{R_2}{(1+r)^2} + \cdots + \frac{R_n}{(1+r)^n}$$

(14.22a)

We write the NPV model with one replacement as:

$$NPV + \frac{NPV}{(1+r)^n} = -V_0 + \frac{R_1}{(1+r)} + \frac{R_2}{(1+r)^2} + \cdots + \frac{R_n}{(1+r)^n}$$
$$+ \frac{1}{(1+r)^n}\left[-V_0 + \frac{R_1}{(1+r)} + \frac{R_2}{(1+r)^2} + \cdots + \frac{R_n}{(1+r)^n}\right]$$

(14.22b)

And we could write the NPV model with enough replacements to equalize their term as:

(14.22c)

$$NPV + \frac{NPV}{(1+r)^n} + \cdots = -V_0 + \frac{R_1}{(1+r)} + \frac{R_2}{(1+r)^2} + \cdots + \frac{R_n}{(1+r)^n}$$
$$+ \frac{1}{(1+r)^n}\left[-V_0 + \frac{R_1}{(1+r)} + \frac{R_2}{(1+r)^2} + \cdots + \frac{R_n}{(1+r)^n}\right] + \cdots$$

Next, factoring, we obtain:

$$NPV \left[1 + \frac{1}{(1+r)^n} + \cdots \right] =$$

$$\left[-V_0 + \frac{R_1}{(1+r)} + \frac{R_2}{(1+r)^2} + \cdots + \frac{R_n}{(1+r)^n}\right]$$

(14.22d)
$$\left[1 + \frac{1}{(1+r)^n} + \cdots \right]$$

Then, canceling the two bracketed terms at the end of each equation, we regain our original one-investment problem:

$$NPV = -V_0 + \frac{R_1}{(1+r)} + \frac{R_2}{(1+r)^2} + \cdots + \frac{R_n}{(1+r)^n}$$

$$= \frac{R}{(1+r)} + \frac{R}{(1+r)^2} + \cdots + \frac{R}{(1+r)^n}$$

(14.22e)

A numerical example that the AE for a single investment is equal to the AE calculated over two investments. Note that the same AE that solved the one-investment problem solves the multiple-replacement problem.

We demonstrate this result in Table 14.5 which calculates AE for one investment and then recalculates the AE for an investment and one replacement.

Table 14.5. Resolving Term Inconsistencies by Calculating AE for an Investment and the Investment and a Replacement Assuming Defender's IRR is 10%

Challenger	V_0	R_1	R_2	R_3	R_4	NPV (rankings)	IRR (rankings)	AE (rankings)
C1	$2,000	$1,200	$1,200			$82.64 (2)	13.1% (1)	$47.65 (1)
C1 plus replacement	$2,000	$1,200	$1,200 - $2,000 = -$800	$1,200	$1,200	$150.95 (1)	13.1% (1)	$47.65 (1)

Table 14.5 illustrates the importance of AE rankings to resolve term (and size) inconsistencies for repeatable investments. Note first that term inconsistencies produce different NPVs. The NPVs are positive because the challenger earns a higher rate of return than the defender. Furthermore, collecting these returns for two challengers, the challenger and its replacement, earns more than just one investment. Hence, the NPV for the challenger and its replacement is greater than the NPV for just one

challenger. On the other hand, both the IRR and the AE rank the investments the same, because their calculations are adjusted for the term of the investment. These results are also helpful because they confirm that the IRR of a single defender can be used to discount the challenger and still maintain consistency.

So what is our best advice? Resolve term inconsistencies for repeatable investments by calculating AE for the first investment or the IRR for the first investment.

So, what have we learned about ranking repeatable investments? When asked to rank two challengers that are repeatable but have unequal term and their reinvestment rate is the defender's IRR, rank them by their respective first investment's AE.

Finding AE that account for technologically improved replacements. Suppose that one of the challengers will be replaced by a technologically improved replacement that perhaps costs more, but also produces higher returns. For $\gamma > 1$ the investment problem takes the following form:

$$NPV + \frac{(1+\gamma)NPV}{(1+r)^n} + \cdots$$

(14.23)

Including enough replacement to equalize terms, we find the sum of the discounted NPVs. Call this sum S which is equal to:

$$S = NPV \left[1 + \frac{1+\gamma}{(1+r)^n} + \frac{(1+\gamma)^2}{(1+r)^{2n}} + \cdots\right]$$

$$= NPV \left[\frac{1}{1 - \frac{1+\gamma}{(1+r)^n}}\right]$$

(14.24)

The details of the derivation are not included here, but require nothing more that the summation of geometric series. The interpretation of equation (14.24) is that technological improvements result in NPV increases in the first replacement by γ percent. The second replacement's NPV increase by $(1 + \gamma)(1 + \gamma)$—over the first one. Thus, the NPVs increased from NPV to $(1 + \gamma)NPV (1 + \gamma)^2$ NPV etc. We demonstrate the effect of technologically improved replacement on the ranking of investments in Table 14.6. To simplify our calculations, we assume that we have already found the NPV of the two challengers equal to $100 for the first investment and $150 for the second investment. The term differences of the two investments are $n_1 = 10$ for the first investment and $n_2 = 20$ for the second investment. The rate of technological improvements are 5% for investment one and 3% for investment two. To demonstrate the importance of accounting for technological improvements, we find the AE unadjusted for technological improvement and the AE accounting for technological improvement.

Table 14.6. Ranking Adjusted for Term Differences and Technologically Improved Replacements. Rankings Assuming Defender's IRR is 10%

Challenger	NPV (rankings)	Terms	Technological change coefficient γ	Adjustment coefficient $\left[\dfrac{1}{1 - \dfrac{1+\gamma}{(1+r)^n}} \right]$	AE not adjusted for technological change (rankings)	NPVs adjusted for technological change (rankings)
C1	$NPV_1 =$ $100 (2)	$n_1 =$ 10	$\gamma_1 = 5\%$	1.68	$16.27 (2)	$100(1.68) = $168 (1)
C2	$NPV_2 =$ $150 (2)	$n_2 =$ 20	$\gamma_2 = 3\%$	1.18	$17.62 (1)	$150(1.18) = $177.12 (2)

It is useful to note in Table 14.6 that NPV and AE unadjusted for technological change are consistent as our theory implies. However, once we account for technological change, the investment rankings based on the investments AE are reversed. Investment one is preferred even though its NPV is less than that of challenger's two NPV.

Inconsistent rankings were not caused by failing to adjust for differences in size and terms. As we have already demonstrated, these can be rationalized using AE. What produced the inconsistencies was comparing the rankings without technologically improved replacements (unadjusted AE) versus including the assumption of technologically improved replacements (adjusted for technology rankings).

Capitalizing AE to find the present value of a stream of repeatable investments. If we are comparing repeatable investments with different terms, then the comparisons are not between individual investments but with the present value sum of all the investments in each cash flow stream. In this regard we could compare the AE since the AE ordering of investment is the same as the NPV orderings. Or, we could capitalize the AE to find the present value sum of all of the investments. To understand how to capitalize the AE, that is, to find its value over an infinite number of repeatable investments, we write equation (14.25):

$$NPV \left[1 + \frac{1}{(1+r)^n} + \cdots \right] =$$

$$\left[\frac{R}{(1+r)} + \frac{R}{(1+r)^2} + \cdots + \frac{R}{(1+r)^n} \right] \left[1 + \frac{1}{(1+r)^n} + \cdots \right]$$

$$= \frac{R}{(1+r)} + \frac{R}{(1+r)^2} + \cdots + \frac{R}{(1+r)^{mn}}$$

$$= \lim_{m \to \infty} \frac{R}{r} \left[1 - \frac{1}{(1+r)^{mn}} \right] = \frac{R}{r}$$

(14.25)

To get some idea of how fast convergent to the capitalization formula R/r occurs in equation (14.25), if $n = 10$ and $r = 10\%$, then for $m = 2$, then $[1 - 1/(1 + r)^{mn}] = .85$; for $m = 3$, then $[1 - 1/(1 + r)^{mn}] = .94$, and for $m = 4$, then $[1 - 1/(1 + r)^{mn}] = .98$. Finally, then $m = 5$, then $[1 - 1/(1 + r)^{mn}] = .991$.

Finding the Optimal Replacement Age for Different Repeatable Investments

The condition that identifies the optimal replacement age for a repeatable investment. The optimal age for each repeatable investment in a stream of repeatable investments is that age that maximizes the NPV for the entire stream of repeatable investments. Finding the optimal age of a repeatable investment is a ranking problem. Only in this case, each challenger is defined by its replacement age, and each age-differentiated investment is considered to be a different challenger. Our goal is to find optimal replacement age.

The key to understanding when to replace repeatable investments (without employing a lot of calculus) is to think about averages—or in our case, AE. We want to maximize the present value sum of NPVs for the entire stream of repeatable investments—not just the NPV for an individual investment.

If the investments in a series of repeatable investments have identical cash flow patterns, then the rule for maximizing the NPV of the present value sum for all repeatable investment is to find the term that maximizes the AE for a single investment. Thus, for a repeatable investment, if holding the investment for an additional period increases the AE for the challenger, then the investment should be held for at least another period—until holding the investment another period decreases the AE. Of course, the periodic cash flows could still be positive and NPV increasing even though AE are decreasing. Thus holding the investment for the term that maximizes its NPV is definitely not the same rule as holding the investment for the term that maximizes its AE.

The pattern of cash flows is the ultimate determinant of an investment's optimal life. Since the calculus requires a smooth inverted cup-like shape for maximization, we typically assume investment cash flows have corresponding patterns. However, the pattern for an investment's periodic cash flows are not the same as the pattern of AE for an investment at different ages. Consider some different kinds of investments and cash flow patterns and their corresponding optimal lives.

Finding the optimal replacement age for a growth and decay type investment. The growth and decay type of investment, after the initial investment, is identified by increasing periodic cash flows followed by decreasing periodic cash flows. Specifically, suppose that we have a repeatable investment with cash flows reported for 6 periods. Assuming the reinvestment rate and the discount rate are 10%, we find the NPV for each investment assuming it has an economic life of one period, two periods, three periods, and up to six periods. Then we find the AE for the investments at their alternative economic lives. Finally, we capitalized the AE by 10% (divide the AE by .1) to find the lifetime present value of the multiple investments at their alternative ages. The results are reported in Table 14.7.

Table 14.7. An Example of a Growth and Decay Type Investment.

Time period	Cash flow per period	NPV per investment for alternative investment lives discounted at 10%	AE per investment for alternative investment lives discounted at 10%	Present value sum of an infinite number of repeatable investments
0	($300.00)	($300.00)		
1	$150.00	($163.64)	($180.00)	($18,000.00)
2	$275.00	$63.64	$36.67	$3,667.00
3	$130.00	$161.31	$64.87	$6,487.00
4	$70.00	$209.12	$65.97	$6,597.00
5	$30.00	$227.75	$60.08	$6,008.00
6	($10.00)	$222.10	$51.00	$5,100.00

If our goal were to maximize the NPV for one of the repeatable investments, we would hold the investment until it no longer produced positive cash flows—in our example until period 5 with a cash flow of $30 and lifetime present earnings of $6,008.00. But if our goal is to optimize our lifetime earnings from a large number of repeatable investments, then we would hold each investment until they reach age 4 with a cash flow of $70 and lifetime earnings of $6,597.00. Another way to report the results of Table 14.7 is to note that as long as the periodic cash flow exceeds the AE in a period, adding that period to the life of the investment will increase the AE and the lifetime earnings of the repeatable investments.

Finding the optimal replacement age for a light bulb type investment. Recall that the "light bulb" type of investment describes a category of investments which, after the initial investment, produce a nearly constant level of services that are virtually undiminished over its economic life. Then, at some point, the investment stops providing services and the investment dies a sudden death. An example cash flow pattern for this investment assumes that the investment dies in period 5. The investment is described in Table 14.8.

Table 14.8. An Example of a Light Bulb Type Investment.

Time period	Cash flow per period	NPV per investment for alternative investment lives discounted at 10%	AE per investment for alternative investment lives discounted at 10%	Present value sum of an infinite number of repeatable investments
0	($300.00)	($300.00)		
1	$100.00	($209.09)	($230.00)	($23,000.00)
2	$100.00	($126.45)	($72.86)	($7,286.00)
3	$100.00	($51.31)	($20.63)	($2,063.00)
4	$100.00	$16.99	$5.36	$536.00
5	$0	$16.99	$4.48	$448.00
6	$0	$16.99	$3.90	$390.00

The light bulb type investment has an important pattern that is easily recognized. It is that as long as its constant cash flows are positive, it's NPV and AE are increasing. However, once the investment dies and its positive cash flows end, its NPV is constant but its AE is continually decreasing. Thus, the optimal life of a light bulb is to keep it until it dies. Of course, this recommendation could be modified if there were serious costs associated with an interruption of services and that the exact period in which the investment died was not known with certainty.

Finding the optimal replacement age for a continuous decay type investment. The continuous decay type investment is one in which the investment performs best when new and then, with use and time, its service capacity decreases and its maintenance requirements increase so that its periodic cash flows exhibit a continuous decay. An example of such a periodic cash flow pattern is described in Table 14.9.

Table 14.9. An Example of the Continual Decay Type Investment.

Time period	Cash flow per period	NPV per investment for alternative investment lives discounted at 10%	AE per investment for alternative investment lives discounted at 10%	Present value sum of an infinite number of repeatable investments
0	($4300.00)	($300.00)		
1	$190.00	($127.27)	($139.96)	($13,996.00)
2	$152.00	($1.65)	($.95)	($95.00)
3	$129.00	$95.27	$38.31	$3,831.00
4	$85.00	$153.32	$48.37	$4,837.00
5	$38.00	$175.92	$46.41	$4,641.00
6	$8.00	$181.43	$41.66	$4,166.00

In the continual decay model, after the cost of the initial investment is paid, the periodic cash flows of the investment continually decrease. Still they increase the NPV of the investment as long as they are positive. At some point, the value of earning high returns during the early life of the investment swamps the cost of acquiring a new investment and the AE decrease indicating the optimal age of the investment. In this example, the optimal life of the investment is 4 periods with a corresponding present value sum of earnings over an infinite number of repeatable investments equal to $4,837.00.

Finding the optimal replacement age for an investment with irregular periodic cash flows. The last category of investments considered are those whose cash flow patterns are unique. That is, the cash flow pattern for an investment owned one year is different than the same investment owned two years, three years, and so on. To illustrate this type of investment, consider a machinery owner who custom hires using his machine to perform services for customers. The cash flow pattern for the machine begins with a capital purchase followed by three years of nearly constant cash flows which then decrease by 25% per year—mostly because of repairs but also because the demand for custom hires using older machines decreases. In the year the machine is replaced, the old machine earns a liquidation value that depends on the age of the machine. In this problem, the machine at each age is considered a unique challenger even though it is the same machine differentiated by age. A description of the cash flows for this problem follows.

Table 14.10. Investments With Irregular Cash Flow Characterized by Constant and then Declining Cash Flow with an Income Spike in the last Period of the Investment's Economic Life. The Discount and Reinvestment Rates are Assumed to Equal 10%.

Period	3 year old challenger	4 year old challenger	5 year old challenger	6 year old challenger	7 year old challenger	8 year old challenger
0	($100)	($100)	($100)	($100)	($100)	($100)
1	$40	$40	$40	$40	$40	$40
2	$40	$40	$40	$40	$40	$40
3	liquidation = $64	$32	$32	$32	$32	$32
4	0	liquidation = $51.20	$25.60	$25.60	$25.60	$25.60
5	0	0	liquidation = $40.96	$20.48	$20.48	$20.48
6	0	0	0	liquidation = $32.77	16.38	$16.38
7	0	0	0	0	liquidation = $26.21	$13.11
8	0	0	0	0	0	liquidation = $20.97
Summary Measures						
NPVs	$17.51	$28.43	$36.38	$42.16	$46.36	$49.42
AE	$7.04	$8.97	$9.60	$9.68	$9.52	$9.26
Capitalized AE	$70.40	$89.70	$96.00	$96.80	$95.20	$92.60

Note that NPVs are increasing with the age of the challengers. The maximum AE is earned in the sixth period and declines for each of the older challengers. Thus the optimal age for the challengers is age 6.

Summary and Conclusions

In Chapter 13, we found two sufficient conditions for consistently ranking mutually exclusive investments. The two conditions are that initial investment sizes and periodic cash flows are equal except for their last common period. In this chapter we extended the results of Chapter 13 by developing methods to rank investments of unequal terms. Ranking unequal term investments are problematic because unequal terms create unequal periodic cash flows, violating the second of two sufficient conditions for consistently ranking investments using IRRs and NPVs.

In our efforts to find methods for ranking investments of unequal terms, we found that MNPV and MIRR models would rank investments equally. But we also found that under some conditions, IRR and NPV models could produce equal rankings. In this chapter, we emphasized that adjusting for term differences by reinvesting and discounting by the defender's IRR that NPV and MNPV and MIRR models would produce consistent rankings. These results would not hold when some other reinvestment rate applies. These findings led to some important practical results: when the reinvestment rate and the discount rate are the same, rank investments using NPVs. When the reinvestment rates are the investments' IRRs, rank using investments' IRRs.

In the second part of this chapter, we considered repeatable investments. If by repeating investments for a required number of times the investments had a common ending date, then individual investment term differences could be ignored. In effect, the entire stream of repeatable investments could be considered to be a single investment. Of course, if the number of repeatable investments was considered to be infinite then the term problem is resolved.

Assuming equal initial investment sizes, we found that the repeatable investment's optimal age was the age that maximized AE for a single investment. Thus, we can find the optimal replacement age for repeatable investments in a stream of replacements by finding the age that maximizes AE for any one investment. Capitalizing the AE provides us with an estimate of the present value of the earnings from the stream of repeatable investments.

Questions

1. Describe the three sufficient conditions required for consistent IRR and NPV rankings for one-time investments? Explain how investment term differences violate one of the two sufficient conditions.
2. Some investments are one-time investments. Others are repeatable. Describe what conditions produce one-time investments. Then describe what conditions produce repeatable investments. Give examples of one-time and repeatable investments.
3. One way to resolve term differences is to reinvest the periodic cash flows of both investments to a common ending period. Explain the implications of assuming that the reinvestment rates are

the defender's IRR, the investments' IRR, or some other rate.

4. Explain the effects on an investment's NPV if term differences are resolved by reinvesting its periodic cash flows to some common period using the defender's IRR, while discounting the reinvested funds over the changed terms by the same rate, the defender's IRR.

5. Explain the difference, if any, between an investment's IRR and its MIRR if the reinvestment rate is the investment's IRR. Depending on your answer, what practical recommendation would you offer to financial managers wanting to rank investments whose earnings would be reinvested in themselves?

6. In the table below, term differences are resolved by reinvesting periodic cash flows to the common ending period assuming the reinvestment rate and the discount rate is the defender's IRR of 10%. Produce a similar table assuming the same initial investment sizes and cash flows, only assume the defender's IRR is 5% not 10%. Then associate your results with the ranking possibilities described in Table 14.1 by declaring which of the four models correspond to your table.

Table Q14.1. The influence of periodic size and term differences created by differential withdrawals assuming a reinvestment rate equal to the defender's IRR of 10%. The discount rate for the NPV and MNPV models equal the defender's IRR. The discount rate for the IRR and MIRR models are the IRRs and MIRRs

Challengers	Initial Outlay	Cash Flow in period one	Cash Flow in period two	NPV (rankings)	IRR (rankings)	MNPV (rankings)	MIRR (rankings)
C1	$900	$1090	0	$90.91 (2)	$21.11% (1)	$90.91 (2)	15.42% (2)
C2	$900	$160	$1050	$113.22 (1)	17.27% (2)	$113.22 (1)	16.71% (1)

7. In the table below, term differences are resolved by reinvesting periodic cash flows to the common ending period assuming the reinvestment rates are the investments' IRRs and the discount rate is 10%. Produce a similar table assuming the same initial investment sizes and cash flows, only assume the defender's IRR is 5% not 10%. Then associate your results with the ranking possibilities described in Table 14.1 by declaring which of the four models correspond to your table.

Table Q14.2. The influence of periodic size and term differences created by differential withdrawals assuming a reinvestment rate equal to the challenger's IRRs. The discount rate for the NPV and MNPV models equal the defender's IRR. The discount rate for the IRR and MIRR models are the IRRs and MIRRs.

Challengers	Initial Outlay	Cash Flow in period one	Cash Flow in period two	NPV (rankings)	IRR (rankings)	MNPV (rankings)	MIRR (rankings)
C1	$900	$1090	$0	$90.91 (2)	$21.11% (1)	$190.91 (1)	21.11% (1)
C2	$900	$160	$1050	$113.22 (1)	17.27% (2)	$122.83 (2)	17.27% (2)

8. Referring to the completed tables in Questions 6 and 7, please answer the following. Why are NPV and MNPV ranking consistent and equal in amounts in the Question 6 table but inconsistent and different in amounts in the Question 7 table? And why are IRR and MIRR rankings inconsistent and unequal in the Question 6 table but consistent and equal in amount in the Question 7 table? What are the practical implications of these results?

9. Annuity equivalents are elements in a stream of constant periodic cash flows whose present value

equals the present value of some fixed amount or the present value of a non-constant cash flow stream. What is the arithmetic mean of a series of AE? If the discount rate is 8% and the term is 10 periods, find the AE for the periodic cash flows 21, 34, 5, and 13. Then find the AE for a fixed present value amount of $199 assuming the same discount rate and term. Finally, recalculate the AE if the term is decreased from 10 periods to 5 periods.

10. A potential Uber driver can purchase a new car for $18,000. Then the car is expected to earn constant periodic cash flows for the next three years of $6,000. After that, mostly because of decreased demand for rides in older cars and higher repair costs, periodic cash flows decrease by 25% per year. The liquidation value of the new car after three years is $9,000 and then declines each year thereafter by 25%. Find the optimal age at which the Uber driver should replace cars. Then find the capitalized value of an investment in one car assuming each car is owned until its optimal age.

15. "Tax Considerations: Analyzing Investments with Homogeneous Tax Rates"

LINDON ROBISON

Learning goals. After completing this chapter, you should be able to: (1) construct effective tax rates on defending and challenging investments; (2) describe how effective tax rates depend on investment types; compute (3) find effective after-tax IRR by finding and adjusting effective investments by calculating a defending investment's tax adjustment coefficient.

Learning objectives. To achieve your learning goals, you should complete the following objectives:
- Learn how to compute the tax adjustment coefficient for a single period.
- Learn how to compare the average effective tax rate for an investment.
- Learn how to find the tax adjustment coefficient for loans and investments with increasing (decreasing) cash flow.
- Learn how taxes and tax adjustment coefficients influence investment rankings.

Introduction

According to Benjamin Franklin, taxes are one of the two constants in life (the other one is death). Taxes need to be included in present value (PV) models because only what the firm earns and keeps after paying taxes really matters. Therefore, proper construction of PV models requires that taxes be consistently applied to defending and challenging investments.

A single-equation PV model compares two investments: a challenger, described by time-dated cash flow, and a defender, usually described by its internal rate of return (IRR) of its time-dated cash flow. Homogeneous tax rates require that the same units are used when describing the cash flow of the challenger as the cash flow used when finding the IRR of the defender. And in particular, homogeneous tax rates require that when the cash flow of the challenger are adjusted for taxes, the IRR of the defender must also be adjusted for taxes. This chapter shows how to find homogeneous tax rates in PV models.

It is popular to adjust a defender's before-tax IRR to an after-tax IRR by multiplying it by $(1 - T)$, where T is the average tax rate applied to the investment. This chapter points out that this method for adjusting the defender's IRR for taxes is only appropriate in a few special cases. Finally, this chapter shows how to find appropriate tax rates for adjusting the defender's IRR for taxes in a variety of tax environments.

After-tax PV Models for Defenders and Challengers

The goal is to find a defender's after-tax IRR. The first step is to find the defender's before-tax IRR. Recall that the defender's before-tax IRR is that rate of return such that the NPV of the defender's before-tax net cash flow is zero. The defender's after-tax IRR discounts the defender's after-tax cash flow so that its NPV remains equal to zero.

There is an easy test to determine if taxes have been properly introduced into a PV model. First consider the defender's cash flow stream and its IRR. Then introduce taxes into the defender's cash flow stream and its IRR. If taxes have been properly introduced, then the NPV of the defender's after-tax cash flow stream discounted by its after-tax IRR is still zero.

To illustrate, consider a defending investment that earns constant net cash flow of R dollars per period in perpetuity. The maximum bid (minimum sell) price V_0 for this defending investment whose before-tax IRR is r. We describe this investment in equation (15.1).

$$
(15.1) \quad V_0 = \frac{R}{(1+r)} + \frac{R}{(1+r)^2} + \cdots = \frac{R}{r}
$$

where $r = R/V_0$ is the before-tax IRR. Now suppose that we describe the defender's cash flow and the IRR for this same investment on an after-tax basis. We do so by introducing the constant marginal income tax rate T into the model:

$$
(15.2) \quad V_0 = \frac{R(1-T)}{[1+r(1-T)]} + \frac{R(1-T)}{[1+r(1-T)]^2} + \cdots = \frac{R}{r}
$$

Income R and the before-tax IRR of the defender are both adjusted for taxes by multiplying by $(1-T)$. We can be sure that $r(1-T)$ is the after-tax IRR, since V_0 is the same in the before and after-tax models. However, we need to be aware that only in the special case of constant infinite income can we multiply r by $(1-T)$ to obtain the after-tax IRR.

A General Approach for Finding the Defender's After-tax IRR

A general approach for finding the defender's after-tax IRR follows. Consider a defender that has a market-determined value of V_0 and earns a before-tax cash flow stream of R_1, R_2, ..., and whose defender's before-tax IRR is r. A before-tax PV model for this defender can be written as:

$$V_0 = \frac{R_1}{(1+r)} + \frac{R_2}{(1+r)^2} + \cdots$$

$$= \frac{R_1}{(1+r)} + \frac{1}{(1+r)}\left[\frac{R_2}{(1+r)} + \frac{R_3}{(1+r)^2} + \cdots\right]$$

(15.3)

Now we express the PV model for the defender one period later as:

$$V_1 = \frac{R_2}{(1+r)} + \frac{R_3}{(1+r)^2} + \cdots$$

(15.4)

Note that the bracketed expression in equation (15.3) equals the right-hand side of equation (15.4). This equality allows us to substitute V_1 for the bracketed expression in equation (15.3). After making the substitution in equation (15.3) we solve for capital gains equal to:

(15.5) $\quad V_1 - V_0 = rV_0 - R_1$

Using the expression in equation (15.5) we can solve for the defender's before-tax IRR equal to:

$$r = \frac{(V_1 - V_0) + R_1}{V_0}$$

(15.6)

We now want to find the after-tax IRR for the defender described in equation (15.6). To do so, the IRR and the cash flow for the defender must be adjusted for taxes in such a way that V_0 in equation (15.3) is not changed (and the defender's NPV is still zero). The defender's cash flow is adjusted for taxes by multiplying them by $(1 - T)$. The defender's before-tax IRR is adjusted for taxes by multiplying it by $(1 - \theta T)$ where θ, a tax adjustment coefficient, adjusts r to its after-tax equivalent such that V_0 is the same whether calculated on a before-tax or after-tax basis. Besides these tax adjustments, let T_j equal other taxes applied to the defender's cash flow that may include property taxes in the case of land, depreciation tax credits in the case of depreciable investments, and capital gains taxes when appropriate for assets earning capital gains. What all these taxes have in common is their functional dependence on the previous period's asset value.

The after-tax PV model corresponding to equation (15.3) that leaves V_0 unchanged can be written as:

$$V_0 = \frac{R_1(1-T) + T_j f(V_0)}{[1 + r(1 - \theta T)]}$$

$$+ \frac{1}{[1 + r(1 - \theta T)]}\left[\frac{R_2(1-T) + T_j f(V_1)}{[1 + r(1 - \theta T)]} + \frac{R_3 + T_j f(V_2)}{[1 + r(1 - \theta T)]^2} + \cdots\right]$$

(15.7)

Similarly, V_1 can be expressed as:

$$V_1 = \frac{R_2(1-T) + T_j f(V_1)}{[1 + r(1 - \theta T)]} + \frac{R_3 + T_j f(V_2)}{[1 + r(1 - \theta T)]^2} + \cdots$$
(15.8)

Replacing the bracketed expression in equation (15.7) with V_1, we find the after-tax IRR for the defender as:

$$r(1 - \theta T) = \frac{(V_1 - V_0) + R_1(1-T) + T_j f(V_0)}{V_0}$$
(15.9)

Finally, substituting for r in equation (15.9) from the right-hand side of equation (15.6) and solving for θ, we obtain:

$$\theta = \frac{R_1 - \left(\dfrac{T_j}{T}\right) f(V_0)}{R_1 + (V_1 - V_0)}$$
(15.10)

The value for θ in equation (15.10) adjusts the defender's before-tax IRR to obtain homogeneity of measures between the defender's after-tax IRR and the defender's after-tax cash flow in equation (15.7). When homogeneity of measures is maintained, the defender's NPV is still zero whether calculated on a before-tax or after-tax basis. We now find some specific after-tax IRRs for various types of defenders.

Case 15.1. $(V_1 - V_0) = 0$ and $T_j f(V_0) = 0$. In this case, the defender earns neither capital gains nor suffers capital losses, in which case $T_j = 0$. This case is illustrated by an infinite constant cash flow series, described in equations 15.1 and 15.2. Because the cash flow is constant, capital gains are zero. Furthermore, the defender's return in each period is equal to its cash receipts, which is fully taxed at income tax rate T. Therefore, the entire before-tax rate of return must be adjusted by $(1 - T)$. In equation (15.10), substituting zero for capital gains and depreciation or capital gains tax results in:

$$\theta = \frac{R_1 - \left(\dfrac{T_j}{T}\right) f(V_0)}{R_1 + (V_1 - V_0)} = \frac{R_1}{R_1} = 1$$
(15.11)

Case 15.2. $(V_1 - V_0) > 0$ and $T_j f(V_0) = 0$. In this case the investment earns capital gains that are not taxed, which lowers the defender's effective tax rate. Thus, $\theta < 1$ and $(1 - \theta T) < (1 - T)$. The greater the capital gains, the lower the effective tax rate in period t. We illustrate this type of model next.

Consider a defending investment whose before-tax cash flow grows geometrically at rate g. Then before-tax cash flow in period t, R_t, equals: $R_0 (1 + g)^t$, and we write the investment's IRR model as:

$$V_0 = \frac{R_0(1+g)}{(1+r)} + \frac{1}{(1+r)} \left[\frac{R_0(1+g)^2}{(1+r)} + \frac{R_0(1+g)^3}{(1+r)^2} + \cdots \right]$$

$$= \frac{R_0(1+g)}{(r-g)}$$

(15.12)

One period later, we can write:

(15.13)
$$V_1 = \frac{R_0(1+g)^2}{(1+r)} + \frac{R_0(1+g)^3}{(1+r)^2} + \cdots = V_0(1+g)$$

and capital gains equal:

(15.14) $\quad V_1 - V_0 = V_0(1+g) - V_0 = gV_0$

Then, substituting the right-hand side of equation (15.12) for V_0 in equation (15.14), we obtain:

$$gV_0 = \frac{gR_0(1+g)}{r-g}$$

(15.15)

Now we are ready to find the tax-adjustment coefficient in this model. Substituting into equation (15.10) for capital gains and first period cash flow, we obtain:

$$\theta = \frac{R_1 - \left(\dfrac{T_j}{T}\right) f(V_0)}{R_1 + (V_1 - V_0)} = \frac{R_0(1+g)}{R_0(1+g) + gV_0}$$

$$= \frac{R_0(1+g)}{R_0(1+g) + \dfrac{gR_0(1+g)}{r-g}} = \frac{r-g}{r}$$

(15.16)

Suppose that we naively introduced taxes into the growth model described in equation (15.12) and obtained:

$$V_0 = \frac{R_0(1+g)(1-T)}{[1+r(1-T)]} + \frac{R_0(1+g)^2(1-T)}{[1+r(1-T)]^2} + \cdots$$

$$= \frac{R_0(1+g)(1-T)}{r(1-T)-g}$$

(15.17)

In this case, an increase in T increases V_0:

$$\frac{dV_0}{dT} = \frac{R_0(1+g)g}{[r(1-T)-g]^2} > 0.$$

(15.18)

Since increasing T increases V_0, we know that $r(1-T)$ cannot equal the after-tax IRR for the defending investment.

> So what have we learned? We learned how to interpret θ in the geometric growth model. Earlier we demonstrated that in the geometric growth model, capital gains are earned at rate g. But in this model, capital gains are not converted to cash, and so they are not taxed. Therefore, not all earnings on the investment are taxed, only the portion earned as cash. As a result, the effective tax rate is not T but θT, where θ is the percentage of returns earned as cash.

If, for example, r = 8%, g = 3%, then

$$\theta = \frac{.08 - .03}{.08} = .63.$$

(15.19)

Furthermore, for an investor in the 35% tax bracket whose cash flow is increasing at 3%, the effective tax rate would be θT = (.63)(.35) = 22%.

Case 15.3. $(V_1 - V_0) < 0$ and $T_f f(V_0) = 0$. In this case the investment suffers capital losses for which no tax savings are allowed, which increases the defender's effective tax rate. Thus, $\theta > 1$ and $(1 - \theta T) > (1 - T)$. The greater the capital losses, the higher is the effective tax rate in period t. We illustrate this type of model next.

Consider a defending investment whose before-tax cash flow declines geometrically at rate $d > 0$. Then before-tax cash flow in period t, R_t, equals: $R_0(1-d)^t$, and we write the investment's maximum bid price as:

(15.20)

$$V_0 = \frac{R_0(1-d)}{(1+r)} + \frac{1}{(1+r)}\left[\frac{R_0(1-d)^2}{(1+r)} + \frac{R_0(1+d)^3}{(1+r)^2} + \cdots\right] = \frac{R_0(1-d)}{(r+d)}$$

One period later, we can write:

$$V_1 = \frac{R_0(1-d)^2}{(1+r)} + \frac{R_0(1+d)^3}{(1+r)^2} + \cdots = V_0(1-d)$$

(15.21)

and capital losses equal:

(15.22) $\quad V_1 - V_0 = V_0(1-d) - V_0 = -dV_0$

Then, substituting the right-hand side of equation (15.20) for V_0 in equation (15.22) we obtain:

$$dV_0 = \frac{dR_0(1-d)}{r+d}$$

(15.23)

Now we are ready to find the tax-adjustment coefficient in this model. Substituting into equation (15.10) for capital losses and first period cash flow, we obtain:

$$\theta = \frac{R_1 - \left(\frac{T_j}{T}\right)f(V_0)}{R_1 + (V_1 - V_0)} = \frac{R_0(1-d)}{R_0(1-d) - dV_0}$$

$$= \frac{R_0(1-d)}{R_0(1-d) + \dfrac{dR_0(1-d)}{r+d}} = \frac{r+d}{r}$$

(15.24)

helpful later on to distinguish between growth in cash receipts $g\%$ and book value depreciation $d\%$.

If for example, $r = 8\%$, $d = 3\%$, then,

$$\theta = \frac{.08 + .03}{.08} = 1.375.$$
(15.25)

Furthermore, for an investor in the 35% tax bracket, the effective tax rate on cash flow described by a geometric growth pattern would be $\theta T = (1.375)(.35) = 48\%$. The conclusion of Case 15.3 is that suffering losses on investments which are not used to shield income from taxes increases the investor's effective tax rate.

Case 15.4. $(V_1 - V_0) > 0$ and $T_{jf}(V_0) = -T_p(1 - T)V_0$. In this model, the defending investment earns capital gains but pays property tax on its previous period's value times the property tax rate T_p. However, property taxes are tax deductible, so we can write the after-tax IRR model for the defending land investment as:

$$
\begin{aligned}
V_0 &= \frac{R_0(1+g)(1-T) - T_p(1-T)V_0}{[1 + r(1 - \theta T)]} \\
&\quad + \frac{R_0(1+g)^2(1-T) - T_p(1-T)V_0(1+g)}{[1 + r(1 - \theta T)]^2} + \cdots \\
&= \frac{R_0(1+g)(1-T)}{r(1-\theta T) - g} - \frac{V_0(1+g)T_p(1-T)}{r(1-\theta T) - g}
\end{aligned}
$$
(15.26)

We can sum the IRR model above by recognizing that it consists of two geometric sums. However, after summing, V_0 appears on both sides of the equation. Therefore, we solve for V_0 using equation (15.26) and obtain:

$$V_0 = \frac{R_0(1+g)(1-T)}{r(1-\theta T) - g + T_p(1-T)}$$
(15.27)

Capital gains and V_0 in this model are the same as in Case 15.2, which allows us to write:

$$\theta = \frac{R_1 - \left(\dfrac{T_f}{T}\right) f(V_0)}{R_1 + (V_1 - V_0)} = \frac{R_0(1+g) + \left(\dfrac{T_p(1-T)}{T}\right) V_0}{R_0(1+g) + gV_0}$$

$$= \frac{R_0(1+g) + \left(\dfrac{T_p(1-T)}{T}\right) \dfrac{R_0(1+g)}{r-g}}{R_0(1+g) + \dfrac{gR_0(1+g)}{r-g}} = \frac{r - g + \dfrac{T_p(1-T)}{T}}{r}$$

(15.28)

Consider the effect of property taxes compared to the geometric model without property taxes. In Case 15.2, we assumed that r = 8% and g = 3%, so that θ = (.08 − .05) / .08 = .63. We continue with the assumption that the decision maker is in the 35% tax bracket and add the assumption that the property tax rate is 2%. We now substitute into equation (15.28) and find:

$$\theta = \frac{r - g + \dfrac{T_p(1-T)}{T}}{r}$$

$$= \frac{.08 - .03 + \dfrac{.02(1 - .35)}{.35}}{.08} = 1.09$$

(15.29)

So what have we learned? We learned that property taxes increase the effective tax rate. To illustrate, for an investor in the 35% tax bracket, the effective tax rate on cash flow described by a geometric growth pattern with property taxes would be θT = (1.09)(.35) = 38%. Obviously, property taxes increase an investor's effective tax rate.

Case 15.5. $(V_1 - V_0) > 0$ and $T_f f(V_0) = T d V_0$. A most fortuitous tax environment is an investment that appreciates but is considered to depreciate at rate d for tax purposes. In this case the investor is not required to pay taxes on the capital gains and is allowed a tax credit for depreciation that occurs only on the books. An example of such a model is the following:

(15.30)

$$V_0 = \frac{R_0(1+g)(1-T) - TdV_0}{[1 + r(1 - \theta T)]} + \frac{R_0(1+g)^2(1-T) + TdV_0(1-d)}{[1 + r(1 - \theta T)]^2} + \cdots$$

$$= \frac{R_0(1+g)(1-T)}{r(1 - \theta T) - g} + \frac{V_0Td}{r(1 - \theta T) + d}$$

Because the before-tax model is the geometric growth model, we can write:

$$\theta = \frac{R_1 - \left(\dfrac{T_f}{T}\right) f(V_0)}{R_1 + (V_1 - V_0)} = \frac{R_0(1+g) - dV_0}{R_0(1+g) + gV_0}$$

$$= \frac{R_0(1+g) - d + \dfrac{R_0(1+g)}{r-g}}{R_0(1+g) + \dfrac{gR_0(1+g)}{r-g}} = \frac{r - g - d}{r}$$

(15.31)

> So what have we learned? We learned that the effective tax rate for depreciable assets whose value is actually increasing while the investor is able to claim a tax deduction for book value depreciation results in a significant reduction in the investor's effective tax rate.

To illustrate, suppose that d = 5%. Then, using numbers from our previous example, we substitute into equation (15.31) and find:

$$\theta = \frac{r - g - d}{r} = \frac{.08 - .03 - .05}{.08} = 0\%$$

(15.32)

In other words, the tax rate for the investment is effectively zero.

Tax Adjustment Coefficients in Finite Models

So far we have obtained tax adjustment coefficient models for infinite time examples. As a result, the tax adjustment coefficients have been the same for each period. This approach has been convenient for exposition purposes. However, this result is not generally applicable. In practice, the tax adjustment coefficients vary by time period. We demonstrate using a finite time horizon model, a loan model in which the interest paid is tax deductible.

In many applications, the defender is a loan. When a loan is the defender, we immediately want to know if the interest paid is tax deductible. To keep our analysis simple, assume a constant-payment loan made for n periods at an interest rate of i percent. In which case, loan amount L_0 at interest rate i with annuity payments A can be written as:

$$L_0 = \frac{A}{(1+i)} + \frac{A}{(1+i)^2} + \cdots + \frac{A}{(1+i)^n}$$

(15.33)

And the firm's before-tax IRR is i. The loan balance after one period can be written as:

$$L_1 = \frac{A}{(1+i)} + \frac{A}{(1+i)^2} + \cdots + \frac{A}{(1+i)^{n-1}}$$

(15.34)

Furthermore, capital loss for loans can be expressed as:

$$L_1 - L_0 = -\frac{A}{(1+i)^n}$$

(15.35)

The after-tax IRR model can be expressed as:

$$L_0 = \frac{A - AT\left[1 - \dfrac{1}{(1+i)^n}\right]}{[1 + i(1 - \theta T)]} + \frac{A - AT\left[1 - \dfrac{1}{(1+i)^{n-1}}\right]}{[1 + i(1 - \theta T)]^2}$$

$$+ \cdots + \frac{A - AT\left[1 - \dfrac{1}{(1+i)}\right]}{[1 + i(1 - \theta T)]^n}$$

$$= \frac{A(1 - T) + \left[\dfrac{AT}{(1+i)^n}\right]}{[1 + i(1 - \theta T)]} + \frac{A(1 - T) + \left[\dfrac{AT}{(1+i)^{n-1}}\right]}{[1 + i(1 - \theta T)]^2}$$

$$+ \cdots + \frac{A(1 - T) + \left[\dfrac{AT}{(1+i)}\right]}{[1 + i(1 - \theta T)]^n}$$

(15.36)

With equation (15.36) in a familiar form, we can write θ as:

$$\theta = \frac{R_1 - \left(\dfrac{T_f}{T}\right) f(V_0)}{R_1 + (V_1 - V_0)} = \frac{A - \dfrac{A}{(1+i)^n}}{A - \dfrac{A}{(1+i)^n}} = 1$$

(15.37)

In words, the effective after-tax IRR for a loan whose interest is tax-deductible is (1 – T).

Ranking Investments and Taxes

In this section, we acknowledge that the effective tax rates vary by the different types of investments being considered. Furthermore, if the effective tax rate for defenders and challengers differ, then before and after-tax investment rankings may be changed. To make this point, consider the following example. Assume the defender's before-tax IRR is 8%, the income tax rate is 35%, the rate of growth in net cash flow is 3%, and the last year's before-tax net cash flow was $100. The maximum bid price for this investment with geometric growing income is:

$$V_0^b = \frac{R_0(1+g)}{r-g} = \frac{\$100(1.03)}{(.08-.03)} = \$2,060.$$

(15.38)

If the minimum sell price is $3,000, then the NPV for the investment is a negative $940 and the challenger is rejected.

Now suppose we introduce taxes into the model and recalculate the investment's NPV. To simplify we assume an infinite life for the investment and assume $\theta = 1$ for the defender and find:

$$
\begin{aligned}
NPV &= -V_0 + \frac{R_0(1+g)(1-T)}{[1+r(1-T)]} + \frac{R_0(1+g)^2(1-T)}{[1+r(1-T)]^2} \\
&\quad + \frac{R_0(1+g)^3(1-T)}{[1+r(1-T)]^3} + \cdots \\
&= -V_0 + \frac{R_0(1+g)(1-T)}{r(1-T)-g} \\
&= -\$3,000 + \frac{\$100(1.03)(1-.35)}{.08(1-.35)-.03} = \$43.18
\end{aligned}
$$

(15.39)

Now the challenger's NPV is positive. Introducing taxes into the NPV model has reversed the ranking: the challenger is now preferred to the defender. These results should alert financial managers to the importance of after-tax rankings.

Summary and Conclusions

Taxes are important when valuing and ranking investments because what really matters is the amount of your earnings you get to keep after paying taxes. It's not the before-tax IRR that matters but the after-tax IRR that counts because that's the rate you really earned on your defending investment.

In this chapter, we have introduced a method for finding a defender's after-tax IRR. The method required that when a defender's cash flow adjusted for taxes and was discounted by its after-tax IRR its change in NPV was zero. Then we used the equality to find the after-tax discount rate IRR. The implied tax rate in the after-tax IRR was compared to the firm's average marginal income tax-rate.

While the usual practice is to multiply the defender's before-tax IRR by $(1 - T)$ to obtain the defender's after-tax IRR, this chapter demonstrated that this cannot be generally relied on to obtain the defender's properly adjusted after-tax IRR. Indeed, we demonstrated that capital gains that are not taxed can lower the effective tax rate. Capital losses that do not create tax shields can increase the effective tax rate. Property tax paid on land and other real property increases the effective tax rate paid. Allowing investors to write off an investment's depreciation lowers the effective tax rate.

> So what have we learned? We learned that when comparing defenders and challengers, it is important to find the correct after-tax IRR of the defender to discount the challenger's after-tax cash flow. Other things being equal, we prefer challengers whose effective tax rate is less than the effective tax rate of the defender.

Finally, this chapter has employed simplifying assumptions, such as large values for n and average depreciation and growth rates, to find effective after-tax discount rates that have nice, closed-form solutions. Usually, this is not the case. It is often more difficult to find effective after-tax discount rates, and often these are not closed-form solutions.

Questions

1. Describe the appropriate test for determining whether or not taxes have been properly introduced into the defender's IRR.
2. When finding after-tax IRRs for defenders, we solve for θ and claim that θT is the defender's effective tax rate. Interpret the meaning of θ.
3. Under what condition is the defender's effective tax rate equal to its income tax rate T or that $\theta = 1$?
4. Assume that a defending investment's price is V_0, that d is the defender's book value depreciation rate, that R is the constant stream of income earned by the defender, that T is the income tax rate, and that r is the defender's before-tax IRR. Also assume that the defender is allowed to write off book value depreciation even though its income stream is constant. We write such a model as:

(Q15.1)
$$V_0 = \frac{R(1 - T) + TdV_0}{[1 + r(1 - \theta T)]} + \frac{R_0(1 - T) + TdV_0}{[1 + r(1 - \theta T)]^2} + \cdots$$

In this model, the depreciation is constant for $100/d$ periods beyond which the discounted cash flow is small enough to be ignored. The before-tax IRR model can be written as:

$$V_0 = \frac{R}{(1+r)} + \frac{R}{(1+r)^2} + \cdots = \frac{R}{r}$$

(Q15.2)

Solve for θ in the after-tax IRR model by substituting for V_0 the right hand side of the second model R/r. Next, solve for a numerical value for θ assuming that d = 3% and r = 8%.

5. Suppose that you have found the NPV for a challenger. What impact will an increase in the defender's effective tax rate have on the challenger's IRR? Please explain your answers.

6. Calculate the effective tax rate θT for a depreciating challenger where d is the depreciation rate, T is the income tax rate, r is the defender's before-tax IRR, and V_0 is the price of defender. The IRR model is written below. (Hint: find θ by setting the right hand side of the equation below to the equivalent model without taxes (T = 0) and solve for θ.

$$V_0 = \frac{R_0(1-d)(1-T) + TdV_0}{[1+r(1-\theta T)]}$$
$$+ \frac{R_0(1-d)^2(1-T) + TdV_0(1-d)}{[1+r(1-\theta T)]^2} + \cdots$$
$$= \frac{R_0(1-d)(1-T) + TdV_0}{r(1-\theta T) + d} +$$

(Q15.3)

7. Discuss the following. Suppose that cash flow was constant ($R_t = R_0$), yet tax laws allowed the owner of the durable to claim depreciation at rate d. Without solving for θ, can you deduce whether it would be equal to, less than, or greater than one? Defend your answer.

8. Assume you are investing in land and that you borrow money to finance its purchase. Also assume that you pay property taxes on the land. In other words, land is the challenger and the loan is the defender. Which investment has the higher effective tax rate under three scenarios: g = 0, g > 0, and g < 0? What do you need to know about the property tax rate T_p to answer this question?

9. In this chapter, five different investment tax scenarios were described. Please provide an example of each type of investment and how the tax scenario might change its rankings compared to before-tax rankings.

16. "Managing Liquidity and Currency: Assessing Homogeneous Financial Assets"

LINDON ROBISON

Learning goals. 1. Learn how to measure an investment's liquidity. 2. Learn how to compare liquidity
for a firm versus liquidity for an investment. 3. Learn how to rank investments according to their
liquidity using capital gains (losses) measures.

- Learn how to distinguish between a firm's liquidity and an investment's liquidity.

Learning objectives. To achieve your learning goals, you should complete the following objectives:

- Learn how to describe an investment's liquidity at a point in time by using its current-to-total
  returns (CTR) ratio.
- Learn how to describe an investment's liquidity over time by using its inter temporal CTR ratio.
- Learn how to connect CTR ratios to price-to-earnings (PE) ratios.
- Learn how PE ratios can be used to infer the liquidity of an investment.
- Learn how coverage (C) ratios can be used to infer the liquidity of an investment.
- Learn how to evaluate investments whose cash flow are in foreign currencies.

Introduction

An investment may earn two types of returns (losses) for investors: (1) time-dated cash flow called current returns, and (2) capital gains (losses). This chapter demonstrates that capital gains earned on an
investment depend on the investment's pattern of future cash flow.

This chapter also demonstrates that the combination of current returns versus capital gains (losses)
has important liquidity implications for investors, especially when an investment is financed with debt
capital. Debt-financed investments whose earnings are expected to grow over time may experience a
cash shortfall called a financing gap, in which the cash returns are less than the scheduled payments of
principal plus interest. This gap is most likely to occur early in the investment's life and is exacerbated
by inflation. As time passes and the cash returns grow in size, they will eventually exceed the repayment obligation, and the liquidity problem is solved.

The term liquidity is used to describe "near-cash investments" because of the similarity between liq-
uids and liquid investments. A liquid such as water can fill the shape of its container and is easily transferred from one container to another. Similarly, liquid funds easily meet the immediate financial needs
of their owners. Illiquid investments such as land and buildings, like solids, are not easily accessed to
meet financial needs because their ownership and control are not easily transferred.

A firm's liquidity reflects its capacity to generate sufficient cash to meet its financial commitments as they come due. A firm's failure to meet its financial commitments results in bankruptcy, even though the firm might be profitable and have positive equity. Consequently, firms must account for an investment's liquidity in addition to earning positive net present value (NPV).

There are several measures that reflect a firm's or an investment's liquidity. One measure used to reflect the liquidity of the firm is the current ratio, the ratio of current assets divided by current liabilities. Because current assets can be quickly converted to cash, they are an important source of liquidity for the firm.

While the current ratio measures the liquidity of the firm, we want a liquidity measure specific to an investment, and one that describes the liquidity of an investment over time—what we will refer to as a periodic liquidity measure. The liquidity measure that provides investment-specific liquidity information over time is the current-to-total returns (CTR) ratio. The CTR ratio is derived from market equilibrium conditions where NPV is zero and represents the ratio of current (cash) returns to total returns. The price-to-earnings (PE) ratio is a commonly reported ratio reflecting the price of an investment reflected by its current earnings. A liquidity measure related to the CTR ratio is the coverage (C) ratio. A C ratio is the ratio of cash returns to loan payments or other debt obligations in any particular period.

Current-to-Total-Returns (CTR) Ratio

The current-to-total returns (CTR) ratio is a periodic liquidity measure derived from the relationship in a given period between an investment's current (cash) returns, its capital gains (losses), and its total return, or the sum of current returns and capital gains (losses). To derive the CTR measure, we begin with an expression of an investment's total returns:

Total investment returns = current returns + capital gains (losses)

The above relationship is expressed symbolically as follows. Let the investment's total return equal the investment's internal rate of return r times the value of the investment at the beginning of the period V_0 or rV_0. Meanwhile, let R_1 be defined as the asset's net cash, or current returns earned at the end of the first period. In addition, let V_0 and V_1 equal the investment's beginning and end-of-period values respectively, while their difference ($V_1 - V_0$) is equal to the investment's capital gains (losses) in the first period. Summarizing, we write the investment's total returns as:

$$(16.1) \quad rV_0 = R_1 + (V_1 - V_0)$$

Next we solve for the investment's internal rate of return earned in each period, r. We solve for this measure by dividing the investment's total returns by the investment's value at the beginning of the period V_0:

$$r = \frac{R_1}{V_0} + \frac{(V_1 - V_0)}{V_0}$$

(16.2)

A useful measure obtained from equation (16.2) is the ratio of current returns R_1 divided by total returns rV_0. This ratio indicates the percentage of total returns the firm receives as cash. The higher this ratio, the greater the likelihood that the firm has the liquidity required to meet its debt obligations in the current period. Rearranging the previous equation yields the ratio of current to total returns in the first period, equal to CTR_1:

$$CTR_1 = \frac{R_1}{r_1 V_0} = 1 - \frac{\left(\dfrac{V_1 - V_0}{V_0}\right)}{r_1} = 1 - \frac{\eta_1}{r_1}$$

(16.3)

where $\eta_1 = (V_1 - V_0) / V_0$ is the capital gains (loss) rate in period one.

To illustrate the CTR ratio, we now derive the CTR ratio for the geometric series of cash flow. Consider an investment that is expected to generate a perpetual series of cash flow that grow at average geometric rate of g percent per period. If R_0 is the initial net cash flow, and r is the IRR of the investment, then the PV of the growth model can be expressed as:

$$V_0 = \frac{R_0(1+g)}{(1+r)} + \frac{R_0(1+g)^2}{(1+r)^2} + \frac{R_0(1+g)^3}{(1+r)^3} + \cdots$$

(16.4a)

One year later:

$$V_1 = \frac{R_0(1+g)^2}{(1+r)} + \frac{R_0(1+g)^3}{(1+r)^2} + \frac{R_0(1+g)^4}{(1+r)^3} + \cdots = V_0(1+g)$$

(16.4b)

and in general

$$V_t = V_0(1+g)^t$$

(16.4c)

and the capital gains rate for the geometric growth model is found to equal:

$$\eta = \frac{V_t - V_{t-1}}{V_{t-1}} = \frac{V_{t-1}(1+g) - V_{t-1}}{V_0} = g$$

(16.4d)

Using our results from equation (16.3) we can find our CTR ratio as:

$$CTR_1 = \frac{R_1}{r_1 V_0} = 1 - \frac{\eta_1}{r_1} = 1 - \frac{g}{r} = \frac{r-g}{r}$$

(16.5)

To illustrate, if an investment earns cash flow in perpetuity described by R_0, r = 10% and g = 5%, the investment's CTR ratio can be found equal to:

$$CTR_1 = \frac{.1 - .05}{.1} = 50\%$$

(16.6)

It is left as an exercise to demonstrate that if the CTR ratio is constant over time, the CTR ratio is 1. Namely, that:

$$CTR_1 = \frac{r-g}{r} \: for \: t = 1, 2, \cdots, n.$$

(16.7a)

To illustrate equation (16.7a), if in period one, r = 10% and g = 5%, then 50% of the investment's returns will be earned in the form of capital gains. On the other hand, if the geometric mean of changes in future cash flow was negative, ($g < 0$), the current returns to total returns would exceed total returns. If g = −5%, the CTR1 ratio would equal:

$$CTR = \frac{r-g}{r} = \frac{.15}{.1} = 150\%$$

(16.7b)

In words, equation (16.7b) informs us that 150% of the investment's return in period one will be received as current returns in order to compensate for the 50% capital losses experienced by the investment.

So, what have we learned? It means that the investments with increasing cash flow are less liquid than those with decreasing cash flow. A less (more) liquid investment means that a part of its return in each period is earned in capital gains (losses) that are not converted to cash until the investment is liquidated.

Liquidity, Inflation, and Real Interest Rates

Prices reflect the ratio of money exchanged for a unit of a good. For example, assume that the price for gasoline is $3.00 per gallon. If you purchased 10 gallons of gasoline, you would pay $30.00 ($3.00 x 10). Conversely, the ratio of $30.00 expended for gas divided by the gallons of gas purchased is the price of gas: $30.00/10 equal to $3.00.

Now suppose that last year you purchased roughly $50,000 worth of goods. For convenience, let p_j be the price of good j where $j = 1, ..., n$. Furthermore, let q_j represent the quantity of good j purchased. Multiplying the price times the quantity of each good purchased equals your total expenditures of $50,000. To summarize, $\$50,000 = \sum_{j=1}^{n} p_j q_j$ equals the sum of price times quantity of all of the goods you purchased.

In case you had not noticed, prices for goods and services change over time. Consider the price of a dozen large eggs. The price of a dozen of large eggs over the past 38 years is graphed in Figure 16.1 ranging from less than $1 per dozen in 1980 to almost $3 per dozen in 2016.

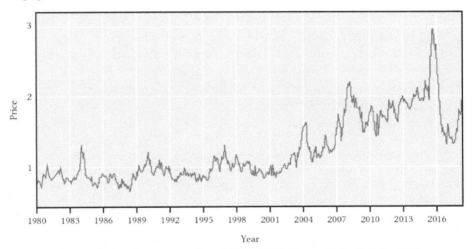

Figure 16.1. *The price of a dozen large eggs over the period 1980 to 2016. (Bureau of Labor Statistics, 2016)*

Prices over time for an individual good can change for several reasons. The demand for eggs can rise—more people wanting to consume more eggs will likely cause egg prices to rise. Or the cost of supplying eggs may change—chicken have become more efficient at producing eggs making them cheaper or chicken feed may become more expensive making eggs more expensive to produce.

The quantity theory of money

There is another reason why prices may change over time—there is more money in circulation. This explanation for why prices rise we call the quantity theory of money (QTM). The quantity theory of money states that there is a direct relationship between the quantity of money in an economy and the level of prices of goods and services sold. What constitutes the money supply is a complicated subject that we can avoid here and still make our point.

Returning to our earlier discussion, let the total of goods and services sold times their prices equal the amount of money M in the economy times its velocity (V) or the number of times the same unit of money is used during a time period. We write this relationship as

$$\sum_{j=1}^{n} p_j q_j = MV$$

(16.8)

According to the QTM, if people purchased the same goods in the same quantity and if V were held constant and M increased by i percent, then the price of each individual good must also increase by i percent.

$$\sum_{j=1}^{n} (1+i)p_j q_j = (1+i)MV$$

(16.9)

Finally, if we measured the prices times the same goods in each year and calculated the ratio of the current year by the previous year we could obtain an estimate of the how prices in general have changed or the rate of inflation. Adding a superscript t to the price variable, we find the inflation rate plus one in year t is equal to:

$$\frac{\sum_{j=1}^{n} p_j^t q_j}{\sum_{j=1}^{n} p_j^{t-1} q_j} = (1+i)$$

(16.10)

An index $(1 + i)$ can be computed for all different bundles of purchased goods. One popular inflation index is called the Consumer Price Index (CPI) that measures the rate of increase in prices holding the bundle of goods constant or at least as far as it is possible. Consider how inflation has affected consumer purchases over time. The vertical axis measures the CPI. The horizontal axis measures time. All indices select one year at their base in which the index is one. In Figure 16.2, the base year is somewhere between 1982-1984.

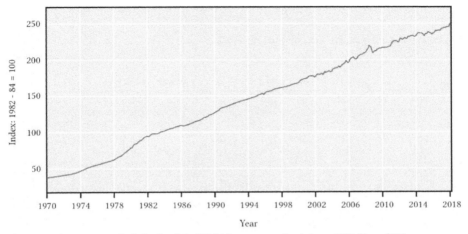

Figure 16.2. The consumer price index for all the U.S. letting average prices between 1982-84 equal 100.

According to Figure 16.2, in 2018 you paid on average two and one-half times as much money to purchase the same good as you did in 1982-1984.

So why is inflation important to our discussion of PV models and profit measures? If your income increases by i percent and the cost of everything you purchase increases by the same percent i, then in real terms what you can actually purchase is the same as before since your income and costs increased by the same rate.

Real interest rates. Let say that your after-tax cash flows increased by rate g% but that g is influenced by the rate of inflation. Then after accounting for inflation, what is left is attributed to other factors besides an increase in the money supply. Let this real growth in after-tax cash flow (ATCF) be g^*. Then we can write:

$$(16.11) \quad (1 + g) = (1 + g^*)(1 + i)$$

Interest rates, discount rates, and inflation. Inflation also influences interest rates paid to borrow money and the discount rate that reflects the opportunity cost for one's resources. To motivate this discussion intuitively, assume you lent a friend $1000 for one year. Also assume that inflation is 5% so that when your friends repays the loan, to make the same purchases at the time the loan was made, they would have to pay back $1,000 * (1.05) = $1,050. But they would have to pay more than 5% for being able to rent your money for a year—let's call this rate the real interest rate and denote it as r^*. To account for both the reduced purchase price of your money because an increase in prices by inflation i and the cost of postponing the use of one's money, the interest rate (and opportunity cost of resources invested in a defender) is r equal to:

(16.12) $(1 + r) = (1 + r^*)(1 + i)$

We graph real interest rates r^* over time in Figure 16.3.

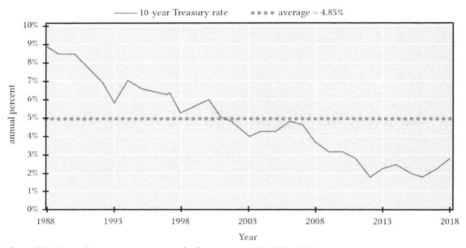

Figure 16.3. *10-year Treasury constant maturity interest rate, U.S., 1988 – 2018*

So, what have we learned? It mean that real interest rates have been falling since 1988 and have recently started to increase. Increasing real interest rates will make long-term investments less liquid because it increases interest rate changes on loans and also increases the rate of growth g that we already demonstrated increases capital gains relative to current earnings.

Liquidity Implications

The mix of capital gains (losses) versus current returns depends directly on the average rate of growth ($g > 0$) or decline ($g < 0$) in future cash flow. As inflation increases the average rate of growth g, then inflation also reduces an investment's liquidity, especially during the investment's initial years.

For geometric decay in earnings ($g < 0$), current returns are more than 100% of total earnings—and current returns have increased in importance relative to capital loss or depreciation. These results clearly show the paradoxical conditions that growth in projected earnings can weaken the liquidity of the investment due to the increasing relative importance of capital gains. In contrast, a decline in projected earnings can strengthen the liquidity due to the increasing relative importance of current returns (See Table 16.1).

Also note in Table 16.1 that increases in the capital gains rate g holding r constant always leads to a reduction in CTR ratio. This is easily explained. Since the total rate of return r is fixed and composed of current rate of returns and capital gains rate of returns, increases in the capital gains rate of return must necessarily decrease the current rate of returns.

Table 16.1. Values of CTR ratios where $CTR_t = (r - g) / r$

g%	r%				
	10	8	6	4	2
-5	150%	163%	183%	225%	350%
-3	130%	138%	150%	175%	250%
0	100%	100%	100%	100%	100%
3	70%	63%	50%	25%	
5	50%	38%	17%		

Price-to-earnings (PE) Ratios

Related to the CTR ratio is the price-to-earnings (PE) ratio equal to:

$$PE = \frac{V_0}{R_1}$$

(16.13)

If we describe the investment using the PV expression in equation (16.4a), then we can write:

$$V_0 = \frac{R_0(1+g)}{(1+r)} + \frac{R_0(1+g)^2}{(1+r)^2} + \frac{R_0(1+g)^3}{(1+r)^3} + \cdots + \frac{R_0(1+g)}{r-g}$$

(16.14)

Next we substitute $R_0(1 + g)$ for R_1, and the right-hand side of equation (16.9) for V_0 into the PE expression in equation (16.8), and obtain:

$$PE = \frac{V_0}{R_1} = \frac{1}{r-g}$$

(16.15)

But from equation (16.7a) we know that $rCTR = (r - g)$, which allows us to connect CTR and PE ratios, namely:

$$PE = \frac{1}{r - g} = \frac{1}{rCTR}$$

(16.16)

In words, what we learn from equation (16.16) is that, in general, higher CTR ratios imply lower PE ratios and lower CTR ratios imply higher PE ratios. These results may at first appear to be somewhat counter intuitive—that, for liquidity purposes, we prefer investments with lower PE. Upon reflection, it makes sense—assets whose returns are mostly capital gains will be earning a lower percentage of current returns compared to their values than assets that earn little or no capital gains.

To make the point that CTR and PE ratios are inversely related, we construct Table 16.2 for PE ratios. Compare the results with those found in Table 16.1 to confirm in your minds the implications of equation (16.16). Note that PE ratios uniformly increase with increases in g and the rate of return earned in the form of capital gains.

Table 16.2. Values of PE ratios where $PE_t = 1/(r - g) = 1 / (rCTR_t)$

g%	r%				
	10	8	6	4	2
−5	6.67%	7.67%	9.11%	11.11%	14.29%
−3	7.69%	9.06%	11.11%	14.29%	20.00%
0	10%	13.50%	16.67%	25.00%	50.00%
3	14.29%	20.00%	33.33%	100.00%	
5	20.00%	33.33%	100.00%		

PE ratios are frequently used to describe the financial condition of an asset. Generally speaking, high PE ratios reflect an expectation of income growth for an asset. Unfortunately, high levels of PE ratios may reflect bubbles or unrealistic expectations for income growth for a particular investment—and high PE ratios are often followed with a market adjustment in which the earnings expectation of an investment are adjusted downward, which reduces the investment's PE ratio. For example, in 1929 for stocks (see Figure 16.4), and 2010 for housing (see Figure 16.5), expected income growth was unrealistic, and in both cases, PE ratios fell when earnings expectations were adjusted downward.

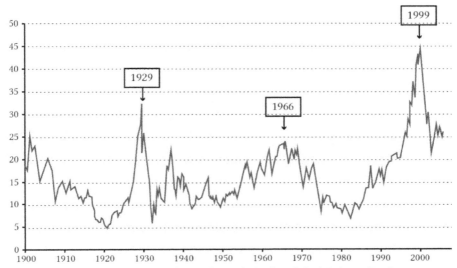

Figure 16.4. Historic PE ratios for stocks described on the Standard and Poor's Stock Exchange. (Earnings are estimated based on a lagged 10-year average.)

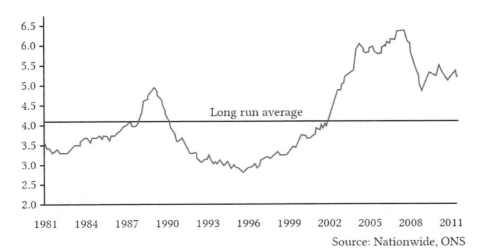

Source: Nationwide, ONS

Figure 16.5. Historic PE ratios for UK housing stock.

Compare the value of the PE ratios in Figures 16.4 and 16.5. PE values for stocks that reflect depreciable assets ($g < 0$) have average values around 20. PE values for housing stock that reflect non-depreciable assets ($g > 0$) have recently averaged around 5. (See Table 16.2.)

Coverage (C) Ratios

Investments can be evaluated according to both profitability and periodic liquidity criteria. Profitability analysis focuses on whether the acceptance of an investment will increase the investor's present wealth. Periodic liquidity measure analysis considers whether an investment will generate cash flow consistent with the terms of financial capital, especially debt capital, that are used to finance the investment. Is an investment capable of generating sufficient net cash flow in each period to satisfy the requirements for repayment of the loan's principal plus interest? If not, then the investment is illiquid because liquid funds drawn from other sources are required to meet cash flow requirements associated with the investment. Thus, a simple test of investment liquidity is to compare the net cash flow generated by the investment in a given period with the debt-servicing requirement.

The ratio of net cash flow in a period t, R_t, divided by the loan plus principal payment in the same period, A_t, is called the coverage ratio, C_t:

$$C_t = \frac{R_t}{A_t}$$
(16.17)

If the coverage ratio is equal to or exceeds 1.0, the investment is liquid in that period. If coverage is less than one, the investment is illiquid in that period. In most cases, the loan payment that includes principal plus interest is a constant "A," that depends on the price of the purchased asset, V_0; the financed proportion of the purchase price γ; the term of the loan n; and the interest rate charged on the loan r^f. Using our previous notation, we can express the relationship between the amount financed, the fixed loan payment, the interest rate on the loan, and the term of the loan as:

$$\gamma V_0 = AUS_0(r^f, n)$$
(16.18)

We solve equation (16.18) for A and substitute the result for A_t in equation (16.19). In the same equation, we also substitute $R_0(1 + g)^t$ for R_t, and obtain:

$$C_t = \frac{R_0(1+g)^t}{\gamma V_0} US_0(r^f, n)$$
(16.19)

Replacing V_0 with $[R_0 (1 + g)]/(r - g)$, we can rewrite equation (16.19) as:

$$C_t = \frac{(r-g)(1+g)^{t-1}}{\gamma} US_0(r^f, n)$$

(16.20)

We illustrate equation (16.20) as follows. Assume $r = 8\%$, $g = 2\%$, $n = 20$, and $r^f = 7\%$. Also assume the investment is 80% financed. Using an Excel spreadsheet, we find that $US_0(7\%, 20) = 10.59$.

Table 16.3. Calculating $US_0(r^f=7\%, n=20)$
Open Table 16.3 in Microsoft Excel

B4			f_x =PV(B1,B2,B3,,0)
	A	B	C
1	rate	7%	
2	nper	20	
3	pmt	-1	
4	NPV	$10.59	=PV(rate,nper,pmt,,0)

Then we find the coverage value for the first year of the investment to equal:

$$C_1 = \frac{(.08 - .02)(1.02)^0 10.59}{.8} = .79$$

(16.21a)

Interpreted, in year one, the investment described above will only pay for 79 percent of the loan payment due. However, 10 years later and half way into the term of the loan, the coverage ratio has increased to:

$$C_{10} = \frac{(.08 - .02)(1.02)^9 10.59)}{.8} = .95$$

(16.21b)

Finally, in the last year of the loan, the coverage ratio is:

$$C_{20} = \frac{(.08 - .02)(1.02)^{19} 10.59)}{.8} = 1.16$$

(16.21c)

In other words, in year 20, the last year of the loan, the investment cash flow not only repays the loan but 16 percent more than the required loan payment. Of course, after the loan is repaid, the periodic cash flow is available to the firm to meet its cash flow requirements.

One word about the term of the investment, it is assumed to be infinite. However, for any one investor, the term may be finite, but since the terminal value for any one owner is simply the present value of the continued cash flow, we can express the investment as having an infinite life. Therefore, we are justified in ignoring the term of the infinite-life investment.

When is the coverage equal to 100 percent? There is another way to approach the issue of coverage. It is to ask in what year is the coverage equal to 1? To answer this question for the geometric growth model with an infinite life and using the already established notation, we set:

(16.22) $$A = R_0(1 + g)^t$$

and solving for t we find:

(16.23a) $$t = \frac{\ln A}{\ln R_0 + \ln(1 + g)}$$

And after making substitutions for A and R_0 and simplifying, we can write:

(16.23b) $$t = \frac{\ln \gamma - \ln(r - g) - \ln US_0(r^f, n)}{\ln(1 + g)}$$

We illustrate equation using numbers from the previous example where: $\gamma = .8$, $r = .08$, $g = .02$, $r^r = .07$, and $n = 20$. We find:

(16.24) $$t = \frac{-.22 + 2.81 - 2.36}{.02} = 11.50$$

In words, what we have found that the 12th payment will be the first period that more than pays for its financing.

So, what have we learned? As the previous example demonstrates, it means that for investments with increasing cash flow, its liquidity increases over time.

Exchange Rates and PV Models

In today's globalized economy, commodity exchanges are likely to occur between countries and involve exchanging dollars for the currency of another country such as Euros, pounds peso, yen, and yuan to name a few. And if we are engaged in some form of international business or travel, we will likely be required to exchange dollars for the currency of the country in which we are doing business or which we are visiting. What follows is intended to describe how to convert measures of foreign currency into our own. We begin with some definitions.

Exchange rate. The exchange rate is the rate at which one currency trades against another currency in the foreign exchange market. To be more precise, an exchange rate is a ratio of the prices of two currencies: the price of the exchange currency being acquired divided by the base currency being sacrificed. During the summer of 2020, the exchange rate for dollars and euros was .89 euros per 1 dollar and, alternatively, 1.12 dollars per 1 euro. Table 16.4 provides a table of several exchange rates in which the dollar is the base currency.

Table 16.4. US Dollar Exchange Rates

US Dollar	1.00 USD
Euro	0.890730
British Pound	0.805050
Indian Rupee	75.521451
Australian Dollar	1.444682
Canadian Dollar	1.357791
Singapore Dollar	1.394211
Swiss Franc	0.948127
Malaysian Ringgit	4.286344
Japanese Yen	107.568396
Chinese Yuan Renminbi	7.067112

Foreign exchange markets. A foreign exchange market is a market in which one currency trades against another. Currencies are continuously traded and currency exchange rates are continuously changing in the foreign exchange market as currency dealers adjust to changing demand and supply for a country's currency. For example, consider the exchange rate between the English pound and the U.S. dollar. Note the drop in the exchange rate (how many dollars an English pound could purchase around the time England's economy experienced difficult times).

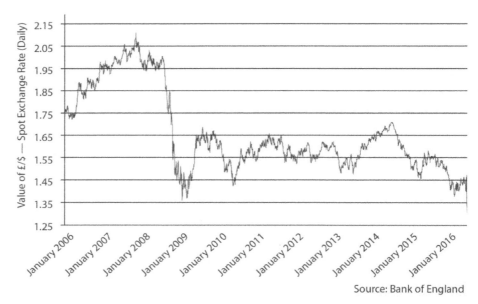

Source: Bank of England

Figure 16.6. Exchange Rate: Pound Sterling to US Dollar

Floating versus fixed exchange rates. The exchange rate influences a country's economy. A high exchange rate makes it more economical for people in the base country to make purchases from or visit the exchange country. A low exchange rate means that it is more expensive for people in the base country to make purchases from or visit the exchange country. As a result, countries often take actions to influence the exchange rate through their monetary policies.

Depending on how countries manage their exchange rates, we describe them as floating or fixed. A floating exchange rate is determined by the supply and demand for currencies in the global currency markets. Therefore, if the demand for the currency is high, its exchange rate will increase. In some extreme cases, some governments may seek to keep the value of their currency fixed at a certain rate compared to other currencies.

What forces influence exchange rates? As Figure 16.6 demonstrates, exchange rates are continually changing. There are several theories that explain the price level of goods and services in a economy and in turn influence their exchange rates with other countries. One such theory already referred to in this chapter is the quantity theory of money. This theory assumes that the quantity of money in an economy is an important determinant on the country's economic activity and that a change in a country's money supply will either increase prices or the supply of its goods and services or both. The quantity theory of money is only one of many theories attempting to explain prices in an economy. We invite students to explore others.

To review the quantity theory of money and apply it to exchange rates, suppose that an economy produces a basket of goods and services G during a period. Moreover, assume that during the period, the money supply is M and used in exchanges for goods G on average V times. The theory adopts the reasonable hypothesis that goods time their prices must equal the money time the number of times it is used in an exchange or PG = MV or that the price of the currency is:

$$P = \frac{MV}{G}$$
(16.25)

Think of the price of money P as the purchasing power of a unit of the country's currency. When P goes down, it requires less of the country's currency to buy the same quantity of the country's goods and services. Then if the country become more productive and G increases, holding everything else constant, people in the country can buy the same amount of goods and services at a lower price P. If the amount of money M in the economy increases, then the currency required to buy the same amount of goods and services increases. (We'll not worry about velocity for now.)

Suppose we have two countries A and B and that people in those countries exchange currency for the purpose of international purchases or to pay expenses when visiting the country or for speculation assuming that one can guess relative changes in the price of each country's currency. Then subscripting the variables in equation (16.25), we can write the exchange rate between the two countries as:

$$\frac{P_A}{P_B} = \frac{G_B}{G_A}\frac{M_A}{M_B}\frac{V_A}{V_B}$$
(16.26)

To apply the quantity theory of money, think of country B as the U.S. and country A as Canada. The exchange rate describes how many Canadian dollars one U.S. dollar can purchase. Assume to begin, that the exchange rate is one Canadian dollar for one U.S. dollar. Then assume that production in the U.S. increases GB. Then holding all other things constant, the exchange rate must increase. One U.S. dollar can now buy more Canadian dollars because those wanting to buy U.S. dollars realize that they can now purchase more than before and are willing to pay more for a U.S. dollar. For an exercise, describe the consequences of an increase in the U.S. money supply.

Now imagine that as a U.S. businessperson, you invest V_0^B in a Canadian business and expect to receive Canadian cash flow for the next n periods of $R_1^A, \cdots, R_n^A$. Assuming your defender's discount rate is r percent and the predicted exchange rate for Canadian and U.S. dollars is $X_1^{A/B}, \cdots, X_n^{A/B}$.

$$NPV = -V_0^B + \frac{R_1^A X_1^{A/B}}{(1+r)} + \cdots + \frac{R_n^A X_n^{A/B}}{(1+r)^n}$$
(16.27)

An example:

Suppose that Lon decides to franchise his business and open Lon's Yard Care Business in Liverpool, England. He wonders what his NPV would equal if an investment in US dollars of $1000 earns three years of £300 British pounds and the exchange rate of pounds for dollars because of the impact of BREXIT is expected to equal: 1.5, 1.4 and 1.3. Also assume that the defender's IRR is 10%.

$$NPV = -\$1,000 + \frac{(300)(1.5)}{1.1} + \frac{(300)(1.4)}{1.1^2} + \frac{(300)(1.3)}{1.1^3} = \$49.21$$
(16.28)

After adjusting for changing exchange rates between the British pound and the U.S. dollar, Lon finds that a three-year investment in a Liverpool franchise would earn $49.21 NPV valued in U.S. dollars.

> So, what have we learned? Suppose that I can exchange 1 dollar for .8 British pound. Then the exchange rate for pounds/dollars is .8. On the other hand if I can exchange 1 British pound for 1.25 dollars, then the exchange rate for dollars/pounds is 1.25. If I am receiving a payment in pounds and I want to know the dollars equivalent of what I am receiving, I multiply the pounds by the dollars/pound exchange rate. So if I were receiving a payment of 300 British pounds, I would multiply by the dollar/pounds exchange rate of 1.25 and compute that I would be receiving the equivalent of $375.

Summary and Conclusions

An investment may earn two types of returns: time dated cash flow and capital gains (losses). Moreover, these returns can be earned over the lifetime of the investment. The relative importance of the two forms of returns, cash flow versus capital gains (losses), will determine the inter temporal liquidity of the asset. The greater the portion of the return is earned as cash, the more liquid will be the investment.

This chapter demonstrated whether an investment earns capital gains (losses) is determined in PV models by its pattern of expected future cash flow. Expected increases (decreases) in the number, frequency, or amount of the expected future cash flow will produce capital gains (losses). Inflation causes long-term investments to become less liquid because they increase the rate of growth in the investment's cash flow.

Investments that earn capital gains are called appreciating investments. Investments that experience capital losses or depreciation are referred to as depreciating investments.

Perhaps paradoxically, investments that earn capital gains are less liquid than investments that experience capital losses. Assuming investments earn similar total rates of return, the greater the cash returns are compared to total returns, the greater are the liquid funds available to meet liquidity needs including repayment of funds and interest required to maintain control of the asset.

In this chapter we developed current-to-total returns (CTR) measures to indicate an investment's liquidity over time. Furthermore, CTR measures were shown to be related to price-to-earnings (PE) ratios which also depended on an investment's liquidity. Finally, one feature of an investment, is its coverage, its ability in any one period to repay principal and interest payments due in any one period. If funds borrowed to purchase an appreciating investment are repaid with a constant loan payment, then initially, it is likely that cash flow generated by the investment will not cover the interest and principal payments. This pattern is very likely during periods of inflation. Coverage ratios will also indicate the liquidity of investments over their productive lives.

This chapter acknowledged that we do business in an increasingly globalized economy. As a result, many investments involve exchanges of foreign currencies. This chapter explored exchange rates and how to perform PV analysis when more than one currency is involved.

In summary, the periodic liquidity of an investment is an important characteristic that should influence the capital decisions of financial managers along with the impact of an investment on the firm's solvency, profitability, efficiency, and leverage.

Questions

1. Please describe three possible appreciating and three depreciating investments that are available for most farm financial managers.
2. Describe the connections between capital gains (losses) with an investment's periodic liquidity.
3. Describe the connection between the inflation rate i and an investment's CTR ratio.
4. How is an investment's periodic liquidity related to its CTR (current-to-total returns) ratio and its C (coverage) ratio? How are the two periodic liquidly measures related to each other?
5. Compare the firms current (CT) ratio and its debt-to-service (DS) ratio with an investment's CTR ratio and C ratio. In what ways are they similar? How do they differ?
6. Consider the CTR ratio described in equation (16.3). Find the CTR ratio for the investment whose anticipated cash flow is a constant R in perpetuity described below:

$$(Q16.1) \quad V_0 = \frac{R}{(1+r)} + \frac{R}{(1+r)^2} + \frac{R}{(1+r)^3} + \cdots$$

(Hint: Observe the CTR ratio described in equation (16.3). Then derive capital gains (losses) measures for the PV model described in this question.)

7. Find the CTR ratio for an investment whose defender's IRR is 8% and its anticipated growth rate is 2%. Then find the PE ratio for the same investment.

8. Assume that PE ratios can be approximated using equation (16.10). What would account for the large swings in PE ratios described in housing stock described in Figure 16.2—changes in expected r or g? Or due to some other influence on the value of housing stock?

9. Find the coverage (C) ratio for year 5 for the investment described in the text where: $\gamma = .7$, $r = .08$, $g = .02$, $r^r = .07$, and $n = 20$. Call the result, the result for the base model.

    a. Recalculate the base model C ratio where $n = 20$ is changed to $n = 15$. Describe how reducing n changed the coverage compared to the base model. Then provide an explanation for the change in coverage.

    b. Recalculate the base model C ratio where $g = .02$ is changed to $g = -.02$. Describe how reducing g changed the coverage compared to the base model. Then provide an explanation for the change in coverage.

    c. Recalculate the base model C ratio when $\gamma = .8$ is changed to $\gamma = .6$. Describe how increasing γ changed the coverage compared to the base model. Then provide an explanation for the change in coverage.

10. In this chapter we derived equation (16.18) which solved for the time period in which the coverage was 100%. Find the time period in which coverage is 100% when $\gamma = .7$, $r = .08$, $g = .02$, $r^f = .06$, and $n = 20$. Call the result, the base model result. Then use equation (16.18) to find how t associated with 100 percent coverage changes for the following cases:

    a. Recalculate the base model and find a new t value associated with 100% coverage where $n = 20$ is changed to $n = 15$. Describe how reducing n changed t and then provide an explanation for the change in t.

    b. Recalculate the base model and find a new t value associated with 100% coverage where $r^f = .06$ is changed to $r^f = .08$. Describe how increasing the interest rate r^f changed t associated with 100% coverage. Then provide an explanation for the change in t.

    c. Recalculate the base model and find a new t value associated with 100% coverage where $r = .08$ is changed to $r = .06$. Describe how decreasing the discount rate r changed t associated with 100% coverage. Then provide an explanation for the change in t.

11. Suppose the firm you managed was facing financial stress due to falling prices. Moreover, the stress is reflected in low liquidity and solvency measures for the firm. It appears that there is no way the firm can survive its current crises without liquidating not only short-term assets, but also long-term investments. Based on what you have learned about investment liquidity, propose a plan for the firm to meet it liquidity crisis.

PART V: PRESENT VALUE MODEL APPLICATIONS

17. "Analyzing Loan Viability: Loan Analysis for Sound Decision-Making"

LINDON ROBISON

Learning goals. After completing this chapter, you should be able to: (1) understand the different ways interest can be calculated on a loan; (2) recognize the different kinds of interest rates that are used to calculate interest costs on loans; (3) compute comparable effective interest rates; (4) use Excel worksheets to calculate the differences between an investment's rate, the utility of an interest rate or the annual schedule for a particular loan (APR), and (5) find the rate of an effective concessionary interest rate loans..

- Learn how to use the loan equality equation to find a loan's effective interest rate, its constant

Learning objectives. To achieve your learning goals, you should complete the following objectives:
payment, its term, and its original loan amount."

- Learn how to find the elasticity relationship between interest rates, loan payments, and the term of the constant payment loan.
- Learn how to create an amortization table for constant payment loans.
- Learn how to find break-even points when refinancing loans.
- Learn how to find the effective rate for several disguised interest rate loans including discount loans and points added loans.

Introduction

1

Loan formulas and PV models have many similarities. Interest rates on loans are like opportunity costs, the loan amount is like an investment, and loan payments are like an investment's cash flow. These and other similarities between PV models and loan formulas allow us to use PV tools to analyze different types of loans and interest rates. The next section focuses on alternative interest rate definitions. This chapter will also identify the relationship between the term of a loan and the size of the loan payment. Finally, this chapter finds break-even points when refinancing loans and effective interest rates for a variety of disguised interest rate loans.

1. Some of the material in this chapter was adapted from Robison, L.J. and P.J. Barry (1996); Present Value Models and Investment Analysis. "Chapter 12: Loan Analysis". MSU Press, East Lansing, Michigan.

Comparing the Actuarial Rate, Annual Percentage Rate (APR), and Effective Interest Rate

Loans charge interest rates of which there are at least three closely related kinds. These rates and their commonly used synonyms are listed below. The interest rate name used in this chapter is italicized. They are:

(1) *actuarial rate*, compound rate, true rate, or periodic rate (r^f);

(2) *Annual Percentage Rate (APR)*, annual rate, or nominal rate (r/m); and

(3) *effective interest rate* or effective annual rate (r^e).

Actuarial Rate. In financial transactions, interest may be computed and charged more than once a year. For example, interest on savings deposits is usually calculated on a daily basis while many corporate bonds pay interest on a semiannual basis. The interest rate used in computations for periods of less than one year is called an actuarial interest rate. The actuarial rate is defined as the interest rate per compounding period or the interest rate per period of conversions. It is the actuarial rate used to charge interest on the principal sum during each successive conversion period. For example, consider a 1% actuarial rate charged monthly on $1,000. In this case, in the first month of the loan, 1% of $1,000 or $10 of interest is charged. In the second month, interest is charged on $1,010 equal to $10.10, etc.

Annual Percentage Rate (APR). Let r^f represent the APR. Let m stand for the number of times during the year the interest is calculated or charged. Thus, m equals the number of compounding periods per year. The ratio of r^f/m is the actuarial rate, the compound rate, the true rate, or the periodic rate.

We find the APR from actuarial rates by expressing the actuarial rate on an annual basis. To convert the actuarial rate to an APR, we multiply the actuarial rate by m. In the previous example, we multiply the actuarial rate of 1% per month by 12 to yield an APR of 12%. When the compound period or conversion period is one year in length, then the actuarial rate and the APR are equal.

Consider two savings institutions, both offering the same APR. The only difference is that institution A offers monthly compounding of interest, while institution B offers annual compounding. Which one should the saver prefer? Obviously, monthly compounding is preferred because the saver earns interest on the interest earned during the same year. With institution B, interest is earned during the year only on the principal saved and on interest earned in previous years.

Effective interest rates. Effective interest rates, designated r^e, are the actual interest charged measured on an annual basis. When APRs have different numbers of compound periods per year, the different actuarial rates should be converted to their effective interest rates for comparison. The effective rate is obtained by compounding the actuarial rate for a period of one year. As the number of compounding periods per year increases, the difference between the APR and the effective rate increases.

Relationship between interest rates. The relationships between an actuarial rate, an APR, and an effective rate can be easily summarized. Let m be the number of compounding periods per year, let r^f be the APR, let r^f/m be the actuarial rate, and let re be the effective rate. The relationship between the effective rate r^e, the APR rate r^f, and the actuarial rate r^f/m can be expressed as:

$$r^e = \left[\left(1 + \frac{r^f}{m}\right)^m - 1 \right]$$

(17.1)

Note that when $m = 1$, the effective interest rate, the APR rate, and the actuarial rate are equal. However, when m is not 1, the rates are no longer equal. For example, suppose we wish to find the re assuming r^f were compounded quarterly. To solve this problem let $m = 4$, and $r^f = 12$. Substituting .12 for r^f and 4 for m in equation (17.1), we obtain the results described in Table 17.1 using Microsoft Excel. In cell B3 we enter the function $f_x = ((1 + (B1 / B2))\wedge B2) - 1$ which returns 12.55%.

Table 17.1. Finding an effective interest rate compounded quarterly.
Open Table 17.1 in Microsoft Excel.

B3			f_x	=(1+B1/B2)^B2 -1
	A		B	C
1	APR		0.12	
2	m		4	
3	effective rate		12.55%	=(1 + APR/m)^m − 1

If m is increased to 12, or monthly compounding periods, the effective rate is found as before. Let $m = 12$, and $r^f = 12$ in equation (17.1). Then

$$\left[\left(1 + \frac{.12}{12}\right)^{12} - 1 \right]$$

(17.2)

To solve this equation in Excel, we change cell B2 to 12 and find the effective interest rate to equal 12.68% as shown in Table 17.2.

Table 17.2. Finding an effective interest rate compounded monthly.
Open Table 17.2 in Microsoft Excel.

B3			f_x	=(1+B2/B3)^B3 -1
	A		B	C
1	APR		0.12	
2	m		12	
3	effective rate		12.68%	=(1 + APR/m)^m − 1

A special compounding formula is obtained by allowing the number of periods compounded to be very large. This idea is expressed as:

$$\lim_{m \to \infty} \left(1 + \frac{r^f}{m}\right)^m$$

(17.3)

which means that as m approaches infinity the effective rate re equals:

$$r^e = \lim_{m \to \infty} \left(1 + \frac{r^f}{m}\right)^m - 1 = e^{r^f} - 1$$

(17.4)

To solve this problem using Excel, we use the EXP function. In Excel, Euler's number "e" is found as the function EXP(1) and 12% compounded continuously can be calculated as f_x = EXP(.12) − 1 = 12.75. Using the previous cell designation, to find the value of continuously compounding of 12% we would enter the formula in B3 as: f_x = EXP(B1) − 1 = 12.75.

Table 17.3. Finding an effective interest rate compounded continuously.
Open Table 17.3 in Microsoft Excel

B3			f_x =EXP(B1) − 1	
	A	B		C
1	APR	0.12		
2	m	Infinite		
3	effective rate	12.75%		=EXP(APR) − 1

Constant Payment Loans

Having defined interest rates in financial models, we now use PV models to analyze the most common type of loan, the constant payment loan. Constant payment loans are repaid with a series of equal payments A at equal time intervals. These payments may occur m times during a year over n years, yielding a total of mn payments.

The fundamental equality is that the sum of the loan payments discounted at the actuarial interest rate must equal the amount loaned. The relationship between loan amount, L_0, received in time-period zero, with payment A, made for mn periods, at actuarial interest rate (r^f/m) beginning in period one, is:

$$L_0 = \frac{A}{1 + \dfrac{r^f}{m}} + \frac{A}{\left(1 + \dfrac{r^f}{m}\right)^2} + \cdots + \frac{A}{\left(1 + \dfrac{r^f}{m}\right)^{mn}}$$

(17.5)

In this formula, the actuarial rate (r^f/m) is the IRR for the PV model, and since loan payments are constant, it is unique.

Fortunately, the calculations described in equation (17.5) can be easily performed using Excel. We calculate L_0 in the following example.

Example 17.1. Loan amount supported by a constant payment loan. Suppose a borrower can make constant payments of $150 per month for 48 months (four years). The borrower wants to know what size loan can be repaid if the APR interest rate is 5% and the actuarial rate is $.05/12 = .42\%$. Using equation (17.5) we can solve for the loan amount supported by the constant loan payment of $150 using the Excel formula in Table 17.4 below:

Table 17.4. Finding the Loan Amount in a Constant Payment Loan
Open Table 17.4 in Microsoft Excel

B5		f_x	=PV(B1/B2,B2*B3,B4,,0)
	A	B	C
1	rate	.05	
2	m	12	
3	n	4	
4	pmt	−150	
5	PV	$6,513.44	=PV(rate/m,mn,pmt,,0)

The answer displayed is: $6,513.44. In other words, 48 monthly payments of $150 on a loan charging a 5% APR interest rate and a monthly actuarial interest rate of .42% will repay a loan in the amount of $6,513.44.

Fortunately, Excel can also solve for the constant payment if the loan amount, term, and interest rate are known. A constant payment loan problem is described in Example 17.2.

Example 17.2. Constant Payment Loan Annuities. Suppose $5,000 is borrowed from a lending institution for five years at an APR of 12% or a monthly actuarial rate of 1%. The loan is to be repaid with 60 equal monthly installments. What is the payment or annuity necessary to retire the loan?

We solve for the loan payment using Excel's PMT function in Table 17.5. The answer displayed is: −$111.22 which means that 60 payments of $111.22 on a loan charging 12% APR interest and a monthly actuarial interest rate of 1% will repay a loan in the amount of $5,000.

Table 17.5. Finding the Constant Loan Payment
Open Table 17.5 in Microsoft Excel

B4			f_x	=PV(B1/B2,B2*B3,B5,,0)
	A	B		C
1	rate	0.12		
2	m	12		
3	n	5		
4	pmt	($111.22)		=PMT(rate/m,mn,PV,,0)
5	PV	$5,000.00		

Finally, consider a loan problem where the unknown variable is the term of the loan. We introduce such a problem in Example 17.3 and the Excel solution in Table 17.6.

Example 17.3. Loan term required to retire a constant payment loan. Suppose a borrower can make constant payments of $150 per month. The borrower wants to know how many monthly payments will be required to retire a loan of $8,000 if the APR interest rate is 6% and the monthly actuarial rate is .5%.

We solve the equation using Excel's NPER function shown in Table 17.6. The answer displayed is 62.19 which means that 62 regular payments and one partial payment will be required to retire a loan of $8,000 if the APR interest rate charged on the loan is 6%.

Table 17.6. Finding the Number of Payments required to Retire a Loan
Open Table 17.6 in Microsoft Excel

B6			f_x	=NPER(B1/B2,B4,B5,,0)
	A	B		C
1	rate	0.06		
2	m	12		
3	n			
4	pmt	-150		
5	PV	$8,000.00		
6	nper	62.18593		=NPER(rate/m,pmt,PV,,0)

Comparing Interest Paid, Loan Term, and Payment Amounts for Constant Payment Loans

An important relationship exists between the loan's term and total interest paid. To illustrate, consider a $30,000 loan at 15% APR to be repaid in monthly payments over 30 years. The monthly payment for this loan is $379.33. Total interest TI paid on a constant payment loan is found by multiplying the constant loan payment A times the term of the loan mn, minus the amount of the loan L_0:

$$(17.6) \quad TI = (A)(mn) - L_0 = (\$379.33)(360) - \$30,000 = \$106,560$$

In this case, the total interest paid is $106,560.

Increasing the payment amount by 10% to $417.27 reduces the term of the loan by 48% to just over 15.36 years (verify the results above using Excel). Meanwhile, total interest paid is reduced by 56% to $46,961.

The term reduction in response to an increased loan payment is not always so significant. For example, if the above loan had an 8% APR, the monthly payment would equal $220.13 instead of $379.22. Increasing the payment by 10% would decrease the term of the loan by only 27% from 30 years to 21.93 years, and the total interest paid would be decreased by 32% from $49,247 to $33,722.

It would be useful to know how changing the term of the loan affects payment size and total interest paid. It can be shown that as mn becomes large, the payment A approaches the interest cost per period, i.e., the smallest payment possible equals the interest charged on the outstanding loan balance. If the borrower wished to minimize his or her payment, the appropriate term is the one that permits the borrower to repay only interest. The shortest repayment period, on the other hand, is one. Obviously, there is a trade-off between the size of the loan payment and the length of the loan.

The point elasticity of term, measured in years n with respect to the payment A, measures the percentage change in the term n in response to a 1% change in the loan payment. The term elasticity, $E_{(n,A)}$, has been calculated as:

$$(17.7) \quad E_{n,A} = \frac{1 - e^{rm}}{rn} < 0$$

For example, a 30-year loan and an APR of 15% would have an elasticity of term equal to:

$$(17.8) \quad E_{n,A} = \frac{1 - e^{(.15)(30)}}{(.15)(30)} = -19.78\% < 0$$

In other words, increasing the payment by 1% would decrease the term by approximately 19.78%. In contrast, the arc elasticity, rather than the point elasticity, compares the percentage change in the loan term to a 10% increase in the loan payment and finds the percentage change in the term to equal 48%, or an arc elasticity of term equal to 4.8%. Note that a point elasticity of 19.78% versus an arc elasticity of 48% is the result of comparing large changes in loan payments of 10% versus comparing tiny changes in loan payments (e.g. .00001%). See Table 17.7 of point elasticities below.

Table 17.7. Point elasticity measures for loans of alternative terms and interest rates.

$n\ /\ r\ \%$	1%	5%	7.5%	10%	15%	20%
1	1.01	1.03	1.04	1.05	1.08	1.11
5	1.08	1.14	1.21	1.30	1.49	1.72
10	1.17	1.30	1.49	1.72	2.32	3.19
15	1.26	1.49	1.85	2.32	3.77	6.36
20	1.37	1.72	2.32	3.19	6.36	13.40
25	1.49	1.99	2.94	4.47	11.07	29.48
30	1.49	2.32	3.77	6.36	19.78	67.07
60	2.99	6.36	19.78	67.07	900.23	13,563.00

Example 17.4. Term and Loan Payment Trade-Offs. Lucy Landlord is financing the renovation of a property. She needs a loan for $28,000. Her lender offers her a loan for 20 years at the current interest rate of 15%. She calculates her annual payment to be $4,473.32. If she increases her payment by 1% to $4,518.05, her term is reduced to 19 years, or a reduction of 5%. This percentage reduction is nearly equal to the tabled value of 6.36 in the Table 17.1, found at the intersection of the row labeled 20 and the column labeled 0.15. Large percentage increases in A, such as 10%, may not be accurately reflected in the table of point elasticities. This is because the percentage changes in n with respect to A are large compared to the very small changes in n with respect to A used to calculate the table.

Creating an Amortization Table for Constant Payment Loans

The word "amortize" originally meant "to kill." Thus when we amortize a loan, we kill or extinguish it by making regular payments—killing the loan if you will. One feature of the constant payment loan is that, while the loan payment is constant, the amount of the payment devoted to paying off the loan—the principal portion of the payment—and the amount of the payment devoted to paying the interest on the loan are constantly changing. As the loan principal is reduced or killed off, the amount of the payment devoted to interest charges is reduced and the amount of the payment devoted to reducing the loan is increased. Lending institutions, when asked, will provide amortization tables that detail the amount of interest and principal paid on each payment during the life of the loan. Fortunately, Excel provides us the tools needed to create our own amortization tables.

Finding principal portion of the tth loan payment using Excel. The Excel PPMT function can be used to find the principal portion of the tth loan payment. The function is expressed as:

$$(17.9) \quad PPMT(rate, per, nper, PV, , 0)$$

To illustrate the PPMT function, consider at $25,000 loan to be repaid in monthly installments for four years. The APR for the loan is 5%. We want to know what portion of the 5th payment (period) will be applied to the loan's principal. The Excel solution is represented in Table 17.8.

Table 17.8. Finding the Loan Principal Paid on the tth Payment
Open Table 17.8 in Microsoft Excel

B6			f_x =PPMT(B1/B2,B4,B2*B3,B5,,0)
	A	B	C
1	rate	0.05	
2	m	12	
3	n	4	
4	period	5	
5	PV	$25,000	
6	Principal paid	($479.47)	=PPMT(rate/m,period,m*n,PV,,0)

It turns out that $479.47 of the 5th payment is applied to the outstanding loan principal. In addition, students may verify that the principal portion of the 25th payment is $521.05. This is because the outstanding principal on which interest is charged decreases over the life of the loan. As interest decreases, more of the loan payment can be applied to the outstanding loan principal.

Finding interest payment IP(t) on the tth loan payment using Excel. The Excel IPMT function can be used to find the interest portion of a loan payment in the tth period and is expressed as:

(17.10) $$IPMT(rate, per, nper, PV,, 0)$$

To illustrate the IPMT function, we return to the earlier example: a loan amount of $25,000, a term of 48 monthly payments, at 5% APR, and a desire to find the interest paid on the 5th loan payment. We illustrate the Excel solution for finding interest paid on the tth period. The solution is entered in cell B8 as $54.68. Table 17.9 describes the solution in more detail.

Table 17.9. Finding the Loan Interest Paid on the tth Payment
Open Table 17.9 in Microsoft Excel.

B6			f_x =IPMT(B1/B2,B4,B2*B3,B5,,0)
	A	B	C
1	rate	0.05	
2	m	12	
3	n	4	
4	period	5	
5	PV	$25,000	
6	Interest paid	($96.26)	=IPMT(rate/m,period,m*n,PV,,0)

Together, the interest payment of $96.26 and the principal payment of $479.47 equals the constant loan payment of $575.73.

PVs of Special Loans

Loans and credit (one's borrowing capacity) make possible a modern economy and successful firms. Sometimes sellers offer special loan arrangements to encourage the potential buyers to purchase their products. These may include concessionary interest rate loans, skip payment loans, skip principal payment loans, variable interest rate loans, and balloon payment loans. Other times firms may want to expand their investment base and need to refinance their loans, or decreases in interest rates may provide them an incentive to refinance. Fortunately, all of these special loans can be analyzed using PV models developed earlier. We consider the benefits and costs of several special loans in what follows.

Concessionary Interest Rate Loans

A concessionary interest rate loan is one whose interest rate is below the market interest rate. Were the issue to exchange an old loan for a new one at a lower interest rate, there wouldn't really be much of a decision to be made. However, concessionary interest rate loans are often involved in trade-offs. For example, a concessionary interest rate loan may be offered as an incentive to make a long-term purchase—and the borrower wants to determine if the NPV of the loan is recaptured in the investment's higher cost? Or, suppose that the economy has exerted downward pressure on interest rates. But in order to refinance, borrowers must pay a percentage of the loan to refinance. In this instance, borrowers may want to know, what percentage of the loan, points, can they afford to pay and still break-even?

Three steps for evaluating concessionary interest rate loans. To evaluate a concessionary interest rate loan, we follow three steps. First, we find the loan payment of the concessionary interest rate loan. Second, we find the PV of the concessionary loan payments using either the market interest rate or the interest rate on the original loan as the defender's IRR. And third, we find the NPV of the concessionary interest rate loan by subtracting from the loan the PV of the concessionary interest rate loan. We now illustrate how to evaluate concessionary interest rate loans.

Example 17.5. Finding the NPV of a concessionary interest rate loan. Suppose that you want to buy a used car whose price is listed at $8,000. To encourage you to make the purchase, the car salesperson offers you a concessionary interest rate loan of $i = 1\%$ while the opportunity costs of capital, your IRR, is $r = 8\%$. If the loan is to be repaid over five years of monthly payments, you ask: what is the NPV of the concessionary rate loan? You might also ask: accounting for the PV of the used car loan, what is the actual price of the used car?

To find the value of the seller's concessionary interest rate loan, we follow the three steps outlined earlier. First, using Excel financial spreadsheet, we calculate the loan payment (PMT) of the concessionary interest rate loan and report our results in Table 17.10 below.

Table 17.10 Finding the loan payment for a concessionary interest rate loan for $8,000 at a concessionary rate of 1%, repaid with five years of monthly payments.
Open Table 17.10 in Microsoft Excel.

B4		f_x	=PMT(B1/B2,B2*B3,B5,,0)	
	A	B		C
1	rate	0.01		
2	m	12		
3	n	5		
4	pmt	($136.75)	=PMT(rate/m,m*n,PV,,0)	
5	PV	$8,000.00		

Our calculations find that a loan payment of $136.75 (pmt) is sufficient to repay an $8,000 loan (PV) at an APR of 1% (rate), with monthly payments (m) over five years (n).

Step two discounts the concessionary interest rate loan payments using the borrower's IRR of 8%/12. The results are summarized in Table 17.11 below.

Table 17.11. Finding the present value of an $8,000 loan at a concessionary interest rate 8%, for monthly payment of $136.75 for five year.
Open Table 17.11 in Microsoft Excel.

B5		f_x	=PV(B1/B2,B2*B3,B4,,0)	
	A	B		C
1	rate	0.08		
2	m	12		
3	n	5		
4	pmt	($136.75)		
5	PV	$6,744.30	=PV(rate/m,m*n,pmt,,0)	

The calculations reported in Table 17.11 find that the present value of the concessionary interest rate loan of $8,000 is equal to $6,744.30.

Step three calculates the NPV for the concessionary interest rate loan by subtracting from the original loan of $8,000 the discounted present value of the concession interest loan equal to $6,744 and finds:

$$(17.11) \quad NPV = \$8,000 - \$6,744.30 = \$1,255.70$$

Once you know the NPV of the concessionary rate loan, you can negotiate—will the seller lower the price by more than the NPV of the concessionary rate loan if you provide your own financing or pay with cash?

The Refinance Problem

A common financial transaction is the refinancing of a constant payment loan. If the current interest rate is less than the interest rate on one's existing loan, a reasonable borrower would refinance. But what if refinancing requires a fee, a percentage of the new loan, to be paid at the loan closing? We want to know what the borrower can afford to pay as a refinancing cost, or points of the loan, to break even. Finding break-even points is what we do next. We will use as our starting point the numbers introduced into the previous example.

The refinance problem is clearly an NPV problem. Its solution requires that we identify the defending and challenging investments. The defender in this case is the borrower current loan. The challenger is the new loan with its reduced interest rate and points charged to close the loan. What the borrower will earn on the loan is not relevant here because we assume that those earnings will be the same regardless of whether they are financed with the new loan or continue to be financed with the old loan.

Example 17.6. Finding break-even points for a refinanced constant payment loan. To solve a refinance problem with points, we recognize that the breakeven points (p) equate the cost of refinancing the loan with the NPV of the refinanced loan. Let the loan (L_0) times points charged to refinance the loan equal the NPV of the new loan. Setting refinancing costs equal to the NPV of the new loan, using data from Example 17.5 we write:

$$(17.12) \quad pL_0 = NPV(\text{new loan}) = \$1,255.70$$

Then solving for points p as a percentage of the refinanced loan, we divide both sides of equation 17.12 by the loan amount L_0 and find:

$$(17.13) \quad p = \frac{NPV(\text{new loan})}{L_0} = \frac{\$1,255.70}{\$8,000} = 15.7\%$$

In words, equation (17.13) computes the points we can pay to refinance an existing loan at a concessionary interest rate and still break even. In this example, break-even points equal 15.7%.

Moderated Payment Loans

Sometimes, we borrow for increased liquidity. Small to medium size firms often face variability of cash receipts that do not coincide with expenses. This means that a firm's liquidity measures such as the current ratio (CT) or the times-interest-earned (TIE) ratio may also vary significantly over time, creating liquidity needs—that are often addressed with increased borrowings. And sometimes, borrowers may apply for loans because the original loan was written for a much shorter period than the investment's productive life creating a mismatch between the term of financing and producing activities of the firm. Whatever the case, liquidity concerns may require the firm to renegotiate the terms of their loans with their lenders to solve liquidity needs.

Increasing a loan's term. Consider a moderated payment loan designed to reduce immediate liquidity needs. We use as our example, the loan described in Example 17.2. In this case the required payment was found to equal $111.22. To improve liquidity, suppose the borrower asks the lender to increase the term of the loan by 12 monthly payments. What would be the new loan payment? Resolving the Excel PMT function returns:

$$(17.14) \quad PMT(rate, nper, PV, , 0) = PMT(.01, 72, 5000, , 0) = \$97.75.$$

Now a loan payment of $97.75 will retire a loan of $5,000 with 72 payments rather than 60 payments at an actuarial rate of 1%. The loan payment is reduced from $111.22 to $97.75. In this example, the term increased by 12, from 60 months to 72 months or 20% while the payment decreased by [($111.22-$97.75)/$111.22] = 12% and the elasticity of term is 20%/12% or 1.67% Compare this result with those in Table 17.7 at the intersection of column headed by 1% and row labeled 60. Can you explain why there is a difference from the results above and those in Table 17.7? (Hint: can you recall the difference between elasticity measured at a point versus elasticity measure over some interval?)

Skip payments and student loans. Sometimes, we borrow funds to accommodate immediate liquidity needs, expecting that sometime in the future our liquidity will improve and allow us to repay our loans. Such an incentive exists for many students whose incentive for borrowing is to delay making interest and loan payments until after graduating from school.

Loans that delay interest and principal payments, we refer to as skip payment loans. The attractive feature of a skip payment loan is that you don't have to make payments until after graduation. The not so nice feature of this loan is that interest is accumulating over those periods that you are not making payments. The effect of accumulating interest cost is that the principal loan balance is increasing—you are in effect borrowing to pay the interest costs on your loan.

Example 17.7. Borrowing to learn. Suppose you obtain a student loan of $12,000 to cover your last year of schooling expenses. No payments are required during your last year in school. After graduation you are required to repay the loan plus accumulated interest over 3 years of monthly payments. Assume the market interest rate is 7.5% which is the interest rate charged on your student loan. What is the NPV of this loan. What is the effective rate on the loan? The timeline for this loan is described in Figure 17.1.

Figure 17.1. *The payment timeline for a 12-month skip payment loan with three years of payments.*

Step 1 for analyzing the skip payment loan is to find the payment A to be made over three years beginning 13 months after the loan was obtained. The amount of the loan to be repaid beginning in month t = 13 is $12,000(1.075), the original amount plus interest charges. This amount must be repaid with 36 payments at an interest rate of 7.5%/12 = 0.625%. What makes the solution to this loan interesting is that we are finding the solution as though we were standing at time period t = 13 where the amount to be repaid equals the discounted value of payments at the beginning of of loan month 13 or the end of loan month 12. We describe the solution using an Excel spreadsheet:

Table 17.12. Finding the loan payment on a skip payment loan.
Open Table 17.12 in Microsoft Excel.

B4		f_x	=PMT(B1/B2,B2*B3,B5,,0)
	A	B	C
1	rate	0.075	
2	m	12	
3	n	3	
4	pmt	($401.27)	=PMT(rate/m,m*n,PV,,0)
5	PV	$12,900.00	$12,900 = 1.075 * $12,000

Our calculations find that to repay a one-year skip payment loan to be repaid over three years of monthly payments at an interest rate of 7.5% is equal to $401.27. We may be interested in what would have been the loan payment if repaid over four years—without one year of skipped payments? Resolving our Excel payment problem by replacing PV of $12,000 with $12,900 and *n* = 3 with *n* = 4, we find:

Table 17.13. Finding the loan payment on the loan without skipping payments.
Open Table 17.13 in Microsoft Excel.

B4			f_x	=PMT(B1/B2,B2*B3,B5,,0)
	A	B		C
1	rate	0.075		
2	m	12		
3	n	4		
4	pmt	($290.15)		=PMT(rate/m,m*n,PV,,0)
5	PV	$12,000.00		

Skipping one year of payments led to an increase payment from $290.15 to $401.27. Was the immediate increase in liquidity equal to the decreased liquidity over the three years of repayment? We can't answer that question, the best financial managers can do is describe the consequences of one's financial choices.

Finally, we ask: what is the difference between the effective interest rate on the old and new loan? There is no difference, None! Can you explain why? For the same reason that we don't change NPVs when we reinvestment and discount at the same interest rate. Acquiring a skip payment loan at the market interest rate may increase future cash flow obligations, but it doesn't change the NPV of the loan.

Disguised Interest Rate Loans

One of the challenges financial managers face when considering borrowing decisions is knowing the actual cost of borrowing—or, stated another way, knowing the effective APR interest rate. Sometimes lenders offer loans that disguise the real cost of their loans. We call loans with disguised interest rates, disguised interest rate loans.

Disguised interest rate loans have effective interest rates than are presented in the loan description. For example, interest costs can be subtracted in the initial period, reducing the actual loan amount received by the borrower (a discount loan). Interest can be charged as though the original loan balance was outstanding throughout the life of the loan (an add-on loan). Alternatively, the lender can charge a loan closing fee, reducing the actual loan balance received by the borrower. Additionally, the interest can compound more frequently than loan payments occur. Each of these methods will increase the effective interest rate above the stated interest rate. Consider several types of disguised interest rate loans.

Discount loan. A borrower approaches his lender for a loan of L_0 for mn periods. The borrower learns that the stated interest rate or disguised interest rate is r^d. When the borrower picks up the check for his loan, the amount he receives equals only:

$$L^d = L(1 - r^d n) \tag{17.15}$$

the amount of the loan requested less the stated interest rate times the term of the loan. Meanwhile, the constant loan payment is calculated as:

$$A = \frac{L_0}{mn} \tag{17.16}$$

To calculate the APR associated with this loan, treat payments of amount A as if they were associated with a constant payment loan that retires a principal of L_0.

Example 17.8. The effective interest rate for a discount loan. To illustrate the discount loan, assume a consumer obtains an installment loan for $10,000, from which $2,500 is deducted for interest costs. The loan is to be repaid over 2 years, with monthly payments equal to $416.67 = ($10,000/24). To solve this problem and find the effective interest rate, we key into our Excel RATE function:

$$RATE(nper, pmt, pv, , 0) = RATE(24, \$416.67, -\$7,5000) = 2.44\%. \tag{17.17}$$

Displayed is the actuarial monthly rate of 2.44% or, after multiplying by 12, we find the corresponding APR rate of 29.3%. The effective rate re is: $r^e = (1.0244)^{12} - 1 = 33.55\%$.

This is quite a difference compared to the stated interest rate of 12.5%. Hence, the discount loan effectively disguises its true APR.

Discounts for on-time payments. Sometimes disguised interest rates can provide opportunities for significant savings. One such opportunity is discounts offered for on-time savings. You may make a purchase on account and be offered a discount for early payment. For example, suppose you are offered a 2% discount if you pay your bill by the 10th day of the month. After 30 days, interest is charged on your account at the rate of 12% per year so by paying early you give up 20 days of free credit. In other words, you are asked to forfeit 20 days of free credit for a discount of 2%.

What is the effective interest rate you would earn by paying your bill by the 10th of the month? The solution requires that we convert the 2% discount to an annual rate by equating 2% is to 20 days as x% is to 365 days.

$$\frac{2\%}{20 \text{ days}} = \frac{x\%}{365 \text{ days}} \tag{17.18}$$

Then solving for x, we find:

$$x = (2\%)\frac{365}{20} = 26.5\% \tag{17.19}$$

And an interest rate of 36.5% for funds paid on time is really an impressive investment.

Points added loans. Earlier we discussed points added to close a loan when refinancing. Now we discuss points added loans in a different view. We ask: what do points added to a loan do to the effective interest rate? In this case, suppose you are quoted an interest rate of r% for a loan amount of L_0 to be repaid over mn periods—and then just before you sign, you are informed that there are p points changed to close the loan adding a transaction charge of pL_0 to obtain the loan. To find the effective rate we simply compare the rate without the refinancing cost with the rate associated with the rate.

For this example, we continue with the loan described in Table 17.8 of $8,000 for monthly payments over 5 years at 1%. The payment for this loan has already been calculated as $136.75. Now suppose that the lender requires an 8% closing fee to close the loan of 8% * $8,000 = $640. In effect what points required to close a loan means that the actual loan amount available to the borrow is reduced by the closing fee, in this case $640 so that the actual loan is $7,460 rather than $8,000. To find the rate associated with the point added loan we employ the Excel Rate function and find:

$$(17.20) \quad RATE(nper, pmt, PV) = RATE(60, \$136.75, \$7,460) = .3175\%$$

Then multiplying the actuarial rate by 12 to find the new APR: 12 * .3175 = 3.8% so that adding points to a loan more than doubled its effective interest rate from 1% to 3.8%.

Future Values

Up until now, we have emphasized the importance of converting future cash flow to their equivalent worth in the present. Hence, the title to this book includes the words, present value. On the other hand, there are times when values in the future deserve our focus. One future focus may be an anticipated event such a future purchase that requires an accumulation of funds and interest. For example, suppose that one anticipates a large capital purchase such as a house or machinery. Or one may be interested in having sufficient funds to generate an annuity at the time of retirement. We represent a future value at the beginning of period n as FV_n.

Example 17.9. Saving for a down payment. Suppose you want to buy a house for $200,000, but to obtain a loan, you must pay a down payment of 10% or $20,000. If you intend to save a monthly amount for 3 years which you reinvest at 5%—what is the amount you must save? To answer this question, we need to distinguish between two different kinds of annuities. Annuities due are annuities paid at the beginning of the period (type = 1 in Excel's PMT function). Ordinary annuities are paid at the end of the period (type = 0 in Excel's PMT function). Knowing when payments (annuities) are paid, at the beginning or end of the period, is important when making payments to achieve some future financial goal.

So, we want to find what amount must we save and invest for 36 monthly payments that earn 5% APR such that their compounded accumulations at the beginning of period n + 1 will equal the $20,000 required for a down payment for a future capital purchase? Suppose you make payments at the beginning of n period so that at the beginning of the n + 1 period or the end of the nth period you have available a future value of FV_{n+1} equal to:

$$(17.21) \quad FV_{n+1} = A(1+r)^n + A(1+r)^{n-1} + \cdots + A(1+r)$$

Table 17.14. Finding annuity due required to save $20,000 in 36 monthly payments.
Open Table 17.14 in Microsoft Excel.

B6			f_x	=PMT(B1/B2,B2*B3,,20000,1)
	A		B	C
1	rate		0.05	
2	m		12	
3	n		3	
4	nper		36	=(m*n) if type = 1
5	rate/m		0.41%	
6	pmt		($513.94)	=PMT(rate/m,m*n,PV=0,FV,type=1)
7	FV		$20,000.00	

Alternatively, we could find the 36 monthly payments required if the payments were made at the end of each period that compound at an APR of 5% APR so that at the beginning of the nth period the accumulated savings will equal $20,000.

$$(17.22) \quad FV_n = A(1+r)^{n-1} + A(1+r)^{n-2} + \cdots + A(1+r) + A$$

Table 17.15. Finding the annuity with payments made at the end of each period.
Open Table 17.15 in Microsoft Excel.

B6			f_x	=PMT(B1/B2,B2*B3,,20000,0)
	A		B	C
1	rate		0.05	
2	m		12	
3	n		3	
4	nper		35	=(m*n)-1 if type = 0
5	rate/m		0.41%	
6	pmt		($516.08)	=PMT(rate/m,m*n,PV=0,FV,type=0)
7	FV		$20,000.00	

Summary and Conclusions

In this chapter we demonstrated the versatility of PV models by using them to analyze loans. For constant payment loans, we used PV models to solve for constant loan payments, terms, loan amounts, and interest rates—remembering that one PV equation can solve for at most one unknown.

Using PV models to analyze loans required that we identify the various kinds of interest rates. This was an important exercise because we discovered the difference between stated interest rates and effective interest rates—the interest rate actually paid on the loan funds made available.

Another important exercise was discovering the sensitivity of the relationship between the size of the loan payment and the term of the loan. In most cases, the relationship is not one-to-one. In other words, a 1% increase in the size of the loan payment rarely leads to a 1% drop in the term. The corresponding percent decline in the term of the loan is usually much, much more. Hence, we discovered that, when applying for loans, it pays to explore various terms and sizes of loan payments and find the best match—the one with the optimal trade-off between term and liquidity.

A common problem is that existing loans often need to be refinanced. Such may be the case when interest rates drop or a project currently financed is expanded and additional funds are required. In the text we considered refinancing existing loans and found break-even loan closing points. In the supplemental materials at the end of this chapter, we will find the more general formula for refinancing when the term, interest rate, and size of the new loan may be different than on the existing loan.

Lastly, we demonstrated how some loans may disguise the true interest rate. While we only illustrated the solution for the discount loan and the points-added loan, there are several other kinds of loans that disguise the true interest rate.

Questions

1. Which would you prefer to earn on your savings? An APR rate of 12.5% or a 1% actuarial rate compounded monthly? Given an APR of r percent, what is the most that the effective rate can earn above the APR rate if it is compounded continuously?

2. Consider a loan of $80,000 at an APR of 13%. What is the loan payment that would retire the loan if repaid in monthly payments for 10 years? If repaid in monthly installments for 9 years? Compare the percentage change in the term versus the percentage change in the loan payment (the arc elasticity). Finally, find the point elasticity $E_{(n,A)}$ on the original loan.

3. Assume a loan of $54,000 with a remaining term of 21 years. The existing loan requires monthly payments at an APR of 11.25%. For a 3% closing fee, the borrowers could refinance their loan at an APR rate of 10% for the same term. What is the effective interest rate on the new loan? What are the break-even points for refinancing the loan? What is the total interest paid on the two loans?

4. A consumer obtains an installment loan of $12,000 from which $2,700 is deducted for interest costs. The loan is to be repaid over two years with monthly payments equal to $500 ($12,000/24). Please determine the effective interest rate re on this loan.

5. A farm supply store offers its customers 30 days same-as-cash arrangements. That is, for bills paid within 30 days after purchases are made, no interest is charged. On the other hand, to encourage early payments, the supply store offers a 2% discount on bills paid with 10 days. Please calculate the effective interest rate the store offers its buyers for giving up 20 days of free credit.

6. Suppose you borrowed $5,000 for 3 years at an APR rate of 8%. Create an amortization table for this loan.

7. Home Depot mailed to some of its customers a coupon entitling them to either a 10% discount on their next purchase or two years of free credit. Under what conditions would you be indifferent between the two options? (Hint: the answer does not depend on the amount purchased.)

8. A farm firm has a mortgage loan for $150,000 at an APR rate of 5%. The term of the loan is 15 years and the payments equal $14,451. Cash flow problems from reduced farm income leaves the firm only able to pay $10,000 on this loan. What would the new term equal if the lender allowed the borrower to repay over a longer term?

18. "Unveiling Land Investments: Evaluating Real Estate Opportunities"

LINDON ROBISON

Learning goals. After completing this chapter, you should be able to: (1) describe land's unique investment characteristics; (2) understand how land's endurable nature affects its price variability; (3) recognize what makes land distinct from other types of investments; and (4) evaluate land investments using present value (PV) models developed earlier.

Learning objectives. To achieve your learning goals, you should complete the following objectives:

- Learn how to distinguish between real and nominal discount rates.
- Learn how to distinguish between inflationary and real growth in earning rates.
- Learn how expected growth rates in earnings from land are capitalized into land values.
- Learn how to find the real growth rate for land.
- Learn how to calculate the maximum bid (minimum sell) price for land.
- Learn how transaction costs associated with buying and selling land influence land's liquidity.
- Learn how taxes influence the maximum bid (minimum sell) price for land.
- Learn how to find the tax adjustment coefficient for investments in land.
- Learn how to use land price-to-earnings ratios to predict adjustments in the price of land.

Introduction

1

Land's immobility and durability make it unique among investments and deserving of special attention in PV analysis. Land's immobility means that it cannot be moved and that its services must be extracted by those physically on site. Durability means that land has the capacity to provide services over time without significant change in its service provision capacity.

Earlier, an asset's liquidity was defined as it nearness to cash. One dimension of an asset's liquidity depends on the form of its earnings—cash versus capital gains (see Chapter 16). In this chapter we discuss a different dimension of liquidity—the cost of converting an asset to cash through its sale. Land's

---

1. Some of the material in this chapter was adapted from Robison, L.J. and P.J. Barry (1996); Present Value Models and Investment Analysis. "Chapter 14: Transaction Costs and Land Purchase/Sale Decision". MSU Press, East Lansing, Michigan.

immobility makes it less liquid than assets that can be moved because it cannot be moved to meet the convenience of the buyer. Land's immobility also limits the potential buyers to those near enough to extract the land's services. Another reason that land is illiquid is because buyers and sellers pay fees to complete its purchase and sale, including Realtor fees, legal costs of changing and recording its title, and other related fees—but not to each other. Evidence of farmland's low liquidity is its infrequent transfer. On average, only 2% to 3% of the privately owned farmland in the United States is sold each year.

On the other hand, lenders prefer land as collateral for loans for the same reason that makes land illiquid—its immobility. Land's immobility reduces the riskiness of it being stolen, hidden, or moved. Lenders also prefer land as collateral for loans because of its durability, which reduces the riskiness of it losing its value as security for loans. To offset some of land's illiquidity, special institutions and programs have developed for financing residential and farm real estate.

The immobility and durability of land also make it a popular object on which to assess taxes. Taxing agencies have easy and indisputable records of the amount of land subject to tax and who owns the land. Thus, most land-owners pay property taxes on land and buildings but pay no similar tax on more mobile and less durable investments. Consequently, land is one of the few investments for which taxes are based on the market value of the investment at the beginning of the period as well as on the earnings of the investment during the period.

This chapter develops PV models to estimate maximum bid (minimum sell) prices for land investments, to describe how transaction costs contribute to land's illiquidity, to understand how land's durability increases its price volatility, and to demonstrate the influence of taxes on maximum bid (minimum sell) prices. We begin by describing the connection between land's durability and its price volatility and why land and other durables are subject to inflationary bubbles and crashes.

Why are land prices so volatile?

Durable price volatility. One interesting feature of farmland and other durables prices such as housing stock, is their historically high swings in values. Figure 18.1 describes year-to-year changes in Michigan farmland values over the 2000 to 2010 period. Figure 18.2 describes changes year-to-year changes in housing values over the same period. Part of these changes can be attributed to capital gains (losses). But there is another explanation for changes in the value of land and other durables, and it has to do with changes in real interest rates and real growth rates.

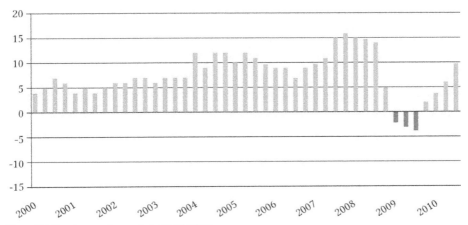

Figure 18.1. Year-to-year changes in farmland values.

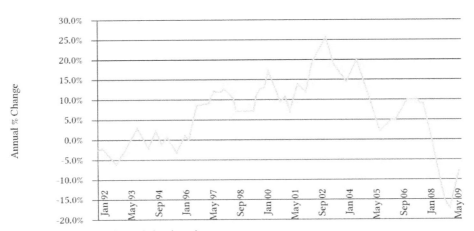

Figure 18.2. Year-to-year changes in housing prices.

Inflationary, nominal, and real interest rates. To understand price volatility of durables, it is necessary to describe inflationary, nominal, and real interest rates. Recall that the inflation rate i is equal to the rate of change in average prices, changes often linked to monetary or fiscal policies of governments. The nominal interest rate r depends on the rate of inflation and a real component that is dependent on factors other than the rate of inflation such as changing market conditions or changes in productivity. To describe the effects of inflation on the nominal interest, let one plus the nominal interest rate r equal one plus the real rate r^* times one plus the inflation rate i so that:

(18.1) $$(1 + r) = (1 + r^*)(1 + i)$$

We solve for the real interest rate in equation (18.1) as:

(18.2) $$r^* = \frac{r - i}{(1 + i)}$$

Historically, real interest rates vary by sectors but are highly correlated. Real interest rates on home loans are described graphically in Figure 18.3:

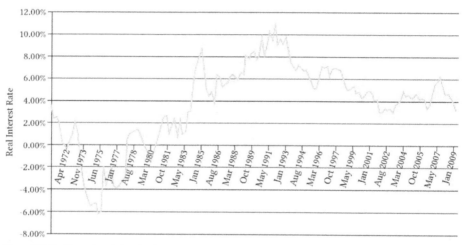

Figure 18.3. Real home loan interest rates.

We can describe the effects of changes in the real growth rate on durable asset prices by letting the nominal growth rate g equal one plus the real growth rate g^* times one plus the inflation rate i, so that:

(18.3) $$(1 + g) = (1 + g^*)(1 + i)$$

We solve for the real growth rate in equation (18.3) as:

(18.4) $$g^* = \frac{g - i}{(1 + i)}$$

To understand the volatility of farmland prices, we build a general PV model where V_0 is land's present value, g is the average nominal growth (decay) rate of net cash flow, r is the nominal interest rate, and R_0 represents initial cash flow. For the moment we ignore taxes and write the relationship between the variables just described in a growth model as:

$$V_0 = \frac{R_0(1+g)}{(1+r)} + \frac{R_0(1+g)^2}{(1+r)^2} + \frac{R_0(1+g)^3}{(1+r)^3} + \cdots = \frac{R_0(1+g)}{(r-g)}$$

(18.5)

We call the result the value in use model because there are no sales or purchases implied. Suppose we replace $(1 + r)$ with the right-hand side of equation (18.1) and $(1 + g)$ with the right-hand side of equation (18.3). After the substitution, we obtain the result:

(18.6)

$$V_0 = \frac{R_0(1+g^*)(1+i)}{(1+r^*)(1+i)} + \frac{R_0[(1+g^*)(1+i)]^2}{[(1+r^*)(1+i)]^2} + \frac{R_0[(1+g^*)(1+i)]^3}{[(1+r^*)(1+i)]^3} + \cdots$$

Notice that the inflationary effects on the discount rate and the growth (decay) rate cancel, so that we can write equation (18.6) as a function of only real rates and initial cash flow:

$$V_0 = \frac{R_0(1+g^*)}{(1+r^*)} + \frac{R_0(1+g^*)^2}{(1+r^*)^2} + \frac{R_0(1+g^*)^3}{(1+r^*)^3} + \cdots = \frac{R_0(1+g^*)}{(r^*-g^*)}$$

(18.7)

Suppose that in equation (18.7), r^* changes. To measure the impact of a change in r^*, we differentiate V_0 with respect to r^* and obtain:

$$\frac{dV_0}{dr^*} = \frac{-R_0(1+g^*)}{(r^*-g^*)^2}$$

(18.8)

The percentage change in V_0, with respect to a change in r^*, equals the change in the asset's value in response to a change in the real interest rate, equation (18.8), divided by the asset's initial value V_0, the right-hand side of equation (18.7):

$$\frac{dV_0/dr^*}{V_0} = \frac{-1}{(r^*-g^*)}$$

(18.9)

Now suppose that g^* changes. To measure the impact of a change in g^* we differentiate V_0 with respect to g^* in equation (18.7) and obtain:

$$\text{(18.10)} \quad \frac{dV_0}{dg^*} = \frac{R_0(1 + g^*)}{(r^* - g^*)^2}$$

The percentage change in V_0 with respect to a change in g^* equals the change in the asset's value in response to a change in the real interest rate, equation (18.10) divided by the asset's initial value V_0 described in equation (18.7).

The percentage change in V_0 with respect to a change in g^* equals:

$$\text{(18.11)} \quad \frac{dV_0/dg^*}{V_0} = \frac{1}{(r^* - g^*)}$$

We now describe the percentage changes in asset values in response to changes in the real discount rate and the real growth rate for alternative real interest rates and real capital gains (capital loss) rates. In the previous chapter we described changes in asset values over time. This analysis is different (and static or timeless). We consider what happens to an asset's value at a point in time if one of the underlying variables that determines its value is changed.

In Table 18.1 calculations are based on equation (18.11). In the calculations we set the percentage change in asset values for alternative values of r^* and g^*. We set r^* equal to 2%, 4%, 6%, 8%, and 10%. We set g^* equal to -20%, -10%, -5%, 0%, 2% and 4%. Negative values for g^* correspond to depreciable durable assets such as buildings and machinery. Positive values of g^* are harder to justify and may reflect speculative bubbles in which asset earnings are expected to grow in real terms in perpetuity—an assumption which is hard to justify.

Table 18.1. Percentage changes in asset values corresponding to small changes in real interest rates for alternative values of r^* and for assets with various degrees of durability characterized by the variable g^*.

	$g^* = -20\%$	$g^* = -10\%$	$g^* = -5\%$	$g^* = 0\%$	$g^* = 2\%$	$g^* = 4\%$
$r^* = 2\%$	-4.5%	-8.3%	-14.3%	-50%	n.a.	n.a.
$r^* = 4\%$	-4.1%	-7.1%	-11.1%	-25%	-50%	n.a.
$r^* = 6\%$	-3.8%	-6.3%	-9.1%	-16.7%	-25%	-50%
$r^* = 8\%$	-3.6%	-5.6%	-7.7%	-12.5%	-16.7%	-25%
$r^* = 10\%$	-3.3%	-5%	-6.7	-10%	-12.5%	-16.7%

Consider Table 18.1. Note that an asset's durability is reflected by its real growth (decay) rate—an asset's durability decreases with its g^* value. Also note that the percentage change in asset values in response to increases in real interest rates decreases with an asset's durability. For example, if the real interest rate were 4%, a small increase in the real interest rate would cause a 4.1% decrease in the value of a depreciable asset with a negative real growth rate of -20%. Meanwhile, a small increase in the real interest rate for a durable asset with a 4% real growth rate would result in a 50% decrease in the value of an asset.

Now consider Table 18.2, which examines the effect of small increases in the real growth rate for the same scenarios described in Table 18.1 and also based on equation (18.11). The difference between Table 18.1 and Table 18.2 is that the signs within the body of the tables are reversed. An increase in the real interest rate reduces asset values because future dollars are worth less with a higher discount rate. In contrast, an increase in the real growth rates means there are more future cash flows to discount—making the change in the value of the assets positive in response to a small increase in the real growth rate.

Table 18.2. Percentage changes in asset values corresponding to 1% changes in real growth rate for alternative values of r^* and for assets with various degrees of durability characterized by the variable g^*.

	$g^* = -20\%$	$g^* = -10\%$	$g^* = -5\%$	$g^* = 0\%$	$g^* = 2\%$	$g^* = 4\%$
$r^* = 2\%$	4.5%	8.3%	14.3%	50%	n.a.	n.a.
$r^* = 4\%$	4.1%	7.1%	11.1%	25%	50%	n.a.
$r^* = 6\%$	3.8%	6.3%	9.1%	16.7%	25%	50%
$r^* = 8\%$	3.6%	5.6%	7.7%	12.5%	16.7%	25%
$r^* = 10\%$	3.3%	5%	6.7	10%	12.5%	16.7%

One interesting feature of Table 18.2 is that the percentage change in asset values in response to small increases in the real growth rate are dampened by higher real interest rates. For that reason, when the economy is "overheated" and prices are rising, one response is to reduce the money supply, increasing the real interest rate and slowing price increases. For example, suppose the real growth rate were zero% and the real interest rate was 2%. If the real growth rate increased slightly, the asset value would increase by 50%. If, instead, the real interest rate were 10% and the real growth rate increased slightly, the asset value would increase by only 10%.

So, what have we learned? We learned that durable assets such as land and houses are subject to significant percentage changes in value in response to changes in real interest rates and real growth rates—much more so than depreciable assets. In addition, changes in the asset's real growth rate in earnings have less effect when real interest rates are high.

To test your understanding of the material just covered, demonstrate that a 1% increase in the real growth rate produces the same percentage changes in asset values as those described in Table 18.1, except opposite in sign.

Maximum Bid (Minimum Sell) Price Models and Transaction Costs

Maximum bid (minimum sell) price models. We now deduce maximum bid price models for buyers and minimum sell price models for sellers. At least two costs differentiate maximum bid price models for buyers and minimum sell price models for sellers: taxes and transactions costs. Let c equal the percentage of land's sale price paid by the buyer to purchase the land—but not paid to the seller. These may include loan closing fees, title examination and registration fees, attorney's costs, and closing points paid by the buyer. Let s equal the percentage of the land's sale price paid by the seller to sell the land—but not paid to the buyer. This may include loan closing fees, Realtor fees, advertising, and other fees.

Denote V_0^b as the buyer's maximum bid price and V_0^s as the seller's minimum sell price. Ignoring taxes, and assuming that the land will never be sold again, the expression for V_0^b can be written as:

(18.12)

$$(1+c)V_0^b = \frac{R_0(1+g)}{(1+r)} + \frac{R_0(1+g)^2}{(1+r)^2} + \frac{R_0(1+g)^3}{(1+r)^3} + \cdots = \frac{R_0(1+g)}{(r-g)}$$

Expression $(1+c)V_0^b$ represents the maximum bid price, including the effect of closing costs. To isolate the maximum bid price, we solve for V_0^b.

$$V_0^b = \frac{R_0(1+g)}{(r-g)(1+c)}$$

(18.13)

In the maximum bid price model, the discounted stream of future cash flow represents the challenging investment—the present value of earnings the buyer will receive if the land is purchased.

Example 18.1: *Finding the Maximum Bid Price for Land.* What is the maximum bid price of a parcel of land if the buyer pays 6% of the acquisition price as a closing fee? To solve the problem, assume last year's net cash flow was $22,000, which is expected to grow in perpetuity at 4.5%. Assume that the buyer's opportunity cost of capital is 12%. The maximum bid price is calculated using equation (18.13):

$$V_0^b = \frac{R_0(1+g)}{(r-g)(1+c)} = \frac{\$22,000(1.045)}{(.12-.045)(1.06)} = \$289,182$$

(18.14)

If closing costs, as a percentage of the price, increase from 6% to 9%, V_0^b decreases to $281,223.

Minimum sell price models. Realtor fees and other closing costs paid by the seller are now introduced into the minimum sell price model. To build the minimum sell price model, let sV_0^s be subtracted from the seller's proceeds. Ignoring taxes and assuming that the land will only be sold one time, we can write the minimum sell price model as:

(18.15)

$$(1-s)V_0^s = \frac{R_0(1+g)}{(1+r)} + \frac{R_0(1+g)^2}{(1+r)^2} + \frac{R_0(1+g)^3}{(1+r)^3} + \cdots = \frac{R_0(1+g)}{(r-g)}$$

Solving for V_0^s, we find the minimum sell price equal to:

$$V_0^s = \frac{R_0(1+g)}{(r-g)(1-s)}$$

(18.16)

In the minimum sell price model, the discounted stream of future cash flow represents the defending investment—it represents the earnings the seller would not earn if the land were sold.

Example 18.2: *Finding the Minimum Sell Price.* Letting s = 2% and using the data from Example 18.1, we find the minimum sell price using equation (18.13):

$$V_0^s = \frac{R_0(1+g)}{(r-g)(1-s)} = \frac{\$22,000(1.045)}{(.12-.045)(.98)} = \$312,789$$

(18.17)

Now, suppose s increases from 2% to 3%. In turn, V_0^s increases to \$316,014. In contrast to the effects of an increase in c that reduced the maximum bid price, an increase in s increases the minimum sell price:

Land Values, Transaction Costs, and Liquidity

Suppose a buyer and a seller had the same earnings expectations and opportunity costs for a durable such as farmland. It must follow that their present-value for the durable in use would be the same. But if the buyer had to pay closing fees to acquire the durable, his maximum bid price would be reduced. And if the seller received only a portion of the present value after the sale, her minimum sell price would increase. Therefore, transaction costs that increase the seller's minimum sell price and reduce the buyer's maximum bid price reduce the liquidity of the durable, even when the buyer and seller have the same earnings expectations and opportunity costs.

In other words, an asset is illiquid if its value in use (V_0) is bounded below by a buyer's maximum bid price (V_0^b) and bounded above by the seller's minimum sell price (V_0^s). We can easily show that assets for individuals with identical expectations of land's value in use are illiquid when transaction costs are imposed on its sale and purchase.

Substitute the value in use from equation (18.5) into the maximum bid price model in equation (18.13), and the result is:

$$(18.18) \quad V_0^b = \frac{R_0(1+g)}{(r-g)(1+c)} = \frac{V_0}{(1+c)} < V_0$$

It should be clear that for c > 0, $V_0^b < V_0$.

Next, substitute the value in use from equation (18.5) into the minimum sell price model in equation (18.16) and the result is:

$$(18.19) \quad V_0^s = \frac{R_0(1+g)}{(r-g)(1-s)} = \frac{V_0}{(1-s)} > V_0$$

It should be clear that for s > 0, $V_0 < V_0^s$. Finally combining these results allows us to express the effects of transaction costs on the maximum bid, minimum sell, and value-in-use models:

$$(18.20) \quad V_0^b < V_0 < V_0^s$$

Despite equal earning expectations, as a result of transaction costs, the maximum bid price is less than the minimum sell price making land illiquid. To make this point another way, suppose that we formed the ratio of the maximum bid price and the minimum sell price for land and assumed that c = 5% and s = 6%. Then the buyer in this example would only be willing to offer 89.2% of the seller's minimum sell price, and a sale would not occur.

$$(18.21) \quad \frac{V_0^b}{V_0^s} = \frac{(1-s)}{(1+c)} = \frac{1-.06}{1+.05} = 89.2\%$$

Other Factors Contributing to Asset Liquidity

Differences in financing costs for buyers and sellers may also contribute to an asset's illiquidity. For example, a loan tied to the ownership of durables at below-market interest rates may create a wedge between the maximum bid price and the minimum sell price. If the loan has a due-on-sale clause, the seller gives up something of value that is not received by the buyer when the investment is sold. Thus, concessionary interest rate loans with due-on-sale clauses may create illiquidity.

Differences in information between the buyer and seller may also contribute to an asset's illiquidity. When two trusted friends exchange a durable, the information costs are insignificant—they freely exchange information. However, when two strangers exchange a durable, the buyer must commit resources to discover the quality of the information provided by the seller. If an investment's service capacity is easily observed, as with certified seed or fertilizer, then the information cost is small and the investment will be more liquid. Durables like used cars or tractors, whose remaining service capacity is not easily observed, will be less liquid. The issuance of a warranty is a signal of higher quality, and thus a warranty is an attempt to reduce information costs for the prospective buyer and to increase the liquidity of the asset.

The cost of gathering information about the asset's service capacity may also contribute to its liquidity. To illustrate, a new asset's service capacity may be well known. Once the durable is used, however, the uncertainty associated with the intensity of use and care of the durable creates an immediate decline in the value of the durable. On the other hand, a used durable whose service extraction is nearly depleted is more liquid, because there is nearly perfect information about the durable's remaining capacity.

The liquidity of durables is also affected by disposal costs. Disposal cost is the cost of removing durables from service paid by its current owner. Most durables are mobile. Buildings, however, must be disassembled at considerable costs. In some cases, the investment is so valuable that assembly and disassembly are warranted. An example is the London Bridge. Most durables with high disposal costs become completely illiquid and remain in service to the first owner until destroyed. Often it is easier to transfer the owner rather than the investment itself. Examples of durables with high disposal costs are land and houses.

Durables whose value increases with time and use are called appreciating durables. Durables whose values decrease with time and use are called depreciating durables. A durable whose value increases with time and use will be more liquid than one whose value declines with time and use, with all other liquidity attributes held constant. Appreciating durables provide greater security for lenders than depreciating durables because their value and the lender's security are increasing. Finally, liquidity is affected by whether or not time or use determines the durables' service capacity. Durables whose service capacity is determined by time have a fixed pattern of changes in service capacity and cannot adjust to changes in the market. Durables whose change in service capacity is determined by use can adjust to changes in the marketplace for the value of its services. Thus, durables whose service capacity is tied to use are more liquid than those whose service capacity is linked to time.

The liquidity of a durable is also influenced by the number of services the durable can provide. Durables become more liquid if the buyer has opportunities for the durables' services that are not available to the seller. A durable is more likely to have multiple uses when it is not fixed geographically. Multiple use capability is also tied to the acquisition characteristics of the durable. If the durable is lumpy in acquisition, potential buyers must take it or leave it. Durables divisible in acquisition, on the other hand, provide options for prospective buyers. They can buy a gallon or a tankful of gas, a sack of seeds or a truckload.

Finally, durables whose service extraction rate is fixed, and hence irreversible, are less liquid than durables whose service extraction rate is variable. Variations in service capacity provide greater adjustment potentials, and thus reduce the differences in perceptions between buyers and sellers. Moreover, durables whose service extraction rates vary tend to have multiple uses, while those with fixed service extraction rates tend to be single-use durables.

Maximum Bid (Minimum Sell) Land Price Models with Taxes

Taxes are now introduced into our maximum bid (minimum sell) price for land models. As mentioned earlier, land is subject to a wide variety of taxes, not all of which are imposed on other assets. Four kinds of taxes must be considered in our maximum bid (minimum sell) price for land models: First, the cash flow stream is taxed at the average income tax rate T. Second, the opportunity cost of capital r is expressed on an after-tax basis. Since the discount rate may reflect the opportunity cost of capital associated with investments that earn both capital gains and cash, the tax rate is θT. Third, property taxes (T_p) are another tax charged against the market price of land in each period. Thus, land's maximum bid price in future periods must be included in each period. The study of capital gains indicated that land prices should increase at the same rate as land earnings. Finally, one tax not included in the land price models is tax-savings rate T_g, resulting from durable depreciation. The reason is simple—land is not considered a depreciable investment.

The Maximum Bid Price Model with Taxes. The expanded maximum bid price model with taxes is written as:

(18.22)

$$(1+c)V_0^b = \frac{R_0(1+g)(1-T) - V_0^b T_p(1-T)}{[1+r(1-\theta T)]}$$
$$+ \frac{R_0(1+g)^2(1-T) - V_0^b(1+g)T_p(1-T)}{[1+r(1-\theta T)]^2} + \cdots = S_1 + S_2$$

The cash flow stream contains two geometric series. In both series, the geometric factor is $(1 + g)/[1 + r(1 - \theta T)]$ and the sums of the two series are equal to:

$$S_1 = \frac{R_0(1+g)(1-T)}{[1+r(1-\theta T)]} + \frac{R_0(1+g)^2(1-T)}{[1+r(1-\theta T)]^2} + \cdots$$

$$= \frac{R_0(1+g)(1-T)}{r(1-\theta T) - g}$$

(18.23)

while

$$S_2 = -\frac{V_0^b T_p(1-T)}{[1+r(1-\theta T)]} - \frac{V_0^b(1+g)T_p(1-T)}{[1+r(1-\theta T)]^2} - \cdots$$

$$= -\frac{V_0^b T_p(1-T)}{r(1-\theta T) - g}$$

(18.24)

Finally, setting $(1+c)V_0^b$ equal to the sum of S_1 and S_2 and solving for V_0^b, the maximum bid price with taxes of land can be written as:

$$V_0^b = \frac{R_0(1+g)(1-T)}{[r(1-\theta T) - g](1+c) + T_p(1-T)}$$

(18.25)

It is still the case that the challenging investment in equation (18.16) is represented by the discounted after-tax cash flow stream while the defender is the maximum bid price plus closing fees, which earns the discount rate r given up to acquire the income earning durable.

Example 18.3: *Maximum Bid Price with Taxes.* An investor is interested in buying a crop farm. According to the financial statements, last year the farm generated a net cash receipts of $48,000. Past data indicated that net cash returns have been growing at 6% per year. The investor's opportunity cost of capital is 11%, and closing fees for the transaction are 3%. The investor's income tax bracket is 30%, the property tax is 2%, and we assume that θ = .75. Using equation (18.25), the maximum bid price for the farm is

$$V_0^b = \frac{\$48,000(1.06)(1-.3)}{\{.11[1-(.75)(.3)] - .06\}(1+.03) + .02(1-.3)} = \frac{\$35,616}{.026+.014}$$

(18.26) $= \$890,400$

The Value in Use model. It will be convenient later on to find the value of what the seller will sacrifice instead of selling his or her land and continuing to extract services from it. In this case there are no transaction costs, and property taxes are associated with its use value as opposed to its maximum bid price. We can derive the value in use with taxes model, V_0^u, by setting $c = 0$ in equation (18.25). The result is:

$$V_0^u = \frac{R_0(1+g)(1-T)}{[r(1-\theta T)-g]+T_p(1-T)}$$

(18.27)

To illustrate, the value in use model for the previous example is:

$$V_0^u = \frac{\$48,000(1.06)(1-.3)}{\{.11[1-(.75)(.3)]-.06\}+.02(1-.3)} = \$913,230$$

(18.28)

One way to interpret the value in use with taxes model is that it represents the defending asset for the seller of land—the present value of future earnings it would receive, provided the land isn't sold.

The Minimum Sell Price Model with Taxes. The minimum sell price model with taxes is similar to the maximum bid price model with taxes, with a few exceptions: First, assume the seller originally bought his or her land t periods earlier at a price of V_{-t}^b. Then, if V_{-t}^b is less than (more than) the current selling price of V_0^s, the seller pays (earns) capital gains taxes (credits) at a rate of α times the average income tax rate of $\alpha T\%$ or αT.

Another difference is the transaction costs. These costs affect taxable capital gains because the capital gains tax is only paid on the net gain from the sale of land. Like the maximum bid price model, however, the property tax rate is assessed against the inflating value in use since there is no benchmark sell price to calibrate its tax value.

The value in use with taxes is the challenging investment for the seller. We equate the after-tax sale price to the value in use with taxes in equation (18.29). We summarize these results in equation (18.29):

$$(1-s)V_0^s - [(1-s)V_0^s - (1+c)V_{-t}^b \alpha T$$
$$= V_0^u = \frac{R_0(1+g)(1-T)}{[r(1-\theta T)-g]+T_p(1-T)}$$

(18.29)

Solving for V_0^s the minimum sell price with taxes we find:

$$V_0^s = \frac{V_0^u - (1+c)V_{-t}^b \alpha T}{(1-s)(1-\alpha T)}$$

(18.30)

Example 18.4: *Minimum Sell Price with Taxes.* ABC Corporation wants to sell a large farm. They want to know their minimum sell price to accept—or the price a buyer would need to offer in order for them to be as well off selling as they would be continuing to farm the land. ABC has already calculated the farm-land's value in use is equal to \$913,230 (see equation 18.27). This is the present value of their defender.

Recognizing its minimum sell price adjusted for transaction costs and capital gains taxes (credits) as its challenger, ABC equates the two, and solves for its minimum sell price with taxes. The result is expressed in equation (18.30). Summarizing the information needed to find ABC's minimum sell price: $V_0^u = \$913{,}230$, c = 3%, $V_{-t}^b = \$600{,}000$, $\alpha = .4$, T = 30%, and s = 5%.

The result is:

$$V_0^s = \frac{V_0^u - (1+c)V_{-t}^b \alpha T}{(1-s)(1-\alpha T)} = \frac{\$913{,}230 - (1.03)(\$600{,}000)(.4)(.3)}{(.95)[1 - (.4)(.3)]}$$

(18.31)
$$= \$1{,}003{,}672$$

Clearly, the buyer and seller in Examples 18.3 and 18.4 would never exchange land—the minimum sell price of \$1,003,672 exceeds the buyer's maximum bid price of \$890,400. What would have to change for land to become liquid—for the buyer to offer the seller at least his or her minimum sell price? Well, for one thing, the buyer would have to expect initial earnings greater than \$48,000. Or the buyer could find means of reducing its property tax rate. Or the buyer could reduce its transaction costs. Or the buyer may have a lower opportunity cost than the seller. Other changes, such as changes in g and T, have ambiguous effects on the maximum bid price V_0^b.

Finding the Tax Adjustment Coefficient θ

The homogeneity of measures principle requires that after-tax cash flow be discounted by an after-tax discount rate—in most cases the IRR of the defender. The question is, how do we find the after-tax IRR that corresponds to the after-tax cash flow of the defender? First, we specify the defender's cash flow stream and PV and solve for the discount rate or the IRR of the investment. We are guaranteed that we have found the IRR of the defender in a maximum bid (minimum sell) price model and value in use model because the NPV in these models is always zero. We demonstrate how to find the defender's IRR first for the simple geometric growth model and then for more complicated models that include taxes.

Now we introduce taxes into equation (18.5), holding V_0 constant, and express the after-tax geometric growth model as:

(18.32)

$$V_0 = \frac{R_0(1+g)(1-T)}{[1+r(1-\theta T)]} + \frac{R_0(1+g)^2(1-T)}{[1+r(1-\theta T)]^2} + \frac{R_0(1+g)^3(1-T)}{[1+r(1-\theta T)]^3} + \cdots$$
$$= \frac{R_0(1+g)(1-T)}{r(1-\theta T)-g}$$

To summarize, because equation (18.32) describes a defender's after-tax cash flow stream, then $r(1 - \theta T)$ is the defender's after-tax IRR—because NPV in equation (18.32) is zero. Another way to summarize the results above is to note that taxes in equation (18.32) are neutral—meaning that they are introduced so that NPV remains zero. Since V_0 is the same in both equations (18.5) and (18.32), we can equate their right-hand sides and write:

(18.33)
$$V_0 = \frac{R_0(1+g)(1-T)}{r(1-\theta T)-g} = \frac{R_0(1+g)}{(r-g)}$$

Up to this point, we have not specified the value of θ. However, we do require that its value be chosen in such a way that $r(1 - \theta T)$ is the after-tax IRR of the defender's after tax cash described using a geometric growth model. We find such a θ for the geometric cash flow model using equation (18.32), which equals:

(18.34)
$$\theta = \frac{r-g}{r}$$

The above results are intuitive. For $g \neq 0$ in equation (18.34), capital gains (losses) are earned (lost) without creating any tax consequences. If the before-tax IRR is r, an after-tax rate of $r(1 - T)$ implies cash and capital gains (losses) are taxed at the average income tax rate T, which is not true because only cash receipts are taxed. Since capital gains (losses) are earned (lost) at rate g, subtracting from r%, g%, makes taxes neutral in the geometric growth model described above. To confirm that θ coefficient makes taxes neutral, the right-hand side of equation (18.34) is substituted into equation (18.33) to obtain the result:

(18.35)
$$V_0 = \frac{R_0(1+g)(1-T)}{\left\{ r\left[1 - \left(\frac{r-g}{r}\right)T\right] - g \right\}} = \frac{R_0(1+g)}{(r-g)}$$

Following a similar procedure, we can find the value for θ in the value in use model for land. In this case, we equate the right-hand side of the value in use land model to the right hand side of the geometric growth model. This new equality can be written as:

$$V_0^u = \frac{R_0(1+g)(1-T)}{[r(1-\theta T)-g]+T_p(1-T)} = \frac{R_0(1+g)}{r-g}$$

(18.36)

As before, θ in equation (18.36) is the coefficient that makes taxes neutral in the land value in use model because it ensures that the effects of taxes on the defender's cash flow are equally offset by changes in the discount rate. Therefore, the discount rate continues to equal the defender's IRR. We can find such a θ for a value in use land model by solving for θ in equation (18.36):

$$\theta = \frac{r-g+(T_p/T)(1-T)}{r}$$

(18.37)

Clearly, property taxes increase the tax adjustment coefficient and the effective tax rate.

Non-neutral taxes. When we calculated the tax-adjustment coefficient, we assumed tax-neutrality. This was an appropriate assumption for finding the after-tax IRR of the defender. In other PV models, there is no reason to assume that the after-tax IRR of the defender used to calculate the maximum bid (minimum sell) price or NPV will be tax-neutral. For example, assume the challenger's cash flow is represented by a geometric growth equation and assume that the tax adjustment coefficient of the defender is one—an assumption consistent with a defender's whose returns are only cash. In this case, we find the value in use as:

$$V_0 = \frac{R_0(1+g)(1-T)}{[1+r(1-T)]} + \frac{R_0(1+g)^2(1-T)}{[1+r(1-T)]^2} + \cdots$$

$$= \frac{R_0(1+g)(1-T)}{r(1-T)-g}$$

(18.38)

To test for tax-neutrality, we differentiate V_0 with respect to T and find:

$$\frac{dV_0}{dT} = \frac{gR_0(1+g)}{[r(1-T)-g]^2} > 0$$

(18.39)

In this particular case, taxes are not neutral, and increasing the tax rate makes the defender less attractive relative to the challenger because the challenger's capital gains are shielded from income taxes.

Price-to-earnings Ratios for Land

An interesting ratio can be derived from the value in use with taxes model, equation (18.32). It is the ratio of land's value in use, divided by the previous period's cash flow, approximated by cash rents. We write the ratio as:

$$(18.40) \quad \frac{V_0}{R_0} = \frac{(1+g)(1-T)}{[r(1-T)-g] + T_p(1-T)}$$

Note that the value-to-earnings ratio for land depends on specific tax rates, opportunity costs, and expected growth rates, and these vary from location to location. Figure 18.4 below describes land values to rent ratios for land in Iowa, Illinois, and Indiana since 1967. Suppose that in equation (18.40) we were to ignore taxes and assume a real growth rate of zero. Then equation (18.40) reduces to the traditional capitalization ratio of:

$$(18.41) \quad \frac{V_0}{R_0} = \frac{1}{r^*}$$

This is how the traditional capitalization ratio is derived. As an earlier graph demonstrated, however, the ratio has not been constant over time.

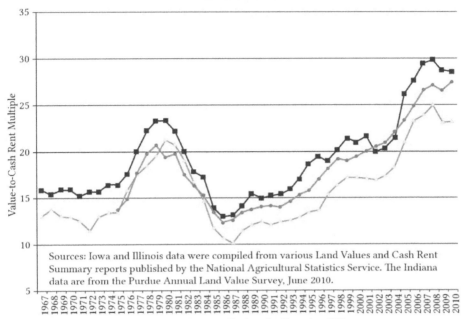

Figure 18.4. *Land values to rent ratios for land in Iowa, Illinois, and Indiana since 1967.*

An interesting exercise would be to approximate the discount rate in equation (18.41) with the real interest rate described in an earlier figure and then compare the results with the ratios described above.

Summary and Conclusions

Land's immobility and durability make it an important asset for securing loans. Its immobility means that lenders know where to find it, and its durability means that it will have the capacity to supply services and earn a return almost undiminished into the future. Both of these characteristics provide assurances to lenders that if they loan money to buy land, they will be able to recover their loans even if the borrowers fail to meet their obligations. On the other hand, land's immobility and durability also mean that its owners' can be easily identified and taxed. Land sales are carefully recorded to establish its value. Thus, land is a favorite source of tax revenue not only for its market value but also at the time of sale if capital gains (losses) are incurred.

Land has another feature. Land is infrequently traded, and transfers of ownership are costly for both buyers and sellers—often requiring the help of outside agents who must be paid for their services. As a result, both buyers and sellers pay funds they do not receive when buying and selling land. These transaction costs, including tax payments, mean that land exchange will likely not occur unless the buyer expects to earn more from land's services than currently earned by sellers. As a result, land is illiquid and its purchase and sale is a very infrequent occurrence.

In this chapter, PV models were used to model three types of prices: maximum bid prices, the most a buyer could offer to purchase the land; minimum sell prices, the least a seller would accept to sell the land; and value in use prices, the value of the land assuming continued use. These models accounted for three different types of taxes (property tax, income tax, and capital gains tax) as well as cash flow. These models provide helpful tools for assisting buyers and sellers in determining investment strategies.

Questions

1. Describe the features that make land an illiquid investment.
2. Why do lenders seem to prefer land to secure their loans? Compare the loan security provided by land compared to that offered by used equipment or breeding livestock?
3. Figures 18.1 and 18.2 compare year-to-year changes in farmland and housing prices. What is similar between those forces contributing to the variability in the prices of land and housing stock?
4. Commodities are nondurable goods and are likely used up in a single period. Meanwhile, land and houses are durables and last for many years. Can you describe how these differences between durable and nondurable goods may contribute to differences in the variability of their prices? Does the fact that the supply of land is relatively fixed versus the supply of commodities that can vary from year to year influence their variability?
5. Equation (18.9) describes the percentage change in the price of a long term asset (in this case land) in response to a change in the real interest rate r^*. Assume that the real growth rate is 3% and the real interest rate is 4%. Find the percentage increase in V_0 if r^* increases by 1%. Find the percentage increase in V_0 if g^* decreases by 1%.
6. Consider the maximum bid price and minimum sell price models. Consider the following data: the closing fee for the buyer is 3%, the closing fee for the seller is 4%, and in the last period land rented for $150 per period. Land is liquid if the maximum bid price is greater than the minimum sell price. Using this data, please answer the following questions. Calculate the ratio of the maximum bid price to the minimum sell price. Is land liquid or illiquid? What must occur for the land to become liquid?
7. An investor is interested in buying a crop farm. According to the financial statements last year, the farm generated a net cash flow of $52,000. Past data indicates that net cash returns have been growing at 3% per year. The investor's opportunity cost of capital, the IRR on its defender, is 8%, and closing fees for the transaction are 4%. The property is taxed at 1.5%, and the investor is in the 35% tax bracket. The tax adjustment coefficient θ is assumed to equal 75%. Find the maxi-

mum bid price for the parcel of land using maximum bid price with taxes model.

8. Farmland owners Rob and Ruthie Bell want to retire and sell their farm. They purchased their farm over 30 years ago for $325,000. They recognize that their minimum sell price must leave them as well off as they would be if they continued to operate their farm. They estimate that closing fees will equal 3%, they are in the 30% tax bracket, and their capital gain tax rate αT is 12%. Finally, they realize that their closing fees will be 5%. Find the minimum sell price for Rob and Ruthie Bell. (Hint: first find the value in use with taxes for the farmland. Then using the value in use with taxes and data described in this question, calculate the minimum sell price using the minimum sell price with taxes model.)

9. In previous problems, the tax adjustment coefficient was assumed to be 75%. Using the data supplied for calculating the maximum bid price for land with taxes, find the tax adjustment coefficient using equation (18.37).

10. Use equation (18.41) and land value to cash rent data described in Figure 18.4 to approximate real interest rates over time for Iowa, Indiana, or Illinois. If you believe that real interest rates are constant, what other explanations can you offer for time varying land value to rent ratios?

19. "Leasing Strategies: Understanding the Implications of Leases"

LINDON ROBISON

Learning goals. After completing this chapter, you should be able to: (1) understand how leasing can provide an alternative method for gaining control of and access to capital resources and (2) evaluate leases using present value (PV) models developed earlier.

Learning objectives. To achieve your learning goals, you should complete the following objectives:

- Distinguish between the different forms of leases including the sale and leaseback lease, the operating lease, and the financial or capital lease.
- Learn the differences between leases and rental agreements.
- Learn how lease agreements are taxed.
- Learn the advantages and disadvantages of entering a lease agreement versus owning a capital resource.
- Learn how to find the break-even purchase price when compared to a leasing option.

Introduction

1

Control of a durable can be transferred between parties in several ways. A lease agreement is one important way. A lease is a contract through which control over the right to use a durable is transferred from one party, the lessor, to another party, the lessee who acquires control of the durable. In exchange for the right to use or control a durable for a specified time period, the lessee pays the lessor a rental payment or share in the output produced by the leased durable. The lease payment or shared output must cover the opportunity cost of funds invested in the leased item, depreciation of the durable, and other incidental ownership costs incurred by the lessor. Thus, leasing is a method of financing the control of a durable that separates its use from its ownership.

There are several kinds of lease arrangements and several kinds of durables that are leased. Farmland is frequently leased as are machines, houses, cars, computers, coping equipment, buildings, breeding

---

1. Some of the material in this chapter was adapted from Robison, L.J. and P.J. Barry (1996). *Present Value Models and Investment Analysis.* "Chapter 18, Leasing Decision." Michigan State University Press.

livestock, and many kinds of management services. In this chapter, we describe various types of leases, evaluate their advantages and disadvantages, and apply present value (PV) tools to analyze leasing benefits for both the lessor and the lessee.

Types of Lease Agreements

Sale and leaseback. Under the sale-and-leaseback agreement, a firm owning a durable to be leased sells the durable to a financial institution and simultaneously executes an agreement to lease the durable back. Thus, the lease becomes the alternative to a purchase with a specific advantage to the lessee: namely, he or she is allowed to write off the entire lease payment as an expense instead of just interest costs and depreciation. The lessor will not enter into this type of lease agreement unless the lease payments are sufficient to return the full purchase price plus a return on the investment to the lessor.

Operating leases. Operating leases, sometimes called service leases, provide for both financing and maintenance. These leases ordinarily call for the lessor to maintain the leased equipment. The cost of the maintenance is built into the lease payment. Computers and office copiers, together with cars and trucks, are the primary types of equipment involved in operating leases.

In the case of operating leases, lease payments are often insufficient to recover the full cost of the equipment. To offset this feature, the lease is written for a time period considerably less than the expected life of the leased equipment, leaving the lessor to recover his or her investment in renewal payments of the lease or through disposal of the leased equipment.

One of the main advantages of the operating lease for lessees is the cancellation of the short lease period which allows them to adopt and bring into use more advanced equipment. Thus, for durables subject to rapid changes in technology, an operating lease is often a preferred method for gaining control of a durable.

Financial or capital leases. A financial lease is a fully amortized lease whose PV of the lease payments equals the full price of the leased equipment. It does not provide for maintenance service nor may it be canceled. The financial lease begins with a lessee selecting the specific items it requires and agreeing with the lessor about the price and the delivery of the item. The lessor arranges with a bank or another financial institution to purchase the equipment and simultaneously executes a financial lease with the lessee intending to use the equipment. The purchase of the equipment builds into the lease payments a rate of return equivalent to what would be charged on a loan, and the lease is canceled when the purchase price of the durable plus a return for the lessor is paid.

Under financial leases, lessees generally pay property taxes and insurance and, in many cases, can acquire ownership of the durable at the end of the lease. The significant difference between the sale-and-leaseback lease and the financial lease is that the lessee purchases the durable directly from the manufacturer rather than from the lessor under the terms of the financial lease.

Lease Agreements and Taxes

One of the major effects of the lease is to alter the tax obligations of the lessee and lessor. Therefore, special attention is required to make sure that lease agreements are acceptable under current tax codes as interpreted in the United States by the Internal Revenue Service. There is an important distinction between a lease agreement and a loan for tax purposes. If the lease agreement cannot be distinguished from an ordinary loan agreement, then any special tax provisions associated with the lease agreement are lost.

To distinguish a lease from a sale agreement, the term over which the investment durable is leased must be less than 75 percent of the economic life of the durable. Nor should the lessee be granted any special repurchase option not available to others not involved in the lease. There are other conditions as well; tax codes are evolving documents that are constantly being updated.

Lease Liquidity and Risk

Normally, the decision to acquire the durable is not at issue in the typical lease analysis. The issue at hand is whether to acquire control of the durable through a lease or by purchasing it—often by borrowing funds to finance the purchase. The decision requires a careful examination of the advantages of leasing. Leasing offers several possible advantages relative to owning a durable that we describe next.

Release of cash and credit. When a firm leases or sells a durable on a leaseback arrangement, the lessee avoids the cash down payment required to purchase the investment. More generally, the liquidity of a lease versus the liquidity of a purchase depends on which option requires the most accelerated payments.

Some texts discuss in detail the effect on the firm's credit reserve as a result of leasing. If leasing uses up credit at a slower rate than borrowing, there may be credit incentives for leasing rather than borrowing. However, lenders are likely to recognize that long-term lease agreements place the same requirements on the firm's future cash flow as loans do.

Obsolescence risk. Investments may experience significant obsolescence risks. In addition, there is some risk that the need for durables' services will change before the durables' service capacity is exhausted. Part of this obsolescence and use risk may be reduced through a lease arrangement for a short time period, especially if the lessor is less subject to obsolescence risk than the lessee. This is likely the case where the leased equipment has alternative uses in other firms or industries and where the risk can be spread over many lessees.

Idle capacity risk. Another risk that can often be reduced through lease arrangement is the risk of holding idle equipment. If the demand for services from a durable is not sufficient to employ the durable full time, the lessee can reduce idle capacity risk by leasing rather than owning the durable. From the lessor's point of view, the durable can be completely employed because many lessees will use the equipment.

Foreclosure risk. In many respects, leasing is similar to borrowing because it represents an obligation of the firm to a series of future cash payments. There is one significant difference between agreeing to lease and borrowing to purchase the durable. In the case of financial difficulties, the lessor simply takes back the equipment because he or she holds the legal title. In the case of a loan, inability to meet loan payments may result in more complex foreclosure proceedings.

Tax advantages. A tax advantage may be gained when the term of the lease is shorter than the allowable tax depreciation period for ownership. However, tax incentives for the lessee must be a result of a lower total tax burden for the lessee and lessor. This situation implies that the lease arrangement has legitimately allowed for a reduction in the total amount of taxes paid. Needless to say, the Internal Revenue Service imposes conditions on what does and does not constitute a legal lease.

Net Present Cost of Leasing versus Purchasing

The decision to lease or to buy a durable depends on the net present cost (NPC) of leasing versus NPC of purchasing the durable. Since the size and timing of the cash flow, influence of taxes, and risks associated with buying and leasing are different, they represent two different investment opportunities which are amenable to analysis using PV models. In the following discussion, the after-tax cash flow is considered risk-adjusted, and the problem is treated as riskless.

To compare the lease with the purchase option, the firm considers itself in both roles—that of a lessee and lessor—and finds the maximum lease payment it could pay and be indifferent between purchasing or leasing the durable. We begin by describing the NPC of the lease (NPC^L). Because we are describing the NPC of the lease, cash costs are treated as positive flow, and income that reduces the cost of leasing is treated as negative cash flow. For simplicity, we will assume a maximum constant lease payment equal to C. Then we assume the lease payment at age t is C_t, the lessee's constant marginal tax rate is T, the lessee's before-tax opportunity cost of capital is r, and the lessee's tax adjustment coefficient is θ as described in Chapter 11. With these definitions in place, the net present cost of a lease for n periods, NPC^L, can be expressed as:

$$NPC^L = C(1-T) + \frac{C(1-T)}{[1-r(1-\theta T)]} + \cdots + \frac{C(1-T)}{[1-r(1-\theta T)]^{n-1}}$$

(19.1)

Notice in equation (19.1) that the first lease payment is made at the beginning of the lease payment rather than at the end of the lease period, which would be the case of a loan. Therefore, leases can be viewed as an annuity due type of financial arrangement. Multiplying both sides of equation (19.1) by [1 + r(1 - θT)] and summing the resulting geometric series, we write the result as:

(19.2) $$NPC^L = C(1-T)\{1 + US_0[r(1-\theta T), n-1]\}$$

where:

(19.3) $$US_0[r(1-\theta T), n-1] = \frac{C(1-T)}{[1-r(1-\theta T)]} + \cdots + \frac{C(1-T)}{[1-r(1-\theta T)]^{n-1}}$$

We now consider the net present cost of a cash purchase, NPC^P, for the same financial manager who previously considered the lease option. We begin by assuming that the market value of the durable leased or purchased is equal to V_0. We also assume that V_t^B is the book value of the depreciable durable at age t. We continue to assume that the purchaser's opportunity cost of capital is r, the average tax rate is T, and γ_t is the percentage of the investment's value allowed to be deducted in year t where $t = 1$, ..., n, and the tax adjustment coefficient is θ. Of course, the sum of the amount deducted cannot exceed the value of the investment so that $\gamma_1 + \cdots + \gamma_n \leq 1$. All these assumptions allow us to write the NPC^P as:

(19.4) $$NPC^P = V_0 - \frac{T\gamma_1 V_0}{[1+r(1-\theta T)]} - \cdots$$
$$- \frac{T\gamma_n V_0}{[1+r(1-\theta T)]^n} - \frac{V_n - T\gamma_n V_n}{[1+r(1-\theta T)]^n}$$

The purchaser's cost on the right-hand side of equation (19.4) is the purchase price V_0, less n periods of tax savings from depreciation equal to $T\gamma_t V_0$ in the period discounted to the present period. The liquidation value V_n minus a tax adjustment term $T(V_n - V_n^B)$ reduces the purchaser's cost. The adjustment term accounts for the tax consequences of a difference between the liquidation value and the book value of the investment. If the investment is completely depreciated by the nth period, and the liquidation value is zero, then the NPC^P can be written as:

(19.5) $$NPC^P = V_0 - \frac{T\gamma_1 V_0}{[1+r(1-\theta T)]} - \cdots - \frac{T\gamma_n V_0}{[1+r(1-\theta T)]^n}$$

Finally, if the NPC^L, expressed as the right-hand side of equation (19.2), is equated to NPC^P, expressed as the left-hand side of equation (19.5), we can solve for the lease payment C, a maximum bid lease, which equates the two alternatives for controlling the services from the durable.

(19.6) $$C = \frac{NPC^p}{(1-T)\{1 + US_0[r(1-\theta T), n-1]\}}$$

Consider an example. Go Green is a lawn service that requires a new truck to service its customers. It wants to know the largest lease payment it could afford and still be as well off as it would be if it purchased the truck. The truck in question has a new sticker price of $30,000 and can be depreciated using a straight-line method over five years. At the end of the lease, the truck has a liquidation value of $5,000. To find the maximum bid payment, the following assumptions are used: T = 32%, γ_t = 10% for t = 1, ..., 5, r = 14%, θ = 1, n = 5, V_n = $5,000, and V_n^B = 0. Finally, the after-tax discount rate is r(1 - T) = .14(1 - .32) = .095

To find the maximum bid payment, we first find NPC^P by substituting numerical values into equation (19.6):

$$NPC^P = \$30,000 - (.32)(\$6,000)US_0(0.095,5) - \frac{\$5,000(1-.32)}{(1.0952)^5}$$

(19.7)

We record the solution to this problem using Excel in Table 19.1 below.

Table 19.1. Finding the NPC of the Purchase.
Open Table 19.1 in Microsoft Excel

B9		f_x	=NPV(B2,B3:B8)
	A	B	C
1	Purchase Price	$30,000	
2	rate	.095	
3	Depreciation tax savings period 1	($1,920)	
4	Depreciation tax savings period 2	($1,920)	
5	Depreciation tax savings period 3	($1,920)	
6	Depreciation tax savings period 4	($1,920)	
7	Depreciation tax savings period 5	($1,920)	
8	After-tax salvage value period 6	($3,100)	
9	NPV of depreciation tax savings + after-tax salvage	($9,170.60)	=NPV(rate, value1:value6)
10	NPC: purchase price - PV of tax-savings + salvage value	$20.829.40	=NPV of depreciation tax savings + salvage value + purchase price

In cell B9 we enter the function: = NPV(rate,values) = NPV(B2,B3:B8) which returns the value ($9,170.60). In cell B10 we add the purchase price of $30,000 to the NPV of after-tax depreciation savings plus the liquidation value which returns the NPC of the purchase equal to $20,829.36.

Having found NPC^P equal to $20,829.40, we can find C using equation (19.6).

We solve this problem using Excel in Table 19.2 by finding the present value of Annuity Due with 5 payments of –1. We enter the arguments of the PV function and label the terms in adjacent cells. Excel's PV function has the following arguments listed in column A: rate (rate), number of payments (nper), annuity (pmt), future value (FV), annuity type (type). For this problem, the discount rate is 9.5% = .095, the number of payments equals 5, the payments are –1, the future value FV is zero, and the type of annuity is an annuity due which requires we enter 1.

Table 19.2. Finding the PV of the Annuity Due
Open Table 19.2 in Microsoft Excel

B6			f_x	=PV(B1,B2,B3,B4,B5)
	A	B		C
1	rate	.095		
2	nper	5		
3	pmt	–1		
4	FV	0		
5	type	1		
6	PV	$4.20		=PV(rate,nper,pmt,FV,type)

In cell B6 we type in the PV function: = PV(B1,B2,B3,B4,B5). The result returned is PV = $4.20. Then we multiply by (1 – T) as required in equation (19.6). Finally we find C:

$$(19.8) \quad C = \frac{NPC^P}{(1-T)\{1+US_0[r(1-\theta T), n-1]\}} = \frac{\$20,829.40}{.68(4.2)} = \$7,283.01$$

Now suppose that we wanted to know the number of periods required to reach a future value of $2,000. With the data already entered, we turn to the "goal seek" option in Excel. To access goal seek from the main menu, press the [Data] tab, then on the ribbon menu press the [What-if Analysis] button, and on the drop down menu press [Goal Seek...]. The goal seek menu allow us to identify a target value for a particular cell and a variable to change. In our case the target cell is B6 and the target amount is $2,000. The cell we allow to vary is the number of periods cell, B2. Then entering these into Excel's solver, the solution returned is 19.57. Thus, by continuing to invest for 8.57 periods, we obtain a future value of $2,000 compared to the future value of $1,005.18 reached after 10 years of investing.

Alternatively, we could have asked what is the payment amount required to reach a future value of $2,000 during the original term. In this case we vary the annuity in cell is B3, and the solver returns the value of $182.65. Thus, by increasing our annuity due from $90 to $182.65, we reach a future value amount of $2,000 in the same term required to reach a future value of $1,005.18 with $90 annuity due payments.

What we have found in this example is that we would be indifferent between purchasing the truck for $30,000 and making five lease payments of $7,283.01. Obviously, the high discount rate of 14% and making the payment for the truck up front contributes to the high lease payment. In the questions at the end of this chapter, students will be asked to repeat the problem assuming the same values except that the opportunity cost of capital is 5%.

Comparative Advantages for Leasee and Leasor

So far, we have described the technical properties of leases and how a financial manager may decide between gaining control of a durable through a lease or purchase arrangement. In this section, we allow the lessee and the lessor to be two different persons whose comparative advantages lead them into an exchange arrangement in which one party purchases an asset and then leases it to another party. The solution in this case considers the NPC from the lessee's (lessor's) position, assuming that the lessor (lessee) pays their maximum bid purchase price (lease payment). What makes this an interesting problem is that differences in the lessee's and lessor's tax rates, as well as opportunity costs of capital, can create incentives to exchange.

Comparative advantage. A fundamental principle of economics is that firms should specialize in tasks for which nature, institutions, or luck has granted them an advantage. To illustrate, suppose two farmers, A and B, can both produce dry edible beans and carrots. Also assume A can grow dry edible beans and carrots more profitably than B, and B can grow carrots more profitably than it can grow dry beans. If both beans and carrots must be produced, then A should produce beans, and B should grow carrots. They could then trade to obtain what they did not produce, and both would be better off.

Even though A produced both beans and carrots more profitably than B, it would still be to A's and B's advantage to specialize. They should decide in which product A had the greatest advantage in production, or B had the least comparative disadvantage, and then specialize and trade as before.

An application of the law of comparative advantage explains why two firms may lease. Suppose firm A is able to purchase a durable at a lower price than firm B. But firm B, not firm A, has need of the services of the durable. In this case, firm A's advantage is in purchasing while B's advantage is in using the durable. Thus, A might purchase the durable and either sell or lease to B.

Another reason why A and B might both agree to lease has to do with relative tax rates. Suppose A, the purchaser of a durable, pays taxes at an average rate T^P, which is higher than T^L, the average rate at which B, the lessee, pays taxes. As the durable is depreciated, the depreciation creates a tax shield of greater value to the purchaser than to the lessee. Thus, we might say that A, the purchaser, has a comparative tax advantage over B, the lessee, in claiming tax depreciation. The lease allows the purchaser, A, and the lessee, B, to benefit from their comparative advantages associated with the tax shields created by depreciation.

Still further reasons why A and B might purchase and lease a durable are that they face different opportunity costs of capital, have different opportunities for using the durable's services, or face different marginal costs of credit.

Comparative advantages for lessee and lessor created by different tax rates and opportunity costs of capital. To demonstrate the idea of comparative advantage with a lease agreement, consider that person B, the lessee, will not lease for more than it would cost to control the durable through a purchase agreement. We want to find B's NPC if the durable were purchased. To simplify, assume the purchase price of the durable is V_0, the book value depreciation rate in year t is $\gamma_t = \gamma(1 - \gamma)^t$ where t = 0, ..., n − 1, r^B is B's opportunity cost of capital, T^B is B's average tax rate, and assume the lessee tax adjustment coefficient is 1. The NPC^P of the purchase for B is:

$$NPC^L(\text{purchase}) = V_0 - \frac{T^B \gamma V_0}{[1 + r^B(1 - T^B)]} - \frac{T^B \gamma V_0(1 - \gamma)}{[1 + r^B(1 - T^B)]^2}$$
$$- \frac{T^B \gamma V_0(1 - \gamma)^2}{[1 + r^B(1 - T^B)]^3} - \cdots$$

(19.9)

Equation (19.9) is equivalent to equation (19.4) except that it is expressed in a form that makes it analytically tractable. Obviously, more detailed expressions with finite time horizons could easily be calculated. What makes equation (19.9) tractable is that it is expressed as an infinite series whose solution can be written as:

$$NPC^L(\text{purchase}) = V_0 - \frac{T^B \gamma V_0}{r^B(1 - T^B) + \gamma}$$

(19.10)

Now consider what happens to B's NPC resulting from the purchase if B's tax rate increases. We find the change in B's NPC associated with the purchase of the durable by differentiating NPC^P with respect to T^B. (This operation in essence examines the change in NPC^P with respect to a small change in T^A. The results is that NPC^P decreases with an increase in T^B. Thus, a firm in a higher tax bracket can buy a durable at a lower after-tax cost than someone in a lower tax bracket.

Next, we find B's NPC^L associated with leasing the durable which, after summing geometrically, can be expressed as:

$$NPC^L \text{ (lease)} = \frac{C(1 - T^B)}{[1 + r^L(1 - T^B)]} + \frac{C(1 - T^B)}{[1 + r^L(1 - T^B)]^2}$$

$$+ \frac{C(1 - T^B)}{[1 + r^L(1 - T^B)]^3} + \cdots$$

$$= \frac{C[1 + r^L(1 - T^B)]}{r^L}$$

(19.11)

To illustrate equation (19.10) consider the following example: Suppose Affordable Assets (AA) buys durables and leases them to other firms. As a well-to-do established firm, AA's tax rate, T^A is high—45 percent. On the other hand, the Unendowed User (UU) lacks capital and prefers to lease rather than own in order to protect its limited credit. Because of its lower earnings, UU's average tax rate T^U is 21 percent. In addition, assume that the leased durable wears out at the rate of γ = 10 percent, and assume the market rate of return for both AA and UU is 14 percent. Finally, assume that the purchase price of the durable is $4,000.

Making the appropriate substitutions into equation (19.10), we find the NPC of purchasing the durable for UU is:

$$NPC^{UU} = \$4,000 - \frac{[(.21)(.1)(\$4,000)]}{[(.14)(1 - .21) + .1]} = \$3,600$$

(19.12)

In other words, the after-tax purchase price of the durable for UU is $3,600.

Now consider the after-tax NPC of the purchase for firm AA. Making the appropriate substitutions into equation (19.10), we find the NPC of purchasing the durable for AA is:

$$NPC^{AA} = \$4,000 - \frac{[(.45)(.1)(\$4,000)]}{[(.14)(1 - .45) + .1]} = \$3,000$$

(19.13)

In other words, the after-tax cost of the durable purchase for AA was only $3,000 compared to $3,600 for UU.

Having calculated NPC for purchasing the durable for firms UU and AA, we can find their respective maximum bid lease prices. Making the appropriate substitutions into equation (19.11), we find NPC^{UU} (leasing) = $C^{UU}[1 + (.14)(1 - .21)] / .14 = \$3,600$. Solving for C^{UU} we find $C^{UU} = \$453.81$.

Similarly we find NPC^{AA} (leasing) = $C^{AA}[1 + (.14)(1 - .45)] / .14 = \$3,000$. Solving for C^{AA} we find $C^{AA} = \$389.97$.

Reflections on comparative advantages for firms UU and AA. Because of their differences in tax rates, firms UU and AA have different effective after-tax cost of the durable even though the market price of the durable is the same for each firm. In this case, the effective cost for AA is less than for firm UU—$3,000 versus $3,600. On the other hand and as a result of the differences in the effective after tax cost of the durable, the maximum bid lease price for firm UU is greater than for firm AA: $453.81 versus $389.97.

These results provide opportunities for firms AA and UU to take advantage of their comparative advantages: firm AA purchases the durable at a lower effective cost than is available to UU. UU, on the other hand, is quite willing to pay a higher lease price than AA's maximum bid lease price. Under these arrangements, both firms AA and UU are made better off.

Leases and NPV. Assume that firm AA buys the durable and UU leases the durable from AA. Now the lease price in an expense for firm UU but an income for AA. We may want to ask: what is the minimum lease payment AA could accept from UU and still break even? To find this amount we set AA's NPV as:

$$NPV^{AA} = \frac{C[1 + r(1 - T^{AA})]}{r - NPC^{AA}(\text{purchase})}$$

(19.14)

After making the appropriate substitutions we find

$$C = \frac{NPC^{AA}(\text{purchase})(r^{AA})}{[1 + r^{AA}(1 - T^{AA})]} = \frac{\$3,000(.14)}{[1 + (.14)(1 - .45)]} = \$389.97$$

(19.15)

Thus, any arrangement with UU which generates a lease payment more than $389.97 will result in a positive NPV for AA.

Summary and Conclusions

Trades occur when each party to the exchange gives up something of value in return for something of greater value. In most trades, a physical object or service is exchanged for an agreed-on amount of cash. Moreover, in most cases, ownership is transferred along with the good or service.

This chapter has considered leasing, a different kind of trade, in which the control over the use of a durable is transferred, but ownership of the durable is not. Leasing exists because it provides benefits to the lessee and lessor that might not be realized if control of a durable also required ownership.

Different types of leases described in this chapter include sale-and-leaseback agreements, operating leases, and financial or capital leases. Leases offer particular advantages for lessees including the avoidance of capital requirements associated with a purchase. As a result, lessees may use their limited credit for other purchases or as a credit reserve. Obsolescence risk of ownership is also reduced for lessees. Additionally, leasing offers the chance to better match service requirements to the delivery of services. Ownership of durables may require holding idle capacity—less likely when services of a durable are leased.

Tax considerations are critical in the decision to lease or to purchase. Ownership allows for tax depreciation shields; leasing allows the entire lease payment to be claimed as an expense.

An important principle of comparative advantage is involved in the lease decision. If the tax depreciation from ownership is greater for one firm than for another, leasing permits the firm which can benefit the most from the depreciation shield to claim it by purchasing the asset and leasing it to another firm. Not only can comparative tax advantages be optimally used through leasing, there can also be comparative advantages in acquiring financing. Comparative advantage and the incentive to lease may also result from differences in opportunity costs, access to credit, and use for the durables' services. In essence, leasing is a critical tool that allows firms to benefit from their comparative advantages.

Questions

1. Describe three different lease types and their essential differences.
2. For every lease agreement, there is a lessor and a lessee who both believe they will be better off by executing the lease. Describe how a sale and leaseback agreement might make both the lessor and lessee better off.
3. Assume a lease agreement that requires $100 payments at the beginning of each period for 15 years. The lessee's marginal tax bracket is 25% and opportunity cost of capital is 8%. The tax adjustment coefficient is assumed to equal 80%. Find the NPC of this lease. Now assume that the lessor agreed to accept payments at the end of each period instead of the beginning. What would be the NPC of the lease agreement under the new arrangement?
4. Resolve the Go Green lease problem assuming that the firm's opportunity cost of capital is 5% rather than 14%. Compare your solution with the previous one. Did the lease payment go up or down? Can you explain why?
5. Resolve the Go Green lease problem by assuming that the lessee will lease the durable for an extra period. The lessee will make 6 lease payments instead of 5, but the depreciation schedule will not change. In other words, find the maximum lease payment and explain your results.
6. Explain in your own words the concept of comparative advantage. Provide one example of how the concept of comparative advantage has influenced your choice or the choice of others.
7. Explain how the principle of comparative advantage might explain why two firms may agree to a lease arrangement.
8. In the example of a lessee UU and a lessor AA, the lessee and lessor are in different average tax brackets (45 versus 21 percent) but were assumed to face the same opportunity cost of capital. Resolve the example by assuming UU's opportunity cost of capital is 7% instead of 14%. Find the effective after-tax purchase price of the durable for the two firms. Then find the maximum bid

lease price for the two firms. Do the results allow for the two firms to take advantage of the principle of comparative advantage? Please explain.

9. Consider the case of firms UU and AA described in the text. Since AA has the lowest NPC for purchasing the durable, it should do so. Meanwhile the maximum bid lease price for UU is higher than for AA, so UU should lease rather than purchase the durable. Suppose that UU agrees to pay AA a lease price of $410.00. What is AA's NPV from buying the durable and leasing it back to UU? (Hint: In this arrangement, the lease cost for UU is an income for AA.)

20. "Navigating Financial Markets: Exploring Opportunities in Financial Investments"

LINDON ROBISON

Learning objectives. After completing this chapter, you should be able to distinguish between financial investments and capital investments; (2) recognize the differences in financial investments using methods similar to those used when comparing kinds of financial investments using present value (PV) models developed in earlier chapters.

- Learn to distinguish between financial and nonfinancial objectives.
- Learn the role of brokers, dealers, and financial intermediaries in the securities markets.

Learning objectives. To achieve your learning goals, you should complete the following objectives:

- Learn how to value riskless securities such as time deposits.
- Learn why Albert Einstein called compounding interest "the greatest mathematical discovery of all time".
- Learn the nature of bonds and the variables that determine their value.
- Learn how tax rates affect the value of financial investments.

Introduction

In its broadest meaning, to invest means to give up something in the present for something of greater value in the future. Investments, what we invest in, can differ greatly. They may range from lottery tickets and burial plots to municipal bonds and corporate stocks. It is helpful to organize these investments into two general categories: real and financial. Capital, or real, investments involve the exchange of money for nonfinancial investments that produce services such as storage services from buildings, pulling services from tractors, and growing services from land. Financial investments involve the exchange of money in the present for a future money payment. Financial investments include time deposits, bonds, and stocks.

This chapter applies PV models developed earlier to financial investments. Large corporations and other business organizations require financial investments from a large number of small investors to provide funds for operation and growth. The collection of these funds would be impossible if each investor were required to exercise a managerial role over them. Moreover, the collection of investment funds from a large number of small investors would be impossible unless the investors could be assured of investment safety and limited liability. A number of financial investments have been designed to overcome these and other investment obstacles.

The market in which financial investments are traded is called the securities market or financial market. Activities in the financial markets are facilitated by brokers, dealers, and financial intermediaries. A broker acts as an agent for investors in the securities markets. The securities broker brings two parties together to obtain the best possible terms for his or her client and is compensated by a commission. A dealer, in contrast to a broker, buys and sells securities for his or her own account. Thus, a dealer also becomes an investor. Similarly, financial intermediaries (e.g. banks, investment firms, and insurance companies) play important roles in the flow of funds from savers to ultimate investors. The intermediary acquires ownership of funds loaned or invested by savers, modifies the risk and liquidity of these funds, and then either loans the funds to individual borrowers or invests in various types of financial assets.

Numerous books discuss the institutional arrangements associated with securities trading. In this chapter, the focus in not on the details of trading in the securities market but on how to value financial investments or securities.

Valuation of Riskless Securities

The prices of financial investments, like other prices, are determined in markets—financial markets. The characteristics of financial markets, however, may differ significantly depending on the type of financial investment traded. Common to all financial markets, though, is that prices are established by matching the desires of buyers and sellers. Moreover, in equilibrium there is neither excess demand nor excess supply. However, equilibrium does not mean that all prospective buyers and sellers agree that an investment's price is equal to its value. It only means that a price has been found that, in a sense, balances the different goals of buyers and sellers.

Time deposits. Time deposits are money deposited at a banking institution for a specified period of time. The main difference between different kinds of time deposits is their liquidity. Generally speaking, the less liquid the time deposits are, the greater their yield is.

The most liquid form of time deposits are sometimes known as "on call" deposits. On call deposits can be withdrawn at any time and without any notice or penalty. Examples of on call deposits include money deposited in a savings or checking account in a bank. Another kind of time deposit is a certificate of deposit (CDs). When CDs mature, they can be withdrawn or they can be held for another term. CDs are generally considered to be liquid because they are negotiable and can be re-discounted when the holder needs some liquidity.

Some time deposits must be held until maturity or suffer penalties for early withdrawal. The rate of return for these time deposits is higher than on call deposits because the requirement that the deposits be held for a designated term gives the bank the ability to invest in financial products that earn greater returns. In addition, the return on time deposits is generally lower than the average return on long-term investments in riskier products like stocks and some bonds. Some banks offer market-linked time deposit accounts which offer potentially higher returns while guaranteeing principal.

Investments in time deposits may consist of a one-time investment or a series of deposits. What all time deposits have in common is that the payment(s) is compounded until some ending date at which time they are partially or totally withdrawn. Thus, our interest is not in the present value of the payments but in their future value. The market determined price in the case of financial investments is the compound rate at which time deposits earn interest. Typically, the compound rate of interest earned on time deposits is low—partly because they provide nearly perfect liquidity—especially for time deposits for which there is no penalty nor transaction cost associated with withdrawal of funds.

Ordinary annuities and annuities due. Previously we described an annuity as a time series of constant payments made or received at the end of each period. Annuities paid and received at the end of a period are referred to as ordinary annuities. Annuities paid (or received) at the beginning of each period are referred to as annuity due payments.

To illustrate an annuity due, consider a series of deposits R made every period, the first one occurring in the present. We write the future value V_n of the time series of deposits R compounded at rate $\hat{r}$ for withdrawal in period n as:

$$(20.1) \quad R(1+\hat{r})^n + R(1+\hat{r})^{n-1} + \cdots + R(1+\hat{r})^2 + R(1+\hat{r}) = V_n$$

Note that the first time deposit R is compounded for n periods—and is equal in value to its compounded value at the beginning of period n. Similarly, the second payment is compounded for $n-1$ period and is equal to its compounded value at the beginning of period n. Finally, the last payment is made at the beginning of period $n-1$ and is compounded once to find its compounded value at the beginning of period n.

To illustrate, suppose a saver deposits a $90 payment (PMT) at the beginning of each period for $n = 10$ periods. If the deposits are compounded at a rate of $r = 2\%$, what amount is available for withdrawal at the beginning of period 10? We solve this problem using Excel in Table 20.1. Note that to indicate annuity due payments at the beginning of the period, "type" in the Excel future value FV function is changed from its default of zero to 1. In place of PV in the equation, we enter a blank closed with a comma.

Table 20.1. The Future Value of 10 Annuity Due Payments of $90 Compounded at 2%
Open Table 20.1 in Microsoft Excel

B4		f_x	=FV(B1,B2,B3,,B6)
	A	B	C
1	rate	0.02	
2	nper	10	
3	pmt	($90.00)	
4	FV	$1,005.18	=FV(rate,nper,pmt,[pv],type)
5	PV	0	
6	type	1	

What our calculations determine is that at the beginning of the 10th period, we have $1,005.18 available. However, there are several other interesting questions that we might answer using our Excel formulas. For example, we might want to know how many periods would be required to have $2,000 available at some future date. Continuing with the entries already made in Excel, we add the following:

Table 20.2. Finding the Number of $90 Annuity
Due Payments Compounded at 2% Required to
Earn a Future Value of $2,000
Open Table 20.2 in Microsoft Excel

B2			f_x	=NPER(B1,B3,B4,B6)
	A	B	C	
1	rate	0.02		
2	nper	29.693477	=NPER(rate,pmt,FV,type)	
3	pmt	($90.00)		
4	FV	$2,000.00		
5	PV	0		
6	type	1		

We might be interested in knowing the periodic investment required to have $2,000 available in 10 years if the investments were compounded at 2%. The required Excel formula is represented in Table 20.3.

Table 20.3. Finding the Annuity Due Payment
Compounded at 2% Required to Earn a Future
Value of $2,000 in 10 Years
Open Table 20.3 in Microsoft Excel

B3			f_x	=PMT(B1,B2,B5,B4,B6)
	A	B	C	
1	rate	0.02		
2	nper	10		
3	pmt	$179.07	=PMT(rate,nper,PV,FV,type)	
4	FV	$2,000.00		
5	PV	0		
6	type	1		

To reach one's savings goal of $2,000 in 10 years at a compound rate of 2% would require a periodic payment into a time deposit at the beginning of each period equal to $179.07.

Compound Interest

The magic of compounding. It is claimed that Albert Einstein called compound interest "the greatest mathematical discovery of all time". It is probable that no other concept in finance has more importance for investors than what is sometimes called the "wonder of compound interest." Compounding interest creates earnings not only on the original amount saved or invested but also creates earning on the interest on earnings, and it does so period after period. Another way to describe this process is to say that compounding interest generates earnings on the investment and reinvested earnings from the investment. To realize the power of compound interest requires two things: the re-investment of earnings and time.

Our previous calculations confirm the importance of compound interest. In 10 payments of $90 we accumulated a future value of $1,005.18. By making an additional 8.57 payments, we doubled our future value. We found a similar effect when we increased loan payments and observed significant decreases in term. When finding the effect of increased loan payments on loan terms, we calculated the elasticity of the term of the loan with respect to the size of the loan payment. Similarly, we can find the impact of an increase in the term of periodic savings on future values (FV). We refer to this elasticity as the FV elasticity with respect to term. The derivation of the FV elasticity with respect to term is found in Derivation 20.1 at the end of this chapter. The discrete approximation to the FV elasticity with respect to n is:

$$E_{FV,n} = \frac{dFV}{dn}\frac{n}{FV} \approx \frac{n}{US_0(r,n)}$$

(20.2)

Table 20.4 provides elasticity estimates for alternative reinvestment rates and terms.

Table 20.4. Tabled Values of elasticity $E_{FV,n}$ = $n/US_0(r,n)$

n	$r = .01$	$r = .03$	$r = .05$	$r = .08$	$r = .10$	$r = .15$
1	1.00%	1.03%	1.05%	1.08%	1.10%	1.15%
3	1.02%	1.06%	1.10%	1.16%	1.21%	1.31%
5	1.03%	1.09%	1.15%	1.25%	1.32%	1.49%
10	1.05%	1.17%	1.30%	1.49%	1.63%	1.99%
20	1.08%	1.34%	1.60%	2.04%	2.35%	3.20%
30	1.16%	1.53%	1.95%	2.66%	3.18%	4.57%
60	1.34%	2.17%	3.17%	4.85%	6.02%	9.00%

A related question with a more intuitive answer is how long does it take to double, triple, or quadruple one's investment? The derivation for the equation that answers this question can be found in Derivation 20.2 at the end of this chapter.

Let m be the number of times one wants to multiply his or her FV obtained at period n. Let n_m equal the period in which the last deposit is made. Then we can find the number of periods ($n_m - n$) required to increase the original FV by m times. The formula found in Derivation 20.2 is provided below:

$$(20.3) \quad n_m - n = \frac{\ln\left[m + (1 - m)e^{-rn}\right]}{r}$$

To illustrate, let $r = .1$, $n = 5$, and $m = 2$. The number of periods required to double the FV of one's original investment equals:

$$(20.4) \quad n_2 - n = \frac{\ln\left[2 - e^{-(.1)(5)}\right]}{.1} = \frac{\ln(1.39)}{.1} = 3.3$$

In this example, an investment consisting of 5 equal payment compounded at 10% could be doubled in additional 3.3 payments. And the investment could be tripled in:

$$(20.5) \quad n_3 - n = \frac{\ln\left[3 - e^{-(.1)(5)}\right]}{.1} = \frac{\ln(1.79)}{.1} = 5.8$$

The second example illustrates the power of compounding interest. Starting after 5 periods of investing, in 3.3 more periods the FV of the investment doubled and in 5.8 additional periods the FV of the original investment tripled.

Finally, we conclude this section by constructing Table 20.5 demonstrating the power of compounding interest. The cells of the table indicate the time required to double, triple, and quadruple an initial investment for reinvestment rates of 1%, 3%, 5%, and 10%.

Table 20.5. Periods required to double, triple, or quadruple the FV of an investment consisting of 5 equal payments assuming alternative reinvestment rates.

Alternative re-investment rates	Number of time periods required to increase the FV of the original investment m times		
	$m = 2$ (double the original FV)	$m = 3$ (triple the original FV)	$m = 4$ (quadruple the original FV)
1%	4.8	9.3	13.7
3%	4.4	8.2	11.6
5%	4.0	7.3	10.2
10%	3.3	5.8	7.8

The rule of 72 approximates the amount of time it takes to double your investment at a given rate of return. To apply the rule, you divide the rate of return by 72. For example, assume you invest $1000 at an interest rate of 5%. It would take 14.4 years (72/5) to double your investment to $2000.

Bonds

A bond is a financial asset frequently traded in financial markets. Bonds represent debt claims on the assets and income of the entity issuing the bond. A bond's value is equal to the present value of its future cash flow (interest and principal) discounted at an appropriate interest rate. Bonds usually have a known maturity date at which time the bond holder receives the bond's face or par value. Bonds are unique because their redemption or liquidation value is fixed. Typical redemption amounts are $1,000 or $10,000.

Consider the following example. Suppose a bond can be purchased at a price of V_0 (an initial cash out-flow) and redeemed n periods later at a cash value of V_n, a cash inflow to the bond holder. Moreover, suppose that the bond generates no cash return except when it is sold. Further, assume that the before-tax discount rate is r percent. Ignoring any tax consequences, the NPV of this bond is the sum of the cash outflow plus the present value of the cash inflow.

$$NPV = -V_0 + \frac{V_n}{(1+r)^n}$$
(20.6)

Those who purchase bonds may want to calculate the "yield" on a bond, which is the discount rate that equates the present value of the bond's cash flow to its present market value—the bond's internal rate of return (IRR). If, for example, the bond's market value is $321.97 and its cash flow of $1,000 occurs at the end of year 10, then the bond's yield, or its IRR, is 12 percent.

$$V_0 = \frac{\$1,000}{(1.12)^{10}} = \$321.97$$
(20.7)

Now consider the effect of taxes. First, assume capital gains taxes are paid by the bond purchaser at rate T_g and income taxes are paid at rate T. The after-tax NPV of the bond is calculated by adjusting the discount rate to its after-tax equivalent and by subtracting from the liquidation value of the bond, the capital gains tax:

$$NPV = -V_0 + \frac{V_n - T_g(V_n - V_0)}{[1 + r(1 - \theta T)]^n}$$
(20.8)

where θ is the tax adjustment coefficient defined in Chapter 11. If the NPV in equation (20.5) is zero then $r(1 - \theta T)$ is the bond's after-tax IRR. To find the effective tax rate we set NPV equal to zero in equations (20.8) and (20.6) so that before-tax cash flow discounted by the before-tax IRR in equation (20.6) is equal to the after-tax cash flow discounted by the after-tax IRR in equation (20.8). Then we solve for θ that makes the two equations equal. The result is:

$$\theta = \frac{(1+r)}{rT} \left\{ 1 - \left[1 - T_g + T_g \left(\frac{V_0}{V_n} \right) \right]^{1/n} \right\}$$

(20.9)

To illustrate using the numbers from our previous example, let the before-tax IRR equal 12%, let V_0 equal $321.97, let V_n equal $1,000, and let the income tax and the capital gains tax T and T_g both equal 15 percent. Next making the appropriate substitutions into equation (20.6) we find θ equal to:

$$\theta = \frac{1.12}{(.12)(.15)} \left\{ 1 - \left[1 - .15 + .15 \left(\frac{\$321.97}{\$1,000} \right) \right]^{1/10} \right\} = .66.$$

(20.10)

For $\theta = .66$ the effective tax rate is reduced from 0.15 to $(.66)(0.15) = 0.10$.

In the example, just completed, we were able to deduce a closed form solution for θ. In most cases, closed form solutions are very difficult to obtain. Nevertheless, in most practical cases involving numerical estimates, we can still find estimates for the effective tax rate and after-tax IRRs. We will demonstrate the empirical approach to finding effective tax rates in the next section.

Coupons and Bonds

Most bonds, in addition to capital gains (or losses), provide "coupon" (interest) payments. The number and amount of the coupon payments will alter the NPV as well as the price of the bond. Usually, the coupon rate r^c is a percentage of the redemption value of the bond.

The before-tax NPV of a bond with n coupon payments is:

$$NPV = -V_0 + \frac{r^c V_n}{(1+r)} + \frac{r^c V_n}{(1+r)^2} + \cdots + \frac{r^c V_n + V_n}{(1+r)^n}$$

$$= -V_0 + (r^c V_n) US_0(r, n-1) + \frac{r^c V_n + V_n}{(1+r)^n}$$

(20.11)

To illustrate, suppose an investor wants to find the maximum bid price V_0^b for a three-year $1,000 bond if it offers coupon payments of $r^c V_n = (.05)(1,000) = \$50$, and $r = 10\%$. Then using equation (20.11) and setting NPV equal to zero, find the maximum bid price V_0^b equal to:

$$V_0{}^b = (r^c V_n) U S_0(r, n) + \frac{V_n}{(1+r)^n} = \$50 U S_0(.10, 2) + \frac{\$1,050}{(1+.10)^3}$$

(20.12) $= \$875.65$

Taxes, of course, affect the NPV of bonds with coupon payments. Only now, taxes may or may not be paid on the coupon payments and capital gains. For example, coupon payments of many municipal bonds are not taxed but their capital gains are taxed. Tax exemptions, of course, raise the maximum bid price and NPVs of the bonds for all investors but especially for higher tax bracket investors. The after-tax present value of the bond with tax-exempt coupon payments is written as:

$$NPV = -V_0 + (r^c V_n) U S_0[r(1 - \theta T), n - 1] + \frac{V_n - (V_n - V_0)T_g}{[1 + r(1 - \theta T)]^n}$$

(20.13)

To illustrate, suppose an investor wants to find the maximum bid price $V_0{}^b$ for a three-year \$1,000 bond if it offers coupon payments of $r^c V_n$ = (.05)(1,000) = \$50 and r = 10% and pays capital gains and income taxes at the rate of 10%. Then using equation (20.13) and setting NPV equal to zero, we find the maximum bid price $V_0{}^b$ for the bond whose earlier maximum bid price was calculated equal to \$875.65:

$$V_0{}^b = (r^c V_n) U S_0[r(1 - \theta T), n] + \frac{V_n - (V_n - V_0)T_g}{[1 + r(1 - \theta T)]^n}$$

$$= \$50 U S_0[.10(1 - \theta.20), 3] + \frac{\$1,050 - (\$1,000 - \$875.65)(.10)}{[1 + .1(1 - \theta.2)]^3}$$

(20.14)

In the application of equation (20.13), the discount rate was the IRR—because it was the discount rate that resulted in NPV equal to zero. We introduced taxes into the cash flow, but we don't know the effective after-tax discount rate that would set NPV equal to zero. We have to solve for θ that will adjust the discount rate for taxes in the same magnitude as were the cash flow adjusted for taxes. For equation (20.13), we find the after-tax IRR using Excel:

Open Table 20.6 in Microsoft Excel

Table 20.6. Finding the After-tax IRR

B5			f_x	=IRR(B1:B4)
	A	B	C	
1	Bond's max bid price	-$875.65		
2	First coupon payment	$50.00		
3	Second coupon payment	$50.00		
4	Salvage value ($1,000) + Coupon	$1,037.60		
5	IRR	9.59%	=IRR(B1:B4)	

The IRR calculation of 9.59% equals the after-tax IRR of 9.59% compared to the before tax IRR of 10%. We can find θ and the effective tax rate by setting

$$(20.15) \quad r(1 - \theta T) = .1[1 - \theta(.1)] = .0959.$$

From the above equation we find θ = .41. Thus the effective tax rate is (.2) (.41) = 8%—far less than the actual income tax rate of 20%.

To review the process, we began by solving for the maximum bid price of the bond. This required that the stated discount rate was the before-tax IRR for the bond. Then we reasoned as follows. If the maximum bid price is the same whether calculated on a before-tax or after-tax basis, then the effect of taxes on the cash flow—in this case the capital gains tax—must have the same effect on the discount rate. Thus, we required that the maximum bid price in the after-tax model be the same maximum bid determined in the before-tax model and solved for the after-tax IRR and the tax adjustment coefficient θ.

Common Stocks

In contrast to bonds, common stocks have neither a fixed return nor a fixed cost. The terminal value of bonds is usually fixed, but the terminal value of stocks depends on the market value of the stock at the time of sale. The equity capital generated by the sale of stock is an alternative to debt capital generated by the sale of bonds. It also is a means of sharing risk among numerous investors.

Stocks offer significant benefits for stockholders as well as the companies issuing the stocks. Stockholders have the opportunity for ownership in the major businesses of the world with the consequent share in profits while their liability is limited to their investments. Moreover, stock ownership frees them from decision-making responsibilities in the management of the company, although common stock allows its owners to vote for directors and sometimes other matters of significance facing the company.

Stock owners receive dividend payments on their stocks, usually on a quarterly basis. The amount of dividends paid on stocks is determined by a corporation's board of directors. The board of directors' dividend policies may influence the kinds of stock they issue and the kinds of investors they attract.

The relevant question for a potential stock purchaser is what is the maximum bid price for a particular stock? If r is the nominal discount rate, and R_1, R_2, $\cdots$ are projected dividends paid on the stock in periods 1, 2, $\cdots$, the maximum bid price for the stock is:

$$V_0^b = \frac{R_1}{(1+r)} + \frac{R_2}{(1+r)^2} + \cdots$$

(20.16)

The model above assumes an infinite life. This assumption is consistent with the "life of the investment" principle discussed in Chapter 8 because to know the terminal value of the stock, V_n, we must know the value of the dividends in periods $(n+1)$, $(n+2)$, $\cdots$. Knowing all future dividends converts the problem to one in which the number of periods equals the life of the firm.

A simplified form of equation (20.16) is possible if expected dividends R_1, R_2, $\cdots$ are replaced by their expected annuity equivalent R. Then we can write:

$$V_0^b = RUS_0(r, \infty) = \frac{R}{r}$$

(20.17)

And r, the stock's IRR, is R/V_0. Thus, with long-term constant dividends of $100 and the stock valued at $1000, the rate of return is 10%. Another important ratio derived from equation (20.16) is what is commonly referred to as the price-to-earnings ratio, $V_0/R = 1/r$ which is often viewed as the bellwether of financial irregularities in the financial market. Higher than usual price-to-earnings ratios may signal what has been called "irrational exuberance" for the investment. Lower than usual price-to-earnings ratios may signal that the investment is undervalued.

Finally, debt capital must be repaid regardless of the financial fortunes of the business. However, the return to stockholders depends critically on the performance of the company. This makes NPV analysis of stock investments subject to considerable uncertainty.

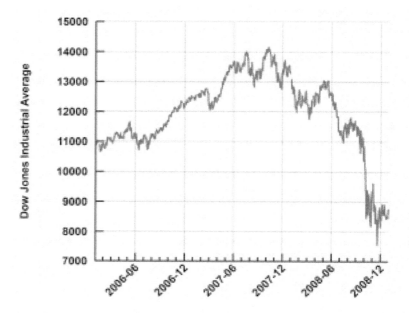

Figure 20.1. Dow Jones crash in 2008.

So, what have we learned? We learned to distinguish between real and financial investments. Earlier chapters in this book focused on real investments. Our focus in this chapter was on financial investments including time deposits, certificates of deposits, bonds, and stocks. The important point is that we can examine both real and financial investments using PV tools.

Summary and Conclusions

This chapter has introduced concepts related to financial investments which involve exchanges of money over time. In relation to financial investments, the focus is on the amount of one's investment available at some future period of time. We find the FV of a financial investment by compounding interest. As we demonstrated in Table 20.1, the power of compounding is truly amazing. Therefore, the advice for most investors is to invest early and continuously, and then let one's investment grow.

Time deposits represent an important financial investment opportunity. These differ mostly in their liquidity—those that are least liquid are also the ones with the higher yields. Bonds are an important class of financial investment. In contrast to most other financial investments, their liquidation value is fixed. What is not fixed is their purchase price which is established in the market and depends on their yield—their expected IRR.

One of the interesting aspects of bonds is the way they are taxed. Often when bonds are issued by municipalities and some other institutions, they receive special tax considerations. In the extreme neither their coupon payments nor their capital gains are taxed. In other circumstances, capital gains are taxed and coupon payments are not. Regardless, an important question is how do special tax provisions provided with some bonds affect their after-tax IRRs. While the effective after-tax IRR can sometimes be found in a formulaic expression, often they are too complicated to be expressed in a closed form solution but can be found numerically by calculating the before and after-tax IRRs.

Finally, we only introduced the concept of common stocks. Investments in common stocks are most often discussed in the context or risk analysis and include discussions of many alternative of risk response strategies. A more complete discussion of investments in stocks is beyond the scope of this financial management text.

Questions

1. To invest means to give up something in the present for something of value in the future. Can you describe three of your most important personal investments? Describe what you sacrificed including money and time, and describe your expected future returns.
2. Describe the difference between real and financial investments. Also describe how the investment settings for real and financial investments may differ.
3. Describe the main characteristics of alternative types of time deposits? What are the rates of return currently offered by major banks or credit unions on alternative types of time deposits?
4. Suppose a saver invests $65 in a time deposit at the beginning of each period for 10 periods. If the deposits are compounded at a rate of 4%, what amount is available for withdrawal at the beginning of period 11?
5. Suppose a young couple now renting an apartment wants to invest in their own home. The average price range of their desired home is approximately $250,000. If they make monthly deposits in a time deposit account at the beginning of the period for 5 years and their deposits earn an APR compound rate of 3%, what would be the required size of their monthly deposit to pay for the 20% required down payment of the price of their home ($50,000)? If they desired to save the required down payment in three years, what would be the required size of their monthly deposits?

6. It is claimed that Albert Einstein called compound interest "the greatest mathematical discovery of all time." What is it about compounding that is so important that he would make such a claim? Do you agree? If so, why? If you disagree, what would be an alternative mathematical discovery of greater importance?

7. Describe in words the meaning of the elasticity of the future value of an investment with respect to its term. Then calculate the elasticity of the future value of an investment compounded at an APR rate of 4% for 12 periods. How would the elasticity measure change if the compound rate were increased to 7%? Can you explain the direction of the change?

8. Find the number of periods required to double the future value of an investment compounded for 5 periods at alternative reinvestment rates of 2%, 4%, and 8%.

9. An investor desires to save $10,000. If the compound rate is 3% per month and the investor plans on saving $200 at the beginning of each month, how many months will be required for the investor to reach her savings goal of $10,000? Once the saving goal is reached, how many addition months will be required for the saver to double the amount saved if she saves at the same rate?

10. Consider an 8-year bond with a par value of $10,000. If the purchase price of the bond is $4,250, what is the yield on the bond? (Ignore the influence of taxes.)

11. What is the relationship between the bond's yield (its IRR) and the bond's purchase price? What would you expect to happen to the bond's purchase price if the expected yield on the bond increased? Please explain.

12. In the example illustrating equation (20.8), the effective tax rate for a bond purchaser was found to equal $\theta T = .66(.15) = 10\%$. Please recalculate the effective tax rate in the example assuming the capital gains tax rate is only 50% of the income tax rate. In other words, if the capital gains tax rate is 7.5%, what is the bond purchaser's effective tax rate? How does lowering the effective tax rate change the firm's effective after-tax IRR?

13. Consider the equation:

$$V_0 = (r^c V_n)(1 - T)USo[r(1 - \theta T), n] + \frac{V_n - (V_n - V_0)T_g}{[1 + r(1 - \theta T)]^n}$$

(Q20.1)

where $r(1 - \theta T)$ is the after-tax IRR of a bond.

Next consider the equation:

$$V_0 = (r^c V_n)USo(r, n) + \frac{V_n}{(1 + r)^n}$$

(Q20.2)

where r is the before-tax IRR of the bond.

Then assume that $V_0 = \$500$, $V_n = \$1000$, $r^c V_n = .04(\$1,000) = \$40$, $T = 20\%$, and $T_g = 10\%$. Find the before-tax and after-tax IRRs using the two equations described in this question and the values listed. Then use the before-tax and after-tax IRRs to find the value of the tax-adjustment coefficient θ.

14. Compare the rule of 72 with the actual time required to double your investment.

Derivation 20.1.

The derivation of the elasticity of future value (FV) with respect to term:

The elasticity of FV with respect to n is defined as:

$$E_{FV,n} = \frac{dFV}{dn}\frac{n}{FV}$$
(20.i)

The future value of n payments compounded at rate r is equal to:

$$FV = \int_0^n Re^{rt}dt = \frac{R}{r}(e^{rn} - 1)$$
(20.ii)

And the derivative of FV with respect to n is:

$$\frac{dFV}{dn} = Re^{rn}$$
(20.iii)

Substituting into the elasticity formula we find:

$$E_{FV,n} = \frac{dFV}{dn}\frac{n}{FV} = \frac{nRe^{rn}}{\frac{R}{r}(e^{rn} - 1)} = \frac{rn}{1 - e^{-rn}}$$
(20.iv)

The discrete approximation of the elasticity of FV with respect to n is:

$$E_{FV,n} = \frac{dFV}{dn}\frac{n}{FV} = \frac{nRe^{rn}}{\frac{R}{r}(e^{rn} - 1)} = \frac{rn}{1 - e^{-rn}} \approx \frac{n}{US_0(r, n)}$$
(20.v)

Derivation 20.2.

Deriving the formula for calculating the number of periods to double the FV of an n period investment reinvested at an interest rate of r%.

To begin, the future value (FV) of an n period investment R compounded at rate r is equal to:

$$FV = \int_0^n Re^{rt}dt = \frac{R}{r}(e^{rn} - 1)$$

(20.vi)

Now m times the FV of the original investment is set equal to the same investment compounded for nm periods:

$$m\int_0^n Re^{rt}dt = \frac{mR}{r}(e^{rn} - 1) = \int_0^{nm} Re^{rt}dt = \frac{R}{r}(e^{rnm} - 1)$$

(20.vii)

and simplifying by equating the two integrated equations above we find:

(20.viii) $\quad m(1 - e^{-rn}) = (e^{rnm-rn} - e^{-rn})$

Then solving for the difference between $(nm - n)$, we find the time it takes to increase the FV of the original investment at period n by m times.

$$nm - n = \frac{\ln[m + (1 - m)e^{-rn}]}{r}$$

(20.ix)

21. "The Dynamics of Interest Rates: Exploring Yield Curves"

LINDON ROBISON

Learning goals. After completing this chapter, you should be able to: (1) understand how interest and earning rates on a variety of debt and investments instruments are related to yield curves and periodic interest rates; (2) describe how yield curves and periodic interest rates defined over future time peri-ods can be used to predict market participants' expectation of future opportunities and threats and to (3) to calculate using single period discount rates investments of varying terms.edict future financial opportunities and threats.ationship between yield curves and single period discount rates.

- Learn how yield curves can be used to predict future financial opportunities and threats.

Learning objectives. To achieve your learning goals, you should complete the following objectives.

Introduction

In most present value (PV) models, the discount rate is a constant even when the term of the model has changed. In reality, each period's discount rate may be different because factors that influence the discount rate are not constant. These factors include the level of economic growth in the economy, the inflation rate, national and international events likely to influence our economy, activities in the stock and bond market, housing and land markets, the unemployment rate, and election outcomes.

One way to observe the difference in period discount rates is to observe the interest rates on loans with different terms. They are not constant. To demonstrate, note the changes in variable interest rate loans. They aren't constant either. Or, relevant to this discussion, notice the difference in average yields on bonds with different maturities even in the same risk class. Alternatively, notice the change in the internal rate of return (IRR) of a bond as its time to maturity changes over times.

In what follows, we pursue two objectives. The first objective is to demonstrate how to calculate the periodic discount rate for no-coupon bonds. The approach we describe can also be used to find peri-odic discount rates implied by bonds that are more complicated as well as other financial instruments. Our second objective is to connect the shapes and patterns of periodic interest rate curves and their corresponding yield curves patterns to predict future economic activity and opportunities and threats. Yield curves, as we will explain in more detail later, are the geometric means of periodic interest rates at a point in time with various maturities.

Geometric Means and Periodic Discount Rates

Geometric means and long-term discount rates.

Suppose we have information that allows us to predict n future periodic discount rates $r_1, r_2, \cdots, r_n$. The geometric mean for the n periodic rates satisfies the following equation:

$$(21.1) \quad (1+r)^n = (1+r_1)(1+r_2)\cdots(1+r_n)$$

In words, one plus the geometric mean multiplied by itself n times would equal the product of 1 plus n periodic discount rates. We can solve for the geometric mean of the n periodic discount rates in equation (21.1) by finding the nth root of the products of the n periodic discount rates and subtracting one:

$$(21.2) \quad r = [(1+r_1)(1+r_2)\cdots(1+r_n)]^{(1/n)} - 1$$

To demonstrate, suppose that periodic discount rates for period one through three were $r_1 = .07$, $r_2 = .03$, and $r_3 = .075$. We can solve for the geometric mean of the three periodic interest rates as:

$$(21.3) \quad r = [(1+.07)(1+.03)(1+.075)]^{(1/3)} - 1 = .058 \text{ or } 5.8\%$$

How to calculate periodic discount rates.

Consider a zero coupon bond that can be purchased for V_0^1 at the beginning of the period and redeemed at the end of the period for its par value of $1,000. The periodic rate of return r_1 for the one-period bond satisfies the PV model:

$$(21.4) \quad V_0^1 = \frac{\$1,000}{(1+r_1)}$$

Solving for the one-period discount rate r_1 we find:

$$(21.5) \quad r_1 = \frac{\$1,000}{V_0^1} - 1$$

For example if $V_0^1 = \$960$ then

$$(21.6) \quad r_1 = \frac{\$1,000}{\$960} - 1 = .042 \text{ or } 4.2\%$$

In the case of a one-period bond, the one-period discount rate is also the geometric mean.

Now consider a zero-coupon bond that matures in two periods with similar risk and tax provisions as the one-period bond described in equation (21.4). Assume the zero-coupon two-period bond can be purchased for V_0^2 at the beginning of the period and redeemed at the end of the period for its par value of $1,000. The periodic rate of return r_2 for the two-period bond satisfies the PV model:

$$V_0^2 = \frac{\$1,000}{(1+r_1)(1+r_2)}$$
(21.7)

Solving for the second period discount rate r_2 we find:

$$r_2 = \frac{\$1,000}{V_0^2(1+r_1)} - 1$$
(21.8)

For example if V_0^2 = $910 then

$$r_2 = \frac{\$1,000}{\$910(1.042)} - 1 = 0.55 \text{ or } 5.5\%$$
(21.9)

When we purchase a two period bond, we acquire a financial instrument with a single yield for two periods. The yield is the geometric mean of the product of the single period discount rates. In our example, the yield or geometric mean is equal to:

$$(21.10) \quad r = [(1+0.42)(1+.055)]^{1/2} - 1 = .048 \text{ or } 4.8\%$$

Continuing our example, if V_0^3 = $855 then

$$r_3 = \frac{\$1,000}{\$855(1.042)(1.055)} - 1 = .064 \text{ or } 6.4\%$$
(21.11)

Finally, consider a zero-coupon n period bond that can be purchased for V_0^n at the beginning of the period and redeemed at the end of the period for its par value of $1,000. The periodic rate of return r_n for the n period bond satisfies the PV model equal to:

$$V_0^n = \frac{\$1,000}{(1+r_1)(1+r_2)\cdots(1+r_n)}$$
(21.12)

Solving for the one-period discount rate r_n we find:

$$(21.13) \quad r_n = \frac{\$1,000}{V_0(1+r_1)(1+r_2)\cdots(1+r_{n-1})} - 1$$

Periodic rates of return and geometric means.

When we purchase a three-period bond, we acquire a single yield for three periods. Consistent with the PV model, the yield is the geometric mean of the product of the single-period discount rates. In our example, the yield or geometric mean for the three-period bond is equal to:

$$(21.14) \quad r = [(1+.042)(1+.055)(1+.064)]^{1/3} - 1 = .054 \text{ or } 5.4\%$$

While one could expect to earn the bond's yield to maturity if the investor held the bond to maturity, a three-year bond becomes a two-year bond after one year, and if sold, the bond's price would reflect the yield on a two-year bond.

Graphing the geometric means of bonds against their varying time to maturity produces the bond's yield curve. In Figure 21.1, we graph the periodic discount rates and the corresponding yield curves for one, two, and three period bonds.

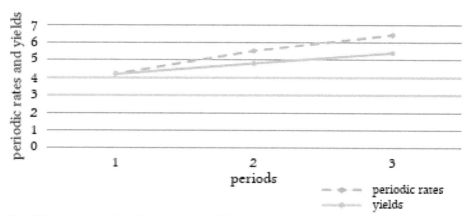

Figure 21.1. A comparison of periodic interest rates and the corresponding yield curves of bonds of varying maturities

Predicting Future Economic Activities and Opportunities and Threats

Marginal periodic rates and average geometric mean yield curves.

The periodic rate is a marginal rate while the yield rate is an average or mean—in this case a geometric mean. In our example, the periodic rate is increasing. As a result, the yield curve is also increasing but at a slower rate because previous and lower values of the periodic rate influence the yield. Therefore, if the yield curve is increasing, it is because the marginal periodic rates added to the series are greater than the geometric mean of the previous values included in the calculation. Moreover, if the yield curve were decreasing, it would require that periodic rates added were less than the geometric mean. To be complete, if the yield curve were constant, it would suggest that the marginal periodic rate were equal to the geometric mean.

Of course, there are many bond yield curves depending on the type of bond considered. When producing a yield curve, it is essential that bonds used to produce the yield curve belong to a similar risk class—even though this may be difficult because term differences produce different risks. To do the best we can to hold risk constant when producing yield curves, government backed debt is often considered. The most frequently reported yield curve compares three-month, two-year, five-year and thirty-year U.S. Treasury debt. We present graphs of U.S. Treasury yield curves at two points in time in Figure 21.2 below

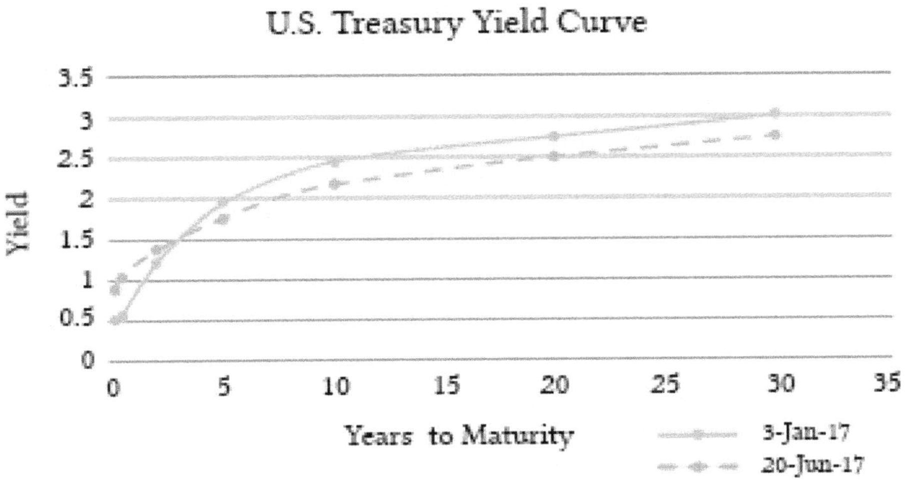

Figure 21.2. Yield curves using U.S. Treasury debt calculated on January 3, 2017 and June 20, 2017

Interpreting the shapes of yield curves.

In the previous section, we described the relationship between the period or marginal interest rates and the yield curve that, according to our PV model, is the geometric mean of the periodic rates. We now suggest some interpretations of the yield curves. Figures of periodic rate calculated from yield curves are not generally available.

- *Positively sloped yield curves.* To invest or lend one's financial capital to another person or entity requires a sacrifice on the part of the lender. Furthermore, the longer the funds are committed to another person or entity, the greater is the sacrifice. As a result, many economists claim that upward sloping yield curves predict a healthy economy in the future where borrowers have a bright view of future earnings and are willing to pay increased interest rates for the privilege of investing in the future. Another explanation is that borrowers expect periodic interest rates in the future to rise that in turn will produce an increasing yield curve. One reason for periodic rates to rise is expected increases in inflation and subsequent response to inflation by the Federal Reserve to increase interest rates on government debt instruments to offset inflationary pressures.
- *Flat or humped yield curves.* A flat yield curve is consistent with constant periodic interest rates so that all bond maturities have similar yields. A humped yield curve implies that periodic interest rates for a period lie above then fall below the yield curve and are constant before and after the hump. Economists generally view constant or humped yield curves as uncertain indicators of the future well-being of the economy.
- *Negatively sloped or inverted yield curves.* During periods when financial market participants expect periodic rates of return to decrease, yield curves have been downward sloping or inverted. Some financial economist connect inverted yield curves with pending downturns in the economy or recessions. In support of this connection, an inverted yield curve has indicated a worsening economic situation in the future 7 times since 1970 (Adrian, 2010). See Table 21.1.

Summary and Conclusions

Previous chapters have treated the multi-period discount rate in PV models (including IRR) as constants. This chapter has emphasized that these constant discount rates are composed of time varying periodic discount rates. Many time-varying factors would prevent periodic discount rates from being constant. Such forces acting on periodic interest rates include monetary and fiscal policies, inflation rates, unemployment rates, and national and international trade and treaties to name a few.

> So, what have we learned? We learned that rate of return expectations built into periodic

discount rates and reflected in yield curves of bonds (and interest rates) of varying maturities reflect expected future economic conditions.

While there is not universal agreement on how to interpret yield curves, and indeed different yield curves may be subject to varying interpretations, there is support for interpreting downward sloping or inverted yield curves as foreshadowing a slow-down in future economic activities.

The goal of this chapter has been to acquaint students with another resource for predicting future opportunities and threats.

Table 21.1. The connection between inverted yield curves and future recessions (1970-2009).

Event	Date of Inversion Start	Date of the Recession Start	Time from Inversion to Recession Start	Duration of Inversion	Duration of Recession
			Months	Months	Months
1970 Recession	Dec-68	Jan-70	13	15	11
1974 Recession	Jun-73	Dec-73	6	18	16
1980 Recession	Nov-78	Feb-80	15	18	6
1981-1982 Recession	Oct-80	Aug-81	10	12	16
1990 Recession	Jun-89	Aug-90	14	7	8
2001 Recession	Jul-00	1-Apr	9	7	8

Questions

1. Compare geometric means and periodic discount rates.
2. Find the geometric mean of three periodic discount rates equal to $r_1 = 8\%$, $r_2 = 6.5\%$, and $r_3 = 2\%$.
3. Suppose the geometric mean of two periodic discount rates was 6%, and the periodic discount rate in the second period was 7%. Find the periodic discount rate in the first period.
4. Suppose a one-year zero-coupon bond with a par value of $1,000 was selling for $962. Find the bond's yield.
5. Suppose the yield curve was decreasing. Some economics would view this as a sign the economy

is slowing down. Do you agree or disagree? Defend your answer.

6. Find data on the yield curve in the economy and discuss what it portends.

22. "Economics in Human Context: Understanding the Relationship between Econs and Humans"

LINDON ROBISON

Learning goals. After completing this chapter, you should be able to: (1) understand that, as humans, our needs include distinct motives for purchasing goods—those goods that can be purchased with money and (2) difference between commodities and relational goods to achieve both economic as well as social-emotional goals exchange goods on terms and levels that econs view as irrational.

- Learn how including relational goods in our models explains exchanges that many econs would call irrational.

Learning objectives. To achieve your learning goals, you should complete the following objectives:

Introduction

The famous Beatles singing group titled one of their hit songs, "Can't Buy Me Love." While coming from an unlikely source of philosophical insight, their song title did proclaim an important truth: money can't buy love nor most any other goods whose value depends on relationships. So, the purpose of this chapter is to remind us that relationships and the intangible goods produced in relationships may be our most important resources that need careful managing.

Econs versus humans. The behavioral economist Richard Thaler (2008) described two types of decision makers: "econs" and "humans." Econs, according to Thaler, make decisions like persons described in graduate school economic textbooks. They are perfectly selfish, possess perfect information about the outcome of their choices, and their will power is absolute. Humans, on the other hand, fail to satisfy any of those assumptions. Their choices are influenced by relationships with other humans that lead them to unselfish choices. They lack complete information about the outcomes of their choices and about alternative choices. Finally, they sometimes overeat, drink too much, and also often don't follow through on their choices.

Motives. A homework question at the end of Chapter 1 asked you what are your motives for wanting a college degree? The list of possible motives are reported below.

- I want a college degree so I can increase my lifetime earnings and get a better job.
- I want a college degree so important people in my life will be pleased with my achievements.

- I want a college degree to live up to the expectations I have for myself.
- I want a college degree so I will feel part of groups to which I want to belong.
- I want a college degree so that, in the future, I will be better able to help others.

An econ would have said that 100% of his or her motive was to increase lifetime earnings. Assuming your responses were not those of an econ, then you undoubtedly make decisions like a human. Your selection of motives can be used to infer that you care about and are motivated by other considerations than your desire to obtain a college degree to increase your potential income. The evidence from past surveys supports the conclusion that we are all human.

Anomalies

One outcome of managers behaving like humans instead of econs is that we observe behavior that is inconsistent with the prediction of profit and net present value (NPV) maximizing behavior associated with econs. One such example occurs regularly in the sale and purchase of farmland. Some of the anomalies we observe in the farmland market include terms and level of trade and selection of trading partners that depend on relationships, unselfish exchanges where sellers sacrifice higher prices for lower ones, and prefer to sell to friends and family rather than strangers and unfriendly neighbors.

To illustrate anomalies in the U.S. farmland markets, consider the minimum sell price of land. Compared to the arm's length market price, fifteen hundred farmland owner-operators in Illinois, Michigan, and Nebraska were surveyed. They reported discounting farmland prices to friends and family members by 5.57% and 6.78% respectively. These same owner-operators reported that they would require a minimum sell price premium of 18.4% to sell their land to their unfriendly neighbors (Siles, et. al., 2000).

Another farmland market study found that strangers entering the Linn County, Oregon, farmland market were at a decided disadvantage because they were forced to rely on public advertisements and Realtors to gain access to farmland sales information. Friendly neighbors and family of sellers accessed farmland purchase opportunities directly from the sellers. One consequence of this differential information access was that a stranger buying an 80-acre parcel of Class II non-irrigated farmland though a Realtor was projected to pay $2,535 per acre while a neighbor of the seller buying the same land was projected to pay 20% less (Perry and Robison, 2001).

Finally, as a result of premiums and discounts and preferential access to farmland markets that depend on relationships, farmland sellers reported that less than 2% of their sales were to unfriendly neighbors while up to 70% of land sales were to friendly neighbors and family. Others reported similar observations in which relationships altered the terms and level of farmland trades. Indeed, terms and level of trade and selection of trading partners in farmland exchanges that are not influenced by relationships have a special name, "arm's length sales."

How do we explain the regular anomalies we observe in farmland markets? One explanation follows. Econs trade and consume only commodities. Humans trade and consume both commodities and relational goods. When we ignore relational goods in human exchanges and consumption, the results appear as anomalies. Consider next the nature of relational goods.

Commodities and Relational Goods

Expanding the decision maker's choice set. For the most part, economic theory focuses on physical goods and services that decision makers obtain for themselves and whose values do not depend on their connection to a particular person(s). We call these goods commodities. Describing this focus on commodities, Becchetti, Pelloni and Rossetti (2008) wrote: "in mainstream economics agents are mostly considered in isolation as they impersonally interact through markets, and consumption goods and leisure are assumed to be 'sufficient statistics' of their utility."

Nothing in economic theory, however, prevents us from expanding the set of properties used to describe goods in decision makers' choice sets. For example, we could add the goods' relational properties to the description of those goods. Relational properties of goods include the identity of persons who produce, exchange, consume, and store goods in the choice set. Furthermore, this added description of goods could be justified if it were shown that decision makers' preference ordering depended on the relational properties of goods.

Social scientists in the past have connected a good's relational properties to its preference orderings (Bruni and Stanca, 2008). Indeed, Adam Smith may have foreshadowed the concept of relational goods when he described fellow-feeling or sympathy as essential for human happiness.

Emphasizing that the identity of exchange partners matters when defining relational goods, Uhlaner (1989) wrote, "goods which arise in exchanges where anyone could anonymously supply one or both sides of the [exchange] are not relational". Luigino and Stanca (2008) concluded in their review of relational goods that "genuineness" is foundational, and the identity of the other person is essential for the value, and in some cases even for the existence, of the relational good. Gui and Sugden (2005) defined relational goods as "the affective components of interpersonal relations [that] are usually perceived as having value through their sincerity or genuineness".

Defining relational goods. Relational goods are those goods whose value depends at least in part on their connections to people who produce, exchange, consume, and store them. Three concepts describe relational goods. The flow of relational goods is called socio-emotional goods (SEG). The stock or inventory of relational goods is called attachment value goods (AVG). SEG embedded in persons are said to create investments in social capital (Robison and Flora, 2003). Finally, social capital is required to produce SEG. We describe these, SEG, AVG, and social capital, in more detail in what follows.

SEG are intangible goods that satisfy socio-emotional needs. While there is no universally accepted list of socio-emotional needs that relational goods are expected to satisfy, generally accepted needs include the need for internal validation or self-actualization, the need for external validation, the need for connectedness (belonging, love and friendship), and the need for knowing (Robison, Schmid, and Siles, 2002). SEG differ from other intangible goods and services because they are produced by social capital—sympathy (empathy), regard, or trust that one person has for another person or group.

SEG like other intangible goods can become attached to, associated with, or embedded in durable goods and change the meaning and value of the durable goods they act on. Durable goods embedded with SEG are called attachment value goods (AVG) and represent a stock of SEG. Since SEG and AVG "spring out of interpersonal relationships, and comprise the often intangible, interpersonal side of economic interactions", they qualify as relational goods (Robison and Ritchie, 2010).

In mainstream economics, the production of commodities employs manufactured capital (tools and implements), natural capital, human capital, and financial capital. All of these contribute to the creation of a good or service valued for its mostly observable physical properties. In contrast, relational goods are produced in sympathetic (empathetic), trusting, and high regard relationships referred to here and by others as social capital. While there are other definitions of social capital, many of these do not satisfy the requirement of being capital or social. Instead they focus on where social capital lives (networks), what it can produce (cooperation), the rules that organize its use (institutions) and how to produce it (Robison, Schmid and Siles, 2002).

Human needs are satisfied by commodities and relational goods. The distinguishing properties of commodities and relational goods are described next.

Distinguishing properties of commodities. The properties that describe commodities have little or no connection to people or relationships among people and are described next. (1) Commodities are exchanged in impersonalized markets. (2) The terms and level at which commodities are exchanged are determined by the aggregate of market participants and apply generally. (3) Commodities are standardized goods of uniform quality which makes them perfect substitutes for each other so that little or no connection exists between their value and those who produce, exchange, consume, and store them. (4) The value of commodities can be inferred from their (mostly) observable properties. (5) Manufactured, natural, human, and financial capital may all play an important role in the production of commodities. (6) The value of commodities can be altered by changing their form, function, location, or other physical properties. (7) Commodities satisfy mostly physical needs and wants. (8) Commodities are mostly nondurable goods not likely to become embedded with SEG because of their short useful lives. (9) Commodities are most likely to have their quantity and quality certified by arm's length agencies established for that purpose.

Distinguishing properties of relational goods. The properties that describe relational goods are wholly or partially dependent on the good's connection to people who produce, exchange, consume, and store them and are described next. (1) Relational goods are exchanged in personalized settings in which either the buyer or the seller or both are known to each other. (2) The terms and level of relational goods exchanged are influenced by the social capital inherent in the relationships of those producing, exchanging, consuming, and storing them. (3) Relational goods are poor substitutes for each other because they are produced in unique relational settings. (4) The value of relational goods depend on their mostly unobservable intangible properties. (5) While other forms of capital may be used in their production, relational goods cannot be produced without social capital. (6) The value of relational goods can be altered by changing their connections to people who produce, exchange, consume, or store them. (7) Relational goods satisfy mostly socio-emotional needs and wants. (8) Relational goods are mostly durable goods likely to become embedded with SEG because of their extended useful lives. (9) Relational goods are not likely to have their quantity or quality value certified by arm's length agencies established for that purpose.

We summarize the differences between commodities and relational goods in Table 22.1.

Table 22.1. Properties of commodities and relational goods.

Property	Commodities	Relational goods
1. Exchange setting.	Impersonal setting in which buyer and seller are not known to each other.	Personalized setting in which buyer and seller are connected through a social relationship.
2. How terms and level of exchange are determined.	Terms and level of goods exchanged are determined by the aggregate influence of market participants.	Terms and level of goods exchanged are uniquely determined by the social capital inherent in the persons engaged in the exchange.
3. Substitutability of goods.	Standardized goods with uniform quality which allows one commodity to substitute for another.	Unique good with few substitutes because its value is uniquely determined by the social capital involved in its exchange.
4. Value determining properties.	Mostly observable, physical properties.	Mostly unobservable intangible SEG exchanged directly or embedded in an AVG.
5. Capital used in their production.	Manufactured, natural, human, and financial capital may all be important in the production of commodities.	While other forms of capital may be used, social capital is required in the production of relational goods.
6. How the value of the good is changed.	Value is altered by changing the physical properties of the good including its form, function, location, taste, color, and other physical properties.	Value is altered by humanistic acts that produce SEG that may lead to increased investments in social capital or that may become embedded objects creating AVG.
7. Needs satisfied.	Mostly physical	Mostly socio-emotional including the need for validation, belonging, and knowing.
8. Durability.	Mostly nondurable or used infrequently.	Mostly durable or if nondurable, used frequently.
9. Certification.	Arm's length agencies empowered with regulatory and inspection duties.	Within the relationships associated with the good's production, consumption, or exchange.

Two setting for exchanging relational goods

There are two types of relational good exchanges. In the first type of exchange, the focus is on the relationships, and goods exchanged are mostly SEG. In the second type of exchange, the focus is on the good exchanged that is almost always an AVG, a tangible thing embedded with SEG.

Exchanges focused on relationships. In relationship focused exchanges, SEG are exchanged directly between persons in social capital rich relationships and require no object besides the persons involved in the exchange to complete the transaction. For example, two persons with strong feelings of affection for each other may express those feelings, SEG, in any number of settings including meals, cultural events, conferences, religious gatherings, or work settings. And if there is an object exchanged, it is incidental to the exchange of SEG.

Exchanges focused on objects. In object focused exchanges, AVG are exchanged, things or objects embedded with SEG. AVG result from prior or anticipated connections between social capital rich persons in which SEG are produced and embedded in objects. AVG are most likely a durable. However, AVG may sometimes be non durables that are often exchanged repeatedly such as a meal prepared to celebrate special occasion or a song or dance performed to mark milestones.

Anomalies and Isoutilities

At the beginning of this chapter, we claimed that econs and humans made decisions differently. Sometimes these differences are called anomalies. Furthermore, because many human decisions differ from econ choices, human choices are sometimes called irrational. The claim here is that human choices can appear irrational because relational goods are excluded from the analysis.

To illustrate how including relational goods in exchanges can resolve important economic anomalies, consider the following example. Suppose a seller has the option of exchanging his farmland with a stranger for a commodity (the market price) or exchanging his farmland with a friend or family member for a combination of commodities and relational goods. If the seller prefers the combination of relational goods and commodities offered by friends and family members to the commodities only offered by a stranger even though the commodities offered by the stranger exceed those offered by friends and family members, we might consider that an economic exchange anomaly has occurred. The seller accepted a lower commodity price from a friend or family member when a higher commodity price was available from a stranger. This is only an anomaly if the relational goods included in the exchange are ignored.

To explain further how including relational goods in exchanges can resolve anomalies, we consider the concept of an isoutility line. Suppose that a decision maker is offered alternative combinations of two goods, a commodity and a relational good. Furthermore, allow that the amounts of the commodity and relational good can be exchanged at some rate that leaves the well-being of the decision maker unaffected. The combinations of relational goods and commodities that leave the decision maker's well-being unaltered are referred to isoutility combinations and are represented in Figure 22.1 as $P_{buyer}P_{buyer}$. Curve $P_{seller}P_{seller}$ represents the seller's isoutility combinations of relational goods and commodity prices.

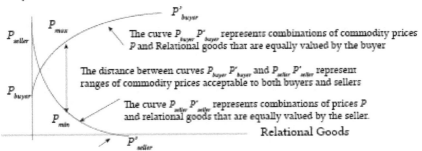

Commodity Price P

P'_{buyer}

P_{seller}

P_{max}

The curve $P_{buyer} P'_{buyer}$ represents combinations of commodity prices P and Relational goods that are equally valued by the buyer

The distance between curves $P_{buyer} P'_{buyer}$ and $P_{seller} P'_{seller}$ represent ranges of commodity prices acceptable to both buyers and sellers

P_{buyer}

The curve $P_{seller} P'_{seller}$ represents combinations of prices P and relational goods that are equally valued by the seller.

P_{min}

Relational Goods

P^0_{seller}

Level of relational goods at which the seller is willing to offer the commodity as a gift

Figure 22.1. Combinations of Commodity Prices and Relational Goods that Leave Buyers' and Sellers' Well-Being Unchanged.

The implication of the graph in Figure 22.1 is that as more of a relational good is received, the seller (buyer) would be willing to accept (offer) a lower (higher) commodity price without suffering a loss in well-being. Furthermore, as relational goods are included in the transaction, the range of commodity prices acceptable to both buyers and sellers increases which also increases the likelihood that persons rich in social capital will exchange. For example, in Figure 22.1 persons without social capital would not trade since, with no relational goods exchanged, the minimum sell price is above the maximum bid price.

In one of the first studies designed to test the influence of relationships on terms and level of exchange, Robison and Schmid (1989) asked faculty and graduate students what would be their minimum sell price of a used car to people who offered them various levels of social capital. Since the Robison and Schmid article was published, the essence of the study has been repeated multiple times with similar results. A recent unpublished survey by Richard Winder found the results reported in Table 22.2. The mode of the distributions of responses by relationship are in bold.

Table 22.2. Average minimum sell price for a used car with a market value of $3,000 reported by 600 survey respondents.

	Nasty neighbor	Stranger	Friend	Family
> $3,500	65			
$3,500	**263**	39	2	
$3,250	21	33	5	1
$3,000	236	**476**	122	29
$2,750	11	30	135	24
$2,500	4	22	**298**	199
< $2,500			38	**348**

Notice that in the absence of social capital (exchanges with a stranger), the distribution of minimum sell prices centers around the commodity exchange price of $3,000. However, when the exchange is conducted with a social capital rich partner such as a friend or family member, the minimum sell price is significantly below the market price with a mode of $2,500 for a friend and a mode price below $2,500 for a family member.

Summary and Conclusions

The material covered in this book is intended to provide instructions about how to behave like an econ. We hope you don't always follow our advice. There are times and places and circumstances when commodity considerations should be softened by social capital and the importance of relational goods. Learning how to make the appropriate trade-offs between commodities and investments in social capital and relational goods, when to behave like an econ versus a human, may be our most important management task. Good luck.

Questions

1. By 2013 Bill and Melinda Gates had donated 38 billion dollars to various charities and especially to fight hunger in Africa. They have donated billions more to these causes since. If Bill and Melinda Gates were to have taken the same survey you took at the beginning of the class where "I want a college degree" is replaced with "We donated billions of dollars...", how do you think they would have answered? To better speak for them, read a brief interview of Bill Gates by Neil Tweedie at: http://www.telegraph.co.uk/technology/bill-gates/9812672/Bill-Gates-interview-I-have-no-use-for-money.-This-is-Gods-work.html. Now answer the survey that follows as though you were channeling either Bill or Melinda Gates by writing the relative importance of each motive using percentages in the blank besides each motive. The sum of the motives must equal 100%.

- ○ _ _ _ _ _ We have donated billions of dollars so that we could increase our lifetime earnings and get a better job.
- ○ _ _ _ _ _ We have donated billions of dollars so that important people in our lives would be pleased with our achievements.
- ○ _ _ _ _ _ We have donated billions of dollars to live up to the expectations we have for ourselves.
- ○ _ _ _ _ _ We have donated billions of dollars so we will feel part of different groups to which we want to belong.
- ○ _ _ _ _ _ We have donated billions of dollars to help others.

2. Consider a hypothetical gas purchase.

   a. You gas tank holds 15 gallons and is nearly empty. You normally fill up your car with gas at a station on your way home. How many additional miles would you drive to fill up your car with gas if you could save 10 cents per gallon? I would drive an additional _ _ _ _ miles to save 10 cents per gallon.

   b. You gas tank holds 15 gallons and is nearly empty. You normally fill up your car with gas at a station on your way home. How many additional miles would you drive to fill up your car with gas at a gas station owned and operated by your favorite uncle? I would drive an additional _ _ _ _ miles to purchase gas at a gas station owned and operated by my favorite uncle.

   c. If your answer to parts a) and b) were different from zero, can you explain why?

3. Summarize the difference between relational goods and commodities as discussed in this chapter. Please list two commodities and two relational goods that you own.

4. An isoutility line describes different combinations of two different goods that provide equal satisfaction. Use the concept of isoutility to explain why you might sell your used car at different prices to a friend, a stranger, a family, member, and someone you disrespect.

5. Commodities are sold in the market place, and their prices are determined by anonymous market forces. The terms of trade of relational goods depend on the relationship between persons exchanging them. Give an example in which you have exchanged relational goods in which relationships altered the terms and level of trade. Then give another example in which you have exchanged commodities in which relationships had no influence on the terms and level of trade.

6. One could donate one's blood or blood plasma at a local Red Cross and receive in return a small amount of juice served in a paper cup and possibly a cookie. One could also sell one's blood at a number of places (the current price is $25 to $60 per bag). Since some people sell their blood for money and others donate it for free, explain the difference in the way these two groups of people dispose of their blood.

7. Suppose you needed a medical procedure that required a skilled physician. Assume that a number of equally skilled physicians were available to perform the procedure. Would your choice of a physician to perform the procedure depend on your relationship to the physician? If he were a family friend? If he were a stranger? If you knew the physician only by reputation—that he performed volunteer work in developing countries? If he was rude to his/her patients, inconsiderate to his/her assistants, and lived a lavish life style? For each of the physicians, answer the questions that follow using the scale included in each question:

a. If the physician were skilled and a family friend, the likelihood I would select this physician to perform my procedure is:

- Not likely   1   3   5   7   Very likely (circle one)

b. If the physician were skilled and a stranger, the likelihood I would select this physician to perform my procedure is:

- Not likely   1   3   5   7   Very likely (circle one)

c. If the physician were skilled and someone I knew only by reputation—that he performed volunteer work in developing countries, the likelihood I would select this physician to perform my procedure is:

- Not likely   1   3   5   7   Very likely (circle one)

d. If the physician were skilled and someone I knew only by reputation—that he was rude to his/her patients, impatient with his assistants, and lived a lavish lifestyle, the likelihood I would select this physician to perform my procedure is:

- Not likely   1   3   5   7   Very likely (circle one)

8. If you were equally likely to select one of the physicians described in question 7, explain why. If you were not equally likely to select one of the physicians described above, explain why.

Appendix

LINDON ROBISON

Introduction

1

This appendix introduces Excel spreadsheets and describes how they can help solve financial management problems discussed in the text. The appendix describes how to input and manipulate data in Excel and illustrates both with a compound interest example. Then, the appendix describes how Excel's "goal seek" tool can test for solution sensitivity and answer "what if" kinds of questions. Finally, the appendix introduces Excel's financial functions and employs them to solve a variety of financial, accounting, and capital budgeting problems.

This appendix assumes readers know how to open, save, print, export, and import an Excel worksheet. In addition, we assume that readers are familiar with functions and number formatting options available in Excel. Having a knowledge of these basic Excel concepts, we are now ready to present Excel tools useful for solving financial management problems. Before doing so, however, we emphasize that what follows is an introduction to Excel. For more Excel details applied to financial management problems, readers should consult such texts as Principles of Finance with Excel by Simon Benninga (2006).

Opening an Excel spreadsheet. To open an Excel spreadsheet, find and press the Excel icon on your desktop. A blank worksheet should appear on your screen. Cells in Excel spreadsheets are identified with letter columns and row numbers. In Figure A.1, for example, the letter x appears in column D and row 5. When the cell with x is selected in the spreadsheet, the cell location is identified in the location tracker cell located in the top left of the spreadsheet as D5. (Try selecting different cells and observe the location tracker cell report the new location.)

1. The figures in the Appendix are screenshots of Microsoft Excel worksheets. The links to open Figures A.1, A.2, A.3, A.4, A.5, A.6, A.7, A.9, A.10, A.14, A.20, A.21, A.22, A.23, and A.24 all open the same Excel file. The worksheet tabs at the bottom of the Excel window can be selected for each figure.

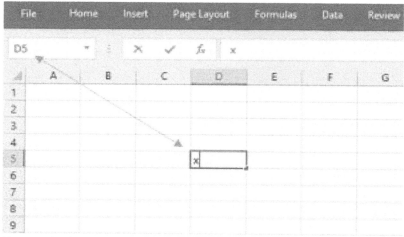

Figure A.1. Identifying cell locations in Excel
Open Example in Microsoft Excel

Users can instruct Excel to perform operations on data in cells by entering a function or calling up an Excel supplied function. Users enter a function to be executed by first pressing the "=" sign. The "=" sign instructs Excel that what follows is a function to be executed.

Entering user supplied functions in Excel. Excel has significant computing capacity that can execute user supplied functions. We illustrate a simple user supplied function in Figure A.2. We enter the numbers 5 and 4 into cells B1 and B2 respectively and in cell B3 instruct Excel to add the two numbers together. Note that the function appears to the right of the Excel function symbol *fx* on the blank space above the letters identifying the columns. After pressing enter, the function calculates the sum of 5 in cell B1 and 4 in cell B2 which is equal to the number 9 displayed in cell B3.

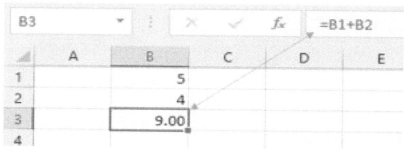

Figure A.2. A user supplied addition function.
Open Example in Microsoft Excel

We can always recover the equation embedded in cell B3 by pointing the cursor to cell B3. One of significant advantage of Excel is that we can replace the numbers in cells B1 and B2 and the function will automatically recalculate their sum. To illustrate, in Figure A.3 we change the number 5 in cell B1 to 7. Excel uses the same function entered earlier to add cells B1 and B2 to return the sum of 11.

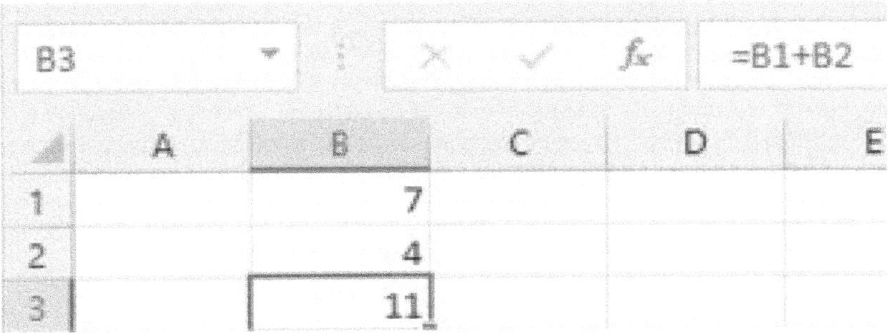

Figure A.3. An Externally supplied addition function with a changed entry.
Open Example in Microsoft Excel

Excel's library of functions. In addition to user supplied functions, Excel has a library of functions capable of operating on data identified in the spreadsheet. To illustrate, we employ Excel's SUM function for adding numbers. The SUM function lists the location of the beginning and ending cell in the string of numbers to be added, separated by a colon. We use the SUM function to solve the example described in Figure A.2 by entering into cell B3 the function SUM(B1:B2).

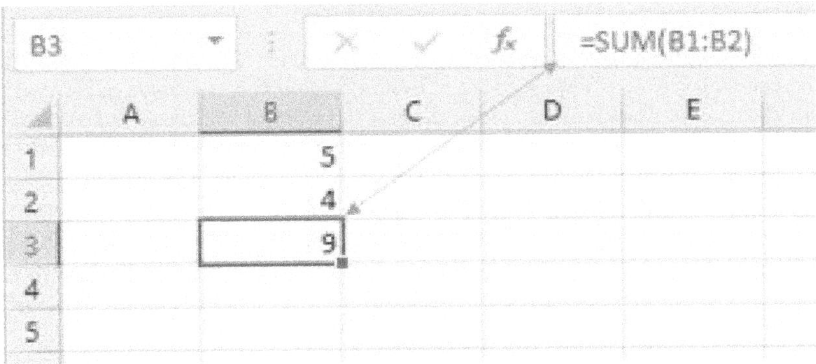

Figure A.4. Adding numbers using Excel SUM function.
Open Example in Microsoft Excel

Excel and handles. A "handle" is powerful Excel tool that enables Excel users to repeat operations or values in a cell by dragging the cell handle to a new location. In the new cell, the function in the handle cell is repeated and updated or the value in the handle cell is repeated. We describe handles next.

In Figure A.4, note the bold lines around cell B3 where the cursor is pointed. At the bottom right corner of the cell is a solid square called the handle. If we click on the handle and drag it to a new cell, B4, the function in cell B3 is repeated in cell B4, and the cell locations in the SUM function will be updated by one row value. In the other words, the function in the original cell SUM(B1:B2) is updated by one row in cell B4 to SUM(B2:B3). Just as the SUM function in cell B3 added the preceding two numbers, so does the SUM function in B4 add the preceding two numbers—4 and 9. We illustrate the use of handles in Figure A.5.

Figure A.5. Dragging the handle in cell B3 to enter the same updated function in cell B4.
Open Example in Microsoft Excel

Fixed cells. The function in B3 was SUM(B1:B2), and the updated function in B4 was SUM(B2:B3). However, there may be occasions when we want to fix a cell's location in a function rather than have it automatically updated when dragged. In our example, suppose that we wanted to add the string of numbers that began in cell B1 rather than having the addition begin with the number in cell B2 when dragged one cell. To do so, we merely fix cell B1's location in our function by preceding the column letter and row number with a "$" sign as in $B$1. Other cells identified in the function that are not fixed are updated when the cell containing the function is dragged by its handle. In our example, the function in B4 updates the cell at the end of the string but keeps fixed the cell B1 at the beginning of the string. To illustrate, in Figure A.6 the SUM function contains a fixed cell B1 but updates the ending cell in the string when the function in B3 is dragged to location B4.

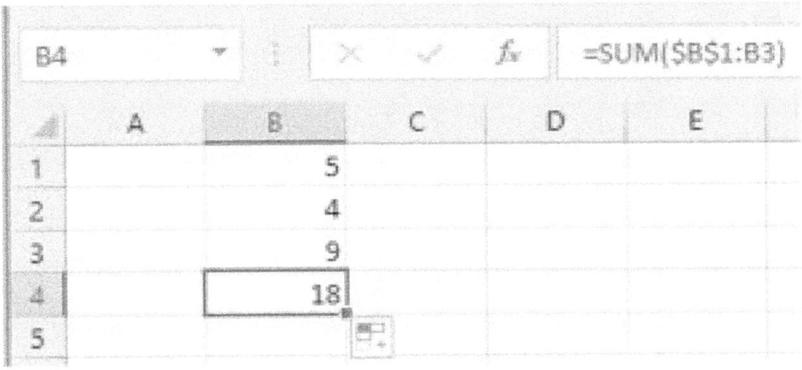

Figure A.6. Using Excel's SUM function to add a string of numbers with the number in the first cell fixed.
Open Example in Microsoft Excel

Formatting cells. Suppose we wanted to indicate that the numbers in the string and function reflect dollars (or percentages, etc.). For the cells to reflect dollar amounts, we must format the cells in the Excel. To format Excel spreadsheet cells, we click "Home" on the main ribbon and then click "Format" on the drop-down menu. Notice that the last entry in the drop down Format menu is labeled "Format Cells" (See Figure A.7.).

Figure A.7. Formatting cells in Excel by accessing the Format cell options.
Open Example in Microsoft Excel

Lastly, we click on "format cells" and note the several format options. After we highlight the cells we wish to reformat, we click the currency line with two decimal places.

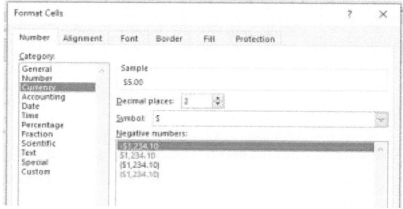

Figure A.8. Cell formatting options.

We display in Figure A.9 the numbers reformatted as currency.

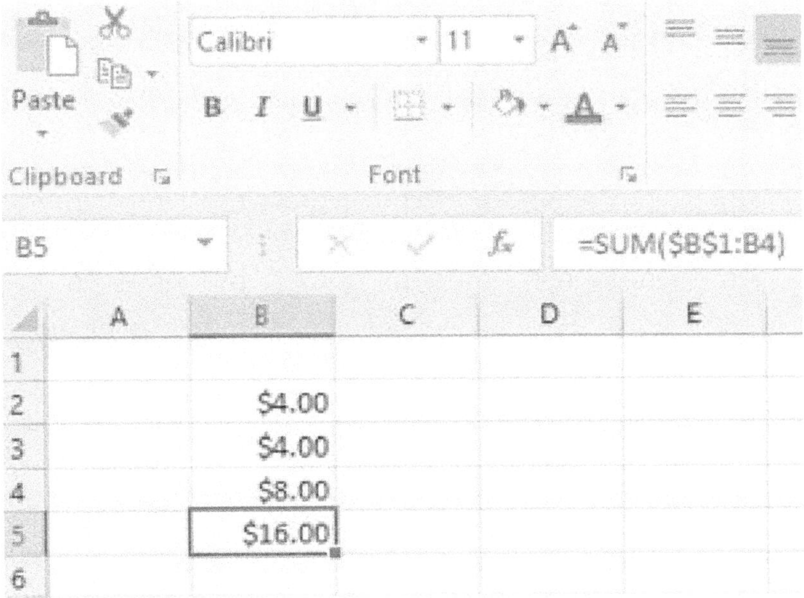

Figure A.9. Currency Formatted cells
Open Example in Microsoft Excel

Excel Financial Functions

Compound interest. We illustrate the important concepts of user supplied functions, handles, and fixed cell locations by calculating compound interest. Suppose we begin in the present, period zero, with an investment of $10,000 that earns 5% per period. Therefore, at the beginning of period 1, our original investment has grown to $10,000(1.05) = $10,500. If we allow the original investment plus interest to grow another period, we have at the beginning of period two an investment of $10,000(1.05)(1.05)=$11,025. It might be interesting, although tedious, to see how our investment would grow over 10 periods following the same procedure. Excel can easily solve this problem using cell handles.

To begin, we label cell A3 "Years" and in cells A4 through A14, we list the number of years for which we want to compute the value of an investment that earns compound interest beginning in the present. We label cell B3, "Compound Values." At the beginning of year 0 in cell B4, we list the original investment amount. At the beginning of year 1 in cell B5, we enter the function for compounding the value in the previous cell—multiplying the previous cell's value by 1.05. Clicking on the handle in cell B5, and dragging it to year 10 in cell B14, we calculate the value of the investment in each of the 10 periods. To make clear this operation, we display the function in each cell to the right of the cell in which the function is embedded. If we wish to explore the effects of compounding with alternative interest rates, we change the interest rate listed in cell C16. For example, compare the investment's value compounded at 5% percent rate compared to the investment's value compounded at 10%. The comparison is reported in Figure A.10.

	A	B	C	D	E
1			Compound Interest and Investment Values		
2					
3	Year		Value	formula	
4		0	$10,000		
5		1	$10,500.00	=C4*(1+$C$16)	
6		2	$11,025.00	=C5*(1+$C$16)	
7		3	$11,576.25	=C6*(1+$C$16)	
8		4	$12,155.06	=C7*(1+$C$16)	
9		5	$12,762.82	=C8*(1+$C$16)	
10		6	$13,400.96	=C9*(1+$C$16)	
11		7	$14,071.00	=C10*(1+$C$16)	
12		8	$14,774.55	=C11*(1+$C$16)	
13		9	$15,513.28	=C12*(1+$C$16)	
14		10	$16,288.95	'=C13*(1+$C$16)	
15					
16	interest rate		5%		
17					

	A	B	C	D	E
1			Compound Interest and Investment Values		
2					
3	Year		Value	formula	
4		0	$10,000		
5		1	$11,000.00	=C4*(1+$C$16)	
6		2	$12,100.00	=C5*(1+$C$16)	
7		3	$13,310.00	=C6*(1+$C$16)	
8		4	$14,641.00	=C7*(1+$C$16)	
9		5	$16,105.10	=C8*(1+$C$16)	
10		6	$17,715.61	=C9*(1+$C$16)	
11		7	$19,487.17	=C10*(1+$C$16)	
12		8	$21,435.89	=C11*(1+$C$16)	
13		9	$23,579.48	=C12*(1+$C$16)	
14		10	$25,937.42	=C13*(1+$C$16)	
15					
16	interest rate		10%		
17					

Figure A.10. Analyzing the Effect of a 5% and a 10% Compound Interest Rate on Investment Values
Open Example in Microsoft Excel

Goal Seek. In the previous example, we found that $10,000 compounded at 5% for 10 periods produced a value of $16,288.95 and $25,937.42 if $10,000 were compounded at 10%. Suppose our goal was to have $20,000 at the end of 10 years of compounding. We might ask: what initial investment, an exogenous variable, compounded for 10 years at 5% would produce a $20,000, an endogenous variable whose value is determined within the system? We could, of course, answer this question by experimenting with alternative investment values in cell C4 where the initial investment amount is stored. However, this would be tedious and may be difficult to find the exact amount.

Excel offers an alternative approach to finding the desired value of an endogenous variable by changing an exogenous variable using an algorithm called "Goal Seek." Excel's Goal Seek algorithm answers "what if" kinds of questions. Specifically, it answers the question "what if" the value of the endogenous variable located in a particular cell has some specified value, then what must be the value of the exogenous variable located in another designated cell? Excel records the new values for endogenous and exogenous variables in the Excel spreadsheet. We illustrate the process using the compounding investment example described in Figure A.10.

To access Goal Seek, press the [Data] tab and the [What If Analysis] button. Finally, press "Goal Seek…" in the drop-down menu. The Data tab, the What If Analysis button, and the drop-down menu displaying the Goal Seek option are displayed in Figure A.11.

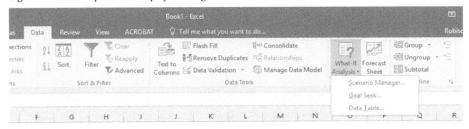

Figure A.11. Accessing Goal Seek in an Excel spreadsheet

The Goal Seek dialogue box asks that the endogenous variable's cell location be identified in the "Set cell" entry field. We enter the desired value of the endogenous variable in the "To value" field. Finally, we identify the cell location of the exogenous variable that is to be changed in the "By changing cell" entry field. After pressing "OK", Goal Seek finds the value of the exogenous variable required to obtain the desired value of the endogenous variable.

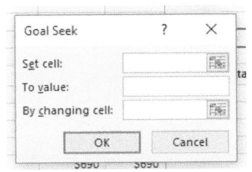

Figure A.12. The Goal Seek dialogue box asking for the endogenous variable location to be recorded in the "Set" field, the desired value of the endogenous variable to be recorded in the "To value" field, and the location of the exogenous variable to be recorded in the "By changing" field.

To illustrate, suppose we wanted to have an investment value of $20,000 at the end of 10 years. Our "what if" question is: What if the value of our original investment compounded at 5% for 10 years were $20,000? Then what would be our required investment amount? To solve this problem, in the

Goal Seek dialogue box we enter cell C14—the endogenous variable location—in the "Set cell" field; we enter $20,000 in the "To value" field; and we enter cell location A4—the exogenous variable—in the "By changing cell" field. The results are recorded in Figure A.13.

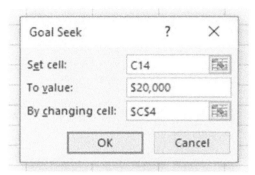

Figure A.13. *A Completed Goal Seek dialogue box that instructs Excel to find the original investment compounded at 5% required to produce a $20,000 investment value at the beginning of period 10.*

Pressing the "OK" button returns the Goal Seek solution reported in Figure A.14.

	A	B	C	D	E
1			Compound Interest and Investment Values		
2					
3	Year		Value	formula	
4		0	$12,278		
5		1	$12,892.18	=C4*(1+$C$16)	
6		2	$13,536.79	=C5*(1+$C$16)	
7		3	$14,213.63	=C6*(1+$C$16)	
8		4	$14,924.31	=C7*(1+$C$16)	
9		5	$15,670.52	=C8*(1+$C$16)	
10		6	$16,454.05	=C9*(1+$C$16)	
11		7	$17,276.75	=C10*(1+$C$16)	
12		8	$18,140.59	=C11*(1+$C$16)	
13		9	$19,047.62	=C12*(1+$C$16)	
14		10	$20,000.00	=C13*(1+$C$16)	
15					
16	interest rate		5%		
17					

Figure A.14. The Goal Seek solution, $12,278, equals the initial Investment compounded at 5% required to produce a $20,000 value at the beginning of period 10.
Open Example in Microsoft Excel

We have determined using Goal Seek that an investment value of $20,000 at the beginning of period 10 requires that we invest $12,278 in the present—an increase of $2,278 over the original investment.

An Application of Goal Seek to HQN's Coordinated Financial Statements (CFS)

In the text, we explored HQN's financial condition reflected by its CFS and associated ratios, DuPont equation, and common size balance sheet and income statements. We now use Goal Seek to find the value of an exogenous variable required to produce the desired value of an endogenous variable. To begin, we copy HQN's original CFS in Figure A.15.

	A	B	C	D	E	F	G	H	I
1		BALANCE SHEET			ACCRUAL INCOME STATEMENT			STATEMENT OF CASH FLOW	
2	DATE	12/31/2017	12/31/2018	DATE		2018	DATE		2018
3	Cash and Marketable Securities	$930	$600	+	Cash Receipts	$38,990	+	Cash Receipts	$38,990
4	Accounts Receivable	$1,640	$1,200	+	Change in Accounts Receivable	($440)	-	Cash Cost of Goods Sold	$27,000
5	Inventory	$3,750	$5,200	+	Change in Inventories	$1,450	-	Cash Overhead Expenses	$11,078
6	Notes Receivable	$0	$0	+	Realized capital gains (losses)	$0	-	Interest paid	$480
7	Total Current Assets	$6,320	$7,000	+	Total Revenue	$40,000	-	Taxes	$68
8							=	Net Cash Flow from Operations	$364
9	Depreciable Assets	$2,990	$2,710	-	Cash Cost of Goods Sold	$27,000			
10	Non-depreciable Assets	$690	$690	+	Change in Accounts. Payable	$1,000	+	Realized Cap. Gains + Depr. Recapture	$0
11	Total Long-Term Assets	$3,680	$3,400	+	Cash Overhead Expenses	$11,078	+	Sales Non-depreciable Assets	$0
12	TOTAL ASSETS	$10,000	$10,400	+	Change in Accrued Liabilities	($78)	-	Purchases Non-depreciable Assets	$0
13				-	Depreciation	$350	-	Sale Depreciable Assets	$30
14	Notes Payable	$1,500	$1,270	=	Total Expenses	$39,350	-	Purchases Depreciable Assets	$100
15	Current Portion Long-Term Debt	$500	$450				=	Net Cash Flow from Investment	($70)
16	Accounts Payable	$3,000	$4,000						
17	Accrued Liabilities	$958	$880		Earnings Before Interest and Taxes (E	$650			
18	Total Current Liabilities	$5,958	$6,600	-	Less Interest Costs	$480	+	Change in Non-Current Long Term Debt	($557)
19	Non-Current Long Term Debt	$2,042	$1,985	=	Earnings Before Taxes (EBT)	$170	+	Change in Current Portion of Long Term Debt	($50)
20	TOTAL LIABILITIES	$8,000	$8,585	-	Less Taxes	$68	+	Change in Notes Payable	($230)
21				=	Net Income After Taxes (NIAT)	$102	-	Less Dividends and Owner Draw	$287
22	Contributed Capital	$1,900	$1,900	-	Less Dividends and Owner Draw	$287	=	Net Cash Flow from Financing	($624)
23	Retained Earnings	$100	($85)	=	Addition to Retained Earnings	($185)			
24	Total Equity	$2,000	$1,815					CHANGE IN CASH POSITION (Q11+Q18+Q24)	($330)
25	TOTAL LIABILITIES AND EQUITY	$10,000	$10,400						

	A	B	C
28	BASE SPELL RATIOS FOR HQN		
29		12/31/2018	Industry
30	SOLVENCY RATIOS		
31	Times Interest Earned (TIE)	1.35	2.5
32	Debt Service Ratio (DSR)	1.02	1.40
33	PROFITABILITY RATIOS		
34	Profit margin (m)	0.43%	1.03%
35	Return on assets (ROA)	6.50%	3.30%
36	After-tax ROA [ROA(1-T*)]	5.82%	
37	Return on equity (ROE)	8.50%	10.70%
38	After-tax ROE [ROE(1-T)]	5.10%	
39	EFFICIENCY RATIOS		
40	Inventory Turnover (ITO)	10.67	7.7
41	ITOT (365/ITO)	34.22	47.4
42	Asset Turnover (ATO)	4.00	3.2
43	ATOT (365/ATO)	91.25	114.1
44	Receivable Turnover (RTO)	24.39	11.41
45	RTOT (365/RTO)	14.97	32
46	Payable Turnover (PTO)	9.33	12.59
47	PTOT (365/PTO)	39.11	29.00
48	LIQUIDITY RATIOS		
49	Current ratio (CR)	1.06	1.30
50	Quick ratio (QR)	0.43	0.70
51	LEVERAGE RATIOS		
52	Debt/Asset (D/A)	0.80	0.91
53	Debt/Equity (D/E)	4.00	2.00
54	Equity multiplier (A/E)	5.00	2.20

CPS template | Exogenous Variables | SPELL Ratios | Common Size Balance Sheets | Common Size Income Statement

Figure A.15. HQN's Coordinated Financial Statements and Embedded Functions and Associated Ratios.
Open CFS Example in Microsoft Excel

Now suppose we are concerned about the low cash receipts efficiency ratio m and ask: what must our cash receipts equal to produce an m efficiency ratio of .8% or 8/10th of a penny on each dollar of sale? To answer this question, we enter the following into our Goal Seek dialogue box.

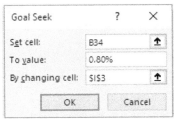

Figure A.16. Solving the "What if" question, how much does cash receipts need to increase to obtain an m ratio of .8% using Goal Seek

After pressing OK, we return the answer to our "What if" question in figure A.17.

	BALANCE SHEET				ACCRUAL INCOME STATEMENT				STATEMENT OF CASH FLOW		
	A	B	C	D	E	F	G	H	I
DATE		12/31/2017	12/31/2018	DATE		2018	DATE			2018
Cash and Marketable Securities		$930	$752	+	Cash Receipts	$39,142	+	Cash Receipts		$39,142
Accounts Receivable		$1,640	$1,200	+	Change in Accounts Receivable	($440)	-	Cash Cost of Goods Sold		$27,000
Inventory		$3,750	$5,200	+	Change in Inventories	$1,450	-	Cash Overhead Expenses		$11,078
Notes Receivable		$0	$0	+	Realized capital gains (losses)	$0	-	Interest paid		$480
Total Current Assets		$6,320	$7,152	=	Total Revenue	$40,152	-	Taxes		$68
							=	Net Cash Flow from Operations		$516
Depreciable Assets		$2,990	$2,710	+	Cash Cost of Goods Sold	$27,000				
Non-depreciable Assets		$690	$690	+	Change in Accounts. Payable	$1,000	+	Realized Cap. Gains + Depr. Recapture		$0
Total Long-Term Assets		$3,680	$3,400	+	Cash Overhead Expenses	$11,078	+	Sales Non-depreciable Assets		$0
TOTAL ASSETS		$10,000	$10,552	+	Change in Accrued Liabilities	($378)	-	Purchases Non-depreciable Assets		$0
				+	Depreciation	$350	+	Sale Depreciable Assets		$30
Notes Payable		$1,500	$1,270	=	Total Expenses	$39,350	-	Purchases Depreciable Assets		$100
Current Portion Long-Term Debt		$500	$450				=	Net Cash Flow from Investment		($70)
Accounts Payable		$3,000	$4,000							
Accrued Liabilities		$958	$880	-	Earnings Before Interest and Taxes (E	$802				
Total Current Liabilities		$5,958	$6,600	-	Less Interest Costs	$480	+	Change in Non-Current Long Term Debt		($57)
Non-Current Long Term Debt		$2,042	$1,985	=	Earnings Before Taxes (EBT)	$322	+	Change in Current Portion of Long Term Debt		($50)
TOTAL LIABILITIES		$8,000	$8,585	-	Less Taxes	$68	+	Change in Notes Payable		($230)
				=	Net Income After Taxes (NIAT)	$254	=	Net Cash Flow from Financing		($624)
Contributed Capital		$1,900	$1,900	-	Less Dividends and Owner Draw	$287				
Retained Earnings		$100	$67	=	Addition to Retained Earnings	($33)				
Total Equity		$2,000	$1,967					CHANGE IN CASH POSITION (Q11+Q18+Q24)		($178)
TOTAL LIABILITIES AND EQUITY		$10,000	$10,552							

A	B	C
BASE SPELL RATIOS FOR HQN		
	12/31/2018	Industry
SOLVENCY RATIOS		
Times Interest Earned (TIE)	1.67	2.5
Debt Service Ratio (DSR)	1.18	1.40
PROFITABILITY RATIOS		
Profit margin (m)	0.80%	1.03%
Return on assets (ROA)	8.02%	3.30%
After-tax ROA [ROA(1-T*)]	7.34%	
Return on equity (ROE)	16.11%	10.70%
After-tax ROE [ROE(1-T)]	12.71%	
EFFICIENCY RATIOS		
Inventory Turnover (ITO)	10.71	7.7
ITOT (365/ITO)	34.09	47.4
Asset Turnover (ATO)	4.02	3.2
ATOT (365/ATO)	90.90	114.1
Receivable Turnover (RTO)	24.48	11.41
RTOT (365/RTO)	14.91	32
Payable Turnover (PTO)	9.33	12.59
PTOT (365/PTO)	39.11	29.00
LIQUIDITY RATIOS		
Current ratio (CR)	1.06	1.30
Quick ratio (QR)	0.43	0.70
LEVERAGE RATIOS		
Debt/Asset (D/A)	0.80	0.91
Debt/Equity (D/E)	4.00	2.00
Equity multiplier (A/E)	5.00	2.20

CFS template   Exogenous Variables   SPELL Ratios   Common Size Balance Sheets   Common Size Income Statement

Figure A.17. The Goal Seek solution to the "What if" question, how much will cash receipts need to increase to produce an m value of .8%?
Open "What if" CFS Example in Microsoft Excel

The Goal Seek answer to the "what if" question described earlier is that cash sales must increase to $39,142 in order for HQN to produce an m ratio equal to .8%. We may also observe that the new level of cash receipts would also increase both ROA and ROE values to well above industry standards. The ROE ratio increases from 8.5% to 16.11%. The ROA increases from 6.50% to 8.02%. Furthermore, increased cash receipts would improve the debt-to-service ratio from 1.02 to 1.18.

An overview of financial functions.

This section discusses how to use Excel financial functions, some of which were discussed in earlier book chapters—particularly Chapter 17 on loan analysis. Obviously, the financial functions discussed in this section are only a sampling of the many financial and other functions available to Excel users. We begin by writing the general present value (NPV) function in equation A.1. The various financial functions we will discuss in what follows are only special cases of equation A.1.

$$NPV = -V_0 + \frac{R_1}{(1+r/m)} + \frac{R_2}{(1+r/m)^2} + \cdots + \frac{R_{mn} + S_{mn}}{(1+r/m)^{mn}}$$

(A.1)

We begin by noting a fundamental algebraic reality. A single equation can solve for at most one unknown variable—although the unknown variable may have more than one solution. Therefore, equation A.1 can produce a solution(s) for at most one unknown. As a result, all of the financial models described in this appendix assume that one of the variables in equation A.1 is unknown. Consider the following financial models that result by assuming one of the variables in A.1 is unknown.

The net present value (NPV) model. The NPV model solves for the net present value of an investment, the present value difference between the cost of the investment V_0 and future cash flows discounted by rate r/m plus the investment's liquidation value V_n.

The internal rate of return (IRR) model. The IRR model finds the value of the discount rate r that makes NPV equal to zero. The variable r is unknown, and because it enters the equation with an exponent, r may have more than one solution.

The maximum bid (minimum sell) price model. The maximum bid price model finds the value of V_0 such that NPV is zero. It represents the most an investor could pay for a future cash flow stream and still break-even. The value of V_0 that makes NPV zero may also represent the least-price an investor could receive in exchange for the investment's future cash flow stream and still break-even.

The annuity equivalent (AE) model. There are two versions of the annuity equivalent model. The first one finds the value of a constant cash flow R received for mn periods whose NPV equals the present value sum of cash flows $R_i(i = 1, ..., mn)$ plus S_{mn}, the equation's NPV.

$$NPV = -V_0 + \frac{R_1}{(1+r/m)} + \frac{R_2}{(1+r/m)^2} + \cdots + \frac{R_{mn} + S_{mn}}{(1+r/m)^{mn}}$$

$$= \frac{R}{(1+r/m)} + \frac{R}{(1+r/m)^2} + \cdots + \frac{R}{(1+r/m)^{mn}}$$

(A.2)

In the second version of the annuity equivalent model, we set NPV equal to zero and find the annuity equivalent whose discounted value is equal to V_0. Cash flows associated with a constant loan payment fit this model where V_0 is the loan amount, R is the constant loan payment, r/m is the interest rate, and mn is the term of the loan.

$$V_0 = \frac{R_1}{(1+r/m)} + \frac{R_2}{(1+r/m)^2} + \cdots + \frac{R_{mn} + S_{mn}}{(1+r/m)^{mn}}$$

$$= \frac{R}{(1+r/m)} + \frac{R}{(1+r/m)^2} + \cdots + \frac{R}{(1+r/m)^{mn}}$$

(A.3)

Break-even models. In some cases, we might be interested in a particular value of R_i or the liquidation value S_{mn} that reduces NPV to zero. In these cases, we often employ Goal Seek to find that particular R_i or S_{mn} value.

The term model. There are two term models considered in this book. In the first, the unknown variable is the term, mn, and its solution depends on the other known variables in the equation. In the second term model, called the optimal term model, the solution for mn depends on a calculus-defined condition requiring that we solve the model for various values of mn until the optimal conditions are satisfied. This is a difficult model to solve because it requires that we know additional future values of variables. Forecasting the future values of variables is discussed in Chapter 11.

The future value model. The future value model solves for S_{mn}, the liquidation value of the investment, assuming NPV is equal to zero. The uniqueness of this model is that instead of discounting future cash flows to their present value, we compound cash flows to their future value in the mn^{th} period

Excel functions.

Corresponding to the general NPV equation variables described in A.1 are several Excel functions. Excel's PV function finds NPV and V_0. Its PMT function finds R, an AE. Its NPER function finds mn. Its RATE function finds r/m, and its FV function finds the value of S_{mn} after setting NPV equal to zero.

Corresponding to the Excel functions PV, RATE, NPER, PMT, and FV are the arguments pv, rate, nper, pmt, and fv. Functions are capitalized. Arguments corresponding to functions are lowercased. When we solve for a particular function, the corresponding argument is eliminated from the function's list of arguments. We list the following Excel functions, their arguments, and the order in which the arguments appear. In addition to the list of arguments, functions call for "type" variables which tells the function whether cash flows occur at the beginning of the period in which case type=1 or at the end of the period in which case type=0. If values are not entered for "type" and "fv", Excel assumes they are both equal to zero. Excel financial functions and their arguments are listed next.

- The PV function is =PV(rate, nper, pmt, fv, type).
- The FV function is= FV(rate, nper, pmt, pv, type).

- The RATE function is =RATE(nper, pmt, pv, fv, type).
- The NPER function is =NPER(rate, pmt, pv, fv, type).
- The PMT function is =PMT(rate, nper, pv, fv, type).

To solve the functions listed above, we enter the cell locations of the argument values and enter them into the Excel function. For example, if the value for rate were listed in cell C4, nper were listed in cell C5, pmt were listed in cell C6, and fv and type were both zero, we would write the PV function as =PV(C4, C5, C6, 0, 0).

Calling up Excel Functions.

There are two ways to call up Excel functions. The first way is to write the function with its argument values in a designated location. For example, assume the value for rate were listed in cell C4, nper were listed in cell C5, pmt were listed in cell C6, and fv and type were both zero and listed in cells C8 and C9. Then, we would write the PV function in cell C7 as =PV(C4, C5, C6, C8, C9).

A second way to call up an Excel function, particularly if the name of the function or its arguments are not known, is to click on the Formulas tab on the main ribbon and the Financial button that produces a drop-down menu with a list of financial functions. The financial functions NPER, RATE, PV, FV, and PMT are included in the list. To illustrate, we find and click the PV function in Figure A.18 below.

Figure A.18. Opening the Excel PV function.

After clicking on PV in the drop-down menu, the PV function dialogue box with its list of arguments is displayed in Figure A.19.

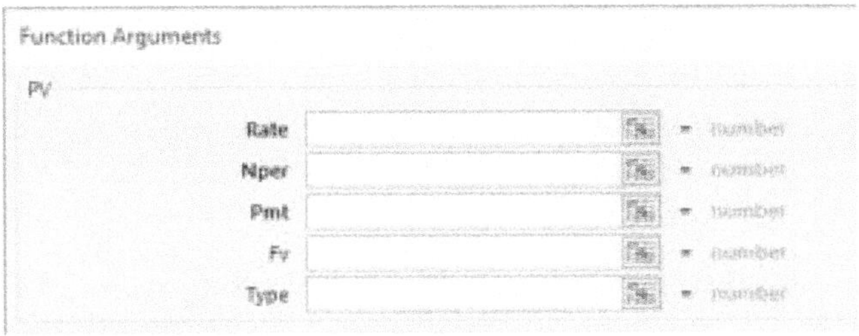

Figure A.19. The PV functions and its arguments.

To review, the PV function arguments correspond to variables in equation A.1. Rate corresponds to "r/m", the discount rate in an NPV model or the interest rate in a constant loan model. Nper corresponds to the product of mn, the number of periods we compound interest in equation A.1. Pmt corresponds to the annuity equivalent R. FV corresponds to future value. One other argument not explicitly described in equation A.1, type, identifies if cash flows occur at the beginning of the period, in which case we enter the number 1, or if calculated at the end of the period, in which case we enter the number 0.

To illustrate, we solve for pv using the PV function. We begin by listing value for all of the PV arguments and in the cell that calls for a pv value, we enter the PV function. Our example in Figure A.21 corresponds to the example in Chapter 17. The annual percentage rate r equals 5%. The number of compound periods per year m is 12. The number of years n is 4. And the annuity equivalent R entered with a negative sign is $-R = -150$. We now transform the numbers corresponding to equation A.1 into PV function arguments. Rate equals r/m = .05/12=.004; Nper equals mn = 12 x 4 = 48. In cell C7 we enter the function PV with its arguments. For the first argument of the PV function we list the location of rate in cell C4. The second argument of the PV function is nper located in cell C5. The third argument is pmt located in cell C6. The fourth argument is pv in cell C7. Since pv is an endogenous variable in the PV function, we enter the PV function is cell C7. Finally, type is equals to zero in cell C8 and fv is also zero located in cell C9. The PV formula in cell C7 is expressed as =PV(C4, C5, C6, C8, C9). The solution to the PV equation with argument values described in Chapter 17 and repeated above are illustrated in Figure A.20.

C7	▾ ⁝	× ✓	f_x	=PV(C4,C5,C6,C8,C9)

	A	B	C
1	Excel PV functions and arguments		
2			
3	Excel arguments	Eqn. A.1 variables	Excel argument values
4	rate	r/m	0.0040
5	nper	mn	48
6	pmt	R	($150.00)
7	pv	NPV+Vo	6539.14
8	type	beg = 0	0.00
9	fv	Vn=0	$0.00
10			

Figure A.20. An Excel PV function solution for equation A.1 where A.1 variables are described in cells C4 through C9.
Open Example in Microsoft Excel

Notice that the argument values for the PV function are listed in cells C4, C5, C6, C8, and C9. The unknown (endogenous variable) pv is located in cell C7. So in cell C7 we list the PV function and its arguments described in the function box located at the top of the figure.

To illustrate another function, suppose that we knew that pv=$5,000 but that nper was unknown. In which case we would enter $5000 in cell C7 and enter the NPER function in cell C5: =NPER(C4, C6, C7, C8, C9). The solution is described in cell C5, and the NPER function is entered in the function box. These results are described in Figure A.21.

| C5 | | | × | ✓ | f_x | =NPER(C4,C6,C7,C8,C9) |

◢	A	B	C
1	Excel NPER function and arguments		
2			
3	Excel arguments	Eqn. A.1 variables	Values
4	rate	r/m	0.0040
5	nper	mn	35.85
6	pmt	R	($150.00)
7	pv	NPV+Vo	5000.00
8	type	beg = 0	0.00
9	fv	Vn=0	$0.00
10			

Figure A.21. Answering the "what if" the nper was unknown.
Open Example in Microsoft Excel

Of course, we can explore "what if" questions by changing arguments values of the function NPER and noting the consequences on nper. For example, what if we change the variable r in cell B4 to 8% so that r/m = 8% / 12 = .0067. Then we ask, what is the new value of nper? The worksheet with the revised value for rate is described in Figure A.22.

| C5 | | | × | ✓ | f_x | =NPER(C4,C6,C7,C8,C9) | |

◢	A	B	C	D
1	Excel NPER function and arguments			
2				
3	Excel arguments	Eqn. A.1 variables	Excel argument Values	
4	rate	r/m	0.0067	
5	nper	mn	37.85	
6	pmt	R	($150.00)	
7	pv	NPV+Vo	5000.00	
8	type	beg = 0	0.00	
9	fv	Vn=0	$0.00	

Figure A.22. Answering the question: "what if" rate were 8%, then what would be the value of nper?
Open Example in Microsoft Excel

To this point, we have assumed time varying cash flows in equation A.1 have been replaced by their AE equal to R. But in some cases, it is important to consider the time varying cash flow rather than the AE cash flow. Excel's NPV function allows us to do just that—consider time varying cash flows. Excel's NPV and IRR function considers the complete A.1 equation including its time varying cash flow.

The NPV function. The NPV function has only two arguments: the rate argument and the stream of periodic cash flows that can be entered individually separated by commas or entered as the first and last value in the cash flow stream beginning in period 1 and ending in period *mn* separated by a constant. The original investment value is not included in the function but added separately to the function value. We illustrate the NPV function using data from the Green and White Services investment problem.

Green and White Services wants to know the NPV of an investment of $40,000 in lawn care equipment with expected cash flow during its four years of operation equal to: $9,800, $16,200, $17,840, and $19,600. In period five, Green and White intend to liquidate their investment and receive an after-tax cash flow liquidation value of $8,000. We enter these values in Figure A.23 and point the cursor at cell C12 where the NPV function is inserted. The first argument of the function is the discount rate of 8% recorded in cell C4. The second argument is the periodic cash flow in cells C7 through C11 separated by a colon. To the NPV function value we add the investment amount of ($40,000) located in cell C6. After pressing enter, the NPV function returns an NPV value of $17,061.91.

C12			f_x	=NPV(C4,C7:C11)+C6		
	A	B		C	D	E
1	Excel NPV function and arguments					
2						
3	Excel arguments	Eqn. A.1 variables	Excel argument values			
4	rate	r		0.08		
5	after-tax cash flow					
6		Va		(40,000.00)		
7		R1		9,800.00		
8		R2		16,300.00		
9		R3		17,840.00		
10		R4		19,600.00		
11		R5		8,000.00		
12		NPV		$17,061.91		
13		IRR		23%		
14						
15						

Figure A.23. The NPV function for Green and White Services' investment of $40,000 that produces four periods of return and then is salvaged in year 5.
Open Example in Microsoft Excel

The IRR function with time varying cash flows. The IRR function finds the discount rate such that NPV is zero. The IRR function has only two arguments. The first argument is investment value. The second argument is the stream of periodic cash flows that can be entered individually separated by commas or entered as the first and last value in the cash flow stream beginning in period 1 and ending in period *mn* separated by a constant. We illustrate the IRR function using data from the Green and White investment problem. We enter the investment value in cell C6 and periodic cash flows in cells C7 through C11. We enter the IRR function is cell C13. Its first argument is the initial investment of ($40,000). The second argument is the periodic cash flow in cells C7 through C11 separated by a colon. After pressing enter, the IRR function returns an IRR value of 23%. We summarize this IRR example in Figure A.24.

	A	B	C	D	E
C13			f_x	=IRR(C6:C11,0.12)	
1	Excel NPV function and arguments				
2					
3	Excel arguments	Eqn. A.1 variables	Excel argument values		
4	rate	r	0.08		
5	after-tax cash flow				
6		V0	(40,000.00)		
7		R1	9,800.00		
8		R2	16,300.00		
9		R3	17,840.00		
10		R4	19,600.00		
11		R5	8,000.00		
12		NPV	$17,061.91		
13		IRR	23%		
14					
15					
16					

Figure A.24. *The IRR function for Green and White Services' investment of $40,000 that produces four periods of return and then is salvaged in year 5.*
Open Example in Microsoft Excel

Excel spreadsheets provide a powerful means for computing what otherwise would be tedious calculations. However, their ability to provide solutions to complex equations rapidly and repeatedly allows for a potential problem. The problem is that we may not spend sufficient time and effort to carefully specify the calculations we need Excel to perform. Cars are valuable means of getting us from point A to point B, but we still need to know the location of point A and point B. Excel spreadsheets provide valuable solutions to complex equations, but we still need to carefully define the problem to be solved and carefully derive the appropriate equation that solves the problem. Then, we are ready to enjoy the benefits of powerful Excel spreadsheets and formulas.

References

LINDON ROBISON

Adrian, Tobias, Arturo Estrella, and Shin Hyun Song. January 1, 2010. "Monetary Cycles, Financial Cycles and the Business Cycle." *FRB of New York Staff Report* No. 421. pp. 1-19.

Becchetti, L.A. Pelloni, and F. Rossetti. 2008. "Relation Goods, Sociability, and Happiness." *Center for Economic and International Studies* 6 (4) No. 117, 1-27.

Bruni, L. and L. Stanca. 2008. "Watching alone: Relational goods, television and happiness." *Journal of Economic Behavior and Organization.* Vol. 65:506-528.

Bureau of Labor Statistics. n.d. "The price of a dozen large eggs over the period 1980 to 2016." Accessed 2016. https://data.bls.gov

Chart of the Day. n.d. "S&P 500 PE Ratio" www.chartoftheday.com

Graham, J.R. and C.R. Harvey. 2001. "The Theory and Practice of Corporate Finance: Evidence from the Field," *Journal of Financial Economics* 60, 187-243.

Gui, B. and R. Sugden. 2005. *Economics and Social Interaction.* Cambridge: Cambridge University Press.

Lieberman, M. D. 2013. *Social: Why our brains are wired to connect.* Crowne Publishers.

Luigino, B. and L. Stanca. 2008. "Watching Alone: Relational goods, television and happiness." *Journal of Economic and Behavioral Organization,* Vol 65, Issues 3-4:506-528.

Maslow, A.H. 1943. "A Theory of Human Motivation." *Psychological Review,* 50(4), 370-96.

Monson, Thomas S. October 1970. Conference Report, 107.

Perry, G.M. and L.J. Robison. 2001. "Evaluating the Influence of Personal Relationships on Land Sale Prices: A Case Study in Oregon." *Land Economics.* 77(3):385-98.

Robison, L.J. and P.J. Barry 1987. *The Competitive Firm's Response to Risk.* New York: Macmillan Publishing Co.

Robison, L.J. and P.J. Barry 2020. *Accrual Income Statements and Present Value Models.* Agricultural Finance Review.

Robison, L.J. and P.J. Barry 1996. *Present Value Models and Investment Analysis.* Michigan Statement University Press.

Robison, L.J., P.J. Barry, and R.J. Myers. 2015. "Consistent IRR and NPV Rankings." *Agricultural Finance Review,* 75(4): 499-513.

Robison, L.J., and J.L. Flora. 2003. "The Social Capital Paradigm: Bridging Across Disciplines." *American Journal of Agricultural Economics,* 85(5): 1187-1193.

Robison, L.J. and B.K. Ritchie. 2010. *Relationship Economics: The Social Capital Paradigm and its Application to Business, Politics, and Other Transactions*. Grower Publishers, 272 pages.

Robison, L.J., A.A. Schmid, and M.E. Siles. 2002. "Is Social Capital Really Capital?" *Review of Social Economy* 60:1-21.

Robison, L.J. and A.A. Schmid. 1991. "Interpersonal relationships and preferences: Evidence and implications", *Handbook of behavioral economics* 2, 347-358.

Siles, M., L.J. Robison, B. Johnson, G.D. Lynne, and M. D. Beveridge. 2000. "Farmland Exchanges: Selection Of Trading Partners, Terms of Trade, And Social Capital." *Journal of the American Society of Farm Managers and Rural Appraisers*, 127-140.

Smith, Adam. 1759, 1976. *The Theory of Moral Sentiments*. Indianapolis: Liberty Classics.

Thaler, Richard, Cass R. Sunstein. 2008. *Nudge*. New Haven: Yale University Press.

Uhlaner, C.J. 1989. "Relational Goods And Participation: Incorporating Sociability into A Theory of Rational Action," *Public Choice*. 62: 253-285

USDA Census of U.S. Agriculture. 2007. "Farms in US " https://www.agcensus.usda.gov/

Wolters Kluwer. n.d. "S and C Corporations Create Different Tax Consequences." Accessed August 1, 2018. http://www.bizfilings.com/toolkit/sbg/tax-info/fed-taxes/s-c-corporations-create-different-tax-consequences.aspx

Wikipedia. March 7, 2018. "Yield Curves." https://en.wikipedia.org/wiki/Yield_curve

Winder, Richard. n.d. "Average minimum sell price for a used car with a market value of $3,000 reported by 600 survey respondents." Unpublished survey.

Index Topics

LINDON ROBISON

Milton Keynes UK
Ingram Content Group UK Ltd.
UKHW040646050923
428087UK00001B/290